Michael Reeve-Fowkes

The Yachtsman's

MANUAL OF TIDES

Fastnet and Brest to

The Wash and Den Helder

THOMAS REED PUBLICATIONS
A division of The ABR Company Limited

Part 1
A detailed explanation of tidal cause and effect and the theory and practice of navigating in tidal waters

Part 2
The Yachtsman's Tidal Atlases
Comprehensive tidal information presented in an easily read form in diagrams and tables:

Western Channel

Southern North Sea and Eastern Channel

Central Channel and the Solent

Channel Ports and Approaches

Cherbourg Tide Tables for use with this manual are available from the publishers on receipt of a stamped and addresses envelope:
Thomas Reed Publications, The Barn, Ford Farm,
Bradford Leigh, Bradford-on-Avon, BA15 2RP

Published by
Thomas Reed Publications
The Barn, Ford Farm
Bradford Leigh
Bradford-on-Avon
Wiltshire BA15 2RP England
Tel. 01225 868821   Fax. 01225 868831
E-mail: sales@abreed.demon.co.uk

REED'S is the trade mark of The ABR Company Limited

Copyright © J. Reeve-Fowkes and Thomas Reed Publications
All rights reserved. No part of this publication may be reproduced, stored in a retrieval system or transmitted, in any form or by any means, electronic, mechanical, photocopying, recording or otherwise, without the prior permission of Thomas Reed Publications.

First published 1983
New edition 1992
Revised edition 2002

ISBN 0 901281 54 9
Produced by Omega Profiles Limited, SP11 7RW
Printed and bound in Great Britain

The information which appears in this atlas has been derived from a number of different sources. In addition, the author has used his expert knowledge and experience to interpolate and make assumptions where the sources were incomplete. Neither the author nor the publishers can accept any responsibility for any errors or inaccuracies which may be present.

Contents

		Page
Part 1		5
Chapter 1	Tidal Cause and Effect	7
Chapter 2	Tidal Publications	15
Chapter 3	Single-Port Phasing	21
Chapter 4	Tide and Weather	25
Chapter 5	Tidal Chartwork	29
Chapter 6	Coastal Passages	33
Chapter 7	Cross-Channel Passages	39
Chapter 8	Windward Passages	45
Chapter 9	Tides and Electronic Position-Fixing Systems	51
Part 2		55
Instructions for use: Tidal Atlases		56
The Yachtsman's Tidal Atlas: Western Channel		59
The Yachtsman's Tidal Atlas: Southern North Sea and Eastern Channel		87
The Yachtsman's Tidal Atlas: Central Channel and the Solent		115
The Yachtsman's Tidal Atlas: Channel Ports and Approaches: Section 1		145
	Section 2	173
Instructions for use: Tidal Ranges		188
Tidal Range Tables: Western Channel		189
	Eastern Channel	190
	Central Channel	191
Index		192

Introduction

The **Yachtsman's Manual of Tides** is a two-part manual covering every aspect of the understanding of tides and their application to the navigation of small craft within tidal waters.

Part 1 of the Manual deals comprehensively with: the cause and effect of tides as well as giving a guide to the theory and practice of navigating in tidal waters: passage planning for short coastal passages and cross-channel passages: tidal chart-work and the use of electronic position-fixing systems.

Part 2 contains the four Yachtsman's Tidal Atlases which give tidal stream rate and tidal height predictions in an easily read form in diagrams and tables. The four tidal atlases cover the cruising area from Fastnet and Brest in the west to the Wash and Den Helder in the east. The diagrams and tables offer instant tidal information for nearly 200 ports throughout the area, together with numerous offshore locations.

There are two atlases for passage making: the **Western Channel** and the **Southern North Sea and Eastern Channel** atlases. The atlas **Central Channel and The Solent** gives greater detail of the Solent and across the English Channel to the Channel Islands and Cherbourg, while **Channel Ports and Approaches** gives larger scale detail of ports and places in some of the popular cruising areas.

TIME

The Tidal Atlases are based upon the time of HW at Cherbourg. The predicted height of the tide at Cherbourg is used to indicate the magnitude of each tidal oscillation: Cherbourg has been selected as the reference port for the atlases because it has a suitable tidal range and it is a place that is relatively free from the fluctuations in mean sea level that can be prevalent at Dover and other ports.

Cherbourg tide tables are supplied free by the publishers and can also be found in all the Almanacs.

Most tide tables for Cherbourg will show the HW times in "Time Zone −0100" which is one hour ahead of UT (GMT). British Summer Time is also one hour ahead of UT so when cruising home waters in the summer time, the actual time read from the tide tables will be the same as the actual clock time. Outside the dates of BST, Time Zone −0100 times will have to have one hour subtracted to equal UT (GMT).

If your Cherbourg tide tables are in UT (GMT) simply add one hour during BST to obtain clock time. Watch out if using local Cherbourg tide tables which list HW in local clock time: French Summer Time is one hour ahead of British Summer Time (and two hours ahead of UT). French Summer Time also operates between different dates to British.

UT	= Universal Time i.e. GMT
Zone −0100	= UT + one hour
British Summer Time	= UT + one hour
French Summer Time	= Zone −0100 + one hour (i.e. UT + two hours)

Take care to establish at the outset the correct time of Cherbourg HW in relation to the time on the ship's clocks and watches.

Part 1

1 Tidal Cause and Effect

THE ORIGIN AND NATURE OF TIDES

Four-fifths of the earth's surface is covered by water, which is split into huge oceans by great dividing land masses. The waters are held firmly to the surface of the earth by gravity, but are relatively free to move about horizontally. If the world were a dead mass with no influence of sun, moon or wind then the water might stay still in the depressions of the earth's surface, but the world is very much alive. The sun warms the tropical seas causing currents to flow both on the surface and in the deeps; the warmed water rises and spreads, and is replaced by cold water from the depths, which in turn draws water from the polar regions. The Trade Winds produce other great ocean currents, moving the surface of the water down wind. It is thus that the water, though held firmly to the surface of the earth by gravity is free to move about under whatever influences may be brought to bear, either from the sun, the wind or in the case of tidal movement, the gravitational pull of our own moon and the lesser pull of the enormous, though more distant, sun.

To the observer on earth, the gravitational pull of the moon and the sun is minute compared with that of the earth, and the actual lifting of water away from the earth towards these heavenly bodies can be discounted. The earth rotates on its axis once each day, carrying around with it the oceans and accompanied by the moon in its own orbit; together they move through space with great regularity and precision. As the earth rotates it presents an ever-changing face to the moon and the surface water is attracted, first one way, then the other, in a rocking motion.

Tidal movement is therefore developed in the oceans where the rocking movement is promoted by the rotation of the earth in relatively close proximity to the moon. The sun also exerts a gravitational pull, but because the moon is itself rotating around the earth, the sun serves to increase the rocking motion when the two bodies are *in conjunction* (on the same side of the earth at the same time), or *in opposition* (when they are on opposite sides at the same time). Thus during periods of full and new moon the sun and the moon work together to produce large tides, known as *spring tides*, the biggest oscillations occurring a day or two after full or new moon since there is a time lag while inertia is overcome. The phases of the moon are about fourteen days apart, so that spring tides occur about every fortnight. The lesser tides, *neap tides*, occur when the sun and moon are out of synchronization with the moon in quarter phases, midway between springs.

The earth moves around the sun and the moon moves around the earth in elliptical orbits, which add to the complexity of tidal predictions, since they will have a greater attraction for one another when they are in close proximity. Furthermore, the orbits are not in the same plane because our earth does not rotate on its axis in the same plane as its orbit round the sun. These influences all affect the magnitude of the tidal oscillation, so that there are times when all the factors combine to produce exceptionally large oscillations, for example at the spring and autumn equinoxes, as well as at other times each year. The horizontal movements of the water caused by tides are known as *streams*, which on the surface of the oceans are quite insignificant, being completely overwhelmed by the ocean currents caused by wind and convection. It is only when this vast mass of deep water, gently rocking, comes into contact with the continental shelf that it causes oscillations to be carried through the English Channel and around our land masses, creating significant tidal streams. The movement of water is still essentially horizontal and would remain so were it not for geographical obstructions which cause the waters to rise. As they reach into the Gulf of St Malo and the Bristol Channel, with no immediate place to go they mount up to reach the highest levels in European waters. The streams surge through the English Channel and around the coast piling up against the headlands and islands, creating races and turbulent overfalls, filling the harbours and estuaries and then scouring them as the water pours out. In the central part of the English Channel, while the level of the sea rises some twenty feet in 6½ hours, the billions of tons of water between the French and English coast also moves bodily eastwards some 10 or 12 miles. As the level of the sea falls during the next 6½ hours, so the same mass of water moves back westwards, this sequence repeating itself nearly twice each day, year after year. There will be little change in this pattern in a thousand years although some headlands may disappear, some spits extend or some land be reclaimed, affecting a local regime that has been in operation since the Ice Age.

The orbits of the earth and the moon relative to the sun are complex, and the tractional forces on the oceans vary from day to day both in direction and magnitude, so that no two tides will be exactly alike. Yet once the oscillations are contained within the channels and straits around the British Isles and adjacent continental coast, the direction of the streams is largely determined by the geography of the land and of the sea bed. For practical purposes it is usually assumed that the direction of the streams will remain the same for both spring and neap tides. Although the direction remains approximately the same, the speed of the streams, known as the *rate*, varies greatly: springs in the principal channels can attain rates nearly double those of neaps. In the central part of the English Channel and in the Dover Strait an average spring rate is about 3 knots, whereas at neaps the rate will be just over half — about 1.7 knots. In the Channel Islands, along the Brittany Coast and in the Solent, tidal streams tend to run much faster which means that spring rates are usually more than double the neap rates. For example, in the main channels between Guernsey and Sark an average neap rate is less than 2 knots while the spring rate will be about 4½ knots. In the approaches to Le Havre and in the Dutch delta areas, the difference between rates at springs and neaps is much less marked and the rates are generally less great.

THE DISCERNIBLE PATTERN

Since spring tides occur when the sun and the moon are in conjunction or in opposition, it follows that spring tides occur everywhere for the same two or three days. Likewise, when the quarter phases of the moon occur, neap tides prevail everywhere.

The moon plays the major part in creating our tides and it is convenient to assume that the sun's role is that of shaping them into springs or neaps. Because the sun can be assumed to perform this role and because we also set our clocks in relation to the sun, it follows that spring tides always occur in any one locality at the same time of day. Thus along the south coast of England from Dover to the Isle of Wight and along the French coast from Calais to Dieppe, when high water occurs at midday or midnight the tides are always springs and when low water is at midday or midnight the tides are always neaps. In south-west Ireland, the Scilly Isles, the West Country and the north-west Brittany coast the opposite applies; low water at midday or midnight when spring tides prevail and high water at these times during neaps.

The pattern thus emerges, that when it is high water at Newhaven and Brighton it will always be low water at St. Mary's and Morlaix. When it is low water at Brighton it will always be high water at Morlaix. When it is unusually high at Brighton it will be unusually low at Morlaix and when it is rising at Brighton it will be falling at Morlaix. In the Thames Estuary high water occurs about an hour later than at Dover and so on. Thus at all other localities throughout our waters tides can be studied and observations taken so that a complete pattern is formed, ruled strictly by the gyrations of the earth and moon around the sun. This pattern can be exactly timed, with only unusual weather conditions causing a significant deviation from the pattern.

STREAMS AND CURRENTS

As explained previously the horizontal movements of water brought about by the moon and sun are known as streams. The movements caused by wind and convection are termed *currents*. Obviously it is important to differentiate between the two, one of which is associated with oscillations to and fro, the other with a permanent or semi-permanent movement in one direction, and the terms should be used correctly. Unfortunately, perhaps the most famous of all the currents is called the Gulf Stream; however, in the normal course of navigation there is no risk of confusion amongst yachtsmen sailing our European waters where currents rarely need to be considered.

The speed of streams is expressed in knots, usually to one decimal place. On tidal stream atlases (which are described in the next chapter) the Admiralty, French and Dutch hydrographers leave out the decimal point, since they aim to show spring and neap rates together and the inclusion of a decimal pont would be confusing. For example, a rate shown as 20.35 would indicate 2 knots at neaps and 3.5 knots at springs. The tidal stream charts in Part 2 of this manual, **The Yachtsman's Tidal Atlases**, use a different system of computing rates and show only the mean rate, which in this case would be 2.7 knots, simply shown as 2.7.

FLOOD AND EBB STREAMS

The flood stream enters estuaries and harbours, the in-going waters rising to cover the foreshore as it progresses, and the ebb reverses the process. The flood stream used to be the basis for our buoyage system, with port-hand buoys to port and starboard-hand buoys to starboard as seen from a vessel moving inwards on the flood stream. But the terms flood and ebb cause some confusion because many channel harbours and estuaries are quite obviously ebbing while half a mile outside, the English Channel is equally obviously still flooding eastwards towards Dover. To make the system work it was necessary to define, where doubt might exist, where the flood stream went. Even so, catastrophic accidents occurred. The IALA system largely retains the old system for channels approaching and entering harbours, but discontinues the system offshore in favour of cardinal marks, which means it is no longer important to define the flood stream. Nevertheless, flood is a term which is still in use although preferable terms are those such as *in-going* or *east-going*.

ROTARY AND RECTILINEAR STREAMS

Streams in the English Channel generally oscillate back and forth, but investigation will show that in open waters the streams often change direction slowly, sometimes going right round the compass so that each particle of water travels in a circle (or more likely, an ellipse) arriving back in the same position after one complete tidal oscillation lasting an average of 12 hours and 25 minutes. These streams are known as *rotary*, and often each particle of water will be permanently on the move. Streams in the waters surrounding Guernsey, Herm and Sark are rotary in an anti-clockwise direction, while those surrounding the Scilly Isles are rotary in a clockwise direction. In both groups of islands the streams between the islands cannot possibly be rotary since they are restricted to narrow channels and are bound to move first in one direction and then in the opposite direction; these streams are called *rectilinear*. Such streams occur in estuaries, between islands, in the central English Channel, the Bristol and St. Georges Channels and in the Dover Strait and many other places. Rectilinear streams may also have rotary components, for example when a predominantly rectilinear stream becomes rotary at the end of an oscillation before returning in the opposite direction. However, these terms are mainly of academic interest; in practice the yachtsman will turn the pages of the tidal stream atlases, noting the direction of the streams and where they change and planning passages accordingly.

SLACK WATER

When streams slow down and stop before changing direction, they are said to be *slack*. Rotary streams do not usually have a slack period, though they may have them in certain combinations with rectilinear streams. Slack is a relative term: a rectilinear stream which attains a rate of 5 knots may be regarded as slack when the rate drops to half a knot, whereas a 2 knot stream may only be regarded as slack when its movement becomes negligible. The Admiralty tidal stream atlases use the term slack, the French use the term *nul* together with symbols while the Dutch use only symbols. All the tidal stream charts in Part 2 of this manual use the descriptive terms *nil* and *weak*.

RACES, OVERFALLS AND TIDE RIPS

These terms describe tidal conditions which are sometimes so similar as to be indistinguishable. The Alderney Race is easily and safely navigated by small boats although there are patches of heavy overfalls which should be avoided, and as in all other areas where streams run fast, strong winds opposed to the direction of the stream will throw up steep seas (as discussed later in Chapter 4). On the other hand the Portland Race has a central and dominant area of extremely violent seas which all mariners are careful to avoid. The Admiralty Channel Pilot describes overfalls over St. Alban's Ledge, a race over Peveril Ledge and off Handfast Point and rips are mentioned elsewhere. If in some misguided moment you take a boat into these turbulent areas, you cannot avoid noticing similarities in their character. The Mariner's Handbook does little to differentiate, describing *overfalls* or *tide rips* as "turbulence associated with the flow of strong tidal streams over abrupt changes in depth, or with the meeting of tidal streams flowing from different directions", and a *race* as "a fast running stream, usually tidal, caused by water passing through a restricted channel or over shallows or by convergent streams, or in the vicinity of headlands".

The yachtsman should treat all races, overfalls and rips with respect, seeking out information about them before approaching. To find oneself unprepared and unexpectedly in an area of turbulent and confused seas could result in a disaster. The chart symbol for overfalls and rips and used to indicate turbulence in races is:

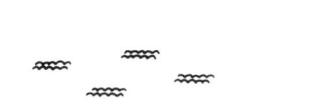

Figure 1.1

However, these symbols may not be very conspicuous on a small-scale chart of a complex area. The exact position of the overfalls may alter as streams change direction and they will generally disappear altogether at slack water although the seas may continue to be disturbed. More detailed information can be found in "Admiralty Sailing Directions", which however, are difficult to read. These show the times at which streams start to run on the ebb and on the flood, related to a Standard Port for that area and to Dover, and the cycle of the streams with their rates and how they affect the overfalls. Other pilots written for yachtsmen may quite simply advise the yachtsman what time to depart from a particular port to avoid the worst of the overfalls, what areas to avoid on passage and what conditions to expect on approach and arrival. Many of the lesser areas of turbulence are not charted or reported in the pilots, but in daytime they can often be seen and avoided. In fresh winds when white horses are present they are not so easily spotted, and at night there may be no hope of avoiding them. Under such circumstances the yacht should be put onto a comfortable point of sailing to attain good steering speed and control, and be carefully eased through.

EDDIES

Tidal streams create eddies behind headlands, islands and underwater obstructions. These eddies take many forms, the most significant being swirls of water less than a hundred yards across, but which are sometimes quite fierce and will grab a yacht, causing it to yaw violently. These are innocuous in otherwise calm water, but they are probably a major constituent of overfalls and races. Other eddies are of enormous proportions, as for instance the eddies which form first on one side and then on the other, behind the Bill of Portland and which at springs cause a massive swirl some 8 to 10 miles in diameter, affecting the direction of the inshore stream for miles around. Eddies form almost everywhere behind headlands and are most noticeable where streams run fastest. As a general rule, eddies do not take shape until their parent main streams have gained full velocity and are beginning to wane. Thus a north-east-going stream in the Alderney Race runs for about three hours before a chain of inshore eddies joins to create an opposing inshore stream from Cherbourg to Cap de la Hague.

Eddies are very numerous and many are not recorded, but are often known to locals. The more prominent ones are used regularly by yachtsmen who, by keeping close inshore, can find a favourable stream going in one direction or sail offshore to find another favourable stream if they wish to go in the opposite direction. In Part 2 of this manual some of these eddies are illustrated, but there are many others. A good rule-of-thumb when stemming an unfavourable stream is to get close inshore behind headlands where the main stream will often be less strong and where there is a chance that a favourable eddy will be found to assist the yacht in the required direction perhaps two or three hours before the main stream changes direciton. One cautionary note is necessary: the most powerful streams produce strong eddies, but somewhere within the system the eddy is likely to converge again with its parent stream, causing a race or overfalls, which for a comfortable passage should be avoided. Small eddies near overfalls, or in the vicinity of shoals and ledges are shown on charts as follows:

Figure 1.2

On tidal stream atlases, large tidal eddies are indicated in exactly the same way as the main streams, by arrows and where possible their rates are given.

TIDAL SET AND DRIFT

Small cruising yachts propelled by sail and perhaps with only a modest auxiliary engine may be capable of an average speed through the water of no more than 5 or 6 knots. Most yachtsmen will encounter streams which reach at least 3 or 4 knots, and in some localities streams will exceed the top speed of the yacht through the water. It is important therefore that yachtsmen understand tides and tidal streams.

Any vessel in tidal waters will be carried along by the stream even though the vessel may be heading in quite a different direction. It is important to appreciate that an entire body of water, which could be as wide as the English Channel and about half its length, may move as a whole at a speed of say, 2 or 3 knots, carrying with it all vessels navigating on its surface whether they are supertankers or small yachts and irrespective of the various speeds and headings they may be making. All vessels are affected by the tidal stream, and the direction they are being borne in is known as the *set* while the distance they are being carried is known as the *drift*. These terms, when used to describe the effect of a tidal stream upon a vessel can be illustrated as follows:

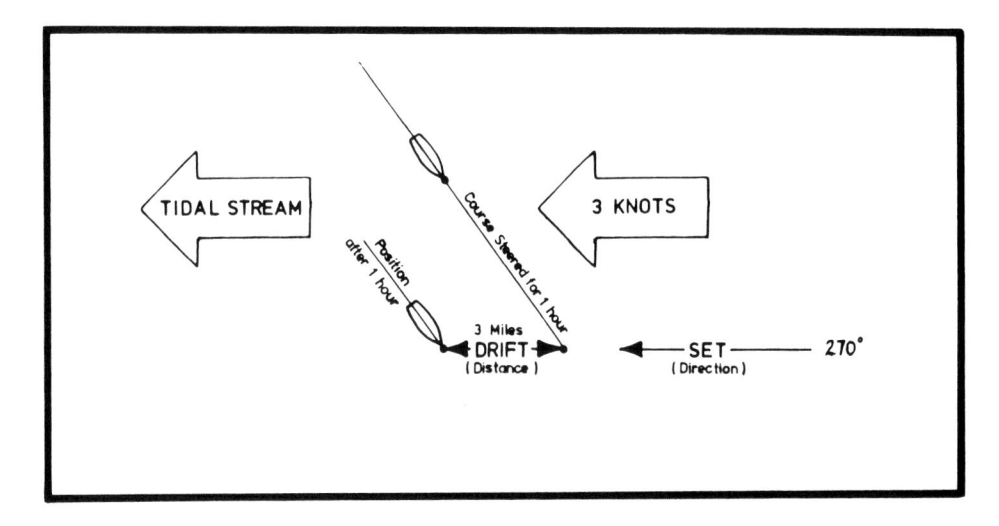

Figure 1.3

The term *set* can refer not only to the influence of streams upon a vessel, but also to the direction of the streams themselves: a stream setting 090° is going towards the east, unlike easterly winds which go towards the west. Thus it may be said that a vessel is set southwards off a course steered, by a southerly tidal stream. It may also be said that a stream sets onto islands or rocks, meaning that it is going in the direction of those dangers.

INSET
The term *inset* describes the tendency of a vessel bound along a coast to be drawn into bays, which can result in serious errors of navigation during bad visibility. The tendency is well known and very real, but an adequate explanation is difficult and is not often attempted. Tidal stream atlases display arrows showing that streams enter bays and further arrows indicate that these same streams follow the contours of the coastline to the far headland where they rejoin the main stream. On the face of it, the navigator may well conclude that the streams setting into a bay are negated by the streams which, at the other end of the bay, are setting out, and conclude that no allowance for inset is therefore necessary. Quite clearly the atlases, including those in Part 2 of this manual, must sometimes lack important information. Each bay and each headland will have individual peculiarities, so it is not possible to pinpoint the causes, but it is likely that they fall into one of two categories. Firstly, all streams running along a coastline, whether of bays, headlands or straight stretches of coastline, will be slowed by friction against the shallowing bottom and the shoreline. The stream will be turned shorewards in much the same way as waves are turned, with the upper levels of water rolling over the sluggish lower levels. These in turn will be displaced towards deeper water so that although the average movement of the water at the upper and lower levels may run parallel to the coast, the upper level upon which boats float will be edged towards the shore. The second explanation touches upon the peculiarities of bays, which of geographical necessity must stand between headlands and which therefore are almost certain to be the site of eddies as already described. Some of these eddies are very well documented, as is demonstrated in the tidal stream charts of Part 2, Channel Ports and Approaches; there are others, almost certainly in existence, which are not documented. As has been explained, these eddies form behind headlands and set up inshore streams running contrary to the direction of the main offshore stream. By their very nature, eddies are circular movements, and the movement running contrary to the main stream is powered by this same offshore stream; here then is a clear source of inshore sets, often poorly documented but likely to be present during considerable periods of each tidal oscillation.

HIGH AND LOW WATER AND STANDS
High water and *low water* are the highest and lowest levels reached in one tidal cycle. In some places, for example at Poole and Le Havre, the level of water remains almost constant for a few hours, and this static period is known as a *stand*.

RANGE
Tides rise and fall, rising above mean level to high water and then falling about an equal amount below mean level to low water. The difference in height between low water and high water of one tide is the *range*. The range is important to those using Admiralty or Dutch tidal stream atlases as in the systems adopted in these publications it is the range which is used to calculate the rate of tidal streams. Mean neap range is the average range at neap tides and mean spring range is the average at spring tides. Mean range is the average range of all tides, but this figure is of no practical interest. All neap tides are, as far as the yachtsman is concerned, of rather similar range, but there is a great variation in spring ranges. One spring can be of enormous proportions, producing ranges (and streams) of over 2½ times those at neaps; other springs can be quite small, producing ranges

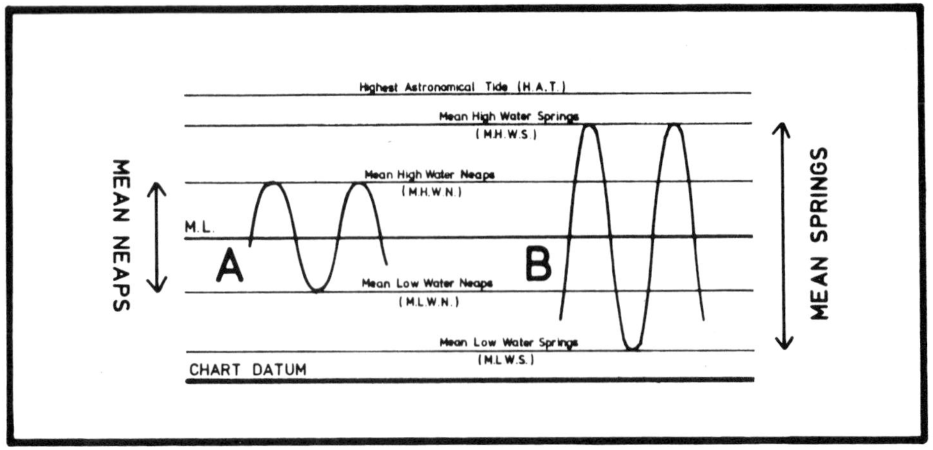

These curves indicate the pattern of tidal heights at Cherbourg, which are reasonably typical and without the oddities found at some places. Curve A gives an impression of the magnitude of neap tides, this being an average or mean neap curve. Curve B shows an average or mean spring tide to the same scale: note that it is slightly more than double the size of neaps.

Figure 1.4

(and streams) little more than 1½ times those at neaps. To give a practical example, on the coast near Cherbourg a rock which has 2.3 metres of water over it at low water neaps will have about 1 metre over it at low water on a lesser spring, but will be awash at low water of a large spring tide. In the Bristol Channel and in the Gulf of St. Malo the comparison is even more dramatic. The occasions when the lesser and greater spring tides occur seem to most of us to be quite random: one cannot look at the moon and declare it to be fuller or newer than usual and therefore expect a greater spring tide, but the magnitude of springs is far from random, being precisely controlled by the astronomical clock. In practice, tide tables can be consulted to obtain the precise figures needed for navigation.

LAT AND HAT
The biggest range of tide occurs when all the favourable astronomical influences coincide, producing the highest predictable high tide and the lowest predictable low tide, the two tending to occur over the same short period. These are known as *highest astronomical tide* (HAT) and *lowest astronomical tide* (LAT).

MEAN LEVELS
It is said to be a *neap* tide when the tidal range is small, and about a week later there is a *spring* tide when the range is large. The average level of high water at neaps is calculated over a typical year, and this level is known as *mean high water neaps* (MHWN). Similarly the level of low water at neaps is calculated and is known

as *mean low water neaps* (MLWN). Springs are treated in the same way, producing figures for *mean high water springs* (MHWS) and *mean low water springs* (MLWS).

Mean sea level (MSL) and *mean tide level* (MTL) amount to very much the same; they are differing methods of determining the average level of the sea. Mean tide level is calculated by averaging the levels of MHWS, MHWN, MLWS and MLWN and is usually known to the yachtsman as *mean level* (ML).

Mean high water (MHW) and *mean low water* (MLW) describe the average of all the high and all the low waters, but these terms are of little use to the yachtsman.

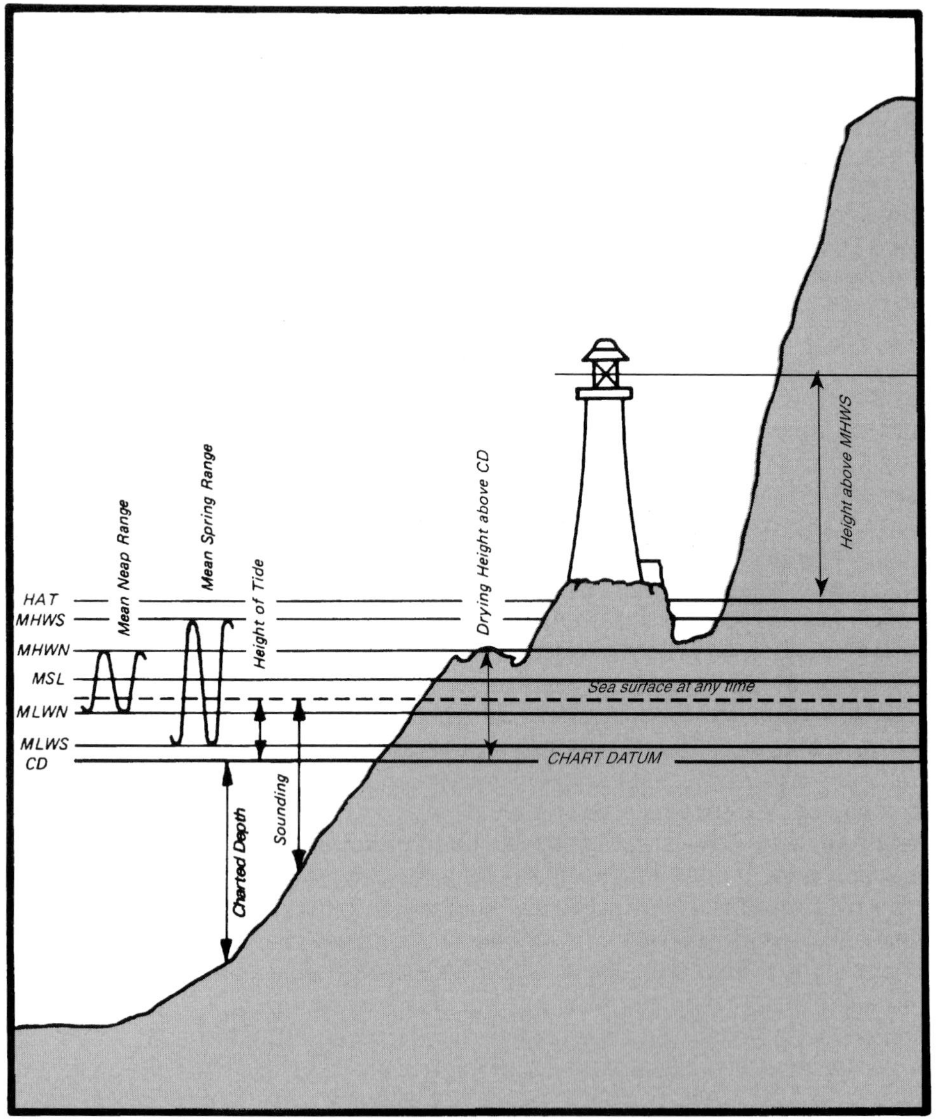

Figure 1.5

CHART DATUM

The tide rises in some places much more than in others, and in rare localities known as *amphidromic points*, there is no rise at all. But wherever tides rise and fall, they will always fall lowest at the biggest springs; at the false amphidromic points near Poole and Arklow the lowest level to which the tide will fall (LAT) will only be about one metre below the sea's mean level. At places such as St. Malo and Avonmouth the lowest level to which the tide will fall will be 6½ or 7 metres below mean level. The lowest predictable level of the tide varies from place to place, but it is this lowest level (LAT) which is used for the datum of all our modern charts, datum being the level from which all measurements of the sea, both upwards and downwards, are made. Thus *Chart Datum* is established, which is as near as is conveniently possible the same level as LAT on all metric charts (old fathoms charts have a datum which approximates to MLWS and which can make quite a large difference in some areas, resulting in less water than calculations indicate). All tidal heights are measured from this level upwards and since the main concern of the navigator is the depth of water required for his vessel, all soundings are measured from this level downwards. In this way the depth of water at any particular location can be found by reference to the sounding marked on the chart, to which is added the height of tide at that time, to give the total depth of water.

MAKING AND TAKING OFF

Tides which are increasing their range, day by day, towards springs are described as *making*, and those which are decreasing in range are *taking off*.

RISE

The vertical distance between Chart Datum and the level of high water is known as *rise*; however this term must not be confused with range, which is the vertical distance between low and high water. The alternative phrase *height of high water*, meaning the same as rise, is preferable.

AWASH

In the strictest sense, the term *awash* refers to rocks or other objects whose topmost level is the same (or very nearly the same) as Chart Datum; this means that they only show on the surface at times of very low spring tides (LAT). However, the term is often very loosely used, for instance to describe a feature "awash two hours after high water". The Admiralty use the term to mean the approximate level of Chart Datum and when the word is encountered elsewhere care should be taken to understand the context.

DRYING HEIGHTS, COVERED AND UNCOVERED

Rocks and other features which are covered and then uncovered by the tide are said to *dry*. The actual height of drying features is measured from Chart Datum, and on metric charts is shown to one decimal place with the metre figure underlined. The height given will obviously never exceed the height of high water at springs otherwise the feature would not then fulfil the requirement that it should cover. All the symbols for features which cover and uncover are illustrated in Admiralty Chart 5011.

HEIGHTS

Heights, other than the drying heights already mentioned, are given in metres above MHWS; these heights include terrestrial objects such as lighthouses, headlands, islands and rocks, which in almost all instances are never covered by the tide. There are a few slightly confusing instances where a rock is shown, for example as 0.3 metres high, which means that it is 0.3 metres above MHWS, yet the rock is below the level of HAT, which means that it actually covers. However these instances occur very rarely, and deserve only the briefest mention. There are methods of finding the distance of a vessel from an object of known height, this distance being known as *distance off*. One method is by the use of a sextant, and another is by the dipping distance of lights — the taller a lighthouse the further away it can be seen; the position where it disappears or *dips* below the horizon is the *dipping distance* and this can be a very useful navigational aid to yachtsmen. Obviously as the tide goes down, the lighthouse in effect gets taller and will be seen from further away, increasing the dipping distance.

HEIGHTS EXPOSED BY FALL OF TIDE

The extent of the fall of tide below MHWS may be called *height exposed by fall of tide* or *exposed height*. In practice this is found by consulting the Tidal Heights charts and tables in Part 2 of this manual to discover the height of tide (in metres above Chart Datum) for the required time. This figure is subtracted from MHWS (found from the chart or almanac) to give the exposed height, which is the figure by which charted heights are adjusted to allow for the tidal fall. Remembering that objects get *taller* as the tide goes down, this figure is *added* to the charted height. The adjusted charted height figure can then be applied to the tables in the almanacs to determine the dipping distance.

STANDARD AND SECONDARY PORTS

Each successive tidal oscillation is accompanied by a wave producing tidal heights, varying in size with the astronomical conditions. The heights at various ports along the coasts are calculated and tabulated to form tide tables, and the ports selected for these predictions are the *Standard Ports*. In the area covered by this manual the British Admiralty have 30 Standard Ports, 18 of which are in the British Isles, 11 on the continent and 1 in the Channel Islands; the times and heights of high and low waters are predicted and published each year for all these ports.

There are a great number of ports and other places where tidal heights will follow a pattern similar to that of a nearby Standard Port, and these locations are known as *secondary ports*. They are so named, not because of any secondary importance either geographically or otherwise, but because it is convenient to link them with a nearby tidal regime. The times and heights of high and low water at secondary ports are found by modifying Standard Port figures, using time and height differences supplied. Most yachtsmen's almanacs use this system, the selected ports often being those of most interest to the yachtsman.

It is the contention of the author that the profusion of Standard Ports is undesirable, because data quite adequate for the yachtsman can be obtained by phasing upon just one Standard Port, provided that this port is carefully selected. In this manual the port used is Cherbourg, which is central to the area covered; it has a height of high water (rise) suitable for tabulation of related data, the regime is uncomplicated and above all, the mean level is relatively stable. Single-port phasing is described in detail in Chapter 3.

2 Tidal Publications

PUBLICATIONS

The British Admiralty and the French and Dutch hydrographic authorities carry out surveys and publish data for the area covered by this manual, and the excellence of this material cannot be overstated. Clearly, the publications are intended to provide a means of safe navigation for commercial shipping and for naval vessels; that some of the publications are useful for yachtsmen is fortuitous, and where it is necessary to point out the inadequacies or to criticise the intricacies of some of these publications, that is only because they are not designed primarily for our use.

CHARTS

Tidal stream information is given on most charts, and is therefore readily to hand for the navigator. The majority of charts for our home waters are now in metric form with Chart Datum at approximate LAT and are therefore suitable for use with all the published tide tables and with the tidal height tables in Part 2.

Featured on many of the charts are "diamond" symbols at certain locations, each symbol containing a letter which relates to tabulated information elsewhere on the face of the chart. These tables give the direction and rate of spring and neap streams at the chosen locations for each hour of the tidal cycle, from 6 hours before to 6 hours after high water at a convenient Standard Port. The diamond symbols can be difficult to find among all the other charted information and it may be necessary to refer first to the tables and then to plot the position of the diamond from the latitude and longitude given in the table. The tidal stream information extracted from these tables is of limited use to the yachtsman for two reasons: firstly, the data refers to specific places, with no indication about where streams have come from or what course they take when they leave and although in the Solent or the Thames Estuary the diamonds are fairly numerous, in the approaches to other ports such as Poole, St. Helier or St. Malo they are sparse and often in unhelpful positions. Secondly, and much more importantly, no means are provided for interpolating or extrapolating between springs and neaps, which at some time or another may lead to considerable error, particularly at periods near springs.

TIDAL STREAM ATLASES

The hydrographic authorities of Britain, France and Holland publish tidal stream atlases. These consist of small scale charts of specific areas in book form, each book having 13 charts depicting the changing pattern of streams at hourly intervals throughout the tidal cycle, similar in general arrangement to the charts contained in **The Yachtsman's Tidal Atlases** in Part 2 of this manual. The British Admiralty's contribution is the greatest, and they offer some ten atlases covering the area under discussion, whereas the French have only three. The Dutch atlases are rather

special: they offer a range of splendid quality atlases in a large size (A3) and are ideal for yachtsmen; no-one visiting Holland should be without them. Their only drawback is that they lack one important ingredient — a means of computing stream rates, but this may be overlooked because in the eastern North Sea and in the Dutch delta areas the difference between spring and neap rates is much less marked. The British Admiralty and French stream atlases all contain, on the inside front covers, a means of computing the rate of streams between neaps and springs, which is of great importance to a slow moving yacht, but which is missing from other sources of tidal stream data. The streams are shown by arrows and their direction is determined by the use of a protractor. The rates of streams are shown in these atlases for both neaps and springs, for example, 19,33 indicating 1.9 knots at neaps and 3.3 knots at springs. An irritating difficulty immediately arises when using these atlases because one rarely finds oneself in the precise location of the figures; more often than not it is necessary to interpolate between two, or even three, sets of adjacent figures. These may be 20 or more miles apart, and therefore pose a problem as follows:

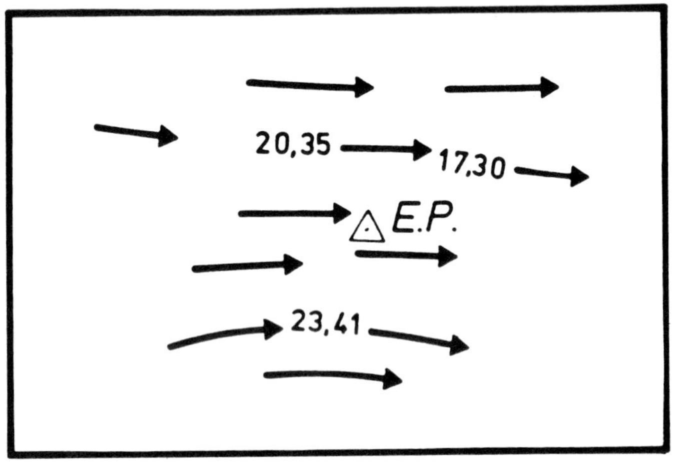

Figure 2.1

If the estimated position or fix is as indicated, then one would take advantage of all three sets of figures and come up with a mean of 20,35. But if the estimated position were further to the north then the modified mean of, say, 19,33 is rather more difficult to obtain by mental interpolation. Note that to complete the task accurately by using the computation facility provided inside the front cover, it is necessary to search out both the neap and the spring figures, since both are required (this is a problem which does not arise with the tidal stream atlases in

Part 2). Having reached the modified mean of 19.33 for the neap and spring rates, these figures are applied to the diagram for computation of rates. Also needed, in the case of Admiralty atlases, is the mean range of tide for that day at the relevant Standard Port (Dover for most atlases). When applied to the diagram as shown, the actual rate of stream in knots for the required location and time is thus found:

we rely on surveys which were carried out many decades ago. With the increased size and draught of commercial shipping there is a need to concentrate new surveys on the channels capable of carrying this monster traffic, but the latest Dutch stream atlases show us that data is still being collected about tidal movements, and its excellent quality reflects the techniques now available.

But how accurate are tidal predictions? Differences are evident when comparisons

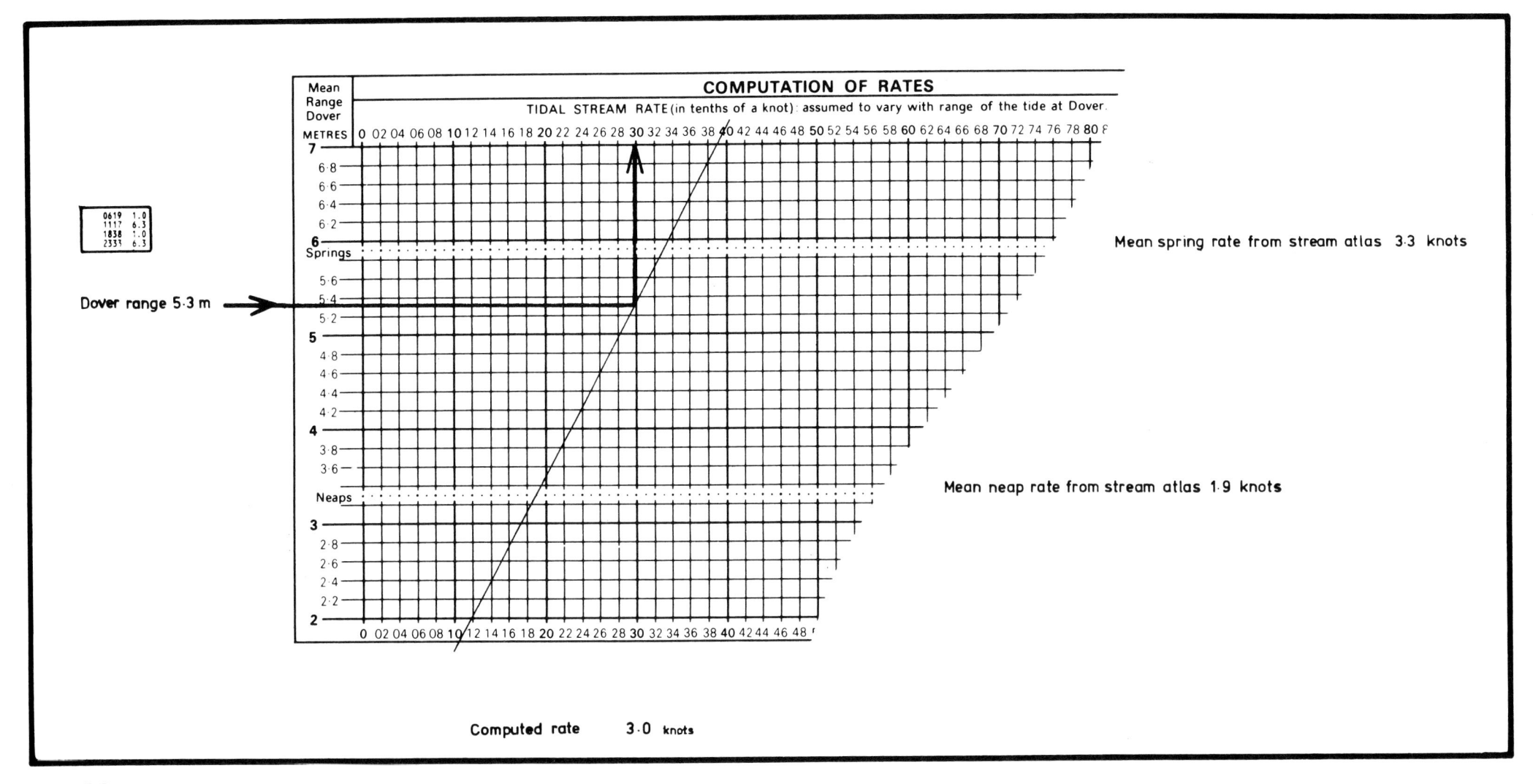

Figure 2.2

QUALITY OF PREDICTIONS

Survey ships containing highly qualified personnel and all the latest in technical aids investigate and record, as a continual process, all the features of the sea and the seabed, but for a great deal of the published data about tidal streams of tidal predictions are made. These differences can be exaggerated where interpolation becomes necessary. The conclusion reached must be that all predictions have their limitations and must be recognised as very useful approximations and averages.

We hear of rivers changing their course for no apparent reason, despite the banks which must inevitably have been formed, so the meandering of streams within the sea itself is fairly likely. Many yachtsmen have encountered surprising and unexpected surges of streams in the Solent, the surges lasting no more than 20 or 30 minutes before reverting to their predicted pattern. Similar surges probably occur in all our waters, some on a much larger scale. The French, in their volume "Courants de Maree" warn thus: "one may finally admit that, in good weather, and for streams of a maximum of 2 or 3 knots, the predicted speed at springs presents an approximation of 15% to 20% and the direction a possible error of 20 degrees. At neaps the relative errors on the speed are greater, but the streams being slower, the absolute error is comparable to that of springs".

It would be foolish to ignore tidal predictions on the grounds that they were inaccurate; they do at least give a good picture of the overall pattern and there is a reasonable chance that during a passage one vigorous surge may be counteracted by a weak one and that when averaged out the predictions will prove very reliable. The sensible approach is to use whatever figures are available, adjusting them meticulously to the best of our ability and applying them intelligently to our passage planning and chartwork, thus preventing any additional errors from magnifying those already present.

What has been said here about the reliability of stream predictions applies also to a great extent to height predictions, about which the Dutch publish interesting "probability graphs" for certain Dutch ports — these demonstrate that the greatest hazard to accuracy of predictions is the weather. This is discussed more fully in Chapter 4.

TIDAL HEIGHTS
The cruising yachtsman is concerned with tidal heights as he moves from coast to coast, entering many ports where passage may be restricted by bars, or where entry through locks or sills is governed by tidal height. Furthermore when previously unvisited small harbours and bays have to be approached, possibly in an emergency, tidal height information could be important and the lack of it a recipe for disaster.

The value of soundings as an aid to navigation, particularly in conditions of poor visibility, is often underestimated by the novice, though never by the yachtsman who has experience of their use. The echo-sounder is an accurate and reliable aid and with the flick of a switch, instant information about the depth of water is available; this information can be related to the chart as soon as adjustment is made for the height of tide. The figure presented by the echo-sounder can be divided into two elements: the depth of water from the sea-bed to Chart Datum (the charted depth) and the rise of tide from the level of Chart Datum to the surface. Before the figure obtained from the echo-sounder can be used on the chart the height of tide must therefore be subtracted. A method is propounded of determining position by recording corrected soundings, taken at intervals along a constant track, then comparing these soundings with those shown on the chart along a similar bearing. In theory at least this should be possible, particularly in areas where there are distinct changes in depth, as for instance when crossing the Hurd Deep. But usually it will be found that soundings, corrected for tidal height, are best used to establish a position on a "position line" of soundings shown on the chart (for example on a 10 metre line) and is especially valuable if a second position line is available to establish a fix. If soundings are used to corroborate fixes on every occasion, even in good visibility, then confidence and peace of mind is established for the occasions when conditions worsen.

SPRING AND NEAP CURVES
Speaking very generally, the Western Approaches are exposed to the unmodified forces of the tides, which does not necessarily mean that all tides will be higher, but often means that spring tides will rise very much higher than neaps. In areas not so geographically exposed the differences are much less. Thus at St. Helier, the spring range is 2.45 times that at neaps, whereas at Le Havre it is only 1.84 times the neap range, and even less than this in areas of the North Sea.

The various patterns of rise and fall are demonstrated by the *mean spring* and *mean neap* curves in the Admiralty tide tables (and the Dutch equivalents). Examples of mean spring and neap curves are shown in Figure 2.3.

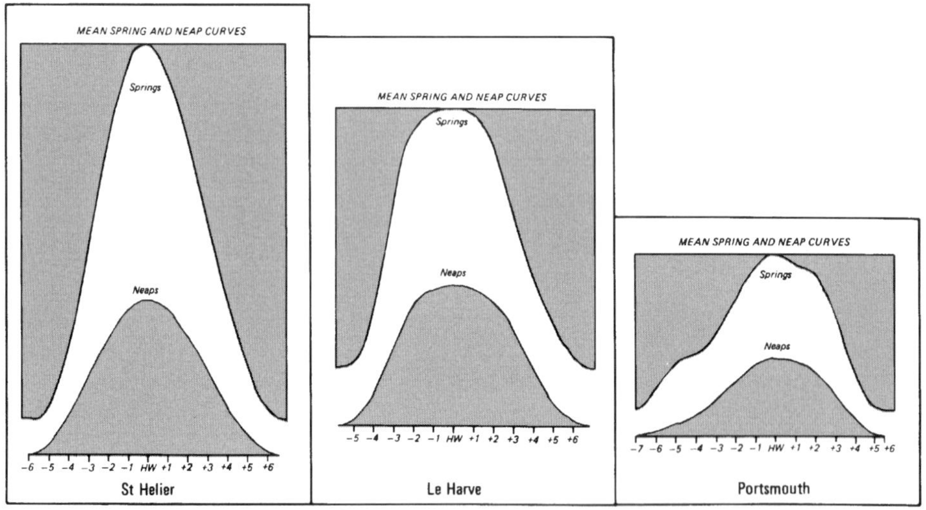

Figure 2.3

St. Helier has a steep curve, with no stand at high or low water, and the curve is nicely symmetrical. Le Havre has by comparison, a full curve; the port is fed by the main Channel flood and by the Seine ebb, creating a stand at high water which in its turn produces a powerful wave which travels some 70 miles up the Seine Maritime to Rouen in a single tide and which sometimes on a big spring will give birth to a bore. At Portsmouth there is a slow rise to high water, then a hesitation and a suggestion of the double high water which occurs throughout the Solent proper and which is more marked at Southampton. This is followed by a very rapid fall during the two and a half hours before low water, causing very strong ebb streams in the rivers and harbour mouth. From these curves the variations in the pattern of rise and fall can be seen. The normal curves, which occur in open waters away from geographical influences and which are predominant in many coastal areas, are similar to a simple cosine curve and form the basis of many systems for determining the heights of tide between the times of high and low water. Only the Admiralty and the Dutch provide spring and neap curves, and with them a means of predicting with any accuracy the heights at intermediate times.

CALCULATION OF TIDAL HEIGHTS

Navigational courses for yachtsmen generally use a system which is based on Admiralty tide tables or those contained in yachtsman's almanacs, for finding heights between high and low water. In theory, these meticulous calculations provide an accurate method of finding tidal heights but they are unlikely to be undertaken even on a normal fair-weather passage. Under fraught conditions or in deteriorating weather when answers are needed in a hurry, their very complexity makes them prone to error and slow to use.

TWELFTHS RULE

A rule-of-thumb method for gauging tidal heights is often recommended and is so simple that the calculations can be done mentally, though yachtsmen would be well advised to use pencil and paper since even the most simple arithmetic can go stupidly wrong under stress or fatigue.

The rule is that during the first hour of rise or fall from low water or high water the extent of rise or fall will be $1/12$ of the range; during the second hour it will be $2/12$ and during the third hour the rise or fall will be $3/12$ of the range:

LW + 1 hour	rise = $1/12$ of range
LW + 2 hours	rise = $2/12$ of range
LW + 3 hours	rise = $3/12$ of range
HW − 3 hours	rise = $3/12$ of range
HW − 2 hours	rise = $2/12$ of range
HW − 1 hour	rise = $1/12$ of range

To apply this rule it is therefore necessary to find the heights of high and low water for the required location and subtract one from the other to find the range. This is then divided by twelve and the rule applied. It must be remembered that the rule is applied to the *range* and the resulting figure must first be subtracted from the high water height or added to the low water height before being applied to Chart Datum to be of use for navigation.

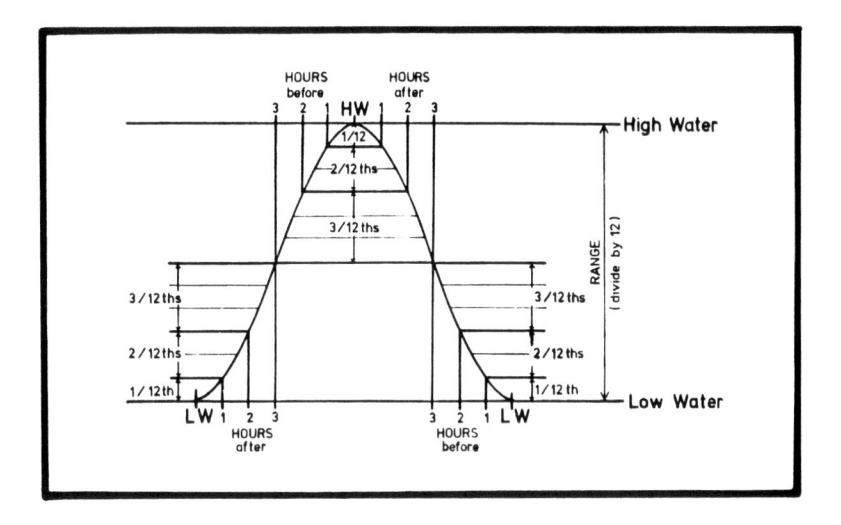

Figure 2.4

This method gives only approximations, which are infinitely better than guesswork or ignorance. It takes no account of the variations in the tidal curves or in the duration of the rise or fall, as it is assumed that both the rise and fall will take six hours and that the pattern of the tide will follow approximately that of a simple cosine curve. It also calls for adding and subtracting which, although simple, can still go wrong under difficult conditions.

MANUAL OF TIDES PART 2 — TIDAL HEIGHTS

The tidal heights tables in the four **Yachtsman's Tidal Atlases** which make up Part 2 of this manual present tidal information for nearly 200 ports and places together with numerous offshore locations. The information presented provides intant tidal heights for these locations for every hour of every day of the year and needs no calculation to use and apply. Although these predictions do not quite match the superb precision of other calculation-based systems, they are certainly adequate for most yachtsmen. They are very quick and simple to use, and as they need no calculation at all are not so prone to error, making them ideal for use in small craft.

19

3 Single-Port Phasing

SINGLE-PORT PHASING

A mass of tidal data has accumulated over the years, and in this computer age, the predictions pour onto paper, year after year. The French produce annual figures for British ports referred to French Standard Ports, and the Admiralty produce figures for French ports referred to British Standard Ports. In the Thames Estuary there are five standard ports and in the Dover Strait there are two more, whereas in the West Country from Bridport in Dorset to St. Mary's in the Scilly Isles, 150 miles westward, there is only one. The Admiralty tidal stream atlas for the Thames Estuary is referred principally to the time of HW at Sheerness, whereas the atlas for the Irish Sea is referred principally to the time of HW at Dover. The endless repetition of tidal oscillations, all essentially alike except for their magnitude, tends to be obscured by a multiplicity of publications and an over-enthusiasm for exactitude. Precision is of course necessary in navigation, except where it becomes so tedious and involved that short cuts and guesswork creep in. It was therefore inevitable that at some time this mass of information would be looked at with a view to reassembling it in a simpler way: one which is more suitable for use by the yachtsman. This has been the aim in compiling the **Yachtsman's Tidal Atlases.**

High water at Avonmouth in the Bristol Channel is, at springs, about 3 hours 47 minutes before high water at Dover and will never deviate from this by much more than 10 minutes and even this deviation is related to the magnitude of the oscillation. Thus the time difference of 3 hours 47 minutes will decrease to, say 3 hours 38 minutes on a big spring tide and increase to 3 hours 56 minutes on a small spring tide. This pattern continues as the range reduces to neaps, when the time difference increases steadily to 4½ hours or more. The essential point is that, given any specific magnitude of oscillation, the difference in times of high and low water at places throughout the area from the Western Approaches to the English Channel to the Wash and Den Helder can be calculated as constants to within an accuracy of a very few minutes.

At St. Helier, spring tides always reach high water in the morning and evening, and if a spring tide of truly average proportions attains high water there at 2100 hours, then 52 minutes later (to within 10 minutes) it will be high water at Avonmouth, and 40 minutes later at approximately 22.32 hours it will be high water at Cherbourg. The maximum variation in timing in areas where the range of tide is appreciable is, at high springs, predicted to be in the order of about plus or minus 5 minutes either side of the average. It is this precision in timing which makes it possible to phase all tidal movement upon the time of high water at one Standard Port. It is of course important to select a port where the tidal regime is regular and undistorted. From there, it is only a short step to decide that the measurement of the size of the oscillation shall be the height attained by the tide at that same Standard Port. Thus all that is needed to use the system is the time and height of high water at the one selected Standard Port. Neap tides, and tides in areas where the range is very small behave with less discipline, but since the rise and fall is much less, the precise timing is less important and the overall accuracy of height prediction is much the same as for springs.

In his earlier work the author selected Dover as the Standard Port for single-port phasing. Dover has the advantage that traditionally it is the port upon which British tidal constants have been calculated, and Dover tide tables are readily available in a dozen or more almanacs and diaries. However, when considering single-port phasing for a large area from the Western Channel to the Southern North Sea, the disadvantage of Dover becomes apparent. When big springs are just taking off, vessels sailing in the West Country or Brittany can be experiencing one tidal oscillation, but be using height and stream measurements based upon the magnitude of the previous oscillation. Although this introduces only very slight errors since succeeding oscillations change in magnitude only very gradually, it is still a source of error which can be reduced (though not entirely eliminated) by using a more centrally situated port. There are also occasional fluctuations of sea level at Dover, due to the interaction of tidal streams in the English Channel and the North Sea, which can introduce further errors.

A port of reference upon which predictions of greater accuracy can be made for the many ports and places covered in the tidal atlases of Part 2, is Cherbourg. It lies approximately midway between Fastnet and Den Helder and has a tidal regime comparatively free from oddities and sea level fluctuations. It is therefore from Cherbourg tidal data that the author has calculated times for the various magnitudes of oscillation and then applied them to spring and neap curves (often modified or redrawn) to complete the tidal height detail. The figures thus assembled are given in the Tidal Height tables adjacent to the charts in Part 2 of this manual.

INSTANT TIDAL HEIGHTS

It is the contention of the author, and no doubt the conviction of every experienced yachtsman, that soundings and their related tidal heights are of prime importance to navigation, particularly when making landfalls. Indeed, there can be nothing that is more important, since the vessel is designed for water and any lack of this commodity is a threat to its safety. Although soundings may have only a minor role in verifying positions and fixes, they have a major role in preserving the safety of the vessel and its crew. Bear in mind that any combination of position lines can constitute a fix, and even a single position line can be of immense value. Soundings can provide a position line at the flick of a switch, and the yachtsman needs only to know the tidal height to relate these soundings to his chart. For this reason the author has given special attention to the supply of instant tidal height information, which is contained in the Part 2 tidal atlases.

It must be appreciated that by using a system of single-port phasing for tidal height predictions one is departing from the intricate exactitude of computerised results, adopting instead a vast string of averages: average times differences, average height differences and average sea levels. Such averages would be very accurate indeed if every tide of the same magnitude behaved in exactly the same fashion, but this would call for some slight re-arrangement of the heavenly bodies! As this is obviously not a possibility, the tide-generating forces will continue to be complex. It is therefore, a question of the degree of accuracy which is acceptable to the yachtsman: if the Twelfths Rule, or any system which does not employ spring and neap curves, is acceptable, then the system of single-port phasing must be acceptable on the ground of accuracy alone. There is however, a further enormous advantage: single-port phasing calls for no calculation and therefore allows less room for the slips and stupid mistakes which are almost inevitable when carried out on a dimly lit, moving chart table. The figures are read off for each hour of the tidal cycle, only requiring occasional simple mental interpolation between two columns of figures (and perhaps between successive hourly predictions) — an expertise which in all the other systems is required to a much greater degree. The figures extracted are also ready for chartwork, as they are related to Chart Datum.

INSTANT TIDAL STREAM RATES

At high springs, high water at Avonmouth occurs at about 3¾ hours before high water at Dover, while at neaps it occurs 45 minutes earlier at about 4½ hours before high water at Dover. Anyone producing a tidal stream atlas referred to Dover (for example, the Admiralty) and showing the direction of stream with an arrow, is faced with a problem. At 4 hours before high water at Dover a neap tide will have reached its peak at Avonmouth half an hour earlier and will already be ebbing, whereas a spring tide will not yet have reached its peak and will still be flooding. In a case like this there has to be a compromise, since to show a neap arrow ebbing and a spring arrow flooding would be confusing and impracticable. This is resolved by indicating that the streams are *slack*. This sort of compromise often has to be made in tidal stream atlases, and those in Part 2 are no exception. A similar compromise is made in connection with tidal heights where the terms *high water* and *low water* may have to describe an average between neaps and springs.

Tidal stream information contained in the Part 2 atlases is presented in much the same way as in traditional atlases except for the use of the *mean* or average figure for the rate of stream rather than the double set of figures showing neap and spring rates. Thus a mean rate of 2.6 knots may be used where, on Admiralty, French or Dutch tidal atlases the rate may be shown as 19,33 indicating 1.9 knots at neaps and 3.3 knots at springs. The latter method has the advantage of flexibility where spring rates are proportionately greater or lesser than average when compared with neap rates, but suffers the disadvantage, already discussed, of requiring interpolation between two or perhaps even three or four sets of figures. A further disadvantage lies in the temptation to use the spring rate for each and every spring tide, rather than to use the somewhat tiresome diagram for computing the rate accurately. The Part 2 atlases, using only the mean rate, make interpolation between the figures on the chart much easier, and also show many more rates — which is especially helpful to the yachtsman whose boat-speed through the water may, on average, be no more than 5 knots. The rates extracted are converted through tables alongside each tidal stream chart, the correct rate being determined by the height of high water for that particular tidal oscillation at the selected Standard Port on which the atlases are based (which is Cherbourg, for reasons already stated). The conversion tables in the atlases have been calculated to convert for stream regimes prevailing in the areas depicted, and therefore differ slightly from one area to another. In certain restricted waters spring streams sometimes run disproportionately fast, and where this occurs the mean rate shown on the chart has been biased towards the spring rate, so that when applied to the conversion table the error, if there is one, will tend to fall in the neap rates and therefore be of lesser significance.

ORIGIN OF TIDAL DATA

In compiling the Part 2 tidal atlases there have been no restrictions on the author, as there may well be on official hydrographers, to publish only that data which can be authenticated by surveys or records. A private researcher can investigate both official and unofficial publications, collecting information from cruising handbooks, club rule books, articles in magazines, from his own cruising experience and that of colleagues. This, together with the wealth of information contained in charts, pilots and other official publications, enables the investigator to develop a critical eye, looking for evidence of eddies where the signs indicate they should be, interpolating where recorded data fades and applying hourly figures to stream rates based only on the data available of maximum rates. This practice has been adopted where interpolations and assumptions would otherwise have to be made by the yachtsman on passage, perhaps under difficult conditions.

4 Tide and Weather

WIND AND TIDE

Tidal heights and tidal streams are both affected by winds, and for the same basic reason: the wind causes the sea to drift down-wind, thus increasing streams going in that direction and decreasing those going in the opposite direction. The tides flooding into bays, estuaries and harbours are augmented by wind-borne currents when the wind is onshore and reduced when the wind is offshore. Allowance can be made for this effect if the extent of the phenomenon is known, but specific information is very limited.

Admiralty Pilots and the "Mariners Handbook" have sections dealing with natural conditions including wind-induced currents and indicate that if the tidal streams are discounted there is an average residual current running east or north-east through the English Channel and into the North Sea, generally of less than ¼ knot, but which in strong and persistent westerly or south-westerly winds can increase to more than 1 knot. Winds in the opposite direction will slow the residual current and eventually reverse it. It is further stated that winds of Force 6 can produce a fully developed wind-induced current of about ½ knot in about 12 hours and a current of about 1¼ knots if winds of Force 9 continue for about 48 hours. These currents are affected by the rotation of the earth and do not therefore go directly down-wind, but veer to the right of down-wind possibly by as much as 30°. Quite obviously a wind-induced current in our waters will be constricted by geographical features, as are tidal streams, and consequently will be enhanced or reduced. While Admiralty figures suggest that wind-induced currents have a potential of variously, $1/30$th, $1/40$th or $1/70$th of wind speed when mature, the Dutch suggest a figure of $1/50$th.

If the wind is not simply a summer onshore breeze, but a feature of a weather pattern, then it would not be unreasonable, despite the conflicting data, to assume that these down-wind drifts are very real. In Chapter 5, methods of determining leeway are suggested, but these methods will probably not show up the allowance necessary to combat wind-induced currents which may only be present in open waters further offshore. Properly, the tidal stream set and drift should be adjusted to compensate for this movement of water, but if the veer to the right is discounted as being a relatively insignificant factor of dubious magnitude and if the movement may therefore always be considered as down-wind, then it is much more convenient to class it as an additional leeway constituent. A study of all the figures available suggests that a rule-of-thumb method is possible: for each wind force of the Beaufort scale, the same number of degrees should be added to leeway compensation. Thus, when winds are part of a steady weather pattern and for example, a Force 4 is blowing, an alteration of course to windward of 4 degrees to compensate for a downwind current would not be unreasonable. This assumes that the yacht has a speed of about 5 knots and the wind is on the beam; lesser allowances should be made on other points of sailing, particularly down-wind.

As has already been mentioned, the wind-induced currents will be constricted by geographical features and when after a considerable fetch a mature current meets a coastline, it will be deflected one way or the other along the coast, the velocity and the direction depending on the shape of the coastline and the influence of it upon the prevailing tidal streams. Where currents are blown into bays, shallow water areas and estuaries, they can increase tidal heights by a foot or more, but usually no more than two feet; offshore winds have the opposite effect to the same degree.

All tidal predictions can be modified by the above conditions, which are variable and complex, but which the yachtsman can solve by sound observation, seamanship and experience.

WAVES AND TIDE

It is well known that wind-against-tide conditions create steep seas, but this phrase tends to put the emphasis on the role of the wind so that one often concludes that the cause is solely the relative speeds of wind and water, whereas a better understanding is reached by examining the behaviour of the waves.

If a 20 knot wind is blowing in the same direction as a 5 knot tidal stream (as can often happen off headlands in the Bristol Channel, the Channel Islands or in the Alderney Race, as well as many other locations), then the wind is travelling over the water at only 15 knots (say Force 4), producing 3 or 4 foot waves. If the same wind is blowing, but now with a stream flowing in the opposite direction at the same 5 knots, then the wind will be passing over the water at 25 knots (say Force 6) producing waves 10 or 12 feet high. However, there is a worse effect which follows on from this.

As the wind blows, so waves are formed, and with the wind and waves appears a wind-induced current which increases steadily to maturity, the waves travelling along a base which is moving in much the same direction. The waves are nicely balanced, only occasionally falling over in a flurry of white water. If a tidal stream is also running in the same direction then the wave behaves in a stable way. If, however, the tidal stream changes direction so that the base on which the wave sits moves in the opposite direction to that of the wave while the crest continues to be blown down-wind, then the wave leans over steeply with the base being pulled out from under it, and it repeatedly falls over. Thus the tide changes a moderate, comfortable sea into a high, steep-fronted or hollow sea, without there being any change in wind force over the area as a whole.

The foregoing supposes winds of 20 knots and streams of 5 knots running first in one direction and then in the other, and describes the enormous differences that will occur in sea state. It should be clear that any combination of wind, wave and tide in opposition, even when the strengths of wind and stream are quite moderate, will produce steep seas immediately, the difference between a normal wave and a steep-fronted wave being a critical difference in its basic structure. Waves will have this steep, threatening character whenever there is resistance to movement of their base, for instance in shallowing water, or when seas are enclosed in a bay, river mouth or estuary without room for a relieving current to develop to leeward. Conditions will be made worse when a backwash forms at lower level.

To illustrate the problems likely to arise, a passage often undertaken by cruising yachtsmen is considered: the passage from Cherbourg to Guernsey via the Alderney Race. The distance is about 40 miles, and it hardly needs to be said that help must be extracted from the tidal streams; by travelling at a speed of about 5 or 6 knots, and even allowing for some tacking, the passage should take little more than 6 or 7 hours. Looking through the tidal stream atlas it is noted that the main stream past Cherbourg begins at about 3 hours after high water, and continues through the Alderney Race and on towards Guernsey for more than 6 hours. In this example the forecast is good but a predicted SW Force 4 will be dead ahead once round Cap de la Hague. Having departed Cherbourg (3 hours after high water) and sailed along the peninsular coast, the Alderney Race will be reached just as it is running at its fastest in the desired direction — towards Guernsey. But a very uncomfortable situation will now be found; with a Force 4 wind (say 14 knots) opposed to a tidal stream of perhaps 6 knots, the seas produced will be those expected in a 20 knot wind: waves 8 or 10 feet high, steep and breaking with patches of turbulent and tumbling seas caused by the rocky bottom. It is these conditions which give the Alderney Race a reputation for being a difficult place — a reputation shared by the Bristol Channel, the Russel Channels, and many other exposed places where streams run fast. But there is no turning back because the tidal stream is as fast, if not faster than the yacht's speed through rough water, even with the wind astern. There is nothing for it but to press on, perhaps edging towards the calmer waters nearer Alderney.

Needless to say, this trauma can be avoided, not only in the Alderney Race but in many other difficult areas, by careful timing. In the Channel Ports & Approaches section of Part 2, there are chartlets showing the streams and eddies along the Cherbourg Peninsula, and from these it can be seen that by leaving Cherbourg at high water, 3 hours earlier than previously described, the yacht, by keeping close inshore, can use these eddies and arrive at the Alderney Race at slack water, then pick up the main ebb just as it starts to run, taking the yacht on to Guernsey, or even Jersey, on one tide. This particular passage is described here as it illustrates very clearly the effect of tidal stream upon sea state.

The sea state which develops when wind and tide run in the same or opposite directions can be fairly easily comprehended. It is less easy to understand that tidal streams running across the path of the wind can also cause changes, often less noticeable, involving the direction in which the waves tend to turn and break towards the oncoming stream. There is also a subtle change in the vessel's attitude. As the wind passes over a moving body of water it causes the direction apparent to the yacht to change, and a close-hauled yacht will make more ground to windward when the tidal stream approaches and runs under the lee side of the yacht. This subject is discussed in detail in Chapter 8 which deals with windward passages across a tidal stream.

STORM SURGES

Storms, sometimes in relatively distant waters, cause surges to sweep along the Channel, often threatening and sometimes very seriously flooding the southern North Sea coast. These surges are usually heralded by a deep depression passing quickly to the north of Britain with storm-force winds driving a mass of water southwards. If this should coincide with a high spring tide, the levels can rise several feet above predictions. Similar surges can occur in the Channel with strong south-easterly winds piling up water against a high spring tide. Negative surges also occur, particularly in the southern North Sea, when levels can fall a long way below those predicted.

BAROMETRIC PRESSURE

The greater the pressure of the atmosphere, the more it depresses the level of the sea. Low pressure has the reverse effect so that during a depression there will be, in theory, a greater depth of water than predicted. However, since low pressure usually brings with it unsettled weather, high winds and rough seas which may in some places reduce the effective depths, it is unwise to rely on such an assumption, especially since any increase due to barometric pressure will usually only amount to a few inches and rarely to more than a foot. Likewise the reduction in levels caused by high barometric pressure will seldom amount to as much as a foot and can therefore be disregarded. Very occasionally at the height of summer, violent storms or line squalls may occur, which, in combination with high barometric pressure, sudden high wind and an ebbing tide, may cause a sudden fall in the level, together with a surge in the streams. If such storms are encountered, then in addition to securing the yacht for strong winds, a watch should be kept for these changes.

RAINFALL

Rivers in spate deposit great quantities of fresh water into estuaries and thence into the sea. This water is lighter than sea water and until it is shaken up it will form an upper layer which will flow seawards, even when the underlying sea water is flooding and causing levels to rise. Some decrease in flood streams and increase in the ebb stream strengths can therefore be expected, and in the upper reaches of tidal rivers the flood stream may disappear altogether, though levels may continue to rise and fall.

5 Tidal Chartwork

CROSSING TIDAL CHANNELS

The cruising or racing yachtsman develops an almost instinctive understanding of the use of *transits* as the eye automatically picks up the changing alignment of buoys or moored boats against the shoreline or other distant features.

Other transits used in this way are coastlines becoming open behind pierheads or headlands and objects lined up with shore features. The experienced sailor goes on to develop a sixth sense, steering courses which may not necessarily follow precise transits but which take into account many near-transits, knowing without conscious calculation his approximate set and drift.

What seems easy and obvious when sailing in well-known waters can be overlooked when cruising in a strange area. Having made calculations for steering a compass course which allows for a cross-track tidal set, a look back at the place just departed will confirm, either by a transit or by a back-bearing, that it is where it should be.

The taking of back-bearings is a valuable check on calculations and it can also be used as a means of adjusting for lesser errors, for example, leeway. The yachtsman who takes advantage of every opportunity for such checking will quickly gain confidence in his ability and will get to know thoroughly the individual characteristics, especially the windward ability, of his boat.

COURSE SETTING ON SHORT PASSAGES

The following calculations show the principle for crossing any narrow tidal channel when it is required to stay on a desired track. Firstly draw a line on the chart from the departure point to the destination; the *track*. Extend the line beyond the destination if the distance to it on the chart is very short. From the tidal stream

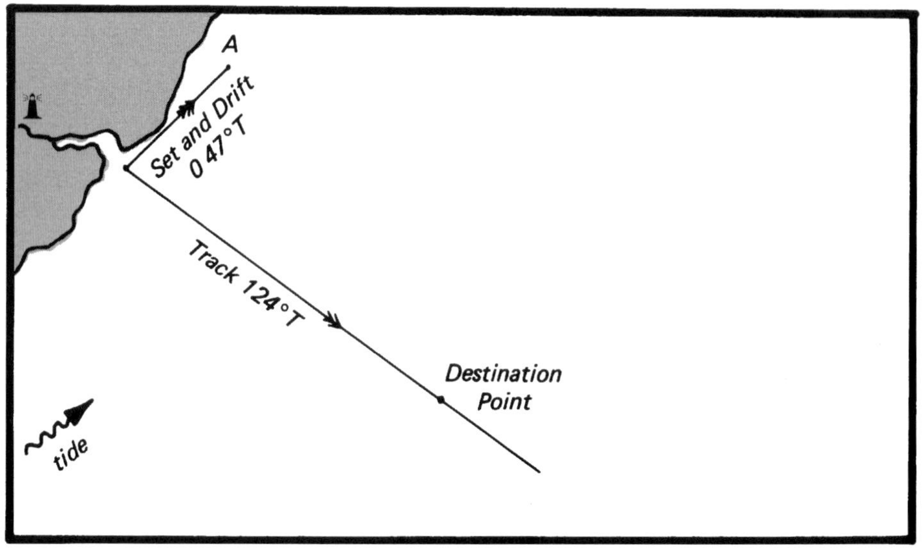

Figure 5.1

atlas obtain the tidal set and drift for the time of the passage. From the point of departure, mark off the set and drift for one hour, as illustrated in Figure 5.1 The estimated distance that will be travelled by the vessel in one hour now has to be decided. For this illustration an estimated speed of 5 knots is assumed, which means that the distance travelled through the water in one hour will be 5 miles. This distance is marked off from Point A using a compass to cut an arc on the track at Point B. Points A and B are now joined, giving the *course to steer*, which can be measured off on the compass rose or by a protractor; in this case the course to steer is 142°T. Where applicable, allowance for the estimated leeway can be applied (into the wind) to find the actual heading that will be required.

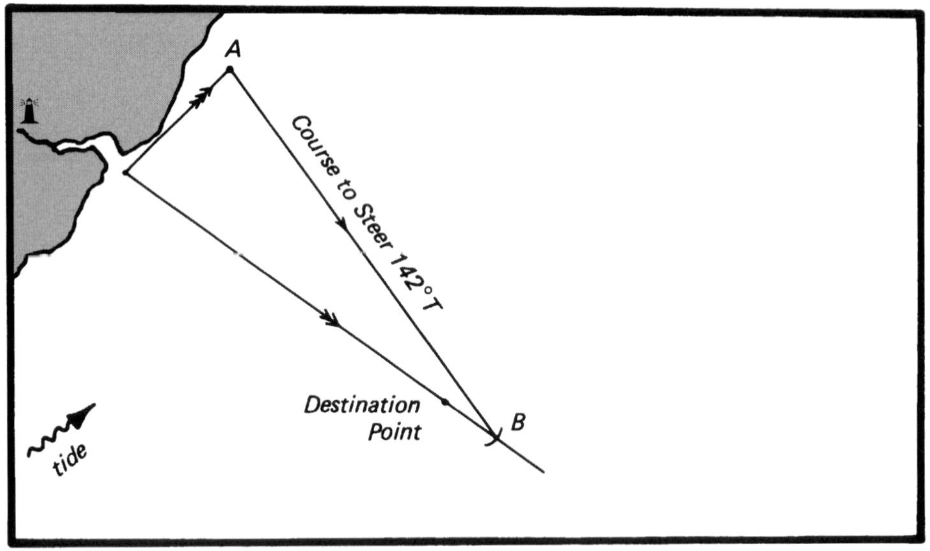

Figure 5.2

Once on passage, if the speed of the vessel is found to be significantly different from that estimated, a fresh arc of appropriate length should be drawn in as soon as possible in order to find the correct course to steer, which can then be adjusted accordingly.

COURSE ADJUSTMENT BY BACK-BEARING

The taking of *back-bearings* can be a valuable check that calculations have been made correctly and that leeway, where applicable, has been estimated and applied correctly, or to correct for leeway once under-way. Adjustments to the course can be made as shown in the following example:

On the chart extend the track backwards and measure the bearing of this line, which is your *anticipated back-bearing*. Take an *actual back-bearing* of your departure point with a hand-bearing compass, soon after departure and at intervals thereafter while it remains in view.

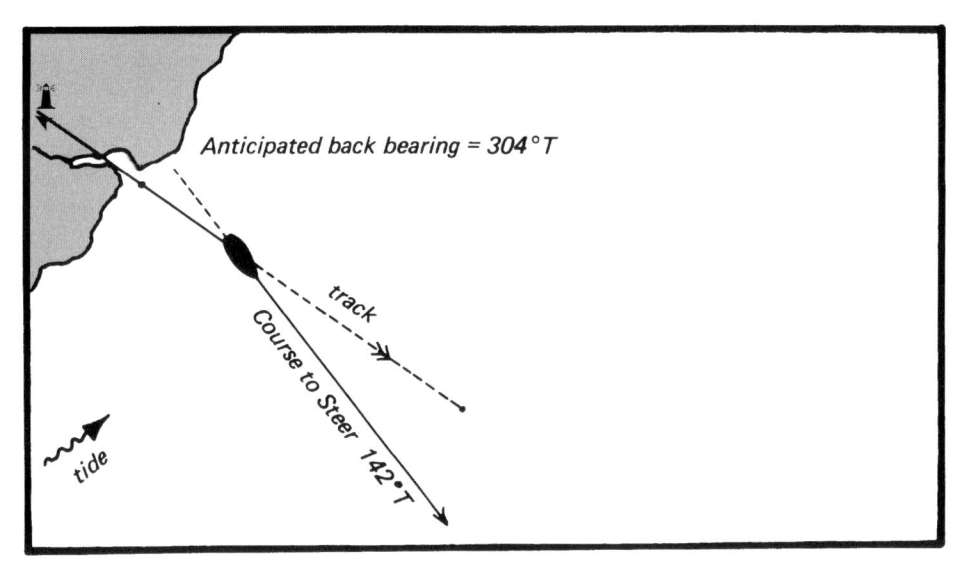

Figure 5.3

If the reading on the hand bearing compass is a *greater* number of degrees than the anticipated bearing, *subtract* this difference from the course. If the reading on the hand-bearing compass is *less* than the anticipated bearing then *add* this number of degrees to the course. Thus in the illustration shown, the anticipated back-bearing is calculated to be 304°T but the actual hand-bearing compass reading is found on passage to be 299°T, which is 5° less. Therefore 5° is added to the calculated course to steer (142°T) to become 147°T.

Carry out this check as soon as reasonably possible after departure in case an adjustment has to be made.

TACKING ANGLES AND LEEWAY

More complex problems arise when the calculated course to steer cannot be achieved because the wind is dead ahead. To be prepared for this eventuality the tacking characteristics of your yacht should if possible be ascertained and noted: each yacht will have different leeway characteristics depending on its shape, rig, trim and helmsmanship, and it is of enormous advantage to know the characteristics of the yacht that you sail. Investigation of leeway characteristics is best done at slack water and should be carried out for varying conditions of wind and sea state. Using a navigational mark as a point of departure, sail on various points of sailing on both port and starboard tacks noting all the headings together with each heading's corresponding back-bearing on the navigational mark (make sure to check the main compass for deviation before these exercises or use a hand-bearing compass to check the headings). The data obtained can then be used to determine two important characteristics of the boat: leeway and tacking angle.

TRACK ESTIMATING WHEN TACKING

Once it has been determined that a particular passage involves tacking because the calculated course cannot be steered, the best course of action is to first sail

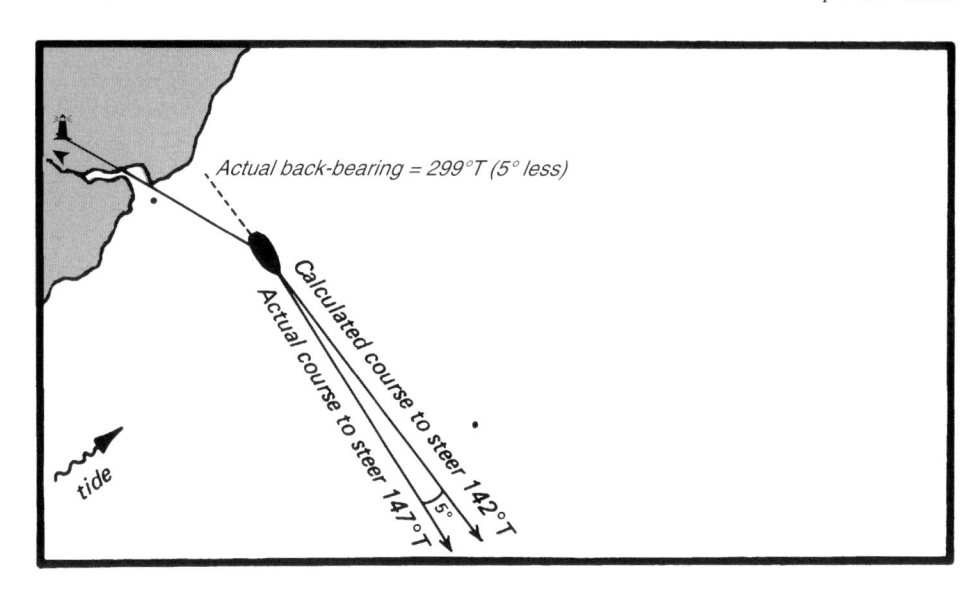

Figure 5.4

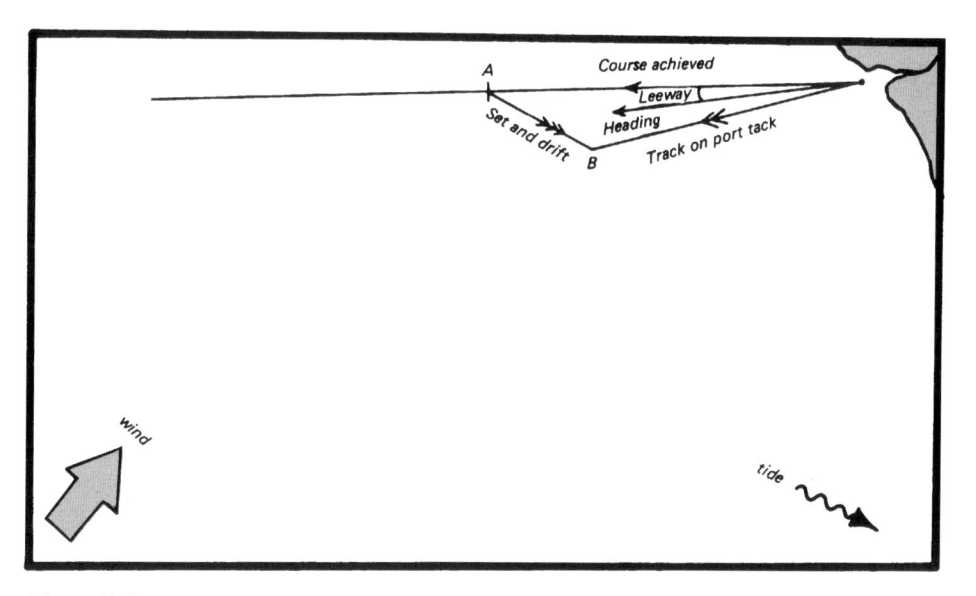

Figure 5.5

as close to the required course as the wind permits (preferably on the tack which is upstream of the course). When you have determined the speed and heading achieved, go to the chart table to plot the likely tracks.

Figure 5.5 illustrates the procedure used to estimate the track when tacking: it is the reverse of the course setting procedure shown in Figures 5.1 and 5.2 as it is the track over the ground that we are now trying to find. Draw on the chart the *course achieved* (i.e. the wake course) which is the actual *heading* with the *estimated*

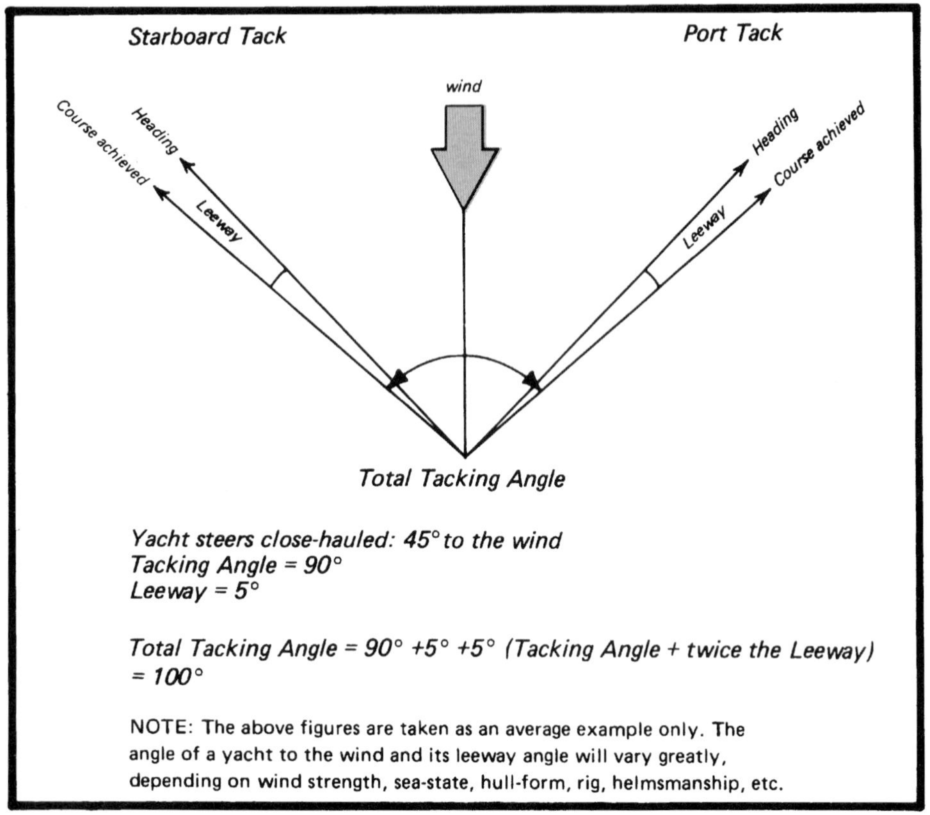

Starboard Tack   wind   Port Tack

Course achieved   Heading   Leeway   Leeway   Heading   Course achieved

Total Tacking Angle

Yacht steers close-hauled: 45° to the wind
Tacking Angle = 90°
Leeway = 5°

Total Tacking Angle = 90° +5° +5° (Tacking Angle + twice the Leeway)
= 100°

NOTE: The above figures are taken as an average example only. The angle of a yacht to the wind and its leeway angle will vary greatly, depending on wind strength, sea-state, hull-form, rig, helmsmanship, etc.

Figure 5.6

leeway applied to it. Mark off on this line the distance that will be covered in one hour, at Point A. From this point plot the set and drift of the tidal stream for one hour, as determined from the tidal stream atlas. Join the departure point to Point B; this line gives the yacht's *track* over the ground.

If it is required to find the likely track on the other tack, the method is as follows: pick any convenient point on the course line to use as an imaginary point of departure for the other tack. From this point draw in the course achieved (the wake course) for the other tack, which is drawn at an angle from the course line which equals the total tacking angle (total tacking angle equals the tacking angle of the yacht plus twice the leeway, as shown in Figure 5.6).

Then apply the required set and drift from the tidal atlas as before, to find the track on the new tack. On the penultimate tack of a passage, the yacht can go about when the destination comes on this bearing. If required, the distance covered on each tack, and therefore the time spent on each tack can be measured off the chart, which could be of importance if visibility is deteriorating.

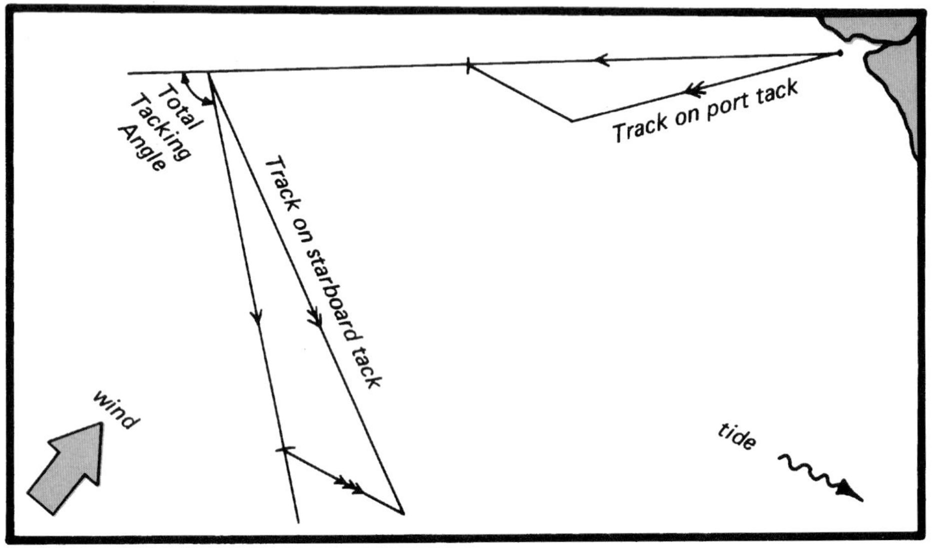

Total Tacking Angle   Track on port tack   Track on starboard tack   wind   tide

Figure 5.7

6 Coastal Passages

LETTING THE TIDES DO THE WORK

If a coastal passage is contemplated then it must be obvious that the time to go is when the tidal streams go with you. The streams around our coasts vary greatly in velocity but 1 or 2 knots is common, with 3 or 4 knot streams near headlands or through channels. If a fairly modest 5 knots through the water can be attained and our destination is approached on a 2 knot tidal stream, then we will progress at a speed of 7 knots over the seabed. If, through mis-timing the 2 knots tidal stream is running against us, one's 5 knots through the water will only amount to 3 knots over the ground. Thus a short coastal passage of say, 10 miles, would take in the first instance 1 hour 26 minutes, or wrongly timed as in the second, 3 hours 20 minutes.

It is easy for the inexperienced navigator to fail to appreciate this quite elementary arithmetic, believing that a 2 knot stream is of no real consequence if, by starting the engine, 5 or 6 knots can be instantly achieved. Indeed, there are some who have great difficulty in understanding the very nature of the phenomenon — that an entire mass of water is on the move, which is a very large force to be countered. Since the majority of cruising yachts have speeds which are limited by their hull forms and by, more often than not, engines which are no more than auxiliaries, there can be no alteration to this basic arithmetic which, when converted to hours and minutes of passage time, presents a very substantial consideration.

SHORT COASTAL PASSAGES

To give an example, using the streams predicted for 30 June (HW Cherbourg 0909 6.6m), if it is intended to sail from Cowes to Yarmouth making the very best of the tidal stream, then departure from Cowes must be made in the early afternoon at about 4½ hours after HW Cherbourg, that is at about 1330; provided that a speed of about 5 knots through the water can be achieved then Yarmouth, almost 9 miles away, will be reached in just over 1 hour having made good a speed over the ground of 8.5 knots. If however tidal streams for the passage had been ignored and Cowes left at 0700, then the opposing stream would have to be stemmed for over 3 hours and the average speed over the ground would work out at only 2.7 knots.

WEATHER AND LUNAR CONSIDERATIONS

To work the tides or make the tides work for us is obviously a very important part of passage planning, but at the same time the strength and direction of the wind and whether it will oppose the stream and thus throw up a steep sea, has to be considered. As has already been pointed out, this is particularly important in notorious places such as the Bristol Channel and Alderney Race where a plan to make best use of a favourable stream could lead to a passage through very steep turbulent seas with unpleasant, if not disastrous results. If the spring curves contained in the almanacs or Admiralty tide tables are consulted then it will be seen that the tide in these areas (the Bristol Channel and the Channel Islands)

rises steeply to high water, and then as steeply falls away. This reflects the speed at which streams can change direction. The rapid change is not confined to these areas: it also occurs where normally rotary streams are confined by geographical outcrops or islands to narrow channels, where streams will quite suddenly change direction and thus quite suddenly change the seastate.

Before contemplating extended cruises, a further and quite fundamental consideration is to decide, in the light of crew knowledge, experience and stamina, whether it is wise to cruise new and hitherto unvisited areas at periods of spring tides. This will apply particularly to the splendid cruising grounds of the Channel Islands and Brittany. Although spring tides bring with them magnificent low water scenery, they also cause powerful streams in many confined channels where navigation often depends upon identification and adherence to transits and where the same streams often set strongly towards dangers. It is much easier to navigate these areas on the first occasion during periods of neap tides. The same applies, though to a lesser degree, to first-time navigation in all strange waters.

LONGER COASTAL PASSAGES

For efficient and sensible cruising it must be understood that passage timing is important, and that for passages of moderate or longer duration the correct departure time must be adhered to. In some cases this may include night sailing, although hazardous passages should not be contemplated in darkness, so should be planned accordingly.

Using the tides predicted for 1 July (HW Cherbourg 0956 6.5m), a passage from Newhaven to Ramsgate is looked at in detail and illustrated with diagrams based on the tidal stream atlases in Part 2.

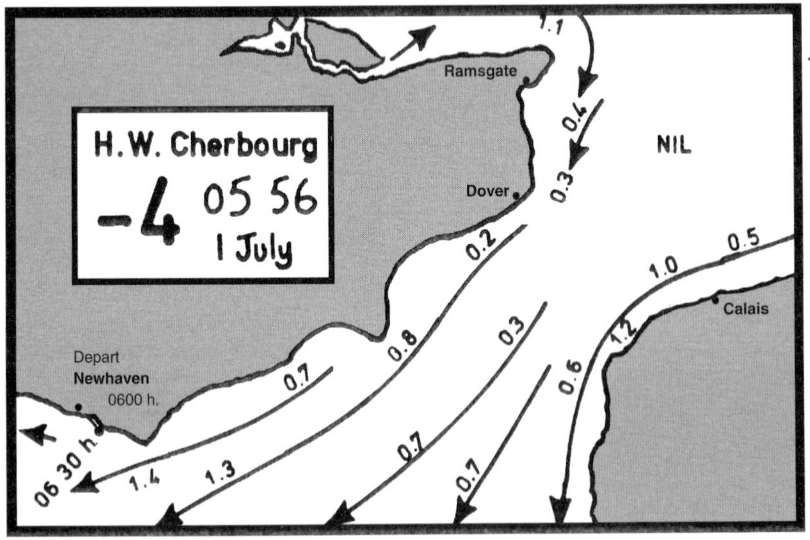

Figure 6.1

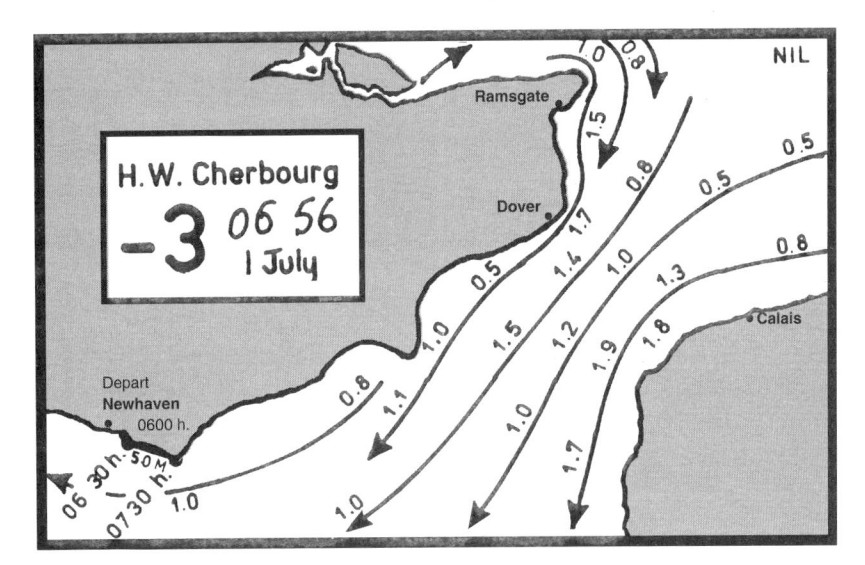

Figure 6.2

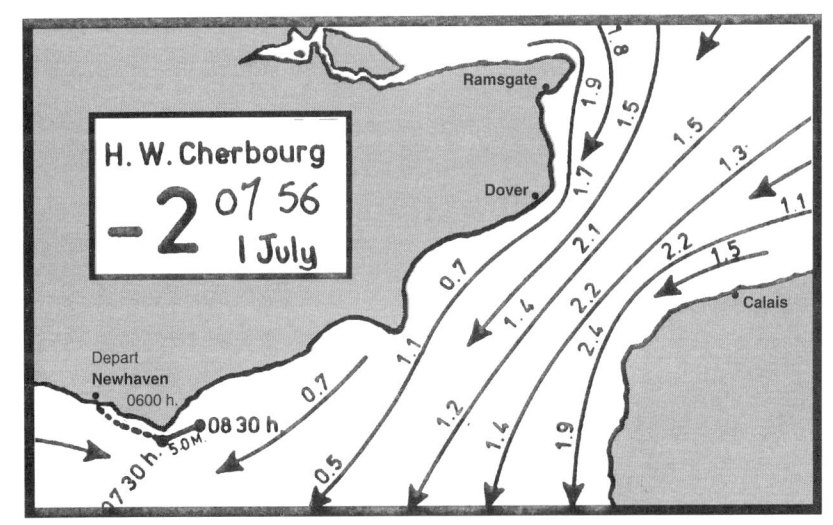

Figure 6.3

A study of the tidal steam atlas for this passage shows that an unusual stream pattern occurs on this stretch of coast. From the yachtsman's point of view this particular area is bleak, with no real ports of refuge or places to shelter from southerly winds whilst between Newhaven and Dover. This eastward passage can be fast because, by careful timing, leaving Newhaven at 0600, a little before local low water (HW Cherbourg −4) the tail end of the Channel ebb can be avoided by making use of a likely eddy behind Beachy Head. The areas of overfalls in that area can be ignored because the tide will be slack. The favourable flood stream can then be picked up, which goes on and on, with only a slight hesitation off Dungeness, where the situation changes from using the original Channel flood, now about to ebb westwards, to the new Dover Strait flood, just beginning.

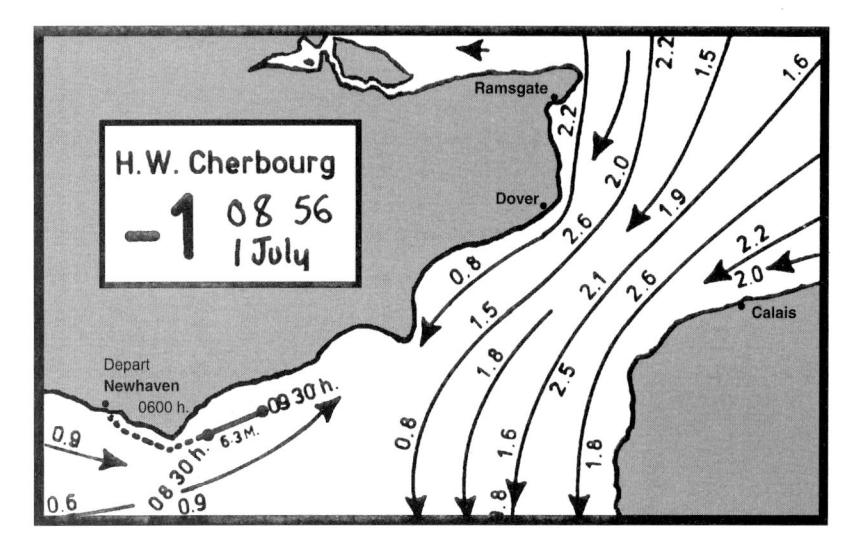

Figure 6.4

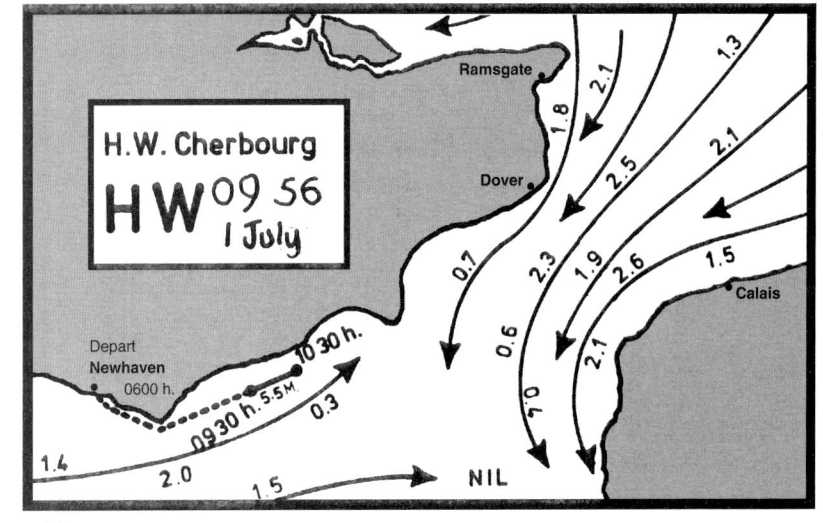

Figure 6.5

35

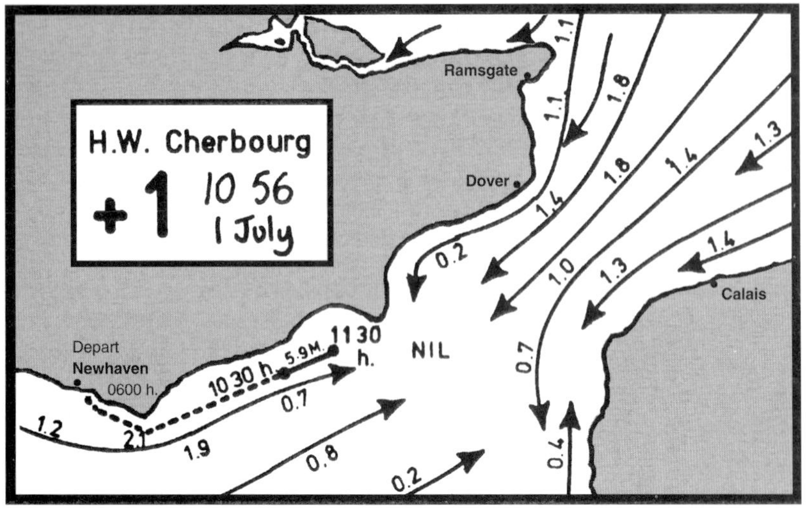

Figure 6.6

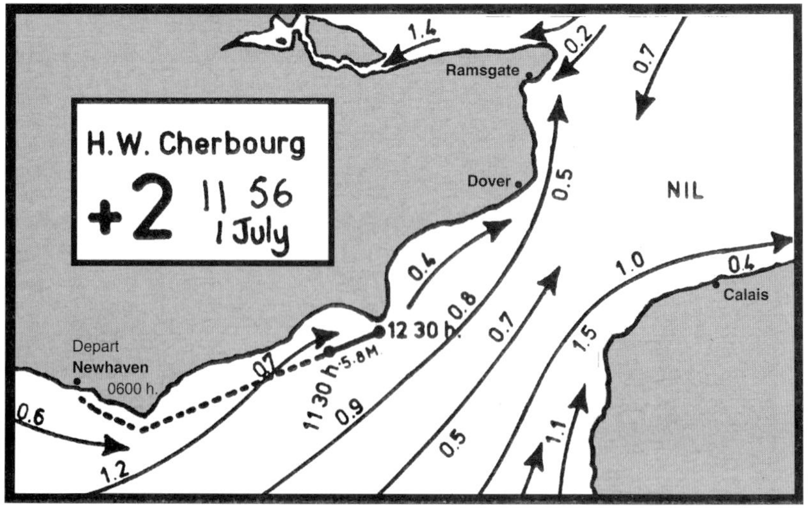

Figure 6.7

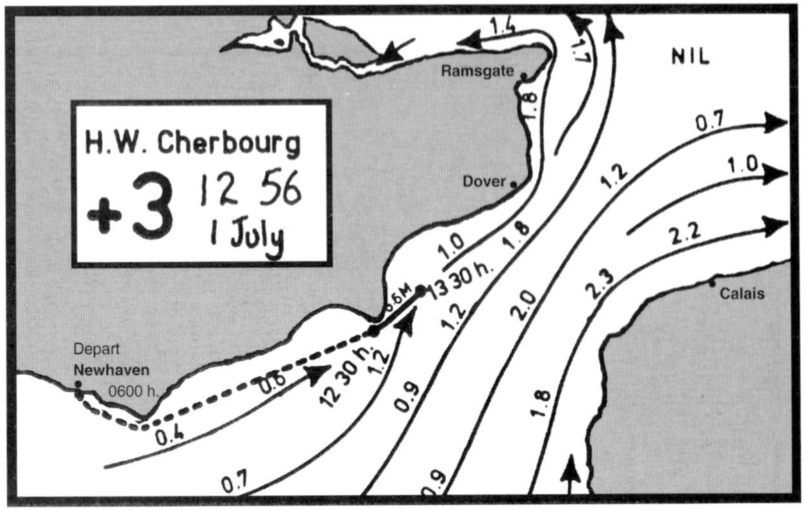

Figure 6.8

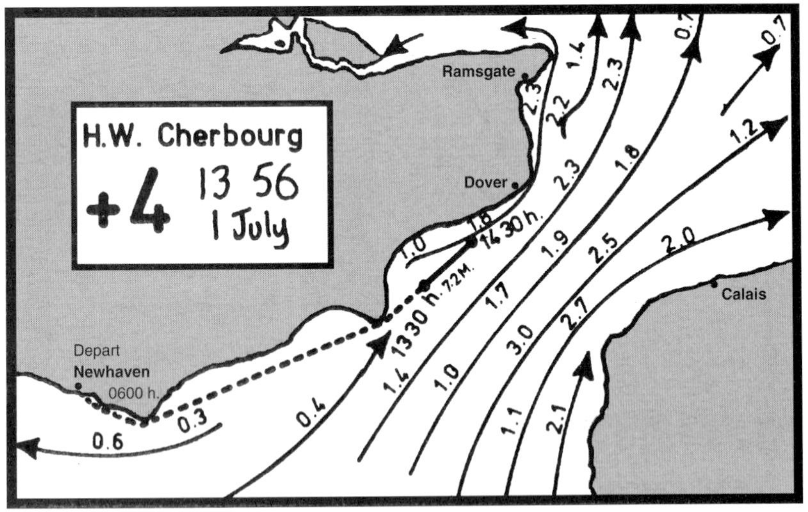

Figure 6.9

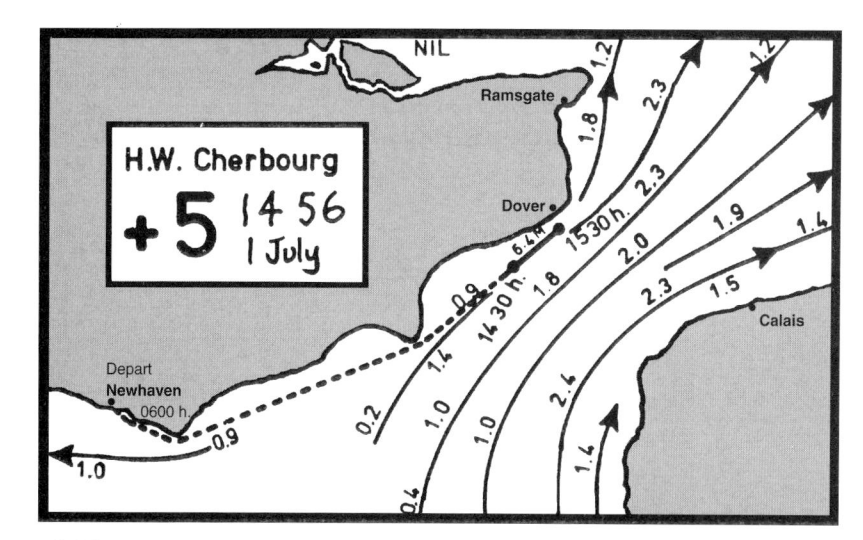

Figure 6.10

The illustrations assume a speed through the water of 5 knots and streams slightly faster than average springs. At neaps the time of departure from Newhaven would need to be earlier to avoid missing the tide gate off Dungeness, the timing of which is quite critical and must be carefully planned in the light of the predicted speed of streams. During small neap tides it is unlikely that a yacht will reach Ramsgate without stemming the first of the south-going stream in the approach so a stop-over at Dover might be considered.

To make the reverse passage from Dover to Newhaven must always involve stemming the tide at one stage or another (except for much faster vessels) and may require either a fair wind or use of the engine if the passage is not to become protracted.

If a yacht which is travelling eastwards is capable of 7 knots or more through the water, then given a fair wind and a spring tide very great distances can be covered, taking a yacht to the French and possibly to the Belgian ports on the North Sea coast in one 12 hour period. Note that at spring tides of any magnitude, this 12 hour period will always be either an all-day or an all-night passage, while at neaps it will be half and half, either starting or ending in darkness. Also note carefully that whatever the destination, the tide will inevitably be falling on arrival and that passing through locks or sills at the port of destination may not be possible, necessitating a wait in an outer harbour. At periods of greater than average spring tides there could be difficulties in the approach and entry to certain ports: the Part 2 atlases give immediately available information about the state of tide, its height and whether it is rising or falling, on every hourly page.

All tidal stream atlases contain chartlets which show the predicted direction and rate of stream for a specified time and it is reasonable to assume that the predictions apply from half an hour before to half an hour after that time; the only complication is between +6, (six hours after) and −6, (six hours before) high water. The time which elapses between the two varies from springs to neaps and has to be ascertained by entering the time of the next HW Cherbourg from the tide tables and completing the tidal cycle (backwards from HW to HW−6) on the chartlets. This is shown in the illustration of the passage from Newhaven, where the +6 chart is timed at 1556 and the −6 chart at 1618 — only 22 minutes later. This time must not be overlooked when assessing streams between tidal cycles. As with all tidal predictions a degree of interpolative skill is required.

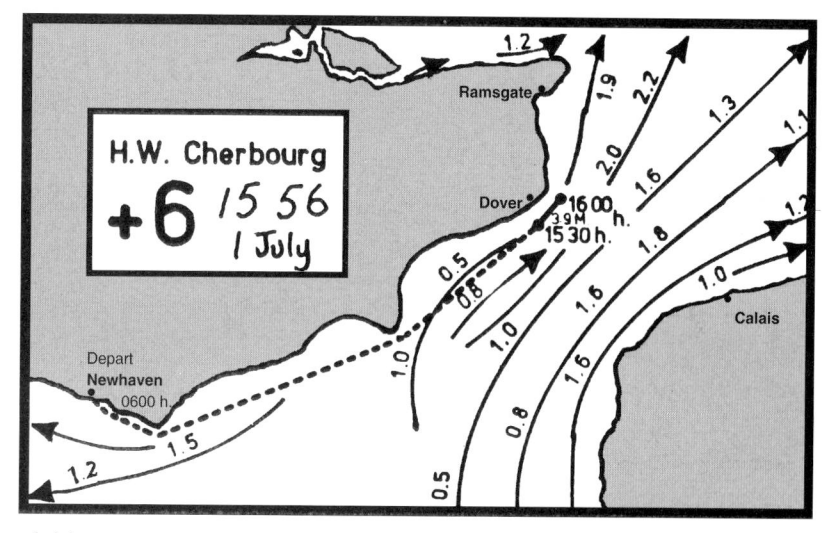

Figure 6.11

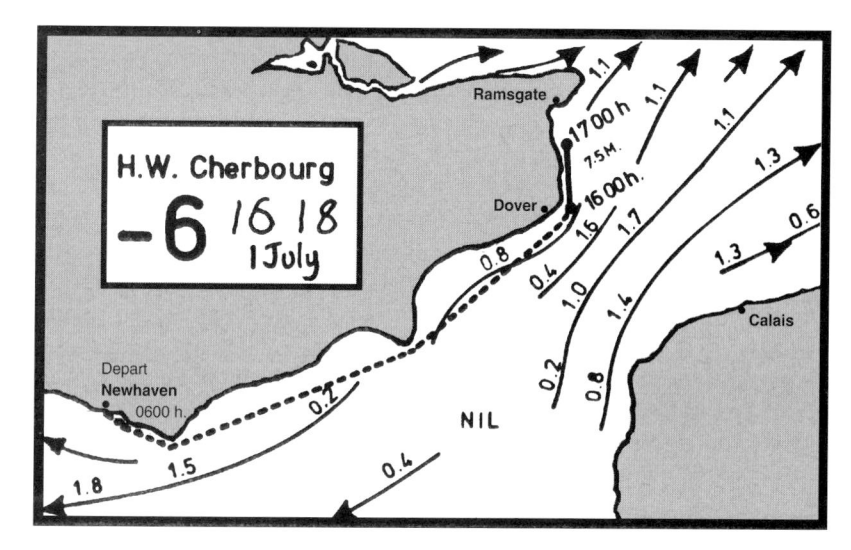

Figure 6.12

37

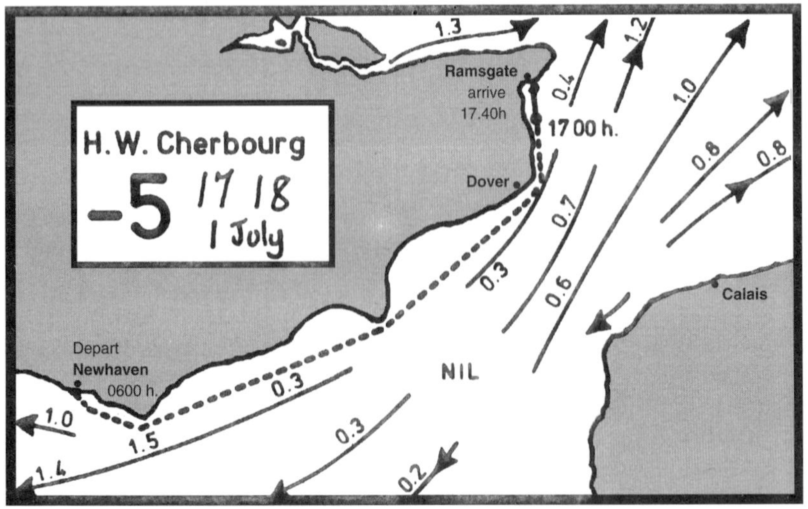

Figure 6.13

The tides can be worked to advantage on many of the passages made in our waters — the passage illustrated here is somewhat exceptional because it exceeds the duration of a normal ebb or flood stream. As in the case of sailing westwards from Dover, most passages of more than 30 or 40 miles will involve stemming the tide for at least part of the time. This disadvantage can usually be reduced by timing the passage to get the yacht into positions where, during periods of adverse streams, those streams are known to be weak. Thus on a coastal passage up or down the Channel it will always be advantageous to ride the streams between Portland Bill and St. Catherine's Point where they run fast, and to stem the streams across Lyme Bay and off the Sussex coast where they are always weaker. It should be borne in mind that tides always run faster in the vicinity of headlands and if stemming the stream, these headlands should be given a wide clearance. However, this factor must be weighed against the advantage of hugging the coast where streams are usually less strong and where favourable eddies may form — a deciding factor in this sort of question will often be the wind strength and direction. There is also a strong possibility that the inshore stream will weaken and perhaps become slack some time before the offshore stream changes.

7 Cross-Channel Passages

TRAVERSING TIDAL WATERS

In tidal waters it is the practice of professional navigators to draw a suitable line on the chart along the intended course, making sure that there is sufficient depth of water and that no wrecks or dangers exist along it, and steering to follow precisely this line, making the necessary course adjustments to compensate for the effects of tidal stream and currents etc. There is usually little need to take heed of tidal height since commercial craft will rarely venture into waters where the chart shows depths of less than adequate under-keel clearance. Most charts show depths at Chart Datum, normally the Lowest Astronomical Tide, so that

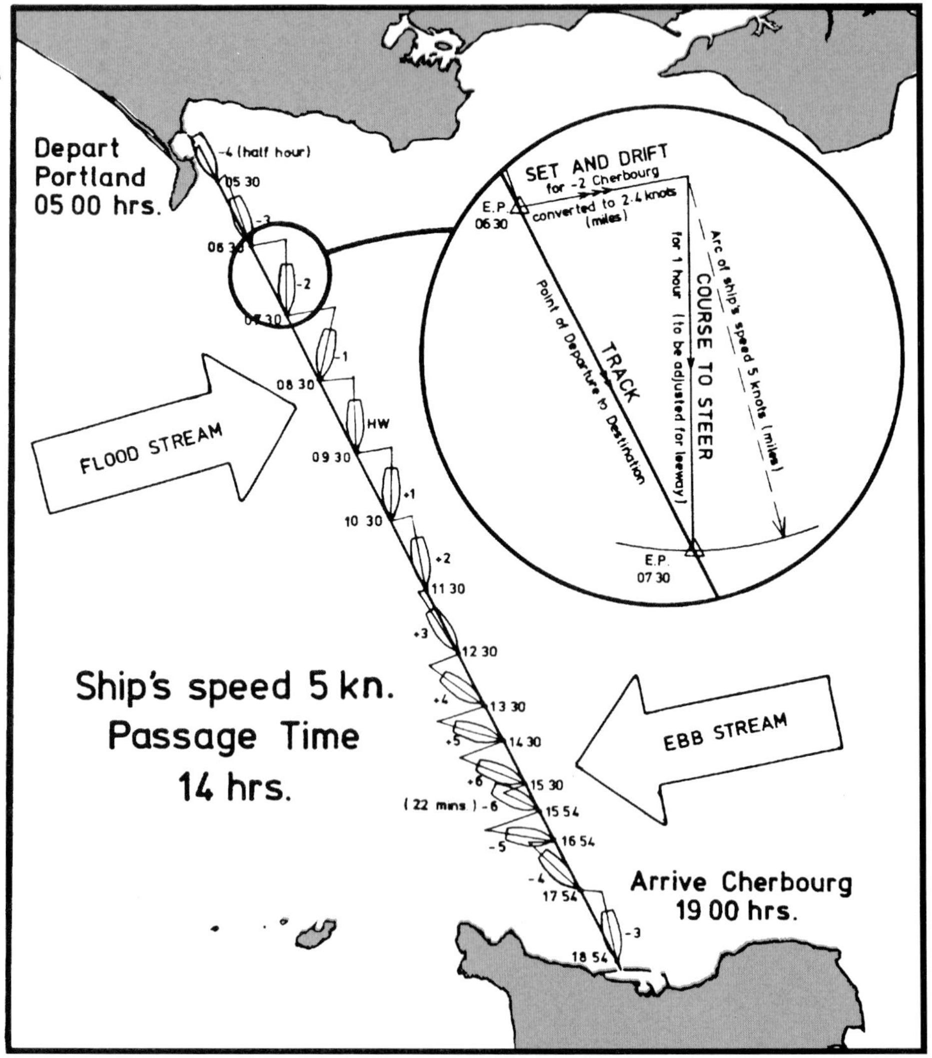

the soundings printed on the chart should always be present, and for the vast majority of the time will be exceeded.

From the yachtman's point of view the situation is quite different. Some navigators of small craft might frequently decide to traverse banks which dry at low water. Others rely on rise of tide to float off a berth or to negotiate bars or sills. Cruising grounds may be more extensive because one is much less constrained by draught and can therefore use depths of water provided fortuitously by rise of tide. Navigation for yachtsmen is in many respects more complicated than that for the larger commercial vessel: the yachtsman needs to take greater cognisance of tidal height and is much more dependent upon the correct usage of streams for successful passage making, since the speed of a yacht through the water is relatively much slower and therefore more influenced by the streams. To illustrate this last point, a 20 knot vessel progressing across a 2 knot tidal stream will need to correct course by a mere 6° into the stream to keep on track, whereas the yachtsman progressing at 5 knots across the same 2 knot stream will need to correct by 23°, whilst the distance made good will be considerably reduced.

Professional navigators have handed down to yachtsmen their navigational principle of following a track drawn across a tidal stream by periodic alterations of course as illustrated in Figure 7.1. It is of course important that the yachtsman should understand the simple geometry of this course-setting process to counter a stream, because many short passages demand it. Indeed for longer passages such as in the Thames Estuary, cluttered by banks, or in the Channel Islands cluttered by rocks, it is often necessary to sail along a track drawn from one point to another in order to avoid these dangers. But for a passage across the Channel such as that illustrated in Figure 7.1 it is doubtful whether any case can be made to support the method, which involves numerous changes of course and therefore much additional chartwork. There also may be difficulty in laying some of the courses because of adverse wind direction. However, the main disadvantage is that the passage takes longer than necessary.

COURSE SETTING — THE SHORTEST DISTANCE

A cruising yacht making relatively slow passages must always be ready to run for shelter should the weather worsen, and although it may be pleasant to take one's time over a passage during good weather, it would be neglectful and even irresponsible if the navigator failed to familiarise himself with the alternative method illustrated in Figures 7.2 and 7.3, which is essential for fast and efficient passage making. It involves steering a straight course through the water while the water itself is ebbing and flooding, causing the resulting track over the ground to be a very distinct curve. The trick is to calculate the course to steer so that one will reach the destination without an alteration of course.

It will be noted in Figure 7.1 that the courses to steer are calculated in the same way as described in Chapter 5 for short passages, except that the point of departure each hour is either a fix by visual or RDF bearings, (perhaps aided by soundings

Depart Portland 05 00 hrs.

FLOOD STREAM

Ship's speed 5 kn. Passage Time 14 hrs.

EBB STREAM

Arrive Cherbourg 19 00 hrs.

SET AND DRIFT for -2 Cherbourg converted to 2.4 knots (miles)

E.P. 06 30

COURSE TO STEER

Arc of ship's speed 5 knots (miles)

for 1 hour (to be adjusted for leeway)

TRACK

Point of Departure to Destination

E.P. 07 30

Figure 7.1

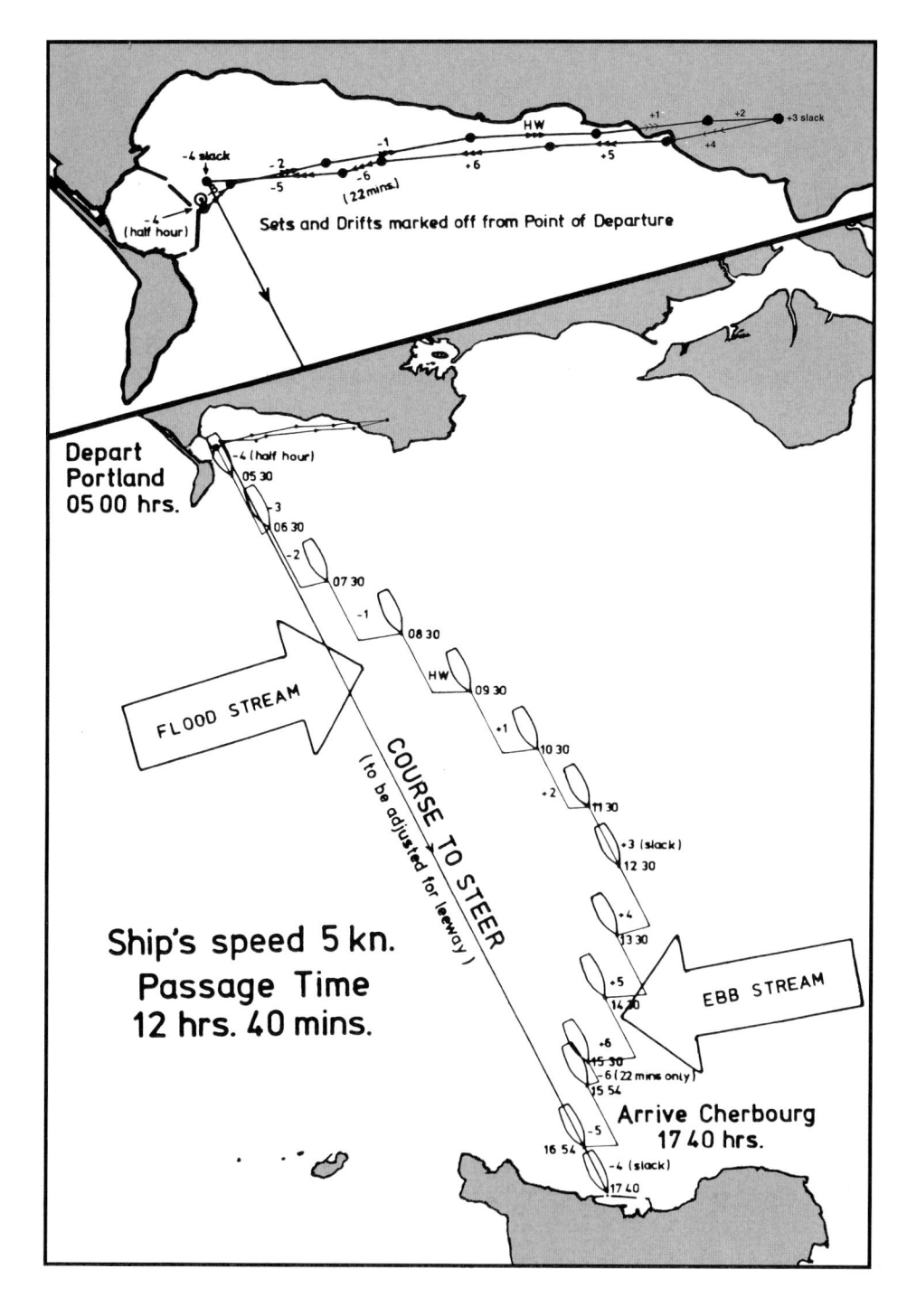

Figure 7.2

(Figure labels: Sets and Drifts marked off from Point of Departure; Depart Portland 05 00 hrs.; FLOOD STREAM; COURSE TO STEER (to be adjusted for leeway); EBB STREAM; Ship's speed 5 kn. Passage Time 12 hrs. 40 mins.; Arrive Cherbourg 17 40 hrs.)

or some other system), or an estimated position by dead reckoning. The method illustrated in Figures 7.2 and 7.3 is basically similar, except that the sets and drifts accumulated for the entire passage are marked off as a whole from one point of departure.

It is something of a coincidence that if a yacht makes 5 knots through the water, then on passages from Poole, Portland, the Needles or the Nab Tower to Cherbourg, the most popular French destination from these places, the course to steer will always approximate to the line of the track. This is because in every case the distance is just a little over 60 miles, which at 5 knots will mean a passage of 12 hours, or one tidal cycle — the east-going and west-going streams more or less negating each other. Thus in Figure 7.2 if the enlargement of the sets and drifts at the top of the illustration is studied, it will be seen that the final set and drift comes back very close to the point of departure.

Planning will, of course, begin with the essentials of weather forecasts, wind direction, visibility etc. and all these being acceptable two arbitrary estimates have to be made: how fast the yacht will travel through the water, and in the light of an initial study of the tidal stream atlas, how many hours the passage will take. With motor vessels the first is a comparatively simple calculation, as it is if one decides to motor-sail should the wind deny the desired speed and direction. Calculation for sailing vessels is more approximate, but becomes easier and more accurate with experience. Having decided the probable speed through the water, the help or hindrance of the tidal streams must be assessed, which calls for careful judgement.

The preliminary gauging of the streams can be approximated in the first instance by adding up the total of east-going streams likely to be encountered, then the west-going streams, and subtracting one from the other. The advantage of one over the other presents an approximation which can be plotted eastwards or westwards of the point of departure and which will give an early picture of the likely influence of the tidal streams upon the passage. The fore-going is a simplified and rough way of performing the process illustrated at the top of Figures 7.2 and 7.3, which at a later stage can be executed more exactly.

The complexity of the problem arises from the number of options open, with time of departure offering widely differing course settings in many instances (though not with the 5 knot passage of 60 miles illustrated in Figure 7.2) and with varying speeds through the water creating a vast number of possibilities. In the illustrated passage from Portland to Cherbourg at 5 knots through the water, no appreciable assistance from the tidal streams can be expected but with a passage at a speed of 7 knots through the water however, the yacht can get a fair bit of help to the eastward.

STATE OF TIDE AT DEPARTURE AND DESTINATION
Tidal streams can influence the duration of the passage, but the state of tide at the ports of departure and destination must also be considered. In the particular examples illustrated there is no significance in the tidal height at either port as

both Portland (Weymouth) and Cherbourg have more than adequate water at all states of the tide. Had the passage been planned from Christchurch or perhaps Chichester, then departure at low water would not be possible. If the passage were planned for a day when spring tides were similar to those upon which the illustrations were based, then a passage commencing at Lymington through the Needles Channel would be a lengthy and frustrating process unless made on the west-going ebb, while exceptionally strong streams would be running through the harbour entrances at Poole, Portsmouth, Chichester and other ports, at certain stages of the tide. On the illustrated passage from Portland a consideration in every yachtsman's mind will be the state of the Portland Race and the associated dangers of the Shambles; it is wise, if only for peace of mind, to leave when the tide will bear the yacht away from these dangers, as it would when the suggested time of departure is 4 hours before high water at Cherbourg. Note that at springs this is always at about 0500, but at neaps a mid-morning or midnight departure would be required. Leaving at HW −4 (Cherbourg) will always be satisfactory for a 5 knot yacht, for arrival will be at a time when the powerful streams of the French coast are slackening and present less of a problem if it is necessary to correct errors which have accumulated on passage. For the 7 knot yacht, departure at this time will shorten the passage by making full use of the east-going streams whilst the minimum of the undesirable west-going streams will be felt. The 7 knot yacht will arrive off the French coast as the west-going stream is reaching full strength, but a 7 knot yacht will have little difficulty in correcting errors in the approach. However, in this case a prudent cruising yachtsman might well decide to make for the eastern entrance to the Cherbourg Rade, and thus provide an alternative down-tide objective should his navigational calculations prove to be at fault.

ACCUMULATED SETS AND DRIFTS

Having decided upon the speed of the yacht, the probable duration of the passage and the most advantageous time to depart, the estimated positions for each hour throughout the passage must be pinpointed on each relevant page of the tidal stream atlas in order to find the set and drift for each hour of the passage. The edge of a sheet of paper, marked off into the expected hourly divisions of the passage and laid along the line from the departure point to the destination on the chart will help to decide the anticipated position for each hour. The sets and drifts thus established are then plotted on the passage chart from the point of departure, and the course to steer thus found. Reference to Figure 7.4 which illustrates a passage from Dover to Calais shows the process more amply illustrated by drawings similar to the chartlets in the Yachtsman's Tidal Atlases, and shows the extraction of rates of drifts. *Mean rates* thus extracted from the tidal atlases in Part 2 should be converted to *actual rates* for plotting on the chart by use of the conversion tables adjacent to the tidal stream charts. The same process is used for the Portland to Cherbourg passage under discussion.

The Dover/Calais illustration in Figure 7.4 not only demonstrates the method for assessing the direction of sets and rates of drifts but also highlights one other

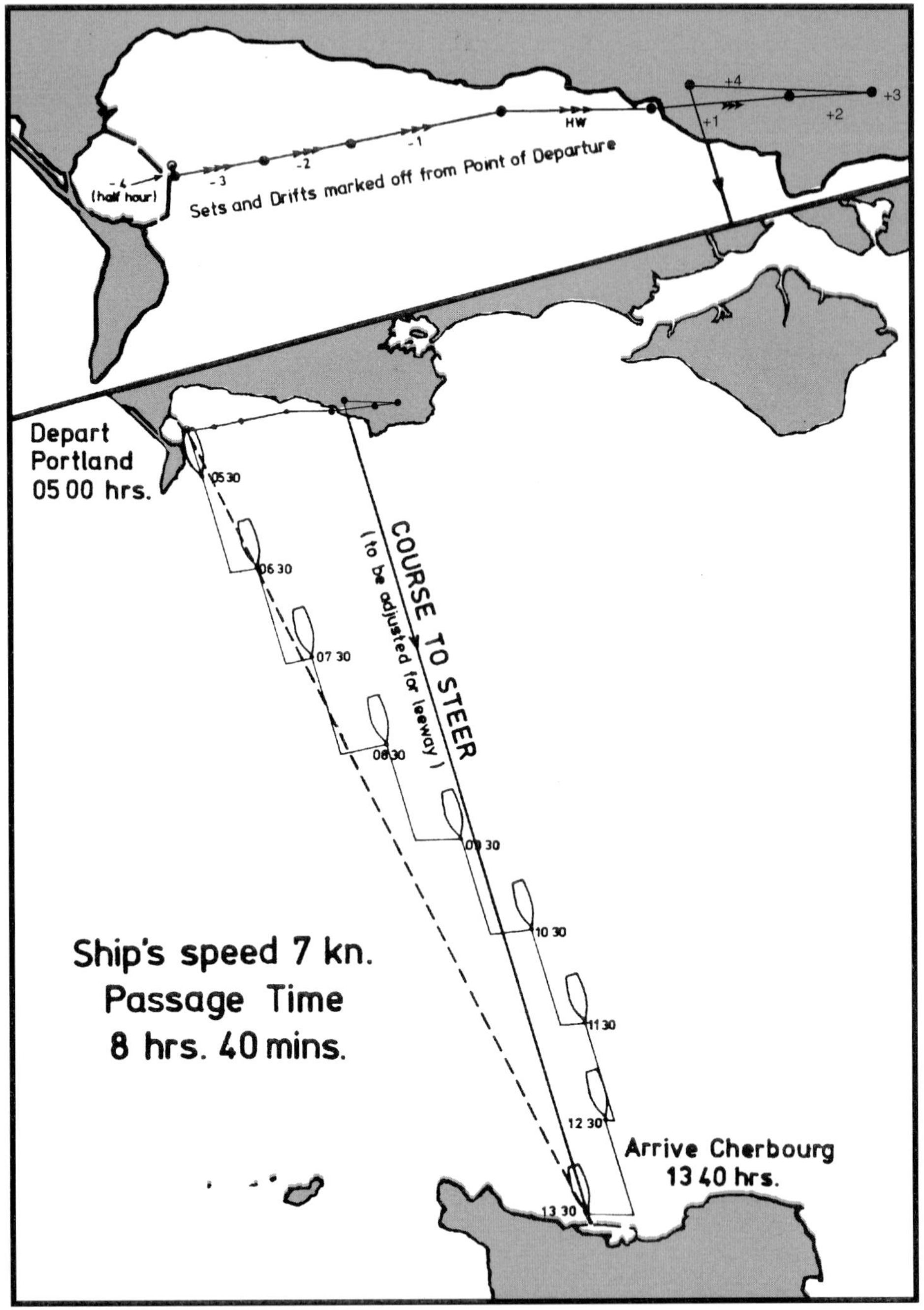

Figure 7.3

point. The distance from Dover to Calais is just over 21 miles and the streams run through the Strait at considerable speed, first in one direction and then in the other. It will already be clear that setting a course into the stream to combat that stream and keep the yacht on the desired track causes a loss of speed over the ground and one might therefore believe that the best time to cross the Dover Strait would be at or near slack water when 5 miles through the water would more closely register 5 miles over the ground, and when one would confidently expect to complete the 21 mile passage in little more than 4 hours. The illustration demonstrates however, that by making the passage on the east-going flood the passage time can be reduced to 3 hours and 40 minutes, and highlights the advantage to be gained by using streams which go even remotely in the desired direction. In this instance, Calais lies ESE of Dover and the flood stream is NE going, so there is an easterly element which is beneficial. It may be said that the saving of half an hour is neither here nor there and of little consequence; in many situations this might be true. Nevertheless it is good planning and seamanlike to make maximum use of the tides, especially in the passage across the Dover Strait where there is the added urgency presented by the Traffic Separation Zones, stiff with the world's shipping and certainly no place to loiter. Note that the course to steer also lies conveniently at right-angles to the separation zones, as required by the IRPCS (International Rules for the Prevention of Collision at Sea).

The foregoing examples show that advantages can be gained by careful timing of cross-Channel passages, and one other instance deserves special mention — the passage between Alderney and the Solent. The prudent skipper might well choose to cross first to Cherbourg, then make the onward passage to Alderney and thus be able to time his arrival at Braye Harbour with greater accuracy and certainty, to avoid any possibility of being borne through the rock-infested waters to the west or through the fast-running streams of the Alderney Race to the east. It is clearly desirable to arrive at slack water, whether making passage from Cherbourg or directly from the Solent. There are of course two slack periods: one at the end of the flood (Cherbourg HW +2½) and the other at the end of the ebb (Cherbourg HW −3½). At first glance it would seem immaterial which of these two to choose. It has already been noted that when making passage from Cherbourg, taking advantage of the eddy behind Cap de la Hague means an arrival in the vicinity of Alderney at the end of the ENE-going flood.

But if making passage from the Solent (or from Poole) there is a distinct advantage in arriving 6 hours earlier or later, on the tail end of the WSW-going ebb, as this is a fast-moving stream containing a fair southerly element to speed the yacht towards the island; much too useful to ignore. For similar reasons it is wise to leave Alderney for the Solent at about the time when the ENE-going flood starts (Cherbourg HW −3½), thus taking advantage of the northerly element in the stream. If the alternatives are studied carefully, it will be found that two or more hours can be cut off the passage time by adopting this tactic, the only other consideration being the possibility, if making for the Needles, of meeting a foul stream in the Needles Channel. This would call for some adjustment in the time of departure and would depend upon the anticipated speed of the yacht through the water.

These passages show how in some cases where timing at first sight seems immaterial, a more careful study reveals that considerable gain can be extracted by the correct use of tidal streams. In the examples described above the essence lay in a slight element of advantage in the set of a stream. It would be convenient if, when wanting to go north, one could simply await the arrival of a north-going stream, but our atlases show us that streams do not alter their courses to suit our needs, and that we must search out the best available. If, wanting to go north, the choice is between an ENE and a WSW stream, then one must go on the former because it contains a northerly element, and will cut minutes, if not hours, from our passage times and will make for much more efficient and enjoyable passage making.

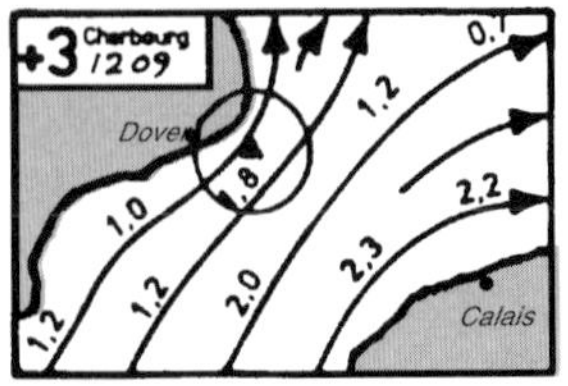

EP First hour 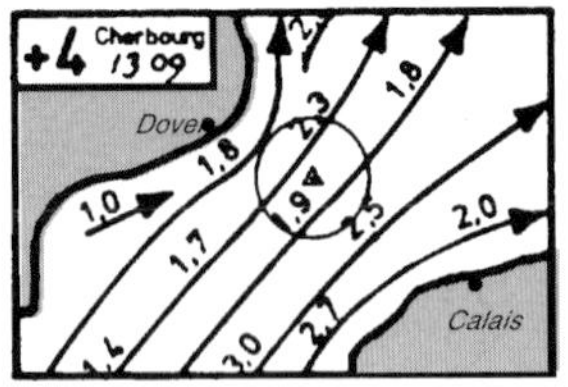 EP Second hour 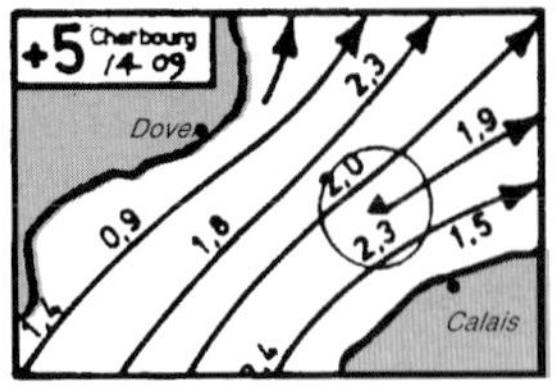 EP Third hour 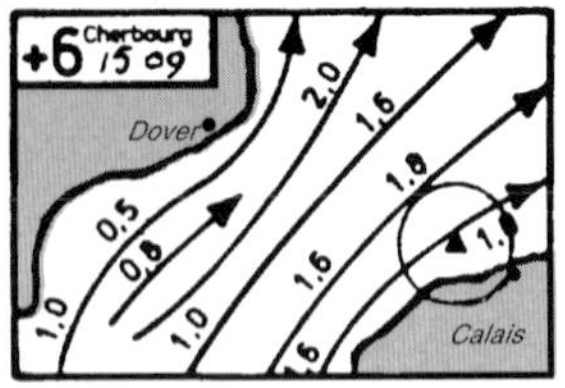 EP Fourth hour (for ½ hour only)

Stream Rate Conversion Table

Mean Rate Figure from Chart ▼	Pencil-in height of HW Cherbourg — Read from column below pencil mark											
	4.8	5.0	5.2	5.4	5.6	5.8	6.0	6.2	6.4	6.6	6.8	
0.1	0.1	0.1	0.1	0.1	0.1	0.1	0.1	0.1	0.1	0.1	0.1	0.2
0.2	0.1	0.1	0.2	0.2	0.2	0.2	0.2	0.2	0.3	0.3	0.3	0.3
0.3	0.2	0.2	0.2	0.3	0.3	0.3	0.3	0.4	0.4	0.4	0.4	0.5
0.4	0.2	0.3	0.3	0.3	0.4	0.4	0.4	0.5	0.5	0.5	0.6	0.6
0.5	0.3	0.3	0.4	0.4	0.5	0.5	0.6	0.6	0.6	0.7	0.7	0.8
0.6	0.4	0.4	0.5	0.5	0.6	0.6	0.7	0.7	0.8	0.8	0.9	0.9
0.7	0.4	0.5	0.5	0.6	0.7	0.7	0.8	0.8	0.9	0.9	1.0	1.1
0.8	0.5	0.5	0.6	0.7	0.7	0.8	0.9	0.9	1.0	1.1	1.1	1.2
0.9	0.5	0.6	0.7	0.8	0.8	0.9	1.0	1.1	1.1	1.2	1.3	1.4
1.0	0.6	0.7	0.8	0.9	0.9	1.0	1.1	1.2	1.3	1.4	1.4	1.5
1.1	0.7	0.8	0.8	0.9	1.0	1.1	1.2	1.3	1.4	1.5	1.6	1.7
1.2 (4th Hour: ½ only)	0.7	0.8	0.9	1.0	1.1	1.2	1.3	1.4	1.5	1.6	1.7	1.8	1.6 for ½ hour = 0.8
1.3	0.8	0.9	1.0	1.1	1.2	1.3	1.4	1.5	1.7	1.8	1.9	2.0
1.4	0.8	1.0	1.1	1.2	1.3	1.4	1.5	1.7	1.8	1.9	2.0	2.1
1.5	0.9	1.0	1.2	1.3	1.4	1.5	1.7	1.8	1.9	2.0	2.2	2.3
1.6 (1st Hour)	1.0	1.1	1.2	1.4	1.5	1.6	1.8	1.9	2.0	2.2	2.3	2.4	= 2.2
1.7	1.0	1.2	1.3	1.5	1.6	1.7	1.9	2.0	2.2	2.3	2.4	2.6
1.8	1.1	1.2	1.4	1.5	1.7	1.8	2.0	2.1	2.3	2.4	2.6	2.7
1.9	1.2	1.3	1.5	1.6	1.8	1.9	2.1	2.3	2.4	2.6	2.7	2.9
2.0 (2nd Hour)	1.2	1.4	1.5	1.7	1.9	2.0	2.2	2.4	2.5	2.7	2.9	3.0	= 2.8
2.1	1.3	1.4	1.6	1.8	2.0	2.1	2.3	2.5	2.7	2.8	3.0	3.2
2.2 (3rd Hour)	1.3	1.5	1.7	1.9	2.1	2.2	2.4	2.6	2.8	3.0	3.2	3.3	= 3.1
2.3	1.4	1.6	1.8	2.0	2.2	2.3	2.5	2.7	2.9	3.1	3.3	3.5
2.4	1.5	1.7	1.9	2.1	2.3	2.4	2.6	2.8	3.0			
2.5	1.5	1.7	1.9	2.1	2.3	2.6	2.?					
2.6	1.6	1.8	2.0									
2.7	1.?											

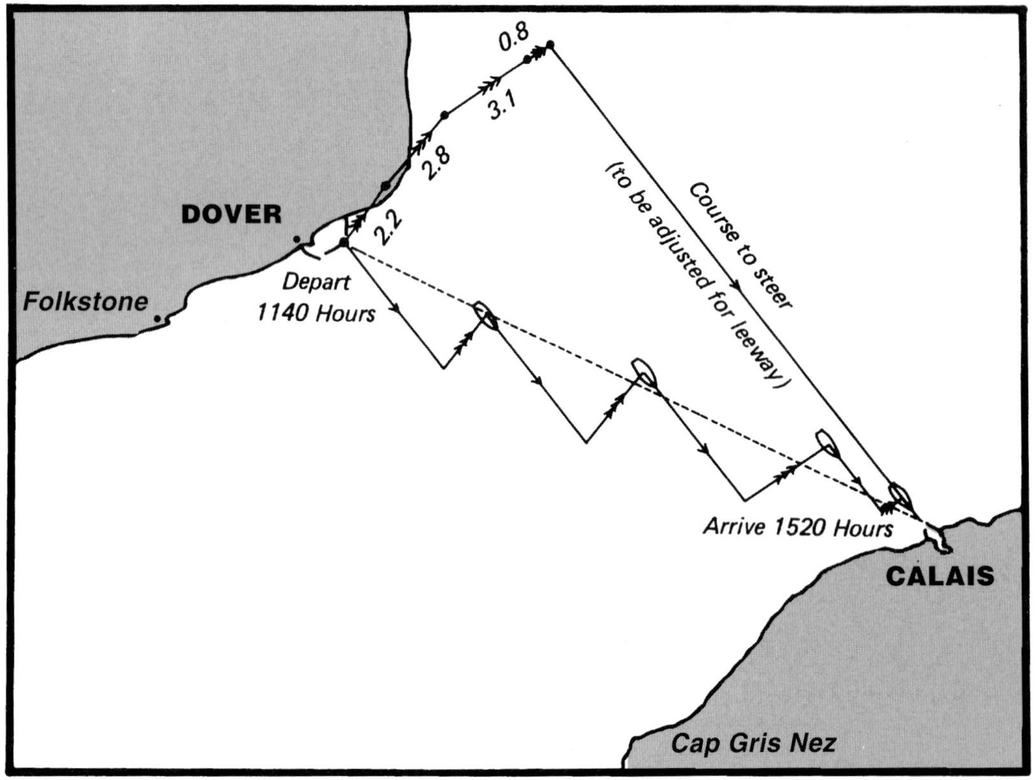

Since Calais lies east of Dover, it is advantageous to cross as the stream floods NE through the Strait. The estimated positions for each hour of the passage are located on the tidal stream atlas chartlets. The directions of sets are noted. The mean rates are converted through the adjacent conversion table using the columns of figures which is indicated·by the height of HW Cherbourg (6.6m). The sets and drifts are then plotted on the passage chart from the point of departure (Dover) and the course to steer is thus established.

Figure 7.4

8 Windward Passages

WINDWARD TACTICS

Cruising by sail is generally undertaken for pleasure, and it is very rewarding and relaxing to travel using only the wind and tide as motive power. However, the prospect of a long beat to one's destination does not have universal appeal, and in some cases a downwind alternative may therefore be selected. If however, one is committed to a particular destination which happens to be upwind, then a beat is unavoidable. Some thoughts on windward tactics may therefore be helpful.

APPARENT WIND

If a motor boat is making a passage on a windless day, at 10 knots, then its ensign will stream astern as shown in Figure 8.1. Should a 10 knot wind spring up on the port beam, then the ensign will stream as shown in Figure 8.2.

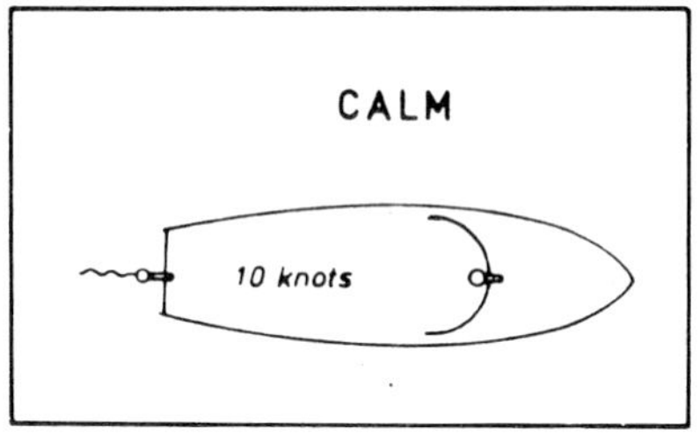

Figure 8.1

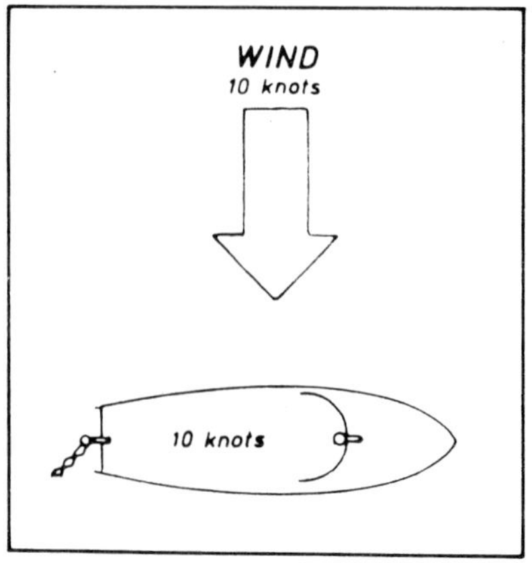

Figure 8.2

The wind apparent to those on board will be the wind that is indicated by the ensign, which is called the *apparent wind*. It is known that, whether close-hauled or reaching, the apparent wind changes direction and strength as the yacht gathers speed: the wind generated by the boat's forward speed combines with the *true wind*, and the burgees, telltales and ensign stream to the new *apparent wind*. If the speeds and directions of the true wind and the yacht are known, a simple vector diagram, as shown in Figure 8.3, will show the shift of direction from true to apparent and will also indicate the wind velocity experienced by the crew aboard the yacht.

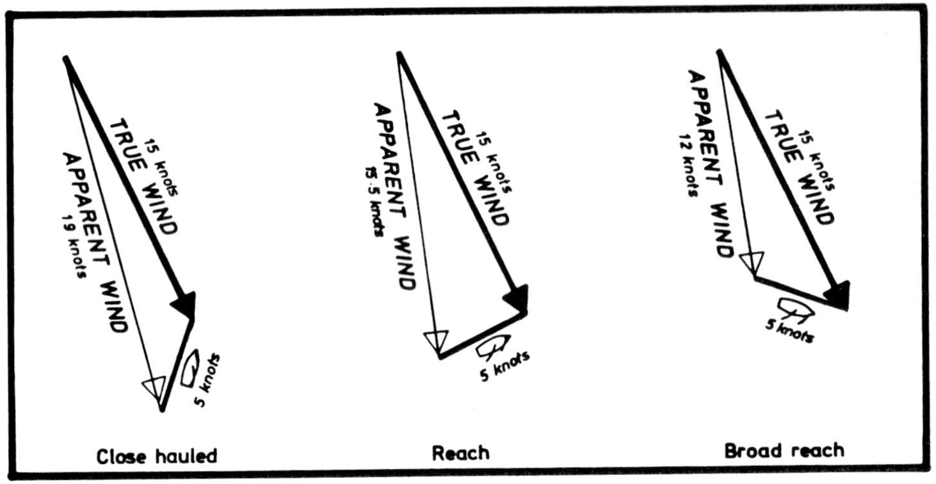

Figure 8.3

Figure 8.3 shows the important points of this phenomenon: note that when close-hauled, the apparent wind speed is 19 knots, whereas on a broad reach it is only 12 knots and on a dead run it will fall to the difference between the yacht's speed and the speed of the true wind — in this case 10 knots — with the direction of the apparent wind coinciding with that of the true wind. Note also that the greater the speed of the yacht across the direction of the true wind, as when reaching, the greater the deflection of the apparent wind. The experienced yachtsman and particularly one of the racing fraternity, will be quite familiar with the principles of apparent wind and indeed may well have electronic instruments to assess it. The skilled helmsman faces the critical problem that the faster he sails close-hauled, the more the apparent wind shifts towards the bow, requiring him to bear away to keep more wind in his sails, which seems to defeat the object of gaining more speed. Meanwhile, the yacht's attitude to the wind will be recorded and tacking angles and leeway angles will be established in order to give the navigator data which he can use for course setting and plotting. There is however another factor, often overlooked, which will affect the course made good, and which must be considered when making to windward on offshore passages.

AIR AND SEASTATE

The influence of the air tends to be underrated because it is invisible. Sea and air are obviously in the closest contact and when one moves, the other gets disturbed. It is this disturbed surface of the sea that we observe, in the form of waves, because the air is not visible. We are accustomed to the idea that waves will be created by air moving over the surface of still water, but cannot so readily appreciate that they can equally be caused by water moving under still air. It is the interaction of the two moving bodies which disturbs the surface, and the conditions observed result from this combination of forces. There are of course many other factors concerned with the formation of seastate: the changing velocity and direction of the wind when it gusts, the right-hand trend of moving bodies in the northern hemisphere, the losses caused by drag between the surfaces, and the effect of shallowing water — but these additional influences can be ignored, as they are difficult to quantify and the variables under discussion are complex enough.

If a 7 knot wind moving over the sea produces 2 foot waves, then on a completely windless day a sea surface moving at 7 knots, as in the Alderney Race or the Swinge, will create a very similar seastate. In these two cases, as in many others, the situation is aggravated by the turbulence associated with water passing over a rocky uneven bottom; the sea presents to the still air above it a surface akin to a giant cheese-grater, ensuring more than ordinary friction and therefore waves in good measure. This can occur on a totally windless day.

TIDE-WIND

As a yacht moves across the wind close-hauled or on a reach, the wind changes its apparent direction and is known as the apparent wind. A similar change occurs as the sea, motivated by tidal forces, moves as an entire sheet across the wind, carrying the yacht which floats upon it. The mass of moving water is in contact with the mass of moving air, and the yacht on the surface will experience the *apparent tide-wind* resulting from the moving components. Figure 8.4 shows the construction of the vector diagram of the apparent tide-wind.

TIDE-WIND AND SEASTATE

Wind against tide causes steep-fronted seas while wind with tide flattens the sea. Winds from points between these extremes flatten or roughen the seas, as one might imagine, in proportion to their proximity to the down-tide or up-tide direction. Ignoring the complexities of gusting winds, drag and right-hand drift — which in any case will affect the conditions in much the same way and do not therefore have much influence on the comparisons we wish to examine — the waves follow the dictates of the apparent tide-wind.

As the tidal stream slowly changes rate, so the apparent tide-wind slowly changes direction and the waves follow steadily the dictates of this change. But waves contain a lot of energy and momentum and therefore do not respond immediately to these changes. In areas where rectilinear streams run fast and change direction quickly, as they do in the confined waters of the Dover Strait and Bristol Channel, off headlands and in narrows between islands and outcrops where rotary streams are forced into linear paths, they change direction with a suddenness akin to a switch being thrown, and a wind driving across the stream can throw up a nasty sea. The relics of old waves are overtaken and overpowered by a new generation from a new direction, and the resultant corkscrew sea can be very uncomfortable. It can also put unusual strains on the keel and rig of a tuned racing yacht. These conditions can last for long periods where a long fetch across a relatively tideless sea produces trains of well-developed waves which then travel into an area of fast-moving streams. The critical wave structure is undermined by the movement of the wave bases, and at the same time the effective wind has changed direction and confused seas are the inevitable result, becoming particularly wild when fast streams quite suddenly change direction.

TIDE-WIND: LEE-BOWING THE TIDE

For practical purposes, when sailing and plotting courses at the chart-table, known tacking angles can be applied to the apparent tide-wind diagram as shown in Figure 8.5 which illustrates the following: A yacht which can sail at 45° to the wind and makes 5° of leeway has a total tacking angle of 100° in a situation where there is no tide. However, by changing tack with the changing tidal stream as shown, and thereby keeping the tidal stream running under the leeside of the yacht, the total tacking angle is effectively reduced, in this particular example to 77°, due to the effect of apparent tide-wind.

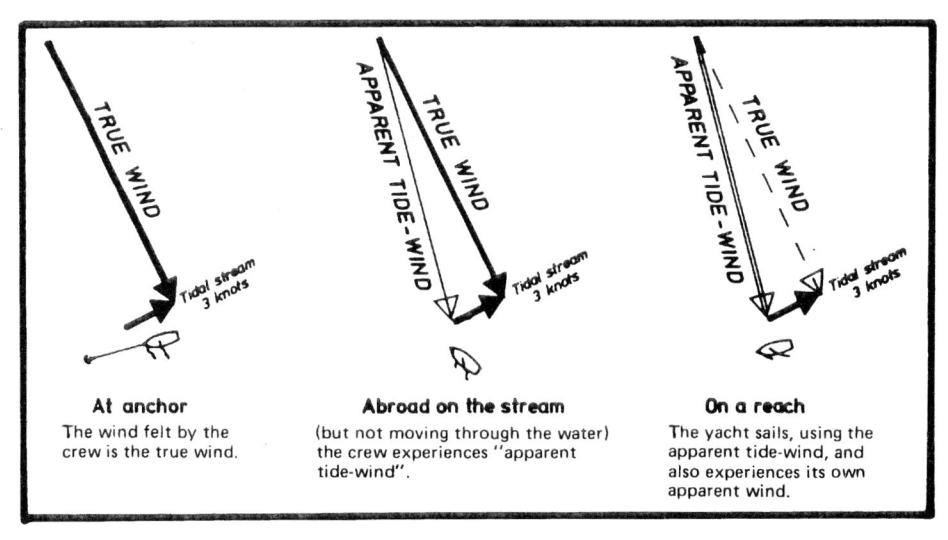

Figure 8.4

At anchor
The wind felt by the crew is the true wind.

Abroad on the stream
(but not moving through the water) the crew experiences "apparent tide-wind".

On a reach
The yacht sails, using the apparent tide-wind, and also experiences its own apparent wind.

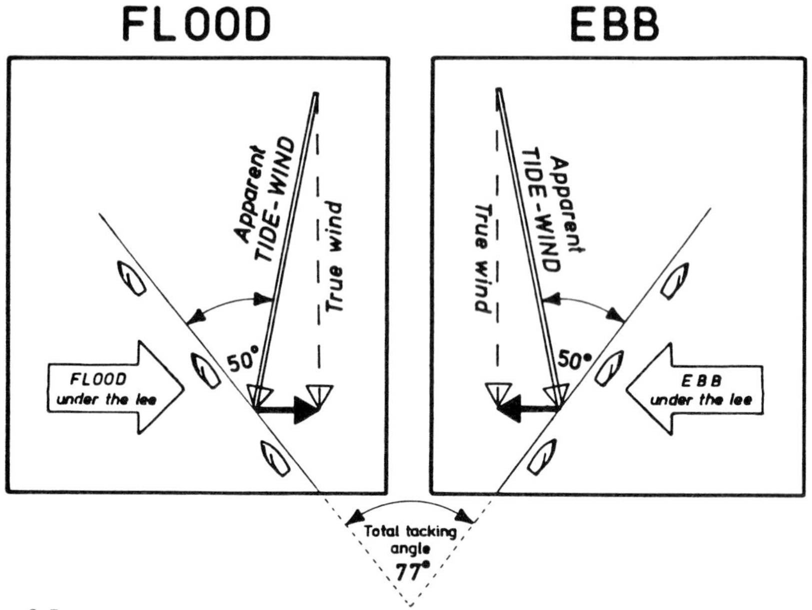

FLOOD

EBB

Figure 8.5

WINDWARD PASSAGES

If a destination is not directly to windward, but can be attained by sailing predominantly on one tack only, with perhaps just one or two alternate tacks, then if it is possible to make these tacks when the tidal stream will be running at its maximum rate under the lee bow, the apparent tide-wind will be at its most advantageous. Under these circumstances, the gain over the ground towards one's destination may seem disappointingly small, but the advantage becomes evident when the alternative is considered: sailing off to leeward with the stream adding to the fast leeward progress. Figure 8.6 illustrates this point.

The passage illustrated shows a departure from Cherbourg timed to make use of two ebb streams, and a plan to sail predominantly on port tack in a NNW wind of about 15 knots; the speed of the yacht is estimated to be 5 knots. In the previous chapter dealing with the same type of passage with the wind free, the aim of the passage planning was to find a constant heading on which to sail across the channel. In a situation demanding close-hauled sailing, the yacht's heading must constantly change, even on the same tack, to accommodate the advantageous changing of the apparent tide-wind. During the flood stream on this passage, the new direction of the apparent tide-wind favours going about onto starboard tack (shown at A); progress over the ground will seem disappointingly slow (3 knots in this illustration) but the alternative (shown at B) is obviously unacceptable.

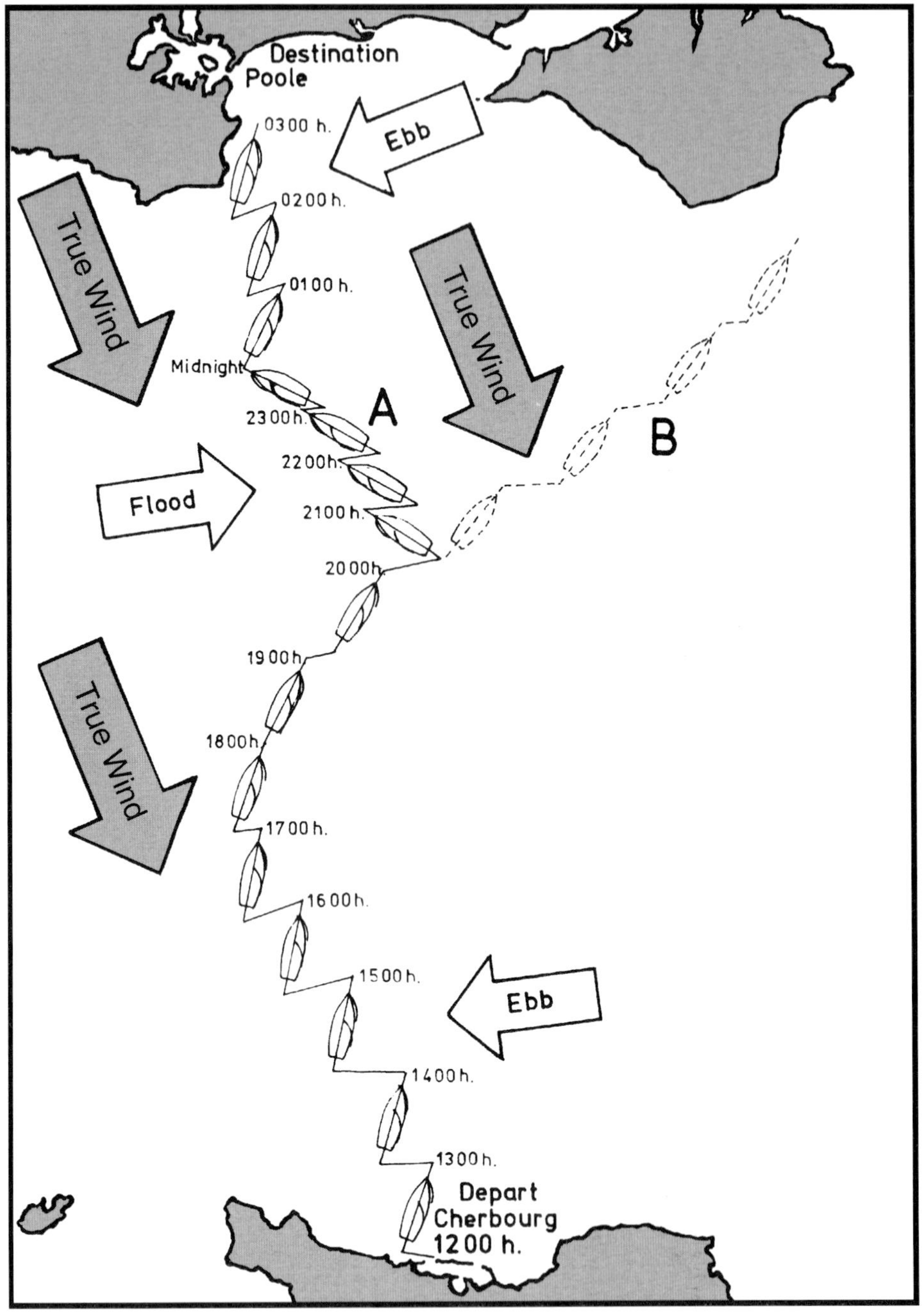

Figure 8.6

PASSAGE PLANNING

A caution is necessary here: the variables involved in planning windward passages are very complex and can make a nonsense of any simple rule which may be expounded. One of the major problems lies in predicting the true wind direction, even for a short time ahead, as changes are constantly occurring and can be quite dramatic if for example, a front goes through. Even less predictable are changes in wind direction as a result of summer sea-breezes. Unfortunately, even a small change in the true wind can mean quite a radical re-think of one's strategy. To add to the problem, there is an almost infinite choice of departure times, each of which alters the picture.

For the theoretical yachtsman, the vector diagrams of: course-to-steer, set, drift, and track; true wind, boat-speed and apparent wind; true wind, tidal stream and apparent tide-wind, can all be plotted as a classroom exercise. But for the practical yachtsman, the best advice is simply to apply a rule-of-thumb extracted from the above, which is: *make the best possible use of apparent tide-wind by keeping the tide running under the lee bow.*

9 Tides and Electronic Position-Fixing Systems

LIMITATIONS

Increasingly, yachts are fitted either with GPS (Global Positioning System), or some other type of electronic position-fixing system. These systems provide a diversity of information and give great advantages for the navigator: at the press of a button, whether in fog, rain or sunshine, a position is available. Perhaps there is a danger of over-reliance upon the instrument, with even the safety-conscious being lulled into dependence on it in conditions of bad visibility. However, it must be said that these instruments are an excellent aid to navigation, especially when used correctly in conjunction with normal navigational practices.

Position-fixing by electronics is a great aid to navigation as it is immediate and precise. When a fix is required on passage, either because one needs to know one's position due to a nearby hazard or one needs a fix as a departure point for a new tack or a new leg of the passage, these electronic instruments provide a fix that is accurate, not prone to human error, and one which is obtained quickly and easily. However, electronic instruments must be used in conjunction with normal navigational practices and not as a replacement for chart-work. The GPS owner is advised to refer once again to Chapters 5, 6 and 7, remembering that however good electronic instruments are at providing accurate information, they can in no way alter the effects of tide upon one's vessel

SHORT PASSAGES – CROSS-TRACK ERROR

Where a passage or part of a passage is to be made using the *stay-on-track* course-setting procedure (as described and illustrated in Chapter 5) the cross-track error facility can be used. The *course-to-steer* to allow for tide is calculated in the same way as described in Chapter 5, and the points of departure and destination are entered into the GPS set. Once on passage, the set will show up any departure from the *track* (either due to leeway or due to an error in calculations) as a *cross-track error*. The actual course being steered can then be adjusted accordingly if necessary.

The departure and destination points need not be visible points, but may be a fix from the set, or by other methods, which is then plotted on the chart. In areas such as the Thames Estuary or the Channel Islands it is essential to navigate in short legs, calculating a course to steer to stay on track for each leg. Electronics, used in this way, are an invaluable aid. The method for each leg is as follows:

1. The departure and destination points for each leg, plotted on the chart, are entered into the GPS set.
2. From the tidal stream atlas, obtain the set and drift for a suitable period of time, such as one hour, which is marked off from the point of departure for the leg.
3. Estimate the speed of the vessel to find the distance that will be travelled through the water for the same period of time; this distance is then marked off to find the course to steer.
4. Where applicable the estimated leeway is applied (into the wind) to find the actual heading that will be required.

5. Check that the yacht is staying on the track by reference to the cross-track error display. Adjust the course being steered as necessary to stay on track.

Remember that the bearing and distance to the destination is not the same as the course-to-steer for it to compensate for a tidal stream.

Figure 9.1 illustrates an example of the chart-work for this procedure.

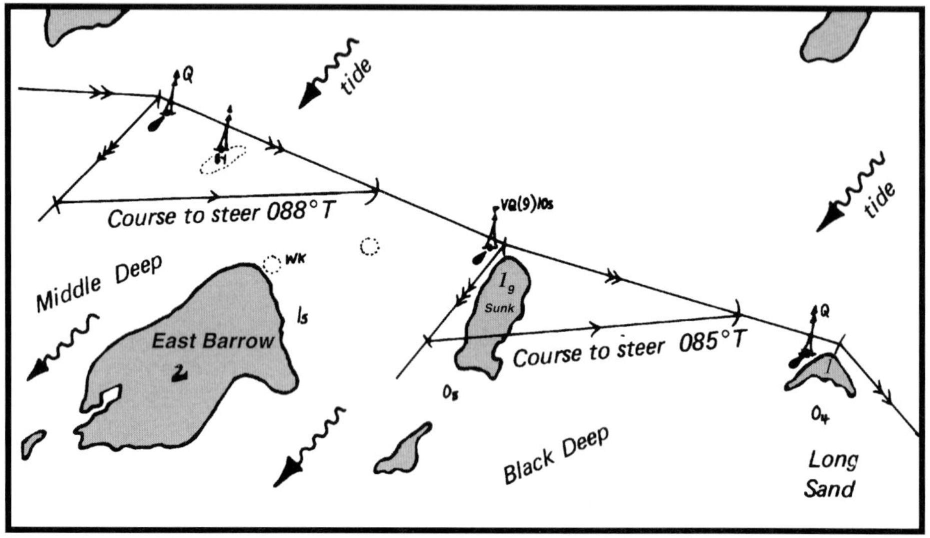

Figure 9.1

COURSE SETTING — LONGER PASSAGES

The temptation to avoid when making longer passages, such as across the Channel, is that of slavishly following an electronic navigator from departure to destination by constantly correcting for cross-track error to keep the yacht on the rhumb line. This will result in a much slower passage than necessary. Passages of several hours or more across a changing tidal stream, where the aim is to steer a straight course for the whole passage would be planned as described in Chapter 7: COURSE SETTING — THE SHORTEST DISTANCE. It cannot be emphasised too much that, where a whole sheet of water is moving (as in the English Channel or North Sea), the shortest distance between two points is achieved by steering through the water *on a constant heading* with as little course alteration as possible. The moving mass of water means that the vessel actually travels in a distinct curve over the ground. This will inevitably cause the vessel to depart many miles off the *rhumb line*, or track, which means that the cross-track error display should be ignored as it is of no help when one is not actually attempting to steer the vessel along a set track.

To illustrate this point, a simple example is considered: To cross from Portland to Cherbourg at 5 knots should take 12 hours. Let us assume that for the first 6 hours the tidal stream will be running westwards at about 2 knots, and for the

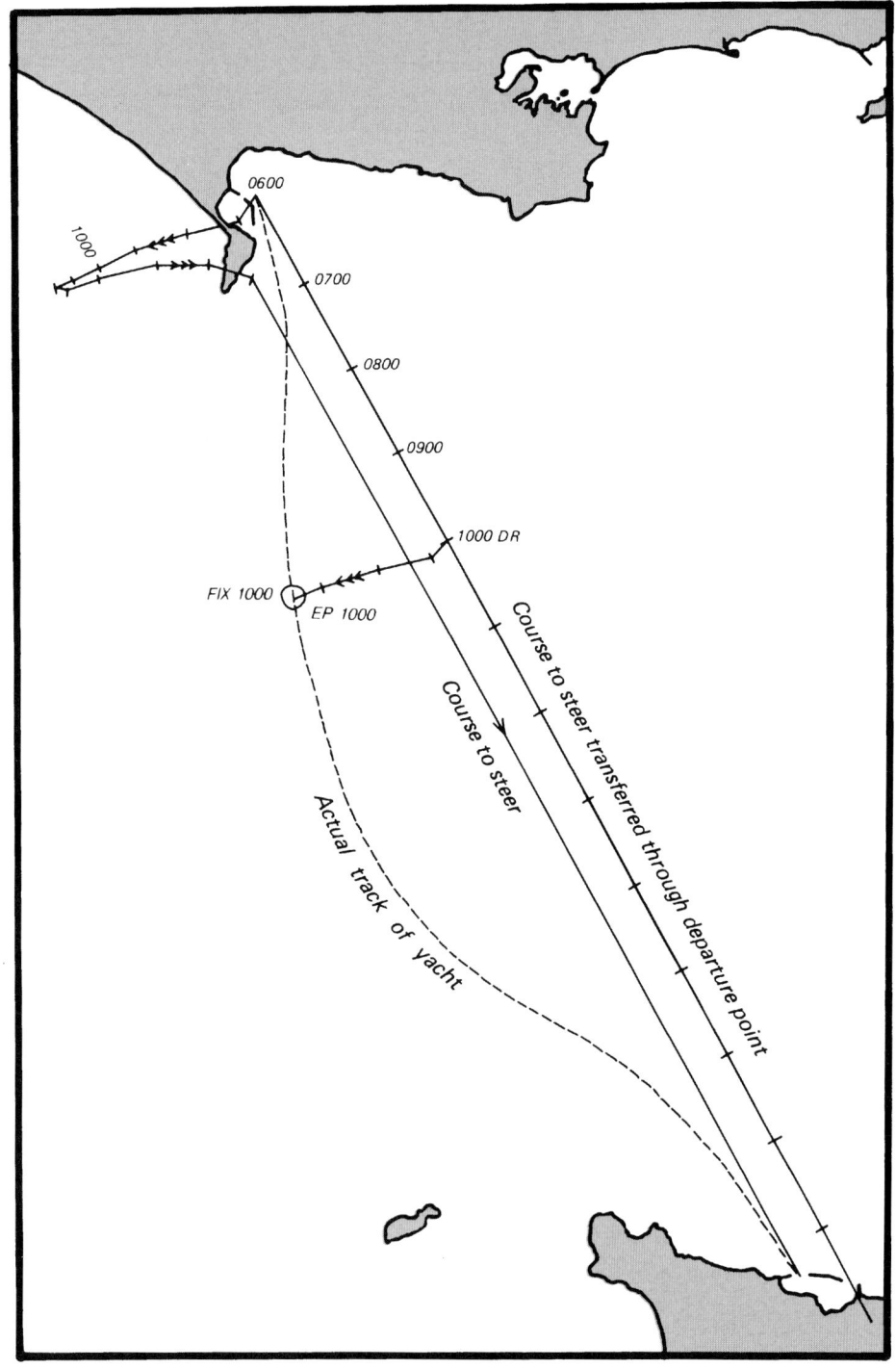

Figure 9.2

last 6 hours it will be running eastwards at about 2 knots. If one starts by heading through the water towards Cherbourg and maintains that heading for the first 6 hours, then the stream will take one 10 or 12 miles westwards, down-channel. But this does not matter because for the next 6 hours it will bring one back eastwards, up-channel. It is nonsensical to waste time and reduce progress towards Cherbourg by trying to stick to the rhumb line by fighting the west-going stream when a later east-going stream will inevitably bring one back to the rhumb line and into Cherbourg.

If when this stay-on-course course-setting method is followed it is required to make a check that all is going according to plan, one's tidal calculations can be verified as follows: obtain a fix from one's electronic navigator and then plot as illustrated in Figure 9.2:

First transfer the course-to-steer line through the departure point using parallel rules. For the time that the fix was taken, transfer the accumulated tidal set and drift so far, marking it off from the DR position for the same time. This will give an EP for the same time as the fix was taken. The position of the EP and the fix should obviously correspond; if they do not, then the error (which may be due either to incorrect estimation of leeway or a slight error in tidal predictions or calculations) can be compensated for by a slight adjustment to the course being steered.

Once these few basic principles are understood, it will be realised that passage-planning still has to be completed before setting off – there is no alternative, since GPS cannot actually do the passage-planning. Navigation in tidal waters is in no way altered by the use of electronics: it is simply made much easier, quicker and more precise.

Part 2

ILE D'OUESSANT AND CHENAL DU FOUR
The channels between Ile d'Ouessant and the mainland are beset with dangers and with strong and sometimes violent streams, particularly when wind is opposed to tide. The Passage du Fromveur on the south-eastern side of the Ile d'Ouessant has very fast streams, attaining 8 or 9 knots at maximum springs, and the seas can be very turbulent. The Chenal du Four, close to the mainland, is the usual passage for yachtsmen. All the other channels between the Passage du Fromveur and Chenal du Four should only be attempted with local knowledge and in good weather. Winds from a northerly direction substantially increase the velocity of the south-going ebb streams through all these channels.

THE SWINGE AND ORTAC CHANNEL
Race conditions with overfalls will prevail in these channels during the flood and ebb and it is therefore advisable to negotiate them at slack water.

ALDERNEY RACE
Passage through the race should if possible be avoided when wind against tide conditions prevail. On windless days passages south or southwest through the Alderney Race on the ebb stream will be comfortable. However, when heading north or northeast on the flood stream, small areas of turbulence occur as Alderney is approached and passed, coinciding with changes in the depth of water. As a yacht passes north of a line from Quenard Point to Cap de la Hague, observations by the author indicate an area of confused water which extends 6 or 7 miles northwards into the English Channel during the period −2 to +1½ hour HW Cherbourg; it is also likely that the rate of flood streams in this area exceeds predictions. These uncomfortable conditions can be avoided if a passage is planned so as to pass through the area at slack water.

OFFSHORE TIDAL HEIGHTS: LE HAVRE
Offshore tidal heights shown in "broad arrows" on each page of the tidal atlases are calculated from co-tidal and co-range lines compiled by the Deutsches Hydrographisches Institut and published by the Admiralty. The author advises caution in their use, particularly in the sea area near Le Havre during the period −2 to HW Cherbourg, when the rise of tide is very rapid and can be as much as one metre in 20 minutes. Under these circumstances any small error in the data can result in a magnified error in the height prediction.

EFFECT OF RAINFALL: SEINE MARITIME
Streams in the Seine Maritime can be very much influenced by rainfall and in particular by the spate of water in the Spring which is caused by thawing snow in the mountains. The effect is to delay the flood stream and to reduce the effective speed of a vessel proceeding upstream, although it is usually possible even under these circumstances for a yacht to reach Rouen on a single tide.

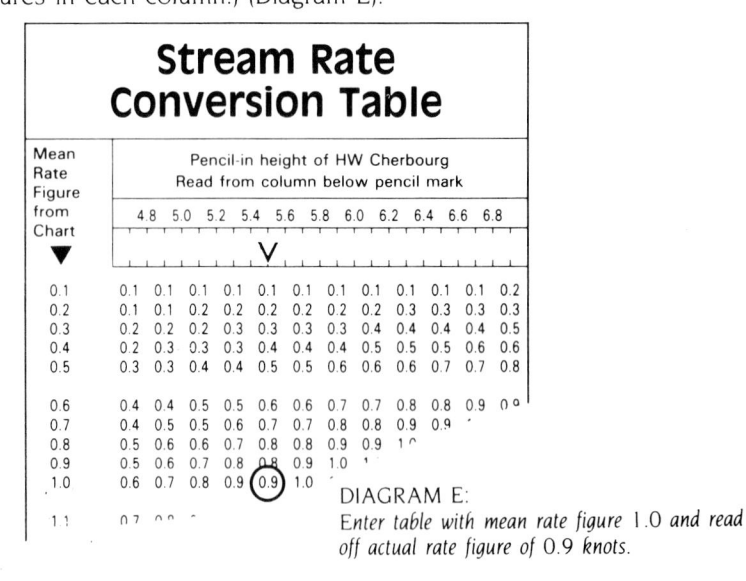

Instructions for use

BEFORE SAILING

1. Establish the time printed in your Cherbourg tide tables in relation to your ship's actual clock time (see previous page).
2. From the Cherbourg tide table extract the time of HW for the passage required (Diagram A). Enter this time in pencil in the box provided on the page for HW Cherbourg (Diagram B).

		Time	Ht	Time	Ht
Sa	1	0729	5.5	1959	5.5
Su	2	0810	5.8	2036	5.7
M	3	0846	6.0	2109	5.9
Tu	4	0919	6.1	2140	6.0
W	5	0950	6.2	2209	6.0
Th	6	1020	6.2	2237	6.0
F	7	1050	6.2	2307	
Sa	8	1120	6.0	2330	
Su	9	1149	5.		
M	10	0000			
Tu	11				
W					

DIAGRAM A:
Time and height for Saturday 1st used here.

HW Cherbourg **HW**

Time 0729 (to be inserted)

DIAGRAM B

3. Turning backwards page by page enter the appropriate times in the boxes from ''HW −1'' to ''HW −6''. Then enter the appropriate times in the boxes ''HW +1'' to ''HW +6'' turning forwards page by page. If the passage is expected to exceed one tidal cycle, repeat this process for the next HW as well: to avoid confusion a note of the date may be added by the pencilled time.
4. From the Cherbourg tide table, also extract the height of Cherbourg HW for the relevant time (Diagram A). Mark this height in pencil on the scale that appears at the top of every table; use a vertical arrow or other similar mark. Mark each page in this way from ''HW −6'' through to ''HW +6'' (Diagram C). It is the position of this arrow that indicates the correct vertical column of figures to use when referring to the tables. If the arrow falls between two vertical columns it will be necessary to interpolate between the figures shown in each column.

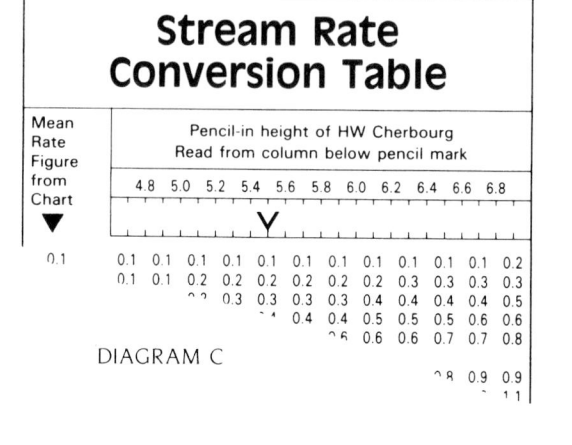

Stream Rate Conversion Table

Mean Rate Figure from Chart ▼	Pencil-in height of HW Cherbourg Read from column below pencil mark											
	4.8	5.0	5.2	5.4	5.6	5.8	6.0	6.2	6.4	6.6	6.8	
0.1	0.1	0.1	0.1	0.1	0.1	0.1	0.1	0.1	0.1	0.1	0.1	0.2
	0.1	0.1	0.2	0.2	0.2	0.2	0.2	0.2	0.3	0.3	0.3	0.3
			0.2	0.3	0.3	0.3	0.3	0.4	0.4	0.4	0.4	0.5
					0.4	0.4	0.5	0.5	0.5	0.6	0.6	
					0.6	0.6	0.6	0.7	0.7	0.8		
						0.8	0.9	0.9				
							1.1				

DIAGRAM C

TO FIND THE DIRECTION AND RATE OF A TIDAL STREAM

1. Turn to the page on which your pencilled time is nearest to the required time.
2. Mark your DR position or EP on the Tidal Streams Chart and find the nearest arrow to your marked position (or interpolate between two arrows) (Diagram D).
3. Measure the direction of the arrow using a Douglas protractor or similar instrument to obtain (in True) the direction of the tidal stream.
4. Stream rates shown on the Tidal Streams Chart are mean rates: to obtain the actual rate of the tidal stream note this mean rate figure shown by your chosen arrow (or interpolate as necessary). (Diagram D)

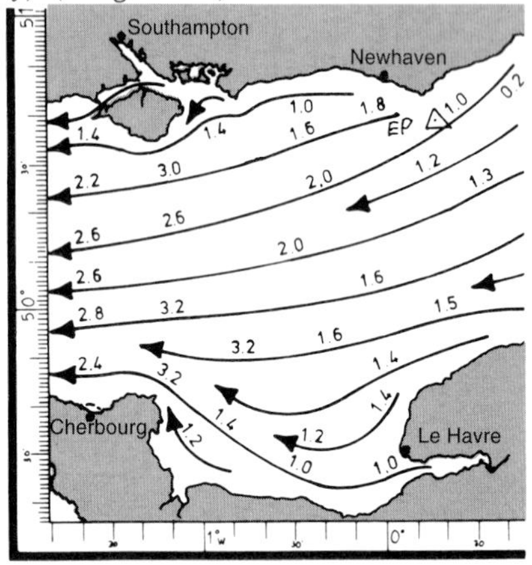

DIAGRAM D:
Direction of flow 236°T, mean rate figure 1.0.

5. In the Stream Rate Conversion Table, find this mean rate figure in the left-hand column and then read across the table to the column of figures underneath your pencilled mark on the top scale. The figure thus found gives the actual rate of tidal stream in knots. (If your pencil mark is between two vertical columns, interpolate between the figures in each column.) (Diagram E).

Stream Rate Conversion Table

Mean Rate Figure from Chart ▼	Pencil-in height of HW Cherbourg Read from column below pencil mark											
	4.8	5.0	5.2	5.4	5.6	5.8	6.0	6.2	6.4	6.6	6.8	
0.1	0.1	0.1	0.1	0.1	0.1	0.1	0.1	0.1	0.1	0.1	0.1	0.2
0.2	0.1	0.1	0.2	0.2	0.2	0.2	0.2	0.2	0.3	0.3	0.3	0.3
0.3	0.2	0.2	0.2	0.3	0.3	0.3	0.3	0.4	0.4	0.4	0.4	0.5
0.4	0.2	0.3	0.3	0.3	0.4	0.4	0.4	0.5	0.5	0.5	0.6	0.6
0.5	0.3	0.3	0.4	0.4	0.5	0.5	0.6	0.6	0.6	0.7	0.7	0.8
0.6	0.4	0.4	0.5	0.5	0.6	0.6	0.7	0.7	0.8	0.8	0.9	0.9
0.7	0.4	0.5	0.5	0.6	0.7	0.7	0.8	0.8	0.9	0.9		
0.8	0.5	0.6	0.6	0.7	0.8	0.8	0.9	0.9	1.0			
0.9	0.5	0.6	0.7	0.8	0.8	0.9	1.0					
1.0	0.6	0.7	0.8	0.9	0.9	1.0						
1.1	0.7	0.8										

DIAGRAM E:
Enter table with mean rate figure 1.0 and read off actual rate figure of 0.9 knots.

TO FIND THE HEIGHT OF TIDE AT THE LISTED PORTS AND PLACES
1. Turn to the page on which your pencilled time is nearest to the required time.
2. From the place listed in the left-hand column of the table "Tidal Heights — Ports and Places", read across the table to the column of figures underneath your pencilled mark on the top scale. The figure thus found gives the height of tide, in metres, above Chart Datum, for the time pencilled in the box on that page (Diagram F).

TIDAL HEIGHTS — PORTS & PLACES

Pencil-in height of HW Cherbourg ▶	4.8	5.0	5.2	5.4	5.6	5.8	6.0	6.2	6.4	6.6	6.8
ENGLAND											
Kings Lynn	2.2	2.1	1.9	1.8	1.7	1.5	1.4	1.2	1.1	1.1	1.1
Blakeney Bar	3.0	2.8	2.6	2.4	2.2	2.1	1.9	1.8	1.6	1.5	1.4
Cromer	2.4	2.3	2.1	2.0	1.8	1.7	1.5	1.4	1.2	1.1	1.0
Gt. Yarmouth (Gorleston)	1.1	1.0	1.0	0.9	0.8	0.8	0.7	0.6	0.5	0.4	0.3
Lowestoft	1.1	1.0	1.0	1.0	0.9	0.8	0.8	0.7	0.7	0.6	0.5
Southwold Haven	1.0	1.0	1.0	1.0	1.0	0.9	0.9	0.9	0.9	0.8	0.7
Orford Haven appr'ch	1.6	1.6	1.6	1.6	1.6	1.6	1.6	1.6	1.6	1.7	1.7
Woodbridge Haven	1.9	1.9	1.9	1.9	1.9	2.0	2.0	2.0	2.0	2.1	2.1
Felixstowe	2.0	2.0	2.0	2.0	2.0	2.0	2.0	2.0	2.1	2.2	2.2
Harwich	2.2	2.2	2.2	2.2	2.3	2.3	2.3	2.4	2.4	2.4	2.4
Walton-on-the-Naze	2.2	2.2	2.2	2.3	2.3	2.4	2.4	2.5	2.5	2.6	2.6
Brightlingsea	2.4	2.5	2.7	2.8	2.9	3.1	3.2	3.4	3.5	3.6	3.8
Bradwell	2.8	2.9	3.1	3.2	3.3	3.5	3.6	3.8	3.9		
Burnham	3.2	3.3	3.5	3.6	3.7	3.9	4.0				
Leigh, Southend	3.3	3.4	3.6	3.7	3.8	3.9					
London Bridge	4.9	5.2	5.4	5.7	6.0						
Sheerness	3.4	3.5	3.7	3.8							
Chatham	3.4	3.6	3.8	4.0							
Rochester	3.5	3.7	3.9								
Whitstable approach	3.5	3.6									
Edinburgh Channels	2.8										
Margate											
Ramsgate											

DIAGRAM F:
Enter table at place required, Cromer, and read off height 1.8m in the column underneath the pencil mark.

OFFSHORE HEIGHTS
Information about offshore tidal heights is shown in the "Tidal Heights Offshore" diagram for every hour either side of HW. These heights are quite closely related to the heights of tide at nearby ports and places.

TO FIND THE HEIGHT OF TIDE OFFSHORE
1. Turn to the page on which your pencilled time is nearest to the required time.
2. Find the broad arrow nearest to your position. This arrow gives you the following information:

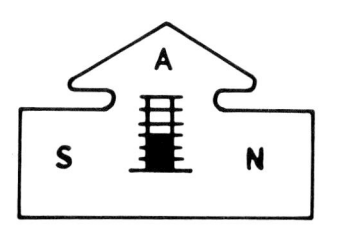

A Average Height of Tide at that time. This is the height of tide, in metres, above Chart Datum, for the time pencilled in the box on that page. Although only an average, this figure is sufficiently accurate to use for most coastal navigation.

S Height of Tide at Springs for the time pencilled in the box on that page.

N Height of Tide at Neaps for the time pencilled in the box on that page. The Tidal Gauge gives a visual display of the approximate state of the tide with the vertical movement of the tide described briefly above or below.

The Yachtsman's Tidal Atlas
WESTERN CHANNEL

TIDAL STREAM RATES & TIDAL HEIGHTS
for the area including
Channel Islands
Western Approaches to Fastnet Rock
St. Georges Channel (South)
Bristol Channel

-6
6 hours before HW Cherbourg

Tidal Heights

Copyright © J Reeve-Fowkes and
Thomas Reed Publications.
No copying without permission

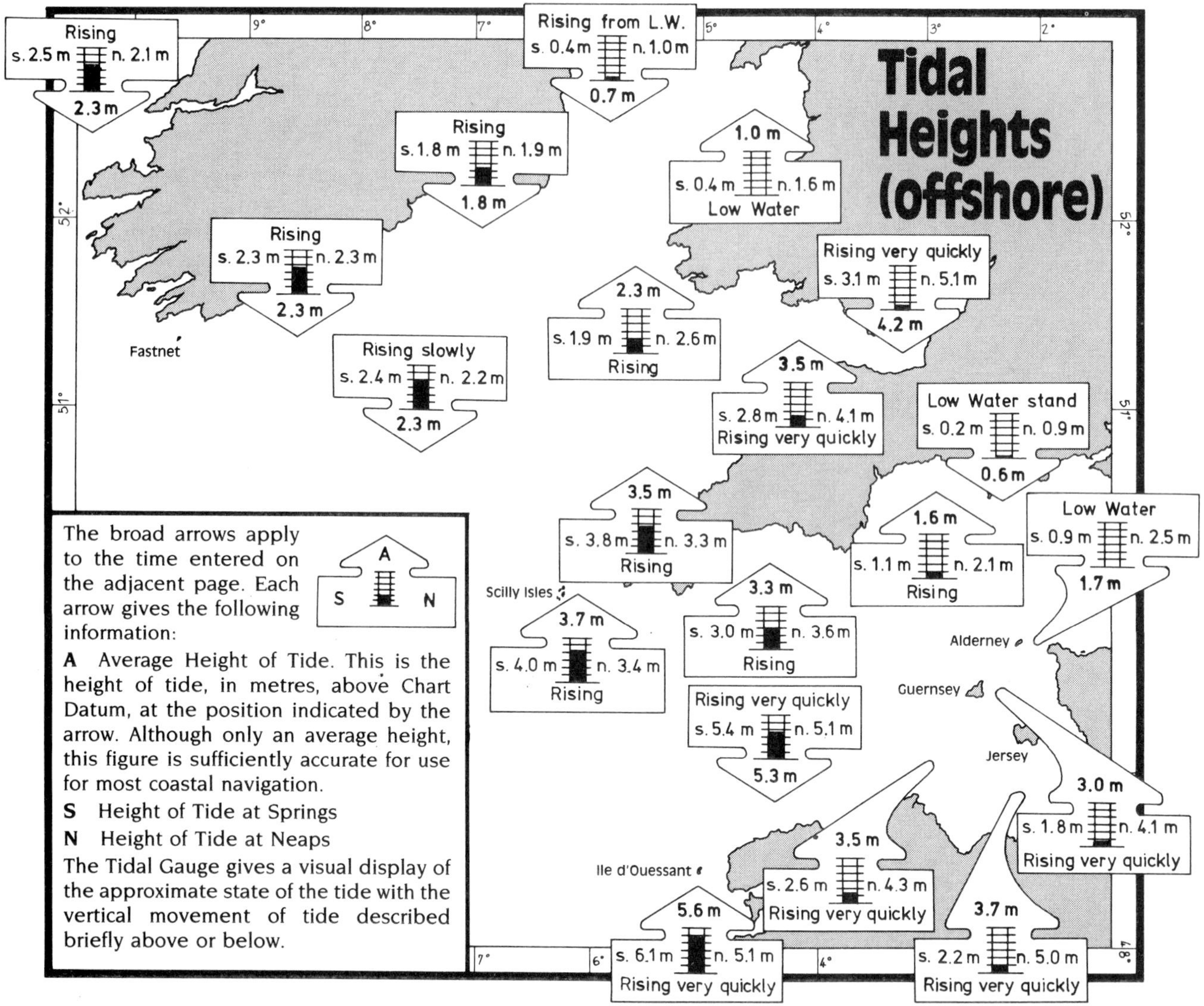

Tidal Heights (offshore)

Rising
s. 2.5 m n. 2.1 m
2.3 m

Rising from L.W.
s. 0.4 m n. 1.0 m
0.7 m

Rising
s. 1.8 m n. 1.9 m
1.8 m

1.0 m
s. 0.4 m n. 1.6 m
Low Water

Rising
s. 2.3 m n. 2.3 m
2.3 m

Rising slowly
s. 2.4 m n. 2.2 m
2.3 m

2.3 m
s. 1.9 m n. 2.6 m
Rising

Rising very quickly
s. 3.1 m n. 5.1 m
4.2 m

3.5 m
s. 2.8 m n. 4.1 m
Rising very quickly

Low Water stand
s. 0.2 m n. 0.9 m
0.6 m

3.5 m
s. 3.8 m n. 3.3 m
Rising

3.3 m
s. 3.0 m n. 3.6 m
Rising

1.6 m
s. 1.1 m n. 2.1 m
Rising

Low Water
s. 0.9 m n. 2.5 m
1.7 m

3.7 m
s. 4.0 m n. 3.4 m
Rising

Rising very quickly
s. 5.4 m n. 5.1 m
5.3 m

3.0 m
s. 1.8 m n. 4.1 m
Rising very quickly

3.5 m
s. 2.6 m n. 4.3 m
Rising very quickly

5.6 m
s. 6.1 m n. 5.1 m
Rising very quickly

3.7 m
s. 2.2 m n. 5.0 m
Rising very quickly

Fastnet
Scilly Isles
Ile d'Ouessant
Alderney
Guernsey
Jersey

The broad arrows apply to the time entered on the adjacent page. Each arrow gives the following information:

A Average Height of Tide. This is the height of tide, in metres, above Chart Datum, at the position indicated by the arrow. Although only an average height, this figure is sufficiently accurate for use for most coastal navigation.

S Height of Tide at Springs

N Height of Tide at Neaps

The Tidal Gauge gives a visual display of the approximate state of the tide with the vertical movement of tide described briefly above or below.

TIDAL HEIGHTS — PORTS & PLACES

Pencil-in height of HW Cherbourg ►	4.8	5.0	5.2	5.4	5.6	5.8	6.0	6.2	6.4	6.6	6.8
WALES											
Pwllheli, Barmouth.......	2.0	1.9	1.7	1.6	1.4	1.3	1.1	1.0	0.8	0.7	0.6	0.5
Aberystwth	2.1	1.9	1.7	1.5	1.3	1.1	0.9	0.7	0.5	0.3	0.2	0.0
Fishguard, P.Cardigan ..	2.4	2.2	2.0	1.8	1.6	1.4	1.3	1.1	0.9	0.8	0.6	0.5
Milford Haven	3.5	3.3	3.1	2.9	2.7	2.6	2.4	2.2	2.0	1.9	1.8	1.7
Burry Inlet approach	4.1	3.9	3.7	3.5	3.3	3.1	2.9	2.7	2.5	2.4	2.2	2.1
Swansea	4.4	4.2	4.0	3.8	3.6	3.3	3.1	2.9	2.7	2.5	2.4	2.2
P. Talbot, Porthcawl	5.0	4.7	4.5	4.2	4.0	3.7	3.5	3.2	3.0	2.9	2.7	2.6
Barry....................	5.6	5.3	4.9	4.6	4.3	4.0	3.6	3.3	3.0	2.9	2.8	2.7
Cardiff, Penarth..........	5.6	5.3	4.9	4.4	3.9	3.5	3.0	2.6	2.1	1.7	1.3	0.9
IRELAND											
Arklow	0.5	0.5	0.5	0.5	0.4	0.4	0.4	0.3	0.3	0.3	0.2	0.2
Rosslare	0.9	0.9	0.9	0.9	0.9	1.0	1.0	1.0	1.0	1.0	1.1	1.1
Waterford Hbr. entr.	1.9	1.9	1.9	1.9	1.9	1.8	1.8	1.8	1.8	1.8	1.7	1.7
Cork	1.9	1.9	1.9	1.9	1.8	1.8	1.8	1.7	1.7	1.6	1.6	1.5
Kinsale, Baltimore Bay .	2.2	2.2	2.2	2.2	2.2	2.2	2.2	2.2	2.2	2.2	2.2	2.2
ENGLAND-WEST											
Avonmouth	5.2	4.7	4.1	3.6	3.1	2.5	2.0	1.4	0.9	0.8	0.6	0.5
Weston-super-Mare	4.7	4.5	4.3	4.1	3.9	3.6	3.4	3.2	3.0	3.0	2.9	2.9
Watchet	5.5	5.2	5.0	4.7	4.5	4.2	4.0	3.7	3.5	3.4	3.4	3.3
Minehead	5.2	5.0	4.8	4.6	4.4	4.2	4.0	3.8	3.6	3.5	3.5	3.4
Porlock Bay	5.2	5.0	4.9	4.6	4.5	4.3	4.1	4.0	3.8	3.8	3.7	3.7
Ilfracombe	4.8	4.6	4.4	4.2	4.0	3.8	3.6	3.4	3.2	3.1	3.1	3.0
Appledore...............	3.3	3.1	2.9	2.7	2.5	2.3	2.1	1.9	1.7	1.6	1.6	1.5
Padstow, Newquay	4.2	4.1	3.9	3.8	3.7	3.6	3.5	3.4	3.3	3.3	3.2	3.2
St. Ives Bay.............	3.5	3.5	3.5	3.5	3.5	3.5	3.5	3.5	3.5	3.5	3.6	3.6
ISLANDS OFF											
Lundy Island	4.1	4.0	3.8	3.7	3.6	3.4	3.3	3.1	3.0	2.9	2.9	2.8
St. Mary's, Scilly Isles .	3.5	3.6	3.6	3.7	3.8	3.9	3.9	4.0	4.1	4.2	4.4	4.4
ENGLAND-SOUTH											
Falmouth, Helford R.....	3.5	3.4	3.4	3.3	3.2	3.1	3.1	3.0	2.9	2.9	2.9	2.9
Mevagissey, Looe.......	3.5	3.4	3.4	3.3	3.2	3.1	3.0	2.9	2.8	2.8	2.7	2.7
Plymouth, Yealm R......	3.7	3.6	3.4	3.3	3.2	3.1	2.9	2.8	2.7	2.6	2.6	2.5
Salcombe	3.5	3.4	3.2	3.1	3.0	2.8	2.7	2.5	2.4	2.4	2.3	2.3
Dartmouth	3.0	2.9	2.7	2.6	2.4	2.3	2.1	2.0	1.8	1.7	1.7	1.6
Brixham, Teignmouth...	2.8	2.7	2.5	2.4	2.2	2.1	1.9	1.8	1.6	1.5	1.4	1.3
Exmouth approach.......	2.6	2.4	2.2	2.0	1.8	1.7	1.5	1.3	1.1	1.1	1.0	1.0
Lyme Regis	2.3	2.2	2.0	1.9	1.8	1.6	1.5	1.3	1.2	1.1	1.1	1.0
Portland, Weymouth	0.9	0.8	0.8	0.7	0.6	0.5	0.5	0.4	0.3	0.3	0.2	0.2
Lulworth Cove	1.1	1.0	1.0	0.9	0.8	0.7	0.6	0.5	0.4	0.4	0.3	0.3
Swanage................	1.3	1.2	1.2	1.1	1.1	1.0	0.9	0.8	0.7	0.6	0.6	0.5
Poole Town	1.6	1.5	1.5	1.4	1.4	1.4	1.3	1.3	1.2	1.2	1.1	1.1
Christchurch Hbr........	0.8	0.8	0.8	0.8	0.8	0.8	0.8	0.7	0.7	0.7	0.7	0.7
CHANNEL ISLANDS											
Braye Hbr...............	2.7	2.5	2.3	2.1	1.8	1.6	1.4	1.1	0.9	0.7	0.6	0.4
St. Peter Port, Sark	4.6	4.3	3.9	3.6	3.3	3.0	2.6	2.3	2.0	1.7	1.5	1.2
St. Helier...............	5.5	5.1	4.7	4.3	3.9	3.4	3.0	2.6	2.2	1.9	1.6	1.3
Les Minquiers	5.2	4.9	4.5	4.2	3.9	3.5	3.2	2.8	2.5	2.3	2.0	1.8
FRANCE											
Cherbourg	2.8	2.6	2.4	2.2	2.0	1.8	1.6	1.4	1.2	0.9	0.7	0.4
Omonville	2.9	2.7	2.5	2.3	2.0	1.8	1.6	1.3	1.1	0.8	0.6	0.3
Iles Chausey	6.2	5.7	5.3	4.8	4.3	3.9	3.4	3.0	2.5	2.2	1.9	1.6
Carteret	5.2	4.8	4.4	4.0	3.7	3.3	2.9	2.6	2.2	1.9	1.7	1.4
Granville................	6.4	5.9	5.4	5.0	4.5	4.0	3.5	3.0	2.5	2.2	1.9	1.6
St Malo	6.2	5.7	5.3	4.8	4.3	3.8	3.3	2.8	2.3	2.0	1.7	1.4
All Hbrs. St Brieuc Bay	5.9	5.6	5.2	4.9	4.6	4.3	3.9	3.6	3.3	3.1	2.9	2.7
Ile de Bréhat	5.8	5.4	5.0	4.6	4.1	3.7	3.3	2.8	2.4	2.2	2.0	1.8
Lezardrieux	5.1	4.9	4.7	4.5	4.2	4.0	3.8	3.5	3.4	3.2	3.0	2.9
Tréguier	5.0	4.9	4.7	4.6	4.5	4.4	4.2	4.1	4.0	3.9	3.9	3.8
Morlaix, Primel Bay	5.7	5.6	5.4	5.3	5.2	5.1	5.0	4.9	4.8	4.7	4.6	4.5
Roscoff, Ile de Batz	5.5	5.4	5.4	5.3	5.2	5.2	5.1	5.1	5.0	4.9	4.9	4.8
L'Aberwrach	5.0	5.1	5.1	5.2	5.3	5.4	5.5	5.6	5.7	5.8	5.8	5.9
All Hbrs. Ch. du Four ...	4.8	4.9	5.1	5.2	5.3	5.5	5.6	5.8	5.9	6.0	6.0	6.1
Brest...................	4.9	5.0	5.2	5.3	5.4	5.6	5.7	5.9	6.0	6.1	6.2	6.3
Camaret, Douarnenez...	4.5	4.7	4.9	5.1	5.2	5.4	5.6	5.7	5.9	6.0	6.1	6.2

Stream Rate Conversion Table

Mean Rate Figure from Chart ▼	\multicolumn{12}{c}{Pencil-in height of HW Cherbourg — Read from column below pencil mark}
	4.8	5.0	5.2	5.4	5.6	5.8	6.0	6.2	6.4	6.6	6.8
0.2	0.1	0.1	0.1	0.1	0.2	0.2	0.2	0.2	0.3	0.3	0.3	0.3
0.4	0.2	0.2	0.2	0.3	0.3	0.4	0.4	0.5	0.5	0.6	0.6	0.7
0.6	0.2	0.3	0.4	0.4	0.5	0.6	0.7	0.7	0.8	0.9	0.9	1.0
0.8	0.4	0.4	0.5	0.6	0.7	0.8	0.9	1.0	1.1	1.1	1.2	1.3
1.0	0.4	0.5	0.6	0.7	0.9	1.0	1.1	1.2	1.3	1.4	1.5	1.7
1.2	0.5	0.6	0.7	0.9	1.0	1.2	1.3	1.4	1.6	1.7	1.9	2.0
1.4	0.6	0.7	0.9	1.0	1.2	1.4	1.5	1.7	1.8	2.0	2.2	2.3
1.6	0.6	0.8	1.0	1.2	1.4	1.6	1.7	1.9	2.1	2.3	2.5	2.7
1.8	0.7	0.9	1.1	1.3	1.5	1.7	2.0	2.2	2.4	2.6	2.8	3.0
2.0	0.8	1.0	1.2	1.5	1.7	1.9	2.2	2.4	2.6	2.9	3.1	3.3
2.2	0.9	1.1	1.4	1.6	1.9	2.1	2.3	2.6	2.9	3.2	3.4	3.7
2.4	0.9	1.2	1.5	1.8	2.1	2.3	2.6	2.9	3.2	3.4	3.7	4.0
2.6	1.0	1.3	1.6	1.9	2.2	2.5	2.8	3.1	3.4	3.7	4.0	4.3
2.8	1.1	1.4	1.7	2.1	2.4	2.7	3.0	3.4	3.7	4.0	4.3	4.7
3.0	1.2	1.5	1.9	2.2	2.6	2.9	3.2	3.6	4.0	4.3	4.6	5.0
3.2	1.3	1.6	2.0	2.4	2.7	3.1	3.4	3.8	4.2	4.6	4.9	5.3
3.4	1.3	1.7	2.1	2.5	2.9	3.3	3.7	4.1	4.5	4.9	5.3	5.7
3.6	1.4	1.8	2.2	2.7	3.1	3.5	3.9	4.3	4.7	5.2	5.6	6.0
3.8	1.5	1.9	2.4	2.8	3.3	3.7	4.1	4.6	5.0	5.4	5.9	6.3
4.0	1.6	2.0	2.5	3.0	3.4	3.9	4.3	4.8	5.3	5.7	6.2	6.7
4.2	1.7	2.1	2.6	3.1	3.6	4.1	4.6	5.0	5.5	6.0	6.5	7.0
4.4	1.7	2.2	2.7	3.3	3.8	4.3	4.8	5.3	5.8	6.3	6.8	7.3
4.6	1.8	2.3	2.9	3.4	3.9	4.5	5.0	5.5	6.1	6.6	7.1	7.7
4.8	1.9	2.4	3.0	3.6	4.1	4.7	5.2	5.8	6.3	6.9	7.4	8.0
5.0	2.0	2.5	3.1	3.7	4.3	4.9	5.4	6.0	6.6	7.2	7.7	8.3
5.2	2.0	2.6	3.2	3.8	4.4	5.0	5.6	6.2	6.8	7.4	8.0	8.6
5.4	2.1	2.8	3.4	4.0	4.6	5.2	5.7	6.5	7.1	7.7	8.4	9.0
5.6	2.2	2.9	3.5	4.1	4.8	5.4	6.1	6.7	7.4	8.0	8.7	9.3
5.8	2.3	3.0	3.6	4.3	5.0	5.6	6.3	7.0	7.6	8.3	9.0	9.6
6.0	2.4	3.0	3.7	4.4	5.1	5.8	6.5	7.2	7.9	8.6	9.3	9.9

Tidal Stream Rates

Copyright © J Reeve-Fowkes and Thomas Reed Publications.
No copying without permission

6 hours before HW Cherbourg **-6**

Time (to be inserted)

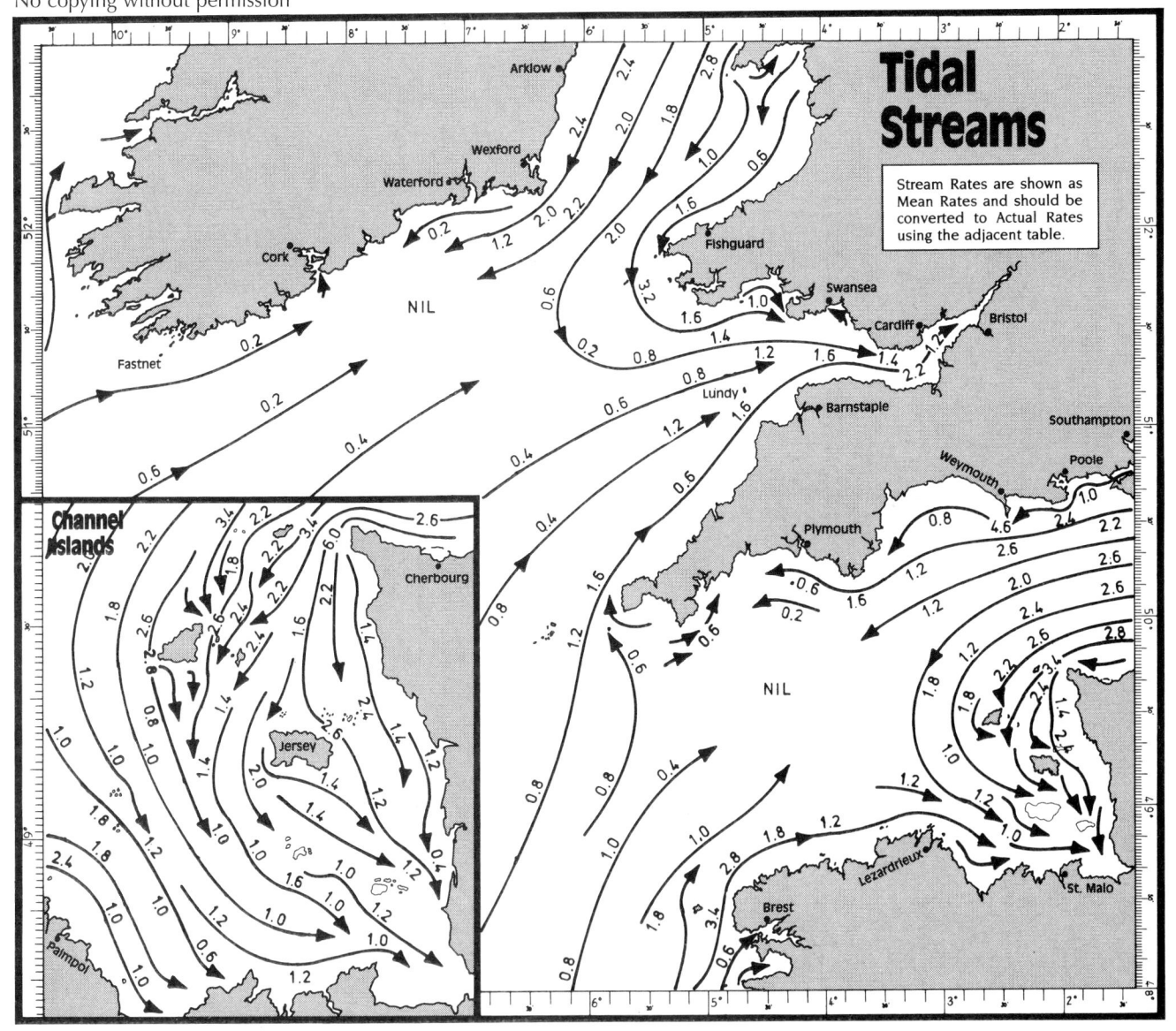

Tidal Streams

Stream Rates are shown as Mean Rates and should be converted to Actual Rates using the adjacent table.

61

-5 5 hours before HW Cherbourg

Tidal Heights

Copyright © J Reeve-Fowkes and
Thomas Reed Publications.
No copying without permission

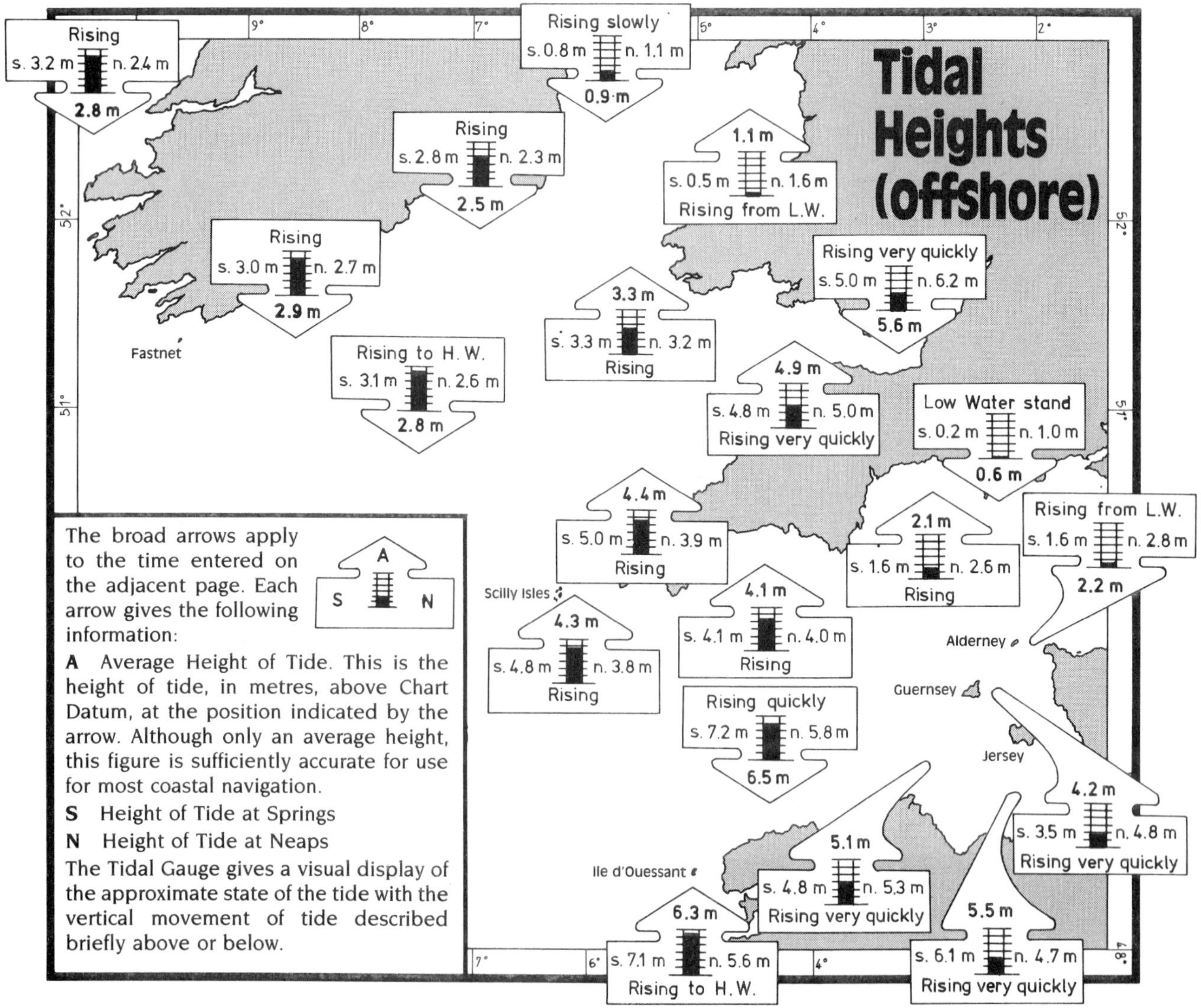

Tidal Heights (offshore)

Rising
s. 3.2 m n. 2.4 m
2.8 m

Rising slowly
s. 0.8 m n. 1.1 m
0.9 m

Rising
s. 2.8 m n. 2.3 m
2.5 m

1.1 m
s. 0.5 m n. 1.6 m
Rising from L.W.

Rising
s. 3.0 m n. 2.7 m
2.9 m

Rising very quickly
s. 5.0 m n. 6.2 m
5.6 m

Fastnet

Rising to H.W.
s. 3.1 m n. 2.6 m
2.8 m

3.3 m
s. 3.3 m n. 3.2 m
Rising

4.9 m
s. 4.8 m n. 5.0 m
Rising very quickly

Low Water stand
s. 0.2 m n. 1.0 m
0.6 m

4.4 m
s. 5.0 m n. 3.9 m
Rising

2.1 m
s. 1.6 m n. 2.6 m
Rising

Rising from L.W.
s. 1.6 m n. 2.8 m
2.2 m

Scilly Isles

4.1 m
s. 4.1 m n. 4.0 m
Rising

Alderney

4.3 m
s. 4.8 m n. 3.8 m
Rising

Guernsey

Rising quickly
s. 7.2 m n. 5.8 m
6.5 m

Jersey

4.2 m
s. 3.5 m n. 4.8 m
Rising very quickly

Ile d'Ouessant

5.1 m
s. 4.8 m n. 5.3 m
Rising very quickly

6.3 m
s. 7.1 m n. 5.6 m
Rising to H.W.

5.5 m
s. 6.1 m n. 4.7 m
Rising very quickly

Arrow key

A — Average Height of Tide
S — Height of Tide at Springs
N — Height of Tide at Neaps

The broad arrows apply to the time entered on the adjacent page. Each arrow gives the following information:

A Average Height of Tide. This is the height of tide, in metres, above Chart Datum, at the position indicated by the arrow. Although only an average height, this figure is sufficiently accurate for use for most coastal navigation.
S Height of Tide at Springs
N Height of Tide at Neaps
The Tidal Gauge gives a visual display of the approximate state of the tide with the vertical movement of tide described briefly above or below.

TIDAL HEIGHTS — PORTS & PLACES

Pencil-in height of ► HW Cherbourg	4.8	5.0	5.2	5.4	5.6	5.8	6.0	6.2	6.4	6.6	6.8
WALES											
Pwllheli, Barmouth....	1.8	1.7	1.5	1.4	1.2	1.1	0.9	0.8	0.6	0.5	0.3	0.2
Aberystwth	2.2	2.0	1.8	1.6	1.5	1.3	1.1	1.0	0.8	0.7	0.5	0.4
Fishguard, P.Cardigan ..	2.6	2.5	2.3	2.2	2.1	2.0	1.9	1.8	1.7	1.6	1.5	1.4
Milford Haven	3.9	3.8	3.8	3.7	3.7	3.6	3.6	3.5	3.5	3.5	3.5	3.5
Burry Inlet approach	4.8	4.7	4.7	4.6	4.5	4.5	4.4	4.4	4.3	4.3	4.3	4.3
Swansea	5.2	5.1	5.1	5.0	4.9	4.8	4.8	4.7	4.6	4.5	4.5	4.4
P. Talbot, Porthcawl...	5.6	5.5	5.5	5.4	5.3	5.3	5.2	5.2	5.1	5.1	5.1	5.1
Barry......................	6.4	6.2	6.0	5.8	5.6	5.4	5.2	5.0	4.8	4.8	4.7	4.7
Cardiff, Penarth..........	6.6	6.3	5.9	5.6	5.3	5.0	4.7	4.4	4.1	3.8	3.6	3.3
IRELAND											
Arklow	0.5	0.5	0.5	0.5	0.4	0.4	0.4	0.3	0.3	0.3	0.2	0.2
Rosslare	1.3	1.3	1.3	1.3	1.3	1.4	1.4	1.4	1.4	1.5	1.5	1.5
Waterford Hbr. entr. ...	2.5	2.5	2.5	2.5	2.6	2.6	2.6	2.7	2.7	2.7	2.8	2.8
Cork	2.5	2.5	2.5	2.6	2.6	2.6	2.6	2.7	2.7	2.7	2.7	2.7
Kinsale, Baltimore Bay .	2.6	2.7	2.7	2.8	2.9	2.9	3.0	3.0	3.1	3.1	3.2	3.2
ENGLAND-WEST											
Avonmouth...............	6.8	6.3	5.7	5.2	4.7	4.1	3.6	3.0	2.5	2.1	1.8	1.4
Weston-super-Mare	5.8	5.7	5.7	5.6	5.5	5.5	5.4	5.4	5.3	5.4	5.4	5.5
Watchet	6.2	6.1	6.1	6.0	5.9	5.8	5.7	5.6	5.5	5.5	5.6	5.6
Minehead	6.0	5.9	5.9	5.8	5.7	5.6	5.6	5.5	5.4	5.4	5.5	5.5
Porlock Bay	5.9	5.8	5.8	5.7	5.6	5.6	5.5	5.5	5.4	5.4	5.5	5.5
Ilfracombe	5.4	5.4	5.4	5.4	5.3	5.3	5.3	5.2	5.2	5.3	5.3	5.4
Appledore................	3.8	3.8	3.8	3.8	3.7	3.7	3.7	3.6	3.6	3.7	3.8	3.9
Padstow, Newquay	4.6	4.7	4.7	4.8	4.8	4.9	4.9	5.0	5.0	5.1	5.1	5.2
St. Ives Bay.............	3.9	4.0	4.2	4.3	4.4	4.6	4.7	4.9	5.0	5.1	5.3	5.4
ISLANDS OFF											
Lundy Island	4.7	4.7	4.7	4.7	4.7	4.8	4.8	4.8	4.8	4.9	4.9	5.0
St. Mary's, Scilly Isles .	3.6	3.8	4.0	4.2	4.3	4.5	4.7	4.8	5.0	5.1	5.3	5.4
ENGLAND-SOUTH											
Falmouth, Helford R.....	3.7	3.8	3.8	3.9	3.9	4.0	4.0	4.1	4.1	4.1	4.2	4.2
Mevagissey, Looe.......	3.8	3.8	3.8	3.8	3.9	3.9	3.9	4.0	4.0	4.0	4.1	4.1
Plymouth, Yealm R......	3.9	3.9	3.9	3.9	3.9	3.9	3.9	3.9	3.9	3.9	3.9	3.9
Salcombe	3.7	3.7	3.7	3.7	3.7	3.6	3.6	3.6	3.6	3.7	3.7	3.8
Dartmouth	3.1	3.1	3.1	3.1	3.0	3.0	3.0	2.9	2.9	2.9	3.0	3.0
Brixham, Teignmouth...	3.3	3.2	3.0	2.9	2.8	2.6	2.5	2.3	2.2	2.2	2.1	2.1
Exmouth approach.......	2.9	2.8	2.6	2.5	2.4	2.3	2.1	2.0	1.9	1.9	1.9	1.9
Lyme Regis...............	2.8	2.7	2.5	2.4	2.3	2.1	2.0	1.8	1.7	1.7	1.6	1.6
Portland, Weymouth	1.0	0.9	0.9	0.8	0.7	0.6	0.5	0.4	0.3	0.3	0.2	0.2
Lulworth Cove	1.3	1.2	1.0	0.9	0.8	0.7	0.6	0.5	0.4	0.4	0.3	0.3
Swanage	1.2	1.1	1.1	1.0	0.9	0.8	0.7	0.5	0.4	0.3	0.3	0.1
Poole Town	1.5	1.4	1.4	1.3	1.3	1.2	1.1	0.9	0.8	0.7	0.7	0.6
Christchurch Hbr.........	0.7	0.7	0.7	0.7	0.7	0.7	0.7	0.6	0.6	0.6	0.6	0.6
CHANNEL ISLANDS											
Braye Hbr.................	3.0	2.9	2.7	2.6	2.5	2.3	2.2	2.0	1.9	1.8	1.7	1.6
St. Peter Port, Sark.....	5.1	4.9	4.7	4.5	4.3	4.2	4.0	3.8	3.6	3.4	3.3	3.1
St. Helier.................	6.2	5.9	5.7	5.4	5.2	4.9	4.7	4.4	4.2	4.1	3.9	3.8
Les Minquiers	5.7	5.6	5.4	5.3	5.2	5.0	4.9	4.7	4.6	4.5	4.4	4.3
FRANCE											
Cherbourg	2.9	2.7	2.5	2.3	2.1	1.9	1.7	1.5	1.3	1.0	0.8	0.5
Omonville	3.1	2.9	2.7	2.5	2.3	2.1	1.9	1.7	1.5	1.2	1.0	0.7
Iles Chausey	7.3	7.0	6.8	6.5	6.2	5.9	5.6	5.3	5.0	4.9	4.7	4.6
Carteret	5.9	5.7	5.5	5.3	5.1	4.8	4.6	4.4	4.2	4.1	3.9	3.8
Granville	7.4	7.1	6.9	6.6	6.3	6.0	5.8	5.5	5.2	5.1	5.0	4.9
St Malo	7.1	6.8	6.6	6.3	6.0	5.7	5.4	5.1	4.8	4.6	4.5	4.3
All Hbrs. St Brieuc Bay	6.4	6.3	6.3	6.2	6.1	6.1	6.0	6.0	5.9	5.8	5.8	5.7
Ile de Bréhat	6.7	6.4	6.2	5.9	5.7	5.4	5.2	4.9	4.7	4.6	4.6	4.5
Lezardrieux	6.0	5.9	5.9	5.8	5.8	5.7	5.7	5.6	5.6	5.6	5.6	5.6
Tréguier	6.0	6.0	6.0	6.0	6.1	6.1	6.1	6.2	6.2	6.3	6.3	6.4
Morlaix, Primel Bay.....	6.2	6.3	6.3	6.4	6.5	6.6	6.7	6.8	6.9	7.0	7.0	7.1
Roscoff, Ile de Batz	6.0	6.1	6.3	6.4	6.5	6.6	6.8	6.9	7.0	7.1	7.1	7.2
L'Aberwrach	5.4	5.6	5.8	6.0	6.2	6.5	6.6	6.8	7.1	7.3	7.5	7.7
All Hbrs. Ch. du Four...	5.2	5.4	5.6	5.8	6.1	6.3	6.5	6.8	7.0	7.1	7.3	7.4
Brest	5.3	5.5	5.7	5.9	6.1	6.4	6.6	6.8	7.0	7.2	7.4	7.6
Camaret, Douarnenez...	4.9	5.1	5.3	5.5	5.8	6.0	6.2	6.5	6.7	6.9	7.0	7.2

Stream Rate Conversion Table

Mean Rate Figure from Chart ▼	\multicolumn{11}{c}{Pencil-in height of HW Cherbourg — Read from column below pencil mark}
	4.8	5.0	5.2	5.4	5.6	5.8	6.0	6.2	6.4	6.6	6.8
0.2	0.1	0.1	0.1	0.1	0.2	0.2	0.2	0.2	0.3	0.3	0.3
0.4	0.2	0.2	0.2	0.3	0.3	0.4	0.4	0.5	0.5	0.6	0.7
0.6	0.2	0.3	0.4	0.4	0.5	0.6	0.7	0.7	0.8	0.9	1.0
0.8	0.4	0.4	0.5	0.6	0.7	0.8	0.9	1.0	1.1	1.2	1.3
1.0	0.4	0.5	0.6	0.7	0.9	1.0	1.1	1.2	1.3	1.4	1.5	1.7
1.2	0.5	0.6	0.7	0.9	1.0	1.2	1.3	1.4	1.6	1.7	1.9	2.0
1.4	0.6	0.7	0.9	1.0	1.2	1.4	1.5	1.7	1.8	2.0	2.2	2.3
1.6	0.6	0.8	1.0	1.2	1.4	1.6	1.7	1.9	2.1	2.3	2.5	2.7
1.8	0.7	0.9	1.1	1.3	1.5	1.7	2.0	2.2	2.4	2.6	2.8	3.0
2.0	0.8	1.0	1.2	1.5	1.7	1.9	2.2	2.4	2.6	2.9	3.1	3.3
2.2	0.9	1.1	1.4	1.6	1.9	2.1	2.3	2.6	2.9	3.2	3.4	3.7
2.4	0.9	1.2	1.5	1.8	2.1	2.3	2.6	2.9	3.2	3.4	3.7	4.0
2.6	1.0	1.3	1.6	1.9	2.2	2.5	2.8	3.1	3.4	3.7	4.0	4.3
2.8	1.1	1.4	1.7	2.1	2.4	2.7	3.0	3.4	3.7	4.0	4.3	4.7
3.0	1.2	1.5	1.9	2.2	2.6	2.9	3.2	3.6	4.0	4.3	4.6	5.0
3.2	1.3	1.6	2.0	2.4	2.7	3.1	3.4	3.8	4.2	4.6	4.9	5.3
3.4	1.3	1.7	2.1	2.5	2.9	3.3	3.7	4.1	4.5	4.9	5.3	5.7
3.6	1.4	1.8	2.2	2.7	3.1	3.5	3.9	4.3	4.7	5.2	5.6	6.0
3.8	1.5	1.9	2.4	2.8	3.3	3.7	4.1	4.6	5.0	5.4	5.9	6.3
4.0	1.6	2.0	2.5	3.0	3.4	3.9	4.3	4.8	5.3	5.7	6.2	6.7
4.2	1.7	2.1	2.6	3.1	3.6	4.1	4.6	5.0	5.5	6.0	6.5	7.0
4.4	1.7	2.2	2.7	3.3	3.8	4.3	4.8	5.3	5.8	6.3	6.8	7.3
4.6	1.8	2.3	2.9	3.4	3.9	4.5	5.0	5.5	6.1	6.6	7.1	7.7
4.8	1.9	2.4	3.0	3.6	4.1	4.7	5.2	5.8	6.3	6.9	7.4	8.0
5.0	2.0	2.5	3.1	3.7	4.3	4.9	5.4	6.0	6.6	7.2	7.7	8.3
5.2	2.0	2.6	3.2	3.8	4.4	5.0	5.6	6.2	6.8	7.4	8.0	8.6
5.4	2.1	2.8	3.4	4.0	4.6	5.2	5.7	6.5	7.1	7.7	8.4	9.0
5.6	2.2	2.9	3.5	4.1	4.8	5.4	6.1	6.7	7.4	8.0	8.7	9.3
5.8	2.3	3.0	3.6	4.3	5.0	5.6	6.3	7.0	7.6	8.3	9.0	9.6
6.0	2.4	3.1	3.7	4.4	5.1	5.8	6.5	7.2	7.9	8.6	9.3	9.9

Tidal Stream Rates

Copyright © J Reeve-Fowkes and Thomas Reed Publications.
No copying without permission

5 hours before HW Cherbourg   **−5**

Time (to be inserted)

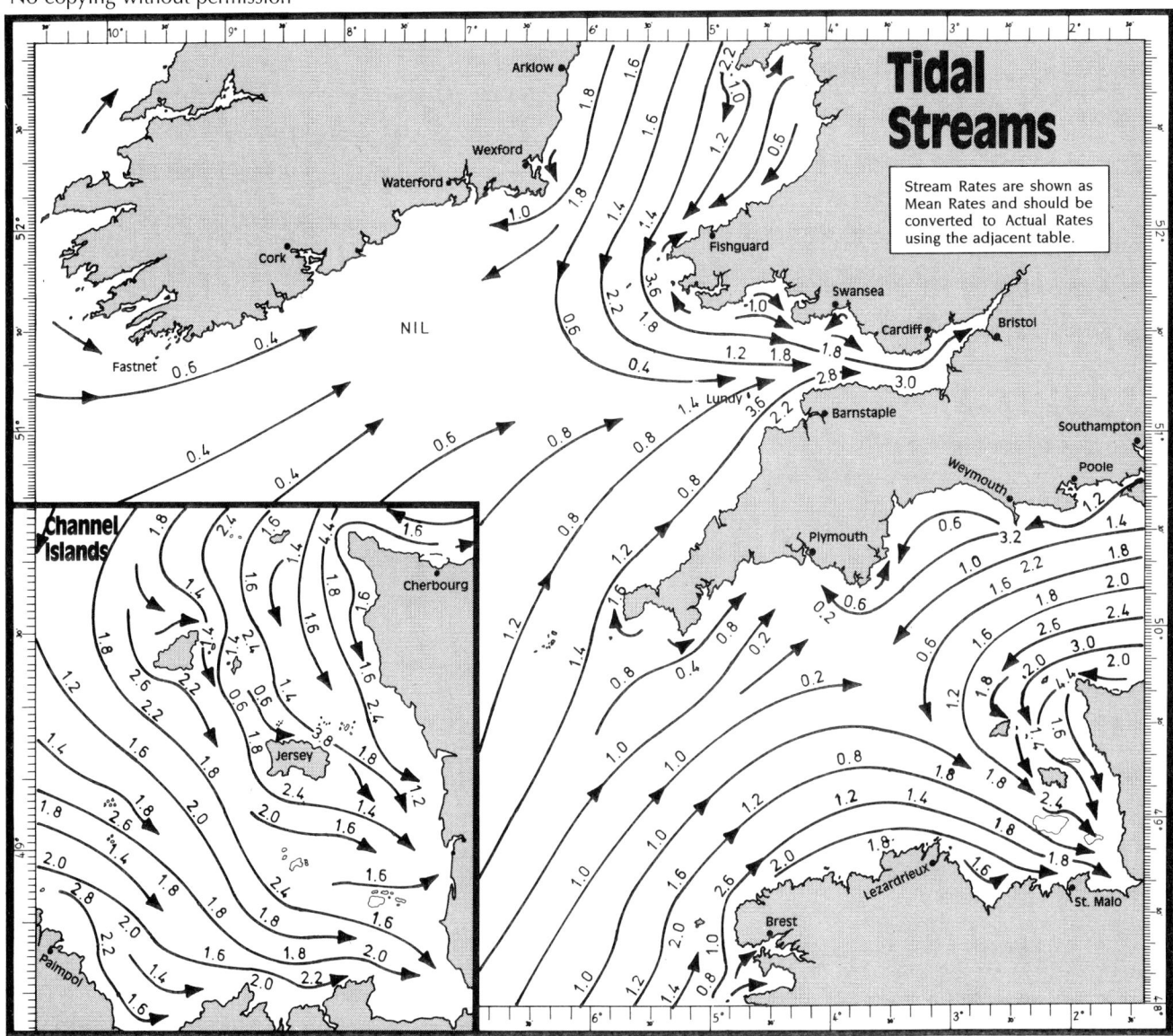

Tidal Streams

Stream Rates are shown as Mean Rates and should be converted to Actual Rates using the adjacent table.

63

-4
4 hours before HW Cherbourg

Tidal Heights

Copyright © J Reeve-Fowkes and Thomas Reed Publications.
No copying without permission.

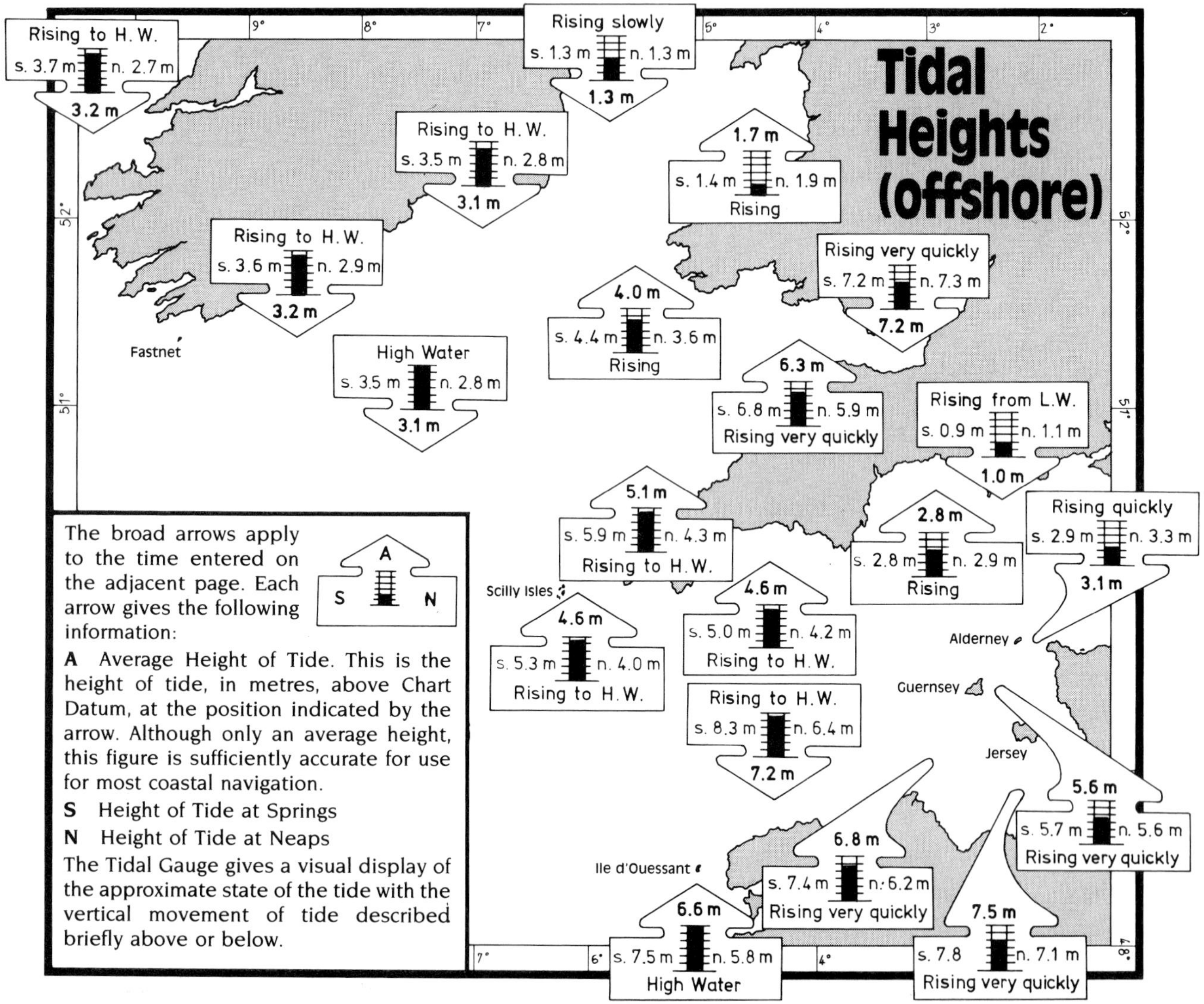

Tidal Heights (offshore)

Rising to H.W. — s. 3.7 m n. 2.7 m — **3.2 m**

Rising slowly — s. 1.3 m n. 1.3 m — **1.3 m**

Rising to H.W. — s. 3.5 m n. 2.8 m — **3.1 m**

1.7 m — s. 1.4 m n. 1.9 m — Rising

Rising to H.W. — s. 3.6 m n. 2.9 m — **3.2 m**

Rising very quickly — s. 7.2 m n. 7.3 m — **7.2 m**

4.0 m — s. 4.4 m n. 3.6 m — Rising

High Water — s. 3.5 m n. 2.8 m — **3.1 m**

6.3 m — s. 6.8 m n. 5.9 m — Rising very quickly

Rising from L.W. — s. 0.9 m n. 1.1 m — **1.0 m**

5.1 m — s. 5.9 m n. 4.3 m — Rising to H.W.

2.8 m — s. 2.8 m n. 2.9 m — Rising

Rising quickly — s. 2.9 m n. 3.3 m — **3.1 m**

4.6 m — s. 5.3 m n. 4.0 m — Rising to H.W.

4.6 m — s. 5.0 m n. 4.2 m — Rising to H.W.

Rising to H.W. — s. 8.3 m n. 6.4 m — **7.2 m**

5.6 m — s. 5.7 m n. 5.6 m — Rising very quickly

6.6 m — s. 7.5 m n. 5.8 m — High Water

6.8 m — s. 7.4 m n. 6.2 m — Rising very quickly

7.5 m — s. 7.8 n. 7.1 m — Rising very quickly

Fastnet
Scilly Isles
Alderney
Guernsey
Jersey
Ile d'Ouessant

The broad arrows apply to the time entered on the adjacent page. Each arrow gives the following information:

A — Average Height of Tide. This is the height of tide, in metres, above Chart Datum, at the position indicated by the arrow. Although only an average height, this figure is sufficiently accurate for use for most coastal navigation.

S Height of Tide at Springs
N Height of Tide at Neaps

The Tidal Gauge gives a visual display of the approximate state of the tide with the vertical movement of tide described briefly above or below.

TIDAL HEIGHTS — PORTS & PLACES

Pencil-in height of HW Cherbourg ▶	4.8	5.0	5.2	5.4	5.6	5.8	6.0	6.2	6.4	6.6	6.8
WALES											
Pwllheli, Barmouth.......	1.9	1.8	1.8	1.7	1.6	1.5	1.4	1.3	1.2	1.1	1.1	1.0
Aberystwth	2.4	2.3	2.3	2.2	2.1	2.1	2.0	2.0	1.9	1.8	1.8	1.7
Fishguard, P.Cardigan ..	2.8	2.8	2.8	2.8	2.8	2.7	2.7	2.7	2.7	2.7	2.7	2.7
Milford Haven	4.4	4.5	4.5	4.6	4.7	4.8	4.8	4.9	5.0	5.1	5.2	5.3
Burry Inlet approach	5.6	5.7	5.7	5.8	5.9	5.9	6.0	6.0	6.1	6.3	6.5	6.7
Swansea	6.0	6.1	6.1	6.2	6.3	6.4	6.5	6.6	6.7	6.8	6.8	6.9
P. Talbot, Porthcawl....	6.2	6.3	6.5	6.6	6.7	6.8	7.0	7.1	7.2	7.4	7.5	7.7
Barry................	7.2	7.2	7.2	7.2	7.1	7.1	7.1	7.0	7.0	7.1	7.2
Cardiff, Penarth.........	7.6	7.5	7.3	7.2	7.1	7.0	6.8	6.7	6.6	6.5	6.3	6.2
IRELAND											
Arklow....................	0.5	0.5	0.5	0.5	0.5	0.4	0.4	0.4	0.4	0.4	0.3	0.3
Rosslare	1.4	1.4	1.4	1.4	1.5	1.5	1.5	1.6	1.6	1.7	1.8	1.8
Waterford Hbr. entr.	2.8	2.9	2.9	3.0	3.1	3.2	3.3	3.4	3.5	3.5	3.6	3.6
Cork	2.9	3.0	3.0	3.1	3.2	3.3	3.4	3.5	3.6	3.7	3.7	3.8
Kinsale, Baltimore Bay .	2.8	2.9	3.1	3.2	3.3	3.4	3.5	3.6	3.7	3.8	3.8	3.9
ENGLAND-WEST											
Avonmouth................	7.8	7.5	7.1	6.8	6.5	6.2	5.9	5.6	5.3	5.1	4.9	4.7
Weston-super-Mare	6.9	7.0	7.0	7.1	7.1	7.2	7.2	7.3	7.3	7.4	7.6	7.7
Watchet	7.1	7.1	7.2	7.2	7.3	7.3	7.3	7.4	7.4	7.5	7.7	7.7
Minehead	6.7	6.8	6.8	6.9	7.0	7.1	7.1	7.2	7.3	7.4	7.6	7.7
Porlock Bay	6.6	6.7	6.8	6.8	6.9	6.9	7.0	7.1	7.1	7.2	7.4	7.5
Ilfracombe	6.0	6.1	6.3	6.4	6.5	6.5	6.7	6.8	7.0	7.1	7.3	7.5	7.7
Appledore................	4.3	4.4	4.6	4.7	4.9	5.0	5.2	5.3	5.5	5.7	6.0	6.2
Padstow, Newquay	5.0	5.2	5.4	5.6	5.7	5.9	6.1	6.2	6.4	6.6	6.7	6.9
St. Ives Bay	4.2	4.5	4.7	5.0	5.2	5.5	5.7	6.0	6.2	6.4	6.6	6.8
ISLANDS OFF											
Lundy Island	5.1	5.3	5.5	5.7	5.8	6.0	6.2	6.3	6.5	6.7	6.9	7.1
St. Mary's, Scilly Isles .	3.9	4.1	4.3	4.5	4.7	4.9	5.1	5.3	5.5	5.7	5.9	6.1
ENGLAND-SOUTH											
Falmouth, Helford R....	3.9	4.0	4.2	4.3	4.4	4.5	4.6	4.7	4.8	4.9	5.0	5.1
Mevagissey, Looe........	4.0	4.1	4.1	4.2	4.3	4.4	4.5	4.6	4.7	4.8	4.9	5.0
Plymouth, Yealm R......	4.1	4.2	4.2	4.3	4.4	4.4	4.5	4.6	4.7	4.8	4.9	5.0
Salcombe	3.8	3.9	3.9	4.0	4.1	4.2	4.3	4.4	4.5	4.6	4.7	4.8
Dartmouth................	3.3	3.4	3.4	3.5	3.5	3.6	3.6	3.7	3.7	3.8	3.9	4.0
Brixham, Teignmouth....	3.4	3.4	3.4	3.4	3.4	3.3	3.3	3.3	3.3	3.4	3.4	3.5
Exmouth approach.......	3.1	3.1	3.1	3.1	3.1	3.0	3.0	3.0	3.0	3.1	3.1	3.1
Lyme Regis...............	2.9	2.9	2.9	2.9	2.9	2.8	2.8	2.8	2.8	2.8	2.9	2.9
Portland, Weymouth	1.0	1.0	1.0	1.0	0.9	0.9	0.9	0.8	0.8	0.8	0.9	0.9
Lulworth Cove	1.2	1.2	1.2	1.2	1.2	1.1	1.1	1.1	1.1	1.2	1.2	1.2
Swanage	1.3	1.2	1.2	1.1	1.0	0.9	0.8	0.7	0.6	0.5	0.5	0.4
Poole Town	1.3	1.2	1.2	1.1	1.0	0.9	0.8	0.6	0.5	0.4	0.3	0.2
Christchurch Hbr.........	0.7	0.7	0.7	0.7	0.6	0.6	0.5	0.5	0.4	0.4	0.3	0.3
CHANNEL ISLANDS											
Braye Hbr.	3.4	3.4	3.4	3.4	3.4	3.5	3.5	3.5	3.5	3.5	3.5	3.5
St. Peter Port, Sark	5.6	5.6	5.6	5.6	5.6	5.7	5.7	5.7	5.7	5.7	5.8	5.8
St. Helier...............	6.7	6.7	6.8	6.9	6.9	7.0	7.0	7.1	7.1	7.2	7.2	7.3
Les Minquiers	7.1	7.2	7.2	7.3	7.3	7.4	7.4	7.5	7.5	7.6	7.6	7.7
FRANCE											
Cherbourg	3.2	3.1	2.9	2.8	2.7	2.5	2.4	2.2	2.1	1.9	1.8	1.6
Omonville	3.5	3.4	3.2	3.1	3.0	2.8	2.7	2.5	2.4	2.2	2.1	1.9
Iles Chausey	8.1	8.2	8.2	8.3	8.3	8.4	8.4	8.5	8.5	8.6	8.7	8.8
Carteret	6.7	6.7	6.7	6.7	6.8	6.8	6.8	6.9	6.9	6.9	7.0	7.0
Granville	8.2	8.3	8.3	8.4	8.5	8.6	8.6	8.7	8.8	8.9	9.0	9.1
St Malo	7.9	7.9	7.9	7.9	7.9	8.0	8.0	8.0	8.0	8.1	8.1	8.2
All Hbrs. St Brieuc Bay	7.3	7.5	7.7	7.9	8.0	8.2	8.4	8.5	8.7	8.8	9.0	9.1
Ile de Bréhat	7.3	7.3	7.3	7.3	7.4	7.4	7.4	7.5	7.5	7.6	7.7	7.8
Lezardrieux	6.6	6.7	6.9	7.0	7.1	7.3	7.4	7.6	7.7	6.8	8.0	8.1
Tréguier	6.4	6.6	6.8	7.0	7.2	7.5	7.7	7.9	8.1	8.3	8.5	8.7
Morlaix, Primel Bay....	6.5	6.7	6.9	7.1	7.4	7.6	7.8	8.1	8.3	8.5	8.6	8.8
Roscoff, Ile de Batz	6.6	6.8	7.0	7.2	7.5	7.7	7.9	8.2	8.4	8.5	8.7	8.8
L'Aberwrach	5.7	6.0	6.2	6.5	6.8	7.1	7.3	7.6	7.9	8.1	8.4	8.6
All Hbrs. Ch. du Four...	5.3	5.6	5.8	6.1	6.3	6.6	6.8	7.1	7.3	7.5	7.6	7.8
Brest....................	5.4	5.7	5.9	6.2	6.4	6.7	6.9	7.2	7.4	7.6	7.8	8.0
Camaret, Douarnenez...	5.1	5.3	5.5	5.7	6.0	6.2	6.4	6.7	6.9	7.1	7.2	7.4

Stream Rate Conversion Table

Mean Rate Figure from Chart ▼	Pencil-in height of HW Cherbourg — Read from column below pencil mark										
	4.8	5.0	5.2	5.4	5.6	5.8	6.0	6.2	6.4	6.6	6.8
0.2	0.1	0.1	0.1	0.1	0.2	0.2	0.2	0.2	0.3	0.3	0.3	0.3
0.4	0.2	0.2	0.2	0.3	0.3	0.4	0.4	0.5	0.5	0.6	0.6	0.7
0.6	0.2	0.3	0.4	0.4	0.5	0.6	0.7	0.7	0.8	0.9	0.9	1.0
0.8	0.4	0.4	0.5	0.6	0.7	0.8	0.9	1.0	1.1	1.1	1.2	1.3
1.0	0.4	0.5	0.6	0.7	0.9	1.0	1.1	1.2	1.3	1.4	1.5	1.7
1.2	0.5	0.6	0.7	0.9	1.0	1.2	1.3	1.4	1.6	1.7	1.9	2.0
1.4	0.6	0.7	0.9	1.0	1.2	1.4	1.5	1.7	1.8	2.0	2.2	2.3
1.6	0.6	0.8	1.0	1.2	1.4	1.6	1.7	1.9	2.1	2.3	2.5	2.7
1.8	0.7	0.9	1.1	1.3	1.5	1.7	2.0	2.2	2.4	2.6	2.8	3.0
2.0	0.8	1.0	1.2	1.5	1.7	1.9	2.2	2.4	2.6	2.9	3.1	3.3
2.2	0.9	1.1	1.4	1.6	1.9	2.1	2.3	2.6	2.9	3.2	3.4	3.7
2.4	0.9	1.2	1.5	1.8	2.1	2.3	2.6	2.9	3.2	3.4	3.7	4.0
2.6	1.0	1.3	1.6	1.9	2.2	2.5	2.8	3.1	3.4	3.7	4.0	4.3
2.8	1.1	1.4	1.7	2.1	2.4	2.7	3.0	3.4	3.7	4.0	4.3	4.7
3.0	1.2	1.5	1.9	2.2	2.6	2.9	3.2	3.6	4.0	4.3	4.6	5.0
3.2	1.3	1.6	2.0	2.4	2.7	3.1	3.4	3.8	4.2	4.6	4.9	5.3
3.4	1.3	1.7	2.1	2.5	2.9	3.3	3.7	4.1	4.5	4.9	5.3	5.7
3.6	1.4	1.8	2.2	2.7	3.1	3.5	3.9	4.3	4.7	5.2	5.6	6.0
3.8	1.5	1.9	2.4	2.8	3.3	3.7	4.1	4.6	5.0	5.4	5.9	6.3
4.0	1.6	2.0	2.5	3.0	3.4	3.9	4.3	4.8	5.3	5.7	6.2	6.7
4.2	1.7	2.1	2.6	3.1	3.6	4.1	4.6	5.0	5.5	6.0	6.5	7.0
4.4	1.7	2.2	2.7	3.3	3.8	4.3	4.8	5.3	5.8	6.3	6.8	7.3
4.6	1.8	2.3	2.9	3.4	3.9	4.5	5.0	5.5	6.1	6.6	7.1	7.7
4.8	1.9	2.4	3.0	3.5	4.1	4.7	5.2	5.8	6.3	6.9	7.4	8.0
5.0	2.0	2.5	3.1	3.7	4.3	4.9	5.4	6.0	6.6	7.2	7.7	8.3
5.2	2.0	2.6	3.2	3.8	4.4	5.0	5.6	6.2	6.8	7.4	8.0	8.6
5.4	2.1	2.8	3.4	4.0	4.6	5.2	5.7	6.5	7.1	7.7	8.4	9.0
5.6	2.2	2.9	3.5	4.1	4.8	5.4	6.1	6.7	7.4	8.0	8.7	9.3
5.8	2.3	3.0	3.6	4.3	5.0	5.6	6.3	7.0	7.6	8.3	9.0	9.6
6.0	2.4	3.1	3.7	4.4	5.1	5.8	6.5	7.2	7.9	8.6	9.3	9.9

Tidal Stream Rates

Copyright © J Reeve-Fowkes and Thomas Reed Publications.
No copying without permission

4 hours before HW Cherbourg **−4**

Time (to be inserted)

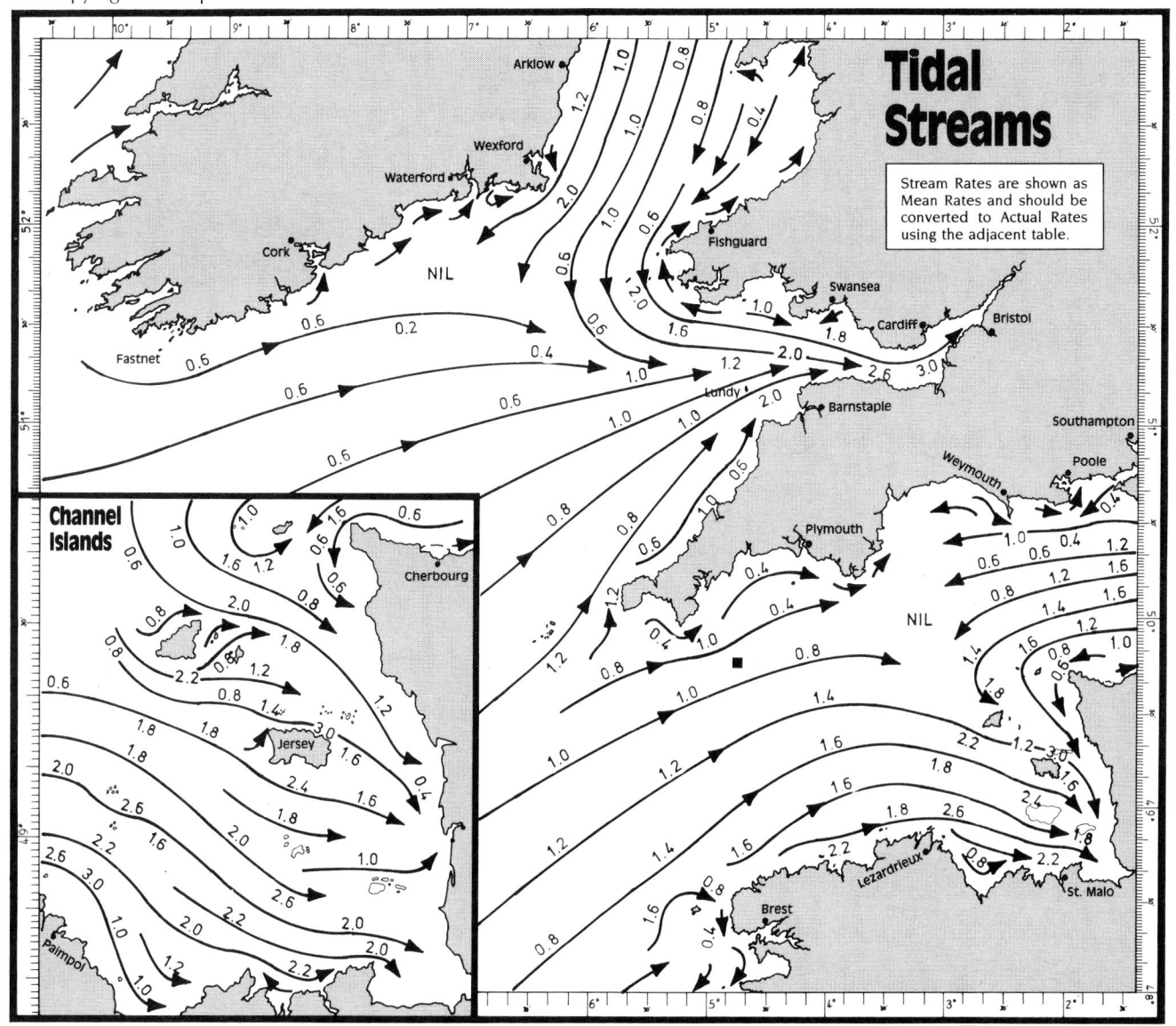

Tidal Streams

Stream Rates are shown as Mean Rates and should be converted to Actual Rates using the adjacent table.

65

-3
3 hours before HW Cherbourg

Tidal Heights

Copyright © J Reeve-Fowkes and
Thomas Reed Publications.
No copying without permission

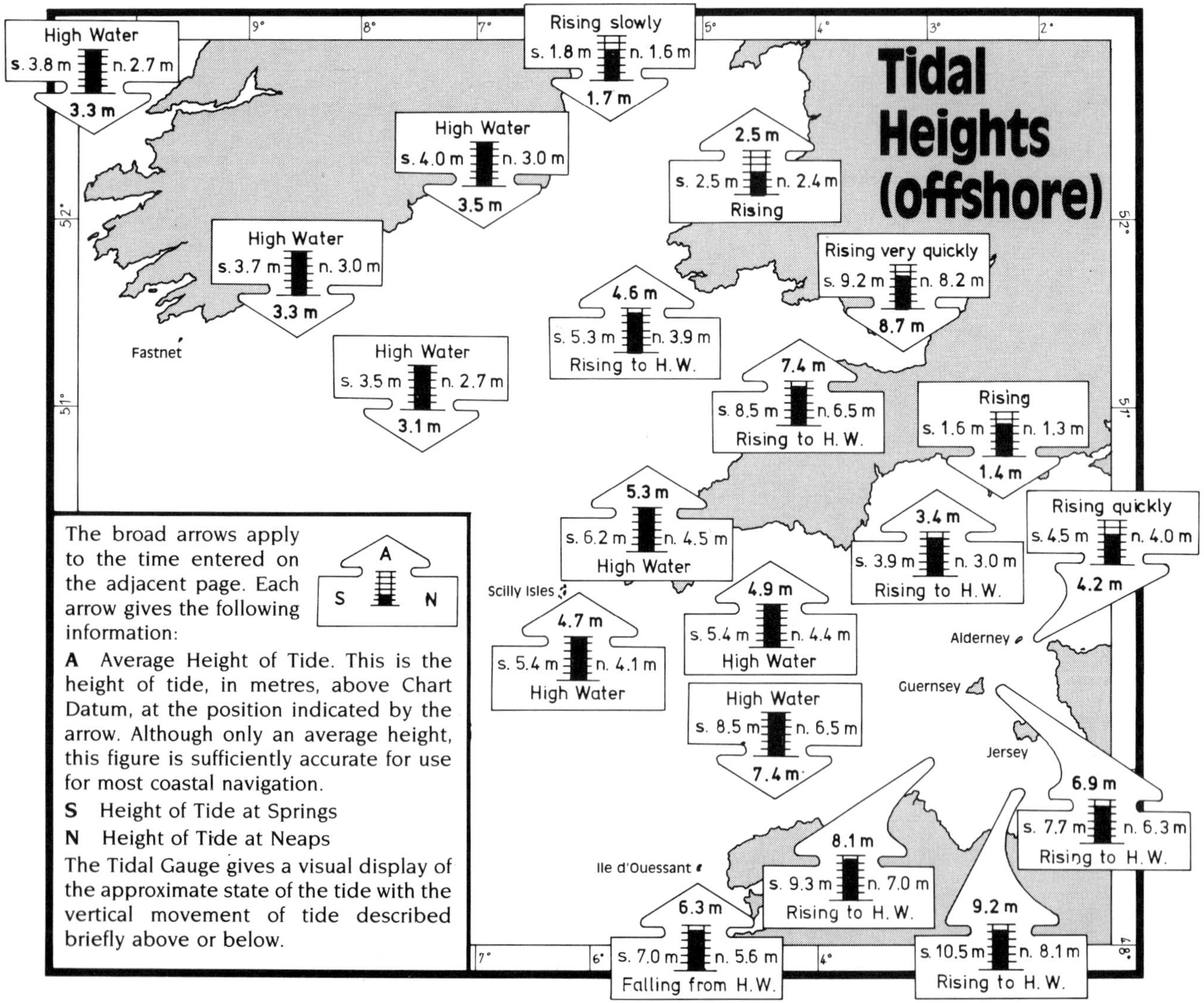

Tidal Heights (offshore)

High Water — s. 3.8 m n. 2.7 m — 3.3 m

Rising slowly — s. 1.8 m n. 1.6 m — 1.7 m

2.5 m — s. 2.5 m n. 2.4 m — Rising

High Water — s. 4.0 m n. 3.0 m — 3.5 m

High Water — s. 3.7 m n. 3.0 m — 3.3 m

Fastnet

High Water — s. 3.5 m n. 2.7 m — 3.1 m

4.6 m — s. 5.3 m n. 3.9 m — Rising to H.W.

Rising very quickly — s. 9.2 m n. 8.2 m — 8.7 m

7.4 m — s. 8.5 m n. 6.5 m — Rising to H.W.

Rising — s. 1.6 m n. 1.3 m — 1.4 m

5.3 m — s. 6.2 m n. 4.5 m — High Water

4.9 m — s. 5.4 m n. 4.4 m — High Water

3.4 m — s. 3.9 m n. 3.0 m — Rising to H.W.

Rising quickly — s. 4.5 m n. 4.0 m — 4.2 m

Scilly Isles

4.7 m — s. 5.4 m n. 4.1 m — High Water

High Water — s. 8.5 m n. 6.5 m — 7.4 m

Alderney

Guernsey

Jersey

6.9 m — s. 7.7 m n. 6.3 m — Rising to H.W.

Ile d'Ouessant

8.1 m — s. 9.3 m n. 7.0 m — Rising to H.W.

6.3 m — s. 7.0 m n. 5.6 m — Falling from H.W.

9.2 m — s. 10.5 m n. 8.1 m — Rising to H.W.

The broad arrows apply to the time entered on the adjacent page. Each arrow gives the following information:

A Average Height of Tide. This is the height of tide, in metres, above Chart Datum, at the position indicated by the arrow. Although only an average height, this figure is sufficiently accurate for use for most coastal navigation.
S Height of Tide at Springs
N Height of Tide at Neaps
The Tidal Gauge gives a visual display of the approximate state of the tide with the vertical movement of tide described briefly above or below.

TIDAL HEIGHTS — PORTS & PLACES

Pencil-in height of ► HW Cherbourg	4.8	5.0	5.2	5.4	5.6	5.8	6.0	6.2	6.4	6.6	6.8
WALES											
Pwllheli, Barmouth.......	2.3	2.3	2.3	2.3	2.3	2.4	2.4	2.4	2.4	2.4	2.4
Aberystwth	2.8	2.8	2.8	2.8	2.9	2.9	2.9	3.0	3.0	3.0	3.0
Fishguard, P.Cardigan ..	3.0	3.1	3.1	3.2	3.3	3.4	3.5	3.6	3.7	3.8	3.9
Milford Haven	4.7	4.9	5.1	5.3	5.5	5.7	5.9	6.1	6.3	6.5	6.7
Burry Inlet approach	6.0	6.3	6.5	6.8	7.0	7.3	7.5	7.8	8.0	8.2	8.4
Swansea	6.5	6.9	7.1	7.4	7.7	7.9	8.2	8.4	8.7	8.9	9.0
P. Talbot, Porthcawl	6.8	7.1	7.3	7.6	7.9	8.2	8.4	8.7	9.0	9.3	9.5
Barry.....................	8.0	8.1	8.1	8.2	8.3	8.4	8.5	8.6	8.7	8.9	9.1
Cardiff, Penarth..........	8.2	8.3	8.5	8.6	8.7	8.9	9.0	9.2	9.3	9.3	9.3
IRELAND											
Arklow	0.6	0.6	0.6	0.6	0.6	0.6	0.6	0.6	0.6	0.6	0.5
Rosslare	1.4	1.5	1.5	1.6	1.7	1.7	1.8	1.8	1.9	2.0	2.1
Waterford Hbr. entr.....	3.0	3.1	3.3	3.4	3.5	3.6	3.8	3.9	4.0	4.1	4.1
Cork	3.1	3.2	3.4	3.5	3.6	3.8	3.9	4.1	4.2	4.3	4.4
Kinsale, Baltimore Bay .	3.0	3.1	3.3	3.4	3.5	3.6	3.8	3.9	4.0	4.1	4.1
ENGLAND-WEST											
Avonmouth...............	8.8	8.7	8.7	8.6	8.6	8.5	8.5	8.4	8.4	8.4	8.4
Weston-super-Mare	7.9	8.1	8.3	8.5	8.7	8.9	9.1	9.3	9.5	9.7	10.0
Watchet	7.6	7.8	8.0	8.2	8.5	8.7	8.9	9.2	9.4	9.6	9.9
Minehead	7.2	7.5	7.7	8.0	8.2	8.5	8.7	9.0	9.2	9.4	9.6
Porlock Bay	7.1	7.3	7.5	7.7	8.0	8.2	8.4	8.7	8.9	9.1	9.4
Ilfracombe	6.4	6.7	6.9	7.2	7.5	7.8	8.0	8.3	8.6	8.9	9.2
Appledore................	4.6	4.9	5.3	5.6	5.9	6.2	6.5	6.8	7.1	7.4	7.7
Padstow, Newquay	5.2	5.5	5.7	6.0	6.2	6.5	6.7	7.0	7.2	7.4	7.7
St. Ives Bay..............	4.5	4.8	5.0	5.3	5.6	5.8	6.1	6.3	6.6	6.8	7.1
ISLANDS OFF											
Lundy Island	5.4	5.7	5.9	6.2	6.5	6.8	7.1	7.4	7.7	8.0	8.2
St. Mary's, Scilly Isles .	4.0	4.2	4.4	4.6	4.8	5.1	5.3	5.5	5.7	5.9	6.1
ENGLAND-SOUTH											
Falmouth, Helford R.....	4.0	4.1	4.3	4.4	4.6	4.7	4.9	5.0	5.2	5.3	5.5
Mevagissey, Looe......	4.1	4.2	4.4	4.5	4.6	4.8	4.9	5.1	5.2	5.3	5.5
Plymouth, Yealm R......	4.2	4.3	4.5	4.6	4.7	4.9	5.0	5.2	5.3	5.4	5.5
Salcombe	3.9	4.0	4.2	4.3	4.4	4.6	4.7	4.9	5.0	5.1	5.3
Dartmouth	3.3	3.4	3.6	3.7	3.8	4.0	4.1	4.3	4.4	4.5	4.7
Brixham, Teignmouth...	3.6	3.7	3.7	3.8	3.9	4.0	4.0	4.1	4.2	4.3	4.5
Exmouth approach......	3.0	3.1	3.3	3.4	3.5	3.6	3.7	3.8	3.9	4.0	4.0
Lyme Regis...............	2.8	2.9	3.1	3.2	3.3	3.4	3.6	3.7	3.8	3.9	4.0
Portland, Weymouth	1.3	1.3	1.3	1.3	1.4	1.4	1.4	1.5	1.5	1.6	1.7
Lulworth Cove	1.3	1.4	1.4	1.5	1.6	1.6	1.7	1.7	1.8	1.9	2.0
Swanage	1.3	1.3	1.3	1.3	1.2	1.2	1.2	1.1	1.1	1.1	1.1
Poole Town	1.4	1.3	1.3	1.2	1.1	1.0	0.9	0.9	0.8	0.7	0.7
Christchurch-Hbr.........	0.8	0.8	0.8	0.8	0.8	0.8	0.8	0.7	0.7	0.7	0.7
CHANNEL ISLANDS											
Braye Hbr.................	3.9	4.0	4.2	4.3	4.4	4.5	4.7	4.8	4.9	5.0	5.2
St. Peter Port, Sark.....	6.0	6.4	6.6	6.6	6.8	7.0	7.2	7.4	7.6	7.8	7.9
St. Helier	7.2	7.5	7.7	8.0	8.3	8.6	8.9	9.2	9.5	9.7	10.0
Les Minquiers	7.8	8.1	8.3	8.6	8.9	9.1	9.4	9.6	9.9	10.1	10.3
FRANCE											
Cherbourg	3.7	3.7	3.7	3.7	3.7	3.6	3.6	3.6	3.6	3.6	3.6
Omonville	4.0	4.0	4.0	4.0	4.0	4.0	4.0	4.0	4.0	4.0	4.0
Iles Chausey	8.9	9.2	9.4	9.7	10.0	10.3	10.6	10.9	11.2	11.4	11.7
Carteret	7.3	7.6	7.8	8.1	8.3	8.6	8.8	9.1	9.3	9.6	9.8
Granville	8.8	9.1	9.5	9.8	10.1	10.4	10.8	11.1	11.4	11.7	11.9
St Malo	8.5	8.8	9.0	9.3	9.6	9.8	10.1	10.3	10.6	10.8	11.1
All Hbrs. St Brieuc Bay .	7.8	8.3	8.6	9.0	9.3	9.7	10.1	10.4	10.8	11.0	11.3
Ile de Bréhat	7.6	7.9	8.1	8.4	8.6	8.9	9.1	9.4	9.6	9.8	10.0
Lezardrieux	7.2	7.5	7.7	8.0	8.3	8.5	8.8	9.0	9.3	9.5	9.8
Tréguier	6.8	7.1	7.5	7.8	8.1	8.4	8.8	9.1	9.4	9.7	9.9
Morlaix, Primel Bay.....	6.5	6.8	7.2	7.5	7.8	8.1	8.4	8.7	9.0	9.2	9.4
Roscoff, Ile de Batz	6.5	6.8	7.2	7.5	7.8	8.1	8.4	8.7	9.0	9.2	9.3
L'Aberwrach	5.7	6.0	6.2	6.5	6.8	7.1	7.3	7.6	7.9	8.1	8.3
All Hbrs. Ch. du Four....	5.3	5.5	5.7	5.9	6.1	6.3	6.5	6.7	6.9	7.0	7.2
Brest.....................	5.3	5.5	5.7	5.9	6.1	6.3	6.5	6.7	6.9	7.1	7.2
Camaret, Douarnenez...	4.9	5.1	5.3	5.5	5.7	5.8	6.0	6.2	6.4	6.5	6.7

Rightmost column (6.8 m equivalents shown in chart): Pwllheli 2.4, Aberystwth 3.0, Fishguard 3.9, Milford Haven 6.9, Burry Inlet 8.6, Swansea 9.2, P. Talbot 9.8, Barry 9.3, Cardiff 9.3; Arklow 0.5, Rosslare 2.2, Waterford 4.2, Cork 4.5, Kinsale 4.2; Avonmouth 8.4, Weston-super-Mare 10.2, Watchet 10.1, Minehead 9.8, Porlock Bay 9.6, Ilfracombe 9.5, Appledore 8.0, Padstow 7.9, St. Ives 7.3; Lundy 8.5, St. Mary's 6.3; Falmouth 5.6, Mevagissey 5.6, Plymouth 5.6, Salcombe 5.4, Dartmouth 4.8, Brixham 4.6, Exmouth 4.1, Lyme Regis 4.1, Portland 1.8, Lulworth 2.1, Swanage 1.1, Poole 0.6, Christchurch 0.7; Braye Hbr 5.3, St. Peter Port 8.1, St. Helier 10.2, Les Minquiers 10.5; Cherbourg 3.6, Omonville 4.0, Iles Chausey 11.9, Carteret 10.0, Granville 12.2, St Malo 11.3, St Brieuc 11.5, Ile de Bréhat 10.2, Lezardrieux 10.0, Tréguier 10.2, Morlaix 9.6, Roscoff 9.3, L'Aberwrach 8.5, Ch. du Four 7.3, Brest 7.4, Camaret 6.8.

Stream Rate Conversion Table

Mean Rate Figure from Chart ▼	\multicolumn{11}{c	}{Pencil-in height of HW Cherbourg Read from column below pencil mark}
	4.8	5.0	5.2	5.4	5.6	5.8	6.0	6.2	6.4	6.6	6.8
0.2	0.1	0.1	0.1	0.1	0.2	0.2	0.2	0.2	0.3	0.3	0.3
0.4	0.2	0.2	0.2	0.3	0.3	0.4	0.4	0.5	0.5	0.6	0.7
0.6	0.2	0.3	0.4	0.4	0.5	0.6	0.7	0.7	0.8	0.9	1.0
0.8	0.4	0.4	0.5	0.6	0.7	0.8	0.9	1.0	1.1	1.2	1.3
1.0	0.4	0.5	0.6	0.7	0.9	1.0	1.1	1.2	1.3	1.4	1.7
1.2	0.5	0.6	0.7	0.9	1.0	1.2	1.3	1.4	1.6	1.7	2.0
1.4	0.6	0.7	0.9	1.0	1.2	1.4	1.5	1.7	1.8	2.0	2.3
1.6	0.6	0.8	1.0	1.2	1.4	1.6	1.7	1.9	2.1	2.3	2.7
1.8	0.7	0.9	1.1	1.3	1.5	1.7	2.0	2.2	2.4	2.6	3.0
2.0	0.8	1.0	1.2	1.5	1.7	1.9	2.2	2.4	2.6	2.9	3.3
2.2	0.9	1.1	1.4	1.6	1.9	2.1	2.3	2.6	2.9	3.2	3.7
2.4	0.9	1.2	1.5	1.8	2.1	2.3	2.6	2.9	3.2	3.4	4.0
2.6	1.0	1.3	1.6	1.9	2.2	2.5	2.8	3.1	3.4	3.7	4.3
2.8	1.1	1.4	1.7	2.1	2.4	2.7	3.0	3.4	3.7	4.0	4.7
3.0	1.2	1.5	1.9	2.2	2.6	2.9	3.2	3.6	4.0	4.3	5.0
3.2	1.3	1.6	2.0	2.4	2.7	3.1	3.4	3.8	4.2	4.6	5.3
3.4	1.3	1.7	2.1	2.5	2.9	3.3	3.7	4.1	4.5	4.9	5.7
3.6	1.4	1.8	2.2	2.7	3.1	3.5	3.9	4.3	4.7	5.2	6.0
3.8	1.5	1.9	2.4	2.8	3.3	3.7	4.1	4.6	5.0	5.4	6.3
4.0	1.6	2.0	2.5	3.0	3.4	3.9	4.3	4.8	5.3	5.7	6.7
4.2	1.7	2.1	2.6	3.1	3.6	4.1	4.6	5.0	5.5	6.0	7.0
4.4	1.7	2.2	2.7	3.3	3.8	4.3	4.8	5.3	5.8	6.3	7.3
4.6	1.8	2.3	2.9	3.4	3.9	4.5	5.0	5.5	6.1	6.6	7.7
4.8	1.9	2.4	3.0	3.6	4.1	4.7	5.2	5.8	6.3	6.9	8.0
5.0	2.0	2.5	3.1	3.7	4.3	4.9	5.4	6.0	6.6	7.2	8.3
5.2	2.0	2.6	3.2	3.8	4.4	5.0	5.6	6.2	6.8	7.4	8.6
5.4	2.1	2.8	3.4	4.0	4.6	5.2	5.7	6.5	7.1	7.7	8.4	9.0
5.6	2.2	2.9	3.5	4.1	4.8	5.4	6.1	6.7	7.4	8.0	8.7	9.3
5.8	2.3	3.0	3.6	4.3	5.0	5.6	6.3	7.0	7.6	8.3	9.0	9.6
6.0	2.4	3.1	3.7	4.4	5.1	5.8	6.5	7.2	7.9	8.6	9.3	9.9

Tidal Stream Rates

Copyright © J Reeve-Fowkes and Thomas Reed Publications.
No copying without permission

3 hours before HW Cherbourg   **−3**

Time (to be inserted)

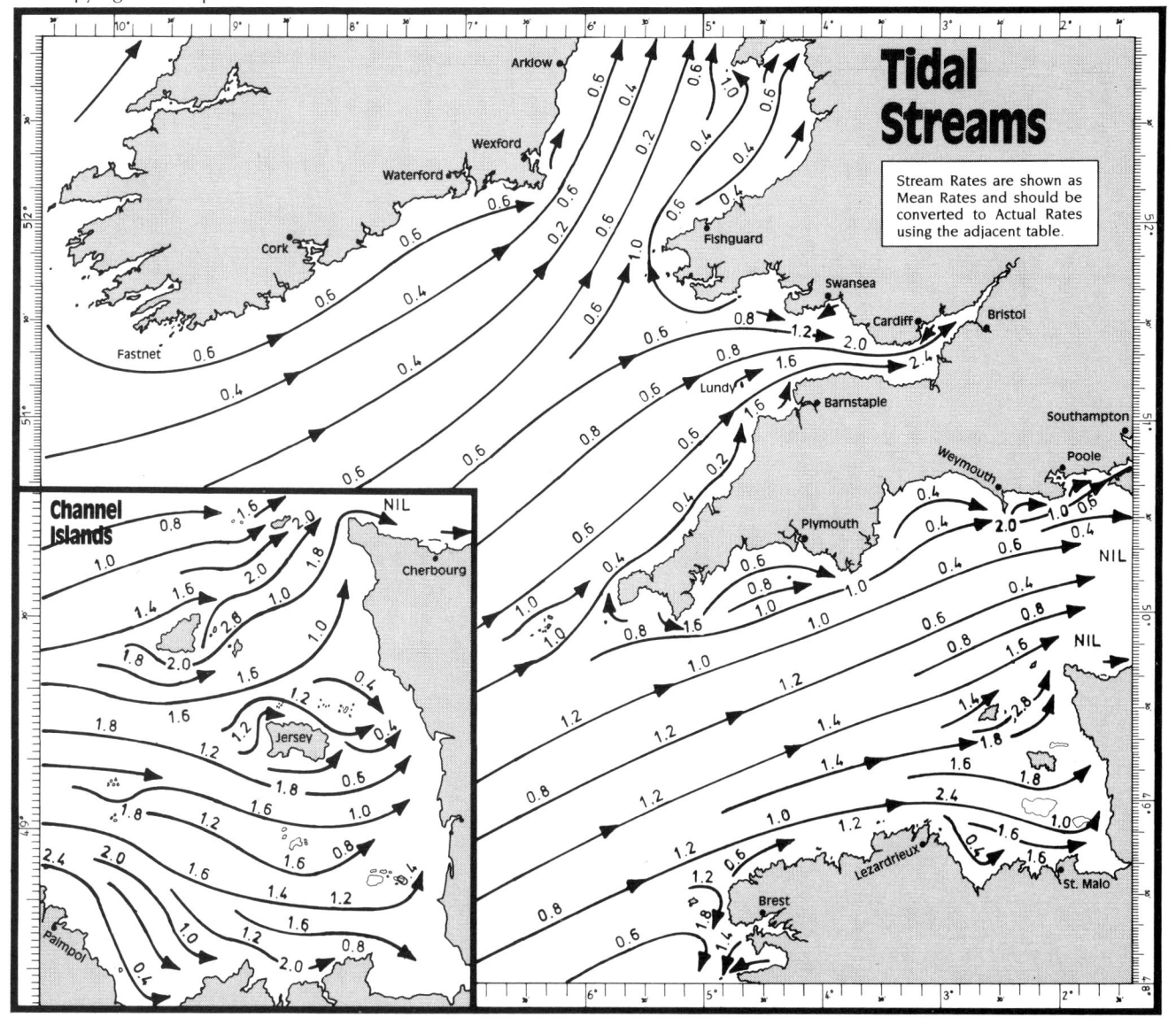

Tidal Streams

Stream Rates are shown as Mean Rates and should be converted to Actual Rates using the adjacent table.

67

-2
2 hours before HW Cherbourg

Tidal Heights

Copyright © J Reeve-Fowkes and
Thomas Reed Publications.
No copying without permission

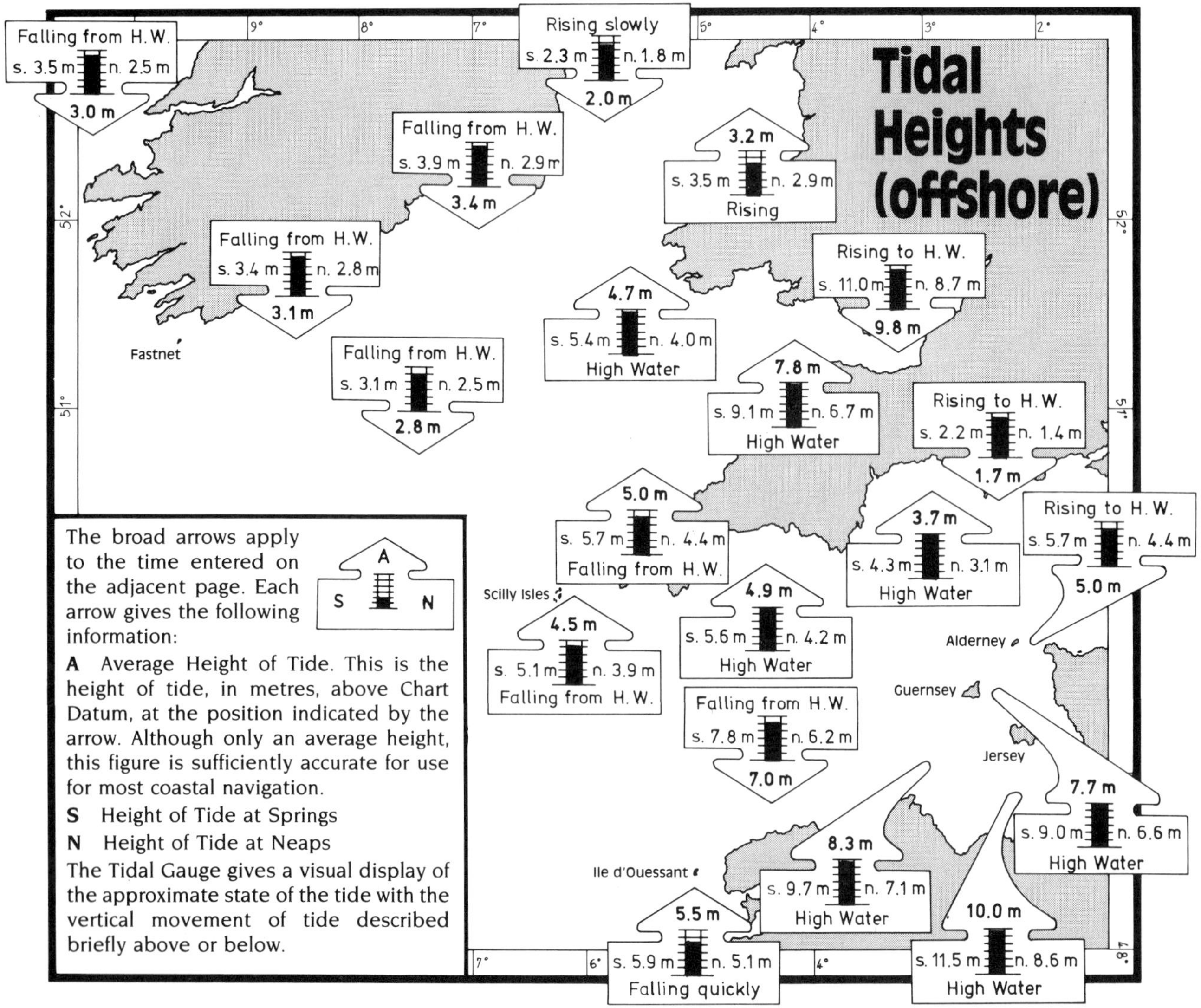

Tidal Heights (offshore)

Falling from H.W.
s. 3.5 m n. 2.5 m
3.0 m

Rising slowly
s. 2.3 m n. 1.8 m
2.0 m

Falling from H.W.
s. 3.9 m n. 2.9 m
3.4 m

s. 3.5 m n. 2.9 m
3.2 m
Rising

Falling from H.W.
s. 3.4 m n. 2.8 m
3.1 m

Rising to H.W.
s. 11.0 m n. 8.7 m
9.8 m

Falling from H.W.
s. 3.1 m n. 2.5 m
2.8 m

Fastnet

4.7 m
s. 5.4 m n. 4.0 m
High Water

7.8 m
s. 9.1 m n. 6.7 m
High Water

Rising to H.W.
s. 2.2 m n. 1.4 m
1.7 m

5.0 m
s. 5.7 m n. 4.4 m
Falling from H.W.

3.7 m
s. 4.3 m n. 3.1 m
High Water

Rising to H.W.
s. 5.7 m n. 4.4 m
5.0 m

Scilly Isles

4.9 m
s. 5.6 m n. 4.2 m
High Water

4.5 m
s. 5.1 m n. 3.9 m
Falling from H.W.

Falling from H.W.
s. 7.8 m n. 6.2 m
7.0 m

Alderney

Guernsey

Jersey

7.7 m
s. 9.0 m n. 6.6 m
High Water

Ile d'Ouessant

5.5 m
s. 5.9 m n. 5.1 m
Falling quickly

8.3 m
s. 9.7 m n. 7.1 m
High Water

10.0 m
s. 11.5 m n. 8.6 m
High Water

The broad arrows apply to the time entered on the adjacent page. Each arrow gives the following information:

A Average Height of Tide. This is the height of tide, in metres, above Chart Datum, at the position indicated by the arrow. Although only an average height, this figure is sufficiently accurate for use for most coastal navigation.

S Height of Tide at Springs

N Height of Tide at Neaps

The Tidal Gauge gives a visual display of the approximate state of the tide with the vertical movement of tide described briefly above or below.

TIDAL HEIGHTS — PORTS & PLACES

Pencil-in height of HW Cherbourg ▶	4.8	5.0	5.2	5.4	5.6	5.8	6.0	6.2	6.4	6.6	6.8
WALES											
Pwllheli, Barmouth.......	2.9	3.0	3.0	3.1	3.2	3.3	3.4	3.5	3.6	3.7	3.7	3.8
Aberystwth	3.1	3.2	3.4	3.5	3.6	3.7	3.8	3.9	4.0	4.1	4.1	4.2
Fishguard, P.Cardigan ..	3.2	3.3	3.5	3.6	3.8	3.9	4.1	4.2	4.4	4.6	4.7	4.9
Milford Haven	4.8	5.1	5.3	5.6	5.9	6.2	6.4	6.7	7.0	7.2	7.5	7.7
Burry Inlet approach	6.2	6.5	6.9	7.2	7.5	7.8	8.1	8.4	8.7	9.0	9.2	9.5
Swansea	6.8	7.1	7.5	7.8	8.2	8.5	8.9	9.2	9.6	9.8	10.0	10.2
P. Talbot, Porthcawl	7.0	7.3	7.7	8.0	8.4	8.7	9.1	9.4	9.8	10.1	10.4	10.7
Barry	8.2	8.5	8.7	9.0	9.3	9.6	9.9	10.2	10.5	10.8	11.1	11.4
Cardiff, Penarth..........	8.7	9.0	9.4	9.7	10.0	10.4	10.7	11.1	11.4	11.6	11.7	11.9
IRELAND											
Arklow	0.7	0.7	0.7	0.7	0.7	0.8	0.8	0.8	0.8	0.8	0.8	0.8
Rosslare	1.4	1.5	1.5	1.6	1.7	1.8	1.8	1.9	2.0	2.1	2.2	2.3
Waterford Hbr. entr.	3.1	3.2	3.4	3.5	3.6	3.8	3.9	4.0	4.1	4.2	4.2	4.3
Cork	3.2	3.3	3.5	3.6	3.8	3.9	4.1	4.2	4.4	4.5	4.6	4.7
Kinsale, Baltimore Bay .	2.9	3.0	3.2	3.3	3.4	3.5	3.6	3.7	3.8	3.9	3.9	4.0
ENGLAND-WEST											
Avonmouth.................	9.3	9.6	9.8	10.1	10.4	10.6	10.9	11.1	11.4	11.6	11.9	12.1
Weston-super-Mare	8.5	8.8	9.2	9.5	9.9	10.2	10.6	10.9	11.3	11.6	11.9	12.2
Watchet	7.9	8.3	8.7	9.1	9.4	9.8	10.2	10.5	10.9	11.2	11.5	11.8
Minehead	7.4	7.8	8.2	8.6	9.0	9.3	9.7	10.1	10.5	10.8	11.1	11.4
Porlock Bay	7.3	7.6	8.0	8.3	8.6	9.0	9.3	9.7	10.0	10.3	10.5	10.8
Ilfracombe	6.4	6.7	7.1	7.4	7.8	8.1	8.5	8.8	9.2	9.5	9.9	10.2
Appledore..................	4.5	4.9	5.3	5.7	6.0	6.4	6.8	7.1	7.5	7.8	8.2	8.5
Padstow, Newquay	5.0	5.3	5.5	5.8	6.1	6.3	6.6	6.8	7.1	7.3	7.6	7.8
St. Ives Bay	4.5	4.7	4.9	5.1	5.3	5.5	5.7	5.9	6.1	6.3	6.6	6.8
ISLANDS OFF											
Lundy Island	5.3	5.6	6.0	6.3	6.6	7.0	7.3	7.7	8.0	8.3	8.6	8.9
St. Mary's, Scilly Isles .	3.8	4.0	4.2	4.4	4.6	4.7	4.9	5.1	5.3	5.5	5.7	5.9
ENGLAND-SOUTH											
Falmouth, Helford R.....	3.7	3.9	4.1	4.3	4.5	4.6	4.8	5.0	5.2	5.3	5.5	5.6
Mevagissey, Looe........	3.8	4.0	4.2	4.4	4.6	4.8	5.0	5.2	5.4	5.5	5.7	5.8
Plymouth, Yealm R......	4.0	4.2	4.4	4.6	4.8	4.9	5.1	5.3	5.5	5.6	5.8	5.9
Salcombe	3.7	3.9	4.1	4.3	4.5	4.7	4.9	5.1	5.3	5.5	5.6	5.8
Dartmouth.................	3.2	3.4	3.6	3.8	4.0	4.1	4.3	4.5	4.7	4.9	5.0	5.2
Brixham, Teignmouth....	3.4	3.6	3.8	4.0	4.2	4.3	4.5	4.7	4.9	5.1	5.2	5.4
Exmouth approach.......	3.1	3.2	3.4	3.5	3.7	3.8	4.0	4.1	4.3	4.4	4.5	4.6
Lyme Regis.................	2.8	3.0	3.2	3.4	3.5	3.7	3.9	4.0	4.2	4.3	4.5	4.6
Portland, Weymouth	1.3	1.4	1.4	1.5	1.6	1.7	1.8	1.9	2,0	2.1	2.2	2.3
Lulworth Cove	1.3	1.4	1.6	1.7	1.8	1.9	2.0	2.1	2.2	2.4	2.5	2.7
Swanage	1.4	1.4	1.4	1.4	1.4	1.4	1.4	1.5	1.5	1.5	1.6	1.6
Poole Town	1.4	1.4	1.4	1.4	1.3	1.3	1.3	1.3	1.3	1.3	1.2	1.2
Christchurch Hbr.	1.0	1.0	1.0	1.0	1.1	1.1	1.1	1.1	1.1	1.1	1.1	1.1
CHANNEL ISLANDS											
Braye Hbr..................	4.3	4.5	4.7	4.9	5.1	5.3	5.5	5.7	5.9	6.1	6.3	6.5
St. Peter Port, Sark	6.2	6.5	6.9	7.2	7.5	7.8	8.2	8.5	8.8	9.0	9.3	9.5
St. Helier	7.5	7.9	8.3	8.7	9.2	9.6	10.0	10.5	10.9	11.3	11.6	12.0
Les Minquiers	8.3	8.7	9.1	9.5	9.8	10.2	10.6	10.9	11.3	11.6	11.9	12.2
FRANCE											
Cherbourg	4.2	4.3	4.5	4.6	4.7	4.8	4.9	5.0	5.1	5.2	5.3	5.4
Omonville	4.3	4.4	4.6	4.7	4.8	4.9	5.1	5.2	5.3	5.4	5.6	5.7
Iles Chausey	9.1	9.5	9.9	10.3	10.8	11.2	11.6	12.1	12.5	12.8	13.2	13.5
Carteret	7.6	8.0	8.4	8.8	9.2	9.5	9.9	10.3	10.7	11.0	11.3	11.6
Granville...................	8.9	9.4	9.8	10.3	10.8	11.3	11.7	12.2	12.7	13.0	13.4	13.7
St Malo	8.4	8.9	9.3	9.8	10.2	10.7	11.1	11.6	12.0	12.3	12.6	12.9
All Hbrs. St Brieuc Bay .	7.9	8.3	8.7	9.1	9.6	10.0	10.4	10.9	11.3	11.6	11.8	12.1
Ile de Bréhat	7.5	7.9	8.3	8.7	9.0	9.4	9.8	10.1	10.5	10.8	11.0	11.3
Lezardrieux	7.1	7.5	7.9	8.3	8.7	9.0	9.4	9.8	10.2	10.5	10.7	11.0
Tréguier	6.7	7.1	7.5	7.9	8.2	8.6	9.0	9.3	9.7	10.0	10.2	10.5
Morlaix, Primel Bay.....	6.2	6.5	6.9	7.2	7.5	7.7	8.1	8.4	8.7	8.9	9.0	9.2
Roscoff, Ile de Batz	6.3	6.6	6.8	7.1	7.4	7.7	7.9	8.2	8.5	8.7	8.8	9.0
L'Aberwrach	5.4	5.6	5.8	6.0	6.2	6.3	6.5	6.7	6.9	7.1	7.2	7.4
All Hbrs. Ch. du Four ...	4.8	4.9	5.1	5.2	5.3	5.5	5.6	5.7	5.8	5.9	5.9	6.0
Brest.......................	4.9	5.0	5.2	5.3	5.4	5.5	5.6	5.7	5.8	5.9	6.0	6.1
Camaret, Douarnenez...	4.6	4.7	4.7	4.8	4.9	5.0	5.1	5.2	5.3	5.4	5.4	5.5

Stream Rate Conversion Table

Pencil-in height of HW Cherbourg
Read from column below pencil mark

Mean Rate Figure from Chart ▼	4.8	5.0	5.2	5.4	5.6	5.8	6.0	6.2	6.4	6.6	6.8
0.2	0.1	0.1	0.1	0.1	0.2	0.2	0.2	0.2	0.3	0.3	0.3
0.4	0.2	0.2	0.2	0.3	0.3	0.4	0.4	0.5	0.5	0.6	0.7
0.6	0.2	0.3	0.4	0.4	0.5	0.6	0.7	0.7	0.8	0.9	1.0
0.8	0.4	0.4	0.5	0.6	0.7	0.8	0.9	1.0	1.1	1.2	1.3
1.0	0.4	0.5	0.6	0.7	0.9	1.0	1.1	1.2	1.3	1.4	1.7
1.2	0.5	0.6	0.7	0.9	1.0	1.2	1.3	1.4	1.6	1.7	2.0
1.4	0.6	0.7	0.9	1.0	1.2	1.4	1.5	1.7	1.8	2.0	2.3
1.6	0.6	0.8	1.0	1.2	1.4	1.6	1.7	1.9	2.1	2.3	2.7
1.8	0.7	0.9	1.1	1.3	1.5	1.7	2.0	2.2	2.4	2.6	3.0
2.0	0.8	1.0	1.2	1.5	1.7	1.9	2.2	2.4	2.6	2.9	3.3
2.2	0.9	1.1	1.4	1.6	1.9	2.1	2.3	2.6	2.9	3.2	3.7
2.4	0.9	1.2	1.5	1.8	2.1	2.3	2.6	2.9	3.2	3.4	4.0
2.6	1.0	1.3	1.6	1.9	2.2	2.5	2.8	3.1	3.4	3.7	4.3
2.8	1.1	1.4	1.7	2.1	2.4	2.7	3.0	3.4	3.7	4.0	4.7
3.0	1.2	1.5	1.9	2.2	2.6	2.9	3.2	3.6	4.0	4.3	5.0
3.2	1.3	1.6	2.0	2.4	2.7	3.1	3.4	3.8	4.2	4.6	5.3
3.4	1.3	1.7	2.1	2.5	2.9	3.3	3.7	4.1	4.5	4.9	5.7
3.6	1.4	1.8	2.2	2.7	3.1	3.5	3.9	4.3	4.7	5.2	6.0
3.8	1.5	1.9	2.4	2.8	3.3	3.7	4.1	4.6	5.0	5.4	6.3
4.0	1.6	2.0	2.5	3.0	3.4	3.9	4.3	4.8	5.3	5.7	6.7
4.2	1.7	2.1	2.6	3.1	3.6	4.1	4.6	5.0	5.5	6.0	7.0
4.4	1.7	2.2	2.7	3.3	3.8	4.3	4.8	5.3	5.8	6.3	7.3
4.6	1.8	2.3	2.9	3.4	3.9	4.5	5.0	5.5	6.1	6.6	7.7
4.8	1.9	2.4	3.0	3.5	4.1	4.7	5.2	5.8	6.3	6.9	8.0
5.0	2.0	2.5	3.1	3.7	4.3	4.9	5.4	6.0	6.6	7.2	8.3
5.2	2.0	2.6	3.2	3.8	4.4	5.0	5.6	6.2	6.8	7.4	8.6
5.4	2.1	2.8	3.4	4.0	4.6	5.2	5.7	6.5	7.1	7.7	9.0
5.6	2.2	2.9	3.5	4.1	4.8	5.4	6.1	6.7	7.4	8.0	9.3
5.8	2.3	3.0	3.6	4.3	5.0	5.6	6.3	7.0	7.6	8.3	9.6
6.0	2.4	3.1	3.7	4.4	5.1	5.8	6.5	7.2	7.9	8.6	9.9

Tidal Stream Rates

Copyright © J Reeve-Fowkes and Thomas Reed Publications.
No copying without permission

2 hours before HW Cherbourg **-2**

Time (to be inserted)

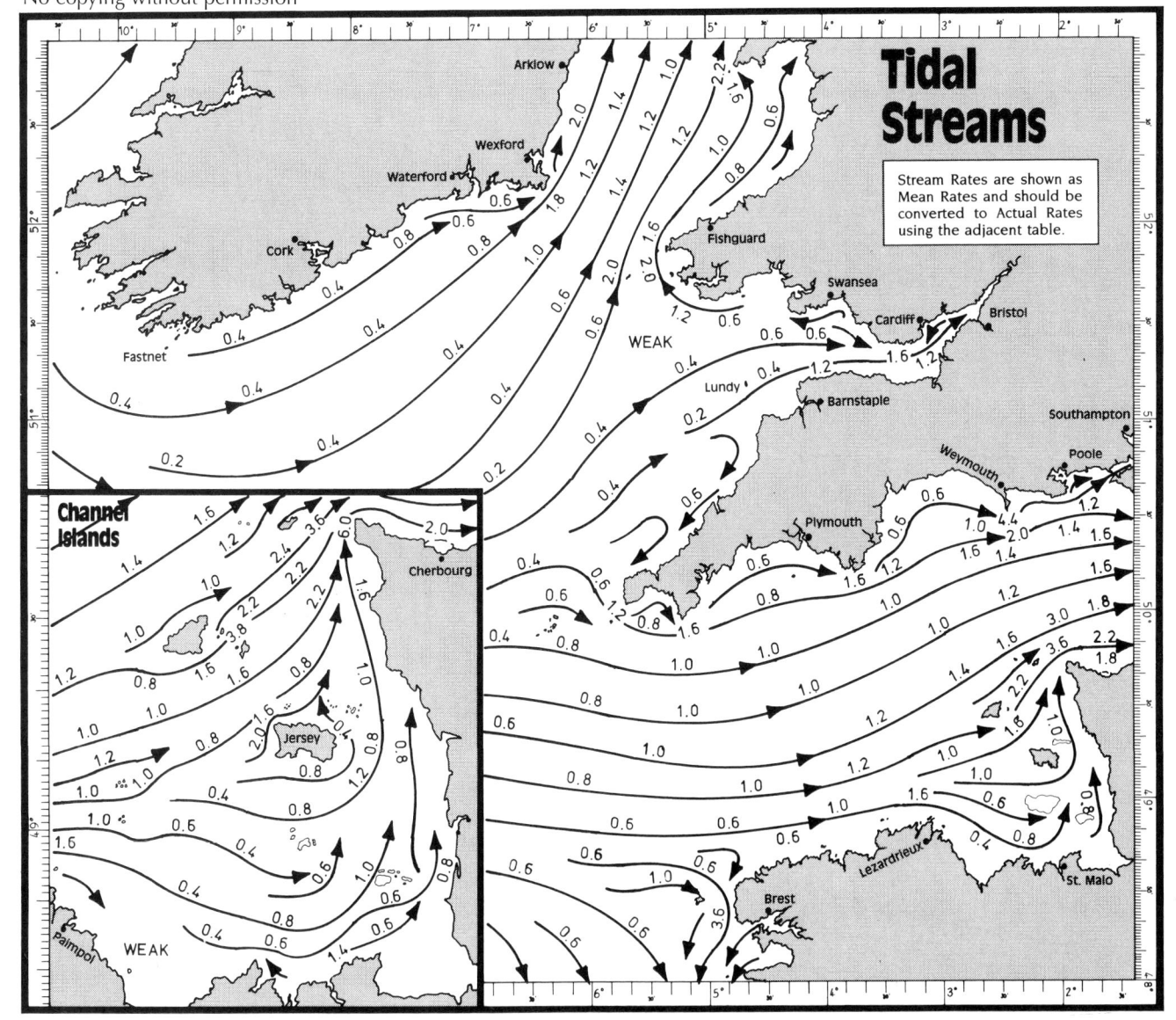

Tidal Streams

Stream Rates are shown as Mean Rates and should be converted to Actual Rates using the adjacent table.

-1 — 1 hour before HW Cherbourg

Tidal Heights

Copyright © J Reeve-Fowkes and
Thomas Reed Publications.
No copying without permission

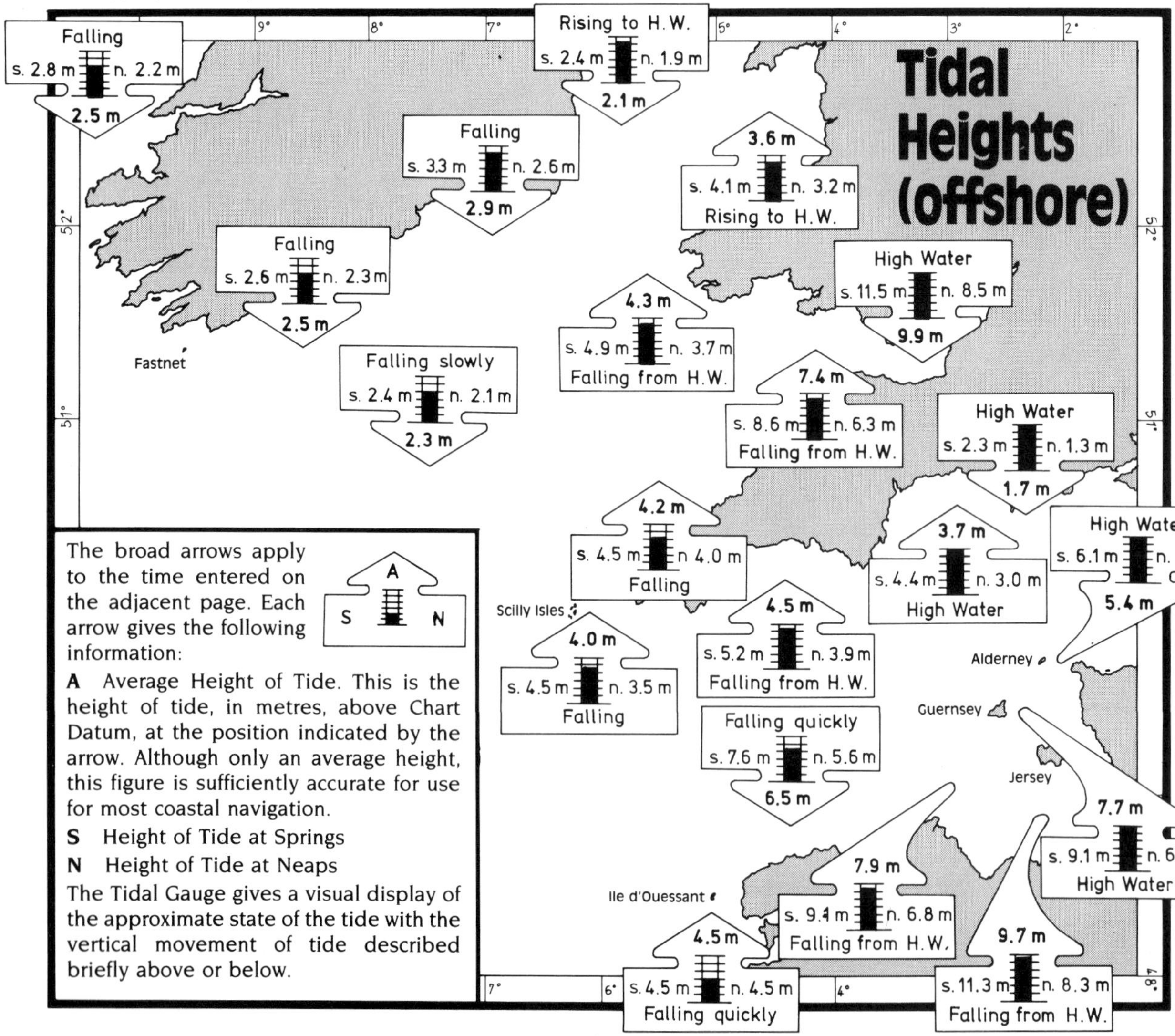

Tidal Heights (offshore)

Falling — s. 2.8 m n. 2.2 m — **2.5 m**

Rising to H.W. — s. 2.4 m n. 1.9 m — **2.1 m**

3.6 m — s. 4.1 m n. 3.2 m — **Rising to H.W.**

Falling — s. 3.3 m n. 2.6 m — **2.9 m**

Falling — s. 2.6 m n. 2.3 m — **2.5 m**

Fastnet

Falling slowly — s. 2.4 m n. 2.1 m — **2.3 m**

4.3 m — s. 4.9 m n. 3.7 m — **Falling from H.W.**

7.4 m — s. 8.6 m n. 6.3 m — **Falling from H.W.**

High Water — s. 11.5 m n. 8.5 m — **9.9 m**

High Water — s. 2.3 m n. 1.3 m — **1.7 m**

4.2 m — s. 4.5 m n. 4.0 m — **Falling**

Scilly Isles

4.0 m — s. 4.5 m n. 3.5 m — **Falling**

4.5 m — s. 5.2 m n. 3.9 m — **Falling from H.W.**

3.7 m — s. 4.4 m n. 3.0 m — **High Water**

High Water — s. 6.1 m n. 4.8 m — **5.4 m**

Alderney

Falling quickly — s. 7.6 m n. 5.6 m — **6.5 m**

Guernsey

Jersey

7.7 m — s. 9.1 m n. 6.6 m — **High Water**

Ile d'Ouessant

7.9 m — s. 9.4 m n. 6.8 m — **Falling from H.W.**

9.7 m — s. 11.3 m n. 8.3 m — **Falling from H.W.**

4.5 m — s. 4.5 m n. 4.5 m — **Falling quickly**

Legend

The broad arrows apply to the time entered on the adjacent page. Each arrow gives the following information:

A Average Height of Tide. This is the height of tide, in metres, above Chart Datum, at the position indicated by the arrow. Although only an average height, this figure is sufficiently accurate for use for most coastal navigation.

S Height of Tide at Springs

N Height of Tide at Neaps

The Tidal Gauge gives a visual display of the approximate state of the tide with the vertical movement of tide described briefly above or below.

TIDAL HEIGHTS — PORTS & PLACES

Pencil-in height of ► HW Cherbourg	4.8	5.0	5.2	5.4	5.6	5.8	6.0	6.2	6.4	6.6	6.8
WALES											
Pwllheli, Barmouth.......	3.0	3.2	3.4	3.6	3.8	3.9	4.1	4.3	4.5	4.6	4.7	4.8
Aberystwth	3.4	3.5	3.7	3.8	4.0	4.1	4.3	4.4	4.6	4.7	4.9	5.0
Fishguard, P.Cardigan ..	3.2	3.4	3.6	3.8	4.0	4.2	4.4	4.6	4.8	5.0	5.1	5.3
Milford Haven	4.6	4.9	5.1	5.4	5.7	5.9	6.2	6.4	6.7	6.9	7.2	7.4
Burry Inlet approach	6.0	6.3	6.5	6.8	7.1	7.4	7.7	8.0	8.3	8.5	8.8	9.0
Swansea	6.6	6.7	7.3	7.6	7.9	8.3	8.6	9.0	9.3	9.5	9.8	10.0
P. Talbot, Porthcawl.....	6.7	7.0	7.4	7.7	8.0	8.4	8.7	9.1	9.4	9.7	9.9	10.2
Barry	7.8	8.3	8.7	9.2	9.6	10.1	10.5	11.0	11.4	11.7	12.1	12.4
Cardiff, Penarth..........	8.6	9.1	9.5	10.0	10.4	10.9	11.3	11.8	12.2	12.5	12.8	13.1
IRELAND											
Arklow	0.9	0.9	0.9	0.9	0.9	0.9	0.9	0.9	0.9	0.9	1.0	1.0
Rosslare	1.3	1.4	1.4	1.5	1.6	1.7	1.7	1.8	1.9	2.0	2.1	2.2
Waterford Hbr. entr.	2.7	2.8	3.0	3.1	3.2	3.3	3.4	3.5	3.6	3.7	3.7	3.8
Cork	3.0	3.1	3.3	3.4	3.5	3.7	3.8	3.9	4.0	4.1	4.1	4.2
Kinsale, Baltimore Bay .	2.7	2.8	2.8	2.9	3.0	3.0	3.1	3.1	3.2	3.2	3.3	3.3
ENGLAND-WEST											
Avonmouth................	9.3	9.8	10.2	10.7	11.2	11.6	12.1	12.5	13.0	13.4	13.7	14.1
Weston-super-Mare	8.3	8.8	9.2	9.7	10.2	10.6	11.1	11.5	12.0	12.3	12.7	13.0
Watchet	7.7	8.1	8.5	8.9	9.4	9.8	10.2	10.7	11.1	11.4	11.7	12.0
Minehead	7.1	7.5	7.9	8.3	8.7	9.1	9.5	9.9	10.3	10.6	10.8	11.1
Porlock Bay	7.0	7.3	7.7	8.0	8.3	8.6	8.9	9.2	9.5	9.8	10.0	10.3
Ilfracombe	5.9	6.2	6.6	6.9	7.2	7.5	7.9	8.2	8.5	8.8	9.0	9.3
Appledore................	4.2	4.5	4.9	5.2	5.5	5.8	6.2	6.5	6.8	7.1	7.4	7.7
Padstow, Newquay	4.7	4.9	5.1	5.3	5.5	5.6	5.8	6.0	6.2	6.4	6.5	6.7
St. Ives Bay	4.3	4.4	4.4	4.5	4.6	4.7	4.8	4.9	5.0	5.1	5.3	5.4
ISLANDS OFF											
Lundy Island	5.0	5.3	5.5	5.8	6.1	6.4	6.6	6.9	7.2	7.5	7.7	8.0
St. Mary's, Scilly Isles .	3.5	3.6	3.8	3.9	4.1	4.2	4.4	4.5	4.7	4.8	5.0	5.1
ENGLAND-SOUTH											
Falmouth, Helford R.....	3.3	3.5	3.7	3.9	4.1	4.2	4.4	4.6	4.8	4.9	5.0	5.1
Mevagissey, Looe.......	3.5	3.7	3.9	4.1	4.3	4.5	4.7	4.9	5.1	5.2	5.3	5.4
Plymouth, Yealm R......	3.7	3.9	4.1	4.3	4.5	4.6	4.8	5.0	5.2	5.3	5.5	5.6
Salcombe	3.4	3.6	3.8	4.0	4.2	4.5	4.7	4.9	5.1	5.2	5.4	5.5
Dartmouth	3.0	3.2	3.4	3.6	3.9	4.1	4.3	4.6	4.8	4.9	5.1	5.2
Brixham, Teignmouth...	3.3	3.5	3.7	3.9	4.1	4.3	4.5	4.7	4.9	5.1	5.3	5.5
Exmouth approach.......	2.9	3.1	3.3	3.5	3.7	3.9	4.1	4.3	4.5	4.6	4.7	4.8
Lyme Regis...............	2.7	2.9	3.1	3.3	3.5	3.7	3.9	4.1	4.3	4.4	4.6	4.7
Portland, Weymouth	1.1	1.2	1.4	1.5	1.6	1.7	1.9	2.0	2.1	2.2	2.4	2.5
Lulworth Cove	1.2	1.3	1.5	1.6	1.7	1.9	2.0	2.2	2.3	2.5	2.6	2.8
Swanage	1.3	1.4	1.4	1.5	1.5	1.6	1.7	1.7	1.8	1.9	1.9	2.0
Poole Town	1.5	1.5	1.5	1.5	1.6	1.6	1.7	1.7	1.8	1.8	1.8	1.8
Christchurch Hbr.	1.0	1.1	1.1	1.2	1.2	1.3	1.4	1.4	1.5	1.5	1.6	1.6
CHANNEL ISLANDS											
Braye Hbr.	4.4	4.6	4.8	5.0	5.3	5.5	5.7	6.0	6.2	6.4	6.7	6.9
St. Peter Port, Sark	6.1	6.4	6.8	7.1	7.5	7.8	8.2	8.5	8.9	9.1	9.4	9.6
St. Helier	7.3	7.8	8.2	8.7	9.1	9.6	10.0	10.5	10.9	11.2	11.6	11.9
Les Minquiers	8.2	8.6	9.0	9.4	9.8	10.1	10.5	10.9	11.3	11.6	11.9	12.2
FRANCE											
Cherbourg	4.6	4.8	5.0	5.2	5.3	5.5	5.7	5.8	6.0	6.2	6.4	6.6
Omonville	4.7	4.8	5.0	5.1	5.3	5.4	5.6	5.7	5.9	6.1	6.3	6.9
Iles Chausey	8.8	9.2	9.6	10.0	10.5	10.9	11.3	11.8	12.2	12.5	12.8	13.1
Carteret	7.6	8.0	8.4	8.8	9.2	9.5	9.9	10.3	10.7	11.0	11.3	11.6
Granville	8.6	9.1	9.5	10.0	10.5	10.9	11.4	11.8	12.3	12.6	12.9	13.2
St Malo	7.9	8.4	8.8	9.3	9.8	10.3	10.7	11.2	11.7	12.0	12.3	12.6
All Hbrs. St Brieuc Bay	7.7	8.0	8.4	8.7	9.1	9.4	9.8	10.1	10.5	10.7	11.0	11.2
Ile de Bréhat	7.1	7.4	7.8	8.1	8.5	8.8	9.2	9.5	9.9	10.2	10.4	10.7
Lezardrieux	7.0	7.3	7.7	8.0	8.3	8.6	9.0	9.3	9.6	9.9	9.9	10.4
Tréguier	6.5	6.8	7.0	7.3	7.6	7.8	8.1	8.3	8.6	8.8	9.0	9.2
Morlaix, Primel Bay......	5.7	5.9	6.1	6.3	6.6	6.8	7.0	7.3	7.5	7.6	7.6	7.7
Roscoff, Ile de Batz.....	5.7	5.9	6.1	6.3	6.5	6.8	7.0	7.2	7.4	7.5	7.5	7.6
L'Aberwrach	5.0	5.1	5.1	5.2	5.3	5.3	5.4	5.4	5.5	5.6	5.6	5.7
All Hbrs. Ch. du Four....	4.4	4.4	4.4	4.4	4.4	4.5	4.5	4.5	4.5	4.5	4.4	4.4
Brest	4.5	4.5	4.5	4.5	4.5	4.5	4.5	4.5	4.5	4.5	4.5	4.5
Camaret, Douarnenez...	4.1	4.1	4.1	4.1	4.1	4.1	4.1	4.1	4.1	4.1	4.0	4.0

Stream Rate Conversion Table

Mean Rate Figure from Chart ▼	\multicolumn{11}{c}{Pencil-in height of HW Cherbourg — Read from column below pencil mark}
	4.8	5.0	5.2	5.4	5.6	5.8	6.0	6.2	6.4	6.6	6.8
0.2	0.1	0.1	0.1	0.1	0.2	0.2	0.2	0.2	0.3	0.3	0.3
0.4	0.2	0.2	0.2	0.3	0.3	0.4	0.4	0.5	0.5	0.6	0.7
0.6	0.2	0.3	0.4	0.4	0.5	0.6	0.7	0.7	0.8	0.9	1.0
0.8	0.4	0.4	0.6	0.6	0.7	0.8	0.9	1.0	1.1	1.2	1.3
1.0	0.4	0.5	0.6	0.7	0.9	1.0	1.1	1.2	1.3	1.5	1.7
1.2	0.5	0.6	0.7	0.9	1.0	1.2	1.3	1.4	1.6	1.7	1.9	2.0
1.4	0.6	0.7	0.9	1.0	1.2	1.4	1.5	1.7	1.8	2.0	2.2	2.3
1.6	0.6	0.8	1.0	1.2	1.4	1.6	1.7	1.9	2.1	2.3	2.5	2.7
1.8	0.7	0.9	1.1	1.3	1.5	1.7	2.0	2.2	2.4	2.6	2.8	3.0
2.0	0.8	1.0	1.2	1.5	1.7	1.9	2.2	2.4	2.6	2.9	3.1	3.3
2.2	0.9	1.1	1.4	1.6	1.9	2.1	2.3	2.6	2.9	3.2	3.4	3.7
2.4	0.9	1.2	1.5	1.8	2.1	2.3	2.6	2.9	3.2	3.4	3.7	4.0
2.6	1.0	1.3	1.6	1.9	2.2	2.5	2.8	3.1	3.4	3.7	4.0	4.3
2.8	1.1	1.4	1.7	2.1	2.4	2.7	3.0	3.4	3.7	4.0	4.3	4.7
3.0	1.2	1.5	1.9	2.2	2.6	2.9	3.2	3.6	4.0	4.3	4.6	5.0
3.2	1.3	1.6	2.0	2.4	2.7	3.1	3.4	3.8	4.2	4.6	4.9	5.3
3.4	1.3	1.7	2.1	2.5	2.9	3.3	3.7	4.1	4.5	4.9	5.3	5.7
3.6	1.4	1.8	2.2	2.7	3.1	3.5	3.9	4.3	4.7	5.2	5.6	6.0
3.8	1.5	1.9	2.4	2.8	3.3	3.7	4.1	4.6	5.0	5.4	5.9	6.3
4.0	1.6	2.0	2.5	3.0	3.4	3.9	4.3	4.8	5.3	5.7	6.2	6.7
4.2	1.7	2.1	2.6	3.1	3.6	4.1	4.6	5.0	5.5	6.0	6.5	7.0
4.4	1.7	2.2	2.7	3.3	3.8	4.3	4.8	5.3	5.8	6.3	6.8	7.3
4.6	1.8	2.3	2.9	3.4	3.9	4.5	5.0	5.5	6.1	6.6	7.1	7.7
4.8	1.9	2.4	3.0	3.6	4.1	4.7	5.2	5.8	6.3	6.9	7.4	8.0
5.0	2.0	2.5	3.1	3.7	4.3	4.9	5.4	6.0	6.6	7.2	7.7	8.3
5.2	2.0	2.6	3.2	3.8	4.4	5.0	5.6	6.2	6.8	7.4	8.0	8.6
5.4	2.1	2.8	3.4	4.0	4.6	5.2	5.7	6.5	7.1	7.7	8.4	9.0
5.6	2.2	2.9	3.5	4.1	4.8	5.4	6.1	6.7	7.4	8.0	8.7	9.3
5.8	2.3	3.0	3.6	4.3	5.0	5.6	6.3	7.0	7.6	8.3	9.0	9.6
6.0	2.4	3.1	3.7	4.4	5.1	5.8	6.5	7.2	7.9	8.6	9.3	9.9

Tidal Stream Rates

Copyright © J Reeve-Fowkes and Thomas Reed Publications.
No copying without permission

1 hour before HW Cherbourg **-1**

Time (to be inserted)

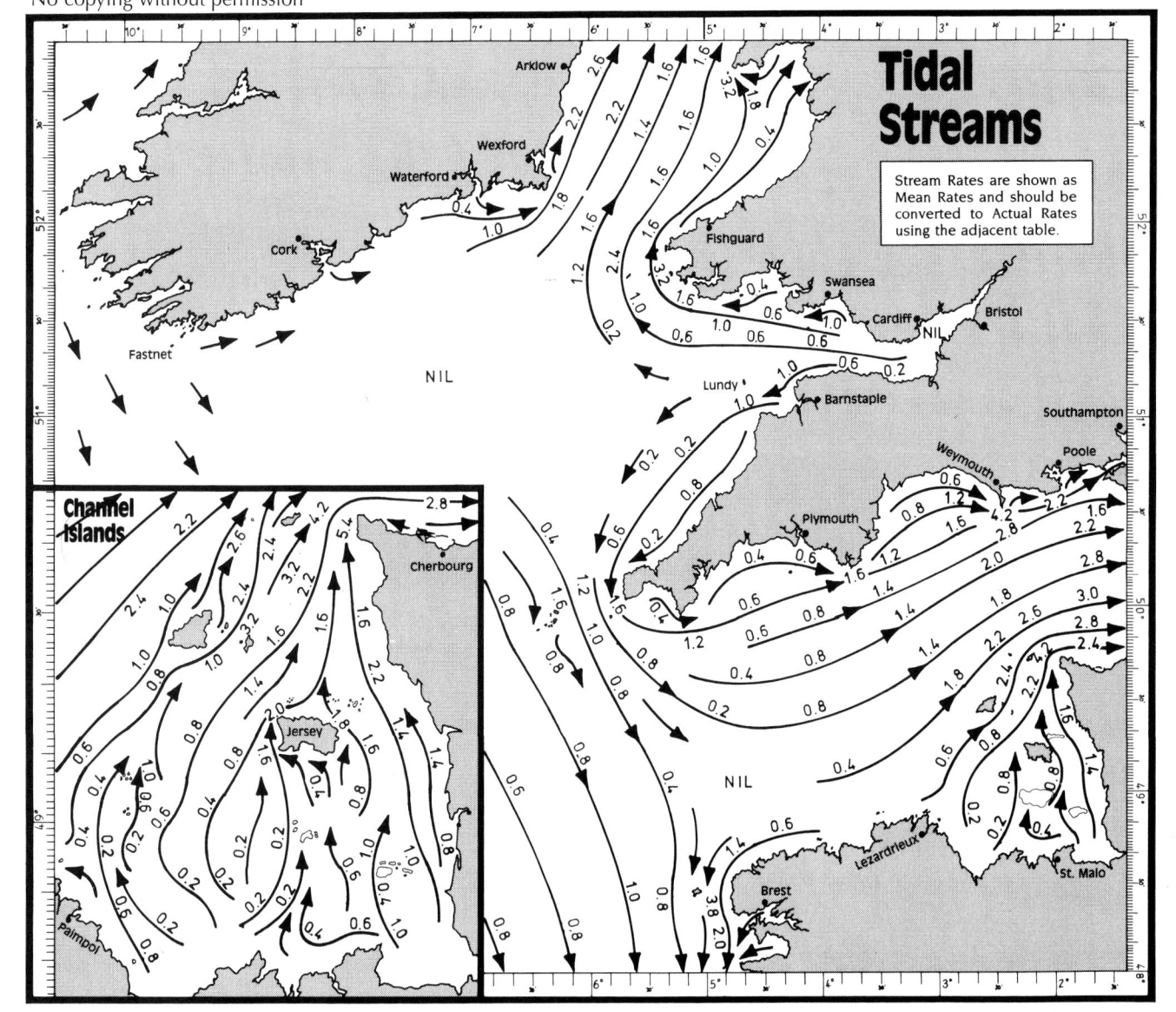

Tidal Streams

Stream Rates are shown as Mean Rates and should be converted to Actual Rates using the adjacent table.

HW
HW Cherbourg

Tidal Heights

Copyright © J Reeve-Fowkes and
Thomas Reed Publications.
No copying without permission

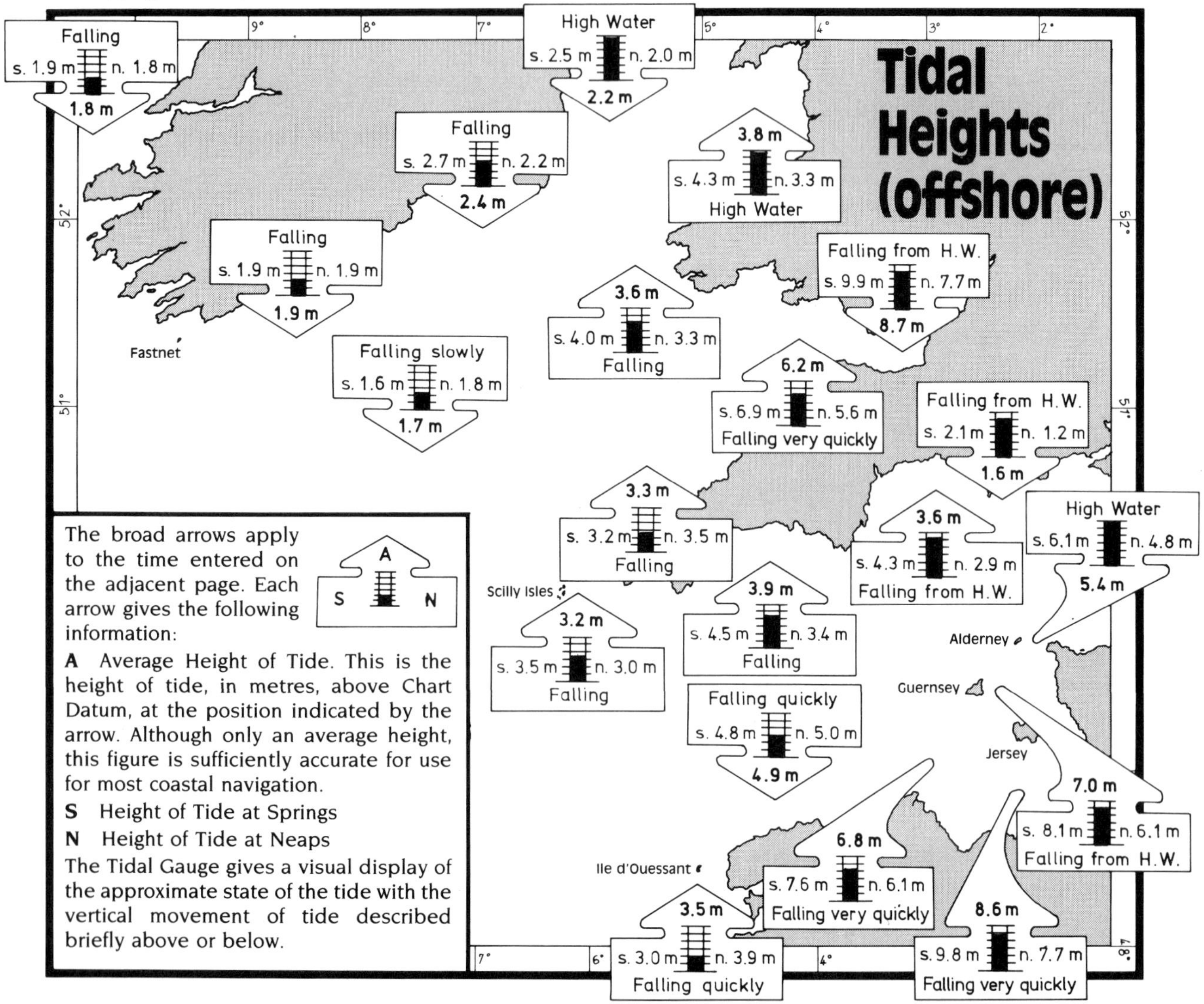

Tidal Heights (offshore)

Falling
s. 1.9 m n. 1.8 m
1.8 m

High Water
s. 2.5 m n. 2.0 m
2.2 m

Falling
s. 2.7 m n. 2.2 m
2.4 m

High Water
3.8 m
s. 4.3 m n. 3.3 m

Falling
s. 1.9 m n. 1.9 m
1.9 m

Fastnet

Falling slowly
s. 1.6 m n. 1.8 m
1.7 m

Falling from H.W.
8.7 m
s. 9.9 m n. 7.7 m

Falling
3.6 m
s. 4.0 m n. 3.3 m

Falling very quickly
6.2 m
s. 6.9 m n. 5.6 m

Falling from H.W.
1.6 m
s. 2.1 m n. 1.2 m

Falling
3.3 m
s. 3.2 m n. 3.5 m

Falling from H.W.
3.6 m
s. 4.3 m n. 2.9 m

High Water
5.4 m
s. 6.1 m n. 4.8 m

Scilly Isles

Falling
3.2 m
s. 3.5 m n. 3.0 m

Falling
3.9 m
s. 4.5 m n. 3.4 m

Alderney

Guernsey

Falling quickly
4.9 m
s. 4.8 m n. 5.0 m

Jersey

Falling from H.W.
7.0 m
s. 8.1 m n. 6.1 m

Ile d'Ouessant

Falling very quickly
6.8 m
s. 7.6 m n. 6.1 m

Falling quickly
3.5 m
s. 3.0 m n. 3.9 m

Falling very quickly
8.6 m
s. 9.8 m n. 7.7 m

The broad arrows apply to the time entered on the adjacent page. Each arrow gives the following information:

A N S

A Average Height of Tide. This is the height of tide, in metres, above Chart Datum, at the position indicated by the arrow. Although only an average height, this figure is sufficiently accurate for use for most coastal navigation.
S Height of Tide at Springs
N Height of Tide at Neaps
The Tidal Gauge gives a visual display of the approximate state of the tide with the vertical movement of tide described briefly above or below.

TIDAL HEIGHTS — PORTS & PLACES

Pencil-in height of HW Cherbourg ▶	4.8	5.0	5.2	5.4	5.6	5.8	6.0	6.2	6.4	6.6	6.8
WALES											
Pwllheli, Barmouth......	3.5	3.7	3.9	4.1	4.2	4.4	4.6	4.7	4.9	5.1	5.2	5.4
Aberystwth	3.4	3.6	3.8	4.0	4.1	4.3	4.5	4.6	4.8	4.9	5.1	5.2
Fishguard, P.Cardigan ..	3.2	3.4	3.6	3.8	3.9	4.1	4.3	4.4	4.6	4.8	4.9	5.1
Milford Haven	4.3	4.5	4.7	4.9	5.0	5.2	5.4	5.5	5.7	5.8	6.0	6.1
Burry Inlet approach	5.5	5.7	5.9	6.1	6.2	6.4	6.6	6.7	6.9	7.1	7.2	7.4
Swansea	6.0	6.3	6.5	6.8	7.1	7.4	7.7	8.0	8.3	8.5	8.6	8.8
P. Talbot, Porthcawl	6.1	6.3	6.5	6.7	6.9	7.2	7.4	7.6	7.8	8.0	8.1	8.3
Barry	7.1	7.5	7.9	8.3	8.7	9.0	9.4	9.8	10.2	10.5	10.7	11.0
Cardiff, Penarth..........	8.0	8.5	8.9	9.4	9.9	10.3	10.8	11.2	11.7	12.0	12.2	12.5
IRELAND											
Arklow.....................	0.9	0.9	0.9	0.9	0.9	1.0	1.0	1.0	1.0	1.0	1.1	1.1
Rosslare	1.2	1.3	1.3	1.4	1.5	1.5	1.6	1.6	1.7	1.8	1.8	1.9
Waterford Hbr. entr.	2.4	2.5	2.5	2.6	2.6	2.7	2.7	2.8	2.8	2.8	2.9	2.9
Cork	2.6	2.7	2.7	2.8	2.9	3.0	3.0	3.1	3.2	3.2	3.3	3.3
Kinsale, Baltimore Bay .	2.4	2.4	2.4	2.4	2.4	2.3	2.3	2.3	2.3	2.3	2.3	2.3
ENGLAND-WEST											
Avonmouth.................	8.5	9.0	9.6	10.1	10.6	11.1	11.7	12.2	12.7	13.0	13.4	13.7
Weston-super-Mare	7.5	7.8	8.2	8.5	8.8	9.1	9.4	9.7	10.0	10.2	10.5	10.7
Watchet	7.1	7.4	7.6	7.9	8.1	8.4	8.6	8.9	9.1	9.3	9.6	9.8
Minehead	6.6	6.8	7.0	7.2	7.4	7.6	7.8	8.0	8.2	8.4	8.6	8.8
Porlock Bay	6.5	6.6	6.8	6.9	7.0	7.2	7.3	7.5	7.6	7.7	7.9	8.0
Ilfracombe	5.3	5.5	5.5	5.9	6.0	6.2	6.4	6.5	6.7	6.9	7.0	7.2
Appledore.................	3.7	3.9	4.1	4.3	4.6	4.8	5.0	5.3	5.5	5.7	6.0	6.2
Padstow, Newquay	4.2	4.3	4.3	4.4	4.5	4.6	4.6	4.7	4.8	4.9	4.9	5.0
St. Ives Bay	3.9	3.9	3.9	3.9	3.9	3.8	3.8	3.8	3.8	3.8	3.9	3.9
ISLANDS OFF											
Lundy Island	4.4	4.6	4.8	5.0	5.1	5.3	5.5	5.6	5.8	5.9	6.1	6.2
St. Mary's, Scilly Isles .	3.1	3.2	3.2	3.3	3.4	3.4	3.5	3.5	3.6	3.7	3.7	3.8
ENGLAND-SOUTH											
Falmouth, Helford R.....	2.9	3.0	3.2	3.3	3.5	3.6	3.8	3.9	4.1	4.2	4.2	4.3
Mevagissey, Looe........	3.0	3.2	3.4	3.6	3.7	3.9	4.1	4.2	4.4	4.5	4.5	4.6
Plymouth, Yealm R......	3.2	3.4	3.6	3.8	3.9	4.1	4.3	4.4	4.6	4.7	4.7	4.8
Salcombe	3.0	3.2	3.4	3.6	3.8	3.9	4.1	4.3	4.5	4.6	4.7	4.8
Dartmouth	2.7	2.9	3.1	3.3	3.5	3.8	4.0	4.2	4.4	4.5	4.7	4.8
Brixham, Teignmouth....	3.0	3.2	3.4	3.6	3.8	4.0	4.2	4.4	4.6	4.8	4.9	5.1
Exmouth approach.......	2.7	2.9	3.1	3.3	3.5	3.7	3.9	4.1	4.3	4.4	4.5	4.6
Lyme Regis................	3.8	3.9	3.9	4.0	4.0	4.1	4.1	4.2	4.2	4.3	4.5	4.6
Portland, Weymouth	1.0	1.1	1.3	1.4	1.5	1.6	1.8	1.9	2.0	2.1	2.3	2.4
Lulworth Cove	1.1	1.2	1.4	1.5	1.6	1.7	1.9	2.0	2.1	2.3	2.4	2.6
Swanage	1.5	1.5	1.5	1.5	1.6	1.6	1.7	1.8	1.9	2.0	2.0	2.1
Poole Town	1.4	1.5	1.5	1.6	1.7	1.8	1.9	2.0	2.1	2.1	2.2	2.2
Christchurch Hbr.	1.1	1.2	1.2	1.3	1.4	1.5	1.6	1.6	1.7	1.7	1.8	1.8
CHANNEL ISLANDS											
Braye Hbr.	4.3	4.5	4.7	4.9	5.1	5.3	5.5	5.7	5.9	6.3	6.4	6.6
St. Peter Port, Sark	5.9	6.1	6.3	6.6	6.9	7.1	7.4	7.6	7.9	8.1	8.3	8.5
St. Helier.................	7.0	7.3	7.7	8.0	8.3	8.7	9.0	9.4	9.7	10.0	10.2	10.5
Les Minquiers	7.9	8.2	8.4	8.7	9.0	9.3	9.6	9.9	10.2	10.4	10.6	10.8
FRANCE											
Cherbourg	4.7	4.9	5.1	5.3	5.5	5.7	5.9	6.1	6.3	6.5	6.7	6.9
Omonville.................	4.7	4.9	5.1	5.3	5.5	5.8	6.0	6.2	6.4	6.7	6.9
Iles Chausey	8.1	8.4	8.8	9.1	9.4	9.7	10.1	10.4	10.7	10.9	11.1	11.3
Carteret	7.3	7.6	7.8	8.1	8.4	8.7	9.0	9.3	9.6	9.8	10.0	10.2
Granville	7.8	8.2	8.6	9.0	9.3	9.7	10.0	10.4	10.8	11.0	11.2	11.4
St Malo	7.2	7.6	8.0	8.4	8.8	9.1	9.5	9.9	10.3	10.5	10.7	10.9
All Hbrs. St Brieuc Bay .	6.9	7.2	7.4	7.7	7.9	8.2	8.4	8.7	8.9	9.0	9.2	9.3
Ile de Bréhat	6.3	6.6	6.8	7.1	7.4	7.7	8.0	8.3	8.6	8.7	8.9	9.0
Lezardrieux	5.9	6.2	6.4	6.7	6.9	7.2	7.4	7.7	7.9	8.1	8.2	8.4
Tréguier	5.8	5.9	6.1	6.2	6.3	6.5	6.6	6.8	6.9	7.0	7.0	7.1
Morlaix, Primel Bay......	5.1	5.2	5.2	5.3	5.4	5.5	5.6	5.7	5.8	5.8	5.7	5.7
Roscoff, Ile de Batz	5.2	5.3	5.3	5.4	5.4	5.5	5.5	5.6	5.7	5.7	5.6	5.6
L'Aberwrach	4.5	4.4	4.4	4.3	4.3	4.2	4.2	4.1	4.0	4.0	3.9	3.9
All Hbrs. Ch. du Four ...	3.9	3.8	3.8	3.7	3.6	3.5	3.4	3.3	3.2	3.1	2.9	2.8
Brest.......................	4.1	4.0	3.8	3.7	3.6	3.4	3.3	3.2	3.1	3.0	3.0	2.9
Camaret, Douarnenez...	3.8	3.7	3.5	3.4	3.3	3.1	3.0	2.9	2.8	2.7	2.6	2.5

Tidal Stream Rates

Stream Rate Conversion Table

Mean Rate Figure from Chart ▼	\multicolumn{11}{c}{Pencil-in height of HW Cherbourg — Read from column below pencil mark}
	4.8	5.0	5.2	5.4	5.6	5.8	6.0	6.2	6.4	6.6	6.8
0.2	0.1	0.1	0.1	0.1	0.2	0.2	0.2	0.2	0.3	0.3	0.3
0.4	0.2	0.2	0.2	0.3	0.3	0.4	0.4	0.5	0.5	0.6	0.7
0.6	0.2	0.3	0.4	0.4	0.5	0.6	0.7	0.7	0.8	0.9	1.0
0.8	0.4	0.4	0.5	0.6	0.7	0.8	0.9	1.0	1.1	1.2	1.3
1.0	0.4	0.5	0.6	0.7	0.9	1.0	1.1	1.2	1.3	1.4	1.5	1.7
1.2	0.5	0.6	0.7	0.9	1.0	1.2	1.3	1.4	1.6	1.7	1.9	2.0
1.4	0.6	0.7	0.9	1.0	1.2	1.4	1.5	1.7	1.8	2.0	2.2	2.3
1.6	0.6	0.8	1.0	1.2	1.4	1.6	1.7	1.9	2.1	2.3	2.5	2.7
1.8	0.7	0.9	1.1	1.3	1.5	1.7	2.0	2.2	2.4	2.6	2.8	3.0
2.0	0.8	1.0	1.2	1.5	1.7	1.9	2.2	2.4	2.6	2.9	3.1	3.3
2.2	0.9	1.1	1.4	1.6	1.9	2.1	2.3	2.6	2.9	3.2	3.4	3.7
2.4	0.9	1.2	1.5	1.8	2.1	2.3	2.6	2.9	3.2	3.4	3.7	4.0
2.6	1.0	1.3	1.6	1.9	2.2	2.5	2.8	3.1	3.4	3.7	4.0	4.3
2.8	1.1	1.4	1.7	2.1	2.4	2.7	3.0	3.4	3.7	4.0	4.3	4.7
3.0	1.2	1.5	1.9	2.2	2.6	2.9	3.2	3.6	4.0	4.3	4.6	5.0
3.2	1.3	1.6	2.0	2.4	2.7	3.1	3.4	3.8	4.2	4.6	4.9	5.3
3.4	1.3	1.7	2.1	2.5	2.9	3.3	3.7	4.1	4.5	4.9	5.3	5.7
3.6	1.4	1.8	2.2	2.7	3.1	3.5	3.9	4.3	4.7	5.2	5.6	6.0
3.8	1.5	1.9	2.4	2.8	3.3	3.7	4.1	4.6	5.0	5.4	5.9	6.3
4.0	1.6	2.0	2.5	3.0	3.4	3.9	4.3	4.8	5.3	5.7	6.2	6.7
4.2	1.7	2.1	2.6	3.1	3.6	4.1	4.6	5.0	5.5	6.0	6.5	7.0
4.4	1.7	2.2	2.7	3.3	3.8	4.3	4.8	5.3	5.8	6.3	6.8	7.3
4.6	1.8	2.3	2.9	3.4	3.9	4.5	5.0	5.5	6.1	6.6	7.1	7.7
4.8	1.9	2.4	3.0	3.6	4.1	4.7	5.2	5.8	6.3	6.9	7.4	8.0
5.0	2.0	2.5	3.1	3.7	4.3	4.9	5.4	6.0	6.6	7.2	7.7	8.3
5.2	2.0	2.6	3.2	3.8	4.4	5.0	5.6	6.2	6.8	7.4	8.0	8.6
5.4	2.1	2.8	3.4	4.0	4.6	5.2	5.7	6.5	7.1	7.7	8.4	9.0
5.6	2.2	2.9	3.5	4.1	4.8	5.4	6.1	6.7	7.4	8.0	8.7	9.3
5.8	2.3	3.0	3.6	4.3	5.0	5.6	6.3	7.0	7.6	8.3	9.0	9.6
6.0	2.4	3.1	3.7	4.4	5.1	5.8	6.5	7.2	7.9	8.6	9.3	9.9

Copyright © J Reeve-Fowkes and Thomas Reed Publications. No copying without permission

HW Cherbourg — **HW Time** (to be inserted)

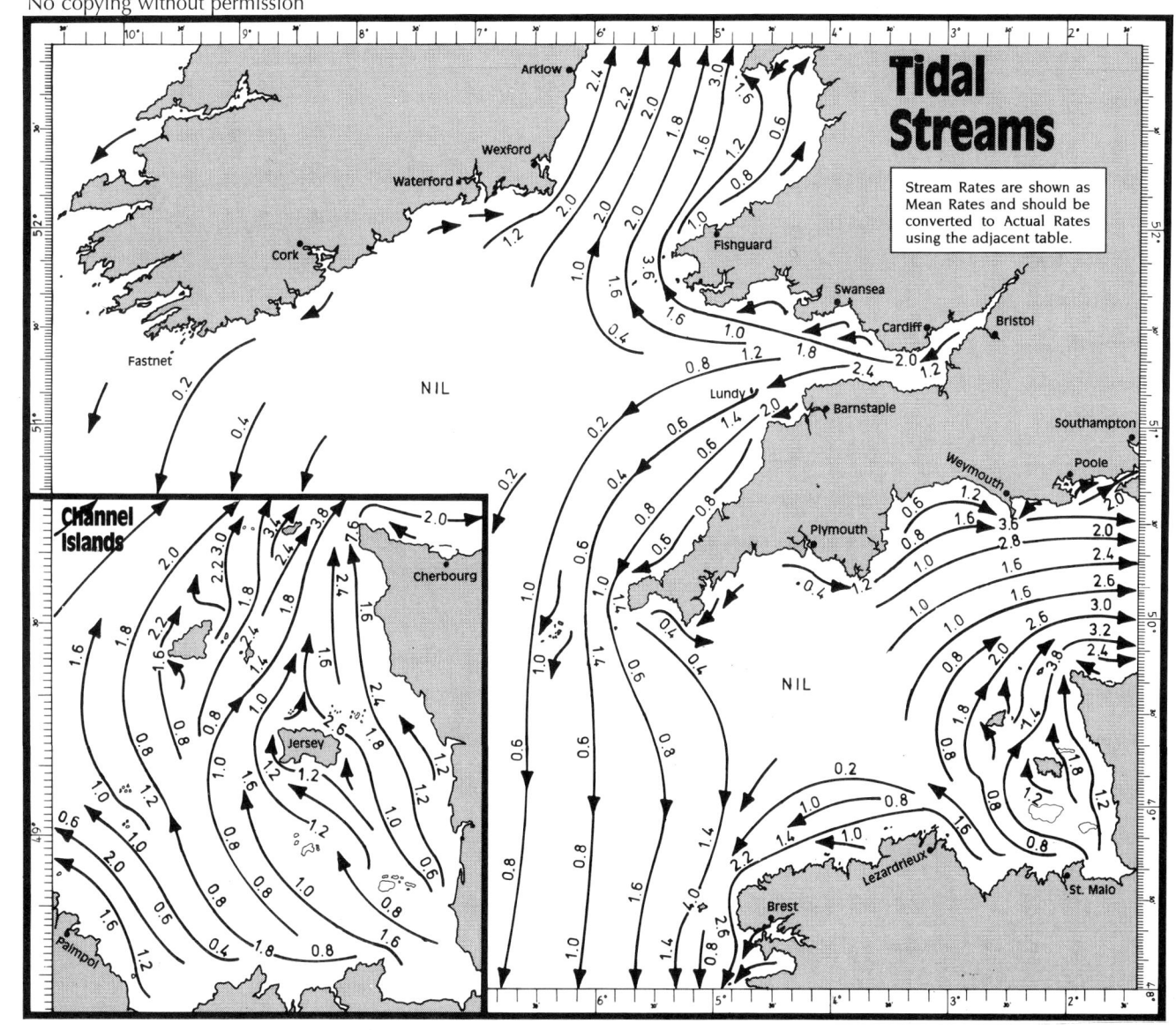

Tidal Streams

Stream Rates are shown as Mean Rates and should be converted to Actual Rates using the adjacent table.

73

+1 — 1 hour after HW Cherbourg

Tidal Heights

Copyright © J Reeve-Fowkes and
Thomas Reed Publications.
No copying without permission

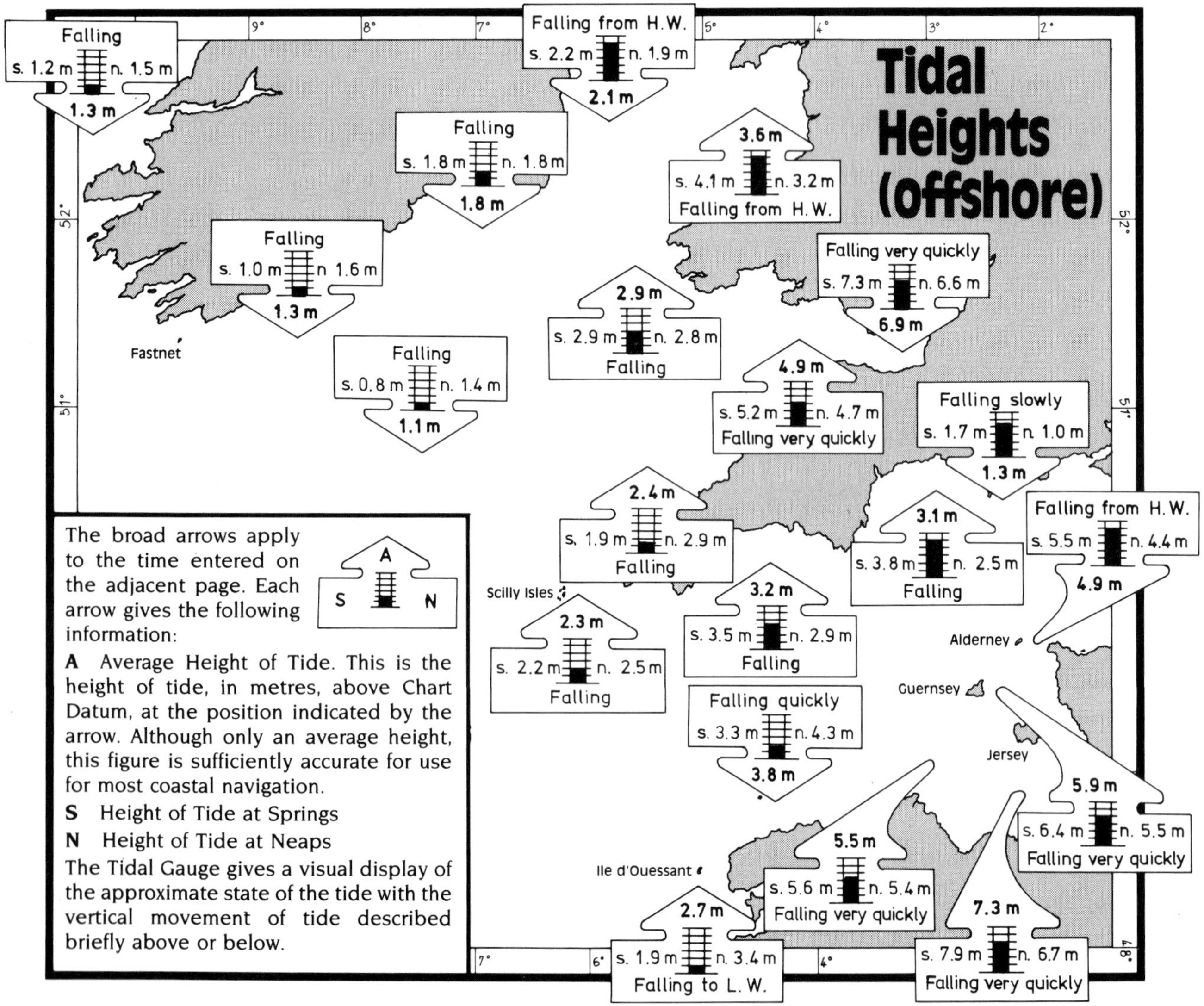

Tidal Heights (offshore)

The broad arrows apply to the time entered on the adjacent page. Each arrow gives the following information:

A Average Height of Tide. This is the height of tide, in metres, above Chart Datum, at the position indicated by the arrow. Although only an average height, this figure is sufficiently accurate for use for most coastal navigation.
S Height of Tide at Springs
N Height of Tide at Neaps
The Tidal Gauge gives a visual display of the approximate state of the tide with the vertical movement of tide described briefly above or below.

Falling — s. 1.2 m n. 1.5 m — 1.3 m
Falling from H.W. — s. 2.2 m n. 1.9 m — 2.1 m
Falling — s. 1.8 m n. 1.8 m — 1.8 m
3.6 m — s. 4.1 m n. 3.2 m — Falling from H.W.
Falling — s. 1.0 m n. 1.6 m — 1.3 m
Falling very quickly — s. 7.3 m n. 6.6 m — 6.9 m
Fastnet
2.9 m — s. 2.9 m n. 2.8 m — Falling
Falling — s. 0.8 m n. 1.4 m — 1.1 m
4.9 m — s. 5.2 m n. 4.7 m — Falling very quickly
Falling slowly — s. 1.7 m n. 1.0 m — 1.3 m
2.4 m — s. 1.9 m n. 2.9 m — Falling
3.1 m — s. 3.8 m n. 2.5 m — Falling
Falling from H.W. — s. 5.5 m n. 4.4 m — 4.9 m
Scilly Isles — 2.3 m — s. 2.2 m n. 2.5 m — Falling
3.2 m — s. 3.5 m n. 2.9 m — Falling
Alderney
Falling quickly — s. 3.3 m n. 4.3 m — 3.8 m
Guernsey
Jersey
5.9 m — s. 6.4 m n. 5.5 m — Falling very quickly
Ile d'Ouessant
5.5 m — s. 5.6 m n. 5.4 m — Falling very quickly
2.7 m — s. 1.9 m n. 3.4 m — Falling to L.W.
7.3 m — s. 7.9 m n. 6.7 m — Falling very quickly

TIDAL HEIGHTS — PORTS & PLACES

Pencil-in height of HW Cherbourg ▶	4.8	5.0	5.2	5.4	5.6	5.8	6.0	6.2	6.4	6.6	6.8
WALES											
Pwllheli, Barmouth.......	3.5	3.6	3.8	3.9	4.1	4.2	4.4	4.5	4.7	4.9	5.0	5.2
Aberystwth	3.3	3.4	3.6	3.7	3.8	4.0	4.1	4.3	4.4	4.5	4.6	4.7
Fishguard, P.Cardigan ..	3.1	3.2	3.4	3.5	3.6	3.7	3.9	4.0	4.1	4.2	4.3	4.4
Milford Haven	3.9	4.0	4.0	4.1	4.1	4.2	4.2	4.3	4.3	4.4	4.4	4.4
Burry Inlet approach	4.9	5.0	5.0	5.1	5.1	5.2	5.2	5.3	5.3	5.3	5.4	5.4
Swansea	5.3	5.4	5.6	5.7	5.8	5.9	6.0	6.1	6.2	6.3	6.3	6.4
P. Talbot, Porthcawl	5.4	5.5	5.5	5.6	5.6	5.7	5.7	5.8	5.8	5.9	5.9	6.0
Barry	6.5	6.6	6.8	6.9	7.1	7.2	7.4	7.5	7.7	7.8	8.0	8.1
Cardiff, Penarth..........	6.9	7.2	7.6	7.9	8.2	8.5	8.8	9.1	9.4	9.7	9.9	10.2
IRELAND											
Arklow	1.0	1.0	1.0	1.0	1.0	1.0	1.1	1.1	1.1	1.1	1.2	1.2
Rosslare	1.2	1.2	1.2	1.2	1.2	1.2	1.3	1.3	1.3	1.3	1.4	1.4
Waterford Hbr. entr.	2.0	2.0	2.0	2.0	2.0	1.9	1.9	1.9	1.9	1.9	1.9	1.9
Cork	2.2	2.3	2.3	2.4	2.4	2.5	2.5	2.6	2.6	2.6	2.6	2.6
Kinsale, Baltimore Bay .	2.1	2.0	2.0	1.9	1.8	1.7	1.7	1.6	1.5	1.5	1.4	1.4
ENGLAND-WEST											
Avonmouth................	7.5	7.9	8.3	8.7	9.1	9.4	9.8	10.2	10.6	10.9	11.1	11.4
Weston-super-Mare	6.5	6.6	6.8	6.9	7.1	7.2	7.4	7.5	7.7	7.9	8.0	8.2
Watchet	6.3	6.4	6.4	6.5	6.5	6.6	6.6	6.7	6.7	6.8	6.8	6.9
Minehead	5.9	5.9	5.9	5.9	5.9	6.0	6.0	6.0	6.0	6.1	6.2	6.3
Porlock Bay	5.8	5.8	5.8	5.8	5.7	5.7	5.7	5.6	5.6	5.7	5.7	5.8
Ilfracombe	4.6	4.6	4.6	4.6	4.6	4.7	4.7	4.7	4.7	4.7	4.8	4.8
Appledore.................	2.8	3.0	3.2	3.4	3.5	3.7	3.9	4.0	4.2	4.3	4.5	4.6
Padstow, Newquay	3.6	3.6	3.6	3.6	3.5	3.5	3.5	3.4	3.4	3.4	3.3	3.3
St. Ives Bay	3.5	3.4	3.2	3.1	3.0	2.8	2.7	2.5	2.4	2.3	2.3	2.2
ISLANDS OFF											
Lundy Island	4.0	4.0	4.0	4.0	4.1	4.1	4.1	4.2	4.2	4.2	4.3	4.3
St. Mary's, Scilly Isles .	2.6	2.6	2.6	2.6	2.5	2.5	2.5	2.4	2.4	2.4	2.4	2.3
ENGLAND-SOUTH											
Falmouth, Helford R.....	2.5	2.6	2.6	2.7	2.8	2.9	2.9	3.0	3.1	3.1	3.1	3.1
Mevagissey, Looe........	2.7	2.8	2.8	2.9	3.0	3.1	3.1	3.2	3.3	3.3	3.3	3.3
Plymouth, Yealm R.	2.8	2.9	3.1	3.2	3.3	3.4	3.5	3.6	3.7	3.7	3.7	3.7
Salcombe	2.6	2.7	2.9	3.0	3.1	3.3	3.4	3.6	3.7	3.7	3.8	3.8
Dartmouth	2.2	2.4	2.6	2.8	2.9	3.1	3.3	3.4	3.6	3.7	3.7	3.8
Brixham, Teignmouth....	2.7	2.8	3.0	3.1	3.3	3.4	3.6	3.7	3.9	4.0	4.2	4.3
Exmouth approach.......	2.3	2.5	2.7	2.9	3.1	3.2	3.4	3.6	3.8	3.9	3.9	4.0
Lyme Regis...............	2.2	2.4	2.6	2.8	3.0	3.1	3.3	3.5	3.7	3.8	3.8	3.9
Portland, Weymouth	0.9	1.0	1.0	1.1	1.2	1.3	1.4	1.5	1.6	1.7	1.8	1.9
Lulworth Cove	1.0	1.1	1.1	1.2	1.3	1.4	1.5	1.6	1.7	1.8	1.9	2.0
Swanage	1.5	1.5	1.5	1.5	1.6	1.6	1.7	1.7	1.8	1.9	1.9	2.0
Poole Town	1.4	1.5	1.5	1.6	1.6	1.7	1.9	2.0	2.2	2.2	2.3	2.3
Christchurch Hbr.	1.1	1.2	1.2	1.3	1.4	1.5	1.6	1.7	1.8	1.8	1.9	1.9
CHANNEL ISLANDS											
Braye Hbr.	3.9	4.0	4.2	4.3	4.4	4.6	4.7	4.9	5.0	5.1	5.3	5.4
St. Peter Port, Sark	5.3	5.4	5.6	5.7	5.8	5.9	6.1	6.2	6.3	6.4	6.4	6.5
St. Helier	6.3	6.5	6.7	6.9	7.1	7.3	7.5	7.7	7.9	8.0	8.1	8.2
Les Minquiers	7.1	7.2	7.4	7.5	7.6	7.7	7.8	7.9	8.0	8.1	8.2	8.3
FRANCE											
Cherbourg	4.6	4.8	5.0	5.2	5.3	5.5	5.7	5.8	6.0	6.2	6.4	6.5
Omonville	4.4	4.6	4.8	5.0	5.1	5.3	5.5	5.6	5.8	6.0	6.2	6.3
Iles Chausey	7.3	7.4	7.6	7.7	7.9	8.0	8.2	8.3	8.5	8.6	8.7	8.8
Carteret	6.6	6.7	6.9	7.0	7.2	7.3	7.5	7.6	7.8	7.9	8.0	8.1
Granville	7.1	7.3	7.5	7.7	7.8	8.0	8.2	8.3	8.5	8.6	8.7	8.8
St Malo	6.5	6.7	6.9	7.1	7.3	7.6	7.8	8.0	8.2	8.3	8.3	8.4
All Hbrs. St Brieuc Bay	6.2	6.3	6.3	6.4	6.4	6.5	6.5	6.6	6.7	6.7	6.7	6.7
Ile de Bréhat	5.5	5.6	5.8	5.9	6.1	6.2	6.4	6.5	6.6	6.7	6.8	6.8
Lezardrieux	5.1	5.2	5.2	5.3	5.4	5.4	5.5	5.5	5.6	5.6	5.6	5.6
Tréguier	5.2	5.1	5.1	5.0	4.9	4.9	4.8	4.8	4.7	4.7	4.6	4.6
Morlaix, Primel Bay.....	4.6	4.5	4.5	4.4	4.3	4.3	4.2	4.2	4.1	3.9	3.8	3.6
Roscoff, Ile de Batz	4.7	4.6	4.6	4.5	4.4	4.3	4.2	4.1	4.0	3.9	3.7	3.6
L'Aberwrach	4.1	3.9	3.7	3.5	3.4	3.2	3.0	2.9	2.7	2.6	2.4	2.3
All Hbrs. Ch. du Four...	3.5	3.3	3.1	2.9	2.7	2.6	2.4	2.3	2.1	1.9	1.7	1.5
Brest......................	3.7	3.5	3.3	3.1	2.9	2.6	2.4	2.2	2.0	1.8	1.7	1.5
Camaret, Douarnenez...	3.4	3.2	3.0	2.8	2.6	2.5	2.3	2.1	1.9	1.7	1.5	1.3

Stream Rate Conversion Table

Mean Rate Figure from Chart ▼	Pencil-in height of HW Cherbourg — Read from column below pencil mark										
	4.8	5.0	5.2	5.4	5.6	5.8	6.0	6.2	6.4	6.6	6.8
0.2	0.1	0.1	0.1	0.1	0.2	0.2	0.2	0.2	0.3	0.3	0.3
0.4	0.2	0.2	0.2	0.3	0.3	0.4	0.4	0.5	0.5	0.6	0.7
0.6	0.2	0.3	0.4	0.4	0.5	0.6	0.7	0.7	0.8	0.9	1.0
0.8	0.4	0.4	0.5	0.6	0.7	0.8	0.9	1.0	1.1	1.1	1.2	1.3
1.0	0.4	0.5	0.6	0.7	0.9	1.0	1.1	1.2	1.3	1.4	1.5	1.7
1.2	0.5	0.6	0.7	0.9	1.0	1.2	1.3	1.4	1.6	1.7	1.9	2.0
1.4	0.6	0.7	0.9	1.0	1.2	1.4	1.5	1.7	1.8	2.0	2.2	2.3
1.6	0.6	0.8	1.0	1.2	1.4	1.6	1.7	1.9	2.1	2.3	2.5	2.7
1.8	0.7	0.9	1.1	1.3	1.5	1.7	2.0	2.2	2.4	2.6	2.8	3.0
2.0	0.8	1.0	1.2	1.5	1.7	1.9	2.2	2.4	2.6	2.9	3.1	3.3
2.2	0.9	1.1	1.4	1.6	1.9	2.1	2.3	2.6	2.9	3.2	3.4	3.7
2.4	0.9	1.2	1.5	1.8	2.1	2.3	2.6	2.9	3.2	3.4	3.7	4.0
2.6	1.0	1.3	1.6	1.9	2.2	2.5	2.8	3.1	3.4	3.7	4.0	4.3
2.8	1.1	1.4	1.7	2.1	2.4	2.7	3.0	3.4	3.7	4.0	4.3	4.7
3.0	1.2	1.5	1.9	2.2	2.6	2.9	3.2	3.6	4.0	4.3	4.6	5.0
3.2	1.3	1.6	2.0	2.4	2.7	3.1	3.4	3.8	4.2	4.6	4.9	5.3
3.4	1.3	1.7	2.1	2.5	2.9	3.3	3.7	4.1	4.5	4.9	5.3	5.7
3.6	1.4	1.8	2.2	2.7	3.1	3.5	3.9	4.3	4.7	5.2	5.6	6.0
3.8	1.5	1.9	2.4	2.8	3.3	3.7	4.1	4.6	5.0	5.4	5.9	6.3
4.0	1.6	2.0	2.5	3.0	3.4	3.9	4.3	4.8	5.3	5.7	6.2	6.7
4.2	1.7	2.1	2.6	3.1	3.6	4.1	4.6	5.0	5.5	6.0	6.5	7.0
4.4	1.7	2.2	2.7	3.3	3.8	4.3	4.8	5.3	5.8	6.3	6.8	7.3
4.6	1.8	2.3	2.9	3.4	3.9	4.5	5.0	5.5	6.1	6.6	7.1	7.7
4.8	1.9	2.4	3.0	3.6	4.1	4.7	5.2	5.8	6.3	6.9	7.4	8.0
5.0	2.0	2.5	3.1	3.7	4.3	4.9	5.4	6.0	6.6	7.2	7.7	8.3
5.2	2.0	2.6	3.2	3.8	4.4	5.0	5.6	6.2	6.8	7.4	8.0	8.6
5.4	2.1	2.8	3.4	4.0	4.6	5.2	5.7	6.5	7.1	7.7	8.4	9.0
5.6	2.2	2.9	3.5	4.1	4.8	5.4	6.1	6.7	7.4	8.0	8.7	9.3
5.8	2.3	3.0	3.6	4.3	5.0	5.6	6.3	7.0	7.6	8.3	9.0	9.6
6.0	2.4	3.1	3.7	4.4	5.1	5.8	6.5	7.2	7.9	8.6	9.3	9.9

Tidal Stream Rates

Copyright © J Reeve-Fowkes and Thomas Reed Publications.
No copying without permission

1 hour after HW Cherbourg **+1**

Time (to be inserted)

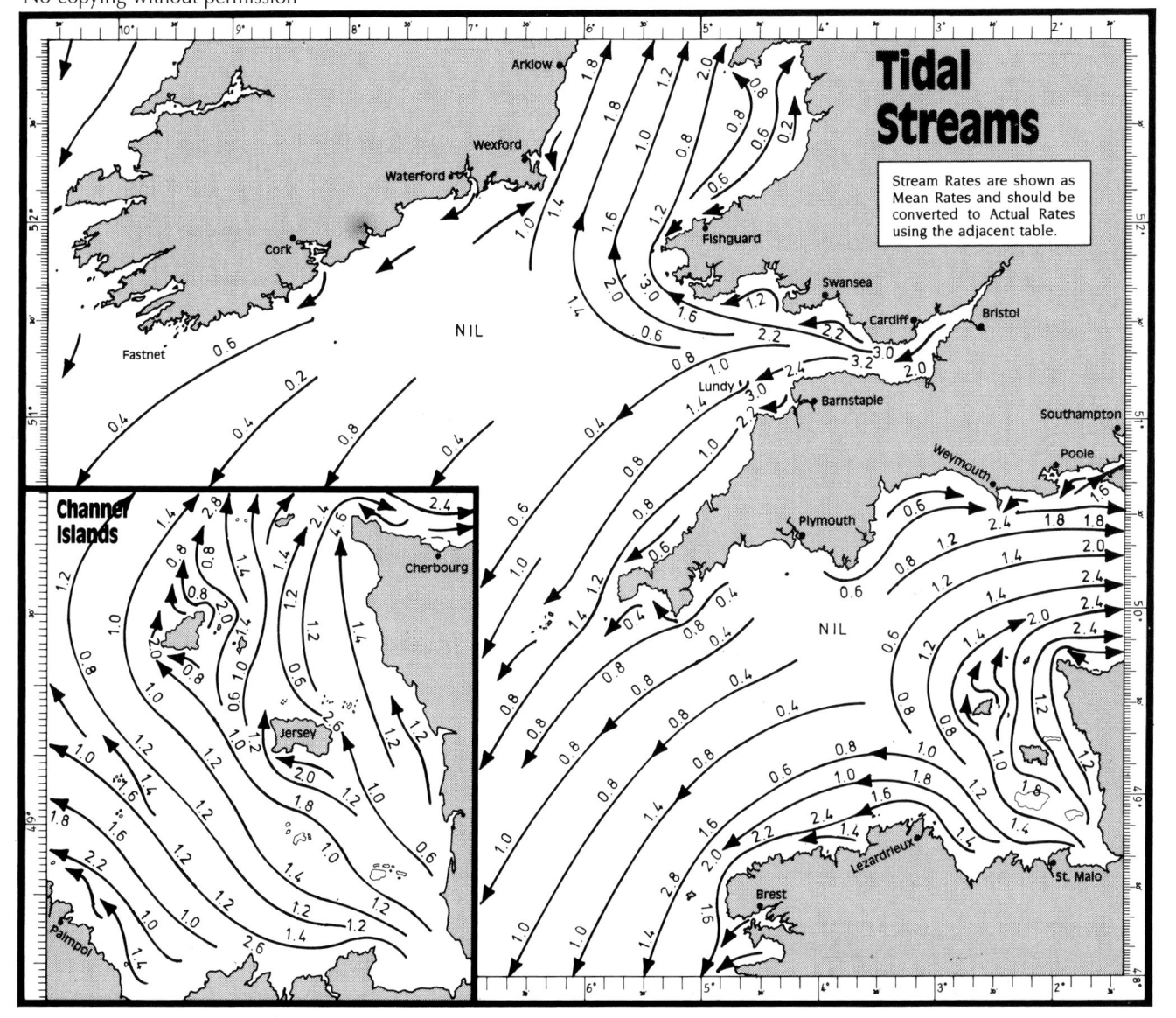

Tidal Streams

Stream Rates are shown as Mean Rates and should be converted to Actual Rates using the adjacent table.

75

+2 — 2 hours after HW Cherbourg

Tidal Heights

Copyright © J Reeve-Fowkes and Thomas Reed Publications.
No copying without permission

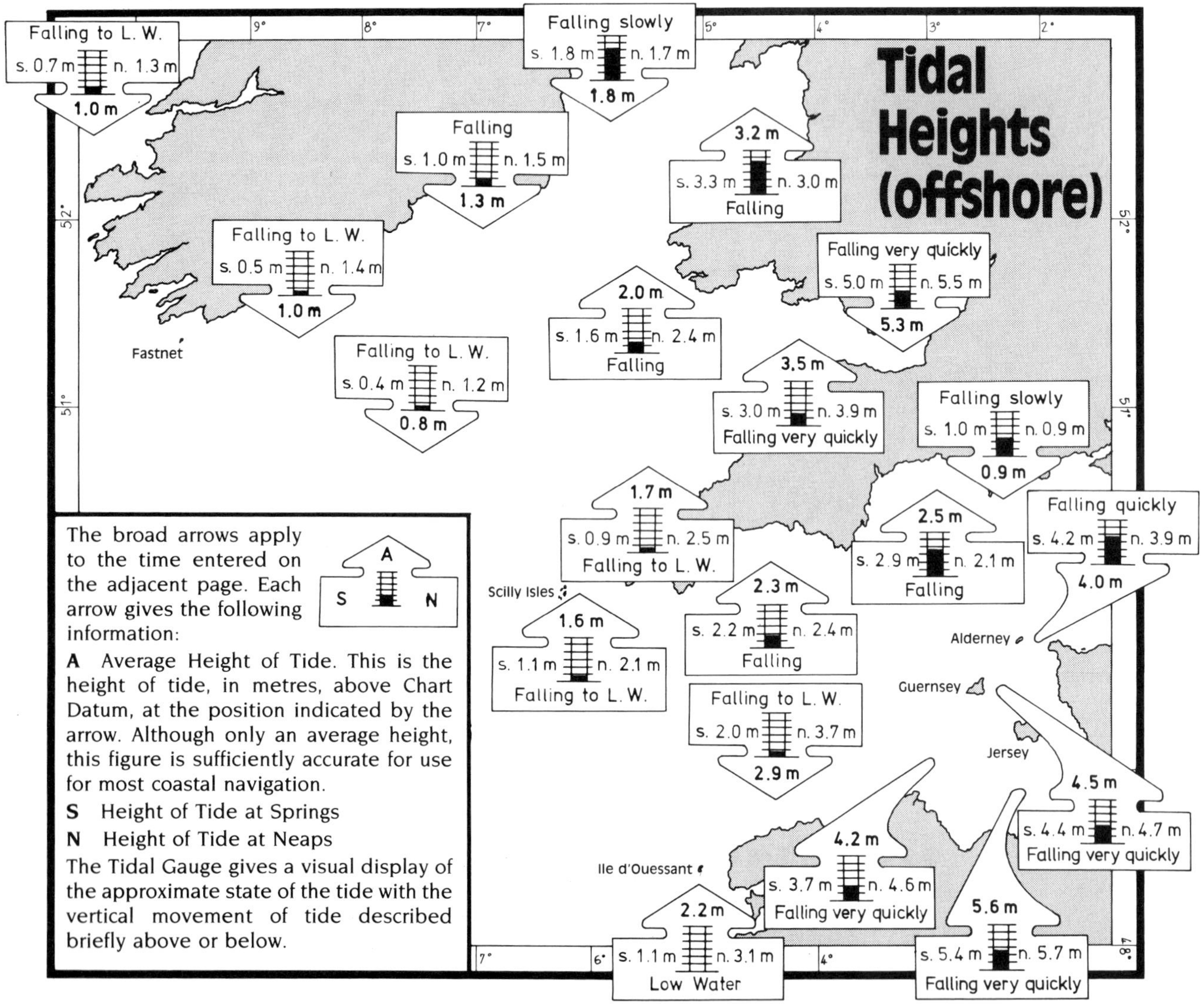

Tidal Heights (offshore)

Falling to L.W. — s. 0.7 m n. 1.3 m — 1.0 m

Falling slowly — s. 1.8 m n. 1.7 m — 1.8 m

Falling — s. 1.0 m n. 1.5 m — 1.3 m

3.2 m — s. 3.3 m n. 3.0 m — Falling

Falling to L.W. — s. 0.5 m n. 1.4 m — 1.0 m

Falling very quickly — s. 5.0 m n. 5.5 m — 5.3 m

Falling to L.W. — s. 0.4 m n. 1.2 m — 0.8 m

2.0 m — s. 1.6 m n. 2.4 m — Falling

3.5 m — s. 3.0 m n. 3.9 m — Falling very quickly

Falling slowly — s. 1.0 m n. 0.9 m — 0.9 m

1.7 m — s. 0.9 m n. 2.5 m — Falling to L.W.

2.5 m — s. 2.9 m n. 2.1 m — Falling

Falling quickly — s. 4.2 m n. 3.9 m — 4.0 m

1.6 m — s. 1.1 m n. 2.1 m — Falling to L.W.

2.3 m — s. 2.2 m n. 2.4 m — Falling

Falling to L.W. — s. 2.0 m n. 3.7 m — 2.9 m

4.5 m — s. 4.4 m n. 4.7 m — Falling very quickly

4.2 m — s. 3.7 m n. 4.6 m — Falling very quickly

2.2 m — s. 1.1 m n. 3.1 m — Low Water

5.6 m — s. 5.4 m n. 5.7 m — Falling very quickly

Fastnet · Scilly Isles · Alderney · Guernsey · Jersey · Ile d'Ouessant

The broad arrows apply to the time entered on the adjacent page. Each arrow gives the following information:

A Average Height of Tide. This is the height of tide, in metres, above Chart Datum, at the position indicated by the arrow. Although only an average height, this figure is sufficiently accurate for use for most coastal navigation.

S Height of Tide at Springs

N Height of Tide at Neaps

The Tidal Gauge gives a visual display of the approximate state of the tide with the vertical movement of tide described briefly above or below.

TIDAL HEIGHTS — PORTS & PLACES

Pencil-in height of HW Cherbourg ▶	4.8	5.0	5.2	5.4	5.6	5.8	6.0	6.2	6.4	6.6	6.8	
WALES												
Pwllheli, Barmouth	3.2	3.3	3.5	3.6	3.7	3.8	3.9	4.0	4.1	4.2	4.3	4.4
Aberystwth	3.1	3.2	3.2	3.3	3.4	3.4	3.5	3.5	3.6	3.7	3.7	3.6
Fishguard, P.Cardigan	3.0	3.0	3.0	3.0	3.1	3.1	3.1	3.2	3.2	3.3	3.3	3.4
Milford Haven	3.5	3.4	3.4	3.3	3.2	3.1	3.0	2.9	2.8	2.8	2.7	2.7
Burry Inlet approach	4.4	4.3	4.1	4.0	3.9	3.8	3.7	3.6	3.5	3.4	3.4	3.3
Swansea	4.2	4.2	4.2	4.2	4.1	4.1	4.1	4.0	4.0	3.9	3.8	3.7
P. Talbot, Porthcawl	4.7	4.6	4.4	4.3	4.2	4.1	4.0	3.9	3.8	3.7	3.6	3.5
Barry	5.6	5.6	5.6	5.6	5.6	5.5	5.5	5.5	5.5	5.5	5.6	5.6
Cardiff, Penarth	5.8	5.9	5.9	6.0	6.1	6.2	6.3	6.4	6.5	6.7	6.9	7.1
IRELAND												
Arklow	0.9	0.9	0.9	0.9	0.9	1.0	1.0	1.0	1.0	1.0	1.0	1.1
Rosslare	0.9	0.9	0.9	0.9	0.9	0.8	0.8	0.8	0.8	0.8	0.8	0.8
Waterford Hbr. entr.	1.7	1.6	1.6	1.5	1.4	1.3	1.3	1.2	1.1	1.1	1.0	1.0
Cork	1.9	1.8	1.8	1.7	1.6	1.6	1.5	1.5	1.4	1.3	1.3	1.2
Kinsale, Baltimore Bay	1.9	1.8	1.6	1.5	1.4	1.3	1.1	1.0	0.9	0.8	0.7	0.6
ENGLAND-WEST												
Avonmouth	6.3	6.6	6.8	7.0	7.3	7.6	7.8	8.1	8.3	8.5	8.7	8.9
Weston-super-Mare	5.3	5.3	5.3	5.3	5.3	5.4	5.4	5.4	5.4	5.5	5.5	5.6
Watchet	5.6	5.5	5.3	5.2	5.1	5.0	4.8	4.7	4.6	4.6	4.6	4.6
Minehead	5.1	5.0	4.8	4.7	4.6	4.4	4.3	4.2	4.1	4.1	4.0	4.0
Porlock Bay	5.1	4.9	4.7	4.5	4.4	4.2	4.0	3.9	3.7	3.7	3.6	3.6
Ilfracombe	3.9	3.8	3.6	3.5	3.3	3.2	3.0	2.9	2.7	2.6	2.4	2.3
Appledore	2.2	2.3	2.3	2.4	2.4	2.5	2.5	2.6	2.7	2.7	2.8	2.8
Padstow, Newquay	3.2	3.1	2.9	2.8	2.6	2.5	2.3	2.2	2.0	1.9	1.7	1.6
St. Ives Bay	3.1	2.9	2.7	2.5	2.2	2.0	1.8	1.5	1.3	1.1	1.0	0.8
ISLANDS OFF												
Lundy Island	3.5	3.4	3.2	3.1	3.0	2.9	2.8	2.7	2.6	2.5	2.5	2.4
St. Mary's, Scilly Isles	2.4	2.3	2.1	2.0	1.9	1.7	1.6	1.4	1.3	1.2	1.1	1.0
ENGLAND-SOUTH												
Falmouth, Helford R.	2.2	2.2	2.2	2.2	2.1	2.1	2.1	2.0	2.0	1.9	1.9	1.8
Mevagissey, Looe	2.4	2.3	2.3	2.2	2.2	2.1	2.1	2.0	2.0	1.9	1.9	1.8
Plymouth, Yealm R.	2.5	2.5	2.5	2.5	2.5	2.4	2.4	2.4	2.4	2.4	2.3	2.3
Salcombe	2.4	2.4	2.4	2.4	2.4	2.4	2.4	2.4	2.4	2.4	2.3	2.3
Dartmouth	2.0	2.1	2.1	2.2	2.2	2.3	2.3	2.4	2.4	2.4	2.3	2.3
Brixham, Teignmouth	2.3	2.4	2.4	2.5	2.6	2.7	2.7	2.8	2.9	3.0	3.0	3.0
Exmouth approach	2.0	2.1	2.3	2.4	2.5	2.6	2.7	2.8	2.9	3.0	3.0	3.0
Lyme Regis	1.9	2.0	2.2	2.3	2.4	2.5	2.6	2.7	2.8	2.8	2.9	2.9
Portland, Weymouth	0.8	0.8	0.8	0.8	0.9	0.9	0.9	1.0	1.0	1.1	1.1	1.2
Lulworth Cove	1.0	1.0	1.0	1.0	1.0	1.1	1.1	1.1	1.1	1.1	1.2	1.2
Swanage	1.5	1.5	1.5	1.5	1.5	1.5	1.5	1.6	1.6	1.6	1.7	1.7
Poole Town	1.6	1.6	1.6	1.6	1.6	1.6	1.7	1.9	2.0	2.0	2.1	2.1
Christchurch Hbr.	1.3	1.3	1.3	1.3	1.4	1.4	1.5	1.5	1.6	1.6	1.7	1.7
CHANNEL ISLANDS												
Braye Hbr.	3.6	3.6	3.6	3.6	3.7	3.7	3.7	3.8	3.8	3.9	3.9	4.0
St. Peter Port, Sark	4.8	4.7	4.7	4.6	4.6	4.5	4.5	4.4	4.4	4.3	4.3	4.2
St. Helier	5.7	5.7	5.7	5.7	5.7	5.6	5.6	5.6	5.6	5.6	5.5	5.5
Les Minquiers	6.1	6.1	6.1	6.1	6.1	6.1	6.0	6.0	6.0	6.0	6.0	6.0
FRANCE												
Cherbourg	4.4	4.5	4.5	4.6	4.7	4.8	4.9	5.0	5.1	5.2	5.3	5.4
Omonville	4.2	4.3	4.3	4.4	4.5	4.6	4.7	4.8	4.9	5.0	5.0	5.1
Iles Chausey	6.3	6.3	6.3	6.3	6.3	6.3	6.3	6.3	6.3	6.2	6.2	6.1
Carteret	5.8	5.8	5.8	5.8	5.7	5.7	5.7	5.6	5.6	5.6	5.5	5.5
Granville	6.3	6.2	6.2	6.1	6.1	6.0	6.0	5.9	5.8	5.7	5.7	5.7
St Malo	5.8	5.8	5.8	5.8	5.8	5.9	5.9	5.9	5.8	5.8	5.7	5.7
All Hbrs. St Brieuc Bay	5.5	5.4	5.2	5.1	5.0	4.9	4.7	4.6	4.5	4.4	4.2	4.1
Ile de Bréhat	4.7	4.7	4.7	4.7	4.7	4.8	4.8	4.8	4.8	4.7	4.7	4.6
Lezardrieux	4.4	4.3	4.1	4.0	3.9	3.8	3.7	3.6	3.5	3.4	3.2	3.1
Tréguier	4.5	4.3	4.1	3.9	3.6	3.4	3.2	2.9	2.7	2.6	2.4	2.3
Morlaix, Primel Bay	4.2	4.0	3.8	3.6	3.4	3.2	3.0	2.8	2.6	2.3	2.1	1.8
Roscoff, Ile de Batz	4.3	4.1	3.9	3.7	3.5	3.2	3.0	2.8	2.6	2.4	2.1	1.9
L'Aberwrach	3.7	3.4	3.2	2.9	2.6	2.4	2.1	1.9	1.6	1.4	1.1	0.9
All Hbrs. Ch. du Four	3.3	3.0	2.8	2.5	2.3	2.0	1.8	1.5	1.3	1.1	0.8	0.6
Brest	3.5	3.2	3.0	2.7	2.4	2.2	1.9	1.7	1.4	1.2	0.9	0.7
Camaret, Douarnenez	3.1	2.9	2.7	2.5	2.2	2.0	1.8	1.5	1.3	1.1	0.8	0.6

Stream Rate Conversion Table

Mean Rate Figure from Chart ▼	\multicolumn{11}{c}{Pencil-in height of HW Cherbourg Read from column below pencil mark}										
	4.8	5.0	5.2	5.4	5.6	5.8	6.0	6.2	6.4	6.6	6.8
0.2	0.1	0.1	0.1	0.1	0.2	0.2	0.2	0.2	0.3	0.3	0.3
0.4	0.2	0.2	0.2	0.3	0.3	0.4	0.4	0.5	0.5	0.6	0.7
0.6	0.2	0.3	0.4	0.4	0.5	0.6	0.7	0.7	0.8	0.9	1.0
0.8	0.4	0.4	0.5	0.6	0.7	0.8	0.9	1.0	1.1	1.2	1.3
1.0	0.4	0.5	0.6	0.7	0.9	1.0	1.1	1.2	1.3	1.4	1.5	1.7
1.2	0.5	0.6	0.7	0.9	1.0	1.2	1.3	1.4	1.6	1.7	1.9	2.0
1.4	0.6	0.7	0.9	1.0	1.2	1.4	1.5	1.7	1.8	2.0	2.2	2.3
1.6	0.6	0.8	1.0	1.2	1.4	1.6	1.7	1.9	2.1	2.3	2.5	2.7
1.8	0.7	0.9	1.1	1.3	1.5	1.7	2.0	2.2	2.4	2.6	2.8	3.0
2.0	0.8	1.0	1.2	1.5	1.7	1.9	2.2	2.4	2.6	2.9	3.1	3.3
2.2	0.9	1.1	1.4	1.6	1.9	2.1	2.3	2.6	2.9	3.2	3.4	3.7
2.4	0.9	1.2	1.5	1.8	2.1	2.3	2.6	2.9	3.2	3.4	3.7	4.0
2.6	1.0	1.3	1.6	1.9	2.2	2.5	2.8	3.1	3.4	3.7	4.0	4.3
2.8	1.1	1.4	1.7	2.1	2.4	2.7	3.0	3.4	3.7	4.0	4.3	4.7
3.0	1.2	1.5	1.9	2.2	2.6	2.9	3.2	3.6	4.0	4.3	4.6	5.0
3.2	1.3	1.6	2.0	2.4	2.7	3.1	3.4	3.8	4.2	4.6	4.9	5.3
3.4	1.3	1.7	2.1	2.5	2.9	3.3	3.7	4.1	4.5	4.9	5.3	5.7
3.6	1.4	1.8	2.2	2.7	3.1	3.5	3.9	4.3	4.7	5.2	5.6	6.0
3.8	1.5	1.9	2.4	2.8	3.3	3.7	4.1	4.6	5.0	5.4	5.9	6.3
4.0	1.6	2.0	2.5	3.0	3.4	3.9	4.3	4.8	5.3	5.7	6.2	6.7
4.2	1.7	2.1	2.6	3.1	3.6	4.1	4.6	5.0	5.5	6.0	6.5	7.0
4.4	1.7	2.2	2.7	3.3	3.8	4.3	4.8	5.3	5.8	6.3	6.8	7.3
4.6	1.8	2.3	2.9	3.4	3.9	4.5	5.0	5.5	6.1	6.6	7.1	7.7
4.8	1.9	2.4	3.0	3.6	4.1	4.7	5.2	5.8	6.3	6.9	7.4	8.0
5.0	2.0	2.5	3.1	3.7	4.3	4.9	5.4	6.0	6.6	7.2	7.7	8.3
5.2	2.0	2.6	3.2	3.8	4.4	5.0	5.6	6.2	6.8	7.4	8.0	8.6
5.4	2.1	2.8	3.4	4.0	4.6	5.2	5.8	6.5	7.1	7.7	8.4	9.0
5.6	2.2	2.9	3.5	4.1	4.8	5.4	6.1	6.7	7.4	8.0	8.7	9.3
5.8	2.3	3.0	3.6	4.3	5.0	5.6	6.3	7.0	7.6	8.3	9.0	9.6
6.0	2.4	3.1	3.7	4.4	5.1	5.8	6.5	7.2	7.9	8.6	9.3	9.9

Tidal Stream Rates

Copyright © J Reeve-Fowkes and Thomas Reed Publications.
No copying without permission

2 hours after HW Cherbourg **+2**

Time (to be inserted)

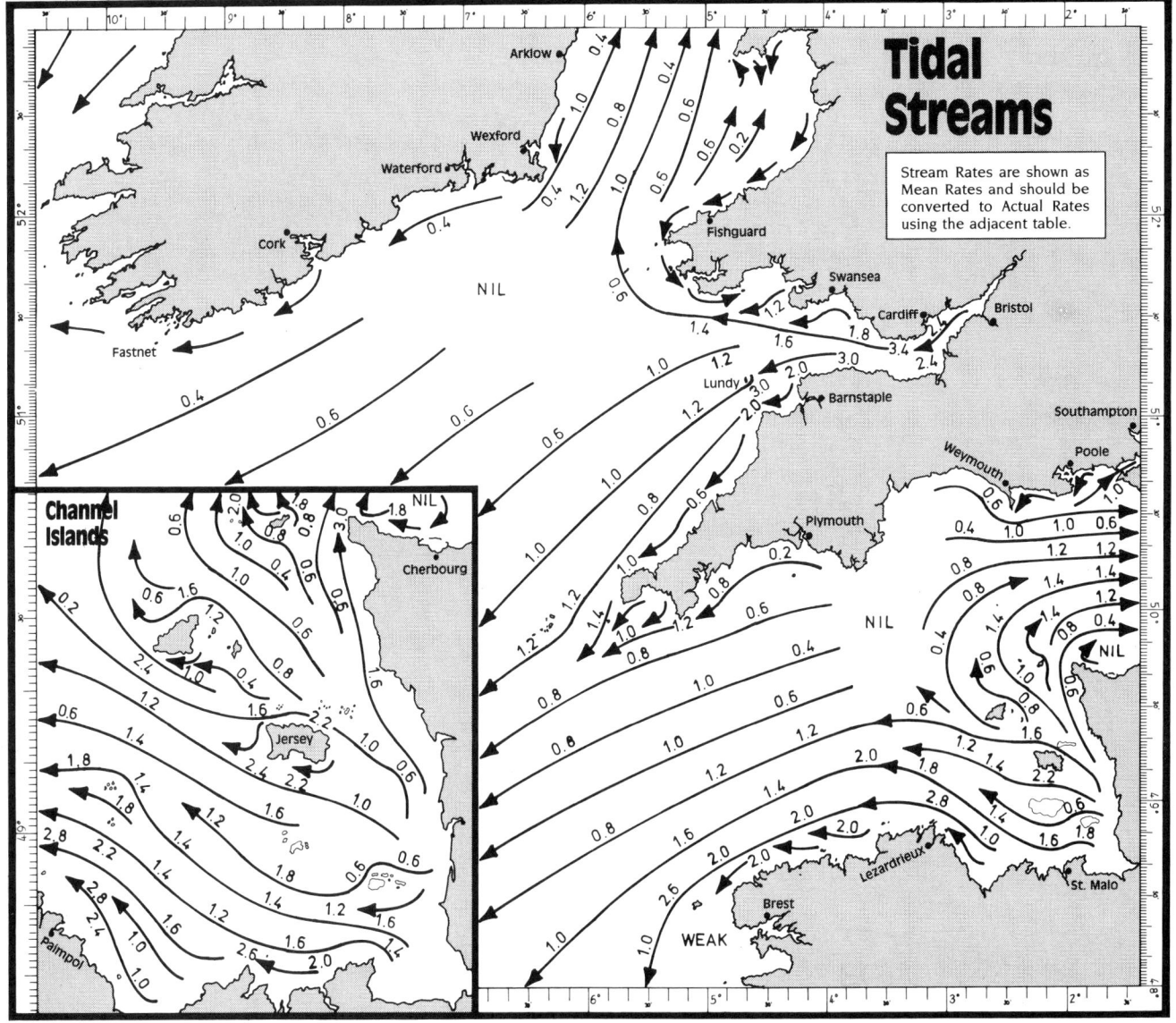

Tidal Streams

Stream Rates are shown as Mean Rates and should be converted to Actual Rates using the adjacent table.

77

+3
3 hours after HW Cherbourg

Tidal Heights

Copyright © J Reeve-Fowkes and
Thomas Reed Publications.
No copying without permission

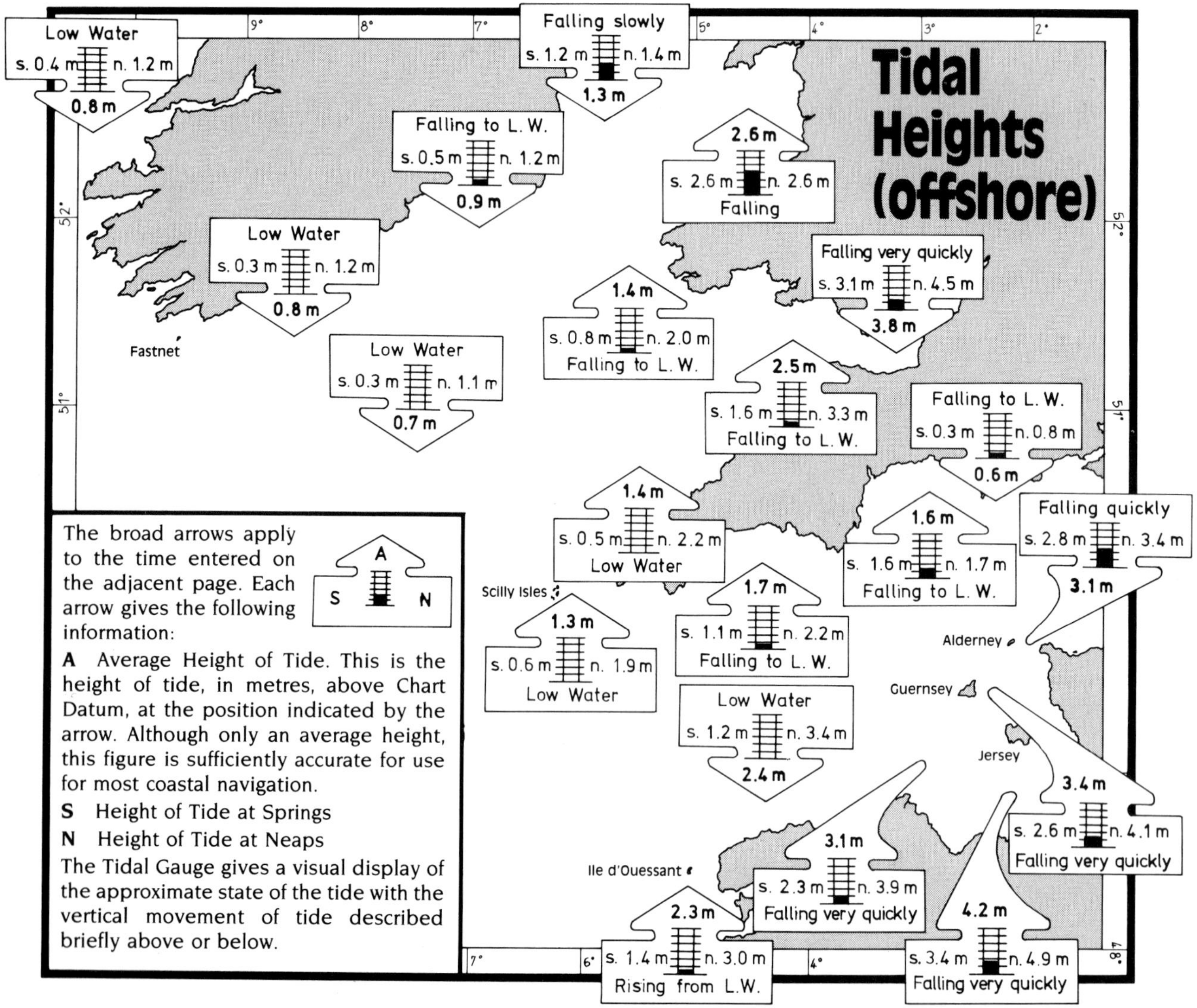

Tidal Heights (offshore)

Low Water
s. 0.4 m   n. 1.2 m
0.8 m

Falling slowly
s. 1.2 m   n. 1.4 m
1.3 m

Falling to L.W.
s. 0.5 m   n. 1.2 m
0.9 m

2.6 m
s. 2.6 m   n. 2.6 m
Falling

Low Water
s. 0.3 m   n. 1.2 m
0.8 m

Fastnet

Falling very quickly
s. 3.1 m   n. 4.5 m
3.8 m

1.4 m
s. 0.8 m   n. 2.0 m
Falling to L.W.

Low Water
s. 0.3 m   n. 1.1 m
0.7 m

2.5 m
s. 1.6 m   n. 3.3 m
Falling to L.W.

Falling to L.W.
s. 0.3 m   n. 0.8 m
0.6 m

1.4 m
s. 0.5 m   n. 2.2 m
Low Water

1.6 m
s. 1.6 m   n. 1.7 m
Falling to L.W.

Falling quickly
s. 2.8 m   n. 3.4 m
3.1 m

Scilly Isles

1.3 m
s. 0.6 m   n. 1.9 m
Low Water

1.7 m
s. 1.1 m   n. 2.2 m
Falling to L.W.

Alderney

Guernsey

Low Water
s. 1.2 m   n. 3.4 m
2.4 m

Jersey

3.4 m
s. 2.6 m   n. 4.1 m
Falling very quickly

Ile d'Ouessant

3.1 m
s. 2.3 m   n. 3.9 m
Falling very quickly

2.3 m
s. 1.4 m   n. 3.0 m
Rising from L.W.

4.2 m
s. 3.4 m   n. 4.9 m
Falling very quickly

The broad arrows apply to the time entered on the adjacent page. Each arrow gives the following information:

A Average Height of Tide. This is the height of tide, in metres, above Chart Datum, at the position indicated by the arrow. Although only an average height, this figure is sufficiently accurate for use for most coastal navigation.
S Height of Tide at Springs
N Height of Tide at Neaps
The Tidal Gauge gives a visual display of the approximate state of the tide with the vertical movement of tide described briefly above or below.

TIDAL HEIGHTS — PORTS & PLACES

Pencil-in height of ▶ HW Cherbourg	4.8	5.0	5.2	5.4	5.6	5.8	6.0	6.2	6.4	6.6	6.8
WALES											
Pwllheli, Barmouth.......	2.9	3.0	3.0	3.1	3.1	3.2	3.2	3.3	3.3	3.3	3.4	3.4
Aberystwth	2.9	2.9	2.9	2.9	2.8	2.8	2.8	2.7	2.7	2.7	2.7	2.7
Fishguard, P.Cardigan ..	2.8	2.7	2.7	2.6	2.6	2.5	2.5	2.4	2.4	2.3	2.3	2.3
Milford Haven	3.2	3.0	2.8	2.6	2.4	2.2	2.0	1.8	1.6	1.5	1.3	1.2
Burry Inlet approach	3.7	3.5	3.3	3.1	2.9	2.6	2.4	2.2	2.0	1.8	1.7	1.5
Swansea	3.8	3.6	3.4	3.2	3.0	2.7	2.5	2.3	2.1	1.9	1.7	1.5
P. Talbot, Porthcawl	4.1	3.8	3.6	3.5	3.1	2.8	2.6	2.3	2.1	1.9	1.6	1.4
Barry.....................	5.0	4.8	4.6	4.4	4.2	4.1	3.9	3.7	3.5	3.4	3.3	3.2
Cardiff, Penarth..........	4.7	4.6	4.6	4.5	4.5	4.4	4.4	4.3	4.3	4.3	4.4	4.4
IRELAND											
Arklow	0.8	0.8	0.8	0.8	0.8	0.9	0.9	0.9	0.9	0.9	0.9	0.9
Rosslare	1.0	0.9	0.9	0.8	0.7	0.7	0.6	0.6	0.5	0.4	0.4	0.3
Waterford Hbr. entr.	1.4	1.3	1.3	1.2	1.1	1.0	0.9	0.8	0.7	0.6	0.5	0.3
Cork	1.7	1.6	1.4	1.3	1.2	1.1	1.0	0.9	0.8	0.7	0.6	0.5
Kinsale, Baltimore Bay .	1.7	1.6	1.4	1.3	1.2	1.0	0.9	0.7	0.6	0.5	0.3	0.2
ENGLAND-WEST											
Avonmouth...............	5.1	5.2	5.4	5.5	5.6	5.7	5.9	6.0	6.1	6.2	6.4	6.5
Weston-super-Mare	4.1	4.0	4.0	3.9	3.8	3.7	3.6	3.5	3.4	3.4	3.4	3.4
Watchet	4.7	4.5	4.3	4.1	3.9	3.6	3.4	3.2	3.0	2.9	2.8	2.7
Minehead	4.5	4.2	4.0	3.7	3.5	3.2	3.0	2.7	2.5	2.4	2.3	2.2
Porlock Bay	4.3	4.1	3.9	3.6	3.3	3.0	2.8	2.5	2.2	2.1	2.0	1.9
Ilfracombe	3.5	3.2	3.0	2.7	2.4	2.1	1.9	1.6	1.3	1.1	0.8	0.6
Appledore...............	1.8	1.7	1.7	1.6	1.6	1.5	1.5	1.4	1.4	1.3	1.3	1.2
Padstow, Newquay	3.1	2.8	2.6	2.3	2.1	1.8	1.6	1.3	1.1	0.9	0.8	0.6
St. Ives Bay	2.9	2.6	2.4	2.1	1.8	1.5	1.2	0.9	0.6	0.4	0.3	0.1
ISLANDS OFF											
Lundy Island	3.1	2.9	2.7	2.5	2.3	2.0	1.8	1.6	1.4	1.2	1.1	0.9
St. Mary's, Scilly Isles .	2.3	2.1	1.9	1.7	1.5	1.3	1.1	0.9	0.7	0.6	0.4	0.3
ENGLAND-SOUTH											
Falmouth, Helford R.....	2.1	2.0	1.8	1.7	1.6	1.4	1.3	1.1	1.0	0.9	0.8	0.7
Mevagissey, Looe......	2.2	2.1	1.9	1.8	1.7	1.5	1.4	1.2	1.1	0.9	0.8	0.6
Plymouth, Yealm R......	2.4	2.3	2.1	2.0	1.9	1.7	1.6	1.4	1.3	1.2	1.0	0.9
Salcombe	2.3	2.2	2.0	1.9	1.8	1.7	1.5	1.4	1.3	1.2	1.1	1.0
Dartmouth	2.0	1.9	1.7	1.6	1.5	1.4	1.3	1.2	1.1	1.1	0.9	0.8
Brixham, Teignmouth ...	2.1	2.0	2.0	1.9	1.9	1.8	1.8	1.7	1.7	1.6	1.5	1.4
Exmouth approach.......	1.8	1.8	1.8	1.8	1.8	1.8	1.8	1.8	1.8	1.8	1.7	1.7
Lyme Regis	1.7	1.7	1.7	1.7	1.6	1.6	1.6	1.6	1.6	1.6	1.5	1.5
Portland, Weymouth	0.8	0.7	0.7	0.6	0.6	0.5	0.5	0.4	0.4	0.4	0.4	0.4
Lulworth Cove	1.0	0.9	0.9	0.8	0.7	0.6	0.6	0.5	0.4	0.4	0.4	0.4
Swanage	1.5	1.5	1.5	1.5	1.5	1.5	1.5	1.4	1.4	1.4	1.5	1.5
Poole Town	1.7	1.7	1.7	1.7	1.7	1.7	1.7	1.7	1.7	1.7	1.7	1.7
Christchurch Hbr.	1.4	1.4	1.4	1.4	1.4	1.4	1.4	1.4	1.4	1.4	1.5	1.5
CHANNEL ISLANDS											
Braye Hbr.	3.2	3.1	3.1	3.0	2.9	2.8	2.8	2.7	2.6	2.5	2.5	2.4
St. Peter Port, Sark	4.4	4.2	4.0	3.8	3.6	3.3	3.1	2.9	2.7	2.5	2.3	2.1
St. Helier.................	5.2	5.0	4.8	4.6	4.4	4.3	4.1	3.9	3.7	3.5	3.4	3.2
Les Minquiers	5.5	5.2	5.0	4.7	4.5	4.2	4.0	3.8	3.5	3.3	3.2	3.0
FRANCE											
Cherbourg	3.9	3.9	3.9	3.9	4.0	4.0	4.0	4.1	4.1	4.1	4.1	4.1
Omonville	3.8	3.8	3.8	3.8	3.8	3.7	3.7	3.7	3.7	3.7	3.7	3.7
Iles Chausey	5.6	5.4	5.2	5.0	4.8	4.6	4.4	4.2	4.0	3.8	3.6	3.4
Carteret	5.1	4.9	4.7	4.5	4.4	4.2	4.0	3.9	3.7	3.5	3.4	3.2
Granville.................	5.7	5.4	5.2	4.9	4.7	4.4	4.2	3.9	3.7	3.5	3.3	3.1
St Malo	5.3	5.1	4.9	4.7	4.5	4.4	4.2	4.0	3.8	3.6	3.4	3.2
All Hbrs. St Brieuc Bay	5.0	4.7	4.5	4.2	3.9	3.6	3.2	3.0	2.7	2.4	2.2	1.9
Ile de Bréhat	4.2	4.1	3.9	3.8	3.6	3.5	3.3	3.2	3.0	2.8	2.7	2.5
Lezardrieux	3.9	3.6	3.4	3.1	2.8	2.6	2.3	2.1	1.8	1.5	1.3	1.0
Tréguier	4.1	3.8	3.4	3.1	2.7	2.4	2.0	1.7	1.3	1.1	0.9	0.7
Morlaix, Primel Bay	3.9	3.6	3.4	3.1	2.8	2.5	2.2	1.9	1.6	1.2	0.9	0.5
Roscoff, Ile de Batz	4.1	3.8	3.4	3.1	2.8	2.5	2.2	1.9	1.6	1.3	1.0	0.7
L'Aberwrach	3.6	3.3	2.9	2.6	2.3	2.0	1.7	1.4	1.1	0.8	0.6	0.3
All Hbrs. Ch. du Four....	3.1	2.9	2.7	2.5	2.3	2.0	1.8	1.6	1.4	1.2	0.9	0.7
Brest	3.3	3.1	2.9	2.7	2.4	2.2	2.0	1.7	1.5	1.3	1.1	0.9
Camaret, Douarnenez...	3.1	2.9	2.7	2.5	2.3	2.2	2.0	1.8	1.6	1.4	1.3	1.1

Tidal Stream Rates

Copyright © J Reeve-Fowkes and Thomas Reed Publications.
No copying without permission

3 hours after HW Cherbourg **+3**

Time (to be inserted)

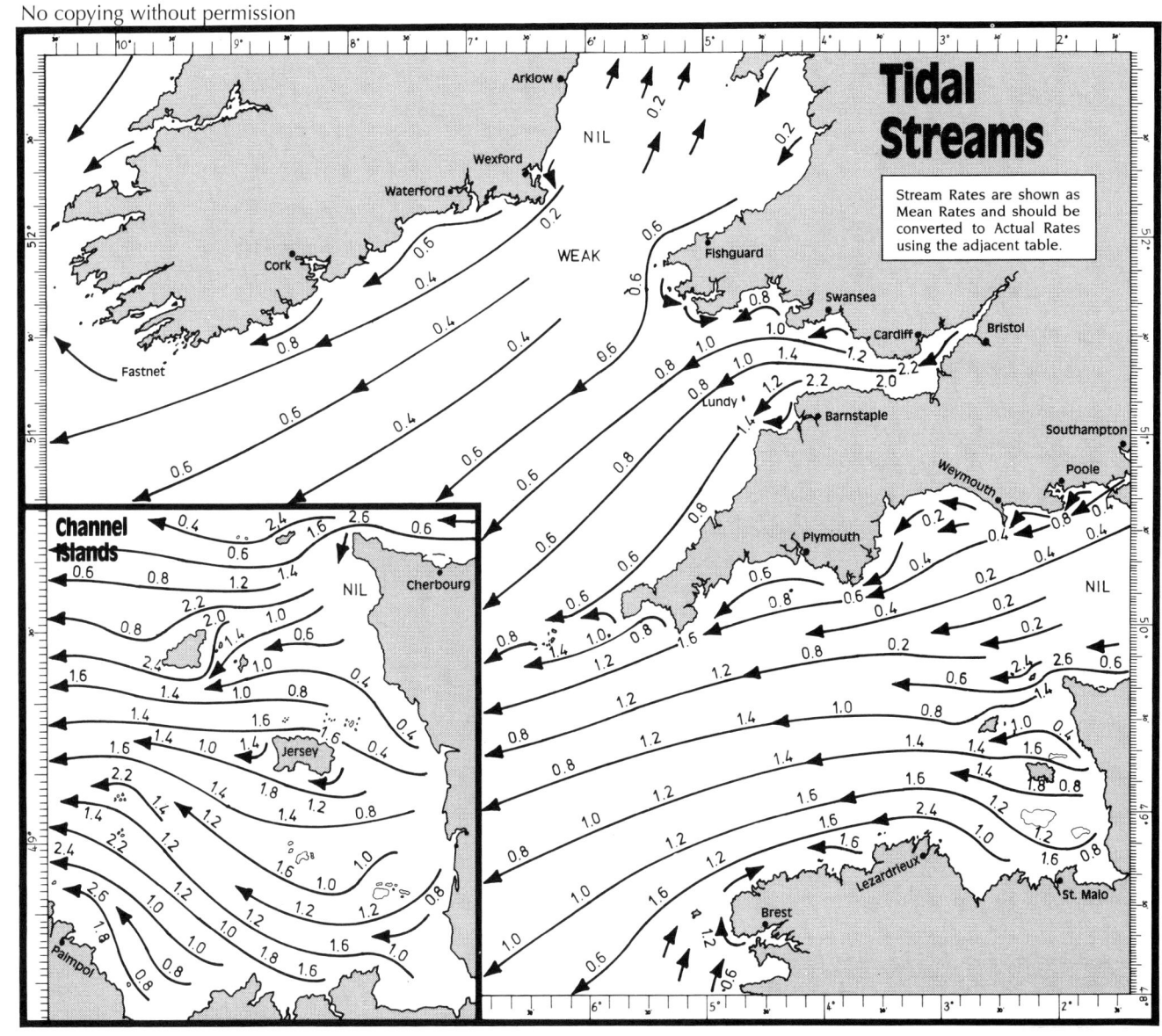

Stream Rate Conversion Table

Mean Rate Figure from Chart ▼	Pencil-in height of HW Cherbourg — Read from column below pencil mark										
	4.8	5.0	5.2	5.4	5.6	5.8	6.0	6.2	6.4	6.6	6.8
0.2	0.1	0.1	0.1	0.1	0.2	0.2	0.2	0.2	0.3	0.3	0.3
0.4	0.2	0.2	0.2	0.3	0.3	0.4	0.4	0.5	0.5	0.6	0.7
0.6	0.2	0.3	0.4	0.4	0.5	0.6	0.7	0.7	0.8	0.9	1.0
0.8	0.4	0.4	0.5	0.6	0.7	0.8	0.9	1.0	1.1	1.2	1.3
1.0	0.4	0.5	0.6	0.7	0.9	1.0	1.1	1.2	1.3	1.4	1.5	1.7
1.2	0.5	0.6	0.7	0.9	1.0	1.2	1.3	1.4	1.6	1.7	1.9	2.0
1.4	0.6	0.7	0.9	1.0	1.2	1.4	1.5	1.7	1.8	2.0	2.2	2.3
1.6	0.6	0.8	1.0	1.2	1.4	1.6	1.7	1.9	2.1	2.3	2.5	2.7
1.8	0.7	0.9	1.1	1.3	1.5	1.7	2.0	2.2	2.4	2.6	2.8	3.0
2.0	0.8	1.0	1.2	1.5	1.7	1.9	2.2	2.4	2.6	2.9	3.1	3.3
2.2	0.9	1.1	1.4	1.6	1.9	2.1	2.3	2.6	2.9	3.2	3.4	3.7
2.4	0.9	1.2	1.5	1.8	2.1	2.3	2.6	2.9	3.2	3.4	3.7	4.0
2.6	1.0	1.3	1.6	1.9	2.2	2.5	2.8	3.1	3.4	3.7	4.0	4.3
2.8	1.1	1.4	1.7	2.1	2.4	2.7	3.0	3.4	3.7	4.0	4.3	4.7
3.0	1.2	1.5	1.9	2.2	2.6	2.9	3.2	3.6	4.0	4.3	4.6	5.0
3.2	1.3	1.6	2.0	2.4	2.7	3.1	3.4	3.8	4.2	4.6	4.9	5.3
3.4	1.3	1.7	2.1	2.5	2.9	3.3	3.7	4.1	4.5	4.9	5.3	5.7
3.6	1.4	1.8	2.2	2.7	3.1	3.5	3.9	4.3	4.7	5.2	5.6	6.0
3.8	1.5	1.9	2.4	2.8	3.3	3.7	4.1	4.6	5.0	5.4	5.9	6.3
4.0	1.6	2.0	2.5	3.0	3.4	3.9	4.3	4.8	5.3	5.7	6.2	6.7
4.2	1.7	2.1	2.6	3.1	3.6	4.1	4.6	5.0	5.5	6.0	6.5	7.0
4.4	1.7	2.2	2.7	3.3	3.8	4.3	4.8	5.3	5.8	6.3	6.8	7.3
4.6	1.8	2.3	2.9	3.4	3.9	4.5	5.0	5.5	6.1	6.6	7.1	7.7
4.8	1.9	2.4	3.0	3.6	4.1	4.7	5.2	5.8	6.3	6.9	7.4	8.0
5.0	2.0	2.5	3.1	3.7	4.3	4.9	5.4	6.0	6.6	7.2	7.7	8.3
5.2	2.0	2.6	3.2	3.8	4.4	5.0	5.6	6.2	6.8	7.4	8.0	8.6
5.4	2.1	2.7	3.3	4.0	4.6	5.2	5.8	6.5	7.1	7.7	8.4	9.0
5.6	2.2	2.8	3.5	4.1	4.8	5.4	6.0	6.7	7.4	8.0	8.7	9.3
5.8	2.3	3.0	3.6	4.3	5.0	5.6	6.3	7.0	7.6	8.3	9.0	9.6
6.0	2.4	3.1	3.7	4.4	5.1	5.8	6.5	7.2	7.9	8.6	9.3	9.9

Tidal Streams

Stream Rates are shown as Mean Rates and should be converted to Actual Rates using the adjacent table.

79

+4
4 hours after HW Cherbourg

Tidal Heights

Copyright © J Reeve-Fowkes and Thomas Reed Publications.
No copying without permission

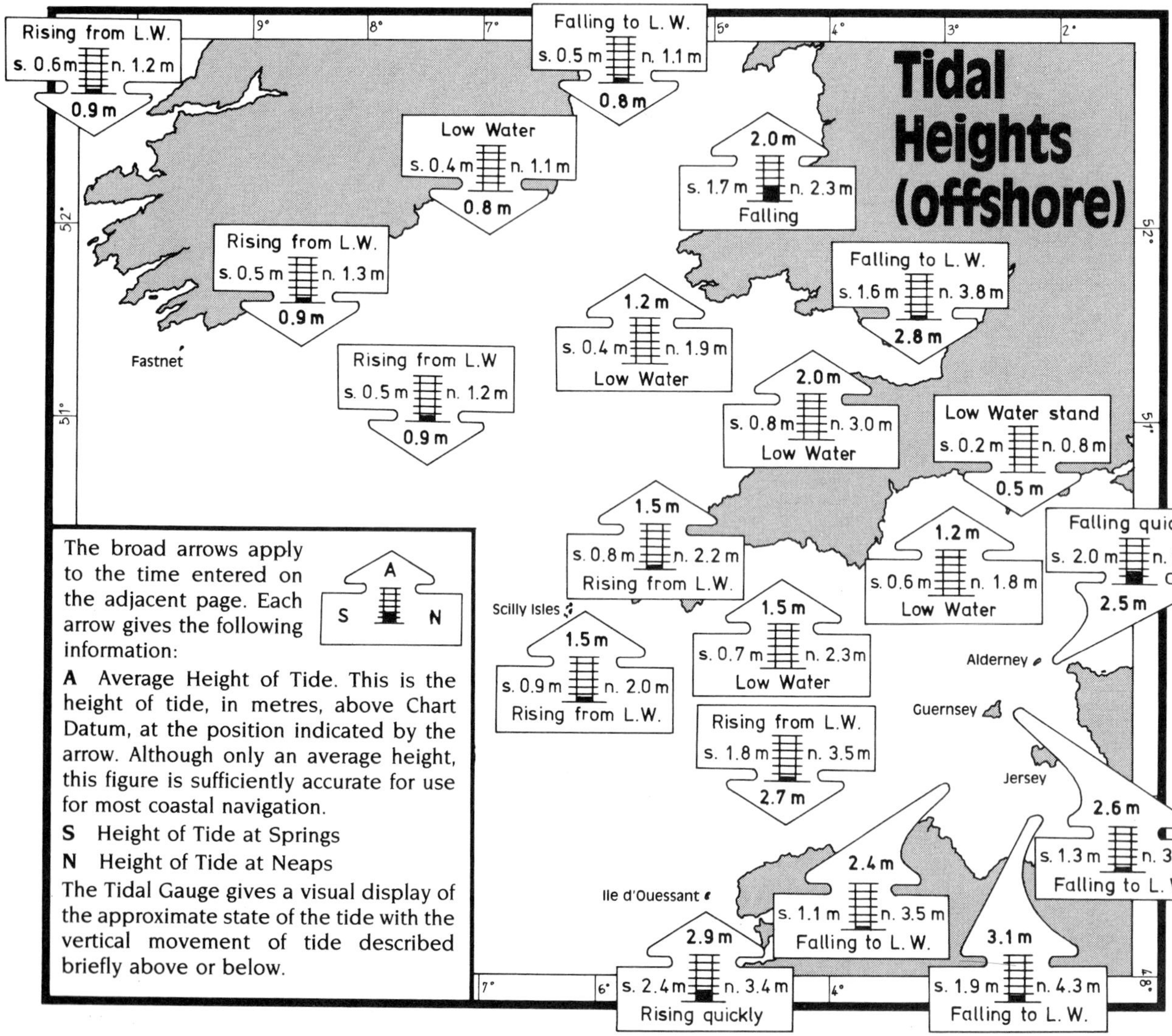

Tidal Heights (offshore)

Rising from L.W.
s. 0.6 m — n. 1.2 m
0.9 m

Falling to L.W.
s. 0.5 m — n. 1.1 m
0.8 m

Low Water
s. 0.4 m — n. 1.1 m
0.8 m

2.0 m
s. 1.7 m — n. 2.3 m
Falling

Rising from L.W.
s. 0.5 m — n. 1.3 m
0.9 m

Falling to L.W.
s. 1.6 m — n. 3.8 m
2.8 m

Rising from L.W.
s. 0.5 m — n. 1.2 m
0.9 m

1.2 m
s. 0.4 m — n. 1.9 m
Low Water

2.0 m
s. 0.8 m — n. 3.0 m
Low Water

Low Water stand
s. 0.2 m — n. 0.8 m
0.5 m

Fastnet

1.5 m
s. 0.8 m — n. 2.2 m
Rising from L.W.

1.2 m
s. 0.6 m — n. 1.8 m
Low Water

Falling quickly
s. 2.0 m — n. 3.0 m
2.5 m

Scilly Isles

1.5 m
s. 0.7 m — n. 2.3 m
Low Water

1.5 m
s. 0.9 m — n. 2.0 m
Rising from L.W.

Alderney

Guernsey

Rising from L.W.
s. 1.8 m — n. 3.5 m
2.7 m

Jersey

2.6 m
s. 1.3 m — n. 3.7 m
Falling to L.W.

Ile d'Ouessant

2.4 m
s. 1.1 m — n. 3.5 m
Falling to L.W.

3.1 m
s. 1.9 m — n. 4.3 m
Falling to L.W.

2.9 m
s. 2.4 m — n. 3.4 m
Rising quickly

The broad arrows apply to the time entered on the adjacent page. Each arrow gives the following information:

A Average Height of Tide. This is the height of tide, in metres, above Chart Datum, at the position indicated by the arrow. Although only an average height, this figure is sufficiently accurate for use for most coastal navigation.
S Height of Tide at Springs
N Height of Tide at Neaps
The Tidal Gauge gives a visual display of the approximate state of the tide with the vertical movement of tide described briefly above or below.

A / S / N

TIDAL HEIGHTS — PORTS & PLACES

Pencil-in height of HW Cherbourg ▶	4.8	5.0	5.2	5.4	5.6	5.8	6.0	6.2	6.4	6.6	6.8
WALES											
Pwllheli, Barmouth......	2.8	2.7	2.7	2.6	2.6	2.5	2.5	2.4	2.4	2.4	2.4	2.4
Aberystwth	2.7	2.6	2.4	2.3	2.2	2.1	2.0	1.9	1.8	1.7	1.7	1.6
Fishguard, P.Cardigan ..	2.6	2.5	2.3	2.2	2.1	1.9	1.8	1.6	1.5	1.4	1.3	1.2
Milford Haven	2.9	2.6	2.4	2.1	1.8	1.6	1.3	1.1	0.8	0.6	0.4	0.2
Burry Inlet approach	3.4	3.1	2.9	2.6	2.3	2.0	1.7	1.4	1.1	0.9	0.6	0.4
Swansea...................	3.7	3.4	3.0	2.7	2.4	2.1	1.7	1.4	1.1	0.8	0.6	0.3
P. Talbot, Porthcawl	3.8	3.5	3.1	2.8	2.5	2.1	1.8	1.4	1.1	0.8	0.6	0.3
Barry.......................	4.4	4.1	3.7	3.4	3.1	2.8	2.5	2.2	1.9	1.8	1.6	1.5
Cardiff, Penarth..........	4.2	4.0	3.8	3.6	3.4	3.1	2.9	2.7	2.5	2.4	2.3	2.2
IRELAND											
Arklow	0.9	0.9	0.9	0.9	0.9	1.0	1.0	1.0	1.0	1.0	1.0	1.0
Rosslare	1.0	0.9	0.9	0.8	0.7	0.6	0.6	0.5	0.4	0.3	0.2	0.2
Waterford Hbr. entr.	1.2	1.1	1.1	1.0	0.9	0.8	0.7	0.6	0.5	0.4	0.3	0.2
Cork	1.5	1.4	1.2	1.1	1.0	0.9	0.7	0.6	0.5	0.4	0.3	0.2
Kinsale, Baltimore Bay .	1.6	1.5	1.3	1.2	1.1	1.0	0.8	0.7	0.6	0.5	0.3	0.2
ENGLAND-WEST											
Avonmouth	4.2	4.2	4.2	4.2	4.2	4.2	4.2	4.2	4.2	4.3	4.3	4.4
Weston-super-Mare	3.3	3.1	2.9	2.7	2.5	2.4	2.2	2.0	1.8	1.7	1.7	1.6
Watchet	4.1	3.9	3.5	3.2	2.9	2.6	2.2	1.9	1.6	1.4	1.3	1.1
Minehead	4.1	3.7	3.3	2.9	2.6	2.2	1.8	1.5	1.1	0.9	0.8	0.6
Porlock Bay	4.1	3.7	3.3	2.9	2.5	2.1	1.7	1.3	0.9	0.7	0.6	0.4
Ilfracombe	3.5	3.2	2.8	2.5	2.1	1.8	1.4	1.1	0.7	0.4	0.2	-0.1
Appledore.................	1.9	1.7	1.5	1.3	1.2	1.0	0.8	0.7	0.5	0.4	0.2	0.1
Padstow, Newquay	3.0	2.7	2.5	2.2	1.9	1.6	1.4	1.1	0.8	0.6	0.4	0.1
St. Ives Bay...............	2.8	2.5	2.3	2.0	1.7	1.5	1.2	1.0	0.7	0.5	0.3	0.1
ISLANDS OFF											
Lundy Island	3.1	2.8	2.6	2.3	2.0	1.7	1.4	1.1	0.8	0.6	0.4	0.1
St. Mary's, Scilly Isles .	2.5	2.3	2.0	1.9	1.7	1.6	1.4	1.3	1.1	1.0	0.8	0.7
ENGLAND-SOUTH											
Falmouth, Helford R.....	2.3	2.1	1.9	1.7	1.5	1.2	1.0	0.8	0.6	0.5	0.3	0.2
Mevagissey, Looe........	2.4	2.2	2.0	1.8	1.5	1.3	1.1	0.8	0.6	0.4	0.3	0.1
Plymouth, Yealm R......	2.5	2.3	2.1	1.9	1.7	1.4	1.2	1.0	0.8	0.7	0.5	0.4
Salcombe	2.5	2.3	2.1	1.9	1.7	1.4	1.2	1.0	0.8	0.6	0.5	0.3
Dartmouth................	2.1	1.9	1.7	1.5	1.3	1.1	0.9	0.7	0.5	0.3	0.2	0.0
Brixham, Teignmouth...	2.4	2.2	2.0	1.8	1.6	1.4	1.2	1.0	0.8	0.7	0.5	0.4
Exmouth approach.......	1.9	1.8	1.6	1.5	1.4	1.4	1.1	0.9	0.8	0.7	0.7	0.6
Lyme Regis	2.1	1.9	1.7	1.5	1.4	1.2	1.0	0.9	0.7	0.6	0.4	0.3
Portland, Weymouth	0.9	0.8	0.8	0.7	0.6	0.5	0.4	0.3	0.2	0.2	0.1	0.1
Lulworth Cove	1.0	0.9	0.9	0.8	0.7	0.6	0.6	0.5	0.4	0.4	0.3	0.3
Swanage	1.7	1.6	1.6	1.5	1.4	1.3	1.4	1.4	1.4	1.4	1.5	1.5
Poole Town	1.8	1.8	1.8	1.8	1.8	1.8	1.7	1.7	1.6	1.6	1.6	1.6
Christchurch Hbr.........	1.4	1.4	1.4	1.4	1.5	1.5	1.5	1.4	1.4	1.4	1.5	1.5
CHANNEL ISLANDS											
Braye Hbr..................	3.0	2.8	2.6	2.4	2.3	2.1	1.9	1.8	1.6	1.4	1.3	1.1
St. Peter Port, Sark	4.2	3.9	3.5	3.2	2.9	2.5	2.2	1.8	1.5	1.2	0.9	0.6
St. Helier..................	4.8	4.5	4.1	3.8	3.5	3.2	2.8	2.5	2.2	1.9	1.6	1.3
Les Minquiers	4.8	4.5	4.1	3.8	3.4	3.1	2.7	2.4	2.0	1.7	1.5	1.2
FRANCE											
Cherbourg	3.6	3.5	3.5	3.4	3.3	3.2	3.2	3.1	3.0	2.9	2.8	2.7
Omonville	3.4	3.3	3.3	3.2	3.1	3.0	2.9	2.8	2.7	2.6	2.4	2.3
Iles Chausey	5.1	4.8	4.4	4.1	3.8	3.4	3.1	2.8	2.4	2.1	1.8	1.5
Carteret	4.7	4.4	4.0	3.7	3.4	3.1	2.8	2.5	2.2	1.9	1.7	1.4
Granville..................	5.3	4.9	4.5	4.1	3.7	3.4	3.0	2.6	2.2	1.9	1.5	1.2
St Malo	4.9	4.6	4.2	3.9	3.6	3.2	2.9	2.5	2.2	1.9	1.6	1.3
All Hbrs. St Brieuc Bay	4.7	4.3	3.9	3.5	3.1	2.7	2.3	1.9	1.5	1.2	0.8	0.5
Ile de Bréhat	4.0	3.7	3.5	3.2	2.9	2.6	2.4	2.1	1.8	1.5	1.3	1.0
Lezardrieux	3.8	3.4	3.0	2.6	2.3	1.9	1.5	1.2	0.8	0.5	0.2	-0.1
Tréguier	3.9	3.5	3.1	2.7	2.4	2.0	1.6	1.3	0.9	0.6	0.4	0.1
Morlaix, Primel Bay......	4.1	3.8	3.4	3.1	2.8	2.5	2.1	1.8	1.5	1.1	0.8	0.4
Roscoff, Ile de Batz	4.0	3.7	3.3	3.0	2.7	2.4	2.1	1.8	1.5	1.2	0.9	0.6
L'Aberwrach	3.7	3.4	3.2	2.9	2.7	2.4	2.2	1.9	1.7	1.5	1.3	1.1
All Hbrs. Ch. du Four....	3.4	3.3	3.1	3.0	2.9	2.7	2.6	2.4	2.3	2.1	2.0	1.8
Brest	3.6	3.5	3.3	3.2	3.1	2.9	2.8	2.6	2.5	2.3	2.2	2.0
Camaret, Douarnenez...	3.3	3.2	3.2	3.1	3.0	2.9	2.8	2.7	2.6	2.5	2.3	2.2

Stream Rate Conversion Table

Mean Rate Figure from Chart ▼	\multicolumn{11}{c}{Pencil-in height of HW Cherbourg Read from column below pencil mark}
	4.8	5.0	5.2	5.4	5.6	5.8	6.0	6.2	6.4	6.6	6.8
0.2	0.1	0.1	0.1	0.1	0.2	0.2	0.2	0.2	0.3	0.3	0.3	0.3
0.4	0.2	0.2	0.2	0.3	0.3	0.4	0.4	0.5	0.5	0.6	0.6	0.7
0.6	0.2	0.3	0.4	0.4	0.5	0.6	0.7	0.7	0.8	0.9	0.9	1.0
0.8	0.4	0.4	0.5	0.6	0.7	0.8	0.9	1.0	1.1	1.1	1.2	1.3
1.0	0.4	0.5	0.6	0.7	0.9	1.0	1.1	1.2	1.3	1.4	1.5	1.7
1.2	0.5	0.6	0.7	0.9	1.0	1.2	1.3	1.4	1.6	1.7	1.9	2.0
1.4	0.6	0.7	0.9	1.0	1.2	1.4	1.5	1.7	1.8	2.0	2.2	2.3
1.6	0.6	0.8	1.0	1.2	1.4	1.6	1.7	1.9	2.1	2.3	2.5	2.7
1.8	0.7	0.9	1.1	1.3	1.5	1.7	2.0	2.2	2.4	2.6	2.8	3.0
2.0	0.8	1.0	1.2	1.5	1.7	1.9	2.2	2.4	2.6	2.9	3.1	3.3
2.2	0.9	1.1	1.4	1.6	1.9	2.1	2.3	2.6	2.9	3.2	3.4	3.7
2.4	0.9	1.2	1.5	1.8	2.1	2.3	2.6	2.9	3.2	3.4	3.7	4.0
2.6	1.0	1.3	1.6	1.9	2.2	2.5	2.8	3.1	3.4	3.7	4.0	4.3
2.8	1.1	1.4	1.7	2.1	2.4	2.7	3.0	3.4	3.7	4.0	4.3	4.7
3.0	1.2	1.5	1.9	2.2	2.6	2.9	3.2	3.6	4.0	4.3	4.6	5.0
3.2	1.3	1.6	2.0	2.4	2.7	3.1	3.4	3.8	4.2	4.6	4.9	5.3
3.4	1.3	1.7	2.1	2.5	2.9	3.3	3.7	4.1	4.5	4.9	5.3	5.7
3.6	1.4	1.8	2.2	2.7	3.1	3.5	3.9	4.3	4.7	5.2	5.6	6.0
3.8	1.5	1.9	2.4	2.8	3.3	3.7	4.1	4.6	5.0	5.4	5.9	6.3
4.0	1.6	2.0	2.5	3.0	3.4	3.9	4.3	4.8	5.3	5.7	6.2	6.7
4.2	1.7	2.1	2.6	3.1	3.6	4.1	4.6	5.0	5.5	6.0	6.5	7.0
4.4	1.7	2.2	2.7	3.3	3.8	4.3	4.8	5.3	5.8	6.3	6.8	7.3
4.6	1.8	2.3	2.9	3.4	3.9	4.5	5.0	5.5	6.1	6.6	7.1	7.7
4.8	1.9	2.4	3.0	3.6	4.1	4.7	5.2	5.8	6.3	6.9	7.4	8.0
5.0	2.0	2.5	3.1	3.7	4.3	4.9	5.4	6.0	6.6	7.2	7.7	8.3
5.2	2.0	2.6	3.2	3.8	4.4	5.0	5.6	6.2	6.8	7.4	8.0	8.6
5.4	2.1	2.8	3.4	4.0	4.6	5.2	5.7	6.5	7.1	7.7	8.4	9.0
5.6	2.2	2.9	3.5	4.1	4.8	5.4	6.1	6.7	7.4	8.0	8.7	9.3
5.8	2.3	3.0	3.6	4.3	5.0	5.6	6.3	7.0	7.6	8.3	9.0	9.6
6.0	2.4	3.1	3.7	4.4	5.1	5.8	6.5	7.2	7.9	8.6	9.3	9.9

Tidal Stream Rates

Copyright © J Reeve-Fowkes and Thomas Reed Publications.
No copying without permission

4 hours after HW Cherbourg **+4**

Time (to be inserted)

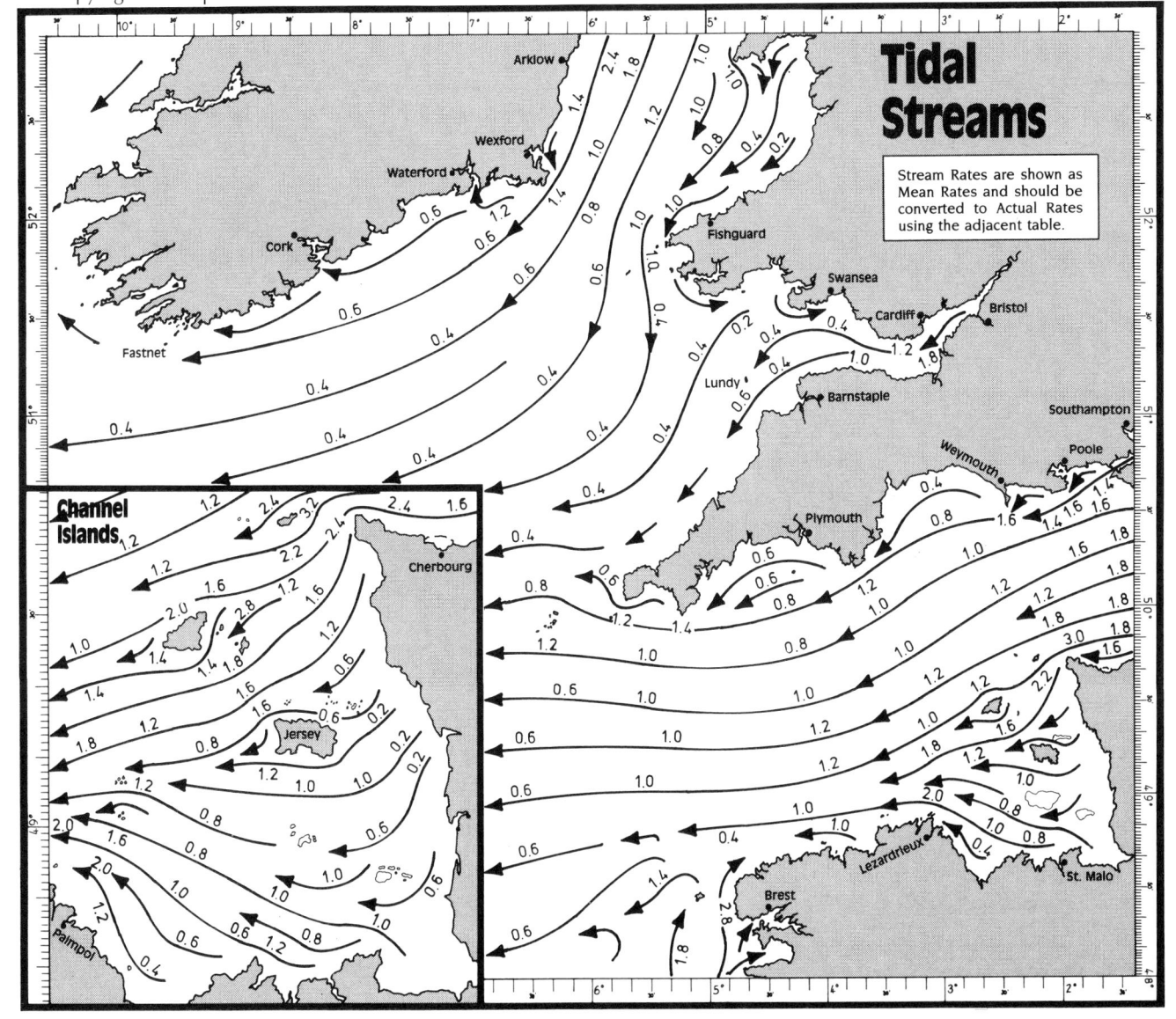

Tidal Streams

Stream Rates are shown as Mean Rates and should be converted to Actual Rates using the adjacent table.

81

Tidal Heights

+5 — 5 hours after HW Cherbourg

Copyright © J Reeve-Fowkes and Thomas Reed Publications.
No copying without permission

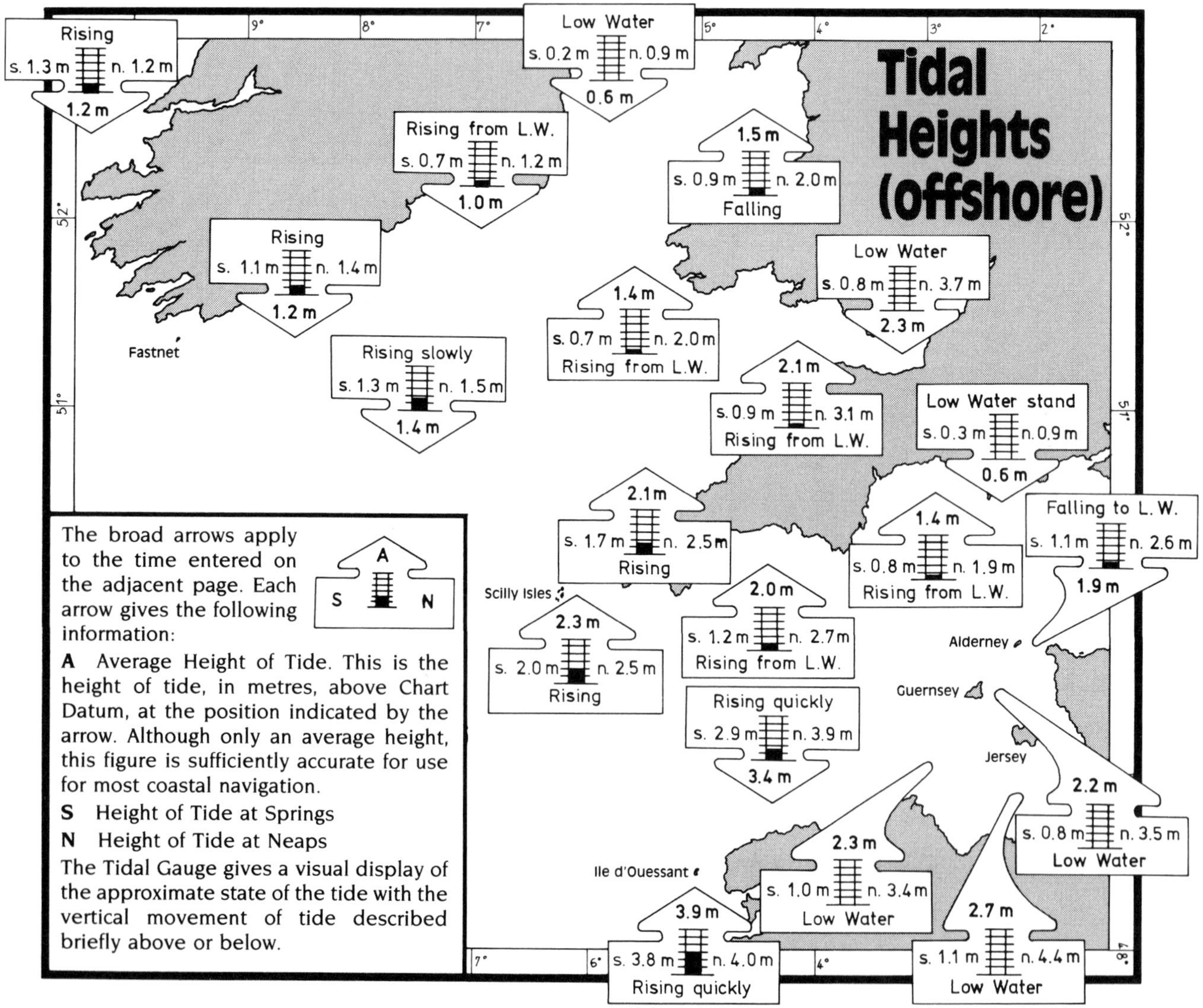

Tidal Heights (offshore)

Map arrow readings:

- Rising — s. 1.3 m n. 1.2 m — **1.2 m**
- Low Water — s. 0.2 m n. 0.9 m — **0.6 m**
- Rising from L.W. — s. 0.7 m n. 1.2 m — **1.0 m**
- Falling — s. 0.9 m n. 2.0 m — **1.5 m**
- Rising — s. 1.1 m n. 1.4 m — **1.2 m** (Fastnet)
- Rising slowly — s. 1.3 m n. 1.5 m — **1.4 m**
- Rising from L.W. — s. 0.7 m n. 2.0 m — **1.4 m**
- Low Water — s. 0.8 m n. 3.7 m — **2.3 m**
- Rising from L.W. — s. 0.9 m n. 3.1 m — **2.1 m**
- Low Water stand — s. 0.3 m n. 0.9 m — **0.6 m**
- Rising — s. 1.7 m n. 2.5 m — **2.1 m**
- Rising from L.W. — s. 0.8 m n. 1.9 m — **1.4 m**
- Falling to L.W. — s. 1.1 m n. 2.6 m — **1.9 m** (Alderney)
- Rising (Scilly Isles) — s. 2.0 m n. 2.5 m — **2.3 m**
- Rising from L.W. — s. 1.2 m n. 2.7 m — **2.0 m**
- Rising quickly — s. 2.9 m n. 3.9 m — **3.4 m** (Guernsey)
- **2.2 m** (Jersey)
- Low Water — s. 0.8 m n. 3.5 m — **2.7 m**
- Rising quickly (Ile d'Ouessant) — s. 3.8 m n. 4.0 m — **3.9 m**
- Low Water — s. 1.0 m n. 3.4 m — **2.3 m**
- Low Water — s. 1.1 m n. 4.4 m — **2.7 m**

The broad arrows apply to the time entered on the adjacent page. Each arrow gives the following information:

A Average Height of Tide. This is the height of tide, in metres, above Chart Datum, at the position indicated by the arrow. Although only an average height, this figure is sufficiently accurate for use for most coastal navigation.

S Height of Tide at Springs

N Height of Tide at Neaps

The Tidal Gauge gives a visual display of the approximate state of the tide with the vertical movement of tide described briefly above or below.

TIDAL HEIGHTS — PORTS & PLACES

Pencil-in height of HW Cherbourg ▶	4.8	5.0	5.2	5.4	5.6	5.8	6.0	6.2	6.4	6.6	6.8
WALES											
Pwllheli, Barmouth	2.4 2.3	2.3	2.2	2.1	2.0	1.9	1.8	1.7	1.7	1.6	1.6
Aberystwth	2.5 2.3	2.1	1.9	1.7	1.6	1.4	1.2	1.0	0.9	0.7	0.6
Fishguard, P.Cardigan	2.5 2.3	2.1	1.9	1.7	1.6	1.4	1.2	1.0	0.8	0.7	0.5
Milford Haven	2.9 2.6	2.4	2.1	1.8	1.6	1.3	1.1	0.8	0.6	0.5	0.3
Burry Inlet approach	3.3 3.0	2.8	2.5	2.2	1.9	1.6	1.3	1.0	0.8	0.5	0.3
Swansea	3.8 3.5	3.1	2.8	2.5	2.2	1.9	1.6	1.3	1.0	0.8	0.5
P. Talbot, Porthcawl	3.9 3.6	3.2	2.9	2.6	2.2	1.9	1.5	1.2	0.9	0.7	0.4
Barry	3.2 2.9	2.7	2.4	2.1	1.8	1.5	1.2	0.9	0.7	0.4	0.2
Cardiff, Penarth	4.5 4.1	3.7	3.3	2.9	2.6	2.2	1.8	1.4	1.2	1.0	0.8
IRELAND											
Arklow	0.7 0.7	0.7	0.7	0.7	0.7	0.6	0.6	0.6	0.6	0.6	0.6
Rosslare	1.1 1.0	1.0	0.9	0.8	0.8	0.7	0.7	0.6	0.6	0.5	0.5
Waterford Hbr. entr.	1.3 1.2	1.2	1.1	1.0	1.0	0.9	0.9	0.8	0.7	0.6	0.5
Cork	1.4 1.3	1.3	1.2	1.1	1.0	0.9	0.8	0.7	0.6	0.5	0.4
Kinsale, Baltimore Bay	1.6 1.5	1.5	1.4	1.3	1.2	1.2	1.1	1.0	0.9	0.8	0.7
ENGLAND-WEST											
Avonmouth	3.7 3.6	3.4	3.3	3.2	3.0	2.9	2.7	2.6	2.6	2.6	2.6
Weston-super-Mare	3.3 3.0	2.6	2.3	2.0	1.7	1.3	1.0	0.7	0.6	0.4	0.3
Watchet	3.0 2.8	2.6	2.4	2.1	1.9	1.7	1.4	1.2	1.0	0.8	0.6
Minehead	4.0 3.7	3.3	3.0	2.6	2.3	1.9	1.6	1.2	1.0	0.9	0.7
Porlock Bay	4.1 3.8	3.4	3.1	2.8	2.4	2.1	1.7	1.4	1.3	1.1	1.0
Ilfracombe	3.8 3.5	3.1	2.8	2.5	2.2	1.8	1.5	1.2	1.0	0.7	0.5
Appledore	2.3 2.0	1.8	1.5	1.2	1.0	0.7	0.5	0.2	0.1	-0.1	-0.2
Padstow, Newquay	3.2 3.0	2.8	2.6	2.3	2.1	1.9	1.6	1.4	1.2	1.1	0.9
St. Ives Bay	2.8 2.7	2.5	2.4	2.2	2.1	1.9	1.8	1.6	1.5	1.3	1.2
ISLANDS OFF											
Lundy Island	3.3 3.0	2.8	2.5	2.2	2.0	1.7	1.5	1.2	1.0	0.8	0.6
St. Mary's, Scilly Isles	2.7 2.6	2.6	2.5	2.5	2.4	2.4	2.3	2.3	2.3	2.2	2.2
ENGLAND-SOUTH											
Falmouth, Helford R.	2.7 2.5	2.3	2.1	1.9	1.7	1.5	1.3	1.1	1.0	0.9	0.8
Mevagissey, Looe	2.8 2.6	2.4	2.2	2.0	1.7	1.5	1.3	1.1	1.0	0.8	0.7
Plymouth, Yealm R.	2.9 2.7	2.5	2.3	2.0	1.8	1.6	1.3	1.1	1.0	0.8	0.7
Salcombe	2.7 2.5	2.3	2.1	1.9	1.6	1.4	1.2	1.0	0.8	0.7	0.5
Dartmouth	2.4 2.2	2.0	1.8	1.5	1.3	1.1	0.8	0.6	0.5	0.3	0.2
Brixham, Teignmouth	2.6 2.4	2.2	2.0	1.8	1.6	1.4	1.2	1.0	0.9	0.7	0.6
Exmouth approach	2.2 2.0	1.8	1.6	1.4	1.1	0.9	0.7	0.5	0.4	0.4	0.3
Lyme Regis	2.1 2.0	1.8	1.7	1.5	1.4	1.2	1.1	0.9	0.8	0.7	0.6
Portland, Weymouth	1.0 0.9	0.9	0.8	0.7	0.6	0.6	0.5	0.4	0.4	0.3	0.3
Lulworth Cove	1.1 1.0	1.0	0.9	0.8	0.7	0.7	0.6	0.5	0.5	0.4	0.4
Swanage	1.6 1.5	1.5	1.4	1.4	1.3	1.3	1.3	1.3	1.3	1.3	1.3
Poole Town	1.8 1.8	1.8	1.8	1.8	1.8	1.8	1.7	1.7	1.7	1.7	1.7
Christchurch Hbr.	1.2 1.2	1.2	1.3	1.3	1.3	1.3	1.3	1.3	1.3	1.4	1.4
CHANNEL ISLANDS											
Braye Hbr.	2.6 2.4	2.2	2.0	1.7	1.5	1.3	1.0	0.8	0.6	0.5	0.3
St. Peter Port, Sark	4.1 3.7	3.3	2.9	2.5	2.2	1.8	1.4	1.0	0.7	0.3	0.0
St. Helier	4.7 4.3	3.9	3.5	3.0	2.6	2.2	1.7	1.3	1.0	0.6	0.3
Les Minquiers	4.6 4.2	3.8	3.4	3.0	2.5	2.1	1.7	1.3	1.0	0.7	0.4
FRANCE											
Cherbourg	3.2 3.1	2.9	2.8	2.6	2.5	2.3	2.2	2.0	1.8	1.7	1.5
Omonville	3.2 3.0	2.8	2.6	2.4	2.3	2.1	1.9	1.7	1.5	1.3	1.1
Iles Chausey	5.0 4.6	4.2	3.8	3.3	2.9	2.5	2.0	1.6	1.2	0.9	0.5
Carteret	4.5 4.1	3.7	3.3	2.9	2.6	2.2	1.8	1.4	1.1	0.7	0.4
Granville	5.3 4.8	4.2	3.7	3.2	2.7	2.2	1.7	1.2	0.8	0.5	0.1
St Malo	5.0 4.5	4.1	3.6	3.2	2.7	2.3	1.8	1.4	1.1	0.7	0.4
All Hbrs. St Brieuc Bay	4.7 4.3	3.9	3.5	3.1	2.6	2.2	1.8	1.4	1.1	0.7	0.4
Ile de Bréhat	4.6 4.2	3.8	3.4	2.9	2.5	2.1	1.6	1.2	0.9	0.7	0.3
Lezardrieux	3.9 3.6	3.2	2.9	2.6	2.3	1.9	1.6	1.3	1.0	0.7	0.4
Tréguier	3.9 3.6	3.4	3.1	2.8	2.5	2.3	2.0	1.7	1.5	1.3	1.1
Morlaix, Primel Bay	4.5 4.2	4.0	3.7	3.5	3.2	3.0	2.7	2.5	2.2	1.9	1.6
Roscoff, Ile de Batz	4.3 4.1	3.9	3.7	3.5	3.3	3.0	2.8	2.6	2.4	2.1	1.9
L'Aberwrach	4.0 3.9	3.7	3.6	3.5	3.4	3.3	3.2	3.1	3.0	2.9	2.8
All Hbrs. Ch. du Four	3.8 3.8	3.8	3.8	3.8	3.8	3.8	3.8	3.8	3.7	3.7	3.6
Brest	4.0 4.0	4.0	4.0	3.9	3.9	3.9	3.8	3.8	3.8	3.8	3.8
Camaret, Douarnenez	3.7 3.7	3.7	3.8	3.8	3.9	3.9	4.0	4.0	4.0	3.9	3.9

Stream Rate Conversion Table

Mean Rate Figure from Chart ▼	Pencil-in height of HW Cherbourg Read from column below pencil mark										
	4.8	5.0	5.2	5.4	5.6	5.8	6.0	6.2	6.4	6.6	6.8
0.2	0.1	0.1	0.1	0.1	0.2	0.2	0.2	0.2	0.3	0.3	0.3
0.4	0.2	0.2	0.2	0.3	0.3	0.4	0.4	0.5	0.5	0.6	0.7
0.6	0.2	0.3	0.4	0.4	0.5	0.6	0.7	0.7	0.8	0.9	1.0
0.8	0.4	0.4	0.5	0.6	0.7	0.8	0.9	1.0	1.1	1.2	1.3
1.0	0.4	0.5	0.6	0.7	0.9	1.0	1.1	1.2	1.3	1.4	1.5	1.7
1.2	0.5	0.6	0.7	0.9	1.0	1.2	1.3	1.4	1.6	1.7	1.9	2.0
1.4	0.6	0.7	0.9	1.0	1.2	1.4	1.5	1.7	1.8	2.0	2.2	2.3
1.6	0.6	0.8	1.0	1.2	1.4	1.6	1.7	1.9	2.1	2.3	2.5	2.7
1.8	0.7	0.9	1.1	1.3	1.5	1.7	2.0	2.2	2.4	2.6	2.8	3.0
2.0	0.8	1.0	1.2	1.5	1.7	1.9	2.2	2.4	2.6	2.9	3.1	3.3
2.2	0.9	1.1	1.4	1.6	1.9	2.1	2.3	2.6	2.9	3.2	3.4	3.7
2.4	0.9	1.2	1.5	1.8	2.1	2.3	2.6	2.9	3.2	3.4	3.7	4.0
2.6	1.0	1.3	1.6	1.9	2.2	2.5	2.8	3.1	3.4	3.7	4.0	4.3
2.8	1.1	1.4	1.7	2.1	2.4	2.7	3.0	3.4	3.7	4.0	4.3	4.7
3.0	1.2	1.5	1.9	2.2	2.6	2.9	3.2	3.6	4.0	4.3	4.6	5.0
3.2	1.3	1.6	2.0	2.4	2.7	3.1	3.4	3.8	4.2	4.6	4.9	5.3
3.4	1.3	1.7	2.1	2.5	2.9	3.3	3.7	4.1	4.5	4.9	5.3	5.7
3.6	1.4	1.8	2.2	2.7	3.1	3.5	3.9	4.3	4.7	5.2	5.6	6.0
3.8	1.5	1.9	2.4	2.8	3.3	3.7	4.1	4.6	5.0	5.4	5.9	6.3
4.0	1.6	2.0	2.5	3.0	3.4	3.9	4.3	4.8	5.3	5.7	6.2	6.7
4.2	1.7	2.1	2.6	3.1	3.6	4.1	4.6	5.0	5.5	6.0	6.5	7.0
4.4	1.7	2.2	2.7	3.3	3.8	4.3	4.8	5.3	5.8	6.3	6.8	7.3
4.6	1.8	2.3	2.9	3.4	3.9	4.5	5.0	5.5	6.1	6.6	7.1	7.7
4.8	1.9	2.4	3.0	3.6	4.1	4.7	5.2	5.8	6.3	6.9	7.4	8.0
5.0	2.0	2.5	3.1	3.7	4.3	4.9	5.4	6.0	6.6	7.2	7.7	8.3
5.2	2.0	2.6	3.2	3.8	4.4	5.0	5.6	6.2	6.8	7.4	8.0	8.6
5.4	2.1	2.8	3.4	4.0	4.6	5.2	5.7	6.5	7.1	7.7	8.4	9.0
5.6	2.2	2.9	3.5	4.1	4.8	5.4	6.1	6.7	7.4	8.0	8.7	9.3
5.8	2.3	3.0	3.6	4.3	5.0	5.6	6.3	7.0	7.6	8.3	9.0	9.6
6.0	2.4	3.1	3.7	4.4	5.1	5.8	6.5	7.2	7.9	8.6	9.3	9.9

Tidal Stream Rates

Copyright © J Reeve-Fowkes and Thomas Reed Publications.
No copying without permission

5 hours after HW Cherbourg **+5**

Time (to be inserted)

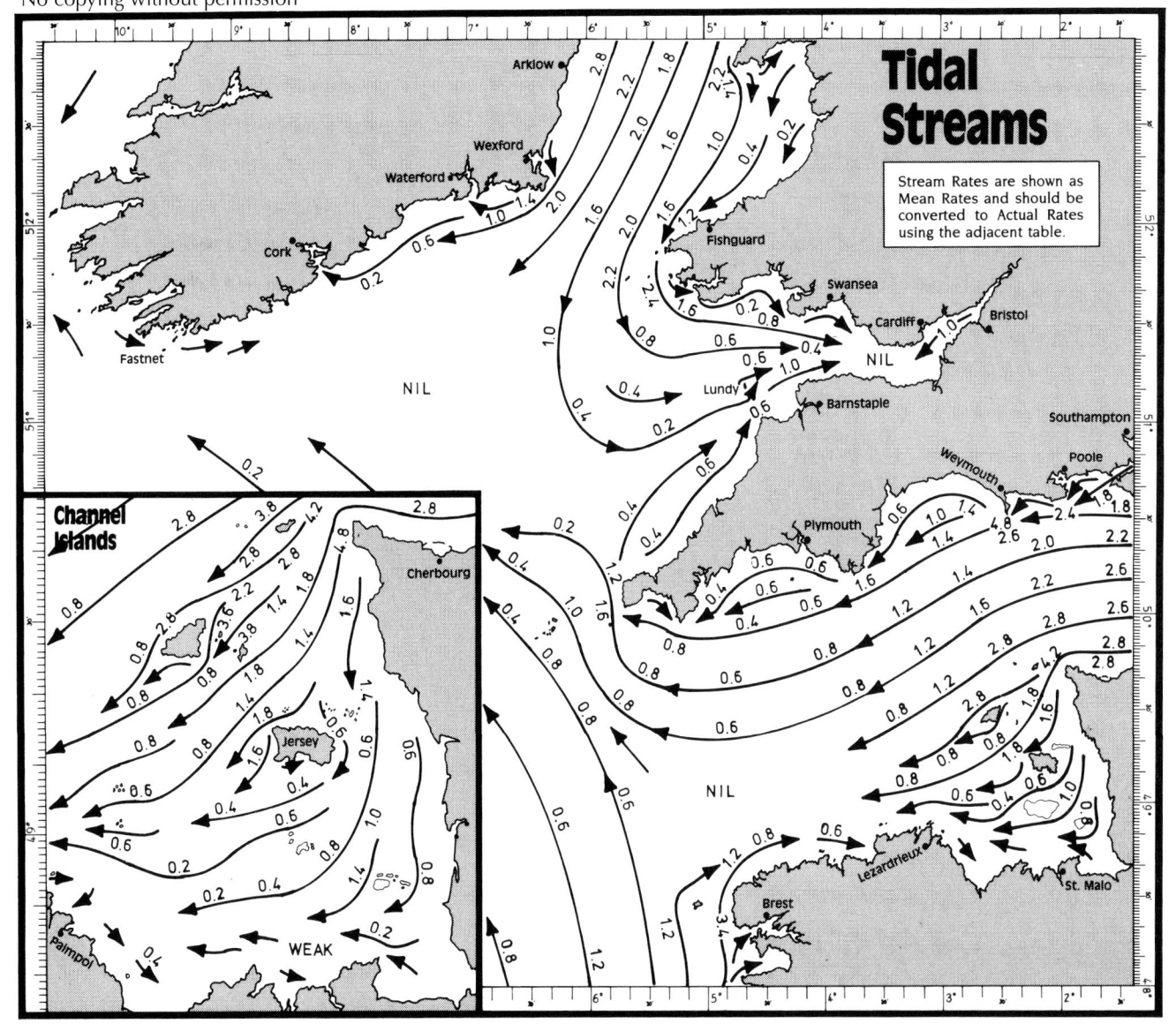

Tidal Streams

Stream Rates are shown as Mean Rates and should be converted to Actual Rates using the adjacent table.

83

+6 — 6 hours after HW Cherbourg

Tidal Heights

Copyright © J Reeve-Fowkes and Thomas Reed Publications.
No copying without permission

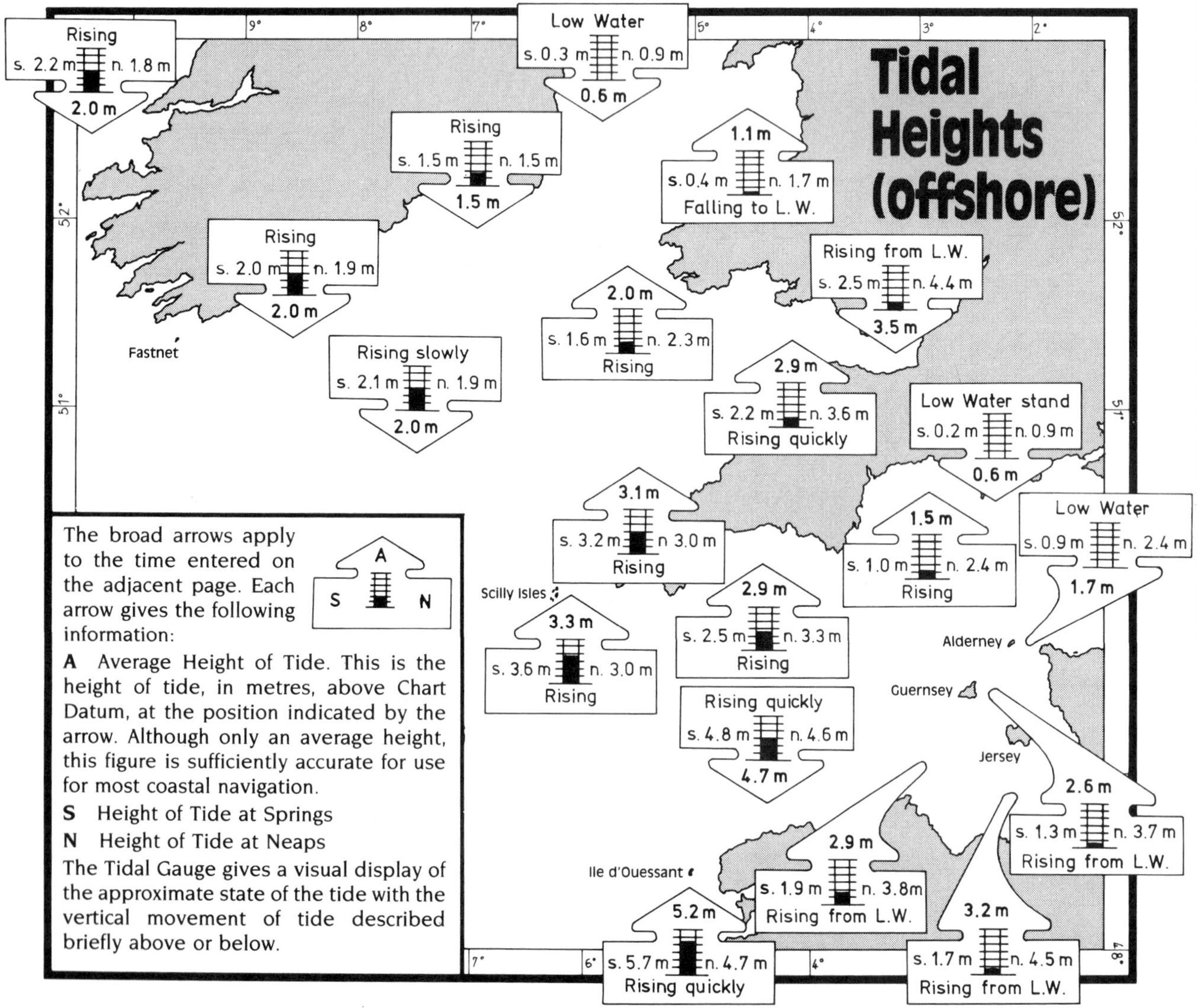

Tidal Heights (offshore)

The broad arrows apply to the time entered on the adjacent page. Each arrow gives the following information:

A Average Height of Tide. This is the height of tide, in metres, above Chart Datum, at the position indicated by the arrow. Although only an average height, this figure is sufficiently accurate for use for most coastal navigation.

S Height of Tide at Springs

N Height of Tide at Neaps

The Tidal Gauge gives a visual display of the approximate state of the tide with the vertical movement of tide described briefly above or below.

Offshore arrows

- Rising — s. 2.2 m n. 1.8 m — **2.0 m**
- Low Water — s. 0.3 m n. 0.9 m — **0.6 m**
- Rising — s. 1.5 m n. 1.5 m — **1.5 m**
- Falling to L.W. — s. 0.4 m n. 1.7 m — **1.1 m**
- Rising — s. 2.0 m n. 1.9 m — **2.0 m**
- Rising from L.W. — s. 2.5 m n. 4.4 m — **3.5 m**
- Rising slowly — s. 2.1 m n. 1.9 m — **2.0 m**
- Rising — s. 1.6 m n. 2.3 m — **2.0 m**
- Rising quickly — s. 2.2 m n. 3.6 m — **2.9 m**
- Low Water stand — s. 0.2 m n. 0.9 m — **0.6 m**
- Rising — s. 3.2 m n. 3.0 m — **3.1 m**
- Rising — s. 1.0 m n. 2.4 m — **1.5 m**
- Low Water — s. 0.9 m n. 2.4 m — **1.7 m**
- Rising — s. 3.6 m n. 3.0 m — **3.3 m**
- Rising — s. 2.5 m n. 3.3 m — **2.9 m**
- Rising quickly — s. 4.8 m n. 4.6 m — **4.7 m**
- Rising from L.W. — s. 1.3 m n. 3.7 m — **2.6 m**
- Rising from L.W. — s. 1.9 m n. 3.8 m — **2.9 m**
- Rising from L.W. — s. 1.7 m n. 4.5 m — **3.2 m**
- Rising quickly — s. 5.7 m n. 4.7 m — **5.2 m**

Fastnet · Scilly Isles · Ile d'Ouessant · Alderney · Guernsey · Jersey

TIDAL HEIGHTS — PORTS & PLACES

Pencil-in height of HW Cherbourg ▶	4.8	5.0	5.2	5.4	5.6	5.8	6.0	6.2	6.4	6.6	6.8
WALES											
Pwllheli, Barmouth	2.2	2.1	1.9	1.8	1.6	1.5	1.3	1.2	1.0	0.9	0.8	0.7
Aberystwth	2.2	2.0	1.8	1.6	1.4	1.2	1.0	0.8	0.6	0.4	0.3	0.1
Fishguard, P.Cardigan	2.4	2.2	2.0	1.9	1.6	1.4	1.2	1.0	0.8	0.6	0.5	0.3
Milford Haven	3.1	2.9	2.7	2.5	2.3	2.2	2.0	1.8	1.6	1.5	1.3	1.2
Burry Inlet approach	3.6	3.4	3.2	3.0	2.8	2.5	2.3	2.1	1.9	1.7	1.6	1.4
Swansea	4.0	3.8	3.6	3.4	3.1	2.9	2.7	2.4	2.2	2.0	1.8	1.6
P. Talbot, Porthcawl	4.4	4.1	3.9	3.6	3.4	3.1	2.9	2.6	2.4	2.2	2.0	1.8
Barry	4.9	4.6	4.2	3.9	3.6	3.3	2.9	2.6	2.3	2.1	2.0	1.8
Cardiff, Penarth	5.2	4.7	4.3	3.8	3.3	2.9	2.4	2.0	1.5	1.1	0.8	0.4
IRELAND											
Arklow	0.6	0.6	0.6	0.6	0.5	0.5	0.5	0.4	0.4	0.4	0.3	0.3
Rosslare	1.1	1.1	1.1	1.1	1.0	1.0	1.0	0.9	0.9	0.9	0.9	0.9
Waterford Hbr. entr.	1.6	1.6	1.6	1.6	1.6	1.5	1.5	1.5	1.5	1.5	1.4	1.4
Cork	1.8	1.7	1.7	1.6	1.5	1.5	1.4	1.4	1.3	1.2	1.2	1.1
Kinsale, Baltimore Bay	1.9	1.9	1.9	1.9	1.9	1.9	1.9	1.9	1.9	1.8	1.8	1.7
ENGLAND-WEST											
Avonmouth	4.7	4.2	3.8	3.3	2.9	2.4	2.0	1.5	1.1	1.0	1.0	0.9
Weston-super-Mare	3.9	3.7	3.5	3.3	3.1	2.9	2.7	2.5	2.3	2.2	2.2	2.1
Watchet	4.8	4.6	4.4	4.2	4.0	3.7	3.5	3.3	3.1	3.0	2.9	2.8
Minehead	4.6	4.4	4.2	4.0	3.8	3.7	3.5	3.3	3.1	3.0	3.0	2.9
Porlock Bay	4.6	4.4	4.2	4.0	3.8	3.7	3.5	3.3	3.1	3.0	3.0	2.9
Ilfracombe	4.3	4.1	3.9	3.7	3.5	3.3	3.1	2.9	2.7	2.6	2.4	2.3
Appledore	2.8	2.6	2.4	2.2	2.0	1.7	1.5	1.3	1.1	1.0	0.9	0.8
Padstow, Newquay	3.7	3.6	3.4	3.3	3.2	3.1	2.9	2.8	2.7	2.6	2.6	2.5
St. Ives Bay	3.1	3.1	3.1	3.1	3.1	3.0	3.0	3.0	3.0	3.0	2.9	2.9
ISLANDS OFF											
Lundy Island	3.8	3.6	3.4	3.2	3.0	2.9	2.7	2.5	2.3	2.2	2.0	1.9
St. Mary's, Scilly Isles	3.1	3.2	3.2	3.3	3.4	3.5	3.5	3.6	3.7	3.8	3.9	4.0
ENGLAND-SOUTH											
Falmouth, Helford R.	3.1	3.0	3.0	2.9	2.8	2.7	2.6	2.5	2.4	2.4	2.3	2.3
Mevagissey, Looe	3.2	3.1	2.9	2.8	2.7	2.6	2.5	2.4	2.3	2.3	2.2	2.2
Plymouth, Yealm R.	3.3	3.2	3.0	2.9	2.8	2.6	2.5	2.3	2.2	2.1	2.1	2.0
Salcombe	3.1	3.0	2.8	2.7	2.5	2.4	2.2	2.1	1.9	1.8	1.8	1.7
Dartmouth	2.8	2.6	2.4	2.2	2.1	1.9	1.7	1.6	1.4	1.3	1.2	1.1
Brixham, Teignmouth	2.6	2.5	2.3	2.2	2.1	1.9	1.8	1.6	1.5	1.4	1.3	1.2
Exmouth approach	2.4	2.2	2.0	1.8	1.6	1.5	1.3	1.1	0.9	0.9	0.8	0.8
Lyme Regis	2.2	2.1	1.9	1.8	1.7	1.5	1.4	1.2	1.1	1.0	1.0	0.9
Portland, Weymouth	1.0	0.9	0.9	0.8	0.7	0.6	0.5	0.4	0.3	0.3	0.3	0.3
Lulworth Cove	1.1	1.0	1.0	0.9	0.8	0.7	0.6	0.5	0.4	0.4	0.3	0.3
Swanage	1.5	1.4	1.4	1.3	1.3	1.3	1.2	1.1	1.1	1.0	1.0	0.9
Poole Town	1.6	1.6	1.6	1.6	1.6	1.6	1.6.	1.5	1.5	1.5	1.5	1.5
Christchurch Hbr.	1.0	1.0	1.0	1.0	1.0	1.0	1.0	0.9	0.9	0.9	0.9	0.9
CHANNEL ISLANDS											
Braye Hbr.	2.6	2.4	2.2	2.0	1.7	1.5	1.3	1.0	0.8	0.6	0.4	0.2
St. Peter Port, Sark	4.2	3.9	3.5	3.2	2.9	2.6	2.2	1.8	1.5	1.2	1.0	0.7
St. Helier	4.8	4.4	4.0	3.6	3.3	2.9	2.5	2.2	1.8	1.5	1.1	0.8
Les Minquiers	4.8	4.4	4.0	3.6	3.3	2.9	2.5	2.2	1.8	1.5	1.3	1.0
FRANCE											
Cherbourg	3.0	2.8	2.6	2.4	2.2	1.9	1.7	1.5	1.3	1.1	0.8	0.6
Omonville	2.9	2.7	2.5	2.3	2.1	1.8	1.6	1.4	1.2	0.9	0.7	0.4
Iles Chausey	5.4	5.0	4.6	4.2	3.8	3.3	2.9	2.5	2.1	1.8	1.4	1.1
Carteret	4.6	4.3	3.9	3.6	3.2	2.9	2.5	2.2	1.8	1.5	1.2	0.9
Granville	5.7	5.2	4.8	4.3	3.8	3.3	2.9	2.4	1.9	1.6	1.3	1.0
St Malo	5.6	5.1	4.7	4.2	3.7	3.2	2.7	2.2	1.7	1.4	1.1	0.8
All Hbrs. St Brieuc Bay	4.9	4.9	4.5	4.2	3.9	3.6	3.3	3.0	2.7	2.4	2.2	1.9
Ile de Bréhat	5.1	4.7	4.3	3.9	3.5	3.1	2.7	2.3	1.9	1.6	1.4	1.1
Lezardrieux	4.5	4.3	4.1	3.9	3.6	3.4	3.2	2.9	2.7	2.5	2.3	2.1
Tréguier	4.3	4.2	4.0	3.9	3.8	3.7	3.5	3.4	3.3	3.2	3.1	3.0
Morlaix, Primel Bay	5.1	5.0	4.8	4.7	4.6	4.5	4.3	4.2	4.1	4.0	3.8	3.7
Roscoff, Ile de Batz	4.9	4.8	4.8	4.7	4.6	4.5	4.5	4.4	4.3	4.2	4.0	3.9
L'Aberwrach	4.4	4.5	4.5	4.6	4.7	4.8	4.8	4.9	5.0	5.0	5.0	5.0
All Hbrs. Ch. du Four	4.3	4.4	4.6	4.8	4.9	5.0	5.2	5.3	5.5	5.5	5.6	5.6
Brest	4.5	4.6	4.8	4.9	5.0	5.2	5.3	5.5	5.6	5.7	5.7	5.8
Camaret, Douarnenez	4.0	4.2	4.4	4.6	4.8	4.9	5.1	5.3	5.5	5.6	5.6	5.7

Stream Rate Conversion Table

Mean Rate Figure from Chart ▼	\multicolumn{11}{c	}{Pencil-in height of HW Cherbourg Read from column below pencil mark}
	4.8	5.0	5.2	5.4	5.6	5.8	6.0	6.2	6.4	6.6	6.8
0.2	0.1	0.1	0.1	0.1	0.2	0.2	0.2	0.2	0.3	0.3	0.3
0.4	0.2	0.2	0.2	0.3	0.3	0.4	0.4	0.5	0.5	0.6	0.7
0.6	0.2	0.3	0.4	0.4	0.5	0.6	0.7	0.7	0.8	0.9	1.0
0.8	0.4	0.4	0.5	0.6	0.7	0.8	0.9	1.0	1.1	1.2	1.3
1.0	0.4	0.5	0.6	0.7	0.9	1.0	1.1	1.2	1.3	1.4	1.5	1.7
1.2	0.5	0.6	0.7	0.9	1.0	1.2	1.3	1.4	1.6	1.7	1.9	2.0
1.4	0.6	0.7	0.9	1.0	1.2	1.4	1.5	1.7	1.8	2.0	2.2	2.3
1.6	0.6	0.8	1.0	1.2	1.4	1.6	1.7	1.9	2.1	2.3	2.5	2.7
1.8	0.7	0.9	1.1	1.3	1.5	1.7	2.0	2.2	2.4	2.6	2.8	3.0
2.0	0.8	1.0	1.2	1.5	1.7	1.9	2.2	2.4	2.6	2.9	3.1	3.3
2.2	0.9	1.1	1.4	1.6	1.9	2.1	2.3	2.6	2.9	3.2	3.4	3.7
2.4	0.9	1.2	1.5	1.8	2.1	2.3	2.6	2.9	3.2	3.4	3.7	4.0
2.6	1.0	1.3	1.6	1.9	2.2	2.5	2.8	3.1	3.4	3.7	4.0	4.3
2.8	1.1	1.4	1.7	2.1	2.4	2.7	3.0	3.4	3.7	4.0	4.3	4.7
3.0	1.2	1.5	1.9	2.2	2.6	2.9	3.2	3.6	4.0	4.3	4.6	5.0
3.2	1.3	1.6	2.0	2.4	2.7	3.1	3.4	3.8	4.2	4.6	4.9	5.3
3.4	1.3	1.7	2.1	2.5	2.9	3.3	3.7	4.1	4.5	4.9	5.3	5.7
3.6	1.4	1.8	2.2	2.7	3.1	3.5	3.9	4.3	4.7	5.2	5.6	6.0
3.8	1.5	1.9	2.4	2.8	3.3	3.7	4.1	4.6	5.0	5.4	5.9	6.3
4.0	1.6	2.0	2.5	3.0	3.4	3.9	4.3	4.8	5.3	5.7	6.2	6.7
4.2	1.7	2.1	2.6	3.1	3.6	4.1	4.6	5.0	5.5	6.0	6.5	7.0
4.4	1.7	2.2	2.7	3.3	3.8	4.3	4.8	5.3	5.8	6.3	6.8	7.3
4.6	1.8	2.3	2.9	3.4	3.9	4.5	5.0	5.5	6.1	6.6	7.1	7.7
4.8	1.9	2.4	3.0	3.6	4.1	4.7	5.2	5.8	6.3	6.9	7.4	8.0
5.0	2.0	2.5	3.1	3.7	4.3	4.9	5.4	6.0	6.6	7.2	7.7	8.3
5.2	2.0	2.6	3.2	3.8	4.4	5.0	5.6	6.2	6.8	7.4	8.0	8.6
5.4	2.1	2.7	3.3	3.9	4.5	5.1	5.7	6.3	6.9	7.5	8.1	8.7
5.4	2.1	2.7	3.3	4.0	4.6	5.2	5.8	6.5	7.1	7.7	8.4	9.0
5.6	2.2	2.9	3.5	4.1	4.8	5.4	6.1	6.7	7.4	8.0	8.7	9.3
5.8	2.3	3.0	3.6	4.3	5.0	5.6	6.3	7.0	7.6	8.3	9.0	9.6
6.0	2.4	3.1	3.7	4.4	5.1	5.8	6.5	7.2	7.9	8.6	9.3	9.9

Tidal Stream Rates

Copyright © J Reeve-Fowkes and Thomas Reed Publications.
No copying without permission

6 hours after HW Cherbourg **+6**

Time (to be inserted)

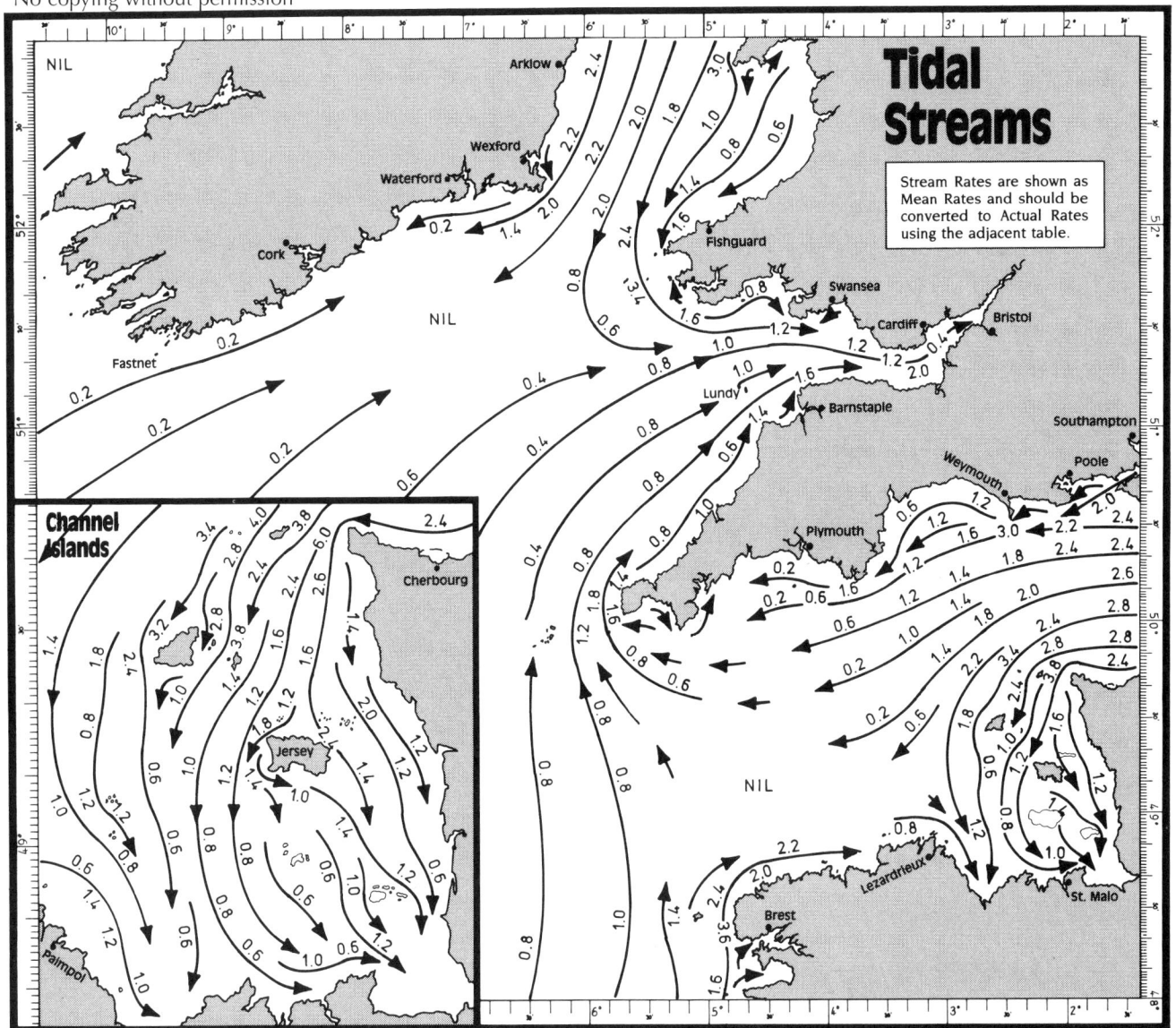

Tidal Streams

Stream Rates are shown as Mean Rates and should be converted to Actual Rates using the adjacent table.

The Yachtsman's Tidal Atlas

SOUTHERN NORTH SEA
&
EASTERN CHANNEL

TIDAL STREAM RATES & TIDAL HEIGHTS
The Solent and Cherbourg to
The Wash and Den Helder

-6
6 hours before HW Cherbourg

Tidal Heights

Copyright © J Reeve-Fowkes and Thomas Reed Publications.
No copying without permission.

Tidal Heights (offshore)

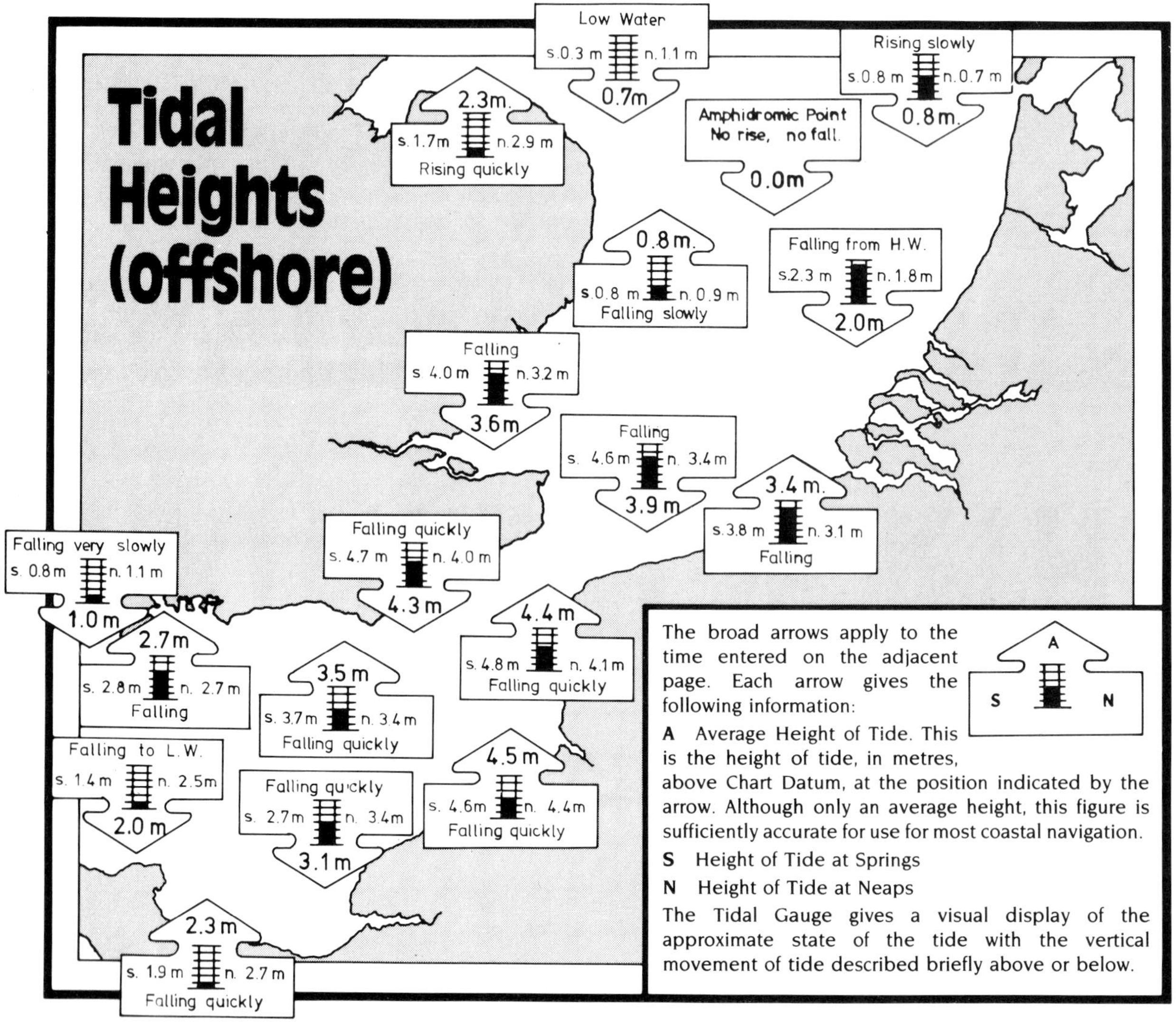

Low Water
s.0.3 m. n.1.1 m
0.7m

2.3m.
s.1.7m n.2.9 m
Rising quickly

Rising slowly
s.0.8 m n.0.7 m
0.8m.

Amphidromic Point
No rise, no fall.
0.0m

0.8 m.
s.0.8 m n.0.9 m
Falling slowly

Falling from H.W.
s.2.3 m n.1.8 m
2.0m

Falling
s 4.0 m n.3.2 m
3.6m

Falling
s. 4.6 m n. 3.4 m
3.9 m

3.4 m.
s.3.8 m n.3.1 m
Falling

Falling very slowly
s. 0.8 m n.1.1 m
1.0 m

Falling quickly
s. 4.7 m n. 4.0 m
4.3 m

4.4 m
s.4.8 m n. 4.1 m
Falling quickly

2.7m
s. 2.8 m n. 2.7 m
Falling

3.5 m
s. 3.7 m n. 3.4 m
Falling quickly

Falling to L.W.
s. 1.4 m n. 2.5 m
2.0 m

Falling quickly
s. 2.7 m n. 3.4 m
3.1 m

4.5 m
s. 4.6 m n. 4.4 m
Falling quickly

2.3 m
s. 1.9 m n. 2.7 m
Falling quickly

The broad arrows apply to the time entered on the adjacent page. Each arrow gives the following information:

A Average Height of Tide. This is the height of tide, in metres, above Chart Datum, at the position indicated by the arrow. Although only an average height, this figure is sufficiently accurate for use for most coastal navigation.

S Height of Tide at Springs
N Height of Tide at Neaps

The Tidal Gauge gives a visual display of the approximate state of the tide with the vertical movement of tide described briefly above or below.

TIDAL HEIGHTS — PORTS & PLACES

Pencil-in height of HW Cherbourg ▶	4.8	5.0	5.2	5.4	5.6	5.8	6.0	6.2	6.4	6.6	6.8
ENGLAND											
Kings Lynn	2.2	2.1	1.9	1.8	1.7	1.5	1.4	1.2	1.1	1.1	1.1
Blakeney Bar	3.0	2.8	2.6	2.4	2.3	2.1	1.9	1.8	1.6	1.5	1.4
Cromer	2.4	2.3	2.1	2.0	1.8	1.7	1.5	1.4	1.2	1.1	1.0
Gt. Yarmouth (Gorleston)	1.1	1.0	1.0	0.9	0.8	0.8	0.7	0.7	0.6	0.5	0.3
Lowestoft	1.1	1.0	1.0	0.9	0.9	0.8	0.8	0.7	0.7	0.6	0.5
Southwold Haven	1.0	1.0	1.0	1.0	1.0	0.9	0.9	0.9	0.9	0.8	0.7
Orford Haven appr'ch	1.6	1.6	1.6	1.6	1.6	1.6	1.6	1.6	1.6	1.6	1.7	1.7
Woodbridge Haven	1.9	1.9	1.9	1.9	1.9	2.0	2.0	2.0	2.0	2.1	2.1
Felixstowe	2.0	2.0	2.0	2.0	2.0	2.0	2.0	2.0	2.0	2.1	2.2
Harwich	2.2	2.2	2.2	2.2	2.3	2.3	2.3	2.4	2.4	2.4	2.4
Walton-on-the-Naze	2.2	2.2	2.2	2.3	2.3	2.4	2.4	2.5	2.5	2.5	2.6	2.6
Brightlingsea	2.4	2.5	2.7	2.8	2.9	3.1	3.2	3.4	3.5	3.6	3.7	3.8
Bradwell	2.8	2.9	3.1	3.2	3.3	3.5	3.6	3.8	3.9	3.9	4.0	4.0
Burnham	3.2	3.3	3.5	3.6	3.7	3.9	4.0	4.2	4.3	4.4	4.5	4.6
Leigh, Southend	3.3	3.4	3.6	3.7	3.8	3.9	4.1	4.2	4.3	4.4	4.6	4.7
London Bridge	4.9	5.2	5.4	5.7	6.0	6.2	6.5	6.7	7.0	7.2	7.5	7.7
Sheerness	3.4	3.5	3.7	3.8	3.9	4.1	4.2	4.4	4.5	4.6	4.7	4.8
Chatham	3.4	3.6	3.8	4.0	4.1	4.3	4.5	4.6	4.8	4.9	5.1	5.2
Rochester	3.5	3.7	3.9	4.1	4.3	4.4	4.6	4.8	5.0	5.2	5.4	5.6
Whitstable approach	3.5	3.6	3.8	3.9	4.0	4.2	4.3	4.5	4.6	4.6	4.7	4.7
Edinburgh Channels	2.8	2.9	2.9	3.0	3.1	3.1	3.2	3.2	3.3	3.3	3.3	3.3
Margate	2.8	2.9	2.9	3.0	3.1	3.2	3.3	3.4	3.5	3.5	3.5	3.5
Ramsgate	2.6	2.7	2.7	2.8	2.9	3.0	3.0	3.1	3.2	3.2	3.3	3.3
Dover	3.7	3.8	3.8	3.9	4.0	4.1	4.1	4.2	4.3	4.3	4.4	4.4
Folkestone	4.0	4.0	4.0	4.0	4.1	4.1	4.1	4.2	4.2	4.2	4.2	4.2
Newhaven	3.3	3.3	3.3	3.3	3.4	3.4	3.4	3.5	3.5	3.5	3.6	3.6
Brighton	3.3	3.3	3.3	3.3	3.4	3.4	3.4	3.4	3.5	3.5	3.5	3.5
Shoreham	3.2	3.3	3.3	3.4	3.4	3.5	3.4	3.6	3.6	3.6	3.6	3.6
Littlehampton Hbr.	3.1	3.2	3.4	3.5	3.7	3.8	4.0	4.1	4.3	4.4	4.5	4.6
Selsey Bill	3.1	3.2	3.4	3.5	3.6	3.7	3.9	4.0	4.1	4.1	4.2	4.2
Chichester entrance	2.8	2.9	3.1	3.2	3.3	3.4	3.6	3.7	3.8	3.9	3.9	4.0
Portsmouth	2.7	2.8	3.0	3.1	3.2	3.3	3.4	3.5	3.6	3.6	3.7	3.7
Southampton	2.4	2.6	2.8	3.0	3.2	3.3	3.5	3.7	3.9	4.0	4.0	4.1
Cowes I. o W.	2.6	2.6	2.6	2.6	2.7	2.7	2.7	2.7	2.7	2.7	2.6	2.6
Yarmouth I. o W.	1.8	1.8	1.8	1.8	1.7	1.7	1.7	1.6	1.6	1.6	1.5	1.5
Lymington	1.9	1.9	1.9	1.9	1.9	1.9	1.9	1.9	1.9	1.9	1.9	1.9
HOLLAND											
Den Helder	1.3	1.2	1.0	0.9	0.8	0.7	0.6	0.5	0.4	0.4	0.4	0.4
IJmuiden	1.6	1.6	1.6	1.6	1.7	1.7	1.7	1.8	1.8	1.8	1.9	1.9
Scheveningen	1.7	1.8	1.8	1.9	1.9	2.0	2.0	2.1	2.1	2.1	2.2	2.2
Hoek van Holland	1.6	1.7	1.7	1.8	1.8	1.9	1.9	2.0	2.0	2.0	2.1	2.1
Rotterdam	1.8	1.8	1.8	1.8	1.8	1.8	1.8	1.8	1.8	1.8	1.9	1.9
Flushing	3.4	3.5	3.7	3.8	3.9	4.0	4.2	4.3	4.4	4.5	4.6	4.7
BELGIUM											
Zeebrugge	3.2	3.3	3.5	3.6	3.7	3.9	4.0	4.2	4.3	4.4	4.4	4.5
Ostende	3.4	3.5	3.5	3.6	3.7	3.8	3.9	4.0	4.1	4.1	4.2	4.2
Nieuwpoort	3.4	3.5	3.5	3.6	3.7	3.8	3.8	3.9	4.0	4.0	4.0	4.0
FRANCE											
Dunkerque	3.5	3.6	3.8	3.9	4.0	4.1	4.3	4.4	4.5	4.5	4.6	4.6
Calais	4.0	4.1	4.2	4.3	4.4	4.5	4.7	4.8	4.9	4.9	4.9	4.9
Boulogne	4.7	4.8	5.0	5.1	5.2	5.4	5.5	5.7	5.8	5.8	5.8	5.8
Somme Estuary	4.7	4.8	5.0	5.1	5.2	5.3	5.4	5.5	5.6	5.6	5.7	5.7
Le Tréport	4.2	4.3	4.4	4.4	4.5	4.5	4.6	4.6	4.7	4.7	4.8	4.8
Dieppe	4.1	4.2	4.2	4.3	4.3	4.4	4.4	4.5	4.5	4.5	4.4	4.4
Fécamp	3.7	3.6	3.6	3.5	3.4	3.3	3.3	3.2	3.1	3.0	3.0	2.9
Le Havre	3.7	3.6	3.5	3.4	3.4	3.3	3.3	3.2	3.1	3.0	3.0	2.9
Ouistreham	3.4	3.3	3.1	3.0	2.9	2.8	2.6	2.5	2.4	2.3	2.1	2.0
Port-en-Bessin	3.2	3.1	2.9	2.8	2.7	2.5	2.4	2.2	2.1	2.0	1.8	1.7
Saint-Vaast-la-Hougue	2.7	2.6	2.4	2.3	2.2	2.1	2.0	1.9	1.8	1.6	1.4	1.2
Barfleur	2.7	2.6	2.4	2.3	2.1	2.0	1.8	1.7	1.5	1.3	1.1	0.9

Stream Rate Conversion Table

Mean Rate Figure from Chart ▼	\multicolumn{12}{c}{Pencil-in height of HW Cherbourg Read from column below pencil mark}
	4.8	5.0	5.2	5.4	5.6	5.8	6.0	6.2	6.4	6.6	6.8
0.1	0.1	0.1	0.1	0.1	0.1	0.1	0.1	0.1	0.1	0.1	0.2
0.2	0.1	0.1	0.2	0.2	0.2	0.2	0.2	0.2	0.3	0.3	0.3
0.3	0.2	0.2	0.2	0.3	0.3	0.3	0.3	0.4	0.4	0.4	0.5
0.4	0.2	0.3	0.3	0.3	0.4	0.4	0.4	0.5	0.5	0.5	0.6
0.5	0.3	0.3	0.4	0.4	0.5	0.5	0.6	0.6	0.6	0.7	0.8
0.6	0.4	0.4	0.5	0.5	0.6	0.6	0.7	0.7	0.8	0.8	0.9
0.7	0.4	0.5	0.5	0.6	0.7	0.7	0.8	0.8	0.9	0.9	1.0	1.1
0.8	0.5	0.6	0.6	0.7	0.8	0.8	0.9	0.9	1.0	1.1	1.1	1.2
0.9	0.5	0.6	0.7	0.8	0.8	0.9	1.0	1.1	1.1	1.2	1.3	1.4
1.0	0.6	0.7	0.8	0.9	0.9	1.0	1.1	1.2	1.3	1.4	1.4	1.5
1.1	0.7	0.8	0.8	0.9	1.0	1.1	1.2	1.3	1.4	1.5	1.6	1.7
1.2	0.7	0.8	0.9	1.0	1.1	1.2	1.3	1.4	1.5	1.6	1.7	1.8
1.3	0.8	0.9	1.0	1.1	1.2	1.3	1.4	1.5	1.7	1.8	1.9	2.0
1.4	0.8	1.0	1.1	1.2	1.3	1.4	1.5	1.7	1.8	1.9	2.0	2.1
1.5	0.9	1.0	1.2	1.3	1.4	1.5	1.7	1.8	1.9	2.0	2.2	2.3
1.6	1.0	1.1	1.2	1.4	1.5	1.6	1.8	1.9	2.0	2.2	2.3	2.4
1.7	1.0	1.2	1.3	1.5	1.6	1.7	1.9	2.0	2.2	2.3	2.4	2.6
1.8	1.1	1.2	1.4	1.5	1.7	1.8	2.0	2.1	2.3	2.4	2.6	2.7
1.9	1.2	1.3	1.5	1.6	1.8	1.9	2.1	2.3	2.4	2.6	2.7	2.9
2.0	1.2	1.4	1.5	1.7	1.9	2.0	2.2	2.4	2.5	2.7	2.9	3.0
2.1	1.3	1.4	1.6	1.8	2.0	2.1	2.3	2.5	2.7	2.8	3.0	3.2
2.2	1.3	1.5	1.7	1.9	2.1	2.2	2.4	2.6	2.8	3.0	3.2	3.3
2.3	1.4	1.6	1.8	2.0	2.2	2.3	2.5	2.7	2.9	3.1	3.3	3.5
2.4	1.5	1.7	1.9	2.1	2.3	2.4	2.6	2.8	3.0	3.2	3.4	3.6
2.5	1.5	1.7	1.9	2.1	2.3	2.6	2.8	3.0	3.2	3.4	3.6	3.8
2.6	1.6	1.8	2.0	2.2	2.4	2.7	2.9	3.1	3.3	3.5	3.7	4.0
2.7	1.6	1.9	2.1	2.3	2.5	2.8	3.0	3.2	3.4	3.7	3.9	4.1
2.8	1.7	1.9	2.2	2.4	2.6	2.9	3.1	3.3	3.6	3.8	4.0	4.3
2.9	1.8	2.0	2.2	2.5	2.7	3.0	3.2	3.4	3.7	3.9	4.2	4.4
3.0	1.8	2.1	2.3	2.6	2.8	3.1	3.3	3.6	3.8	4.1	4.3	4.6
3.1	1.9	2.1	2.4	2.7	2.9	3.2	3.4	3.7	4.0	4.2	4.5	4.7
3.2	1.9	2.2	2.4	2.7	3.0	3.3	3.5	3.8	4.1	4.4	4.7	4.9
3.3	2.0	2.2	2.5	2.8	3.1	3.4	3.7	4.0	4.2	4.5	4.8	5.1
3.4	2.0	2.3	2.6	2.9	3.2	3.5	3.8	4.1	4.4	4.7	5.0	5.3
3.5	2.1	2.3	2.7	3.0	3.3	3.6	3.9	4.2	4.5	4.8	5.1	5.4
3.6	2.1	2.4	2.7	3.1	3.4	3.7	4.0	4.3	4.6	4.9	5.2	5.6
3.7	2.2	2.5	2.8	3.1	3.5	3.8	4.1	4.4	4.7	5.1	5.4	5.8
3.8	2.2	2.6	2.9	3.2	3.6	3.9	4.2	4.5	4.9	5.2	5.5	5.9
3.9	2.3	2.6	2.9	3.3	3.7	4.0	4.3	4.7	5.0	5.3	5.7	6.1
4.0	2.3	2.7	3.0	3.4	3.7	4.1	4.4	4.8	5.1	5.5	5.8	6.2

Tidal Stream Rates

6 hours before HW Cherbourg **−6**

Time (to be inserted)

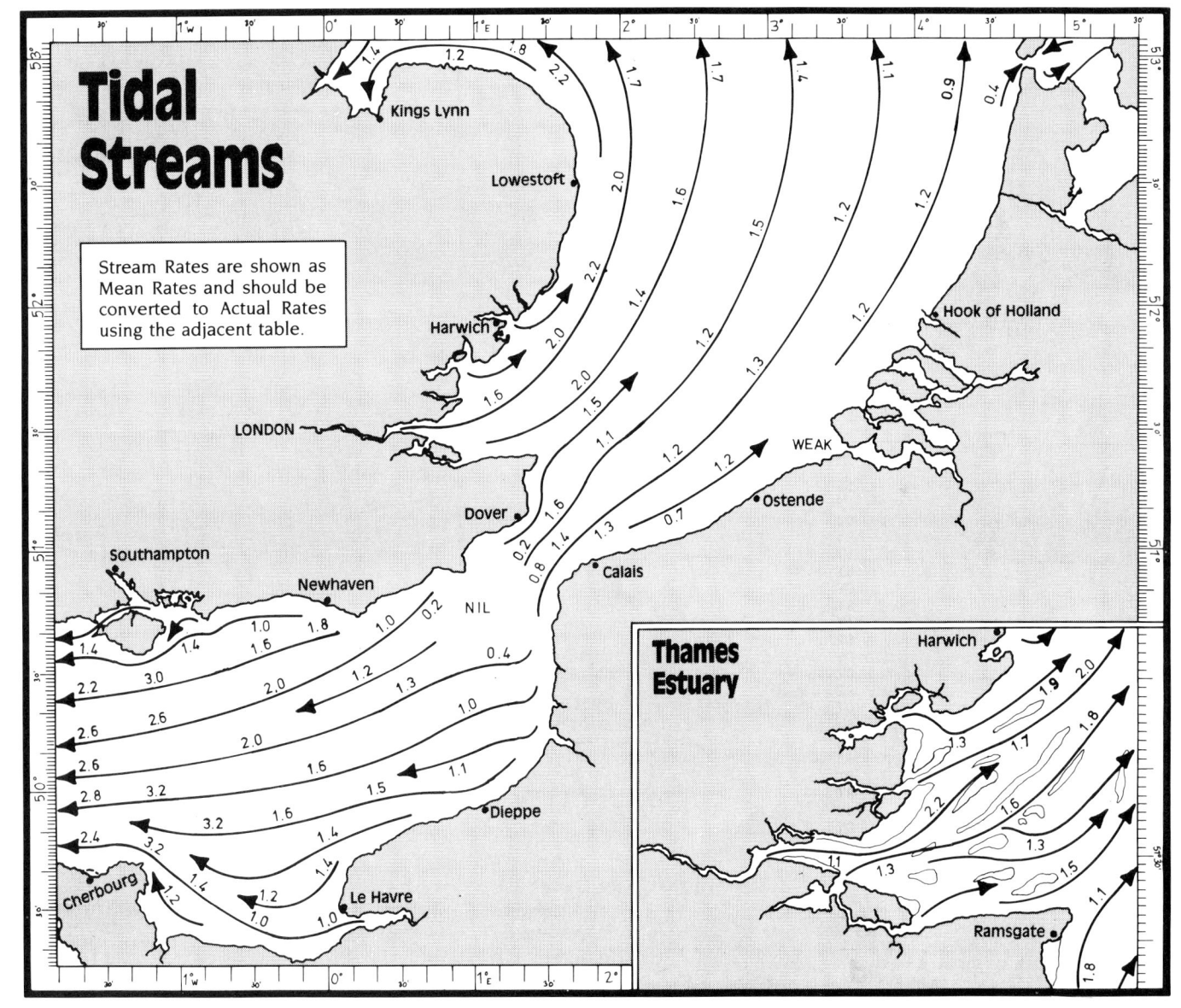

Tidal Streams

Stream Rates are shown as Mean Rates and should be converted to Actual Rates using the adjacent table.

Thames Estuary

-5
5 hours before HW Cherbourg

Tidal Heights

Copyright © J Reeve-Fowkes and Thomas Reed Publications.
No copying without permission.

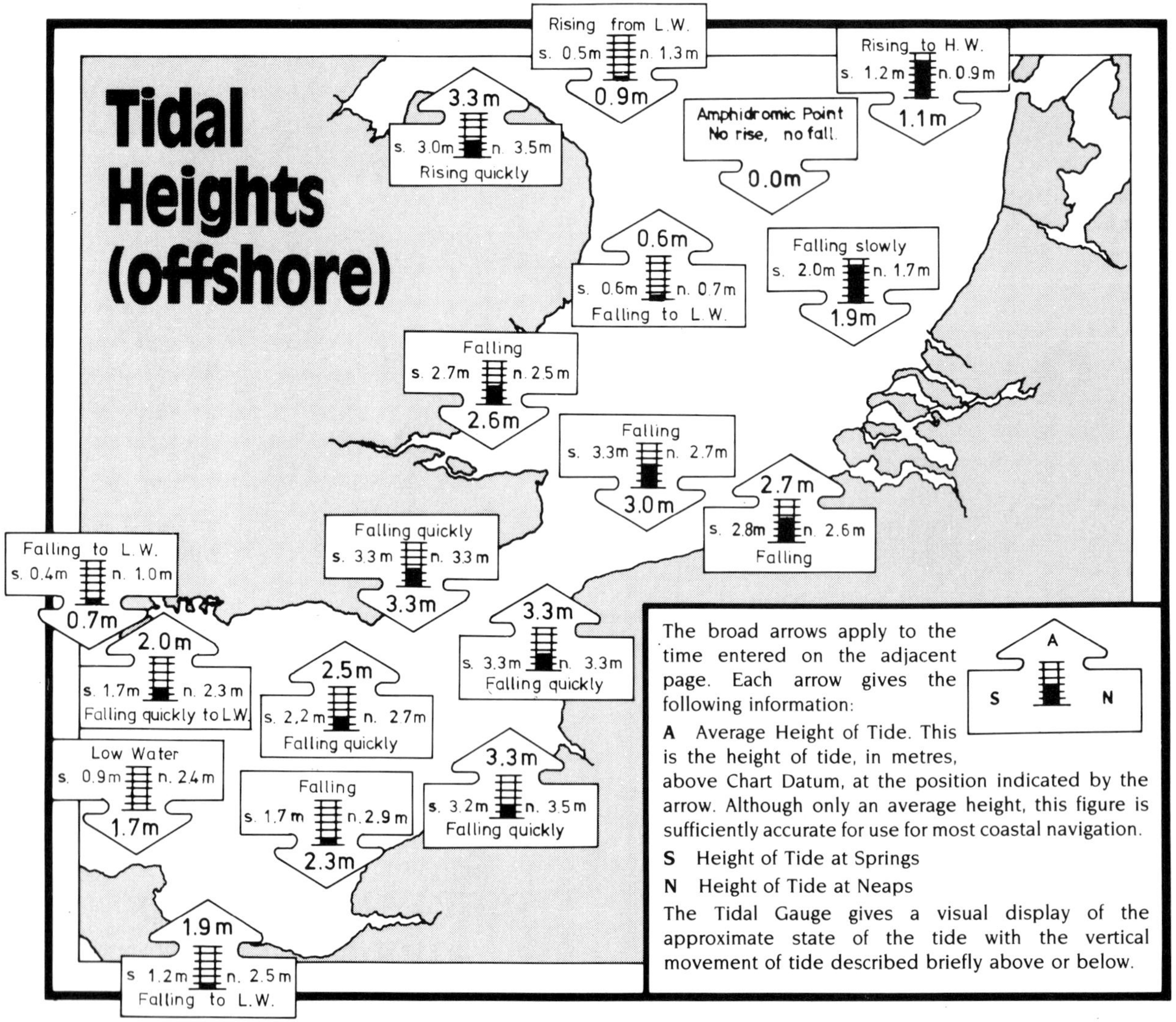

Tidal Heights (offshore)

Rising from L.W.
s. 0.5m n. 1.3m
0.9m

Rising to H.W.
s. 1.2m n. 0.9m
1.1m

3.3m
s. 3.0m n. 3.5m
Rising quickly

Amphidromic Point
No rise, no fall.
0.0m

0.6m
s. 0.6m n. 0.7m
Falling to L.W.

Falling slowly
s. 2.0m n. 1.7m
1.9m

Falling
s. 2.7m n. 2.5m
2.6m

Falling
s. 3.3m n. 2.7m
3.0m

2.7m
s. 2.8m n. 2.6m
Falling

Falling to L.W.
s. 0.4m n. 1.0m
0.7m

Falling quickly
s. 3.3m n. 3.3m
3.3m

3.3m
s. 3.3m n. 3.3m
Falling quickly

2.0m
s. 1.7m n. 2.3m
Falling quickly to L.W.

2.5m
s. 2.2m n. 2.7m
Falling quickly

3.3m
s. 3.2m n. 3.5m
Falling quickly

Low Water
s. 0.9m n. 2.4m
1.7m

Falling
s. 1.7m n. 2.9m
2.3m

1.9m
s. 1.2m n. 2.5m
Falling to L.W.

The broad arrows apply to the time entered on the adjacent page. Each arrow gives the following information:

A Average Height of Tide. This is the height of tide, in metres, above Chart Datum, at the position indicated by the arrow. Although only an average height, this figure is sufficiently accurate for use for most coastal navigation.

S Height of Tide at Springs

N Height of Tide at Neaps

The Tidal Gauge gives a visual display of the approximate state of the tide with the vertical movement of tide described briefly above or below.

TIDAL HEIGHTS — PORTS & PLACES

Pencil-in height of HW Cherbourg ▶	4.8	5.0	5.2	5.4	5.6	5.8	6.0	6.2	6.4	6.6	6.8
ENGLAND											
Kings Lynn	3.1	2.8	2.6	2.3	2.1	1.9	1.6	1.3	1.1	1.1	1.1
Blakeney Bar	3.4	3.3	3.3	3.2	3.1	3.0	2.9	2.8	2.7	2.7	2.6
Cromer	2.8	2.7	2.7	2.6	2.5	2.4	2.4	2.3	2.2	2.2	2.1
Gt. Yarmouth (Gorleston)	1.1	1.0	1.0	0.9	0.8	0.7	0.7	0.6	0.5	0.4	0.3
Lowestoft	1.1	1.0	1.0	0.9	0.8	0.7	0.7	0.6	0.5	0.4	0.3
Southwold Haven	1.1	1.0	1.0	0.9	0.8	0.7	0.7	0.6	0.5	0.4	0.4
Orford Haven appr'ch	1.3	1.2	1.2	1.1	1.1	1.0	1.0	0.9	0.9	0.9	0.9
Woodbridge Haven	1.4	1.4	1.4	1.4	1.4	1.3	1.3	1.3	1.3	1.3	1.4
Felixstowe	1.5	1.5	1.5	1.5	1.4	1.4	1.4	1.3	1.3	1.3	1.3
Harwich	1.7	1.7	1.7	1.7	1.7	1.7	1.7	1.7	1.7	1.7	1.6
Walton-on-the-Naze	1.7	1.7	1.7	1.7	1.7	1.7	1.7	1.7	1.7	1.7	1.7
Brightlingsea	1.9	2.0	2.0	2.1	2.2	2.3	2.3	2.4	2.5	2.5	2.6
Bradwell	2.1	2.2	2.2	2.3	2.4	2.5	2.6	2.7	2.8	2.8	2.8
Burnham	2.7	2.8	2.8	2.9	3.0	3.0	3.1	3.1	3.2	3.3	3.3
Leigh, Southend	2.5	2.6	2.6	2.7	2.8	2.9	2.9	3.0	3.1	3.1	3.2
London Bridge	4.0	4.3	4.5	4.8	5.0	5.3	5.5	5.8	6.0	6.2	6.5
Sheerness	2.6	2.7	2.7	2.8	2.9	3.0	3.1	3.2	3.3	3.3	3.4
Chatham	2.6	2.7	2.9	3.0	3.1	3.2	3.3	3.4	3.5	3.5	3.6
Rochester	2.7	2.8	3.0	3.1	3.2	3.3	3.5	3.6	3.7	3.8	4.0
Whitstable approach	2.7	2.8	3.0	3.1	3.2	3.3	3.4	3.5	3.6	3.6	3.6
Edinburgh Channels	2.3	2.3	2.3	2.3	2.3	2.2	2.2	2.2	2.2	2.2	2.1
Margate	2.3	2.3	2.3	2.3	2.3	2.4	2.4	2.4	2.4	2.4	2.3
Ramsgate	2.1	2.1	2.1	2.1	2.1	2.2	2.2	2.2	2.2	2.2	2.2
Dover	3.1	3.1	3.1	3.1	3.1	3.1	3.1	3.1	3.1	3.0	3.0
Folkestone	3.3	3.2	3.2	3.1	3.1	3.0	3.0	2.9	2.9	2.8	2.7
Newhaven	2.7	2.6	2.6	2.5	2.4	2.3	2.3	2.2	2.1	2.1	2.0
Brighton	2.6	2.5	2.5	2.4	2.3	2.2	2.2	2.2	2.1	2.0	1.9
Shoreham	2.7	2.6	2.6	2.5	2.4	2.4	2.3	2.3	2.2	2.2	2.1
Littlehampton Hbr	2.7	2.7	2.7	2.7	2.8	2.8	2.8	2.9	2.9	2.9	3.0
Selsey Bill	2.7	2.7	2.7	2.7	2.7	2.7	2.8	2.8	2.8	2.8	2.8
Chichester entrance	2.4	2.4	2.4	2.4	2.5	2.5	2.5	2.6	2.6	2.6	2.6
Portsmouth	2.2	2.2	2.2	2.2	2.2	2.2	2.2	2.2	2.2	2.2	2.1
Southampton	1.9	2.0	2.0	2.1	2.2	2.2	2.3	2.4	2.4	2.3	2.3
Cowes I. o W.	2.3	2.2	2.2	2.1	2.1	2.0	1.9	1.9	1.8	1.7	1.5
Yarmouth I. o W.	1.7	1.6	1.6	1.5	1.4	1.3	1.2	1.2	1.1	1.0	0.8
Lymington	1.7	1.6	1.6	1.5	1.5	1.4	1.3	1.3	1.2	1.1	1.0
HOLLAND											
Den Helder	1.4	1.4	1.4	1.4	1.3	1.3	1.3	1.2	1.2	1.2	1.2
IJmuiden	1.6	1.7	1.7	1.8	1.9	1.9	2.0	2.0	2.1	2.1	2.2
Scheveningen	1.5	1.6	1.6	1.7	1.8	1.8	1.9	1.9	2.0	2.0	2.1
Hoek van Holland	1.6	1.6	1.6	1.6	1.7	1.7	1.7	1.8	1.8	1.9	1.9
Rotterdam	1.8	1.9	1.9	2.0	2.0	2.1	2.1	2.2	2.2	2.3	2.3
Flushing	3.1	3.2	3.2	3.3	3.4	3.5	3.6	3.7	3.8	3.9	3.9
BELGIUM											
Zeebrugge	2.8	2.9	2.9	3.0	3.1	3.2	3.3	3.4	3.5	3.5	3.6
Ostende	2.8	2.9	2.9	3.0	3.0	3.1	3.1	3.2	3.2	3.2	3.2
Nieuwpoort	2.8	2.8	2.8	2.8	2.9	2.9	2.9	3.0	3.0	3.0	3.0
FRANCE											
Dunkerque	2.8	2.9	2.9	3.0	3.1	3.2	3.2	3.3	3.4	3.4	3.3
Calais	3.3	3.3	3.3	3.3	3.4	3.4	3.4	3.5	3.5	3.5	3.4
Boulogne	3.9	3.9	3.9	3.9	3.9	4.0	4.0	4.0	4.0	3.9	3.8
Somme Estuary	3.8	3.8	3.8	3.8	3.8	3.8	3.8	3.8	3.8	3.8	3.7
Le Tréport	3.5	3.4	3.4	3.3	3.3	3.2	3.2	3.1	3.1	3.1	3.0
Dieppe	3.5	3.4	3.4	3.3	3.2	3.1	3.0	2.9	2.8	2.7	2.5
Fécamp	3.2	3.1	2.9	2.7	2.6	2.4	2.2	2.1	1.9	1.8	1.5
Le Havre	3.3	3.2	3.0	2.9	2.7	2.6	2.4	2.3	2.1	1.9	1.6
Ouistreham	3.1	2.9	2.7	2.5	2.3	2.2	2.0	1.8	1.6	1.4	1.0
Port-en-Bessin	3.0	2.8	2.6	2.4	2.2	1.9	1.7	1.5	1.3	1.1	0.8
Saint-Vaast-la-Hougue	2.6	2.4	2.2	2.0	1.8	1.7	1.5	1.3	1.1	0.9	0.6
Barfleur	2.7	2.5	2.3	2.1	1.9	1.6	1.4	1.2	1.0	0.8	0.3

Tidal Stream Rates

5 hours before HW Cherbourg   **-5**

Time (to be inserted)

Stream Rate Conversion Table

Mean Rate Figure from Chart ▼	\multicolumn{12}{c}{Pencil-in height of HW Cherbourg — Read from column below pencil mark}
	4.8	5.0	5.2	5.4	5.6	5.8	6.0	6.2	6.4	6.6	6.8
0.1	0.1	0.1	0.1	0.1	0.1	0.1	0.1	0.1	0.1	0.1	0.1	0.2
0.2	0.1	0.1	0.2	0.2	0.2	0.2	0.2	0.2	0.3	0.3	0.3	0.3
0.3	0.2	0.2	0.2	0.3	0.3	0.3	0.3	0.4	0.4	0.4	0.4	0.5
0.4	0.2	0.3	0.3	0.3	0.4	0.4	0.4	0.5	0.5	0.5	0.6	0.6
0.5	0.3	0.3	0.4	0.4	0.5	0.5	0.6	0.6	0.6	0.7	0.7	0.8
0.6	0.4	0.4	0.5	0.5	0.6	0.6	0.7	0.7	0.8	0.8	0.9	0.9
0.7	0.4	0.5	0.5	0.6	0.7	0.7	0.8	0.8	0.9	0.9	1.0	1.1
0.8	0.5	0.6	0.6	0.7	0.8	0.8	0.9	0.9	1.0	1.1	1.1	1.2
0.9	0.5	0.6	0.7	0.8	0.8	0.9	1.0	1.1	1.1	1.2	1.3	1.4
1.0	0.6	0.7	0.8	0.9	0.9	1.0	1.1	1.2	1.3	1.4	1.4	1.5
1.1	0.7	0.8	0.8	0.9	1.0	1.1	1.2	1.3	1.4	1.5	1.6	1.7
1.2	0.7	0.8	0.9	1.0	1.1	1.2	1.3	1.4	1.5	1.6	1.7	1.8
1.3	0.8	0.9	1.0	1.1	1.2	1.3	1.4	1.5	1.7	1.8	1.9	2.0
1.4	0.8	1.0	1.1	1.2	1.3	1.4	1.5	1.7	1.8	1.9	2.0	2.1
1.5	0.9	1.0	1.3	1.4	1.5	1.7	1.8	1.9	2.0	2.2	2.3
1.6	1.0	1.1	1.2	1.4	1.5	1.6	1.8	1.9	2.0	2.2	2.3	2.4
1.7	1.0	1.2	1.3	1.5	1.6	1.7	1.9	2.0	2.2	2.3	2.4	2.6
1.8	1.1	1.2	1.4	1.5	1.7	1.8	2.0	2.1	2.3	2.4	2.6	2.7
1.9	1.2	1.3	1.5	1.6	1.8	1.9	2.1	2.3	2.4	2.6	2.7	2.9
2.0	1.2	1.4	1.5	1.7	1.9	2.0	2.2	2.4	2.5	2.7	2.9	3.0
2.1	1.3	1.4	1.6	1.8	2.0	2.1	2.3	2.5	2.7	2.8	3.0	3.2
2.2	1.3	1.5	1.7	1.9	2.1	2.2	2.4	2.6	2.8	3.0	3.2	3.3
2.3	1.4	1.6	1.8	2.0	2.2	2.3	2.5	2.7	2.9	3.1	3.3	3.5
2.4	1.5	1.7	1.9	2.1	2.3	2.4	2.6	2.8	3.0	3.2	3.4	3.6
2.5	1.5	1.7	1.9	2.1	2.3	2.6	2.8	3.0	3.2	3.4	3.6	3.8
2.6	1.6	1.8	2.0	2.2	2.4	2.7	2.9	3.1	3.3	3.5	3.7	4.0
2.7	1.6	1.9	2.1	2.3	2.5	2.8	3.0	3.2	3.4	3.7	3.9	4.1
2.8	1.7	1.9	2.2	2.4	2.6	2.9	3.1	3.3	3.6	3.8	4.0	4.3
2.9	1.8	2.0	2.2	2.5	2.7	3.0	3.2	3.4	3.7	3.9	4.2	4.4
3.0	1.8	2.1	2.3	2.6	2.8	3.1	3.3	3.6	3.8	4.1	4.3	4.6
3.1	1.9	2.1	2.4	2.7	2.9	3.2	3.4	3.7	4.0	4.2	4.5	4.7
3.2	1.9	2.2	2.4	2.7	3.0	3.3	3.5	3.8	4.1	4.4	4.7	4.9
3.3	2.0	2.2	2.5	2.8	3.1	3.4	3.7	4.0	4.2	4.5	4.8	5.1
3.4	2.0	2.3	2.6	2.9	3.2	3.5	3.8	4.1	4.4	4.7	5.0	5.3
3.5	2.1	2.3	2.7	3.0	3.3	3.6	3.9	4.2	4.5	4.8	5.1	5.4
3.6	2.1	2.4	2.7	3.1	3.4	3.7	4.0	4.3	4.6	4.9	5.2	5.6
3.7	2.2	2.5	2.8	3.1	3.5	3.8	4.1	4.4	4.7	5.1	5.4	5.8
3.8	2.2	2.6	2.9	3.2	3.6	3.9	4.2	4.5	4.9	5.2	5.5	5.9
3.9	2.3	2.6	2.9	3.3	3.7	4.0	4.3	4.7	5.0	5.3	5.7	6.1
4.0	2.3	2.7	3.0	3.4	3.7	4.1	4.4	4.8	5.1	5.5	5.8	6.2

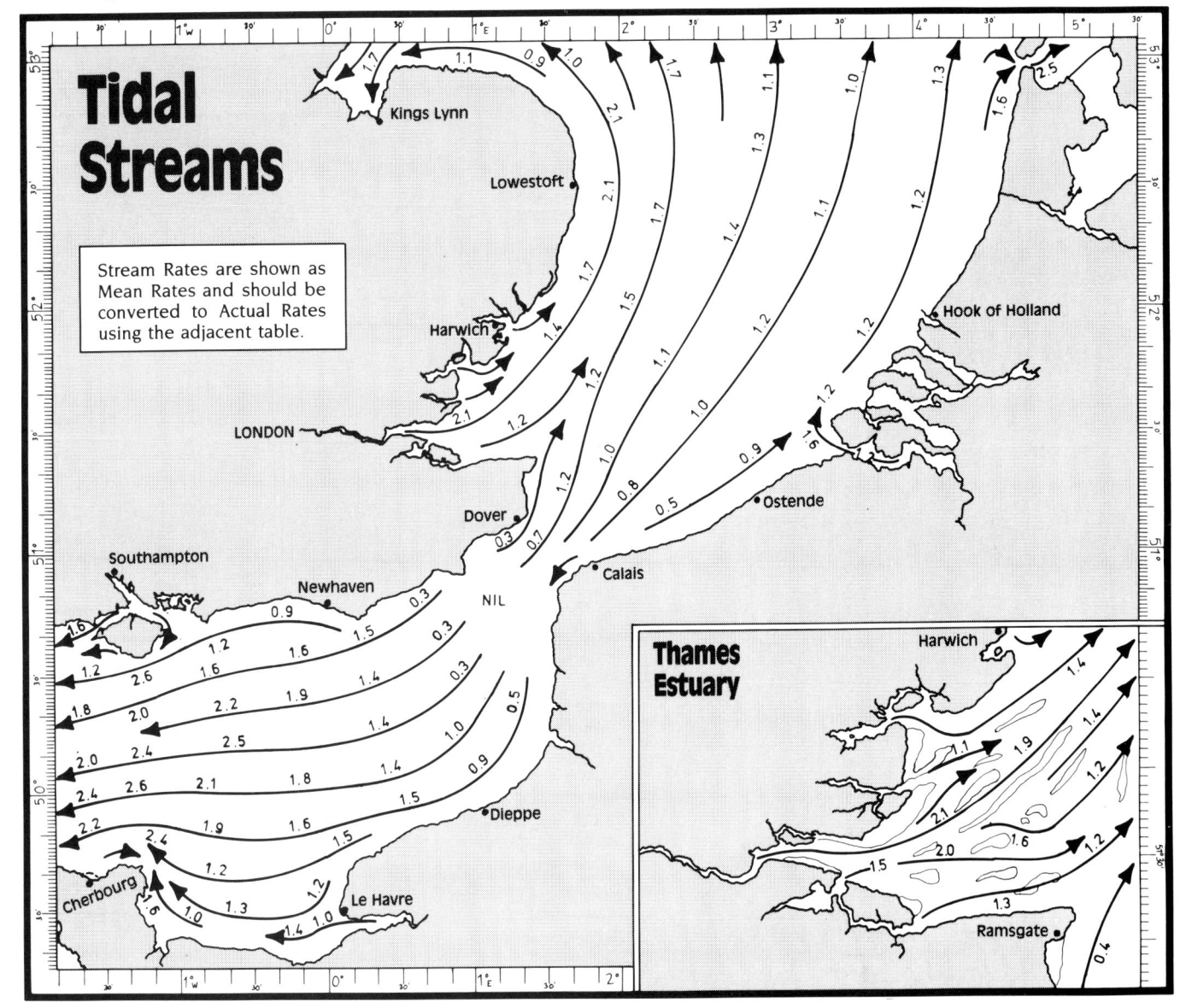

Tidal Streams

Stream Rates are shown as Mean Rates and should be converted to Actual Rates using the adjacent table.

Thames Estuary

91

-4
4 hours before HW Cherbourg

Tidal Heights

Copyright © J Reeve-Fowkes and
Thomas Reed Publications.
No copying without permission.

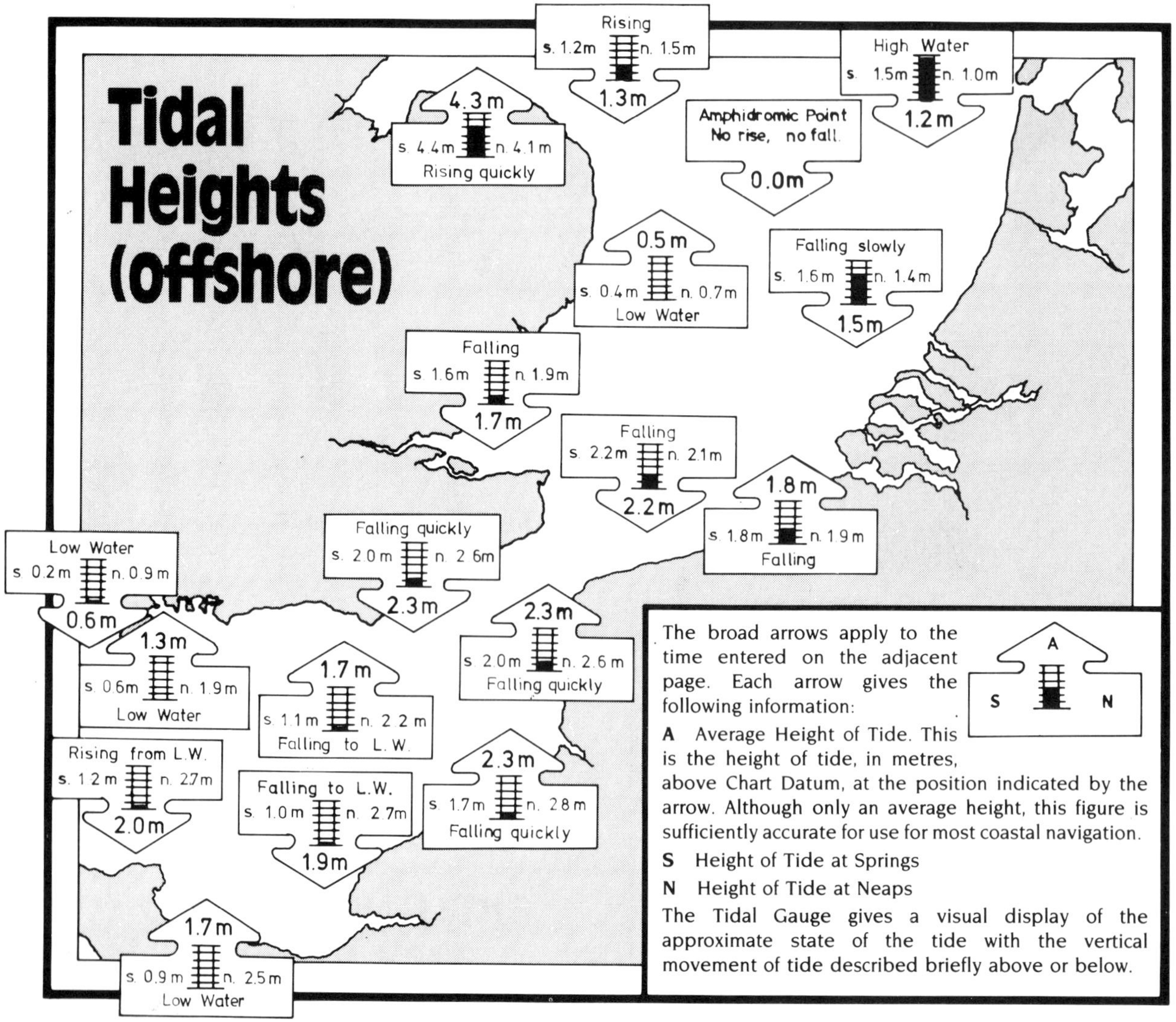

Tidal Heights (offshore)

Rising — s. 1.2m n. 1.5m → 1.3m

High Water — s. 1.5m n. 1.0m → 1.2m

Amphidromic Point — No rise, no fall. → 0.0m

4.3m — s. 4.4m n. 4.1m — Rising quickly

0.5m — s. 0.4m n. 0.7m — Low Water

Falling slowly — s. 1.6m n. 1.4m → 1.5m

Falling — s. 1.6m n. 1.9m → 1.7m

Falling — s. 2.2m n. 2.1m → 2.2m

1.8m — s. 1.8m n. 1.9m — Falling

Low Water — s. 0.2m n. 0.9m → 0.6m

Falling quickly — s. 2.0m n. 2.6m → 2.3m

2.3m — s. 2.0m n. 2.6m — Falling quickly

1.3m — s. 0.6m n. 1.9m — Low Water

1.7m — s. 1.1m n. 2.2m — Falling to L.W.

2.3m — s. 1.7m n. 2.8m — Falling quickly

Rising from L.W. — s. 1.2m n. 2.7m → 2.0m

Falling to L.W. — s. 1.0m n. 2.7m → 1.9m

1.7m — s. 0.9m n. 2.5m — Low Water

The broad arrows apply to the time entered on the adjacent page. Each arrow gives the following information:

A Average Height of Tide. This is the height of tide, in metres, above Chart Datum, at the position indicated by the arrow. Although only an average height, this figure is sufficiently accurate for use for most coastal navigation.

S Height of Tide at Springs

N Height of Tide at Neaps

The Tidal Gauge gives a visual display of the approximate state of the tide with the vertical movement of tide described briefly above or below.

TIDAL HEIGHTS — PORTS & PLACES

Pencil-in height of HW Cherbourg ▶	4.8	5.0	5.2	5.4	5.6	5.8	6.0	6.2	6.4	6.6	6.8
ENGLAND											
Kings Lynn	4.0	3.8	3.6	3.4	3.2	3.0	2.8	2.6	2.4	2.4	2.4
Blakeney Bar	3.8	3.8	3.8	3.8	3.9	3.9	3.9	4.0	4.0	4.0	4.1
Cromer	3.3	3.3	3.3	3.3	3.3	3.3	3.3	3.3	3.3	3.3	3.3
Gt. Yarmouth (Gorleston)	1.1	1.1	1.1	1.1	1.0	1.0	1.0	0.9	0.9	0.8	0.8
Lowestoft	1.2	1.1	1.1	1.0	0.9	0.8	0.8	0.7	0.6	0.5	0.4
Southwold Haven	1.0	0.9	0.9	0.8	0.7	0.6	0.6	0.5	0.4	0.3	0.2
Orford Haven appr'ch	1.1	1.0	1.0	0.9	0.8	0.7	0.7	0.6	0.5	0.5	0.4
Woodbridge Haven	1.2	1.1	1.1	1.0	1.0	0.9	0.9	0.8	0.8	0.8	0.8
Felixstowe	1.3	1.2	1.2	1.1	1.0	0.9	0.9	0.8	0.7	0.7	0.7
Harwich	1.4	1.3	1.3	1.2	1.1	1.1	1.0	1.0	0.9	0.9	0.8
Walton-on-the-Naze	1.4	1.3	1.3	1.2	1.2	1.1	1.1	1.0	1.0	1.0	0.9
Brightlingsea	1.4	1.4	1.4	1.4	1.5	1.5	1.5	1.6	1.6	1.6	1.6
Bradwell	1.6	1.6	1.6	1.6	1.7	1.7	1.7	1.8	1.8	1.7	1.7
Burnham	2.1	2.1	2.1	2.1	2.1	2.2	2.2	2.2	2.2	2.2	2.2
Leigh, Southend	1.9	1.9	1.9	1.9	1.9	1.9	1.9	1.9	1.9	1.9	1.8
London Bridge	3.2	3.4	3.6	3.8	3.9	4.1	4.3	4.4	4.6	4.7	4.7
Sheerness	2.0	2.0	2.0	2.0	2.0	2.1	2.1	2.1	2.1	2.1	2.0
Chatham	2.1	2.1	2.1	2.1	2.1	2.2	2.2	2.2	2.2	2.2	2.1
Rochester	2.0	2.1	2.1	2.2	2.2	2.3	2.3	2.4	2.4	2.4	2.4
Whitstable approach	2.2	2.2	2.2	2.2	2.3	2.3	2.3	2.4	2.4	2.3	2.3
Edinburgh Channels	1.9	1.8	1.8	1.7	1.6	1.5	1.4	1.3	1.2	1.1	1.1
Margate	1.9	1.8	1.8	1.7	1.6	1.6	1.5	1.5	1.4	1.3	1.3
Ramsgate	1.7	1.6	1.6	1.5	1.5	1.4	1.4	1.3	1.3	1.2	1.2
Dover	2.6	2.5	2.5	2.4	2.3	2.2	2.2	2.1	2.0	1.9	1.8
Folkestone	2.7	2.6	2.4	2.3	2.2	2.1	2.0	1.9	1.8	1.7	1.6
Newhaven	2.4	2.2	2.0	1.8	1.7	1.5	1.3	1.2	1.0	0.9	0.8
Brighton	2.2	2.1	1.9	1.8	1.7	1.5	1.4	1.2	1.1	1.0	0.8
Shoreham	2.3	2.2	2.0	1.9	1.7	1.6	1.4	1.3	1.1	1.0	0.9
Littlehampton Hbr	2.1	2.0	2.0	1.9	1.8	1.7	1.6	1.5	1.4	1.4	1.3
Selsey Bill	2.2	2.1	2.1	2.0	1.9	1.8	1.8	1.8	1.7	1.7	1.6
Chichester entrance	2.2	2.1	1.9	1.8	1.7	1.6	1.4	1.3	1.2	1.1	1.1
Portsmouth	2.0	1.9	1.7	1.6	1.4	1.3	1.1	1.0	0.8	0.7	0.6
Southampton	2.0	1.9	1.7	1.6	1.4	1.3	1.1	1.0	0.8	0.7	0.6
Cowes I. o W.	1.9	1.8	1.8	1.6	1.5	1.3	1.1	1.0	0.8	0.6	0.5
Yarmouth I. o W.	1.6	1.5	1.5	1.4	1.3	1.2	1.1	0.9	0.8	0.7	0.5
Lymington	1.5	1.4	1.4	1.3	1.1	1.0	0.9	0.7	0.6	0.5	0.4
HOLLAND											
Den Helder	1.5	1.5	1.5	1.5	1.5	1.6	1.6	1.6	1.6	1.6	1.6
IJmuiden	1.4	1.5	1.5	1.6	1.6	1.7	1.7	1.8	1.8	1.8	1.9
Scheveningen	1.4	1.4	1.4	1.4	1.5	1.5	1.5	1.6	1.6	1.6	1.7
Hoek van Holland	1.3	1.3	1.3	1.3	1.4	1.4	1.4	1.5	1.5	1.5	1.6
Rotterdam	1.6	1.7	1.7	1.8	1.9	2.0	2.0	2.1	2.2	2.2	2.3
Flushing	2.4	2.5	2.5	2.6	2.6	2.7	2.7	2.8	2.8	2.9	3.0
BELGIUM											
Zeebrugge	2.3	2.3	2.3	2.3	2.3	2.4	2.4	2.4	2.4	2.4	2.4
Ostende	2.1	2.1	2.1	2.1	2.1	2.1	2.1	2.1	2.1	2.1	2.1
Nieuwpoort	2.2	2.2	2.2	2.2	2.1	2.1	2.1	2.0	2.0	2.0	1.9
FRANCE											
Dunkerque	2.3	2.3	2.3	2.3	2.3	2.2	2.2	2.2	2.2	2.2	2.1
Calais	2.6	2.6	2.6	2.6	2.5	2.5	2.5	2.4	2.4	2.3	2.2
Boulogne	3.2	3.1	3.1	3.0	2.9	2.8	2.7	2.6	2.5	2.4	2.2
Somme Estuary	3.2	3.1	2.9	2.8	2.7	2.6	2.5	2.4	2.3	2.2	2.2
Le Tréport	2.9	2.8	2.6	2.5	2.3	2.2	2.0	1.9	1.7	1.7	1.6
Dieppe	3.0	2.8	2.6	2.4	2.3	2.1	1.9	1.8	1.6	1.5	1.3
Fécamp	2.9	2.7	2.5	2.3	2.0	1.8	1.6	1.3	1.1	0.9	0.8
Le Havre	3.1	2.9	2.7	2.5	2.2	2.0	1.8	1.5	1.3	1.1	0.9
Ouistreham	3.1	2.8	2.6	2.3	2.0	1.7	1.5	1.2	0.9	0.7	0.5
Port-en-Bessin	3.1	2.8	2.6	2.3	2.0	1.7	1.5	1.2	0.9	0.7	0.5
Saint-Vaast-la-Hougue	2.7	2.5	2.3	2.1	1.9	1.6	1.4	1.2	1.0	0.7	0.5
Barfleur	3.0	2.8	2.6	2.4	2.2	1.9	1.7	1.5	1.3	1.0	0.8

Stream Rate Conversion Table

Mean Rate Figure from Chart ▼	Pencil-in height of HW Cherbourg Read from column below pencil mark										
	4.8	5.0	5.2	5.4	5.6	5.8	6.0	6.2	6.4	6.6	6.8
0.1	0.1	0.1	0.1	0.1	0.1	0.1	0.1	0.1	0.1	0.1	0.2
0.2	0.1	0.1	0.2	0.2	0.2	0.2	0.2	0.2	0.3	0.3	0.3
0.3	0.2	0.2	0.2	0.3	0.3	0.3	0.3	0.4	0.4	0.4	0.5
0.4	0.2	0.3	0.3	0.3	0.4	0.4	0.4	0.5	0.5	0.5	0.6
0.5	0.3	0.3	0.4	0.4	0.5	0.5	0.6	0.6	0.6	0.7	0.8
0.6	0.4	0.4	0.5	0.5	0.6	0.6	0.7	0.7	0.8	0.8	0.9
0.7	0.4	0.5	0.5	0.6	0.7	0.7	0.8	0.8	0.9	1.0	1.1
0.8	0.5	0.6	0.6	0.7	0.8	0.8	0.9	1.0	1.1	1.1	1.2
0.9	0.5	0.6	0.7	0.8	0.8	0.9	1.0	1.1	1.2	1.3	1.4
1.0	0.6	0.7	0.8	0.9	0.9	1.0	1.1	1.2	1.3	1.4	1.5
1.1	0.7	0.8	0.8	0.9	1.0	1.1	1.2	1.3	1.4	1.5	1.7
1.2	0.7	0.8	0.9	1.0	1.1	1.2	1.3	1.4	1.5	1.6	1.8
1.3	0.8	0.9	1.0	1.1	1.2	1.3	1.4	1.5	1.7	1.8	2.0
1.4	0.8	1.0	1.1	1.2	1.3	1.4	1.5	1.7	1.8	1.9	2.1
1.5	0.9	1.0	1.2	1.3	1.4	1.5	1.7	1.8	1.9	2.0	2.3
1.6	1.0	1.1	1.2	1.4	1.5	1.6	1.8	1.9	2.0	2.2	2.3	2.4
1.7	1.0	1.2	1.3	1.5	1.6	1.7	1.9	2.0	2.2	2.3	2.4	2.6
1.8	1.1	1.2	1.4	1.5	1.7	1.8	2.0	2.1	2.3	2.4	2.6	2.7
1.9	1.2	1.3	1.5	1.6	1.8	1.9	2.1	2.3	2.4	2.6	2.7	2.9
2.0	1.2	1.4	1.5	1.7	1.9	2.0	2.2	2.4	2.5	2.7	2.9	3.0
2.1	1.3	1.4	1.6	1.8	2.0	2.1	2.3	2.5	2.7	2.8	3.0	3.2
2.2	1.3	1.5	1.7	1.9	2.1	2.2	2.4	2.6	2.8	3.0	3.2	3.3
2.3	1.4	1.6	1.8	2.0	2.2	2.3	2.5	2.7	2.9	3.1	3.3	3.5
2.4	1.5	1.7	1.9	2.1	2.3	2.4	2.6	2.8	3.0	3.2	3.4	3.6
2.5	1.5	1.7	1.9	2.1	2.3	2.6	2.8	3.0	3.2	3.4	3.6	3.8
2.6	1.6	1.8	2.0	2.2	2.4	2.7	2.9	3.1	3.3	3.5	3.7	4.0
2.7	1.6	1.9	2.1	2.3	2.5	2.8	3.0	3.2	3.4	3.7	3.9	4.1
2.8	1.7	1.9	2.2	2.4	2.6	2.9	3.1	3.3	3.6	3.8	4.0	4.3
2.9	1.8	2.0	2.2	2.5	2.7	3.0	3.2	3.4	3.7	3.9	4.2	4.4
3.0	1.8	2.1	2.3	2.6	2.8	3.1	3.3	3.6	3.8	4.1	4.3	4.6
3.1	1.9	2.1	2.4	2.7	2.9	3.2	3.4	3.7	4.0	4.2	4.5	4.7
3.2	1.9	2.2	2.4	2.7	3.0	3.3	3.5	3.8	4.1	4.4	4.7	4.9
3.3	2.0	2.2	2.5	2.8	3.1	3.4	3.7	4.0	4.2	4.5	4.8	5.1
3.4	2.0	2.3	2.6	2.9	3.2	3.5	3.8	4.1	4.4	4.7	5.0	5.3
3.5	2.1	2.3	2.7	3.0	3.3	3.6	3.9	4.2	4.5	4.8	5.1	5.4
3.6	2.1	2.4	2.7	3.1	3.4	3.7	4.0	4.3	4.6	4.9	5.2	5.6
3.7	2.2	2.5	2.8	3.1	3.5	3.8	4.1	4.4	4.7	5.1	5.4	5.8
3.8	2.2	2.6	2.9	3.2	3.6	3.9	4.2	4.5	4.9	5.2	5.5	5.9
3.9	2.3	2.6	2.9	3.3	3.7	4.0	4.3	4.7	5.0	5.3	5.7	6.1
4.0	2.3	2.7	3.0	3.4	3.7	4.1	4.4	4.8	5.1	5.5	5.8	6.2

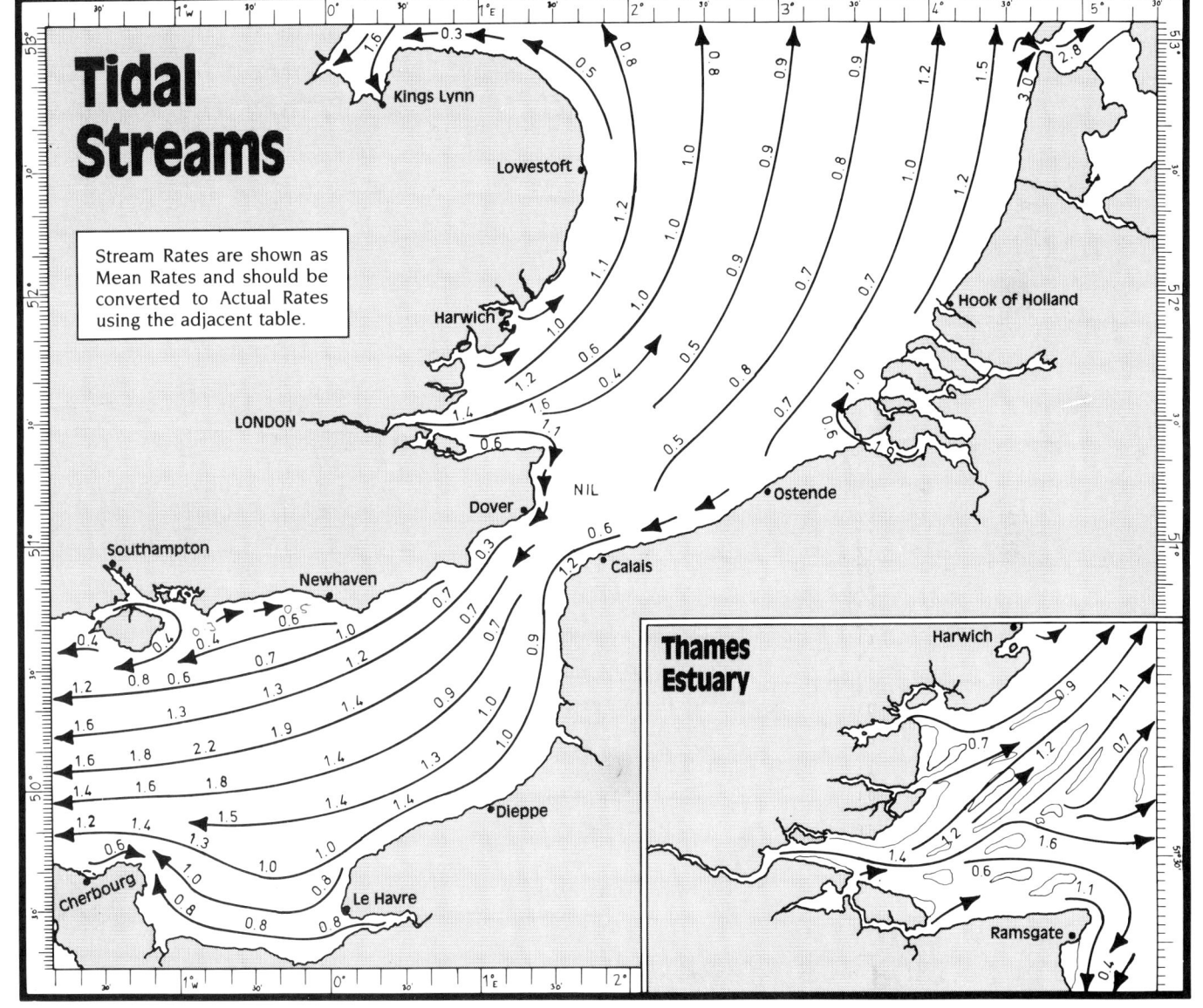

Tidal Stream Rates

4 hours before HW Cherbourg **-4**

Time 9 27 (to be inserted)

Tidal Streams

Stream Rates are shown as Mean Rates and should be converted to Actual Rates using the adjacent table.

Thames Estuary

-3 — 3 hours before HW Cherbourg

Tidal Heights

Copyright © J Reeve-Fowkes and Thomas Reed Publications.
No copying without permission.

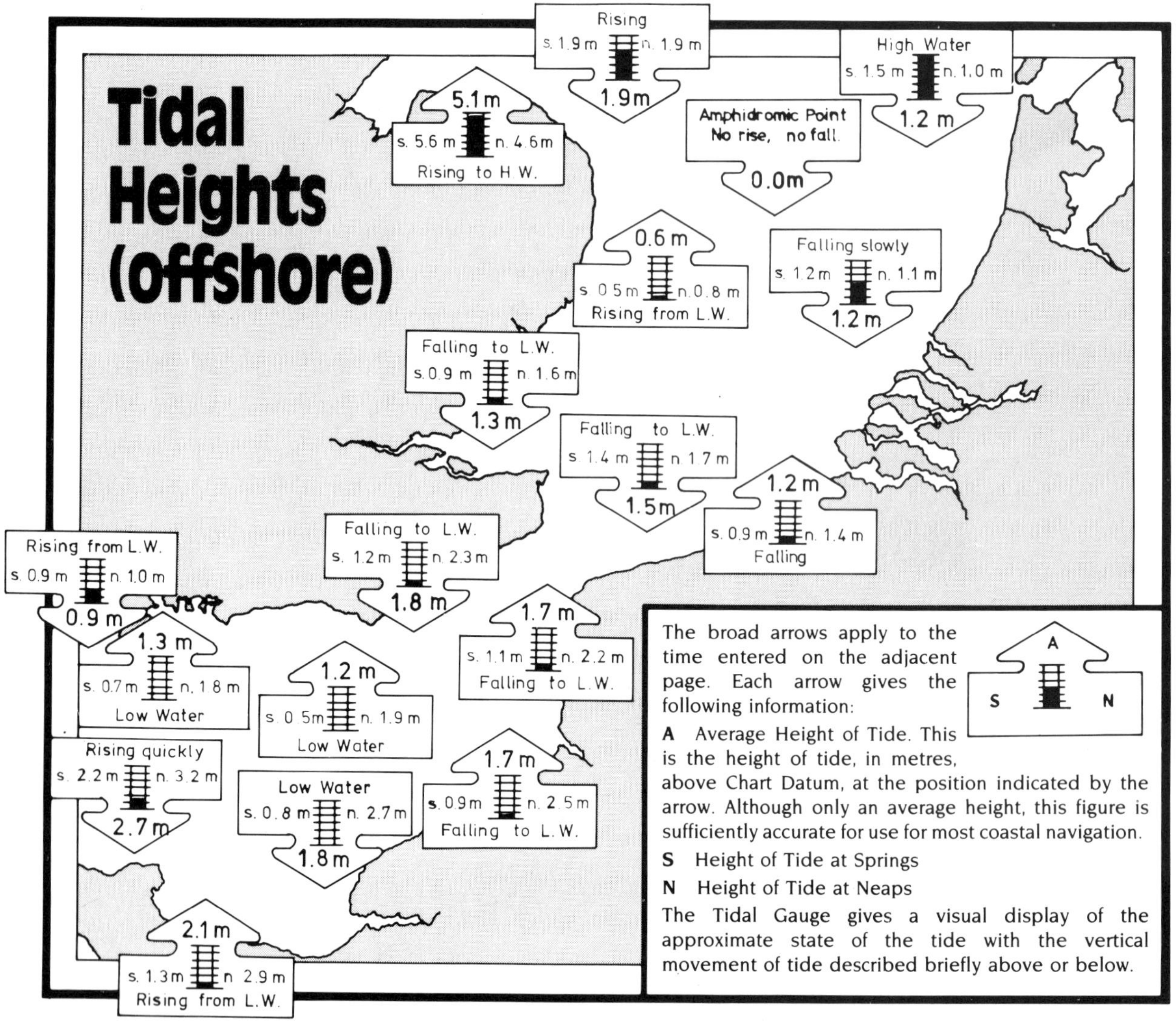

Tidal Heights (offshore)

Rising — s. 1.9 m / n. 1.9 m — **1.9 m**
5.1 m — s. 5.6 m / n. 4.6 m — Rising to H.W.
High Water — s. 1.5 m / n. 1.0 m — **1.2 m**
Amphidromic Point — No rise, no fall. — **0.0 m**
0.6 m — s. 0.5 m / n. 0.8 m — Rising from L.W.
Falling slowly — s. 1.2 m / n. 1.1 m — **1.2 m**
Falling to L.W. — s. 0.9 m / n. 1.6 m — **1.3 m**
Falling to L.W. — s. 1.4 m / n. 1.7 m — **1.5 m**
1.2 m — s. 0.9 m / n. 1.4 m — Falling
Falling to L.W. — s. 1.2 m / n. 2.3 m — **1.8 m**
1.7 m — s. 1.1 m / n. 2.2 m — Falling to L.W.
Rising from L.W. — s. 0.9 m / n. 1.0 m — **0.9 m**
1.3 m — s. 0.7 m / n. 1.8 m — Low Water
1.2 m — s. 0.5 m / n. 1.9 m — Low Water
Rising quickly — s. 2.2 m / n. 3.2 m — **2.7 m**
Low Water — s. 0.8 m / n. 2.7 m — **1.8 m**
1.7 m — s. 0.9 m / n. 2.5 m — Falling to L.W.
2.1 m — s. 1.3 m / n. 2.9 m — Rising from L.W.

The broad arrows apply to the time entered on the adjacent page. Each arrow gives the following information:

A Average Height of Tide. This is the height of tide, in metres, above Chart Datum, at the position indicated by the arrow. Although only an average height, this figure is sufficiently accurate for use for most coastal navigation.

S Height of Tide at Springs

N Height of Tide at Neaps

The Tidal Gauge gives a visual display of the approximate state of the tide with the vertical movement of tide described briefly above or below.

TIDAL HEIGHTS — PORTS & PLACES

Pencil-in height of ▶ HW Cherbourg	4.8	5.0	5.2	5.4	5.6	5.8	6.0	6.2	6.4	6.6	6.8	
ENGLAND												
Kings Lynn	4.6	4.6	4.6	4.6	4.5	4.5	4.5	4.4	4.4	4.5	4.5	4.6
Blakeney Bar	4.1	4.2	4.4	4.5	4.6	4.7	4.9	5.0	5.1	5.2	5.2	5.3
Cromer	3.7	3.8	3.8	3.9	4.0	4.1	4.2	4.3	4.4	4.4	4.5	4.5
Gt. Yarmouth (Gorleston)	1.3	1.3	1.3	1.3	1.4	1.4	1.4	1.5	1.5	1.5	1.5	1.5
Lowestoft	1.3	1.3	1.3	1.3	1.2	1.2	1.2	1.1	1.1	1.1	1.0	1.0
Southwold Haven	1.1	1.0	1.0	0.9	0.9	0.9	0.8	0.7	0.7	0.6	0.6	0.5
Orford Haven appr'ch	1.0	0.9	0.9	0.8	0.7	0.6	0.5	0.4	0.3	0.3	0.2	0.2
Woodbridge Haven	1.1	1.0	1.0	0.9	0.8	0.7	0.7	0.6	0.5	0.5	0.4	0.4
Felixstowe	1.3	1.2	1.0	0.9	0.8	0.7	0.6	0.5	0.4	0.3	0.3	0.2
Harwich	1.2	1.1	1.1	1.0	0.9	0.8	0.7	0.6	0.5	0.4	0.3	0.2
Walton-on-the-Naze	1.3	1.2	1.0	0.9	0.8	0.7	0.6	0.5	0.4	0.3	0.3	0.2
Brightlingsea	1.3	1.2	1.2	1.1	1.1	1.0	1.0	0.9	0.9	0.8	0.8	0.7
Bradwell	1.3	1.3	1.3	1.3	1.2	1.2	1.2	1.1	1.1	1.0	0.9	0.8
Burnham	1.6	1.6	1.6	1.6	1.5	1.5	1.5	1.4	1.4	1.3	1.3	1.2
Leigh, Southend	1.6	1.5	1.5	1.4	1.3	1.2	1.2	1.1	1.0	0.9	0.8	0.7
London Bridge	2.6	2.7	2.7	2.8	2.9	3.0	3.1	3.2	3.3	3.3	3.4	3.4
Sheerness	1.7	1.6	1.6	1.5	1.4	1.4	1.3	1.3	1.2	1.1	1.0	0.9
Chatham	1.7	1.6	1.6	1.5	1.4	1.4	1.3	1.3	1.1	0.9	0.7	0.5
Rochester	1.6	1.5	1.5	1.4	1.4	1.3	1.3	1.2	1.2	1.1	1.1	1.0
Whitstable approach	1.8	1.7	1.7	1.6	1.5	1.5	1.4	1.4	1.3	1.2	1.1	1.0
Edinburgh Channels	1.7	1.6	1.4	1.3	1.2	1.0	0.9	0.7	0.6	0.5	0.3	0.2
Margate	1.7	1.6	1.4	1.3	1.2	1.1	1.0	0.8	0.7	0.5	0.5	0.4
Ramsgate	1.4	1.3	1.3	1.2	1.1	1.0	0.9	0.8	0.7	0.6	0.5	0.4
Dover	2.3	2.2	2.0	1.9	1.8	1.6	1.5	1.3	1.2	1.1	0.9	0.8
Folkestone	2.4	2.2	2.0	1.8	1.7	1.5	1.3	1.2	1.0	0.8	0.6	0.4
Newhaven	2.2	2.0	1.8	1.6	1.4	1.1	0.9	0.7	0.5	0.4	0.2	0.1
Brighton	2.2	2.0	1.8	1.6	1.4	1.2	1.0	0.8	0.6	0.4	0.3	0.1
Shoreham	2.2	2.0	1.8	1.6	1.4	1.3	1.1	0.9	0.7	0.6	0.4	0.3
Littlehampton Hbr	2.0	1.8	1.6	1.4	1.2	1.1	0.9	0.7	0.5	0.4	0.4	0.3
Selsey Bill	2.1	1.9	1.7	1.5	1.3	1.2	1.0	0.8	0.6	0.5	0.4	0.3
Chichester entrance	2.1	1.9	1.7	1.5	1.4	1.2	1.0	0.9	0.7	0.6	0.5	0.4
Portsmouth	2.0	1.9	1.7	1.6	1.4	1.3	1.1	1.0	0.8	0.7	0.5	0.4
Southampton	2.3	2.1	1.9	1.7	1.5	1.3	1.1	0.9	0.7	0.6	0.5	0.4
Cowes I. o W.	1.9	1.8	1.8	1.7	1.5	1.4	1.2	1.1	0.9	0.7	0.6	0.4
Yarmouth I. o W.	1.7	1.6	1.6	1.5	1.5	1.4	1.3	1.2	1.1	1.0	0.9	0.8
Lymington	1.6	1.5	1.5	1.4	1.3	1.2	1.1	0.9	0.8	0.7	0.6	0.5
HOLLAND												
Den Helder	1.6	1.6	1.6	1.6	1.6	1.6	1.6	1.6	1.6	1.6	1.6	1.6
IJmuiden	1.2	1.3	1.3	1.4	1.4	1.5	1.5	1.6	1.6	1.6	1.6	1.6
Scheveningen	1.1	1.1	1.1	1.1	1.1	1.2	1.2	1.2	1.2	1.2	1.2	1.2
Hoek van Holland	1.0	1.0	1.0	1.0	1.0	1.0	1.0	1.0	1.0	1.0	1.0	1.0
Rotterdam	1.3	1.4	1.4	1.5	1.6	1.7	1.7	1.8	1.9	1.9	2.0	2.0
Flushing	1.9	1.9	1.9	1.9	1.9	1.8	1.8	1.8	1.8	1.8	1.9	1.9
BELGIUM												
Zeebrugge	1.9	1.8	1.8	1.7	1.7	1.6	1.6	1.5	1.5	1.4	1.4	1.3
Ostende	1.6	1.5	1.5	1.4	1.3	1.3	1.2	1.2	1.1	1.0	0.9	0.8
Nieuwpoort	1.7	1.6	1.6	1.5	1.4	1.3	1.2	1.1	1.0	0.9	0.9	0.8
FRANCE												
Dunkerque	1.9	1.8	1.8	1.7	1.6	1.6	1.5	1.5	1.4	1.3	1.2	1.1
Calais	2.3	2.2	2.0	1.9	1.8	1.7	1.6	1.5	1.4	1.3	1.2	1.1
Boulogne	3.0	2.8	2.6	2.4	2.2	2.1	1.9	1.7	1.5	1.3	1.1	0.9
Somme Estuary	3.0	2.8	2.6	2.4	2.2	2.0	1.8	1.6	1.4	1.3	1.2	1.1
Le Tréport	2.7	2.5	2.3	2.1	1.8	1.6	1.4	1.1	0.9	0.8	0.8	0.7
Dieppe	2.9	2.6	2.4	2.1	1.8	1.6	1.3	1.1	0.8	0.6	0.5	0.3
Fécamp	2.9	2.6	2.4	2.1	1.9	1.6	1.4	1.1	0.9	0.7	0.5	0.3
Le Havre	3.5	3.2	3.0	2.7	2.4	2.1	1.8	1.5	1.2	1.0	0.7	0.5
Ouistreham	3.5	3.2	2.8	2.5	2.2	1.9	1.6	1.3	1.0	0.8	0.6	0.4
Port-en-Bessin	3.5	3.2	3.0	2.7	2.4	2.2	1.9	1.7	1.4	1.2	1.1	0.9
Saint-Vaast-la-Hougue	3.1	2.9	2.7	2.5	2.3	2.2	2.0	1.8	1.6	1.4	1.2	1.0
Barfleur	3.4	3.3	3.1	3.0	2.9	2.7	2.6	2.4	2.3	2.1	2.0	1.8

Tidal Stream Rates

3 hours before HW Cherbourg **−3**

Time 10 27 (to be inserted)

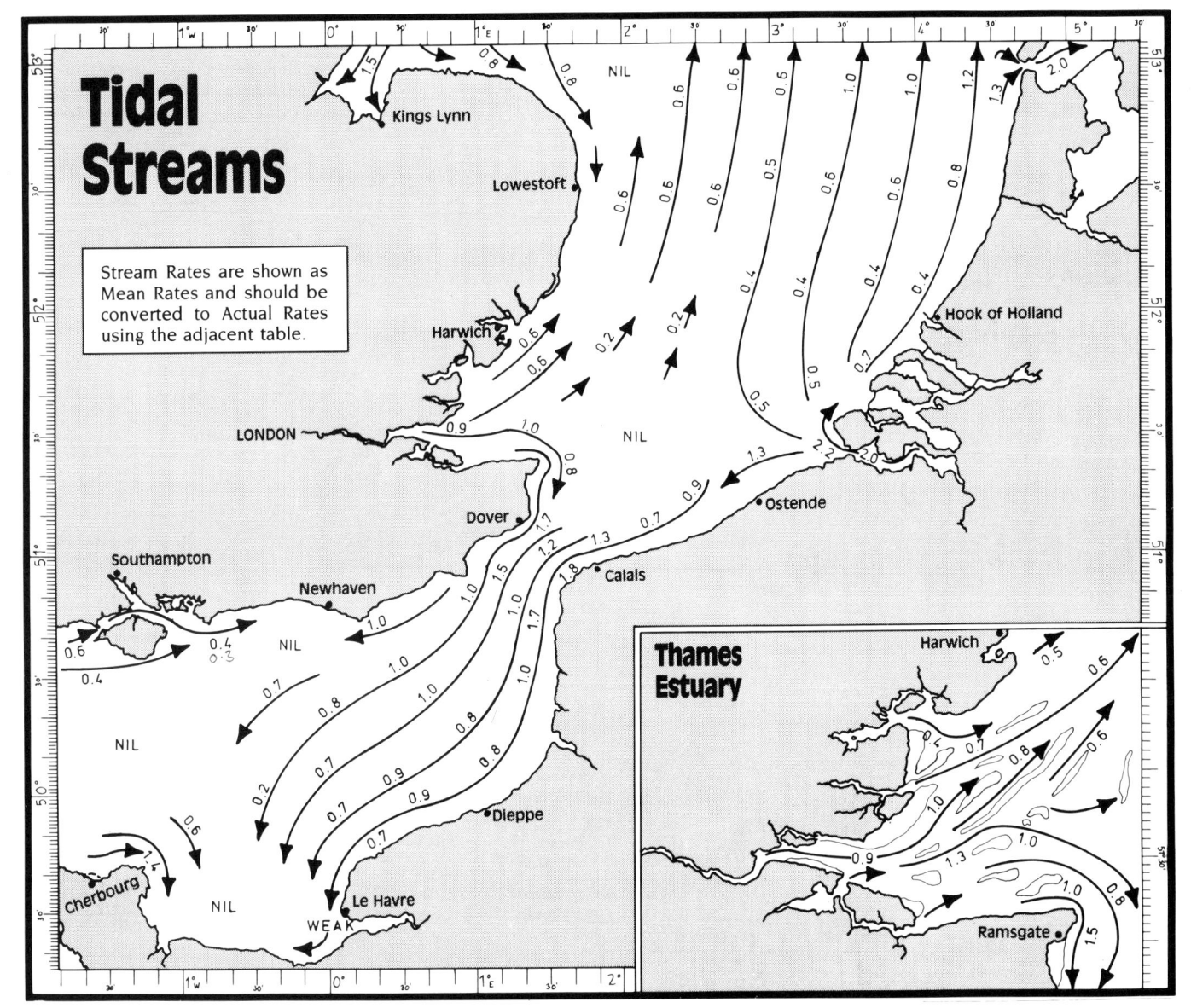

Stream Rate Conversion Table

Mean Rate Figure from Chart ▼	4.8	5.0	5.2	5.4	5.6	5.8	6.0	6.2	6.4	6.6	6.8
0.1	0.1	0.1	0.1	0.1	0.1	0.1	0.1	0.1	0.1	0.1	0.2
0.2	0.1	0.1	0.2	0.2	0.2	0.2	0.2	0.2	0.3	0.3	0.3
0.3	0.2	0.2	0.2	0.3	0.3	0.3	0.3	0.4	0.4	0.4	0.5
0.4	0.2	0.3	0.3	0.3	0.4	0.4	0.4	0.5	0.5	0.6	0.6
0.5	0.3	0.3	0.4	0.4	0.5	0.5	0.6	0.6	0.6	0.7	0.8
0.6	0.4	0.4	0.5	0.5	0.6	0.6	0.7	0.7	0.8	0.8	0.9
0.7	0.4	0.5	0.5	0.6	0.7	0.7	0.8	0.8	0.9	0.9	1.1
0.8	0.5	0.6	0.6	0.7	0.8	0.8	0.9	0.9	1.0	1.1	1.2
0.9	0.5	0.6	0.7	0.8	0.8	0.9	1.0	1.1	1.1	1.2	1.4
1.0	0.6	0.7	0.8	0.9	0.9	1.0	1.1	1.2	1.3	1.4	1.5
1.1	0.7	0.8	0.8	0.9	1.0	1.1	1.2	1.3	1.4	1.5	1.7
1.2	0.7	0.8	0.9	1.0	1.1	1.2	1.3	1.4	1.5	1.6	1.8
1.3	0.8	0.9	1.0	1.1	1.2	1.3	1.4	1.5	1.7	1.8	2.0
1.4	0.8	1.0	1.1	1.2	1.3	1.4	1.5	1.7	1.8	1.9	2.1
1.5	0.9	1.0	1.2	1.3	1.4	1.5	1.7	1.8	1.9	2.0	2.3
1.6	1.0	1.1	1.2	1.4	1.5	1.6	1.8	1.9	2.0	2.2	2.4
1.7	1.0	1.2	1.3	1.5	1.6	1.7	1.9	2.0	2.2	2.3	2.6
1.8	1.1	1.2	1.4	1.5	1.7	1.8	2.0	2.1	2.3	2.4	2.7
1.9	1.2	1.3	1.5	1.6	1.8	1.9	2.1	2.3	2.4	2.6	2.9
2.0	1.2	1.4	1.5	1.7	1.9	2.0	2.2	2.4	2.5	2.7	3.0
2.1	1.3	1.4	1.6	1.8	2.0	2.1	2.3	2.5	2.7	2.8	3.2
2.2	1.3	1.5	1.7	1.9	2.1	2.2	2.4	2.6	2.8	3.0	3.3
2.3	1.4	1.6	1.8	2.0	2.2	2.3	2.5	2.7	2.9	3.1	3.5
2.4	1.5	1.7	1.9	2.1	2.3	2.4	2.6	2.8	3.0	3.2	3.6
2.5	1.5	1.7	1.9	2.1	2.3	2.6	2.8	3.0	3.2	3.4	3.8
2.6	1.6	1.8	2.0	2.2	2.4	2.7	2.9	3.1	3.3	3.5	4.0
2.7	1.6	1.9	2.1	2.3	2.5	2.8	3.0	3.2	3.4	3.7	4.1
2.8	1.7	1.9	2.2	2.4	2.6	2.9	3.1	3.3	3.6	3.8	4.3
2.9	1.8	2.0	2.2	2.5	2.7	3.0	3.2	3.4	3.7	3.9	4.4
3.0	1.8	2.1	2.3	2.6	2.8	3.1	3.3	3.6	3.8	4.1	4.6
3.1	1.9	2.1	2.4	2.7	2.9	3.2	3.5	3.7	4.0	4.2	4.7
3.2	1.9	2.2	2.4	2.7	3.0	3.3	3.5	3.8	4.1	4.4	4.9
3.3	2.0	2.3	2.5	2.8	3.1	3.4	3.7	4.0	4.2	4.5	4.8	5.1
3.4	2.0	2.3	2.6	2.9	3.2	3.5	3.8	4.1	4.4	4.7	5.0	5.3
3.5	2.1	2.3	2.7	3.0	3.3	3.6	3.9	4.2	4.5	4.8	5.1	5.4
3.6	2.1	2.4	2.7	3.1	3.4	3.7	4.0	4.3	4.6	4.9	5.2	5.6
3.7	2.2	2.5	2.8	3.1	3.5	3.8	4.1	4.4	4.7	5.1	5.4	5.8
3.8	2.2	2.6	2.9	3.2	3.6	3.9	4.2	4.5	4.9	5.2	5.5	5.9
3.9	2.3	2.6	2.9	3.3	3.7	4.0	4.3	4.7	5.0	5.3	5.7	6.1
4.0	2.3	2.7	3.0	3.4	3.7	4.1	4.4	4.8	5.1	5.5	5.8	6.2

Pencil-in height of HW Cherbourg — Read from column below pencil mark

Tidal Streams

Stream Rates are shown as Mean Rates and should be converted to Actual Rates using the adjacent table.

-2 — 2 hours before HW Cherbourg

Tidal Heights

Copyright © J Reeve-Fowkes and Thomas Reed Publications.
No copying without permission.

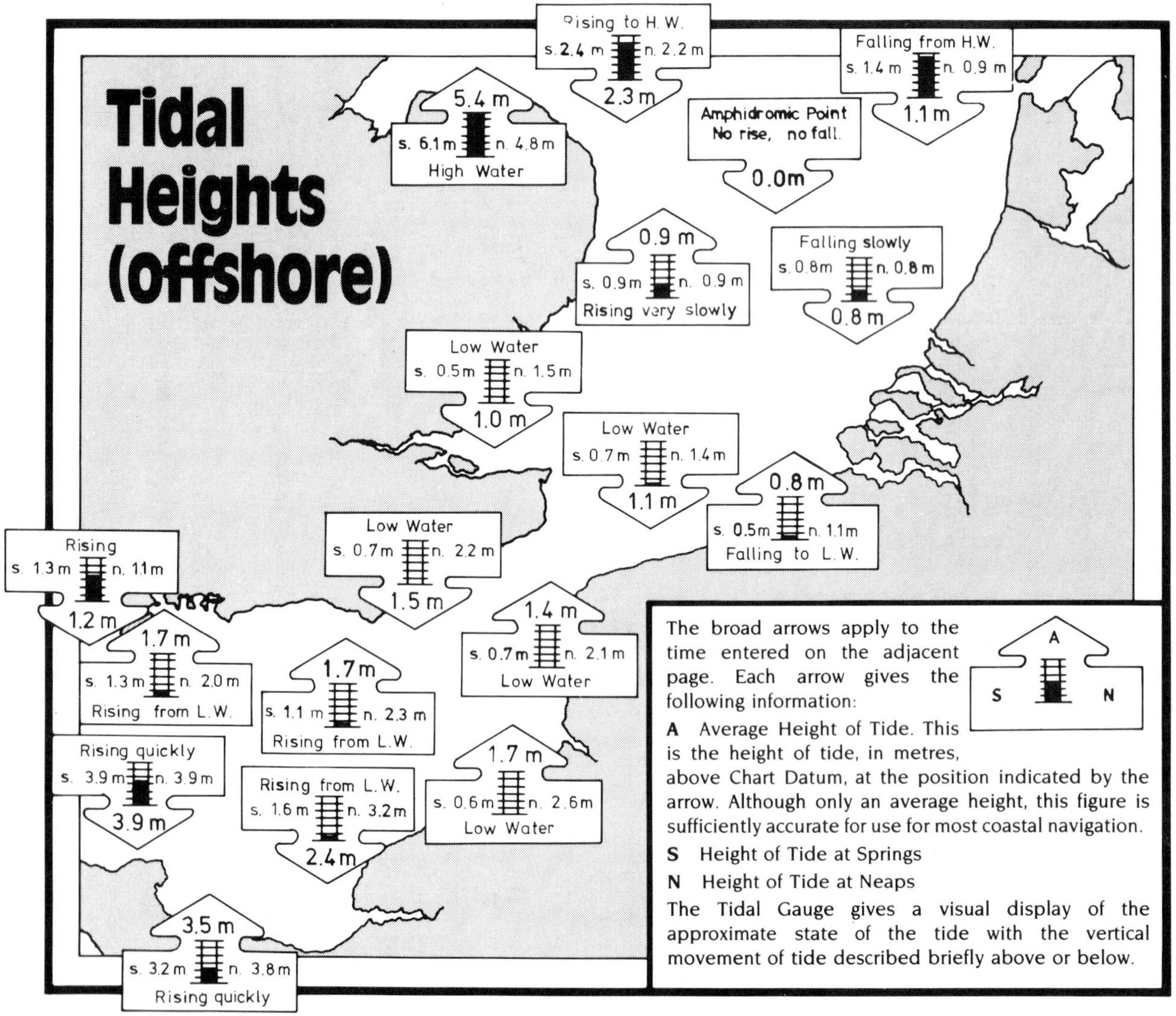

Tidal Heights (offshore)

Rising to H.W. — s. 2.4 m n. 2.2 m — 2.3 m

Falling from H.W. — s. 1.4 m n. 0.9 m — 1.1 m

High Water — 5.4 m — s. 6.1 m n. 4.8 m

Amphidromic Point No rise, no fall. — 0.0 m

0.9 m — s. 0.9 m n. 0.9 m — Rising very slowly

Falling slowly — s. 0.8 m n. 0.8 m — 0.8 m

Low Water — s. 0.5 m n. 1.5 m — 1.0 m

Low Water — s. 0.7 m n. 1.4 m — 1.1 m

0.8 m — s. 0.5 m n. 1.1 m — Falling to L.W.

Low Water — s. 0.7 m n. 2.2 m — 1.5 m

1.4 m — s. 0.7 m n. 2.1 m — Low Water

Rising — s. 1.3 m n. 11 m — 1.2 m

1.7 m — s. 1.3 m n. 2.0 m — Rising from L.W.

1.7 m — s. 1.1 m n. 2.3 m — Rising from L.W.

1.7 m — s. 0.6 m n. 2.6 m — Low Water

Rising quickly — s. 3.9 m n. 3.9 m — 3.9 m

Rising from L.W. — s. 1.6 m n. 3.2 m — 2.4 m

3.5 m — s. 3.2 m n. 3.8 m — Rising quickly

The broad arrows apply to the time entered on the adjacent page. Each arrow gives the following information:

A — Average Height of Tide. This is the height of tide, in metres, above Chart Datum, at the position indicated by the arrow. Although only an average height, this figure is sufficiently accurate for use for most coastal navigation.

S — Height of Tide at Springs

N — Height of Tide at Neaps

The Tidal Gauge gives a visual display of the approximate state of the tide with the vertical movement of tide described briefly above or below.

TIDAL HEIGHTS — PORTS & PLACES

Pencil-in height of HW Cherbourg ▶	4.8	5.0	5.2	5.4	5.6	5.8	6.0	6.2	6.4	6.6	6.8	
ENGLAND												
Kings Lynn	4.7	5.0	5.2	5.5	5.8	6.1	6.3	6.6	6.9	7.1	7.2	7.4
Blakeney Bar	4.2	4.4	4.6	4.8	4.9	5.1	5.3	5.4	5.6	5.7	5.8	5.9
Cromer	3.8	4.0	4.2	4.4	4.5	4.7	4.9	5.0	5.2	5.2	5.3	5.3
Gt. Yarmouth (Gorleston)	1.5	1.6	1.6	1.7	1.8	1.8	1.9	1.9	2.0	2.1	2.1	2.2
Lowestoft	1.4	1.5	1.5	1.6	1.6	1.7	1.7	1.8	1.8	1.8	1.8	1.8
Southwold Haven	1.3	1.3	1.3	1.3	1.3	1.4	1.4	1.4	1.4	1.4	1.4	1.4
Orford Haven appr'ch	1.2	1.1	1.1	1.0	0.9	0.8	0.8	0.7	0.6	0.6	0.6	0.6
Woodbridge Haven	1.2	1.1	1.1	1.0	0.9	0.9	0.8	0.8	0.7	0.7	0.6	0.6
Felixstowe	1.3	1.2	1.2	1.1	1.0	0.9	0.8	0.7	0.6	0.5	0.5	0.4
Harwich	1.4	1.3	1.1	1.0	0.9	0.8	0.6	0.5	0.4	0.3	0.3	0.2
Walton-on-the-Naze	1.4	1.3	1.1	1.0	0.9	0.8	0.7	0.6	0.5	0.4	0.4	0.3
Brightlingsea	1.5	1.4	1.2	1.1	1.0	0.8	0.7	0.5	0.4	0.3	0.2	0.1
Bradwell	1.6	1.5	1.3	1.2	1.1	0.9	0.8	0.6	0.5	0.4	0.2	0.1
Burnham	1.6	1.5	1.3	1.2	1.1	1.0	0.8	0.7	0.6	0.5	0.4	0.3
Leigh, Southend	1.6	1.5	1.3	1.2	1.1	1.0	0.8	0.7	0.6	0.5	0.3	0.2
London Bridge	1.9	2.0	2.0	2.1	2.1	2.2	2.2	2.3	2.3	2.2	2.2	2.1
Sheerness	1.7	1.6	1.4	1.3	1.2	1.1	0.9	0.8	0.7	0.6	0.4	0.3
Chatham	1.6	1.5	1.3	1.2	1.1	1.0	0.8	0.7	0.6	0.5	0.3	0.2
Rochester	1.5	1.4	1.2	1.1	1.0	0.9	0.8	0.7	0.6	0.5	0.3	0.2
Whitstable approach	1.7	1.6	1.4	1.3	1.2	1.1	0.9	0.8	0.7	0.6	0.4	0.3
Edinburgh Channels	1.6	1.5	1.3	1.2	1.0	0.9	0.7	0.6	0.4	0.3	0.1	0.1
Margate	1.6	1.5	1.3	1.2	1.1	0.9	0.8	0.6	0.5	0.4	0.2	0.1
Ramsgate	1.4	1.3	1.1	1.0	0.9	0.8	0.6	0.5	0.4	0.3	0.2	0.1
Dover	2.3	2.1	1.9	1.7	1.5	1.4	1.2	1.0	0.8	0.6	0.5	0.3
Folkestone	2.3	3.1	1.9	1.7	1.5	1.3	1.1	0.9	0.7	0.5	0.4	0.2
Newhaven	2.4	2.2	2.0	1.8	1.6	1.4	1.2	1.0	0.8	0.7	0.5	0.4
Brighton	2.4	2.2	2.1	1.8	1.7	1.5	1.3	1.2	1.0	0.9	0.7	0.6
Shoreham	2.4	2.2	2.0	1.9	1.7	1.5	1.3	1.2	1.0	0.9	0.8	0.7
Littlehampton Hbr	1.9	1.8	1.8	1.7	1.6	1.5	1.4	1.3	1.2	1.1	1.1	1.0
Selsey Bill	2.1	2.0	1.8	1.7	1.6	1.5	1.4	1.3	1.2	1.1	1.1	1.0
Chichester entrance	2.0	1.9	1.9	1.8	1.7	1.7	1.6	1.6	1.5	1.5	1.4	1.4
Portsmouth	2.1	2.0	2.0	1.9	1.8	1.7	1.6	1.5	1.4	1.4	1.3	1.3
Southampton	2.3	2.2	2.2	2.1	2.0	1.9	1.9	1.8	1.7	1.6	1.6	1.5
Cowes I. o W.	2.1	2.0	2.0	1.9	1.8	1.7	1.6	1.6	1.5	1.4	1.2	1.1
Yarmouth I. o W.	1.7	1.7	1.7	1.7	1.7	1.7	1.7	1.6	1.6	1.6	1.5	1.5
Lymington	1.6	1.6	1.6	1.6	1.5	1.5	1.5	1.4	1.4	1.4	1.3	1.3
HOLLAND												
Den Helder	1.6	1.6	1.6	1.6	1.6	1.7	1.7	1.7	1.7	1.7	1.8	1.8
IJmuiden	1.1	1.1	1.1	1.1	1.2	1.2	1.2	1.3	1.3	1.3	1.3	1.3
Scheveningen	0.8	0.8	0.8	0.8	0.8	0.7	0.7	0.7	0.7	0.7	0.7	0.7
Hoek van Holland	0.6	0.6	0.6	0.6	0.5	0.5	0.5	0.4	0.4	0.4	0.5	0.5
Rotterdam	1.0	1.1	1.1	1.2	1.2	1.3	1.3	1.4	1.4	1.4	1.5	1.5
Flushing	1.5	1.4	1.4	1.3	1.2	1.2	1.1	1.1	1.0	1.0	0.9	0.9
BELGIUM												
Zeebrugge	1.4	1.3	1.3	1.2	1.1	1.0	0.9	0.8	0.7	0.6	0.6	0.5
Ostende	1.3	1.2	1.0	0.9	0.8	0.7	0.6	0.5	0.4	0.3	0.3	0.2
Nieuwpoort	1.4	1.3	1.1	1.0	0.9	0.7	0.6	0.4	0.3	0.2	0.1	0.0
FRANCE												
Dunkerque	1.7	1.6	1.4	1.3	1.2	1.1	1.0	0.9	0.8	0.7	0.6	0.5
Calais	2.0	1.9	1.7	1.6	1.4	1.3	1.1	1.0	0.8	0.7	0.5	0.4
Boulogne	3.0	2.7	2.5	2.2	1.9	1.7	1.4	1.2	0.9	0.7	0.5	0.3
Somme Estuary	3.4	3.1	2.9	2.6	2.3	2.0	1.7	1.4	1.1	1.0	0.9	0.8
Le Tréport	3.2	2.9	2.5	2.2	1.9	1.6	1.3	1.0	0.7	0.6	0.6	0.5
Dieppe	3.3	3.0	2.6	2.3	2.0	1.7	1.4	1.1	0.8	0.6	0.5	0.3
Fécamp	3.3	3.1	2.9	2.7	2.5	2.3	2.1	1.9	1.7	1.5	1.4	1.2
Le Havre	4.1	3.9	3.7	3.5	3.3	3.1	2.9	2.7	2.5	2.3	2.2	2.0
Ouistreham	4.1	4.0	3.8	3.7	3.6	3.5	3.3	3.2	3.1	3.0	2.9	2.8
Port-en-Bessin	4.1	4.1	4.1	4.1	4.1	4.1	4.1	4.1	4.1	4.0	4.0	3.9
Saint-Vaast-la-Hougue	3.8	3.7	3.7	3.6	3.6	3.5	3.5	3.4	3.4	3.3	3.3	3.2
Barfleur	3.9	3.9	3.9	3.9	3.9	3.9	3.9	3.9	3.9	3.9	3.9	3.9

Stream Rate Conversion Table

Mean Rate Figure from Chart	\multicolumn{12}{c}{Pencil-in height of HW Cherbourg Read from column below pencil mark}
▼	4.8	5.0	5.2	5.4	5.6	5.8	6.0	6.2	6.4	6.6	6.8
0.1	0.1	0.1	0.1	0.1	0.1	0.1	0.1	0.1	0.1	0.1	0.1	0.2
0.2	0.1	0.1	0.2	0.2	0.2	0.2	0.2	0.2	0.3	0.3	0.3	0.3
0.3	0.2	0.2	0.2	0.3	0.3	0.3	0.3	0.4	0.4	0.4	0.4	0.5
0.4	0.2	0.3	0.3	0.3	0.4	0.4	0.4	0.5	0.5	0.5	0.6	0.6
0.5	0.3	0.3	0.4	0.4	0.5	0.5	0.6	0.6	0.6	0.7	0.7	0.8
0.6	0.4	0.4	0.5	0.5	0.6	0.6	0.7	0.7	0.8	0.8	0.9	0.9
0.7	0.4	0.5	0.5	0.6	0.7	0.7	0.8	0.8	0.9	0.9	1.0	1.1
0.8	0.5	0.6	0.6	0.7	0.8	0.8	0.9	0.9	1.0	1.1	1.1	1.2
0.9	0.5	0.6	0.7	0.8	0.8	0.9	1.0	1.1	1.1	1.2	1.3	1.4
1.0	0.6	0.7	0.8	0.9	0.9	1.0	1.1	1.2	1.3	1.4	1.4	1.5
1.1	0.7	0.8	0.8	0.9	1.0	1.1	1.2	1.3	1.4	1.5	1.6	1.7
1.2	0.7	0.8	0.9	1.0	1.1	1.2	1.3	1.4	1.5	1.6	1.7	1.8
1.3	0.8	0.9	1.0	1.1	1.2	1.3	1.4	1.5	1.7	1.8	1.9	2.0
1.4	0.8	1.0	1.1	1.2	1.3	1.4	1.5	1.7	1.8	1.9	2.0	2.1
1.5	0.9	1.0	1.2	1.3	1.4	1.5	1.7	1.8	1.9	2.0	2.2	2.3
1.6	1.0	1.1	1.2	1.4	1.5	1.6	1.8	1.9	2.0	2.2	2.3	2.4
1.7	1.0	1.2	1.3	1.5	1.6	1.7	1.9	2.0	2.2	2.3	2.4	2.6
1.8	1.1	1.2	1.4	1.5	1.7	1.8	2.0	2.1	2.3	2.4	2.6	2.7
1.9	1.2	1.3	1.5	1.6	1.8	1.9	2.1	2.3	2.4	2.6	2.7	2.9
2.0	1.2	1.4	1.5	1.7	1.9	2.0	2.2	2.4	2.5	2.7	2.9	3.0
2.1	1.3	1.4	1.6	1.8	2.0	2.1	2.3	2.5	2.7	2.8	3.0	3.2
2.2	1.3	1.5	1.7	1.9	2.1	2.2	2.4	2.6	2.8	3.0	3.2	3.3
2.3	1.4	1.6	1.8	2.0	2.2	2.3	2.5	2.7	2.9	3.1	3.3	3.5
2.4	1.5	1.7	1.9	2.1	2.3	2.4	2.6	2.8	3.0	3.2	3.4	3.6
2.5	1.5	1.7	1.9	2.1	2.3	2.6	2.8	3.0	3.2	3.4	3.6	3.8
2.6	1.6	1.8	2.0	2.2	2.4	2.7	2.9	3.1	3.3	3.5	3.7	4.0
2.7	1.6	1.9	2.1	2.3	2.5	2.8	3.0	3.2	3.4	3.7	3.9	4.1
2.8	1.7	1.9	2.2	2.4	2.6	2.9	3.1	3.3	3.6	3.8	4.0	4.3
2.9	1.8	2.0	2.2	2.5	2.7	3.0	3.2	3.4	3.7	3.9	4.2	4.4
3.0	1.8	2.1	2.3	2.6	2.8	3.1	3.3	3.6	3.8	4.1	4.3	4.6
3.1	1.9	2.1	2.4	2.7	2.9	3.2	3.4	3.7	4.0	4.2	4.5	4.7
3.2	1.9	2.2	2.4	2.7	3.0	3.3	3.5	3.8	4.1	4.4	4.7	4.9
3.3	2.0	2.2	2.5	2.8	3.1	3.4	3.7	4.0	4.2	4.5	4.8	5.1
3.4	2.0	2.3	2.6	2.9	3.2	3.5	3.8	4.1	4.4	4.7	5.0	5.3
3.5	2.1	2.3	2.7	3.0	3.3	3.6	3.9	4.2	4.5	4.8	5.1	5.4
3.6	2.1	2.4	2.7	3.1	3.4	3.7	4.0	4.3	4.6	4.9	5.2	5.6
3.7	2.2	2.5	2.8	3.1	3.5	3.8	4.1	4.4	4.7	5.1	5.4	5.8
3.8	2.2	2.6	2.9	3.2	3.6	3.9	4.2	4.5	4.9	5.2	5.5	5.9
3.9	2.3	2.6	2.9	3.3	3.7	4.0	4.3	4.7	5.0	5.3	5.7	6.1
4.0	2.3	2.7	3.0	3.4	3.7	4.1	4.4	4.8	5.1	5.5	5.8	6.2

Tidal Stream Rates

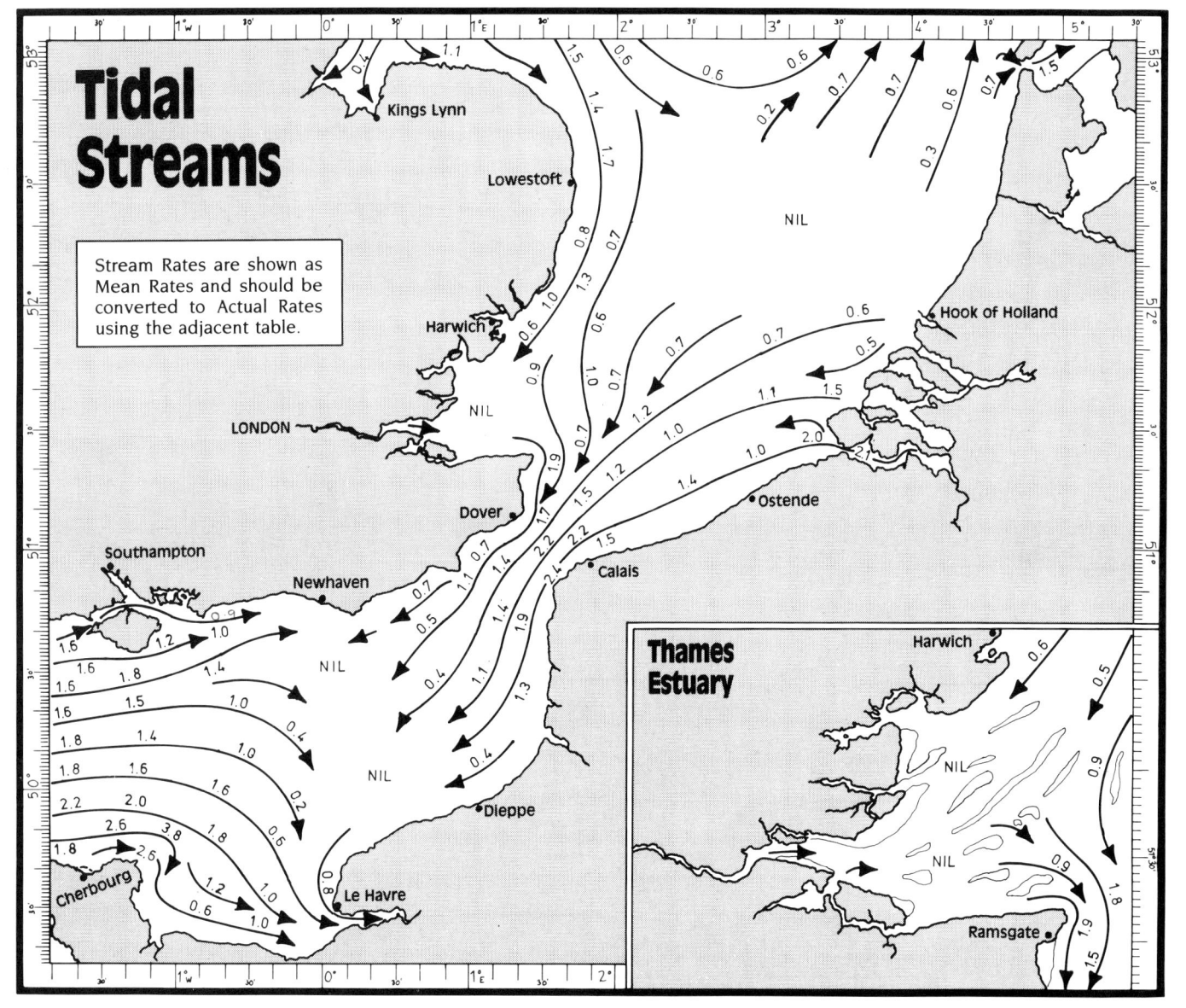

2 hours before HW Cherbourg **-2**

Time (to be inserted) 11 27

Tidal Streams

Stream Rates are shown as Mean Rates and should be converted to Actual Rates using the adjacent table.

Thames Estuary

97

-1 1 hour before HW Cherbourg

Tidal Heights

Copyright © J Reeve-Fowkes and Thomas Reed Publications.
No copying without permission.

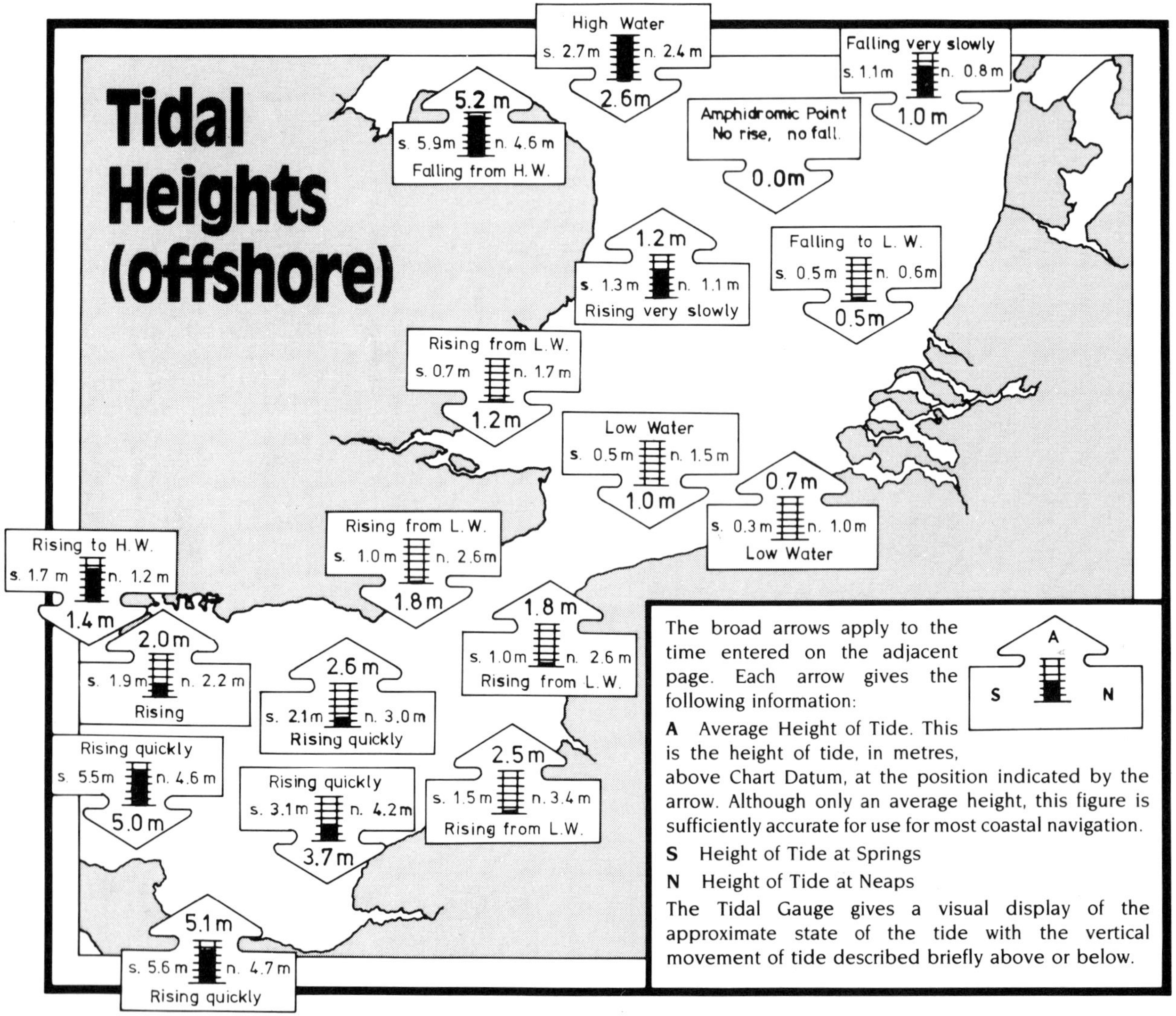

Tidal Heights (offshore)

High Water
s. 2.7m n. 2.4m
2.6m

Falling very slowly
s. 1.1m n. 0.8m
1.0m

5.2 m
s. 5.9m n. 4.6m
Falling from H.W.

Amphidromic Point
No rise, no fall.
0.0m

1.2 m
s. 1.3m n. 1.1m
Rising very slowly

Falling to L.W.
s. 0.5m n. 0.6m
0.5m

Rising from L.W.
s. 0.7m n. 1.7m
1.2m

Low Water
s. 0.5m n. 1.5m
1.0m

0.7m
s. 0.3m n. 1.0m
Low Water

Rising from L.W.
s. 1.0m n. 2.6m
1.8m

Rising to H.W.
s. 1.7m n. 1.2m
1.4m

2.0m
s. 1.9m n. 2.2m
Rising

1.8m
s. 1.0m n. 2.6m
Rising from L.W.

2.6 m
s. 2.1m n. 3.0m
Rising quickly

Rising quickly
s. 5.5m n. 4.6m
5.0m

Rising quickly
s. 3.1m n. 4.2m
Rising from L.W.

2.5 m
s. 1.5m n. 3.4m
Rising from L.W.

3.7m

5.1 m
s. 5.6m n. 4.7m
Rising quickly

The broad arrows apply to the time entered on the adjacent page. Each arrow gives the following information:

A Average Height of Tide. This is the height of tide, in metres, above Chart Datum, at the position indicated by the arrow. Although only an average height, this figure is sufficiently accurate for use for most coastal navigation.

S Height of Tide at Springs
N Height of Tide at Neaps

The Tidal Gauge gives a visual display of the approximate state of the tide with the vertical movement of tide described briefly above or below.

| A |
| S   N |

TIDAL HEIGHTS — PORTS & PLACES

Pencil-in height of HW Cherbourg ▶	4.8	5.0	5.2	5.4	5.6	5.8	6.0	6.2	6.4	6.6	6.8
ENGLAND											
Kings Lynn	4.6	4.9	5.1	5.4	5.7	6.0	6.2	6.5	6.8	7.0	7.1	7.3
Blakeney Bar	4.1	4.3	4.5	4.7	4.9	5.0	5.2	5.4	5.6	5.7	5.7	5.8
Cromer	3.9	4.1	4.3	4.5	4.6	4.8	5.0	5.1	5.3	5.3	5.4	5.4
Gt. Yarmouth (Gorleston)	1.6	1.7	1.7	1.8	1.9	2.0	2.0	2.1	2.2	2.3	2.3	2.4
Lowestoft	1.6	1.7	1.7	1.8	1.8	1.9	1.9	2.0	2.0	2.0	2.1	2.1
Southwold Haven	1.4	1.5	1.5	1.6	1.7	1.7	1.8	1.8	1.9	1.9	2.0	2.0
Orford Haven appr'ch	1.4	1.3	1.3	1.2	1.1	1.1	1.0	1.0	0.9	0.9	0.9	0.9
Woodbridge Haven	1.5	1.4	1.3	1.3	1.3	1.2	1.2	1.1	1.1	1.1	1.1	1.1
Felixstowe	1.6	1.5	1.5	1.4	1.3	1.2	1.2	1.1	1.0	1.0	1.0	1.0
Harwich	1.8	1.7	1.5	1.4	1.3	1.2	1.1	1.0	0.9	0.9	0.8	0.8
Walton-on-the-Naze	1.6	1.5	1.5	1.4	1.3	1.2	1.2	1.1	1.0	1.0	0.9	0.9
Brightlingsea	1.8	1.7	1.5	1.4	1.2	1.1	0.9	0.8	0.6	0.5	0.4	0.3
Bradwell	2.0	1.8	1.6	1.4	1.3	1.1	0.9	0.8	0.6	0.5	0.4	0.3
Burnham	1.7	1.6	1.4	1.3	1.1	1.0	0.8	0.7	0.5	0.4	0.2	0.1
Leigh, Southend	1.8	1.7	1.5	1.4	1.2	1.1	0.9	0.8	0.6	0.5	0.3	0.2
London Bridge	1.6	1.6	1.6	1.6	1.5	1.5	1.5	1.4	1.4	1.3	1.1	1.0
Sheerness	1.9	1.8	1.6	1.5	1.3	1.2	1.0	0.9	0.7	0.6	0.4	0.3
Chatham	1.7	1.6	1.4	1.3	1.2	1.1	0.9	0.8	0.7	0.4	0.2	-0.1
Rochester	1.5	1.4	1.2	1.1	0.9	0.8	0.6	0.5	0.3	0.2	0.0	-0.1
Whitstable approach	1.7	1.6	1.4	1.3	1.1	1.0	0.8	0.7	0.5	0.4	0.2	0.1
Edinburgh Channels	1.8	1.7	1.5	1.4	1.3	1.1	1.0	0.8	0.7	0.6	0.4	0.3
Margate	1.8	1.7	1.5	1.4	1.3	1.1	1.0	0.8	0.7	0.6	0.4	0.4
Ramsgate	1.6	1.5	1.3	1.2	1.1	1.0	0.8	0.7	0.6	0.5	0.4	0.3
Dover	2.5	2.3	2.1	1.9	1.7	1.6	1.4	1.2	1.0	0.8	0.7	0.5
Folkestone	2.6	2.4	2.2	2.0	1.8	1.7	1.5	1.3	1.1	1.0	0.8	0.7
Newhaven	2.8	2.7	2.5	2.4	2.3	2.1	2.0	1.8	1.7	1.6	1.6	1.5
Brighton	2.8	2.7	2.5	2.4	2.3	2.2	2.0	1.9	1.8	1.7	1.7	1.6
Shoreham	2.7	2.6	2.4	2.3	2.2	2.1	1.9	1.8	1.7	1.6	1.6	1.5
Littlehampton Hbr.	2.1	2.1	2.1	2.1	2.1	2.1	2.0	2.0	2.0	2.0	1.9	1.9
Selsey Bill	2.1	2.1	2.1	2.1	2.1	2.1	2.0	2.0	2.0	1.9	1.9	1.8
Chichester entrance	2.1	2.1	2.1	2.1	2.1	2.1	2.0	2.0	2.0	2.0	1.9	1.9
Portsmouth	2.1	2.1	2.1	2.1	2.0	2.0	2.0	1.9	1.9	1.9	1.8	1.8
Southampton	2.3	2.3	2.3	2.3	2.2	2.2	2.2	2.1	2.1	2.1	2.0	2.0
Cowes I. o W.	2.1	2.1	2.1	2.1	2.0	2.0	2.0	2.0	2.0	1.9	1.8	1.7
Yarmouth I. o W.	1.8	1.8	1.8	1.8	1.9	1.9	1.9	1.8	1.8	1.8	1.8	1.8
Lymington	1.7	1.7	1.7	1.7	1.7	1.7	1.7	1.8	1.8	1.8	1.8	1.8
HOLLAND											
Den Helder	1.4	1.5	1.5	1.6	1.6	1.7	1.7	1.8	1.8	1.8	1.9	1.9
IJmuiden	1.0	1.0	1.0	1.0	1.1	1.1	1.1	1.2	1.2	1.2	1.2	1.2
Scheveningen	0.7	0.7	0.7	0.7	0.7	0.6	0.6	0.6	0.6	0.6	0.5	0.5
Hoek van Holland	0.4	0.4	0.4	0.4	0.3	0.3	0.3	0.2	0.2	0.2	0.2	0.2
Rotterdam	0.7	0.7	0.7	0.7	0.8	0.8	0.8	0.9	0.9	0.9	1.0	1.0
Flushing	1.1	1.0	1.0	0.9	0.8	0.7	0.7	0.6	0.5	0.4	0.4	0.3
BELGIUM											
Zeebrugge	1.4	1.3	1.1	1.0	0.9	0.8	0.6	0.5	0.4	0.3	0.2	0.1
Ostende	1.2	1.1	0.9	0.8	0.7	0.6	0.4	0.3	0.2	0.1	0.1	0.0
Nieuwpoort	1.2	1.1	0.9	0.8	0.7	0.6	0.4	0.3	0.2	0.1	-0.1	-0.2
FRANCE											
Dunkerque	1.7	1.6	1.4	1.3	1.2	1.1	0.9	0.8	0.7	0.6	0.4	0.3
Calais	2.3	2.1	1.9	1.7	1.5	1.4	1.2	1.0	0.8	0.7	0.5	0.4
Boulogne	3.6	3.3	2.9	2.6	2.3	2.0	1.7	1.4	1.1	0.9	0.7	0.5
Somme Estuary	4.4	4.1	3.9	3.6	3.3	3.0	2.7	2.4	2.1	2.0	2.0	1.9
Le Tréport	4.1	3.8	3.6	3.3	3.0	2.8	2.5	2.3	2.0	2.0	1.9	1.9
Dieppe	4.1	3.9	3.7	3.5	3.2	3.0	2.8	2.5	2.4	2.2	2.1	2.0
Fécamp	4.1	4.0	4.0	3.9	3.8	3.7	3.7	3.6	3.5	3.4	3.4	3.3
Le Havre	5.1	5.0	5.1	5.1	5.2	5.2	5.2	5.3	5.3	5.3	5.3	5.3
Ouistreham	4.8	5.0	5.2	5.4	5.5	5.7	5.9	6.0	6.2	6.3	6.3	6.4
Port-en-Bessin	4.8	5.0	5.2	5.4	5.6	5.8	6.0	6.2	6.4	6.5	6.6	6.7
Saint-Vaast-la-Hougue	4.3	4.4	4.6	4.7	4.8	4.9	5.0	5.1	5.2	5.3	5.3	5.4
Barfleur	4.4	4.5	4.7	4.8	4.9	5.0	5.2	5.3	5.4	5.5	5.6	5.7

Stream Rate Conversion Table

Mean Rate Figure from Chart ▼	Pencil-in height of HW Cherbourg Read from column below pencil mark										
	4.8	5.0	5.2	5.4	5.6	5.8	6.0	6.2	6.4	6.6	6.8
0.1	0.1	0.1	0.1	0.1	0.1	0.1	0.1	0.1	0.1	0.1	0.2
0.2	0.1	0.1	0.2	0.2	0.2	0.2	0.2	0.2	0.3	0.3	0.3
0.3	0.2	0.2	0.2	0.3	0.3	0.3	0.3	0.4	0.4	0.4	0.5
0.4	0.2	0.3	0.3	0.3	0.4	0.4	0.4	0.5	0.5	0.5	0.6
0.5	0.3	0.3	0.4	0.4	0.5	0.5	0.6	0.6	0.6	0.7	0.8
0.6	0.4	0.4	0.5	0.5	0.6	0.6	0.7	0.7	0.8	0.8	0.9
0.7	0.4	0.5	0.5	0.6	0.7	0.7	0.8	0.8	0.9	0.9	1.1
0.8	0.5	0.6	0.6	0.7	0.8	0.8	0.9	0.9	1.0	1.1	1.2
0.9	0.5	0.6	0.7	0.8	0.8	0.9	1.0	1.1	1.1	1.2	1.4
1.0	0.6	0.7	0.8	0.9	0.9	1.0	1.1	1.2	1.3	1.4	1.5
1.1	0.7	0.8	0.8	0.9	1.0	1.1	1.2	1.3	1.4	1.5	1.7
1.2	0.7	0.8	0.9	1.0	1.1	1.2	1.3	1.4	1.5	1.6	1.8
1.3	0.8	0.9	1.0	1.1	1.2	1.3	1.4	1.5	1.7	1.8	2.0
1.4	0.8	1.0	1.1	1.2	1.3	1.4	1.5	1.7	1.8	1.9	2.1
1.5	0.9	1.0	1.2	1.3	1.4	1.5	1.7	1.8	1.9	2.0	2.3
1.6	1.0	1.1	1.2	1.4	1.5	1.6	1.8	1.9	2.0	2.2	2.4
1.7	1.0	1.2	1.3	1.5	1.6	1.7	1.9	2.0	2.2	2.3	2.6
1.8	1.1	1.2	1.4	1.5	1.7	1.8	2.0	2.1	2.3	2.4	2.7
1.9	1.2	1.3	1.5	1.6	1.8	1.9	2.1	2.3	2.4	2.6	2.9
2.0	1.2	1.4	1.5	1.7	1.9	2.0	2.2	2.4	2.5	2.7	3.0
2.1	1.3	1.4	1.6	1.8	2.0	2.1	2.3	2.5	2.7	2.8	3.2
2.2	1.3	1.5	1.7	1.9	2.1	2.2	2.4	2.6	2.8	3.0	3.3
2.3	1.4	1.6	1.8	2.0	2.2	2.3	2.5	2.7	2.9	3.1	3.5
2.4	1.5	1.7	1.9	2.1	2.3	2.4	2.6	2.8	3.0	3.2	3.6
2.5	1.5	1.7	1.9	2.1	2.3	2.6	2.8	3.0	3.2	3.4	3.8
2.6	1.6	1.8	2.0	2.2	2.4	2.7	2.9	3.1	3.3	3.5	4.0
2.7	1.6	1.9	2.1	2.3	2.5	2.8	3.0	3.2	3.4	3.7	4.1
2.8	1.7	1.9	2.2	2.4	2.6	2.9	3.1	3.3	3.6	3.8	4.3
2.9	1.8	2.0	2.2	2.5	2.7	3.0	3.2	3.4	3.7	3.9	4.4
3.0	1.8	2.1	2.3	2.6	2.8	3.1	3.3	3.6	3.8	4.1	4.6
3.1	1.9	2.1	2.4	2.7	2.9	3.2	3.4	3.7	4.0	4.2	4.7
3.2	1.9	2.2	2.4	2.7	3.0	3.3	3.5	3.8	4.1	4.4	4.9
3.3	2.0	2.2	2.5	2.8	3.1	3.4	3.7	4.0	4.2	4.5	5.1
3.4	2.0	2.3	2.6	2.9	3.2	3.5	3.8	4.1	4.4	4.7	5.3
3.5	2.1	2.3	2.7	3.0	3.3	3.6	3.9	4.2	4.5	4.8	5.4
3.6	2.1	2.4	2.7	3.1	3.4	3.7	4.0	4.3	4.6	4.9	5.2	5.6
3.7	2.2	2.5	2.8	3.1	3.5	3.8	4.1	4.4	4.7	5.1	5.4	5.8
3.8	2.2	2.6	2.9	3.2	3.6	3.9	4.2	4.5	4.9	5.2	5.5	5.9
3.9	2.3	2.6	2.9	3.3	3.7	4.0	4.3	4.7	5.0	5.3	5.7	6.1
4.0	2.3	2.7	3.0	3.4	3.7	4.1	4.4	4.8	5.1	5.5	5.8	6.2

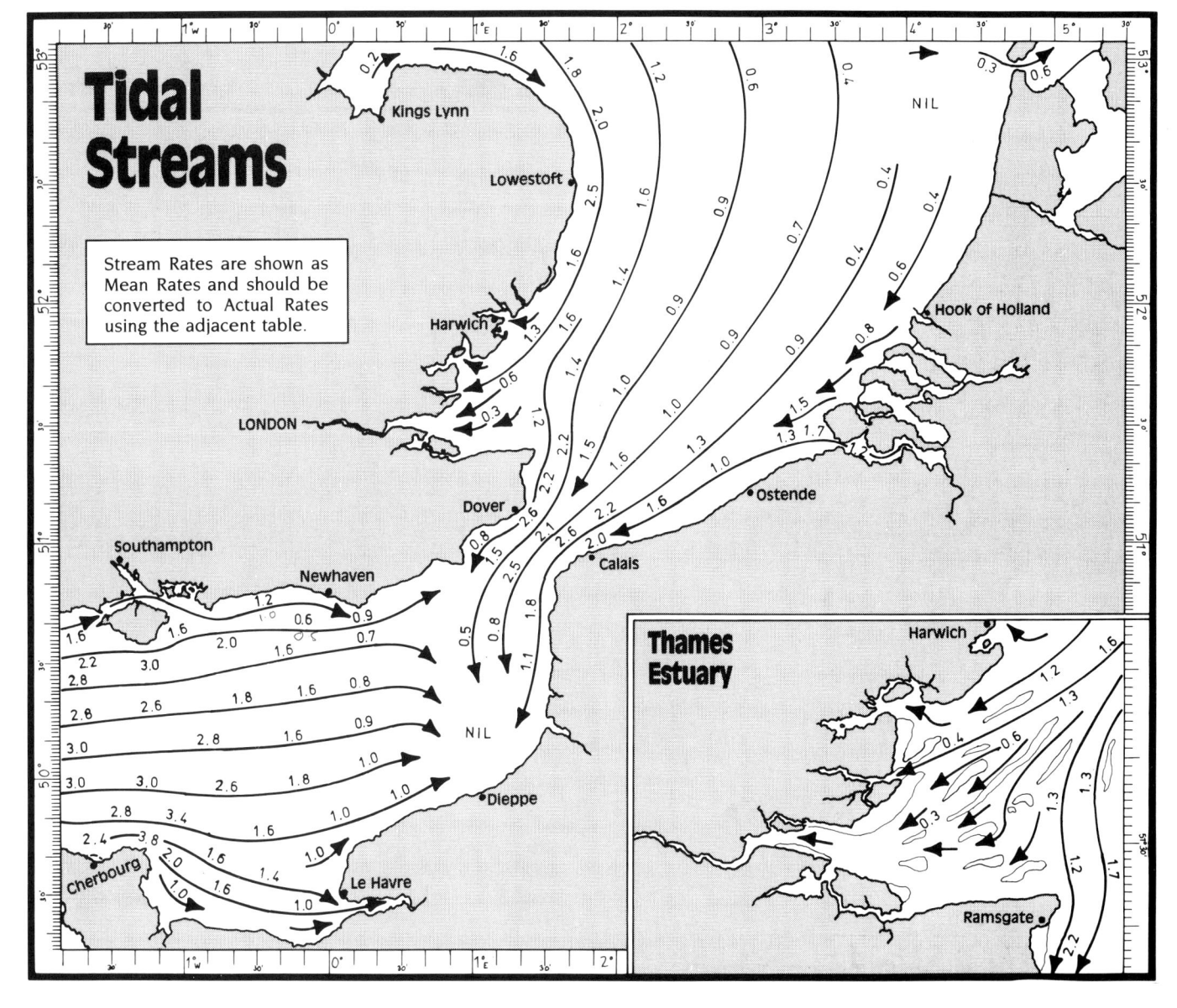

Tidal Stream Rates

1 hour before HW Cherbourg −1

Time 12 27 (to be inserted)

Tidal Streams

Stream Rates are shown as Mean Rates and should be converted to Actual Rates using the adjacent table.

Thames Estuary

Tidal Heights

HW — HW Cherbourg

Copyright © J Reeve-Fowkes and Thomas Reed Publications. No copying without permission.

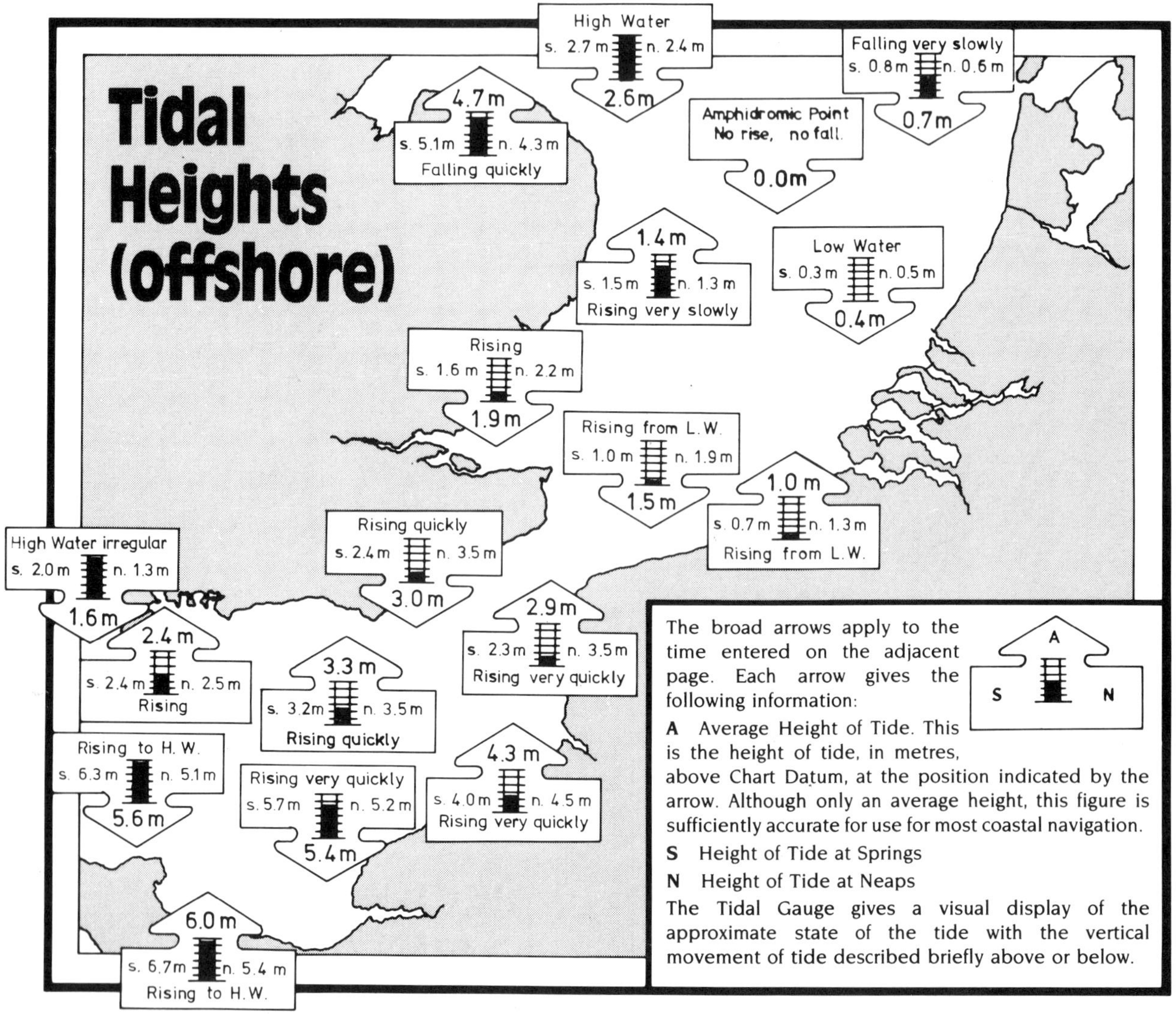

Tidal Heights (offshore)

- **High Water** — s. 2.7 m n. 2.4 m — 2.6 m
- **Falling very slowly** — s. 0.8 m n. 0.6 m — 0.7 m
- **4.7 m** — s. 5.1 m n. 4.3 m — Falling quickly
- **Amphidromic Point** No rise, no fall. — 0.0 m
- **1.4 m** — s. 1.5 m n. 1.3 m — Rising very slowly
- **Low Water** — s. 0.3 m n. 0.5 m — 0.4 m
- **Rising** — s. 1.6 m n. 2.2 m — 1.9 m
- **Rising from L.W.** — s. 1.0 m n. 1.9 m — 1.5 m
- **1.0 m** — s. 0.7 m n. 1.3 m — Rising from L.W.
- **High Water irregular** — s. 2.0 m n. 1.3 m — 1.6 m
- **Rising quickly** — s. 2.4 m n. 3.5 m — 3.0 m
- **2.9 m** — s. 2.3 m n. 3.5 m — Rising very quickly
- **2.4 m** — s. 2.4 m n. 2.5 m — Rising
- **3.3 m** — s. 3.2 m n. 3.5 m — Rising quickly
- **Rising to H.W.** — s. 6.3 m n. 5.1 m — 5.6 m
- **Rising very quickly** — s. 5.7 m n. 5.2 m — 5.4 m
- **4.3 m** — s. 4.0 m n. 4.5 m — Rising very quickly
- **6.0 m** — s. 6.7 m n. 5.4 m — Rising to H.W.

The broad arrows apply to the time entered on the adjacent page. Each arrow gives the following information:

A Average Height of Tide. This is the height of tide, in metres, above Chart Datum, at the position indicated by the arrow. Although only an average height, this figure is sufficiently accurate for use for most coastal navigation.

S Height of Tide at Springs

N Height of Tide at Neaps

The Tidal Gauge gives a visual display of the approximate state of the tide with the vertical movement of tide described briefly above or below.

TIDAL HEIGHTS — PORTS & PLACES

Pencil-in height of HW Cherbourg ▶	4.8	5.0	5.2	5.4	5.6	5.8	6.0	6.2	6.4	6.6	6.8	7.0
ENGLAND												
Kings Lynn	4.3	4.5	4.7	4.9	5.2	5.4	5.6	5.9	6.1	6.2	6.4	6.5
Blakeney Bar	3.9	4.0	4.2	4.3	4.4	4.5	4.7	4.8	4.9	4.9	5.0	5.0
Cromer	3.8	3.9	4.1	4.2	4.3	4.4	4.6	4.7	4.8	4.9	4.9	4.9
Gt. Yarmouth (Gorleston)	1.8	1.9	1.9	2.0	2.1	2.1	2.2	2.2	2.3	2.4	2.5	2.6
Lowestoft	1.8	1.9	1.9	2.0	2.0	2.1	2.1	2.2	2.2	2.3	2.3	2.4
Southwold Haven	1.7	1.8	1.8	1.9	1.9	2.0	2.0	2.1	2.1	2.1	2.2	2.2
Orford Haven appr'ch	1.7	1.7	1.7	1.7	1.6	1.6	1.6	1.5	1.5	1.5	1.6	1.6
Woodbridge Haven	1.8	1.8	1.8	1.8	1.8	1.8	1.8	1.8	1.8	1.8	1.9	1.9
Felixstowe	1.9	1.9	1.9	1.8	1.8	1.7	1.7	1.6	1.6	1.6	1.7	1.7
Harwich	2.1	2.0	2.0	1.9	1.9	1.8	1.8	1.7	1.7	1.7	1.6	1.6
Walton-on-the-Naze	2.0	1.9	1.9	1.8	1.8	1.7	1.7	1.6	1.6	1.6	1.6	1.6
Brightlingsea	2.2	2.1	1.9	1.8	1.7	1.6	1.5	1.4	1.3	1.3	1.2	1.2
Bradwell	2.4	2.3	2.1	2.0	1.9	1.8	1.6	1.5	1.4	1.3	1.2	1.1
Burnham	2.1	2.0	1.8	1.7	1.6	1.5	1.3	1.2	1.1	1.0	0.9	0.8
Leigh, Southend	2.3	2.2	2.0	1.9	1.8	1.7	1.6	1.5	1.4	1.3	1.3	1.2
London Bridge	2.1	1.9	1.7	1.5	1.4	1.2	1.0	0.9	0.7	0.6	0.4	0.3
Sheerness	2.4	2.3	2.1	2.0	1.9	1.8	1.6	1.5	1.4	1.3	1.3	1.2
Chatham	2.3	2.1	1.9	1.7	1.6	1.4	1.2	1.1	0.9	0.8	0.6	0.5
Rochester	2.1	1.9	1.7	1.5	1.4	1.2	1.0	0.9	0.7	0.6	0.5	0.4
Whitstable approach	2.3	2.1	1.9	1.7	1.5	1.4	1.2	1.0	0.8	0.7	0.5	0.4
Edinburgh Channels	2.4	2.3	2.1	2.0	1.9	1.8	1.6	1.5	1.4	1.3	1.3	1.2
Margate	2.3	2.2	2.0	1.9	1.8	1.7	1.6	1.5	1.4	1.3	1.3	1.2
Ramsgate	2.0	1.9	1.9	1.8	1.7	1.7	1.6	1.6	1.5	1.4	1.4	1.3
Dover	3.2	3.1	2.9	2.8	2.7	2.6	2.5	2.4	2.3	2.2	2.1	2.0
Folkestone	3.3	3.2	3.2	3.1	3.0	2.9	2.9	2.8	2.7	2.6	2.6	2.5
Newhaven	3.4	3.3	3.3	3.2	3.1	3.1	3.0	3.0	2.9	2.9	2.9	2.9
Brighton	3.3	3.3	3.3	3.2	3.2	3.1	3.1	3.0	3.0	3.0	2.9	2.9
Shoreham	3.3	3.2	3.2	3.1	3.0	2.9	2.9	2.8	2.7	2.7	2.7	2.7
Littlehampton Hbr	2.5	2.5	2.5	2.5	2.5	2.5	2.4	2.4	2.4	2.4	2.4	2.4
Selsey Bill	2.4	2.4	2.4	2.4	2.4	2.4	2.3	2.3	2.3	2.3	2.2	2.2
Chichester entrance	2.4	2.4	2.4	2.4	2.4	2.4	2.4	2.4	2.4	2.3	2.3	2.3
Portsmouth	2.4	2.4	2.4	2.4	2.3	2.3	2.3	2.2	2.2	2.2	2.2	2.2
Southampton	2.4	2.4	2.4	2.3	2.3	2.3	2.3	2.2	2.2	2.2	2.1	2.1
Cowes I. o W.	2.4	2.4	2.4	2.4	2.3	2.3	2.3	2.3	2.3	2.2	2.2	2.1
Yarmouth I. o W.	1.8	1.9	1.9	2.0	2.0	2.1	2.1	2.1	2.1	2.1	2.2	2.2
Lymington	1.8	1.8	1.8	1.8	1.9	1.9	2.0	2.0	2.1	2.1	2.2	2.2
HOLLAND												
Den Helder	1.3	1.4	1.4	1.5	1.5	1.6	1.6	1.7	1.7	1.7	1.8	1.8
IJmuiden	0.8	0.8	0.8	0.8	0.9	0.9	0.9	1.0	1.0	1.0	1.0	1.0
Scheveningen	0.6	0.6	0.6	0.6	0.6	0.7	0.7	0.7	0.7	0.7	0.6	0.6
Hoek van Holland	0.3	0.3	0.3	0.3	0.3	0.3	0.3	0.3	0.3	0.3	0.3	0.3
Rotterdam	0.5	0.5	0.5	0.5	0.5	0.5	0.5	0.5	0.5	0.5	0.6	0.6
Flushing	1.2	1.1	1.1	1.0	0.9	0.8	0.8	0.7	0.6	0.6	0.5	0.5
BELGIUM												
Zeebrugge	1.7	1.6	1.4	1.3	1.2	1.1	1.0	0.9	0.8	0.7	0.7	0.6
Ostende	1.4	1.3	1.3	1.2	1.1	1.0	0.9	0.8	0.7	0.6	0.6	0.5
Nieuwpoort	1.5	1.4	1.2	1.1	1.0	0.9	0.8	0.7	0.6	0.5	0.5	0.4
FRANCE												
Dunkerque	2.2	2.1	1.9	1.8	1.7	1.6	1.5	1.4	1.3	1.2	1.2	1.1
Calais	3.1	2.9	2.7	2.5	2.3	2.2	2.0	1.8	1.6	1.5	1.3	1.2
Boulogne	4.7	4.4	4.2	3.9	3.6	3.3	3.0	2.7	2.4	2.3	2.1	2.0
Somme Estuary	5.2	5.1	5.1	5.0	4.9	4.8	4.7	4.6	4.5	4.5	4.5	4.5
Le Tréport	4.9	4.9	4.9	4.8	4.8	4.7	4.7	4.6	4.6	4.6	4.7	4.7
Dieppe	4.9	4.9	4.9	4.9	4.9	4.8	4.8	4.8	4.8	4.8	4.7	4.7
Fécamp	4.7	4.8	4.8	4.9	5.0	5.0	5.1	5.1	5.2	5.2	5.3	5.3
Le Havre	5.7	5.9	6.1	6.3	6.4	6.6	6.8	7.0	7.1	7.2	7.3	7.4
Ouistreham	5.6	5.8	6.0	6.2	6.4	6.7	6.9	7.1	7.3	7.4	7.5	7.6
Port-en-Bessin	5.4	5.6	5.8	6.0	6.2	6.4	6.6	6.8	7.0	7.1	7.2	7.3
Saint-Vaast-la-Hougue	4.9	5.1	5.3	5.5	5.6	5.8	6.0	6.1	6.3	6.5	6.6	6.8
Barfleur	4.8	5.0	5.2	5.4	5.5	5.7	5.9	6.0	6.2	6.4	6.5	6.7

Tidal Stream Rates

HW Cherbourg

HW

Time 13.27 (to be inserted)

Stream Rate Conversion Table

Mean Rate Figure from Chart ▼	Pencil-in height of HW Cherbourg — Read from column below pencil mark										
	4.8	5.0	5.2	5.4	5.6	5.8	6.0	6.2	6.4	6.6	6.8
0.1	0.1	0.1	0.1	0.1	0.1	0.1	0.1	0.1	0.1	0.1	0.2
0.2	0.1	0.1	0.2	0.2	0.2	0.2	0.2	0.2	0.3	0.3	0.3
0.3	0.2	0.2	0.2	0.3	0.3	0.3	0.4	0.4	0.4	0.4	0.5
0.4	0.2	0.3	0.3	0.3	0.4	0.4	0.5	0.5	0.5	0.6	0.6
0.5	0.3	0.3	0.4	0.4	0.5	0.5	0.6	0.6	0.6	0.7	0.8
0.6	0.4	0.4	0.5	0.5	0.6	0.6	0.7	0.7	0.8	0.8	0.9
0.7	0.4	0.5	0.5	0.6	0.7	0.7	0.8	0.8	0.9	1.0	1.1
0.8	0.5	0.6	0.6	0.7	0.8	0.8	0.9	1.0	1.1	1.1	1.2
0.9	0.5	0.6	0.7	0.8	0.8	0.9	1.0	1.1	1.2	1.3	1.4
1.0	0.6	0.7	0.8	0.9	0.9	1.0	1.1	1.2	1.3	1.4	1.5
1.1	0.7	0.8	0.8	0.9	1.0	1.1	1.2	1.3	1.4	1.5	1.6	1.7
1.2	0.7	0.8	0.9	1.0	1.1	1.2	1.3	1.4	1.5	1.6	1.7	1.8
1.3	0.8	0.9	1.0	1.1	1.2	1.3	1.4	1.5	1.7	1.8	1.9	2.0
1.4	0.8	1.0	1.1	1.2	1.3	1.4	1.5	1.7	1.8	1.9	2.0	2.1
1.5	0.9	1.0	1.2	1.3	1.4	1.5	1.7	1.8	1.9	2.0	2.2	2.3
1.6	1.0	1.1	1.2	1.4	1.5	1.6	1.8	1.9	2.0	2.2	2.3	2.4
1.7	1.0	1.2	1.3	1.5	1.6	1.7	1.9	2.0	2.2	2.3	2.4	2.6
1.8	1.1	1.2	1.4	1.5	1.7	1.8	2.0	2.1	2.3	2.4	2.6	2.7
1.9	1.2	1.3	1.5	1.6	1.8	1.9	2.1	2.3	2.4	2.6	2.7	2.9
2.0	1.2	1.4	1.5	1.7	1.9	2.0	2.2	2.4	2.5	2.7	2.9	3.0
2.1	1.3	1.4	1.6	1.8	2.0	2.1	2.3	2.5	2.7	2.8	3.0	3.2
2.2	1.3	1.5	1.7	1.9	2.1	2.2	2.4	2.6	2.8	3.0	3.2	3.3
2.3	1.4	1.6	1.8	2.0	2.2	2.3	2.5	2.7	2.9	3.1	3.3	3.5
2.4	1.5	1.7	1.9	2.1	2.3	2.4	2.6	2.8	3.0	3.2	3.4	3.6
2.5	1.5	1.7	1.9	2.1	2.3	2.6	2.8	3.0	3.2	3.4	3.6	3.8
2.6	1.6	1.8	2.0	2.2	2.4	2.7	2.9	3.1	3.3	3.5	3.7	4.0
2.7	1.6	1.9	2.1	2.3	2.5	2.8	3.0	3.2	3.4	3.7	3.9	4.1
2.8	1.7	1.9	2.2	2.4	2.6	2.9	3.1	3.3	3.6	3.8	4.0	4.3
2.9	1.8	2.0	2.2	2.5	2.7	3.0	3.2	3.4	3.7	3.9	4.2	4.4
3.0	1.8	2.1	2.3	2.6	2.8	3.1	3.3	3.6	3.8	4.1	4.3	4.6
3.1	1.9	2.1	2.4	2.7	2.9	3.2	3.4	3.7	4.0	4.2	4.5	4.7
3.2	1.9	2.2	2.4	2.7	3.0	3.3	3.5	3.8	4.1	4.4	4.7	4.9
3.3	2.0	2.2	2.5	2.8	3.1	3.4	3.7	4.0	4.2	4.5	4.8	5.1
3.4	2.0	2.3	2.6	2.9	3.2	3.5	3.8	4.1	4.4	4.7	5.0	5.3
3.5	2.1	2.3	2.7	3.0	3.3	3.6	3.9	4.2	4.5	4.8	5.1	5.4
3.6	2.1	2.4	2.7	3.1	3.4	3.7	4.0	4.3	4.6	4.9	5.2	5.6
3.7	2.2	2.5	2.8	3.1	3.5	3.8	4.1	4.4	4.7	5.1	5.4	5.8
3.8	2.2	2.6	2.9	3.2	3.6	3.9	4.2	4.5	4.9	5.2	5.5	5.9
3.9	2.3	2.6	2.9	3.3	3.7	4.0	4.3	4.7	5.0	5.3	5.7	6.1
4.0	2.3	2.7	3.0	3.4	3.7	4.1	4.4	4.8	5.1	5.5	5.8	6.2

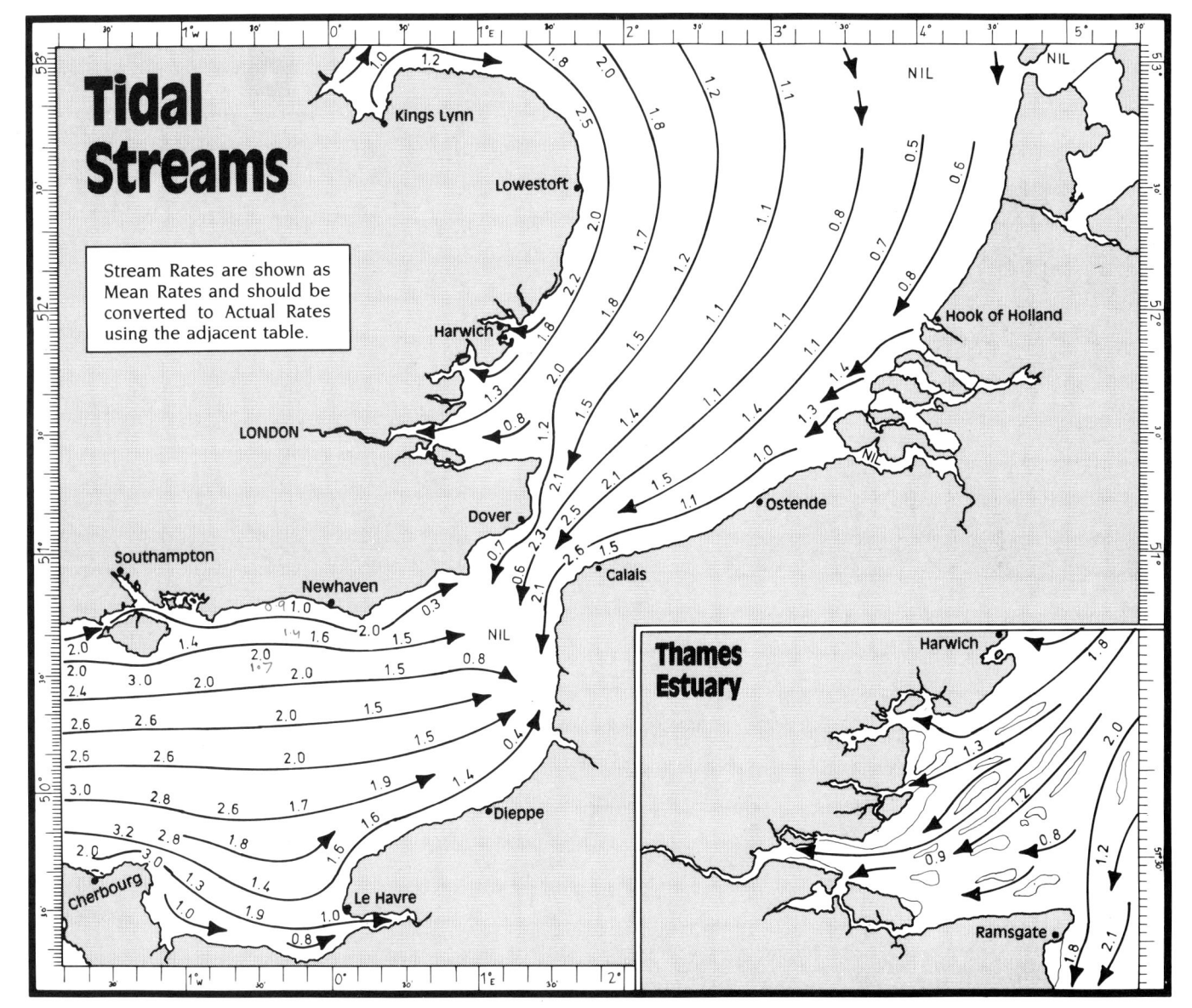

Tidal Streams

Stream Rates are shown as Mean Rates and should be converted to Actual Rates using the adjacent table.

Thames Estuary

101

+1 — 1 hour after HW Cherbourg

Tidal Heights

Copyright © J Reeve-Fowkes and Thomas Reed Publications. No copying without permission.

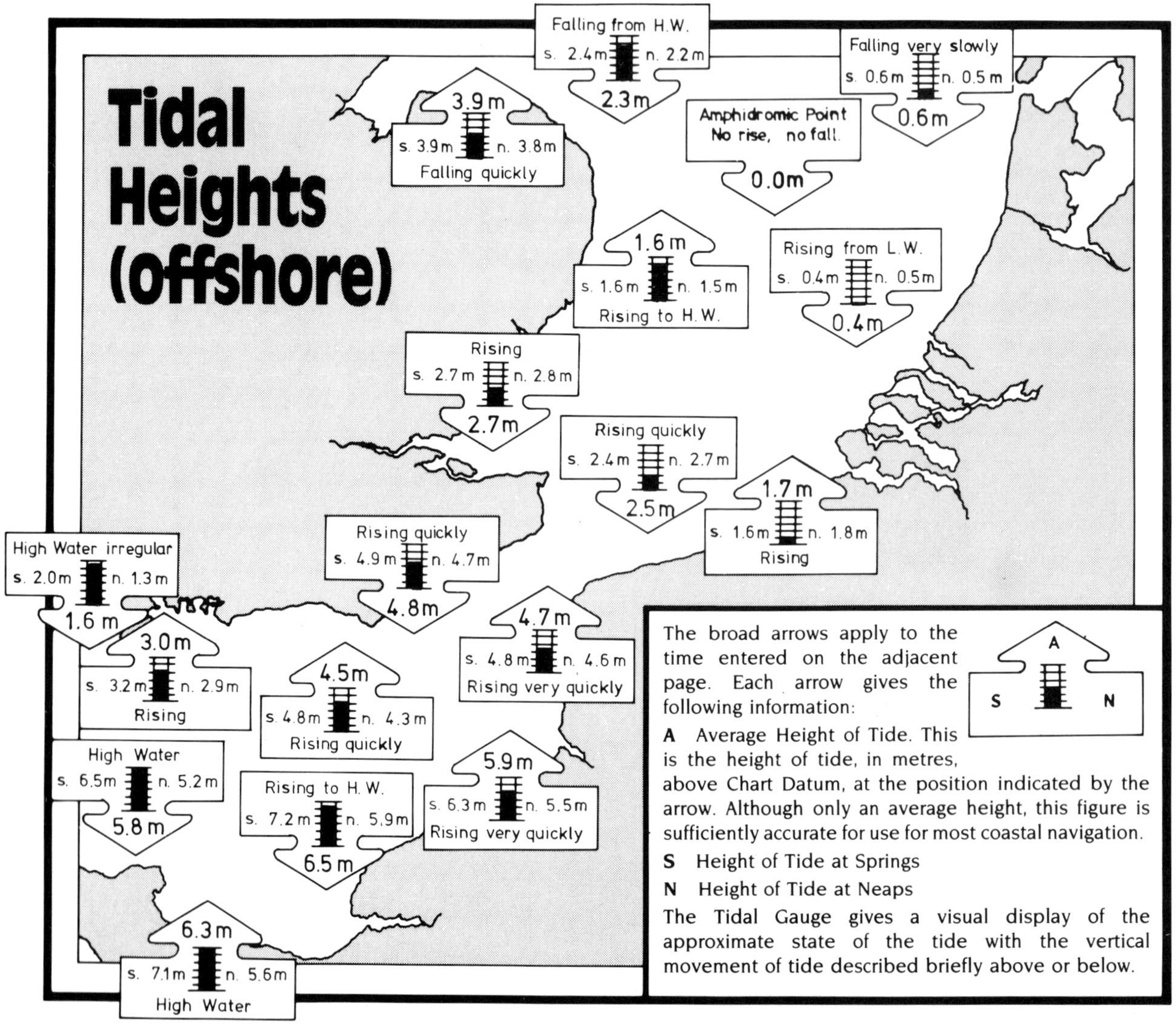

Tidal Heights (offshore)

- Falling from H.W. — s. 2.4m n. 2.2m — **2.3m**
- Falling very slowly — s. 0.6m n. 0.5m — **0.6m**
- 3.9 m — s. 3.9m n. 3.8m — Falling quickly
- Amphidromic Point — No rise, no fall. — **0.0m**
- 1.6 m — s. 1.6m n. 1.5m — Rising to H.W.
- Rising from L.W. — s. 0.4m n. 0.5m — **0.4m**
- Rising — s. 2.7m n. 2.8m — **2.7m**
- Rising quickly — s. 2.4m n. 2.7m — **2.5m**
- 1.7 m — s. 1.6m n. 1.8m — Rising
- Rising quickly — s. 4.9m n. 4.7m — **4.8m**
- High Water irregular — s. 2.0m n. 1.3m — **1.6 m**
- 3.0 m — s. 3.2m n. 2.9m — Rising
- 4.5 m — s. 4.8m n. 4.3m — Rising quickly
- 4.7 m — s. 4.8m n. 4.6m — Rising very quickly
- High Water — s. 6.5m n. 5.2m — **5.8m**
- Rising to H.W. — s. 7.2m n. 5.9m — **6.5 m**
- 5.9 m — s. 6.3m n. 5.5m — Rising very quickly
- 6.3 m — s. 7.1m n. 5.6m — High Water

The broad arrows apply to the time entered on the adjacent page. Each arrow gives the following information:

A Average Height of Tide. This is the height of tide, in metres, above Chart Datum, at the position indicated by the arrow. Although only an average height, this figure is sufficiently accurate for use for most coastal navigation.

S Height of Tide at Springs

N Height of Tide at Neaps

The Tidal Gauge gives a visual display of the approximate state of the tide with the vertical movement of tide described briefly above or below.

TIDAL HEIGHTS — PORTS & PLACES

Pencil-in height of HW Cherbourg ▶	4.8	5.0	5.2	5.4	5.6	5.8	6.0	6.2	6.4	6.6	6.8	7.0
ENGLAND												
Kings Lynn	3.9	4.0	4.2	4.3	4.5	4.6	4.8	4.9	5.1	5.2	5.4	5.5
Blakeney Bar	3.4	3.5	3.5	3.6	3.7	3.7	3.8	3.8	3.9	3.9	3.9	3.9
Cromer	3.5	3.6	3.6	3.7	3.8	3.8	3.9	3.9	4.0	4.0	4.0	4.0
Gt. Yarmouth (Gorleston)	1.9	2.0	2.0	2.1	2.2	2.2	2.3	2.3	2.4	2.5	2.6	2.7
Lowestoft	2.0	2.1	2.1	2.2	2.2	2.3	2.3	2.4	2.4	2.5	2.5	2.6
Southwold Haven	1.9	2.0	2.0	2.1	2.1	2.2	2.2	2.3	2.3	2.4	2.5	2.6
Orford Haven appr'ch	2.0	2.0	2.0	2.0	2.0	2.0	2.0	2.0	2.0	2.1	2.1	2.2
Woodbridge Haven	2.2	2.2	2.2	2.2	2.2	2.2	2.2	2.2	2.2	2.3	2.3	2.4
Felixstowe	2.3	2.3	2.3	2.3	2.3	2.2	2.2	2.2	2.2	2.3	2.3	2.4
Harwich	2.4	2.4	2.4	2.4	2.3	2.3	2.3	2.2	2.2	2.2	2.2	2.2
Walton-on-the-Naze	2.5	2.5	2.5	2.5	2.4	2.4	2.4	2.3	2.3	2.3	2.4	2.4
Brightlingsea	2.7	2.6	2.6	2.5	2.5	2.4	2.4	2.3	2.3	2.3	2.3	2.3
Bradwell	3.1	3.0	2.8	2.7	2.6	2.5	2.4	2.3	2.2	2.2	2.1	2.1
Burnham	2.7	2.6	2.6	2.5	2.4	2.3	2.3	2.2	2.1	2.0	1.9	1.8
Leigh, Southend	2.8	2.8	2.8	2.8	2.7	2.7	2.7	2.6	2.6	2.6	2.5	2.5
London Bridge	3.0	2.7	2.5	2.2	1.9	1.6	1.3	1.0	0.7	0.6	0.4	0.3
Sheerness	2.9	2.8	2.8	2.7	2.7	2.6	2.6	2.5	2.5	2.5	2.5	2.5
Chatham	2.6	2.6	2.6	2.6	2.5	2.5	2.5	2.4	2.4	2.3	2.3	2.2
Rochester	2.6	2.5	2.5	2.4	2.3	2.2	2.2	2.1	2.0	1.9	1.8	1.7
Whitstable approach	3.0	2.8	2.6	2.4	2.3	2.1	1.9	1.8	1.6	1.5	1.4	1.3
Edinburgh Channels	2.9	2.8	2.8	2.7	2.7	2.6	2.6	2.5	2.5	2.5	2.5	2.5
Margate	2.7	2.7	2.7	2.7	2.6	2.6	2.6	2.5	2.5	2.5	2.4	2.4
Ramsgate	2.5	2.6	2.6	2.7	2.7	2.8	2.8	2.9	2.9	2.9	3.0	3.0
Dover	3.9	4.0	4.0	4.1	4.1	4.2	4.2	4.3	4.3	4.3	4.4	4.4
Folkestone	4.1	4.2	4.4	4.5	4.7	4.8	5.0	5.1	5.3	5.4	5.4	5.5
Newhaven	4.1	4.2	4.2	4.3	4.4	4.4	4.5	4.5	4.6	4.7	4.7	4.8
Brighton	3.9	4.0	4.0	4.1	4.2	4.3	4.3	4.4	4.5	4.5	4.6	4.6
Shoreham	3.8	3.9	3.9	4.0	4.0	4.1	4.1	4.2	4.2	4.2	4.3	4.3
Littlehampton Hbr	3.1	3.1	3.1	3.1	3.2	3.2	3.2	3.3	3.3	3.3	3.4	3.4
Selsey Bill	3.0	3.0	3.0	3.0	3.0	3.0	3.1	3.1	3.1	3.1	3.1	3.1
Chichester entrance	2.9	2.9	2.9	2.9	2.9	3.0	3.0	3.0	3.0	3.0	3.0	3.0
Portsmouth	2.8	2.8	2.8	2.8	2.8	2.9	2.9	2.9	3.0	3.0	3.1	3.1
Southampton	2.9	2.9	2.9	2.9	2.9	2.9	2.8	2.8	2.8	2.8	2.8	2.8
Cowes I. o W.	2.8	2.8	2.8	2.8	2.8	2.8	2.9	2.9	3.0	3.0	3.0	3.0
Yarmouth I. o W.	2.1	2.2	2.2	2.3	2.3	2.4	2.5	2.5	2.6	2.6	2.6	2.6
Lymington	2.1	2.1	2.1	2.1	2.2	2.2	2.3	2.3	2.4	2.4	2.5	2.5
HOLLAND												
Den Helder	1.2	1.2	1.2	1.2	1.3	1.3	1.3	1.4	1.4	1.4	1.5	1.5
IJmuiden	0.7	0.7	0.7	0.7	0.7	0.7	0.7	0.7	0.7	0.7	0.7	0.7
Scheveningen	0.6	0.6	0.6	0.6	0.6	0.5	0.5	0.5	0.5	0.5	0.4	0.4
Hoek van Holland	0.4	0.4	0.4	0.4	0.4	0.3	0.3	0.3	0.3	0.3	0.3	0.3
Rotterdam	0.4	0.4	0.4	0.4	0.4	0.5	0.5	0.5	0.5	0.5	0.6	0.6
Flushing	1.5	1.4	1.4	1.3	1.2	1.2	1.1	1.1	1.0	1.0	1.0	1.0
BELGIUM												
Zeebrugge	1.9	1.8	1.8	1.7	1.6	1.6	1.5	1.5	1.4	1.3	1.3	1.2
Ostende	1.9	1.8	1.8	1.7	1.6	1.5	1.5	1.4	1.3	1.2	1.2	1.1
Nieuwpoort	1.9	1.8	1.8	1.7	1.6	1.5	1.4	1.3	1.2	1.1	1.1	1.0
FRANCE												
Dunkerque	2.8	2.7	2.7	2.6	2.5	2.4	2.4	2.3	2.2	2.2	2.1	2.1
Calais	4.0	3.9	3.9	3.8	3.7	3.6	3.5	3.4	3.3	3.3	3.3	3.2
Boulogne	5.7	5.6	5.6	5.5	5.4	5.4	5.3	5.3	5.2	5.2	5.2	5.2
Somme Estuary	5.9	6.0	6.2	6.3	6.4	6.5	6.6	6.7	6.8	6.9	6.9	7.0
Le Tréport	5.9	6.0	6.2	6.4	6.5	6.5	6.7	6.8	6.9	7.0	7.1	7.2
Dieppe	5.8	5.9	6.1	6.2	6.3	6.5	6.6	6.8	6.9	7.0	7.0	7.1
Fécamp	5.6	5.7	5.9	6.0	6.1	6.3	6.4	6.6	6.7	6.8	6.9	7.0
Le Havre	6.1	6.3	6.5	6.7	6.9	7.1	7.3	7.5	7.7	7.8	8.0	8.1
Ouistreham	5.8	6.0	6.2	6.4	6.6	6.9	7.1	7.3	7.5	7.6	7.7	7.9
Port-en-Bessin	5.6	5.8	6.0	6.2	6.4	6.5	6.7	6.9	7.1	7.2	7.3	7.4
Saint-Vaast-la-Hougue	5.1	5.3	5.5	5.7	5.9	6.0	6.2	6.4	6.6	6.8	7.0	7.2
Barfleur	4.9	5.1	5.3	5.5	5.7	5.8	6.0	6.2	6.4	6.6	6.8	7.0

Stream Rate Conversion Table

Mean Rate Figure from Chart ▼	Pencil-in height of HW Cherbourg — Read from column below pencil mark										
	4.8	5.0	5.2	5.4	5.6	5.8	6.0	6.2	6.4	6.6	6.8
0.1	0.1	0.1	0.1	0.1	0.1	0.1	0.1	0.1	0.1	0.1	0.2
0.2	0.1	0.1	0.2	0.2	0.2	0.2	0.2	0.2	0.3	0.3	0.3
0.3	0.2	0.2	0.2	0.3	0.3	0.3	0.3	0.4	0.4	0.4	0.5
0.4	0.2	0.3	0.3	0.3	0.4	0.4	0.4	0.5	0.5	0.5	0.6
0.5	0.3	0.3	0.4	0.4	0.5	0.5	0.6	0.6	0.6	0.7	0.8
0.6	0.4	0.4	0.5	0.5	0.6	0.6	0.7	0.7	0.8	0.8	0.9
0.7	0.4	0.5	0.5	0.6	0.7	0.7	0.8	0.8	0.9	0.9	1.0
0.8	0.5	0.6	0.6	0.7	0.8	0.8	0.9	0.9	1.0	1.1	1.2
0.9	0.5	0.6	0.7	0.8	0.8	0.9	1.0	1.1	1.1	1.2	1.3
1.0	0.6	0.7	0.8	0.9	0.9	1.0	1.1	1.2	1.3	1.4	1.5
1.1	0.7	0.8	0.8	0.9	1.0	1.1	1.2	1.3	1.4	1.5	1.6
1.2	0.7	0.8	0.9	1.0	1.1	1.2	1.3	1.4	1.5	1.6	1.7
1.3	0.8	0.9	1.0	1.1	1.2	1.3	1.4	1.5	1.7	1.8	1.9
1.4	0.8	1.0	1.1	1.2	1.3	1.4	1.5	1.7	1.8	1.9	2.0
1.5	0.9	1.0	1.2	1.3	1.4	1.5	1.7	1.8	1.9	2.0	2.2
1.6	1.0	1.1	1.2	1.4	1.5	1.6	1.8	1.9	2.0	2.2	2.3
1.7	1.0	1.2	1.3	1.5	1.6	1.7	1.9	2.0	2.2	2.3	2.4
1.8	1.1	1.2	1.4	1.5	1.7	1.8	2.0	2.1	2.3	2.4	2.6
1.9	1.2	1.3	1.5	1.6	1.8	1.9	2.1	2.3	2.4	2.6	2.7
2.0	1.2	1.4	1.5	1.7	1.9	2.0	2.2	2.4	2.5	2.7	2.9
2.1	1.3	1.4	1.6	1.8	2.0	2.1	2.3	2.5	2.7	2.8	3.0
2.2	1.3	1.5	1.7	1.9	2.1	2.2	2.4	2.6	2.8	3.0	3.2
2.3	1.4	1.6	1.8	2.0	2.2	2.3	2.5	2.7	2.9	3.1	3.3
2.4	1.5	1.7	1.9	2.1	2.3	2.4	2.6	2.8	3.0	3.2	3.4
2.5	1.5	1.7	1.9	2.1	2.3	2.6	2.8	3.0	3.2	3.4	3.6
2.6	1.6	1.8	2.0	2.2	2.4	2.7	2.9	3.1	3.3	3.5	3.7
2.7	1.6	1.9	2.1	2.3	2.5	2.8	3.0	3.2	3.4	3.7	3.9
2.8	1.7	1.9	2.2	2.4	2.6	2.9	3.1	3.3	3.6	3.8	4.0
2.9	1.8	2.0	2.2	2.5	2.7	3.0	3.2	3.4	3.7	3.9	4.2
3.0	1.8	2.1	2.3	2.6	2.8	3.1	3.3	3.6	3.8	4.1	4.3
3.1	1.9	2.1	2.4	2.7	2.9	3.2	3.4	3.7	4.0	4.2	4.5
3.2	1.9	2.2	2.4	2.7	3.0	3.3	3.5	3.8	4.1	4.4	4.7
3.3	2.0	2.2	2.5	2.8	3.1	3.4	3.7	4.0	4.2	4.5	4.8
3.4	2.0	2.3	2.6	2.9	3.2	3.5	3.8	4.1	4.4	4.7	5.0
3.5	2.1	2.3	2.7	3.0	3.3	3.6	3.9	4.2	4.5	4.8	5.1
3.6	2.1	2.4	2.7	3.1	3.4	3.7	4.0	4.3	4.6	4.9	5.2
3.7	2.2	2.5	2.8	3.1	3.5	3.8	4.1	4.4	4.7	5.1	5.4
3.8	2.2	2.6	2.9	3.2	3.6	3.9	4.2	4.5	4.9	5.2	5.5
3.9	2.3	2.6	2.9	3.3	3.7	4.0	4.3	4.7	5.0	5.3	5.7
4.0	2.3	2.7	3.0	3.4	3.7	4.1	4.4	4.8	5.1	5.5	5.8

Tidal Stream Rates

1 hour after HW Cherbourg +1

Time (to be inserted) 14.27

Tidal Streams

Stream Rates are shown as Mean Rates and should be converted to Actual Rates using the adjacent table.

Thames Estuary (inset)

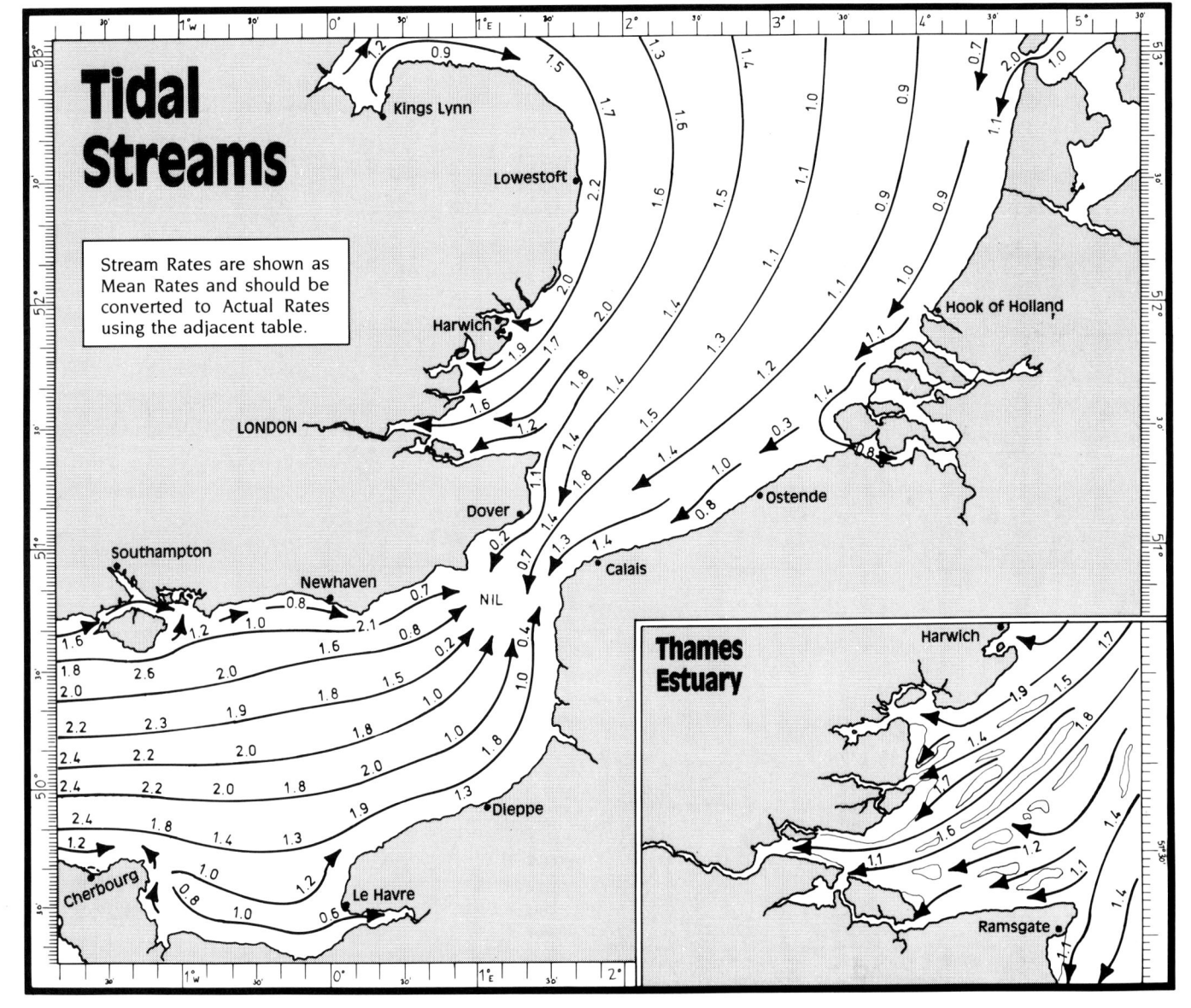

+2 — 2 hours after HW Cherbourg

Tidal Heights

Copyright © J Reeve-Fowkes and Thomas Reed Publications.
No copying without permission.

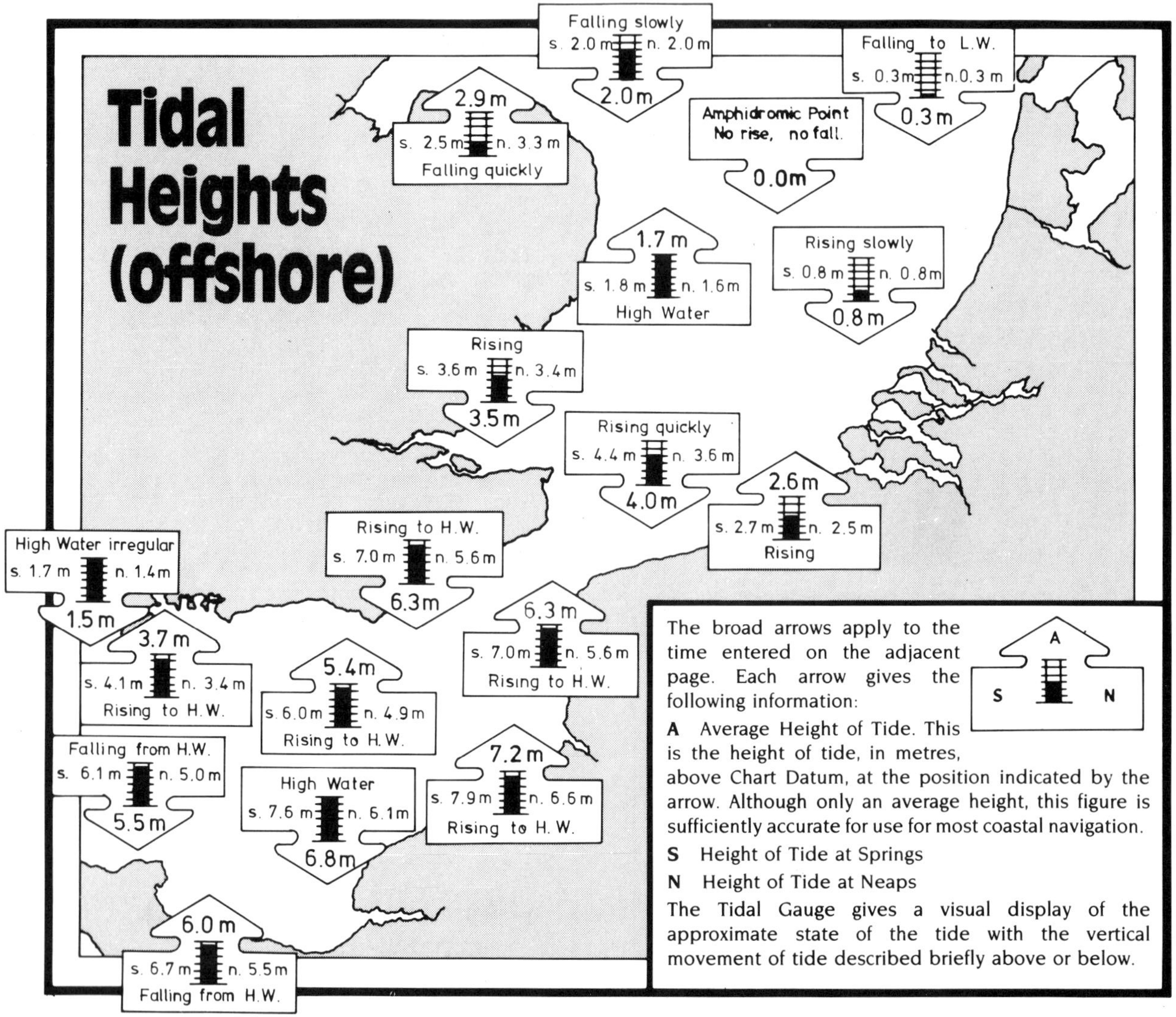

Tidal Heights (offshore)

Falling slowly
s. 2.0m n. 2.0m
2.0m

Falling to L.W.
s. 0.3m n. 0.3m
0.3m

2.9m
s. 2.5m n. 3.3m
Falling quickly

Amphidromic Point
No rise, no fall.
0.0m

1.7m
s. 1.8m n. 1.6m
High Water

Rising slowly
s. 0.8m n. 0.8m
0.8m

Rising
s. 3.6m n. 3.4m
3.5m

Rising quickly
s. 4.4m n. 3.6m
4.0m

2.6m
s. 2.7m n. 2.5m
Rising

High Water irregular
s. 1.7m n. 1.4m
1.5m

Rising to H.W.
s. 7.0m n. 5.6m
6.3m

6.3m
s. 7.0m n. 5.6m
Rising to H.W.

3.7m
s. 4.1m n. 3.4m
Rising to H.W.

5.4m
s. 6.0m n. 4.9m
Rising to H.W.

Falling from H.W.
s. 6.1m n. 5.0m
5.5m

High Water
s. 7.6m n. 6.1m
6.8m

7.2m
s. 7.9m n. 6.6m
Rising to H.W.

6.0m
s. 6.7m n. 5.5m
Falling from H.W.

The broad arrows apply to the time entered on the adjacent page. Each arrow gives the following information:

A Average Height of Tide. This is the height of tide, in metres, above Chart Datum, at the position indicated by the arrow. Although only an average height, this figure is sufficiently accurate for use for most coastal navigation.

S Height of Tide at Springs
N Height of Tide at Neaps

The Tidal Gauge gives a visual display of the approximate state of the tide with the vertical movement of tide described briefly above or below.

TIDAL HEIGHTS — PORTS & PLACES

Pencil-in height of HW Cherbourg ▶	4.8	5.0	5.2	5.4	5.6	5.8	6.0	6.2	6.4	6.6	6.8
ENGLAND											
Kings Lynn	3.2	3.3	3.5	3.6	3.7	3.8	4.0	4.1	4.2	4.3	4.4	4.5
Blakeney Bar	2.9	2.9	2.9	2.9	2.8	2.8	2.8	2.7	2.7	2.7	2.6	2.6
Cromer	3.0	3.0	3.0	3.0	3.0	2.9	2.9	2.9	2.9	2.9	2.9	2.9
Gt. Yarmouth (Gorleston)	1.8	1.9	1.9	2.0	2.0	2.1	2.1	2.2	2.2	2.3	2.3	2.4
Lowestoft	1.9	2.0	2.0	2.1	2.1	2.2	2.2	2.3	2.3	2.4	2.5	2.6
Southwold Haven	2.1	2.2	2.2	2.3	2.3	2.4	2.4	2.5	2.5	2.6	2.6	2.7
Orford Haven appr'ch	2.4	2.4	2.4	2.4	2.5	2.5	2.5	2.6	2.6	2.7	2.7	2.8
Woodbridge Haven	2.5	2.6	2.6	2.7	2.7	2.8	2.8	2.9	2.9	3.0	3.0	3.1
Felixstowe	2.7	2.7	2.7	2.7	2.8	2.8	2.8	2.9	2.9	3.0	3.1	3.2
Harwich	2.8	2.8	2.8	2.8	2.8	2.9	2.9	2.9	2.9	2.9	2.9	2.9
Walton-on-the-Naze	3.0	3.0	3.0	3.0	3.0	3.1	3.1	3.1	3.1	3.2	3.3	3.4
Brightlingsea	3.2	3.2	3.2	3.2	3.2	3.2	3.2	3.2	3.2	3.3	3.3	3.4
Bradwell	3.6	3.5	3.5	3.4	3.4	3.3	3.3	3.2	3.2	3.2	3.2	3.2
Burnham	3.4	3.3	3.3	3.2	3.1	3.1	3.0	3.0	2.9	2.9	3.0	3.0
Leigh, Southend	3.6	3.6	3.6	3.6	3.6	3.6	3.6	3.6	3.6	3.7	3.7	3.8
London Bridge	3.8	3.6	3.4	3.2	3.1	2.9	2.7	2.6	2.4	2.4	2.3	2.3
Sheerness	3.5	3.5	3.5	3.5	3.5	3.6	3.6	3.6	3.6	3.6	3.7	3.7
Chatham	3.4	3.4	3.4	3.4	3.4	3.4	3.4	3.4	3.4	3.4	3.4	3.5
Rochester	3.2	3.2	3.2	3.2	3.2	3.2	3.2	3.2	3.2	3.3	3.3	3.4
Whitstable approach	3.5	3.4	3.4	3.3	3.2	3.2	3.1	3.1	3.0	3.0	3.0	3.0
Edinburgh Channels	3.3	3.4	3.4	3.5	3.5	3.6	3.6	3.7	3.7	3.7	3.8	3.8
Margate	3.2	3.3	3.3	3.4	3.4	3.5	3.5	3.6	3.6	3.6	3.6	3.6
Ramsgate	3.1	3.2	3.4	3.5	3.7	3.8	4.0	4.1	4.3	4.4	4.4	4.5
Dover	4.6	4.8	5.0	5.2	5.4	5.6	5.8	6.0	6.2	6.3	6.5	6.6
Folkestone	5.0	5.2	5.4	5.6	5.9	6.1	6.3	6.6	6.8	7.0	7.1	7.3
Newhaven	4.6	4.8	5.0	5.2	5.4	5.5	5.7	5.9	6.1	6.2	6.4	6.5
Brighton	4.4	4.6	4.8	5.0	5.2	5.3	5.5	5.7	5.9	6.0	6.1	6.2
Shoreham	4.5	4.5	4.7	4.8	4.9	5.1	5.2	5.4	5.5	5.6	5.7	5.8
Littlehampton Hbr	3.7	3.8	4.0	4.1	4.2	4.3	4.4	4.5	4.6	4.7	4.7	4.8
Selsey Bill	3.6	3.7	3.7	3.8	3.9	4.0	4.1	4.2	4.3	4.4	4.4	4.5
Chichester entrance	3.4	3.5	3.5	3.6	3.7	3.8	3.8	3.9	4.0	4.1	4.1	4.2
Portsmouth	3.3	3.4	3.4	3.5	3.6	3.7	3.7	3.8	3.9	4.0	4.0	4.1
Southampton	3.4	3.5	3.5	3.6	3.7	3.7	3.8	3.8	3.9	4.0	4.0	4.1
Cowes I. o W.	3.1	3.2	3.2	3.3	3.3	3.4	3.5	3.7	3.8	3.8	3.9	3.9
Yarmouth I. o W.	2.3	2.4	2.4	2.5	2.5	2.6	2.7	2.8	2.9	3.0	3.2	3.3
Lymington	2.2	2.3	2.3	2.4	2.4	2.5	2.6	2.7	2.8	2.9	2.9	3.0
HOLLAND											
Den Helder	0.9	0.9	0.9	0.9	0.9	1.0	1.0	1.0	1.0	1.0	1.1	1.1
IJmuiden	0.6	0.6	0.6	0.6	0.5	0.5	0.5	0.4	0.4	0.4	0.4	0.4
Scheveningen	0.5	0.5	0.5	0.5	0.5	0.4	0.4	0.4	0.4	0.4	0.3	0.3
Hoek van Holland	0.5	0.5	0.5	0.5	0.4	0.4	0.4	0.3	0.3	0.3	0.3	0.3
Rotterdam	0.4	0.4	0.4	0.4	0.5	0.5	0.5	0.6	0.6	0.6	0.7	0.7
Flushing	1.9	1.9	1.9	1.8	1.8	1.7	1.7	1.6	1.6	1.6	1.6	1.6
BELGIUM											
Zeebrugge	2.5	2.4	2.4	2.3	2.2	2.2	2.1	2.1	2.0	2.0	1.9	1.9
Ostende	2.5	2.5	2.5	2.5	2.4	2.4	2.4	2.3	2.3	2.3	2.2	2.2
Nieuwpoort	2.7	2.6	2.6	2.5	2.5	2.4	2.4	2.3	2.3	2.2	2.1	2.0
FRANCE											
Dunkerque	3.7	3.7	3.7	3.7	3.7	3.8	3.8	3.8	3.8	3.8	3.8	3.8
Calais	4.9	5.0	5.0	5.1	5.2	5.3	5.4	5.5	5.6	5.6	5.7	5.7
Boulogne	6.4	6.6	6.8	7.0	7.2	7.5	7.7	7.9	8.1	8.2	8.3	8.4
Somme Estuary	6.9	7.1	7.3	7.5	7.8	8.0	8.2	8.5	8.7	8.8	8.9	9.0
Le Tréport	6.7	7.0	7.2	7.5	7.7	8.0	8.2	8.5	8.7	8.8	9.0	9.1
Dieppe	6.5	6.8	7.0	7.3	7.5	7.8	8.0	8.3	8.5	8.6	8.8	8.9
Fécamp	6.0	6.2	6.4	6.6	6.8	7.1	7.3	7.5	7.7	7.9	8.0	8.2
Le Havre	6.2	6.4	6.6	6.8	7.0	7.2	7.4	7.6	7.8	7.9	8.1	8.2
Ouistreham	5.9	6.1	6.3	6.5	6.7	6.9	7.1	7.3	7.5	7.6	7.8	7.9
Port-en-Bessin	5.5	5.7	5.9	6.1	6.2	6.4	6.6	6.7	6.9	7.0	7.1	7.2
Saint-Vaast-la-Hougue	5.0	5.1	5.3	5.4	5.6	5.7	5.9	6.0	6.2	6.4	6.5	6.7
Barfleur	4.8	4.9	5.1	5.2	5.4	5.5	5.7	5.8	6.0	6.2	6.3	6.5

Tidal Stream Rates

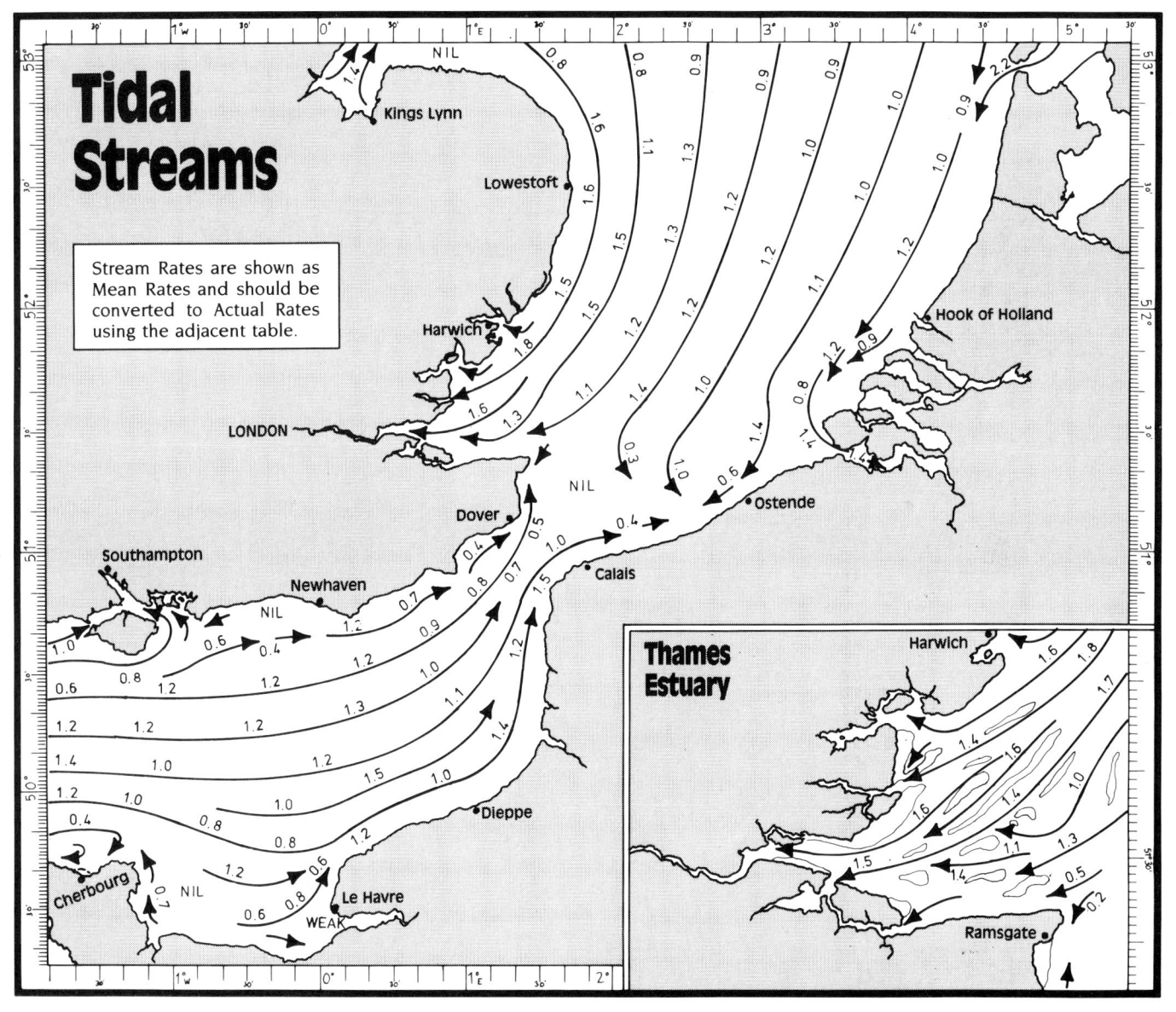

2 hours after HW Cherbourg

+2

Time IS 27 (to be inserted)

Stream Rate Conversion Table

Mean Rate Figure from Chart ▼	\multicolumn{11}{c}{Pencil-in height of HW Cherbourg — Read from column below pencil mark}
	4.8	5.0	5.2	5.4	5.6	5.8	6.0	6.2	6.4	6.6	6.8
0.1	0.1	0.1	0.1	0.1	0.1	0.1	0.1	0.1	0.1	0.1	0.2
0.2	0.1	0.1	0.2	0.2	0.2	0.2	0.2	0.2	0.3	0.3	0.3
0.3	0.2	0.2	0.2	0.3	0.3	0.3	0.3	0.4	0.4	0.4	0.5
0.4	0.2	0.3	0.3	0.3	0.4	0.4	0.4	0.5	0.5	0.5	0.6	0.6
0.5	0.3	0.3	0.4	0.4	0.5	0.5	0.6	0.6	0.6	0.7	0.7	0.8
0.6	0.4	0.4	0.5	0.5	0.6	0.6	0.7	0.7	0.8	0.8	0.9	0.9
0.7	0.4	0.5	0.5	0.6	0.7	0.7	0.8	0.8	0.9	0.9	1.0	1.1
0.8	0.5	0.6	0.6	0.7	0.8	0.8	0.9	0.9	1.0	1.1	1.1	1.2
0.9	0.5	0.6	0.7	0.8	0.8	0.9	1.0	1.1	1.1	1.2	1.3	1.4
1.0	0.6	0.7	0.8	0.9	0.9	1.0	1.1	1.2	1.3	1.4	1.4	1.5
1.1	0.7	0.8	0.8	0.9	1.0	1.1	1.2	1.3	1.4	1.5	1.6	1.7
1.2	0.7	0.8	0.9	1.0	1.1	1.2	1.3	1.4	1.5	1.6	1.7	1.8
1.3	0.8	0.9	1.0	1.1	1.2	1.3	1.4	1.5	1.7	1.8	1.9	2.0
1.4	0.8	1.0	1.1	1.2	1.3	1.4	1.5	1.7	1.8	1.9	2.0	2.1
1.5	0.9	1.0	1.2	1.3	1.4	1.5	1.7	1.8	1.9	2.0	2.2	2.3
1.6	1.0	1.1	1.2	1.4	1.5	1.6	1.8	1.9	2.0	2.2	2.3	2.4
1.7	1.0	1.2	1.3	1.5	1.6	1.7	1.9	2.0	2.2	2.3	2.4	2.6
1.8	1.1	1.2	1.4	1.5	1.7	1.8	2.0	2.1	2.3	2.4	2.6	2.7
1.9	1.2	1.3	1.5	1.6	1.8	1.9	2.1	2.3	2.4	2.6	2.7	2.9
2.0	1.2	1.4	1.5	1.7	1.9	2.0	2.2	2.4	2.5	2.7	2.9	3.0
2.1	1.3	1.4	1.6	1.8	2.0	2.1	2.3	2.5	2.7	2.8	3.0	3.2
2.2	1.3	1.5	1.7	1.9	2.1	2.2	2.4	2.6	2.8	3.0	3.2	3.3
2.3	1.4	1.6	1.8	2.0	2.2	2.3	2.5	2.7	2.9	3.1	3.3	3.5
2.4	1.5	1.7	1.9	2.1	2.3	2.4	2.6	2.8	3.0	3.2	3.4	3.6
2.5	1.5	1.7	1.9	2.1	2.3	2.6	2.8	3.0	3.2	3.4	3.6	3.8
2.6	1.6	1.8	2.0	2.2	2.4	2.7	2.9	3.1	3.3	3.5	3.7	4.0
2.7	1.6	1.9	2.1	2.3	2.5	2.8	3.0	3.2	3.4	3.7	3.9	4.1
2.8	1.7	1.9	2.2	2.4	2.6	2.9	3.1	3.3	3.6	3.8	4.0	4.3
2.9	1.8	2.0	2.2	2.5	2.7	3.0	3.2	3.4	3.7	3.9	4.2	4.4
3.0	1.8	2.1	2.3	2.6	2.8	3.1	3.3	3.6	3.8	4.1	4.3	4.6
3.1	1.9	2.1	2.4	2.7	2.9	3.2	3.4	3.7	4.0	4.2	4.5	4.7
3.2	1.9	2.2	2.4	2.7	3.0	3.3	3.5	3.8	4.1	4.4	4.7	4.9
3.3	2.0	2.3	2.5	2.8	3.1	3.4	3.7	4.0	4.2	4.5	4.8	5.1
3.4	2.0	2.3	2.6	2.9	3.2	3.5	3.8	4.1	4.4	4.7	5.0	5.3
3.5	2.1	2.3	2.7	3.0	3.3	3.6	3.9	4.2	4.5	4.8	5.1	5.4
3.6	2.1	2.4	2.7	3.1	3.4	3.7	4.0	4.3	4.6	4.9	5.2	5.6
3.7	2.2	2.5	2.8	3.1	3.5	3.8	4.1	4.4	4.7	5.1	5.4	5.8
3.8	2.2	2.6	2.9	3.2	3.6	3.9	4.2	4.5	4.9	5.2	5.5	5.9
3.9	2.3	2.6	2.9	3.3	3.7	4.0	4.3	4.7	5.0	5.3	5.7	6.1
4.0	2.3	2.7	3.0	3.4	3.7	4.1	4.4	4.8	5.1	5.5	5.8	6.2

Tidal Streams

Stream Rates are shown as Mean Rates and should be converted to Actual Rates using the adjacent table.

Thames Estuary

+3 — 3 hours after HW Cherbourg

Tidal Heights

Copyright © J Reeve-Fowkes and Thomas Reed Publications.
No copying without permission.

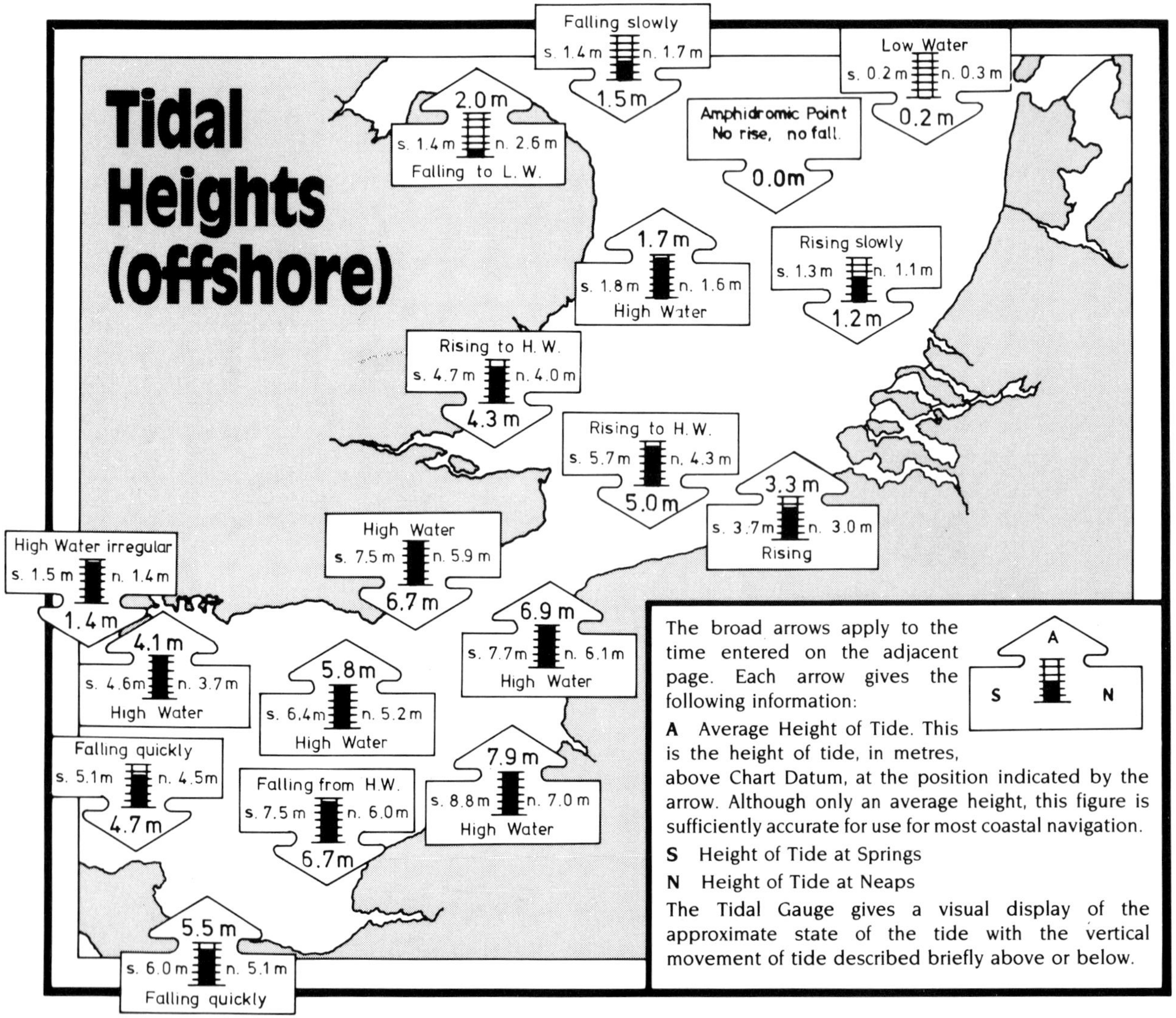

Tidal Heights (offshore)

Falling slowly — s. 1.4 m n. 1.7 m — 1.5 m

Low Water — s. 0.2 m n. 0.3 m — 0.2 m

2.0 m — s. 1.4 m n. 2.6 m — Falling to L.W.

Amphidromic Point No rise, no fall — 0.0 m

1.7 m — s. 1.8 m n. 1.6 m — High Water

Rising slowly — s. 1.3 m n. 1.1 m — 1.2 m

Rising to H.W. — s. 4.7 m n. 4.0 m — 4.3 m

Rising to H.W. — s. 5.7 m n. 4.3 m — 5.0 m

3.3 m — s. 3.7 m n. 3.0 m — Rising

High Water — s. 7.5 m n. 5.9 m — 6.7 m

6.9 m — s. 7.7 m n. 6.1 m — High Water

High Water irregular — s. 1.5 m n. 1.4 m — 1.4 m

4.1 m — s. 4.6 m n. 3.7 m — High Water

5.8 m — s. 6.4 m n. 5.2 m — High Water

Falling quickly — s. 5.1 m n. 4.5 m — 4.7 m

Falling from H.W. — s. 7.5 m n. 6.0 m — 6.7 m

7.9 m — s. 8.8 m n. 7.0 m — High Water

5.5 m — s. 6.0 m n. 5.1 m — Falling quickly

The broad arrows apply to the time entered on the adjacent page. Each arrow gives the following information:

A Average Height of Tide. This is the height of tide, in metres, above Chart Datum, at the position indicated by the arrow. Although only an average height, this figure is sufficiently accurate for use for most coastal navigation.

S Height of Tide at Springs

N Height of Tide at Neaps

The Tidal Gauge gives a visual display of the approximate state of the tide with the vertical movement of tide described briefly above or below.

TIDAL HEIGHTS — PORTS & PLACES

Pencil-in height of HW Cherbourg ▶	4.8	5.0	5.2	5.4	5.6	5.8	6.0	6.2	6.4	6.6	6.8
ENGLAND											
Kings Lynn	2.8	2.9	2.9	3.0	3.1	3.2	3.2	3.3	3.4	3.5	3.5	3.6
Blakeney Bar	2.6	2.5	2.3	2.2	2.1	2.0	1.8	1.7	1.6	1.5	1.4	1.3
Cromer	2.7	2.6	2.4	2.3	2.2	2.1	2.0	1.9	1.8	1.8	1.7	1.7
Gt. Yarmouth (Gorleston)	1.8	1.8	1.8	1.8	1.8	1.8	1.8	1.8	1.8	1.8	1.8	1.8
Lowestoft	1.9	1.9	1.9	1.9	1.9	2.0	2.0	2.0	2.0	2.1	2.1	2.2
Southwold Haven	2.1	2.1	2.1	2.1	2.2	2.2	2.2	2.3	2.3	2.4	2.4	2.5
Orford Haven appr'ch	2.5	2.6	2.6	2.7	2.8	2.9	2.9	3.0	3.1	3.2	3.3	3.4
Woodbridge Haven	2.6	2.7	2.9	3.0	3.1	3.2	3.3	3.4	3.5	3.6	3.8	3.9
Felixstowe	2.9	3.0	3.0	3.1	3.2	3.3	3.3	3.4	3.5	3.7	3.8	4.0
Harwich	3.1	3.2	3.2	3.3	3.3	3.4	3.4	3.5	3.5	3.6	3.6	3.7
Walton-on-the-Naze	3.1	3.2	3.4	3.5	3.6	3.7	3.8	3.9	4.0	4.1	4.2	4.3
Brightlingsea	3.5	3.6	3.6	3.7	3.8	3.9	4.0	4.1	4.2	4.3	4.5	4.6
Bradwell	3.8	3.9	3.9	4.0	4.1	4.1	4.2	4.2	4.3	4.4	4.4	4.5
Burnham	4.0	4.0	4.0	4.0	4.0	4.1	4.1	4.1	4.1	4.2	4.3	4.4
Leigh, Southend	4.2	4.3	4.3	4.4	4.4	4.5	4.5	4.6	4.6	4.7	4.9	5.0
London Bridge	4.5	4.4	4.4	4.3	4.3	4.2	4.1	4.1	4.0	4.1	4.1	4.2
Sheerness	4.3	4.3	4.3	4.3	4.4	4.4	4.4	4.5	4.5	4.6	4.7	4.9
Chatham	4.2	4.2	4.2	4.2	4.3	4.3	4.3	4.4	4.4	4.5	4.6	4.7
Rochester	3.9	4.0	4.0	4.1	4.1	4.2	4.2	4.3	4.3	4.4	4.6	4.7
Whitstable approach	4.1	4.1	4.1	4.1	4.1	4.2	4.2	4.2	4.2	4.2	4.3	4.3
Edinburgh Channels	3.6	3.7	3.9	4.0	4.1	4.2	4.3	4.4	4.5	4.6	4.6	4.7
Margate	3.5	3.6	3.8	3.9	4.0	4.1	4.3	4.4	4.5	4.6	4.6	4.7
Ramsgate	3.4	3.6	3.8	4.0	4.2	4.3	4.5	4.7	4.9	5.0	5.1	5.2
Dover	5.0	5.2	5.4	5.6	5.8	6.1	6.3	6.5	6.7	6.9	7.0	7.2
Folkestone	5.4	5.6	5.8	6.0	6.2	6.5	6.7	6.9	7.1	7.3	7.4	7.6
Newhaven	4.9	5.1	5.3	5.5	5.7	6.0	6.2	6.4	6.6	6.8	6.9	7.1
Brighton	4.8	5.0	5.2	5.4	5.6	5.9	6.1	6.3	6.5	6.6	6.8	6.9
Shoreham	4.7	4.9	5.1	5.3	5.4	5.6	5.8	5.9	6.1	6.3	6.4	6.6
Littlehampton Hbr	4.2	4.4	4.6	4.8	4.9	5.1	5.3	5.4	5.6	5.7	5.9	6.0
Selsey Bill	4.0	4.1	4.3	4.4	4.5	4.7	4.8	5.0	5.1	5.2	5.3	5.5
Chichester entrance	3.7	3.8	4.0	4.1	4.2	4.3	4.5	4.6	4.7	4.8	4.9	5.0
Portsmouth	3.5	3.6	3.8	4.0	4.2	4.3	4.5	4.6	4.7	4.8	4.8	4.9
Southampton	3.5	3.6	3.8	3.9	4.0	4.1	4.3	4.4	4.5	4.6	4.7	4.8
Cowes I. o W.	3.3	3.4	3.4	3.5	3.7	3.8	3.9	4.1	4.2	4.3	4.3	4.4
Yarmouth I. o W.	2.4	2.5	2.5	2.6	2.6	2.7	2.8	2.8	2.9	3.0	3.2	3.3
Lymington	2.4	2.5	2.5	2.6	2.6	2.7	2.8	2.8	2.9	3.0	3.0	3.1
HOLLAND											
Den Helder	0.7	0.7	0.7	0.7	0.7	0.7	0.7	0.7	0.7	0.7	0.7	0.7
IJmuiden	0.5	0.5	0.5	0.5	0.4	0.4	0.4	0.3	0.3	0.3	0.2	0.2
Scheveningen	0.8	0.7	0.7	0.6	0.6	0.5	0.5	0.4	0.4	0.4	0.3	0.3
Hoek van Holland	0.6	0.6	0.6	0.6	0.5	0.5	0.5	0.4	0.4	0.4	0.4	0.4
Rotterdam	0.4	0.4	0.4	0.4	0.4	0.5	0.5	0.5	0.5	0.5	0.6	0.6
Flushing	2.6	2.5	2.5	2.4	2.4	2.3	2.3	2.2	2.2	2.2	2.3	2.3
BELGIUM											
Zeebrugge	3.1	3.1	3.1	3.1	3.1	3.1	3.1	3.1	3.1	3.1	3.2	3.2
Ostende	3.4	3.5	3.5	3.6	3.7	3.2	3.8	3.9	4.0	4.1	4.1	4.2
Nieuwpoort	3.6	3.7	3.7	3.8	3.9	4.0	4.1	4.2	4.3	4.3	4.3	4.3
FRANCE											
Dunkerque	4.3	4.4	4.6	4.7	4.8	5.0	5.1	5.3	5.4	5.5	5.5	5.6
Calais	5.3	5.5	5.7	5.9	6.0	6.2	6.4	6.5	6.7	6.8	6.8	6.9
Boulogne	6.9	7.2	7.4	7.7	7.9	8.2	8.4	8.7	8.9	9.0	9.2	9.3
Somme Estuary	7.3	7.6	8.0	8.3	8.6	8.9	9.2	9.5	9.8	9.9	10.1	10.2
Le Tréport	7.1	7.4	7.6	7.9	8.2	8.5	8.8	9.1	9.4	9.6	9.7	9.9
Dieppe	6.7	7.0	7.4	7.7	8.0	8.3	8.7	9.0	9.3	9.5	9.6	9.8
Fécamp	5.8	6.1	6.3	6.6	6.8	7.1	7.3	7.6	7.8	7.9	8.1	8.2
Le Havre	6.0	6.2	6.4	6.6	6.8	7.1	7.3	7.5	7.7	7.8	8.0	8.1
Ouistreham	5.7	5.9	6.1	6.3	6.4	6.6	6.8	6.9	7.1	7.2	7.3	7.4
Port-en-Bessin	5.5	5.6	5.6	5.7	5.8	5.9	5.9	6.0	6.1	6.2	6.2	6.3
Saint-Vaast-la-Hougue	4.6	4.7	4.7	4.8	4.9	5.0	5.1	5.2	5.3	5.4	5.4	5.5
Barfleur	4.4	4.5	4.5	4.6	4.7	4.8	4.8	4.9	5.0	5.1	5.2	5.3

Stream Rate Conversion Table

Mean Rate Figure from Chart ▼	Pencil-in height of HW Cherbourg Read from column below pencil mark										
	4.8	5.0	5.2	5.4	5.6	5.8	6.0	6.2	6.4	6.6	6.8
0.1	0.1	0.1	0.1	0.1	0.1	0.1	0.1	0.1	0.1	0.1	0.2
0.2	0.1	0.1	0.2	0.2	0.2	0.2	0.2	0.2	0.3	0.3	0.3
0.3	0.2	0.2	0.2	0.3	0.3	0.3	0.3	0.4	0.4	0.4	0.5
0.4	0.2	0.3	0.3	0.3	0.4	0.4	0.4	0.5	0.5	0.6	0.6
0.5	0.3	0.3	0.4	0.4	0.5	0.5	0.6	0.6	0.7	0.7	0.8
0.6	0.4	0.4	0.5	0.5	0.6	0.6	0.7	0.7	0.8	0.8	0.9
0.7	0.4	0.5	0.5	0.6	0.7	0.7	0.8	0.8	0.9	0.9	1.0	1.1
0.8	0.5	0.6	0.6	0.7	0.8	0.8	0.9	1.0	1.1	1.1	1.2
0.9	0.5	0.6	0.7	0.8	0.8	0.9	1.0	1.1	1.1	1.2	1.3	1.4
1.0	0.6	0.7	0.8	0.9	0.9	1.0	1.1	1.2	1.3	1.4	1.4	1.5
1.1	0.7	0.8	0.8	0.9	1.0	1.1	1.2	1.3	1.4	1.5	1.6	1.7
1.2	0.7	0.8	0.9	1.0	1.1	1.2	1.3	1.4	1.5	1.6	1.7	1.8
1.3	0.8	0.9	1.0	1.1	1.2	1.3	1.4	1.5	1.7	1.8	1.9	2.0
1.4	0.8	1.0	1.1	1.2	1.3	1.4	1.5	1.7	1.8	1.9	2.0	2.1
1.5	0.9	1.0	1.2	1.3	1.4	1.5	1.7	1.8	1.9	2.0	2.2	2.3
1.6	1.0	1.1	1.2	1.4	1.5	1.6	1.8	1.9	2.0	2.2	2.3	2.4
1.7	1.0	1.2	1.3	1.5	1.6	1.7	1.9	2.0	2.2	2.3	2.4	2.6
1.8	1.1	1.2	1.4	1.5	1.7	1.8	2.0	2.1	2.3	2.4	2.6	2.7
1.9	1.2	1.3	1.5	1.6	1.8	1.9	2.1	2.3	2.4	2.6	2.7	2.9
2.0	1.2	1.4	1.5	1.7	1.9	2.0	2.2	2.4	2.5	2.7	2.9	3.0
2.1	1.3	1.4	1.6	1.8	2.0	2.1	2.3	2.5	2.7	2.8	3.0	3.2
2.2	1.3	1.5	1.7	1.9	2.1	2.2	2.4	2.6	2.8	3.0	3.2	3.3
2.3	1.4	1.6	1.8	2.0	2.2	2.3	2.5	2.7	2.9	3.1	3.3	3.5
2.4	1.5	1.7	1.9	2.1	2.3	2.4	2.6	2.8	3.0	3.2	3.4	3.6
2.5	1.5	1.7	1.9	2.1	2.3	2.6	2.8	3.0	3.2	3.4	3.6	3.8
2.6	1.6	1.8	2.0	2.2	2.4	2.7	2.9	3.1	3.3	3.5	3.7	4.0
2.7	1.6	1.9	2.1	2.3	2.5	2.8	3.0	3.2	3.4	3.7	3.9	4.1
2.8	1.7	1.9	2.2	2.4	2.6	2.9	3.1	3.3	3.6	3.8	4.0	4.3
2.9	1.8	2.0	2.2	2.5	2.7	3.0	3.2	3.4	3.7	3.9	4.2	4.4
3.0	1.8	2.1	2.3	2.6	2.8	3.1	3.3	3.6	3.8	4.1	4.3	4.6
3.1	1.9	2.1	2.4	2.7	2.9	3.2	3.4	3.7	4.0	4.2	4.5	4.7
3.2	1.9	2.2	2.4	2.7	3.0	3.3	3.5	3.8	4.1	4.4	4.7	4.9
3.3	2.0	2.2	2.5	2.8	3.1	3.4	3.7	4.0	4.2	4.5	4.8	5.1
3.4	2.0	2.3	2.6	2.9	3.2	3.5	3.8	4.1	4.4	4.7	5.0	5.3
3.5	2.1	2.3	2.7	3.0	3.3	3.6	3.9	4.2	4.5	4.8	5.1	5.4
3.6	2.1	2.4	2.7	3.1	3.4	3.7	4.0	4.3	4.6	4.9	5.2	5.6
3.7	2.2	2.5	2.8	3.1	3.5	3.8	4.1	4.4	4.7	5.1	5.4	5.8
3.8	2.2	2.6	2.9	3.2	3.6	3.9	4.2	4.5	4.9	5.2	5.5	5.9
3.9	2.3	2.6	2.9	3.3	3.7	4.0	4.3	4.7	5.0	5.3	5.7	6.1
4.0	2.3	2.7	3.0	3.4	3.7	4.1	4.4	4.8	5.1	5.5	5.8	6.2

Tidal Stream Rates

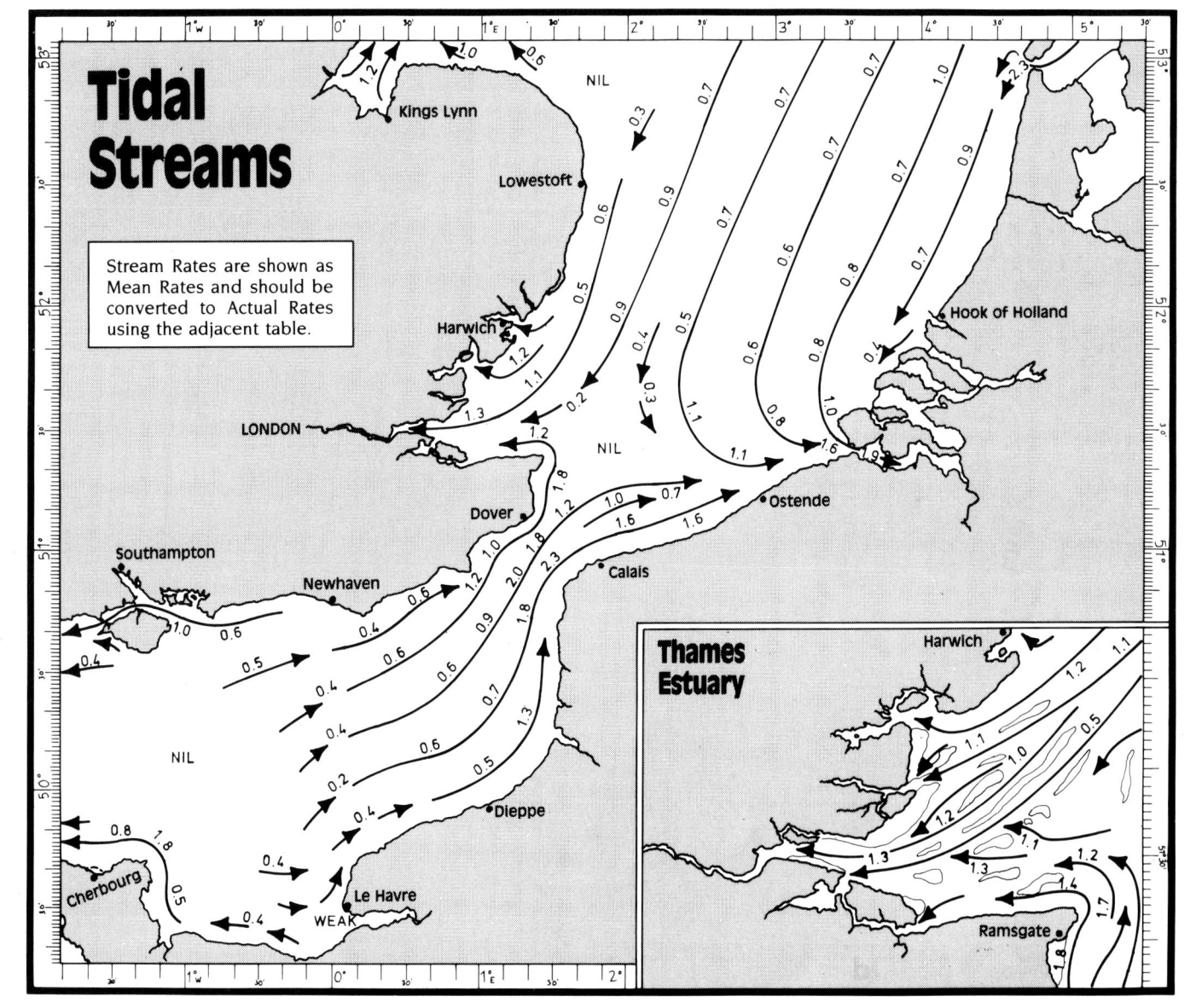

3 hours after HW Cherbourg **+3**

Time 16.27 (to be inserted)

Tidal Streams

Stream Rates are shown as Mean Rates and should be converted to Actual Rates using the adjacent table.

Thames Estuary

+4 — 4 hours after HW Cherbourg

Tidal Heights

Copyright © J Reeve-Fowkes and Thomas Reed Publications.
No copying without permission.

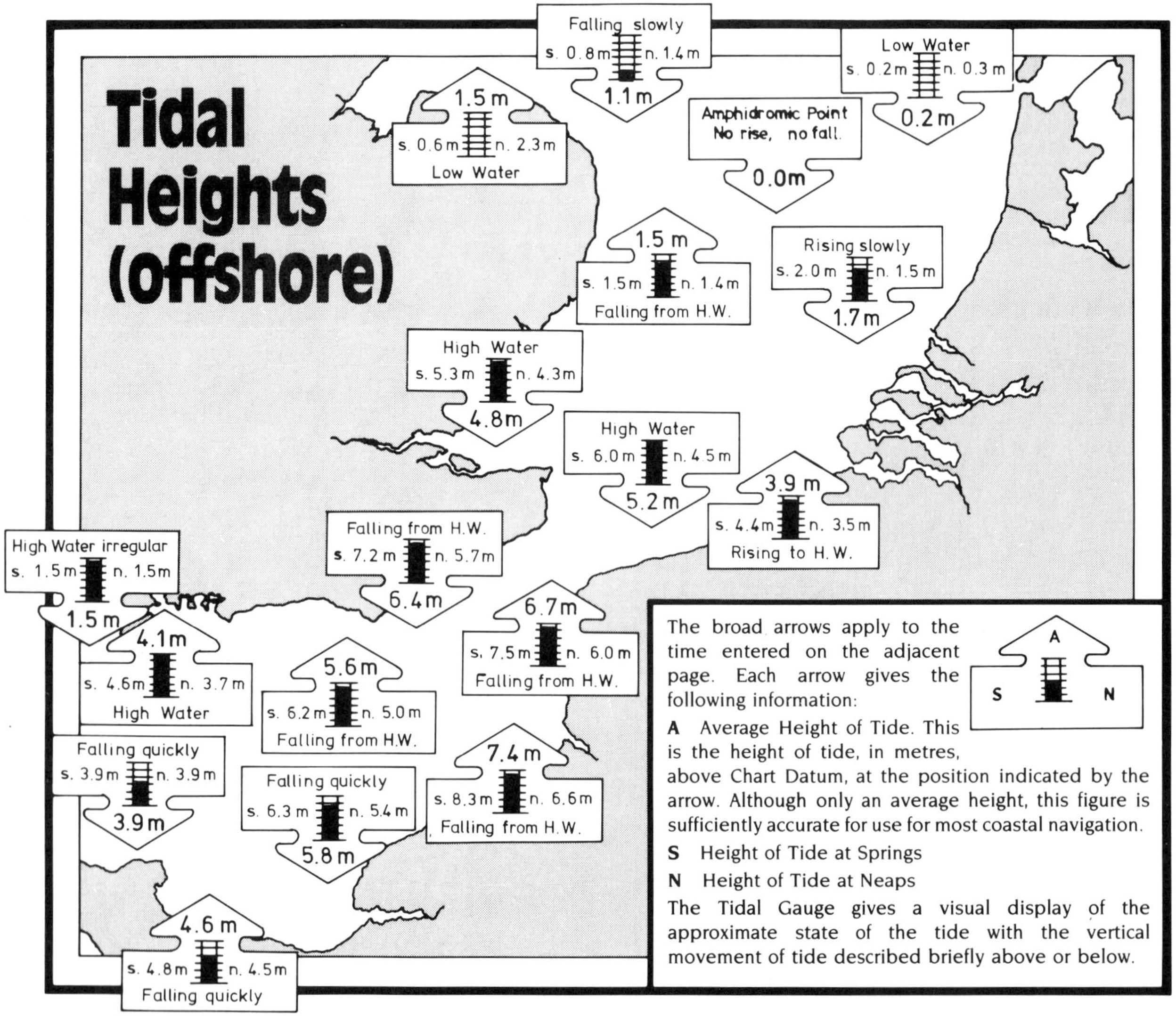

Tidal Heights (offshore)

Falling slowly
s. 0.8m n. 1.4m
1.1 m

Low Water
s. 0.2m n. 0.3m
0.2 m

1.5 m
s. 0.6m n. 2.3m
Low Water

Amphidromic Point
No rise, no fall.
0.0 m

1.5 m
s. 1.5m n. 1.4m
Falling from H.W.

Rising slowly
s. 2.0m n. 1.5m
1.7 m

High Water
s. 5.3m n. 4.3m
4.8 m

High Water
s. 6.0m n. 4.5m
5.2 m

3.9 m
s. 4.4m n. 3.5m
Rising to H.W.

Falling from H.W.
s. 7.2m n. 5.7m
6.4 m

6.7 m
s. 7.5m n. 6.0m
Falling from H.W.

High Water irregular
s. 1.5m n. 1.5m
1.5 m

4.1 m
s. 4.6m n. 3.7m
High Water

5.6 m
s. 6.2m n. 5.0m
Falling from H.W.

Falling quickly
s. 3.9m n. 3.9m
3.9 m

Falling quickly
s. 6.3m n. 5.4m
5.8 m

7.4 m
s. 8.3m n. 6.6m
Falling from H.W.

4.6 m
s. 4.8m n. 4.5m
Falling quickly

The broad arrows apply to the time entered on the adjacent page. Each arrow gives the following information:

A Average Height of Tide. This is the height of tide, in metres, above Chart Datum, at the position indicated by the arrow. Although only an average height, this figure is sufficiently accurate for use for most coastal navigation.

S Height of Tide at Springs

N Height of Tide at Neaps

The Tidal Gauge gives a visual display of the approximate state of the tide with the vertical movement of tide described briefly above or below.

TIDAL HEIGHTS — PORTS & PLACES

Pencil-in height of HW Cherbourg ▶	4.8	5.0	5.2	5.4	5.6	5.8	6.0	6.2	6.4	6.6	6.8
ENGLAND											
Kings Lynn	2.3	2.3	2.3	2.3	2.3	2.4	2.4	2.4	2.4	2.4	2.5	2.5
Blakeney Bar	2.4	2.2	2.0	1.8	1.6	1.4	1.2	1.0	0.8	0.7	0.5	0.4
Cromer	2.3	2.1	1.9	1.7	1.6	1.4	1.2	1.1	0.9	0.9	0.8	0.8
Gt. Yarmouth (Gorleston)	1.5	1.5	1.5	1.5	1.5	1.4	1.4	1.4	1.4	1.4	1.4	1.4
Lowestoft	1.6	1.6	1.6	1.6	1.6	1.6	1.6	1.6	1.6	1.6	1.6	1.6
Southwold Haven	1.9	1.9	1.9	1.9	1.9	1.9	1.9	1.9	1.9	1.9	2.0	2.0
Orford Haven appr'ch	2.4	2.5	2.5	2.6	2.7	2.8	2.9	3.0	3.1	3.2	3.3	3.4
Woodbridge Haven	2.7	2.8	3.0	3.1	3.2	3.3	3.5	3.6	3.7	3.8	4.0	4.1
Felixstowe	2.8	2.9	3.1	3.2	3.3	3.4	3.5	3.6	3.7	3.9	4.0	4.2
Harwich	3.3	3.4	3.4	3.5	3.6	3.7	3.8	3.9	4.0	4.1	4.1	4.2
Walton-on-the-Naze	3.2	3.3	3.5	3.6	3.7	3.8	4.0	4.1	4.2	4.3	4.5	4.6
Brightlingsea	3.5	3.7	3.9	4.1	4.3	4.4	4.6	4.8	5.0	5.2	5.3	5.5
Bradwell	4.0	4.1	4.3	4.4	4.6	4.7	4.9	5.0	5.2	5.3	5.4	5.5
Burnham	4.2	4.3	4.5	4.6	4.7	4.8	5.0	5.1	5.2	5.4	5.5	5.7
Leigh, Southend	4.5	4.6	4.8	4.9	5.0	5.1	5.3	5.4	5.5	5.7	5.8	6.0
London Bridge	5.2	5.2	5.2	5.2	5.2	5.3	5.3	5.3	5.3	5.4	5.6	5.7
Sheerness	4.5	4.6	4.8	4.9	5.0	5.1	5.2	5.3	5.4	5.6	5.7	5.9
Chatham	4.5	4.6	4.8	4.9	5.0	5.1	5.3	5.4	5.5	5.7	5.8	6.0
Rochester	4.4	4.5	4.7	4.8	4.9	5.0	5.1	5.2	5.3	5.5	5.8	6.0
Whitstable approach	4.2	4.3	4.5	4.6	4.7	4.8	5.0	5.1	5.2	5.3	5.3	5.4
Edinburgh Channels	3.8	3.9	4.1	4.2	4.3	4.4	4.6	4.7	4.8	4.9	5.0	5.1
Margate	3.7	3.8	4.0	4.1	4.2	4.4	4.5	4.7	4.8	4.9	4.9	5.0
Ramsgate	3.5	3.7	3.9	4.1	4.2	4.4	4.6	4.7	4.9	5.0	5.1	5.2
Dover	4.9	5.1	5.3	5.5	5.7	5.9	6.1	6.3	6.5	6.7	6.8	7.0
Folkestone	5.2	5.4	5.6	5.8	6.0	6.1	6.3	6.5	6.7	6.9	7.0	7.2
Newhaven	4.7	4.9	5.1	5.3	5.5	5.8	6.0	6.2	6.4	6.5	6.7	6.8
Brighton	4.7	4.9	5.1	5.3	5.5	5.7	5.9	6.1	6.3	6.4	6.6	6.7
Shoreham	4.6	4.8	5.0	5.2	5.3	5.5	5.7	5.8	6.0	6.1	6.3	6.4
Littlehampton Hbr	4.3	4.4	4.6	4.7	4.9	5.0	5.2	5.3	5.5	5.6	5.8	5.9
Selsey Bill	4.2	4.3	4.5	4.6	4.7	4.9	5.0	5.2	5.3	5.4	5.4	5.5
Chichester entrance	3.8	3.9	4.1	4.2	4.3	4.5	4.6	4.8	4.9	5.0	5.1	5.2
Portsmouth	3.6	3.7	3.9	4.0	4.1	4.2	4.4	4.5	4.6	4.7	4.8	4.9
Southampton	3.6	3.7	3.7	3.8	3.9	4.0	4.1	4.2	4.3	4.4	4.5	4.6
Cowes I. o W.	3.3	3.4	3.4	3.5	3.6	3.7	3.8	4.0	4.1	4.2	4.2	4.3
Yarmouth I. o W.	2.4	2.5	2.5	2.6	2.6	2.7	2.7	2.8	2.8	2.9	3.1	3.2
Lymington	2.4	2.5	2.5	2.6	2.6	2.7	2.8	2.8	2.9	3.0	3.0	3.1
HOLLAND											
Den Helder	0.5	0.5	0.5	0.5	0.5	0.4	0.4	0.4	0.4	0.4	0.4	0.4
IJmuiden	0.8	0.7	0.7	0.6	0.6	0.5	0.5	0.4	0.4	0.4	0.3	0.3
Scheveningen	0.9	0.9	0.9	0.9	0.8	0.8	0.8	0.7	0.7	0.7	0.6	0.6
Hoek van Holland	1.1	1.0	1.0	0.9	0.9	0.8	0.8	0.7	0.7	0.7	0.7	0.7
Rotterdam	0.6	0.6	0.6	0.6	0.6	0.5	0.5	0.5	0.5	0.5	0.6	0.6
Flushing	3.3	3.3	3.3	3.3	3.3	3.4	3.4	3.4	3.4	3.5	3.7	3.8
BELGIUM											
Zeebrugge	3.5	3.6	3.8	3.9	4.0	4.1	4.3	4.4	4.5	4.6	4.7	4.8
Ostende	3.8	3.9	4.1	4.2	4.4	4.5	4.7	4.8	5.0	5.1	5.1	5.2
Nieuwpoort	4.0	4.1	4.3	4.4	4.5	4.7	4.8	5.0	5.1	5.1	5.2	5.2
FRANCE											
Dunkerque	4.6	4.7	4.9	5.0	5.2	5.3	5.5	5.6	5.8	5.9	5.9	6.0
Calais	5.5	5.7	5.9	6.1	6.3	6.4	6.6	6.8	7.0	7.1	7.1	7.2
Boulogne	6.7	7.0	7.2	7.5	7.8	8.0	8.3	8.5	8.8	8.9	9.1	9.2
Somme Estuary	7.3	7.6	7.8	8.1	8.4	8.7	9.0	9.3	9.6	9.7	9.8	10.0
Le Tréport	6.6	6.8	7.0	7.2	7.5	7.7	7.9	8.2	8.4	8.5	8.7	8.8
Dieppe	6.2	6.5	6.7	7.0	7.3	7.5	7.8	8.0	8.3	8.4	8.5	8.6
Fécamp	5.4	5.5	5.7	5.8	5.9	6.1	6.2	6.4	6.5	6.6	6.7	6.8
Le Havre	5.8	5.9	6.1	6.2	6.4	6.5	6.7	6.8	7.0	7.1	7.1	7.2
Ouistreham	5.5	5.6	5.6	5.7	5.7	5.8	5.8	5.9	5.9	5.9	6.0	6.0
Port-en-Bessin	5.1	5.1	5.1	5.1	5.0	5.0	5.0	4.9	4.9	4.9	4.8	4.8
Saint-Vaast-la-Hougue	4.0	4.0	4.0	4.0	4.1	4.1	4.1	4.2	4.2	4.2	4.2	4.2
Barfleur	3.9	3.9	3.9	3.9	3.9	3.9	3.9	3.9	3.9	3.9	3.9	3.9

Stream Rate Conversion Table

| Mean Rate Figure from Chart ▼ | Pencil-in height of HW Cherbourg Read from column below pencil mark |||||||||||
	4.8	5.0	5.2	5.4	5.6	5.8	6.0	6.2	6.4	6.6	6.8
0.1	0.1	0.1	0.1	0.1	0.1	0.1	0.1	0.1	0.1	0.1	0.2
0.2	0.1	0.1	0.2	0.2	0.2	0.2	0.2	0.2	0.3	0.3	0.3
0.3	0.2	0.2	0.2	0.3	0.3	0.3	0.3	0.4	0.4	0.4	0.5
0.4	0.2	0.3	0.3	0.3	0.4	0.4	0.4	0.5	0.5	0.5	0.6
0.5	0.3	0.3	0.4	0.4	0.5	0.5	0.6	0.6	0.6	0.7	0.8
0.6	0.4	0.4	0.5	0.5	0.6	0.6	0.7	0.7	0.8	0.8	0.9	0.9
0.7	0.4	0.5	0.5	0.6	0.7	0.7	0.8	0.8	0.9	0.9	1.0	1.1
0.8	0.5	0.6	0.6	0.7	0.8	0.8	0.9	0.9	1.0	1.1	1.1	1.2
0.9	0.5	0.6	0.7	0.8	0.8	0.9	1.0	1.1	1.1	1.2	1.3	1.4
1.0	0.6	0.7	0.8	0.9	0.9	1.0	1.1	1.2	1.3	1.4	1.4	1.5
1.1	0.7	0.8	0.8	0.9	1.0	1.1	1.2	1.3	1.4	1.5	1.6	1.7
1.2	0.7	0.8	0.9	1.0	1.1	1.2	1.3	1.4	1.5	1.6	1.7	1.8
1.3	0.8	0.9	1.0	1.1	1.2	1.3	1.4	1.5	1.7	1.8	1.9	2.0
1.4	0.8	1.0	1.1	1.2	1.3	1.4	1.5	1.7	1.8	1.9	2.0	2.1
1.5	0.9	1.0	1.2	1.3	1.4	1.5	1.7	1.8	1.9	2.0	2.2	2.3
1.6	1.0	1.1	1.2	1.4	1.5	1.6	1.8	1.9	2.0	2.2	2.3	2.4
1.7	1.0	1.2	1.3	1.5	1.6	1.7	1.9	2.0	2.2	2.3	2.4	2.6
1.8	1.1	1.2	1.4	1.5	1.7	1.8	2.0	2.1	2.3	2.4	2.6	2.7
1.9	1.2	1.3	1.5	1.6	1.8	1.9	2.1	2.3	2.4	2.6	2.7	2.9
2.0	1.2	1.4	1.5	1.7	1.9	2.0	2.2	2.4	2.5	2.7	2.9	3.0
2.1	1.3	1.4	1.6	1.8	2.0	2.1	2.3	2.5	2.7	2.8	3.0	3.2
2.2	1.3	1.5	1.7	1.9	2.1	2.2	2.4	2.6	2.8	3.0	3.2	3.3
2.3	1.4	1.6	1.8	2.0	2.2	2.3	2.5	2.7	2.9	3.1	3.3	3.5
2.4	1.5	1.7	1.9	2.1	2.3	2.4	2.6	2.8	3.0	3.2	3.4	3.6
2.5	1.5	1.7	1.9	2.1	2.3	2.6	2.8	3.0	3.2	3.4	3.6	3.8
2.6	1.6	1.8	2.0	2.2	2.4	2.7	2.9	3.1	3.3	3.5	3.7	4.0
2.7	1.6	1.9	2.1	2.3	2.5	2.8	3.0	3.2	3.4	3.7	3.9	4.1
2.8	1.7	1.9	2.2	2.4	2.6	2.9	3.1	3.3	3.6	3.8	4.0	4.3
2.9	1.8	2.0	2.2	2.5	2.7	3.0	3.2	3.4	3.7	3.9	4.2	4.4
3.0	1.8	2.1	2.3	2.6	2.8	3.1	3.3	3.6	3.8	4.1	4.3	4.6
3.1	1.9	2.1	2.4	2.7	2.9	3.2	3.4	3.7	4.0	4.2	4.5	4.7
3.2	1.9	2.2	2.4	2.7	3.0	3.3	3.5	3.8	4.1	4.4	4.7	4.9
3.3	2.0	2.2	2.5	2.8	3.1	3.4	3.7	4.0	4.2	4.5	4.8	5.1
3.4	2.0	2.3	2.6	2.9	3.2	3.5	3.8	4.1	4.4	4.7	5.0	5.3
3.5	2.1	2.3	2.7	3.0	3.3	3.6	3.9	4.2	4.5	4.8	5.1	5.4
3.6	2.1	2.4	2.7	3.1	3.4	3.7	4.0	4.3	4.6	4.9	5.2	5.6
3.7	2.2	2.5	2.8	3.1	3.5	3.8	4.1	4.4	4.7	5.1	5.4	5.8
3.8	2.2	2.6	2.9	3.2	3.6	3.9	4.2	4.5	4.9	5.2	5.5	5.9
3.9	2.3	2.6	2.9	3.3	3.7	4.0	4.3	4.7	5.0	5.3	5.7	6.1
4.0	2.3	2.7	3.0	3.4	3.7	4.1	4.4	4.8	5.1	5.5	5.8	6.2

Tidal Stream Rates

4 hours after HW Cherbourg

+4

Time (to be inserted)

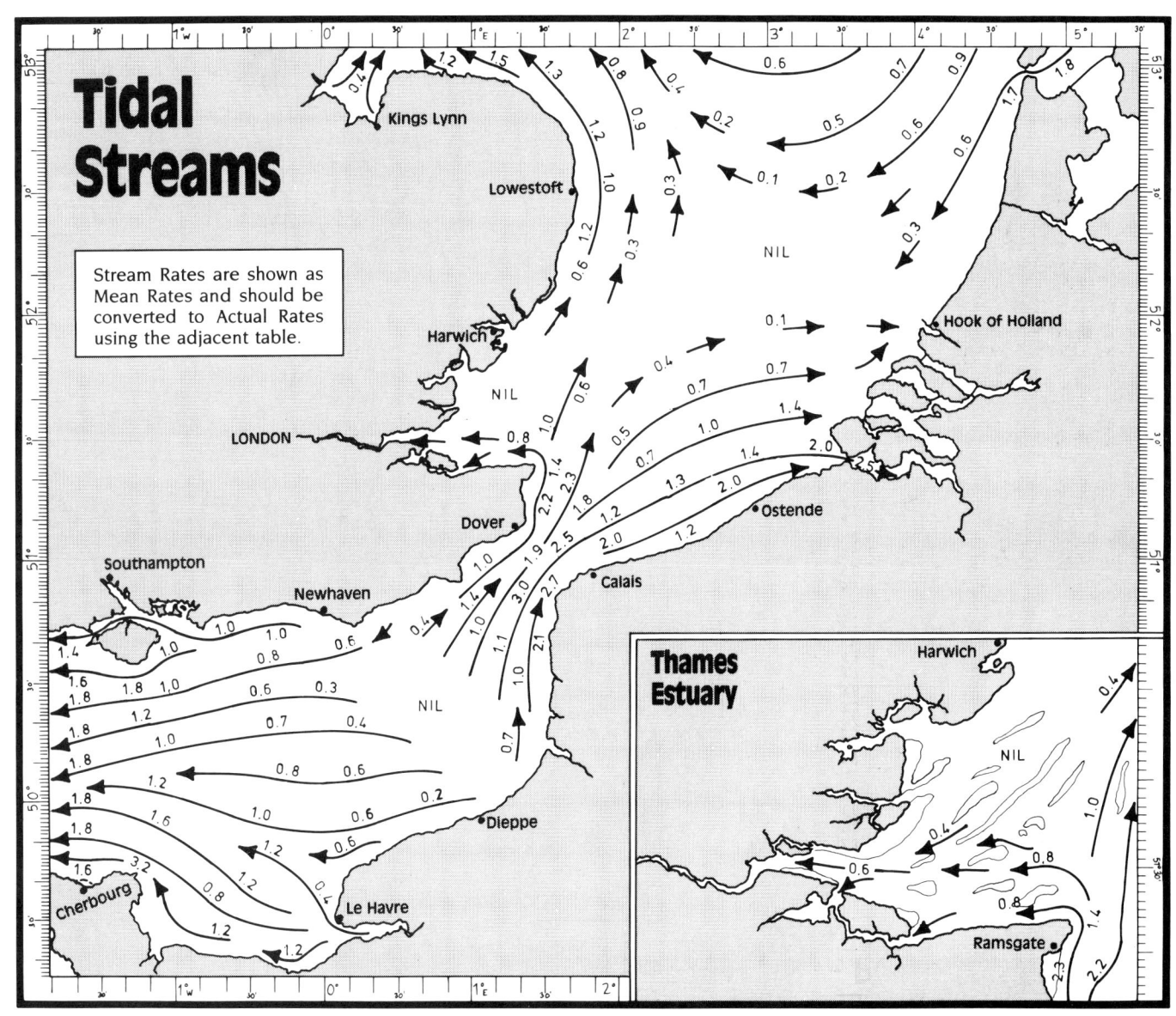

Tidal Streams

Stream Rates are shown as Mean Rates and should be converted to Actual Rates using the adjacent table.

Thames Estuary

+5
5 hours after HW Cherbourg

Tidal Heights

Copyright © J Reeve-Fowkes and
Thomas Reed Publications.
No copying without permission.

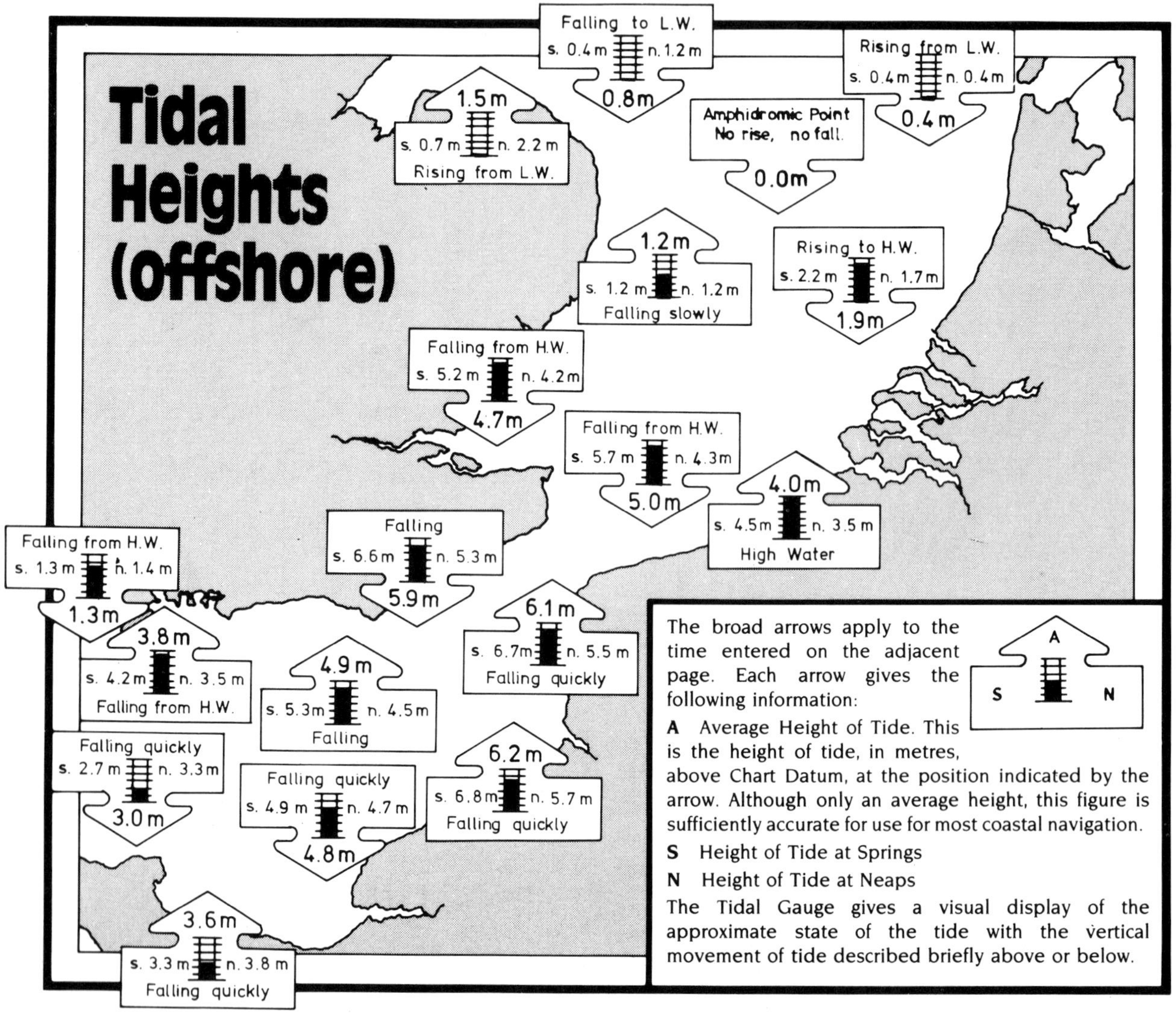

Tidal Heights (offshore)

Falling to L.W.
s. 0.4m   n. 1.2m
0.8m

Rising from L.W.
s. 0.7m   n. 2.2m
1.5m
Rising from L.W.

Amphidromic Point
No rise, no fall.
0.0m

Rising from L.W.
s. 0.4m   n. 0.4m
0.4m

Falling slowly
s. 1.2m   n. 1.2m
1.2m

Rising to H.W.
s. 2.2m   n. 1.7m
1.9m

Falling from H.W.
s. 5.2m   n. 4.2m
4.7m

Falling from H.W.
s. 5.7m   n. 4.3m
5.0m

High Water
s. 4.5m   n. 3.5m
4.0m

Falling from H.W.
s. 1.3m   n. 1.4m
1.3m

Falling from H.W.
s. 4.2m   n. 3.5m
3.8m

Falling
s. 6.6m   n. 5.3m
5.9m

Falling
s. 5.3m   n. 4.5m
4.9m

Falling quickly
s. 6.7m   n. 5.5m
6.1m

Falling quickly
s. 2.7m   n. 3.3m
3.0m

Falling quickly
s. 4.9m   n. 4.7m
4.8m

Falling quickly
s. 6.8m   n. 5.7m
6.2m

Falling quickly
s. 3.3m   n. 3.8m
3.6m

The broad arrows apply to the time entered on the adjacent page. Each arrow gives the following information:

A Average Height of Tide. This is the height of tide, in metres, above Chart Datum, at the position indicated by the arrow. Although only an average height, this figure is sufficiently accurate for use for most coastal navigation.

S Height of Tide at Springs

N Height of Tide at Neaps

The Tidal Gauge gives a visual display of the approximate state of the tide with the vertical movement of tide described briefly above or below.

TIDAL HEIGHTS — PORTS & PLACES

Pencil-in height of HW Cherbourg ▶	4.8	5.0	5.2	5.4	5.6	5.8	6.0	6.2	6.4	6.6	6.8	
ENGLAND												
Kings Lynn	2.0	1.9	1.9	1.8	1.8	1.7	1.7	1.6	1.6	1.6	1.6	1.6
Blakeney Bar	2.4	2.2	2.0	1.8	1.5	1.3	1.0	0.8	0.6	0.5	0.4	0.3
Cromer	2.2	2.0	1.8	1.6	1.4	1.2	1.0	0.8	0.6	0.5	0.5	0.4
Gt. Yarmouth (Gorleston)	1.4	1.3	1.3	1.2	1.2	1.1	1.1	1.0	1.0	0.9	0.9	0.8
Lowestoft	1.3	1.3	1.3	1.3	1.3	1.2	1.2	1.2	1.2	1.2	1.2	1.2
Southwold Haven	1.6	1.6	1.6	1.6	1.6	1.5	1.5	1.5	1.5	1.5	1.5	1.5
Orford Haven appr'ch	2.2	2.3	2.3	2.4	2.4	2.5	2.5	2.6	2.6	2.7	2.7	2.8
Woodbridge Haven	2.5	2.6	2.6	2.7	2.8	2.9	3.0	3.1	3.2	3.3	3.4	3.5
Felixstowe	2.6	2.7	2.7	2.8	2.9	2.9	3.0	3.0	3.1	3.2	3.4	3.5
Harwich	3.0	3.1	3.1	3.2	3.3	3.4	3.4	3.5	3.6	3.6	3.7	3.7
Walton-on-the-Naze	3.0	3.1	3.1	3.2	3.3	3.4	3.5	3.6	3.7	3.8	3.9	4.0
Brightlingsea	3.3	3.5	3.7	3.9	4.0	4.2	4.4	4.5	4.7	4.9	5.1	5.3
Bradwell	3.7	3.9	4.1	4.3	4.4	4.6	4.8	4.9	5.1	5.2	5.3	5.4
Burnham	4.0	4.2	4.4	4.6	4.7	4.9	5.1	5.2	5.4	5.6	5.7	5.9
Leigh, Southend	4.5	4.6	4.8	4.9	5.0	5.2	5.3	5.5	5.6	5.8	6.0	6.2
London Bridge	5.5	5.6	5.8	5.9	6.0	6.1	6.3	6.4	6.5	6.7	6.9	7.1
Sheerness	4.5	4.6	4.8	4.9	5.0	5.2	5.3	5.5	5.6	5.8	6.0	6.2
Chatham	4.5	4.7	4.9	5.1	5.3	5.4	5.6	5.8	6.0	6.2	6.4	6.6
Rochester	4.5	4.7	4.9	5.1	5.2	5.4	5.6	5.7	5.9	6.2	6.4	6.7
Whitstable approach	4.2	4.3	4.5	4.6	4.8	4.9	5.1	5.2	5.4	5.5	5.5	5.6
Edinburgh Channels	3.6	3.7	3.9	4.0	4.1	4.2	4.3	4.4	4.5	4.6	4.7	4.8
Margate	3.5	3.6	3.8	3.9	4.0	4.1	4.3	4.4	4.5	4.6	4.7	4.8
Ramsgate	3.4	3.5	3.7	3.8	3.9	4.1	4.2	4.4	4.5	4.6	4.7	4.8
Dover	4.5	4.7	4.9	5.1	5.2	5.4	5.6	5.7	5.9	6.0	6.1	6.2
Folkestone	4.9	5.0	5.2	5.3	5.4	5.5	5.7	5.8	5.9	6.0	6.2	6.3
Newhaven	4.3	4.4	4.6	4.7	4.8	5.0	5.1	5.3	5.4	5.5	5.7	5.8
Brighton	4.3	4.4	4.6	4.7	4.9	5.0	5.2	5.3	5.5	5.6	5.7	5.8
Shoreham	4.2	4.3	4.5	4.6	4.8	4.9	5.1	5.2	5.4	5.5	5.6	5.7
Littlehampton Hbr	4.1	4.2	4.4	4.5	4.7	4.8	5.0	5.1	5.3	5.4	5.5	5.6
Selsey Bill	4.0	4.1	4.3	4.4	4.5	4.6	4.7	4.8	4.9	5.0	5.1	5.2
Chichester entrance	3.6	3.7	3.9	4.0	4.1	4.2	4.4	4.5	4.6	4.7	4.7	4.8
Portsmouth	3.4	3.5	3.7	3.8	3.9	4.0	4.2	4.3	4.4	4.5	4.5	4.6
Southampton	3.4	3.5	3.7	3.8	3.9	4.0	4.2	4.3	4.4	4.5	4.6	4.7
Cowes I. o W.	3.2	3.3	3.3	3.4	3.5	3.6	3.7	3.8	3.9	3.8	4.0	4.0
Yarmouth I. o W.	2.3	2.4	2.4	2.5	2.5	2.6	2.6	2.7	2.7	2.8	2.9	3.0
Lymington	2.3	2.4	2.4	2.5	2.5	2.6	2.7	2.7	2.8	2.9	2.9	3.0
HOLLAND												
Den Helder	0.6	0.5	0.5	0.4	0.4	0.3	0.3	0.2	0.2	0.2	0.2	0.2
IJmuiden	1.1	1.0	1.0	0.9	0.8	0.8	0.7	0.7	0.6	0.6	0.5	0.5
Scheveningen	1.4	1.4	1.4	1.4	1.3	1.3	1.3	1.2	1.2	1.2	1.2	1.2
Hoek van Holland	1.4	1.4	1.4	1.4	1.4	1.5	1.5	1.5	1.5	1.5	1.6	1.6
Rotterdam	1.0	1.0	1.0	0.9	0.9	0.8	0.8	0.7	0.7	0.7	0.8	0.8
Flushing	3.6	3.7	3.9	4.0	4.1	4.3	4.4	4.6	4.7	4.8	4.9	5.0
BELGIUM												
Zeebrugge	3.8	3.9	4.1	4.2	4.3	4.5	4.6	4.8	4.9	5.0	5.1	5.2
Ostende	3.9	4.0	4.2	4.3	4.4	4.5	4.7	4.8	4.9	4.9	5.0	5.0
Nieuwpoort	3.9	4.0	4.2	4.3	4.4	4.5	4.6	4.7	4.8	4.9	4.9	5.0
FRANCE												
Dunkerque	4.5	4.6	4.8	4.9	5.0	5.2	5.3	5.5	5.6	5.7	5.7	5.8
Calais	5.2	5.3	5.5	5.6	5.8	5.9	6.1	6.2	6.4	6.5	6.5	6.6
Boulogne	6.2	6.4	6.6	6.8	7.0	7.3	7.5	7.7	7.9	8.0	8.1	8.2
Somme Estuary	6.4	6.6	6.8	7.0	7.2	7.4	7.6	7.8	8.0	8.1	8.1	8.2
Le Tréport	5.7	5.8	6.0	6.1	6.2	6.4	6.5	6.7	6.8	6.9	7.0	7.1
Dieppe	5.5	5.6	5.8	5.9	6.0	6.2	6.3	6.5	6.6	6.7	6.7	6.8
Fécamp	4.8	4.8	4.8	4.8	4.9	4.9	4.9	5.0	5.0	5.0	5.1	5.1
Le Havre	5.2	5.2	5.2	5.2	5.3	5.3	5.3	5.4	5.4	5.4	5.4	5.4
Ouistreham	4.7	4.6	4.6	4.5	4.5	4.4	4.4	4.3	4.3	4.3	4.2	4.2
Port-en-Bessin	4.3	4.2	4.2	4.1	4.0	3.9	3.8	3.7	3.6	3.5	3.5	3.4
Saint-Vaast-la-Hougue	3.5	3.4	3.4	3.3	3.3	3.2	3.2	3.1	3.1	3.0	3.0	2.9
Barfleur	3.4	3.3	3.3	3.2	3.1	3.0	3.0	2.9	2.8	2.7	2.5	2.4

Stream Rate Conversion Table

Mean Rate Figure from Chart ▼	Pencil-in height of HW Cherbourg Read from column below pencil mark										
	4.8	5.0	5.2	5.4	5.6	5.8	6.0	6.2	6.4	6.6	6.8
0.1	0.1	0.1	0.1	0.1	0.1	0.1	0.1	0.1	0.1	0.1	0.2
0.2	0.1	0.1	0.2	0.2	0.2	0.2	0.2	0.2	0.3	0.3	0.3
0.3	0.2	0.2	0.2	0.3	0.3	0.3	0.3	0.4	0.4	0.4	0.5
0.4	0.2	0.3	0.3	0.3	0.4	0.4	0.4	0.5	0.5	0.5	0.6
0.5	0.3	0.3	0.4	0.4	0.5	0.5	0.6	0.6	0.6	0.7	0.8
0.6	0.4	0.4	0.5	0.5	0.6	0.6	0.7	0.7	0.8	0.8	0.9
0.7	0.4	0.5	0.5	0.6	0.7	0.7	0.8	0.8	0.9	0.9	1.0	1.1
0.8	0.5	0.6	0.6	0.7	0.8	0.8	0.9	1.0	1.1	1.1	1.2
0.9	0.5	0.6	0.7	0.8	0.8	0.9	1.0	1.1	1.1	1.2	1.3	1.4
1.0	0.6	0.7	0.8	0.9	0.9	1.0	1.1	1.2	1.3	1.4	1.4	1.5
1.1	0.7	0.8	0.8	0.9	1.0	1.1	1.2	1.3	1.4	1.5	1.6	1.7
1.2	0.7	0.8	0.9	1.0	1.1	1.2	1.3	1.4	1.5	1.6	1.7	1.8
1.3	0.8	0.9	1.0	1.1	1.2	1.3	1.4	1.5	1.7	1.8	1.9	2.0
1.4	0.8	1.0	1.1	1.2	1.3	1.4	1.5	1.7	1.8	1.9	2.0	2.1
1.5	0.9	1.0	1.2	1.3	1.4	1.5	1.7	1.8	1.9	2.0	2.2	2.3
1.6	1.0	1.1	1.2	1.4	1.5	1.6	1.8	1.9	2.0	2.2	2.3	2.4
1.7	1.0	1.2	1.3	1.5	1.6	1.7	1.9	2.0	2.2	2.3	2.4	2.6
1.8	1.1	1.2	1.4	1.5	1.7	1.8	2.0	2.1	2.3	2.4	2.6	2.7
1.9	1.2	1.3	1.5	1.6	1.8	1.9	2.1	2.3	2.4	2.6	2.7	2.9
2.0	1.2	1.4	1.5	1.7	1.9	2.0	2.2	2.4	2.5	2.7	2.9	3.0
2.1	1.3	1.4	1.6	1.8	2.0	2.1	2.3	2.5	2.7	2.8	3.0	3.2
2.2	1.3	1.5	1.7	1.9	2.1	2.2	2.4	2.6	2.8	3.0	3.2	3.3
2.3	1.4	1.6	1.8	2.0	2.2	2.3	2.5	2.7	2.9	3.1	3.3	3.5
2.4	1.5	1.7	1.9	2.1	2.3	2.4	2.6	2.8	3.0	3.2	3.4	3.6
2.5	1.5	1.7	1.9	2.1	2.3	2.6	2.8	3.0	3.2	3.4	3.6	3.8
2.6	1.6	1.8	2.0	2.2	2.4	2.7	2.9	3.1	3.3	3.5	3.7	4.0
2.7	1.6	1.9	2.1	2.3	2.5	2.8	3.0	3.2	3.4	3.7	3.9	4.1
2.8	1.7	1.9	2.2	2.4	2.6	2.9	3.1	3.3	3.6	3.8	4.0	4.3
2.9	1.8	2.0	2.2	2.5	2.7	3.0	3.2	3.4	3.7	3.9	4.2	4.4
3.0	1.8	2.1	2.3	2.6	2.8	3.1	3.3	3.6	3.8	4.1	4.3	4.6
3.1	1.9	2.1	2.4	2.7	2.9	3.2	3.4	3.7	4.0	4.2	4.5	4.7
3.2	1.9	2.2	2.4	2.7	3.0	3.3	3.5	3.8	4.1	4.4	4.7	4.9
3.3	2.0	2.2	2.5	2.8	3.1	3.4	3.7	4.0	4.2	4.5	4.8	5.1
3.4	2.0	2.3	2.6	2.9	3.2	3.5	3.8	4.1	4.4	4.7	5.0	5.3
3.5	2.1	2.3	2.7	3.0	3.3	3.6	3.9	4.2	4.5	4.8	5.1	5.4
3.6	2.1	2.4	2.7	3.1	3.4	3.7	4.0	4.3	4.6	4.9	5.2	5.6
3.7	2.2	2.5	2.8	3.1	3.5	3.8	4.1	4.4	4.7	5.1	5.4	5.8
3.8	2.2	2.6	2.9	3.2	3.6	3.9	4.2	4.5	4.9	5.2	5.5	5.9
3.9	2.3	2.6	2.9	3.3	3.7	4.0	4.3	4.7	5.0	5.3	5.7	6.1
4.0	2.3	2.7	3.0	3.4	3.7	4.1	4.4	4.8	5.1	5.5	5.8	6.2

Tidal Stream Rates

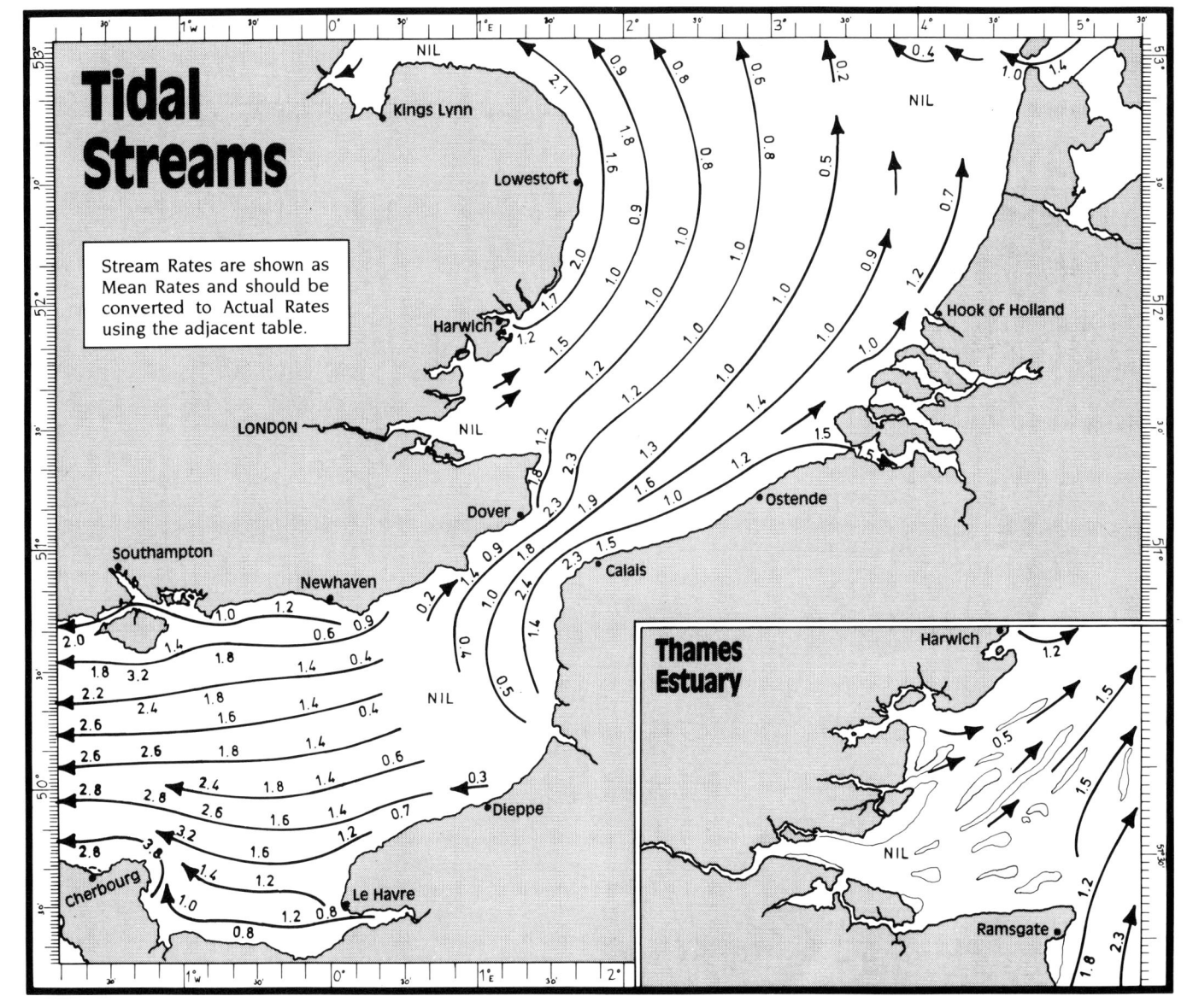

5 hours after HW Cherbourg

+5

Time (to be inserted)

Tidal Streams

Stream Rates are shown as Mean Rates and should be converted to Actual Rates using the adjacent table.

Thames Estuary

+6
6 hours after HW Cherbourg

Tidal Heights

Copyright © J Reeve-Fowkes and Thomas Reed Publications.
No copying without permission.

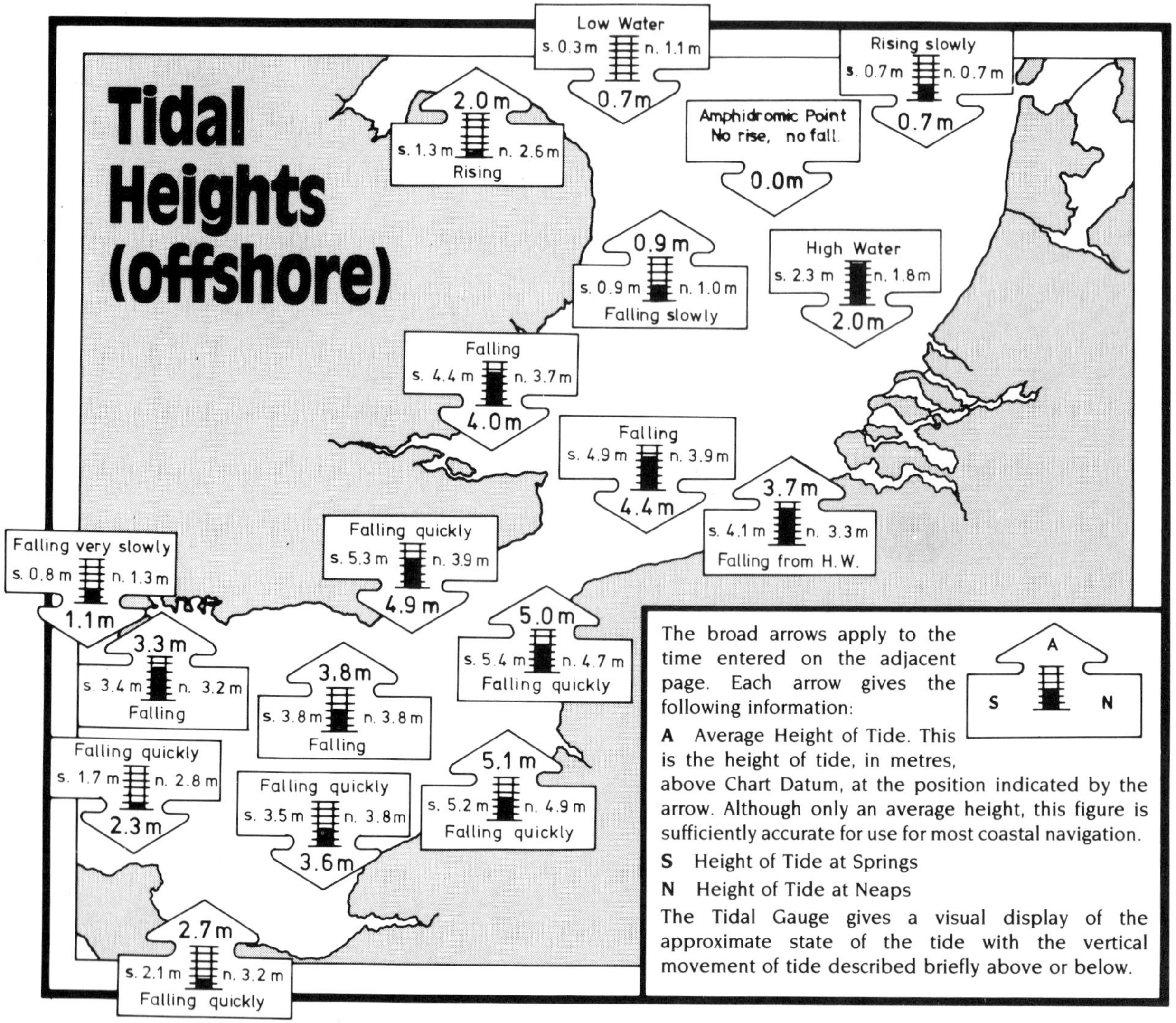

Tidal Heights (offshore)

Low Water
s. 0.3m n. 1.1m
0.7m

Rising slowly
s. 0.7m n. 0.7m
0.7m

2.0 m
s. 1.3m n. 2.6m
Rising

Amphidromic Point
No rise, no fall.
0.0m

0.9 m
s. 0.9m n. 1.0m
Falling slowly

High Water
s. 2.3m n. 1.8m
2.0m

Falling
s. 4.4 m n. 3.7m
4.0m

Falling
s. 4.9m n. 3.9m
4.4 m

3.7 m
s. 4.1m n. 3.3m
Falling from H.W.

Falling very slowly
s. 0.8 m n. 1.3m
1.1m

3.3 m
s. 3.4 m n. 3.2m
Falling

Falling quickly
s. 5.3 m n. 3.9 m
4.9 m

3.8 m
s. 3.8m n. 3.8m
Falling

5.0 m
s. 5.4 m n. 4.7 m
Falling quickly

Falling quickly
s. 1.7m n. 2.8m
2.3 m

Falling quickly
s. 3.5m n. 3.8 m
3.6m

5.1 m
s. 5.2 m n. 4.9 m
Falling quickly

2.7 m
s. 2.1 m n. 3.2m
Falling quickly

The broad arrows apply to the time entered on the adjacent page. Each arrow gives the following information:

A Average Height of Tide. This is the height of tide, in metres, above Chart Datum, at the position indicated by the arrow. Although only an average height, this figure is sufficiently accurate for use for most coastal navigation.

S Height of Tide at Springs
N Height of Tide at Neaps

The Tidal Gauge gives a visual display of the approximate state of the tide with the vertical movement of tide described briefly above or below.

TIDAL HEIGHTS — PORTS & PLACES

Pencil-in height of ► HW Cherbourg	4.8	5.0	5.2	5.4	5.6	5.8	6.0	6.2	6.4	6.6	6.8
ENGLAND											
Kings Lynn	2.0	1.9	1.7	1.6	1.5	1.4	1.3	1.2	1.1	1.1	1.1	1.1
Blakeney Bar	2.7	2.5	2.3	2.1	2.0	1.8	1.6	1.5	1.3	1.2	1.1	1.0
Cromer	2.2	2.1	1.9	1.8	1.6	1.5	1.3	1.2	1.0	0.9	0.9	0.8
Gt. Yarmouth (Gorleston)	1.2	1.1	1.1	1.0	0.9	0.9	0.8	0.8	0.7	0.6	0.5	0.4
Lowestoft	1.1	1.1	1.1	1.1	1.0	1.0	1.0	0.9	0.9	0.8	0.8	0.7
Southwold Haven	1.4	1.3	1.3	1.2	1.2	1.1	1.1	1.0	1.0	1.0	0.9	0.9
Orford Haven appr'ch	1.9	1.9	1.9	1.9	1.9	1.8	1.8	1.8	1.8	1.8	1.9	1.9
Woodbridge Haven	2.2	2.2	2.2	2.2	2.3	2.3	2.3	2.4	2.4	2.5	2.5	2.6
Felixstowe	2.3	2.3	2.3	2.3	2.3	2.3	2.3	2.3	2.4	2.4	2.4	2.5
Harwich	2.5	2.5	2.5	2.5	2.6	2.6	2.6	2.7	2.7	2.7	2.7	2.7
Walton-on-the-Naze	2.6	2.6	2.6	2.6	2.7	2.7	2.7	2.8	2.8	2.9	2.9	3.0
Brightlingsea	2.9	3.0	3.2	3.3	3.4	3.5	3.6	3.7	3.8	3.9	4.1	4.2
Bradwell	3.2	3.3	3.5	3.6	3.7	3.9	4.0	4.2	4.3	4.3	4.4	4.4
Burnham	3.7	3.8	4.0	4.1	4.2	4.3	4.5	4.6	4.7	4.8	5.0	5.1
Leigh, Southend	3.9	4.0	4.2	4.3	4.4	4.5	4.6	4.7	4.8	4.9	5.1	5.2
London Bridge	5.4	5.6	5.8	6.0	6.2	6.5	6.7	6.9	7.1	7.3	7.6	7.8
Sheerness	3.9	4.0	4.2	4.3	4.4	4.5	4.7	4.8	4.9	5.1	5.2	5.4
Chatham	4.1	4.2	4.4	4.5	4.6	4.8	4.9	5.1	5.2	5.4	5.6	5.7
Rochester	4.1	4.2	4.4	4.5	4.7	4.8	5.0	5.1	5.3	5.5	5.8	6.0
Whitstable approach	3.9	4.0	4.2	4.3	4.4	4.6	4.7	4.9	5.0	5.0	5.1	5.1
Edinburgh Channels	3.2	3.3	3.3	3.4	3.4	3.5	3.5	3.6	3.6	3.6	3.7	3.7
Margate	3.2	3.3	3.3	3.4	3.5	3.6	3.6	3.7	3.8	3.8	3.9	3.9
Ramsgate	3.0	3.1	3.1	3.2	3.3	3.3	3.4	3.4	3.5	3.6	3.6	3.7
Dover	4.2	4.3	4.3	4.4	4.5	4.5	4.6	4.6	4.7	4.8	4.8	4.9
Folkestone	4.5	4.5	4.5	4.5	4.5	4.5	4.5	4.5	4.5	4.5	4.6	4.6
Newhaven	3.8	3.8	3.8	3.8	3.9	3.9	3.9	4.0	4.0	4.0	4.1	4.1
Brighton	3.8	3.8	3.8	3.8	3.9	3.9	3.9	4.0	4.0	4.0	4.1	4.1
Shoreham	3.8	3.8	3.8	3.8	3.9	3.9	3.9	4.0	4.0	4.0	4.1	4.1
Littlehampton Hbr	3.6	3.7	3.9	4.0	4.1	4.3	4.4	4.6	4.7	4.8	4.9	5.0
Selsey Bill	3.5	3.6	3.8	3.9	4.0	4.1	4.2	4.3	4.4	4.5	4.5	4.6
Chichester entrance	3.2	3.3	3.5	3.6	3.7	3.8	3.9	4.0	4.1	4.2	4.2	4.3
Portsmouth	3.2	3.3	3.3	3.4	3.5	3.6	3.7	3.8	3.9	4.0	4.0	4.1
Southampton	3.0	3.1	3.3	3.4	3.5	3.7	3.8	4.0	4.1	4.2	4.2	4.3
Cowes I. o W.	2.8	2.9	2.9	3.0	3.0	3.1	3.2	3.3	3.4	3.4	3.4	3.4
Yarmouth I. o W.	2.1	2.1	2.1	2.1	2.2	2.2	2.2	2.2	2.2	2.2	2.3	2.3
Lymington	2.2	2.2	2.2	2.2	2.3	2.3	2.3	2.4	2.4	2.4	2.5	2.5
HOLLAND											
Den Helder	0.9	0.8	0.8	0.7	0.6	0.5	0.4	0.3	0.2	0.2	0.2	0.2
IJmuiden	1.4	1.4	1.4	1.4	1.3	1.3	1.3	1.2	1.2	1.2	1.2	1.2
Scheveningen	1.8	1.8	1.8	1.8	1.9	1.9	1.9	2.0	2.0	2.0	2.1	2.1
Hoek van Holland	1.6	1.7	1.7	1.8	1.8	1.9	1.9	2.0	2.0	2.1	2.1	2.2
Rotterdam	1.5	1.5	1.5	1.5	1.5	1.4	1.4	1.4	1.4	1.4	1.5	1.5
Flushing	3.6	3.7	3.9	4.0	4.1	4.2	4.3	4.4	4.5	4.6	4.7	4.8
BELGIUM											
Zeebrugge	3.5	3.6	3.8	3.9	4.0	4.1	4.2	4.3	4.4	4.5	4.6	4.7
Ostende	3.7	3.8	3.8	3.9	4.0	4.1	4.2	4.3	4.4	4.4	4.5	4.5
Nieuwpoort	3.7	3.8	3.8	3.9	4.0	4.1	4.1	4.2	4.3	4.3	4.4	4.4
FRANCE											
Dunkerque	4.0	4.1	4.3	4.4	4.5	4.6	4.7	4.8	4.9	4.9	5.0	5.0
Calais	4.5	4.6	4.8	4.9	5.0	5.1	5.2	5.3	5.4	5.4	5.4	5.4
Boulogne	5.4	5.5	5.7	5.8	5.9	6.1	6.2	6.4	6.5	6.5	6.5	6.5
Somme Estuary	5.5	5.6	5.6	5.7	5.8	5.9	5.9	6.0	6.1	6.1	6.2	6.2
Le Tréport	4.9	5.0	5.0	5.1	5.1	5.2	5.2	5.3	5.3	5.3	5.4	5.4
Dieppe	4.8	4.8	4.8	4.8	4.9	4.9	4.9	5.0	5.0	5.0	5.0	5.0
Fécamp	4.2	4.1	4.1	4.0	4.0	3.9	3.9	3.8	3.8	3.7	3.5	3.4
Le Havre	4.2	4.1	4.1	4.0	3.9	3.9	3.8	3.8	3.7	3.6	3.5	3.4
Ouistreham	3.9	3.8	3.6	3.5	3.4	3.2	3.1	2.9	2.8	2.7	2.6	2.5
Port-en-Bessin	3.6	3.5	3.3	3.2	3.0	2.9	2.7	2.6	2.4	2.3	2.1	2.0
Saint-Vaast-la-Hougue	3.1	3.0	2.8	2.7	2.6	2.5	2.3	2.2	2.1	1.9	1.8	1.6
Barfleur	3.0	2.9	2.7	2.6	2.4	2.3	2.1	2.0	1.8	1.6	1.4	1.2

Tidal Stream Rates

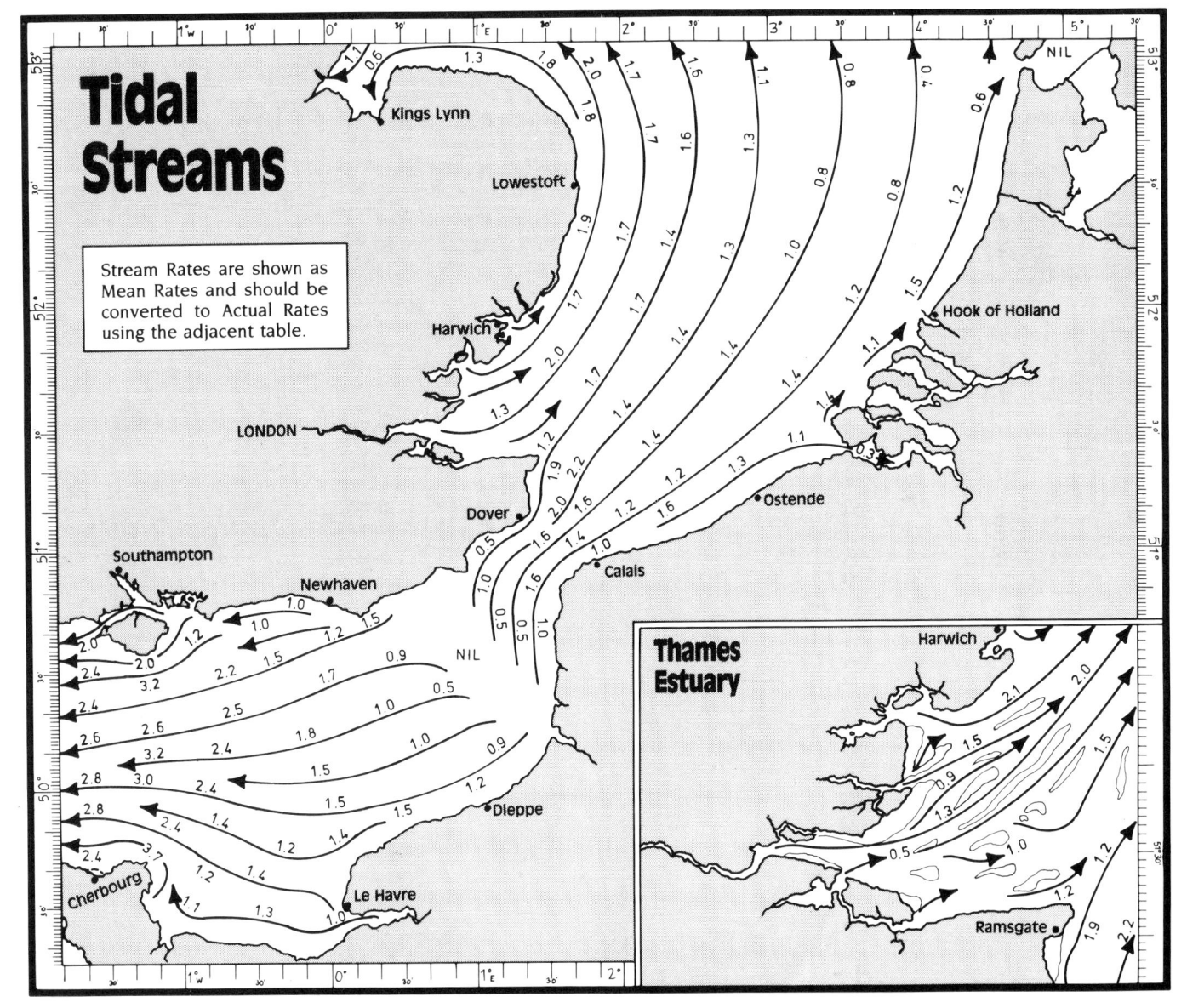

6 hours after HW Cherbourg **+6**

Time (to be inserted)

Stream Rate Conversion Table

Mean Rate Figure from Chart ▼	\multicolumn{11}{c	}{Pencil-in height of HW Cherbourg — Read from column below pencil mark}
	4.8	5.0	5.2	5.4	5.6	5.8	6.0	6.2	6.4	6.6	6.8
0.1	0.1	0.1	0.1	0.1	0.1	0.1	0.1	0.1	0.1	0.1	0.2
0.2	0.1	0.1	0.2	0.2	0.2	0.2	0.2	0.2	0.3	0.3	0.3
0.3	0.2	0.2	0.2	0.3	0.3	0.3	0.3	0.4	0.4	0.4	0.5
0.4	0.2	0.3	0.3	0.3	0.4	0.4	0.4	0.5	0.5	0.5	0.6
0.5	0.3	0.3	0.4	0.4	0.5	0.5	0.6	0.6	0.6	0.7	0.8
0.6	0.4	0.4	0.5	0.5	0.6	0.6	0.7	0.7	0.8	0.8	0.9
0.7	0.4	0.5	0.5	0.6	0.7	0.7	0.8	0.8	0.9	0.9	1.0
0.8	0.5	0.6	0.6	0.7	0.8	0.8	0.9	0.9	1.0	1.1	1.2
0.9	0.5	0.6	0.7	0.8	0.8	0.9	1.0	1.1	1.2	1.3	1.4
1.0	0.6	0.7	0.8	0.9	0.9	1.0	1.1	1.2	1.3	1.4	1.5
1.1	0.7	0.8	0.8	0.9	1.0	1.1	1.2	1.3	1.4	1.5	1.7
1.2	0.7	0.8	0.9	1.0	1.1	1.2	1.3	1.4	1.5	1.6	1.8
1.3	0.8	0.9	1.0	1.1	1.2	1.3	1.4	1.5	1.7	1.8	2.0
1.4	0.8	1.0	1.1	1.2	1.3	1.4	1.5	1.7	1.8	1.9	2.1
1.5	0.9	1.0	1.1	1.3	1.4	1.5	1.7	1.8	1.9	2.0	2.3
1.6	1.0	1.1	1.2	1.4	1.5	1.6	1.8	1.9	2.0	2.2	2.4
1.7	1.0	1.2	1.3	1.5	1.6	1.7	1.9	2.0	2.2	2.3	2.6
1.8	1.1	1.2	1.4	1.5	1.7	1.8	2.0	2.1	2.3	2.4	2.7
1.9	1.2	1.3	1.5	1.6	1.8	1.9	2.1	2.3	2.4	2.6	2.9
2.0	1.2	1.4	1.5	1.7	1.9	2.0	2.2	2.4	2.5	2.7	3.0
2.1	1.3	1.4	1.6	1.8	2.0	2.1	2.3	2.5	2.7	2.8	3.2
2.2	1.3	1.5	1.7	1.9	2.1	2.2	2.4	2.6	2.8	3.0	3.3
2.3	1.4	1.6	1.8	2.0	2.2	2.3	2.5	2.7	2.9	3.1	3.5
2.4	1.5	1.7	1.9	2.1	2.3	2.4	2.6	2.8	3.0	3.2	3.6
2.5	1.5	1.7	1.9	2.1	2.3	2.6	2.8	3.0	3.2	3.4	3.8
2.6	1.6	1.8	2.0	2.2	2.4	2.7	2.9	3.1	3.3	3.5	4.0
2.7	1.6	1.9	2.1	2.3	2.5	2.8	3.0	3.2	3.4	3.7	4.1
2.8	1.7	1.9	2.2	2.4	2.6	2.9	3.1	3.3	3.6	3.8	4.3
2.9	1.8	2.0	2.2	2.5	2.7	3.0	3.2	3.4	3.7	3.9	4.4
3.0	1.8	2.1	2.3	2.6	2.8	3.1	3.3	3.6	3.8	4.1	4.3	4.6
3.1	1.9	2.1	2.4	2.7	2.9	3.2	3.4	3.7	4.0	4.2	4.5	4.7
3.2	1.9	2.2	2.4	2.7	3.0	3.3	3.5	3.8	4.1	4.4	4.7	4.9
3.3	2.0	2.2	2.5	2.8	3.1	3.4	3.7	4.0	4.2	4.5	4.8	5.1
3.4	2.0	2.3	2.6	2.9	3.2	3.5	3.8	4.1	4.4	4.7	5.0	5.3
3.5	2.1	2.3	2.7	3.0	3.3	3.6	3.9	4.2	4.5	4.8	5.1	5.4
3.6	2.1	2.4	2.7	3.1	3.4	3.7	4.0	4.3	4.6	4.9	5.2	5.6
3.7	2.2	2.5	2.8	3.1	3.5	3.8	4.1	4.4	4.7	5.1	5.4	5.8
3.8	2.2	2.6	2.9	3.2	3.6	3.9	4.2	4.5	4.9	5.2	5.5	5.9
3.9	2.3	2.6	2.9	3.3	3.7	4.0	4.3	4.7	5.0	5.3	5.7	6.1
4.0	2.3	2.7	3.0	3.4	3.7	4.1	4.4	4.8	5.1	5.5	5.8	6.2

Tidal Streams

Stream Rates are shown as Mean Rates and should be converted to Actual Rates using the adjacent table.

Thames Estuary

The Yachtsman's Tidal Atlas
CENTRAL CHANNEL & THE SOLENT

TIDAL STREAM RATES & TIDAL HEIGHTS
Lyme Regis and Lézardrieux to
Newhaven and Le Havre

-6
6 hours before HW Cherbourg

Tidal Heights

Copyright © J Reeve-Fowkes and Thomas Reed Publications.
No copying without permission.

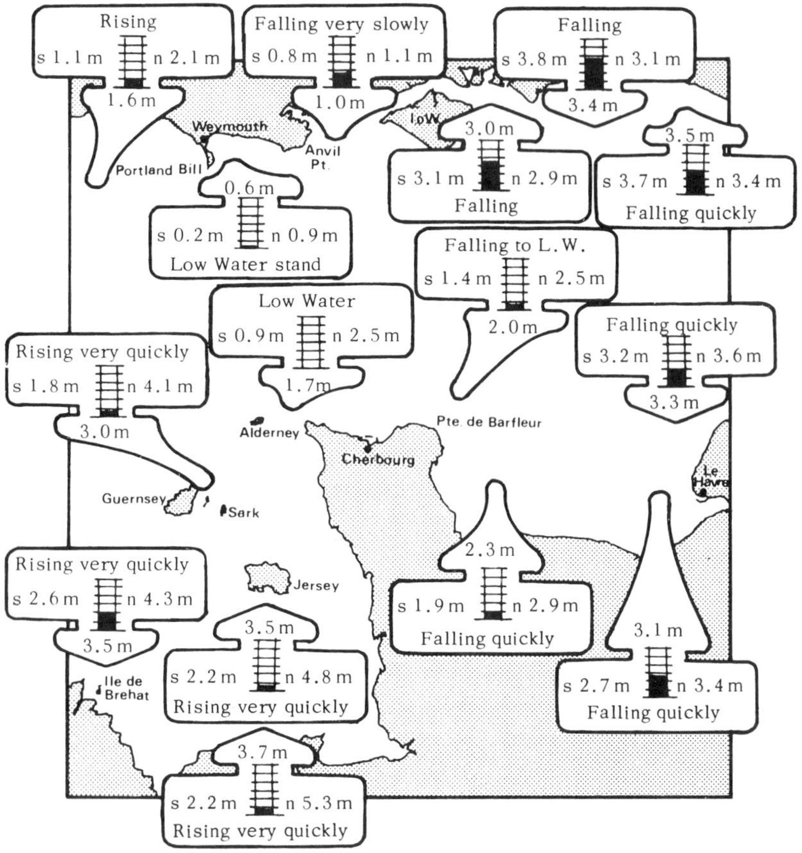

Tidal Heights (offshore)

The broad arrows apply to the time entered on the adjacent page. Each arrow gives the following information:

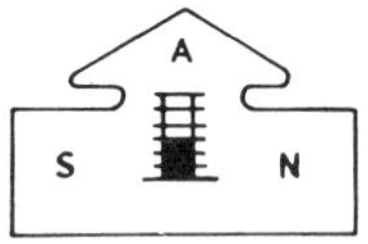

A Average Height of Tide. This is the height of tide, in metres, above Chart Datum, at the position indicated by the arrow. Although only an average height, this figure is sufficiently accurate for use for most coastal navigation.
S Height of Tide at Springs.
N Height of Tide at Neaps.
The Tidal Gauge gives a visual display of the approximate state of the tide with the vertical movement of tide described briefly above or below.

Offshore tidal diagram (map)

- **Rising** — s 1.1 m n 2.1 m — 1.6 m
- **Falling very slowly** — s 0.8 m n 1.1 m — 1.0 m
- **Falling** — s 3.8 m n 3.1 m — 3.4 m
- s 3.1 m n 2.9 m — 3.0 m — **Falling**
- **Falling quickly** — s 3.7 m n 3.4 m — 3.5 m
- **Low Water stand** — s 0.2 m n 0.9 m — 0.6 m
- **Falling to L.W.** — s 1.4 m n 2.5 m
- **Low Water** — s 0.9 m n 2.5 m — 1.7 m / 2.0 m
- **Falling quickly** — s 3.2 m n 3.6 m — 3.3 m
- **Rising very quickly** — s 1.8 m n 4.1 m — 3.0 m
- **Rising very quickly** — s 2.6 m n 4.3 m — 3.5 m
- 2.3 m — s 1.9 m n 2.9 m — **Falling quickly**
- 3.1 m — s 2.7 m n 3.4 m — **Falling quickly**
- 3.5 m — s 2.2 m n 4.8 m — **Rising very quickly**
- 3.7 m — s 2.2 m n 5.3 m — **Rising very quickly**

Place names: Weymouth, Portland Bill, Anvil Pt., IoW, Alderney, Cherbourg, Pte. de Barfleur, Le Havre, Guernsey, Sark, Jersey, Ile de Bréhat.

TIDAL HEIGHTS — PORTS & PLACES

Pencil-in height of HW Cherbourg ▶	4.8	5.0	5.2	5.4	5.6	5.8	6.0	6.2	6.4	6.6	6.8
ENGLAND											
Lyme Regis	2.3	2.2	2.0	1.9	1.8	1.6	1.5	1.3	1.2	1.1	1.1	1.0
Bridport	2.2	2.1	1.9	1.8	1.7	1.6	1.4	1.3	1.2	1.1	1.1	1.0
Portland & Weymouth	0.9	0.8	0.8	0.7	0.6	0.5	0.4	0.4	0.3	0.3	0.2	0.2
Lulworth Cove	1.1	1.0	1.0	0.9	0.8	0.7	0.6	0.5	0.4	0.4	0.3	0.3
Swanage	1.3	1.2	1.2	1.1	1.1	1.0	0.9	0.8	0.7	0.6	0.6	0.5
Poole entrance	1.3	1.2	1.2	1.1	1.1	1.0	0.9	0.9	0.8	0.7	0.6	0.5
Poole Town Quay	1.6	1.5	1.5	1.4	1.4	1.4	1.3	1.3	1.2	1.2	1.1	1.1
Christchurch appr'ch	0.8	0.8	0.8	0.8	0.8	0.8	0.8	0.7	0.7	0.7	0.6	0.6
Christchurch Hbr	0.8	0.8	0.8	0.8	0.8	0.8	0.8	0.7	0.7	0.7	0.7	0.7
Lymington	1.9	1.9	1.9	1.9	1.9	1.9	1.9	1.9	1.9	1.9	1.9	1.9
Yarmouth I. o. W.	1.8	1.8	1.8	1.8	1.7	1.7	1.7	1.6	1.6	1.6	1.5	1.5
Cowes I. o. W.	2.6	2.6	2.6	2.6	2.7	2.7	2.7	2.7	2.7	2.6	2.6	2.6
Sandown I. o. W.	2.3	2.2	2.2	2.1	2.1	2.0	2.0	1.9	1.9	1.9	1.8	1.8
Southampton	2.4	2.6	2.8	3.0	3.2	3.3	3.5	3.7	3.9	4.0	4.0	4.1
Portsmouth	2.7	2.8	3.0	3.1	3.2	3.3	3.4	3.5	3.6	3.6	3.7	3.7
Chichester entrance	2.8	2.9	3.1	3.2	3.3	3.4	3.6	3.7	3.8	3.9	3.9	4.0
Selsey Bill	3.1	3.2	3.4	3.5	3.6	3.7	3.9	4.0	4.1	4.1	4.2	4.2
Littlehampton Hbr	2.9	3.1	3.3	3.5	3.7	3.8	4.0	4.2	4.4	4.5	4.6	4.7
Littlehampton appr'ch	3.1	3.2	3.4	3.5	3.7	3.8	4.0	4.1	4.3	4.4	4.5	4.6
Shoreham	3.2	3.3	3.3	3.4	3.4	3.5	3.5	3.6	3.6	3.6	3.6	3.6
Brighton	3.3	3.3	3.3	3.3	3.4	3.4	3.4	3.5	3.5	3.5	3.5	3.5
Newhaven	3.3	3.3	3.3	3.3	3.4	3.4	3.4	3.5	3.5	3.5	3.6	3.6
FRANCE											
Le Havre	3.7	3.6	3.5	3.4	3.4	3.3	3.2	3.1	3.0	3.0	2.9	2.9
Honfleur	3.7	3.6	3.6	3.5	3.5	3.4	3.4	3.3	3.3	3.2	3.2	3.1
Trouville (Deauville)	3.5	3.4	3.4	3.3	3.2	3.1	3.0	2.9	2.8	2.7	2.5	2.4
Ouistreham	3.4	3.3	3.1	3.0	2.9	2.8	2.6	2.5	2.4	2.3	2.1	2.0
Courseulles	2.7	2.6	2.6	2.5	2.4	2.3	2.2	2.1	2.0	1.9	1.8	1.6
Arromanches	3.4	3.3	3.1	3.0	2.9	2.8	2.6	2.5	2.4	2.3	2.2	2.0
Port-en-Bessin	3.2	3.1	2.9	2.8	2.7	2.5	2.4	2.2	2.1	2.0	1.8	1.7
Saint-Vaast-la-Hougue	2.7	2.6	2.4	2.3	2.2	2.1	2.0	1.9	1.8	1.6	1.4	1.2
Barfleur	2.7	2.6	2.4	2.3	2.1	2.0	1.8	1.7	1.5	1.3	1.1	0.9
Cherbourg	2.8	2.6	2.4	2.2	2.0	1.8	1.6	1.4	1.2	0.9	0.7	0.4
Omonville	2.9	2.7	2.5	2.3	2.0	1.8	1.6	1.3	1.1	0.8	0.6	0.3
Goury	4.1	3.8	3.4	3.1	2.8	2.5	2.1	1.8	1.5	1.2	0.8	0.5
Dielette	4.7	4.3	3.9	3.5	3.2	2.8	2.4	2.1	1.7	1.4	1.1	0.8
Carteret	5.2	4.8	4.4	4.0	3.7	3.3	2.9	2.6	2.2	1.9	1.7	1.4
Granville	6.4	5.9	5.4	5.0	4.5	4.0	3.5	3.0	2.5	2.2	1.9	1.6
Saint Malo	6.2	5.7	5.3	4.8	4.3	3.8	3.3	2.8	2.3	2.0	1.7	1.4
All Hbrs, St Brieuc Bay	5.9	5.6	5.2	4.9	4.6	4.3	3.9	3.6	3.3	3.1	2.9	2.7
Paimpol	5.2	4.9	4.5	4.2	3.9	3.5	3.2	2.8	2.5	2.3	2.1	1.9
Ile de Bréhat	5.8	5.4	5.0	4.6	4.1	3.7	3.3	2.8	2.4	2.2	2.0	1.8
Lezardrieux	5.1	4.9	4.7	4.5	4.2	4.0	3.8	3.5	3.4	3.2	3.0	2.9
ISLANDS OFF											
Braye, Alderney	2.7	2.5	2.3	2.1	1.8	1.6	1.4	1.1	0.9	0.7	0.6	0.4
St Peter Port & Sark	4.6	4.3	3.9	3.6	3.3	3.0	2.6	2.3	2.0	1.7	1.5	1.2
St Helier, Jersey	5.5	5.1	4.7	4.3	3.9	3.4	3.0	2.6	2.2	1.9	1.6	1.3
St Catherine, Jersey	5.3	4.9	4.5	4.1	3.6	3.2	2.8	2.3	1.9	1.6	1.2	0.9
Les Minquiers	5.2	4.9	4.5	4.2	3.9	3.5	3.2	2.8	2.5	2.3	2.0	1.8
Iles Chausey	6.2	5.7	5.3	4.8	4.3	3.9	3.4	3.0	2.5	2.2	1.9	1.6

Tidal Stream Rates

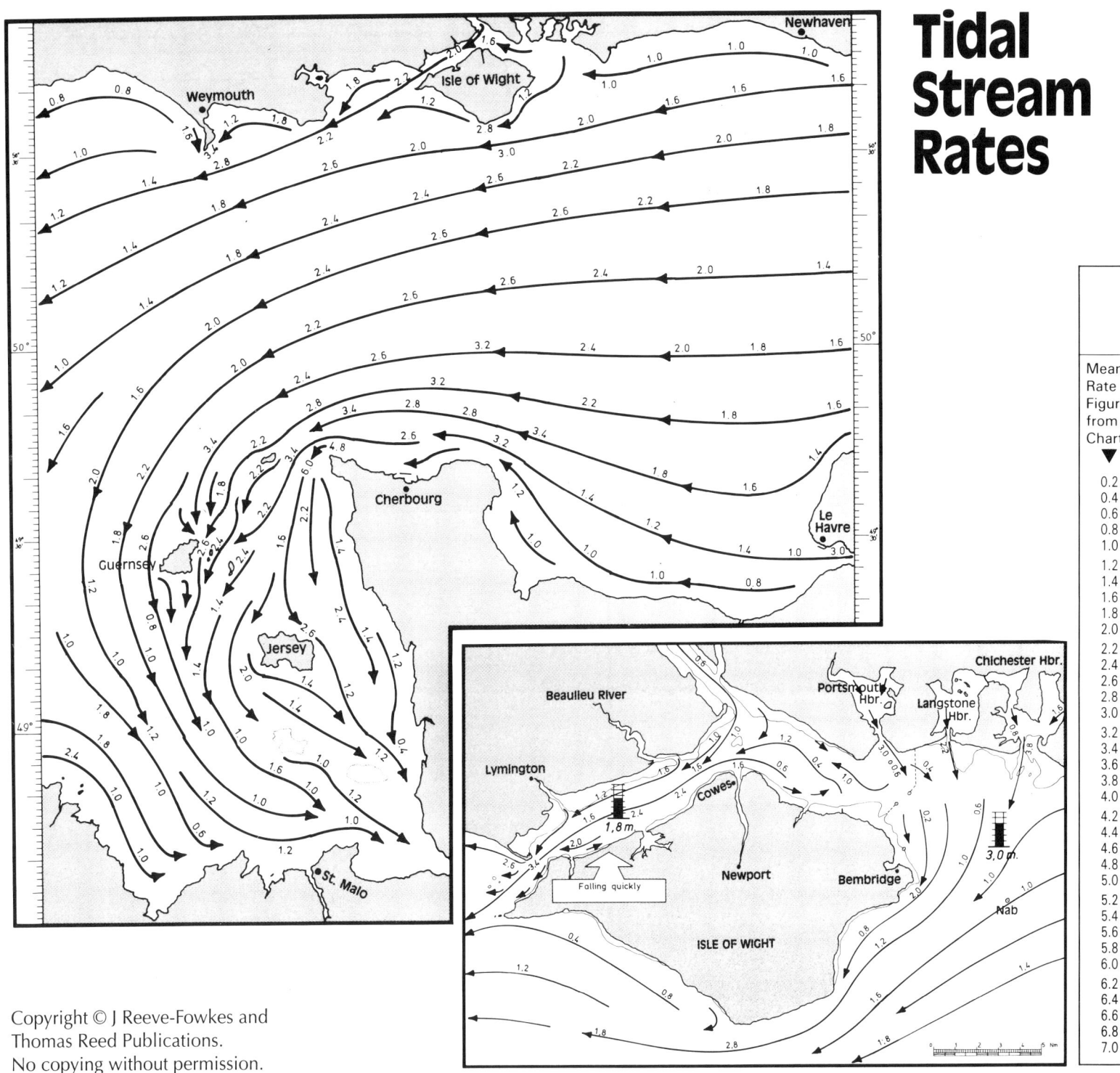

6 hours before HW Cherbourg

Time (to be inserted)

−6

Stream Rate Conversion Table

Mean Rate Figure from Chart ▼	\multicolumn{11}{c}{Pencil-in height of HW Cherbourg — Read from column below pencil mark}
	4.8	5.0	5.2	5.4	5.6	5.8	6.0	6.2	6.4	6.6	6.8
0.2	0.1	0.1	0.2	0.2	0.2	0.2	0.2	0.2	0.3	0.3	0.3
0.4	0.2	0.3	0.3	0.3	0.4	0.4	0.4	0.5	0.5	0.6	0.6
0.6	0.4	0.4	0.5	0.5	0.6	0.6	0.6	0.7	0.7	0.8	0.9
0.8	0.5	0.5	0.6	0.7	0.7	0.8	0.9	1.0	1.1	1.2	1.2
1.0	0.6	0.7	0.8	0.8	0.9	1.0	1.1	1.2	1.3	1.4	1.5	1.5
1.2	0.7	0.8	0.9	1.0	1.1	1.2	1.3	1.4	1.6	1.7	1.9
1.4	0.8	0.9	1.1	1.2	1.3	1.4	1.6	1.7	1.8	1.9	2.0	2.2
1.6	0.9	1.1	1.2	1.4	1.5	1.6	1.8	1.9	2.1	2.2	2.3	2.5
1.8	1.0	1.2	1.4	1.5	1.7	1.8	2.0	2.1	2.3	2.5	2.6	2.8
2.0	1.2	1.3	1.5	1.7	1.9	2.0	2.2	2.4	2.6	2.7	2.9	3.1
2.2	1.3	1.5	1.7	1.9	2.1	2.2	2.4	2.6	2.8	3.0	3.2	3.4
2.4	1.4	1.6	1.8	2.0	2.2	2.5	2.7	2.9	3.1	3.3	3.5	3.7
2.6	1.5	1.8	2.0	2.2	2.4	2.7	2.9	3.1	3.3	3.6	3.8	4.0
2.8	1.6	1.9	2.1	2.4	2.6	2.9	3.1	3.3	3.6	3.8	4.1	4.3
3.0	1.8	2.0	2.3	2.5	2.8	3.1	3.3	3.6	3.8	4.1	4.4	4.6
3.2	1.9	2.2	2.4	2.7	3.0	3.3	3.5	3.8	4.1	4.4	4.7	4.9
3.4	2.0	2.3	2.6	2.9	3.2	3.5	3.8	4.1	4.4	4.7	5.0	5.3
3.6	2.1	2.4	2.7	3.1	3.4	3.7	4.0	4.3	4.6	4.9	5.2	5.6
3.8	2.2	2.6	2.9	3.2	3.6	3.9	4.2	4.5	4.9	5.2	5.5	5.9
4.0	2.3	2.7	3.0	3.4	3.7	4.1	4.4	4.8	5.1	5.5	5.8	6.2
4.2	2.5	2.8	3.2	3.6	3.9	4.3	4.7	5.0	5.4	5.8	6.1	6.5
4.4	2.6	3.0	3.3	3.7	4.1	4.5	4.9	5.3	5.6	6.0	6.4	6.8
4.6	2.7	3.1	3.5	3.9	4.3	4.7	5.1	5.5	5.9	6.3	6.7	7.1
4.8	2.8	3.2	3.6	4.1	4.5	4.9	5.3	5.7	6.2	6.6	7.0	7.4
5.0	2.9	3.4	3.8	4.2	4.7	5.1	5.5	6.0	6.4	6.9	7.3	7.7
5.2	3.0	3.5	4.0	4.4	4.9	5.3	5.8	6.2	6.7	7.1	7.6	8.0
5.4	3.2	3.6	4.1	4.6	5.0	5.5	6.0	6.5	6.9	7.4	7.9	8.3
5.6	3.3	3.8	4.3	4.7	5.2	5.7	6.2	6.7	7.2	7.7	8.2	8.6
5.8	3.4	3.9	4.4	4.9	5.4	5.9	6.4	6.9	7.4	7.9	8.5	9.0
6.0	3.5	4.0	4.6	5.1	5.6	6.1	6.7	7.2	7.7	8.2	8.7	9.3
6.2	3.6	4.2	4.7	5.3	5.8	6.3	6.9	7.4	8.0	8.5	9.0	9.6
6.4	3.8	4.3	4.9	5.4	6.0	6.5	7.1	7.7	8.2	8.8	9.3	9.9
6.6	3.9	4.4	5.0	5.6	6.2	6.7	7.3	7.9	8.5	9.0	9.6	10.2
6.8	4.0	4.6	5.2	5.8	6.4	6.9	7.5	8.1	8.7	9.3	9.9	10.5
7.0	4.1	4.7	5.3	5.9	6.6	7.2	7.8	8.4	9.0	9.6	10.2	10.8

Copyright © J Reeve-Fowkes and Thomas Reed Publications. No copying without permission.

-5
5 hours before HW Cherbourg

Tidal Heights

Copyright © J Reeve-Fowkes and
Thomas Reed Publications.
No copying without permission.

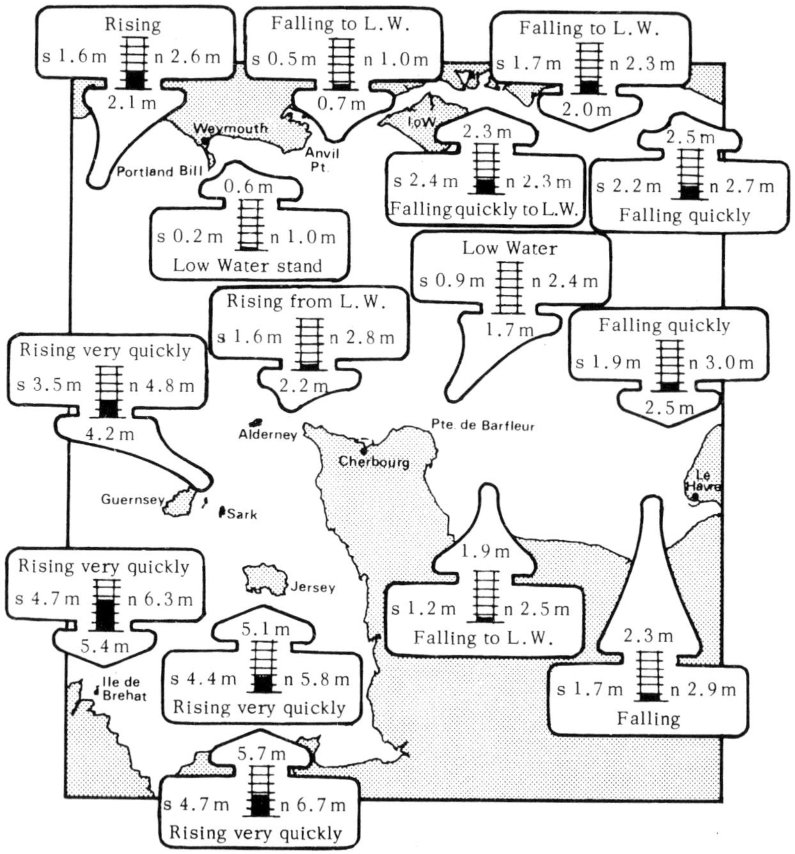

Tidal Heights (offshore)

The broad arrows apply to the time entered on the adjacent page. Each arrow gives the following information:

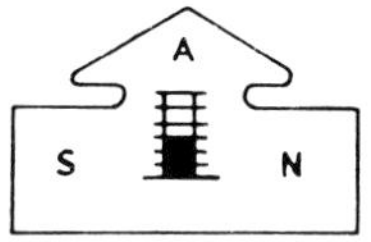

A Average Height of Tide. This is the height of tide, in metres, above Chart Datum, at the position indicated by the arrow. Although only an average height, this figure is sufficiently accurate for use for most coastal navigation.
S Height of Tide at Springs.
N Height of Tide at Neaps.
The Tidal Gauge gives a visual display of the approximate state of the tide with the vertical movement of tide described briefly above or below.

Map labels:
- Rising — s 1.6m n 2.6m — 2.1m
- Falling to L.W. — s 0.5m n 1.0m — 0.7m
- Falling to L.W. — s 1.7m n 2.3m — 2.0m
- 2.3m
- 2.5m
- s 2.4m n 2.3m — Falling quickly to L.W. — 2.4m
- s 2.2m n 2.7m — Falling quickly
- s 0.2m n 1.0m — Low Water stand — 0.6m
- Low Water — s 0.9m n 2.4m — 1.7m
- Rising from L.W. — s 1.6m n 2.8m — 2.2m
- Falling quickly — s 1.9m n 3.0m — 2.5m
- Rising very quickly — s 3.5m n 4.8m — 4.2m
- Rising very quickly — s 4.7m n 6.3m — 5.4m
- 1.9m
- s 1.2m n 2.5m — Falling to L.W. — 5.1m
- 2.3m — s 1.7m n 2.9m — Falling
- Rising very quickly — s 4.4m n 5.8m
- Rising very quickly — s 4.7m n 6.7m — 5.7m

Place names: Weymouth, Portland Bill, Anvil Pt., Alderney, Cherbourg, Pte. de Barfleur, Le Havre, Guernsey, Sark, Jersey, Ile de Bréhat

TIDAL HEIGHTS — PORTS & PLACES

Pencil-in height of HW Cherbourg ▶	4.8	5.0	5.2	5.4	5.6	5.8	6.0	6.2	6.4	6.6	6.8
ENGLAND											
Lyme Regis	2.8	2.7	2.5	2.4	2.3	2.1	2.0	1.8	1.7	1.7	1.6	1.6
Bridport	2.7	2.6	2.4	2.3	2.2	2.0	1.9	1.7	1.6	1.6	1.5	1.5
Portland & Weymouth	1.0	0.9	0.9	0.8	0.7	0.6	0.5	0.4	0.3	0.3	0.2	0.2
Lulworth Cove	1.3	1.2	1.0	0.9	0.8	0.7	0.6	0.5	0.4	0.4	0.3	0.3
Swanage	1.2	1.1	1.1	1.0	0.9	0.8	0.7	0.5	0.4	0.3	0.2	0.1
Poole entrance	1.2	1.1	1.1	1.0	1.0	0.9	0.8	0.6	0.5	0.4	0.2	0.1
Poole Town Quay	1.5	1.4	1.4	1.3	1.3	1.2	1.1	0.9	0.8	0.7	0.7	0.6
Christchurch appr'ch	0.7	0.7	0.7	0.7	0.7	0.7	0.6	0.5	0.4	0.3	0.3	0.6
Christchurch Hbr	0.7	0.7	0.7	0.7	0.7	0.7	0.7	0.6	0.6	0.6	0.6	0.6
Lymington	1.7	1.6	1.6	1.5	1.5	1.4	1.3	1.3	1.2	1.1	1.1	1.0
Yarmouth I. o. W.	1.7	1.6	1.6	1.5	1.4	1.3	1.2	1.2	1.1	1.0	0.9	0.8
Cowes I. o. W.	2.3	2.2	2.2	2.1	2.1	2.0	1.9	1.9	1.8	1.7	1.6	1.5
Sandown I. o. W.	2.0	1.9	1.9	1.8	1.7	1.6	1.5	1.3	1.2	1.1	1.0	0.9
Southampton	1.9	2.0	2.0	2.1	2.2	2.2	2.3	2.3	2.4	2.4	2.3	2.3
Portsmouth	2.2	2.2	2.2	2.2	2.2	2.2	2.2	2.2	2.2	2.2	2.1	2.1
Chichester entrance	2.4	2.4	2.4	2.4	2.5	2.5	2.5	2.6	2.6	2.6	2.6	2.6
Selsey Bill	2.7	2.7	2.7	2.7	2.7	2.7	2.8	2.8	2.8	2.8	2.8	2.8
Littlehampton Hbr	2.2	2.3	2.5	2.6	2.7	2.8	3.0	3.1	3.2	3.2	3.3	3.3
Littlehampton appr'ch	2.7	2.7	2.7	2.7	2.8	2.8	2.8	2.9	2.9	2.9	3.0	3.0
Shoreham	2.7	2.6	2.6	2.5	2.4	2.4	2.3	2.3	2.2	2.2	2.1	2.1
Brighton	2.6	2.5	2.5	2.4	2.3	2.2	2.2	2.2	2.1	2.0	2.0	1.9
Newhaven	2.7	2.6	2.6	2.5	2.4	2.3	2.3	2.2	2.1	2.1	2.0	2.0
FRANCE											
Le Havre	3.3	3.2	3.0	2.9	2.7	2.6	2.4	2.3	2.1	1.9	1.8	1.6
Honfleur	3.3	3.2	3.0	2.9	2.8	2.7	2.5	2.4	2.3	2.2	2.0	1.9
Trouville (Deauville)	3.3	3.1	2.9	2.7	2.5	2.4	2.2	2.0	1.8	1.6	1.5	1.3
Ouistreham	3.1	2.9	2.7	2.5	2.3	2.2	2.0	1.8	1.6	1.4	1.2	1.0
Courseulles	2.7	2.5	2.3	2.1	2.0	1.8	1.6	1.5	1.3	1.1	1.0	0.8
Arromanches	3.2	3.0	2.8	2.6	2.4	2.3	2.1	1.9	1.7	1.5	1.3	1.1
Port-en-Bessin	3.0	2.8	2.6	2.4	2.2	1.9	1.7	1.5	1.3	1.1	1.0	0.8
Saint-Vaast-la-Hougue	2.6	2.4	2.2	2.0	1.8	1.7	1.5	1.3	1.1	0.9	0.6	0.4
Barfleur	2.7	2.5	2.3	2.1	1.9	1.6	1.4	1.2	1.0	0.8	0.5	0.3
Cherbourg	2.9	2.7	2.5	2.3	2.1	1.9	1.7	1.5	1.3	1.0	0.8	0.5
Omonville	3.1	2.9	2.7	2.5	2.3	2.1	1.9	1.7	1.5	1.2	1.0	0.7
Goury	4.6	4.3	4.1	3.8	3.6	3.3	3.1	2.8	2.6	2.4	2.1	1.9
Dielette	5.3	5.0	4.8	4.5	4.2	4.0	3.7	3.5	3.2	3.0	2.8	2.6
Carteret	5.9	5.7	5.5	5.3	5.1	4.8	4.6	4.4	4.2	4.1	3.9	3.8
Granville	7.4	7.1	6.9	6.6	6.3	6.0	5.8	5.5	5.2	5.1	5.0	4.9
Saint Malo	7.1	6.8	6.6	6.3	6.0	5.7	5.4	5.1	4.8	4.6	4.5	4.3
All Hbrs, St Brieuc Bay	6.4	6.3	6.3	6.2	6.1	6.1	6.0	6.0	5.9	5.8	5.8	5.7
Paimpol	6.0	5.9	5.7	5.6	5.5	5.4	5.2	5.1	5.0	5.0	4.9	4.9
Ile de Bréhat	6.7	6.4	6.2	5.9	5.7	5.4	5.2	4.9	4.7	4.6	4.6	4.5
Lezardrieux	6.0	5.9	5.9	5.8	5.8	5.7	5.7	5.6	5.6	5.6	5.6	5.6
ISLANDS OFF											
Braye, Alderney	3.0	2.9	2.7	2.6	2.5	2.3	2.2	2.0	1.9	1.8	1.7	1.6
St Peter Port & Sark	5.1	4.9	4.7	4.5	4.3	4.2	4.0	3.8	3.6	3.3	3.2	3.1
St Helier, Jersey	6.2	5.9	5.7	5.4	5.2	4.9	4.7	4.4	4.2	4.1	3.9	3.8
St Catherine, Jersey	6.0	5.7	5.5	5.2	4.9	4.6	4.4	4.1	3.8	3.6	3.5	3.3
Les Minquiers	5.7	5.6	5.4	5.3	5.2	5.0	4.9	4.7	4.6	4.5	4.4	4.3
Iles Chausey	7.3	7.0	6.8	6.5	6.2	5.9	5.6	5.3	5.0	4.9	4.7	4.6

Tidal Stream Rates

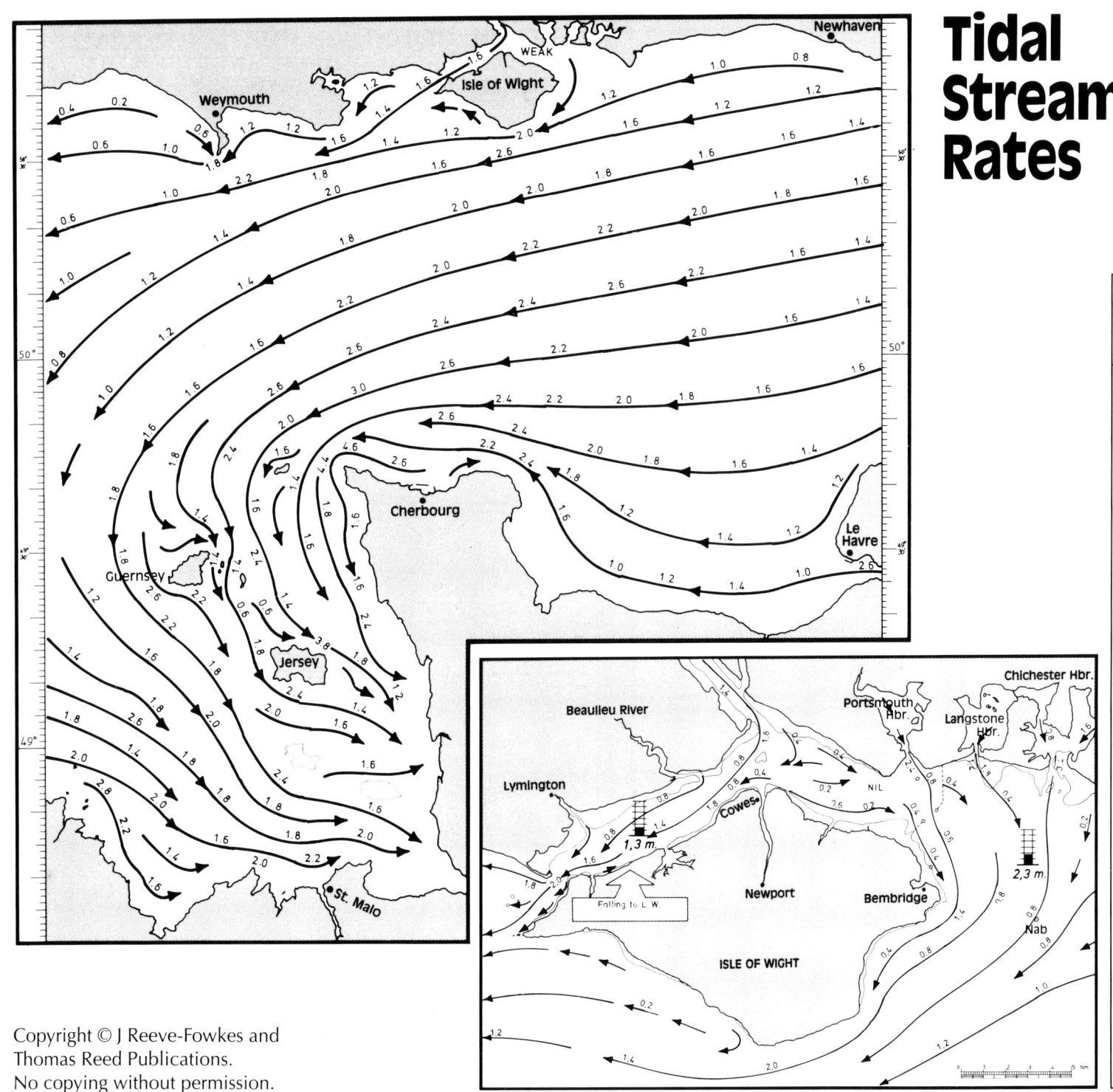

5 hours before HW Cherbourg

-5

Time (to be inserted)

Stream Rate Conversion Table

Mean Rate Figure from Chart ▼	\multicolumn{11}{c}{Pencil-in height of HW Cherbourg — Read from column below pencil mark}										
	4.8	5.0	5.2	5.4	5.6	5.8	6.0	6.2	6.4	6.6	6.8
0.2	0.1	0.1	0.2	0.2	0.2	0.2	0.2	0.2	0.3	0.3	0.3
0.4	0.2	0.3	0.3	0.3	0.4	0.4	0.4	0.5	0.5	0.6	0.6
0.6	0.4	0.4	0.5	0.5	0.6	0.6	0.6	0.7	0.8	0.8	0.9
0.8	0.5	0.5	0.6	0.7	0.7	0.8	0.9	1.0	1.0	1.1	1.2
1.0	0.6	0.7	0.8	0.8	0.9	1.0	1.1	1.2	1.3	1.4	1.5
1.2	0.7	0.8	0.9	1.0	1.1	1.2	1.3	1.4	1.5	1.6	1.7	1.9
1.4	0.8	0.9	1.1	1.2	1.3	1.4	1.6	1.7	1.8	1.9	2.0	2.2
1.6	0.9	1.1	1.2	1.4	1.5	1.6	1.8	1.9	2.1	2.2	2.3	2.5
1.8	1.0	1.2	1.4	1.5	1.7	1.8	2.0	2.1	2.3	2.5	2.6	2.8
2.0	1.2	1.3	1.5	1.7	1.9	2.0	2.2	2.4	2.6	2.7	2.9	3.1
2.2	1.3	1.5	1.7	1.9	2.1	2.2	2.4	2.6	2.8	3.0	3.2	3.4
2.4	1.4	1.6	1.8	2.0	2.2	2.5	2.7	2.9	3.1	3.3	3.5	3.7
2.6	1.5	1.8	2.0	2.2	2.4	2.7	2.9	3.1	3.3	3.6	3.8	4.0
2.8	1.6	1.9	2.1	2.4	2.6	2.9	3.1	3.3	3.6	3.8	4.1	4.3
3.0	1.8	2.0	2.3	2.5	2.8	3.1	3.3	3.6	3.8	4.1	4.4	4.6
3.2	1.9	2.2	2.4	2.7	3.0	3.3	3.5	3.8	4.1	4.4	4.7	4.9
3.4	2.0	2.3	2.6	2.9	3.2	3.5	3.8	4.1	4.4	4.7	5.0	5.3
3.6	2.1	2.4	2.7	3.1	3.4	3.7	4.0	4.3	4.6	4.9	5.2	5.6
3.8	2.2	2.6	2.9	3.2	3.6	3.9	4.2	4.5	4.9	5.2	5.5	5.9
4.0	2.3	2.7	3.0	3.4	3.7	4.1	4.4	4.8	5.1	5.5	5.8	6.2
4.2	2.5	2.8	3.2	3.6	3.9	4.3	4.7	5.0	5.4	5.8	6.1	6.5
4.4	2.6	3.0	3.3	3.7	4.1	4.5	4.9	5.3	5.6	6.0	6.4	6.8
4.6	2.7	3.1	3.5	3.9	4.3	4.7	5.1	5.5	5.9	6.3	6.7	7.1
4.8	2.8	3.2	3.6	4.1	4.5	4.9	5.3	5.7	6.2	6.6	7.0	7.4
5.0	2.9	3.4	3.8	4.2	4.7	5.1	5.5	6.0	6.4	6.9	7.3	7.7
5.2	3.0	3.5	4.0	4.4	4.9	5.3	5.8	6.2	6.7	7.1	7.6	8.0
5.4	3.2	3.6	4.1	4.6	5.0	5.5	6.0	6.5	6.9	7.4	7.9	8.3
5.6	3.3	3.8	4.3	4.7	5.2	5.7	6.2	6.7	7.2	7.7	8.2	8.6
5.8	3.4	3.9	4.4	4.9	5.4	5.9	6.4	6.9	7.4	7.9	8.5	9.0
6.0	3.5	4.0	4.6	5.1	5.6	6.1	6.7	7.2	7.7	8.2	8.7	9.3
6.2	3.6	4.2	4.7	5.3	5.8	6.3	6.9	7.4	8.0	8.5	9.0	9.6
6.4	3.8	4.3	4.9	5.4	6.0	6.5	7.1	7.7	8.2	8.8	9.3	9.9
6.6	3.9	4.4	5.0	5.6	6.2	6.7	7.3	7.9	8.5	9.0	9.6	10.2
6.8	4.0	4.6	5.2	5.8	6.4	6.9	7.5	8.1	8.7	9.3	9.9	10.5
7.0	4.1	4.7	5.3	5.9	6.6	7.2	7.8	8.4	9.0	9.6	10.2	10.8

Copyright © J Reeve-Fowkes and Thomas Reed Publications.
No copying without permission.

-4
4 hours before HW Cherbourg

Tidal Heights

Copyright © J Reeve-Fowkes and Thomas Reed Publications.
No copying without permission.

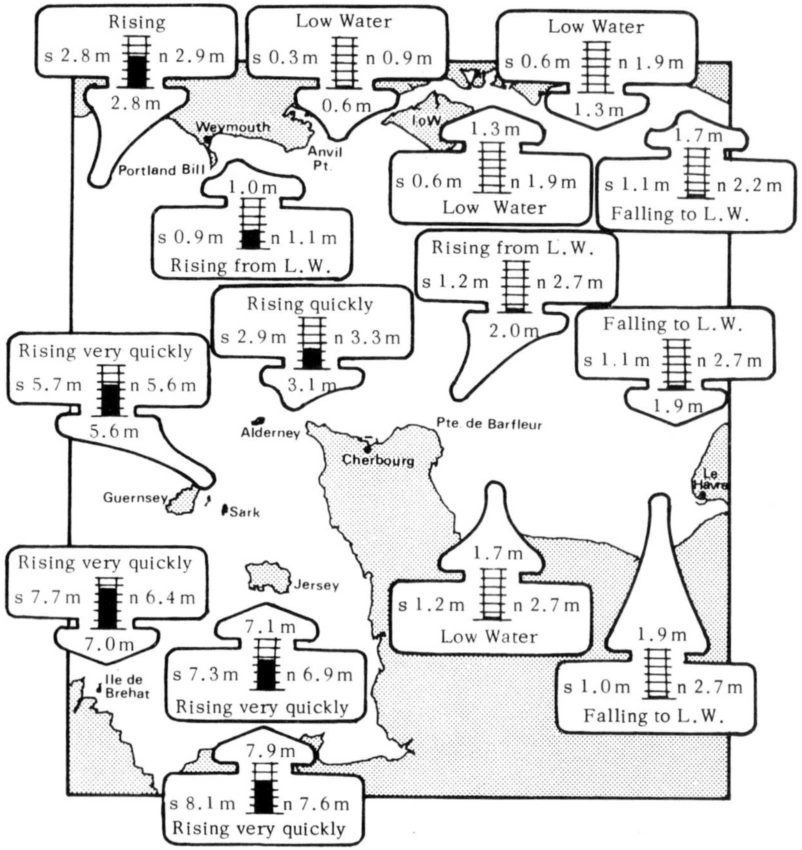

TIDAL HEIGHTS — PORTS & PLACES

Pencil-in height of HW Cherbourg ▶	4.8	5.0	5.2	5.4	5.6	5.8	6.0	6.2	6.4	6.6	6.8
ENGLAND											
Lyme Regis...............	2.9	2.9	2.9	2.9	2.9	2.8	2.8	2.8	2.8	2.8	2.9	2.9
Bridport.....................	2.8	2.8	2.8	2.8	2.8	2.8	2.8	2.8	2.8	2.9	2.9	3.0
Portland & Weymouth..	1.0	1.0	1.0	1.0	0.9	0.9	0.9	0.8	0.8	0.8	0.9	0.9
Lulworth Cove	1.2	1.2	1.2	1.2	1.2	1.2	1.1	1.1	1.1	1.1	1.2	1.2
Swanage	1.3	1.2	1.2	1.1	1.0	0.9	0.8	0.7	0.6	0.5	0.5	0.4
Poole entrance	1.2	1.1	1.1	1.0	1.0	0.9	0.8	0.7	0.6	0.5	0.3	0.2
Poole Town Quay.........	1.3	1.2	1.2	1.1	1.0	0.9	0.8	0.6	0.5	0.4	0.3	0.2
Christchurch appr'ch ...	0.6	0.6	0.6	0.6	0.6	0.6	0.4	0.1	−0.1	−0.1	−0.2	−0.2
Christchurch Hbr.........	0.7	0.7	0.7	0.7	0.6	0.6	0.5	0.5	0.4	0.4	0.3	0.3
Lymington	1.5	1.4	1.4	1.3	1.1	1.0	0.9	0.7	0.6	0.5	0.4	0.3
Yarmouth I. o. W.	1.6	1.5	1.5	1.4	1.3	1.2	1.1	0.9	0.8	0.7	0.5	0.4
Cowes I. o. W.	1.9	1.8	1.8	1.6	1.5	1.3	1.1	1.0	0.8	0.6	0.5	0.3
Sandown I. o. W........	1.9	1.7	1.7	1.5	1.4	1.2	1.0	0.9	0.7	0.6	0.4	0.3
Southampton	2.0	1.9	1.7	1.6	1.4	1.3	1.1	1.0	0.8	0.7	0.6	0.5
Portsmouth................	2.0	1.9	1.7	1.6	1.5	1.3	1.1	1.0	0.8	0.7	0.6	0.5
Chichester entrance.....	2.2	2.1	1.9	1.8	1.7	1.6	1.4	1.3	1.2	1.1	1.1	1.0
Selsey Bill.................	2.2	2.1	2.1	2.0	1.9	1.9	1.8	1.8	1.7	1.7	1.6	1.6
Littlehampton Hbr........	2.0	1.9	1.9	1.8	1.8	1.7	1.7	1.6	1.6	1.6	1.6	1.6
Littlehampton appr'ch ..	2.1	2.0	2.0	1.9	1.8	1.7	1.6	1.5	1.4	1.4	1.3	1.3
Shoreham.................	2.3	2.2	2.0	1.9	1.7	1.6	1.4	1.3	1.1	1.0	0.9	0.8
Brighton	2.2	2.1	1.9	1.8	1.7	1.5	1.4	1.2	1.1	1.0	0.8	0.7
Newhaven..................	2.4	2.2	2.0	1.8	1.7	1.5	1.3	1.2	1.0	0.9	0.8	0.7
FRANCE											
Le Havre	3.1	2.9	2.7	2.5	2.2	2.0	1.8	1.5	1.3	1.1	0.9	0.7
Honfleur	3.1	2.9	2.7	2.5	2.4	2.2	2.0	1.9	1.7	1.6	1.4	1.3
Trouville (Deauville)	3.2	2.9	2.7	2.4	2.2	1.9	1.7	1.5	1.2	1.0	0.8	0.6
Ouistreham	3.1	2.8	2.6	2.3	2.0	1.7	1.5	1.2	0.9	0.7	0.5	0.3
Courseulles................	2.8	2.5	2.3	2.0	1.8	1.5	1.3	1.0	0.8	0.6	0.5	0.3
Arromanches	3.3	3.0	2.8	2.5	2.2	2.0	1.7	1.5	1.2	1.0	0.8	0.6
Port-en-Bessin............	3.1	2.8	2.6	2.3	2.0	1.7	1.5	1.2	0.9	0.7	0.5	0.3
Saint-Vaast-la-Hougue..	2.7	2.5	2.3	2.1	1.9	1.6	1.4	1.2	1.0	0.7	0.5	0.2
Barfleur	3.0	2.8	2.6	2.4	2.2	1.9	1.7	1.5	1.3	1.1	0.8	0.6
Cherbourg	3.2	3.1	2.9	2.8	2.7	2.5	2.4	2.2	2.1	1.9	1.8	1.6
Omonville	3.5	3.4	3.2	3.1	3.0	2.8	2.7	2.5	2.4	2.2	2.1	1.9
Goury	5.1	5.0	5.0	4.9	4.8	4.7	4.6	4.5	4.4	4.3	4.2	4.1
Dielette	6.0	5.9	5.9	5.8	5.7	5.7	5.6	5.6	5.6	5.5	5.5	5.5
Carteret....................	6.7	6.7	6.7	6.7	6.8	6.8	6.8	6.9	6.9	6.9	7.0	7.0
Granville...................	8.2	8.3	8.3	8.4	8.5	8.6	8.6	8.7	8.8	8.9	9.0	9.1
Saint Malo	7.9	7.9	7.9	7.9	7.9	8.0	8.0	8.0	8.0	8.1	8.1	8.2
All Hbrs, St Brieuc Bay	7.3	7.5	7.7	7.9	8.0	8.2	8.4	8.5	8.7	8.8	9.0	9.1
Paimpol	6.7	6.8	7.0	7.1	7.3	7.4	7.6	7.7	7.9	8.0	8.2	8.3
Ile de Bréhat	7.3	7.3	7.3	7.3	7.4	7.4	7.4	7.4	7.5	7.6	7.7	7.8
Lezardrieux	6.6	6.7	6.9	7.0	7.1	7.3	7.4	7.5	7.7	7.8	8.0	8.1
ISLANDS OFF											
Braye, Alderney...........	3.4	3.4	3.4	3.4	3.4	3.5	3.5	3.5	3.5	3.5	3.5	3.5
St Peter Port & Sark	5.6	5.6	5.6	5.6	5.6	5.7	5.7	5.7	5.7	5.7	5.8	5.8
St Helier, Jersey	6.7	6.8	6.8	6.9	7.0	7.0	7.0	7.1	7.1	7.2	7.2	7.3
St Catherine, Jersey	6.7	6.7	6.7	6.7	6.6	6.6	6.6	6.5	6.5	6.5	6.6	6.6
Les Minquiers	7.1	7.2	7.2	7.3	7.3	7.4	7.4	7.5	7.5	7.6	7.6	7.7
Iles Chausey	8.1	8.2	8.2	8.3	8.3	8.4	8.4	8.5	8.5	8.6	8.7	8.8

Tidal Heights (offshore)

The broad arrows apply to the time entered on the adjacent page. Each arrow gives the following information:

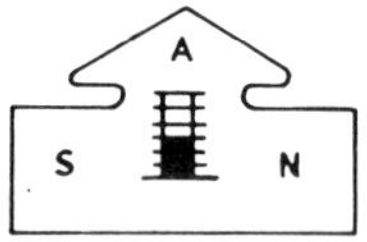

A Average Height of Tide. This is the height of tide, in metres, above Chart Datum, at the position indicated by the arrow. Although only an average height, this figure is sufficiently accurate for use for most coastal navigation.
S Height of Tide at Springs.
N Height of Tide at Neaps.
The Tidal Gauge gives a visual display of the approximate state of the tide with the vertical movement of tide described briefly above or below.

Rising s 2.8 m n 2.9 m — 2.8 m

Low Water s 0.3 m n 0.9 m — 0.6 m

Low Water s 0.6 m n 1.9 m — 1.3 m

Low Water s 0.6 m n 1.9 m — 1.3 m

Falling to L.W. s 1.1 m n 2.2 m — 1.7 m

Rising from L.W. s 0.9 m n 1.1 m — 1.0 m

Rising from L.W. s 1.2 m n 2.7 m — 2.0 m

Falling to L.W. s 1.1 m n 2.7 m — 1.9 m

Rising quickly s 2.9 m n 3.3 m — 3.1 m

Rising very quickly s 5.7 m n 5.6 m — 5.6 m

Rising very quickly s 7.7 m n 6.4 m — 7.0 m

Low Water s 1.2 m n 2.7 m — 1.7 m

Rising very quickly s 7.3 m n 6.9 m — 7.1 m

Falling to L.W. s 1.0 m n 2.7 m — 1.9 m

Rising very quickly s 8.1 m n 7.6 m — 7.9 m

Tidal Stream Rates

4 hours before HW Cherbourg **-4**

Time (to be inserted)

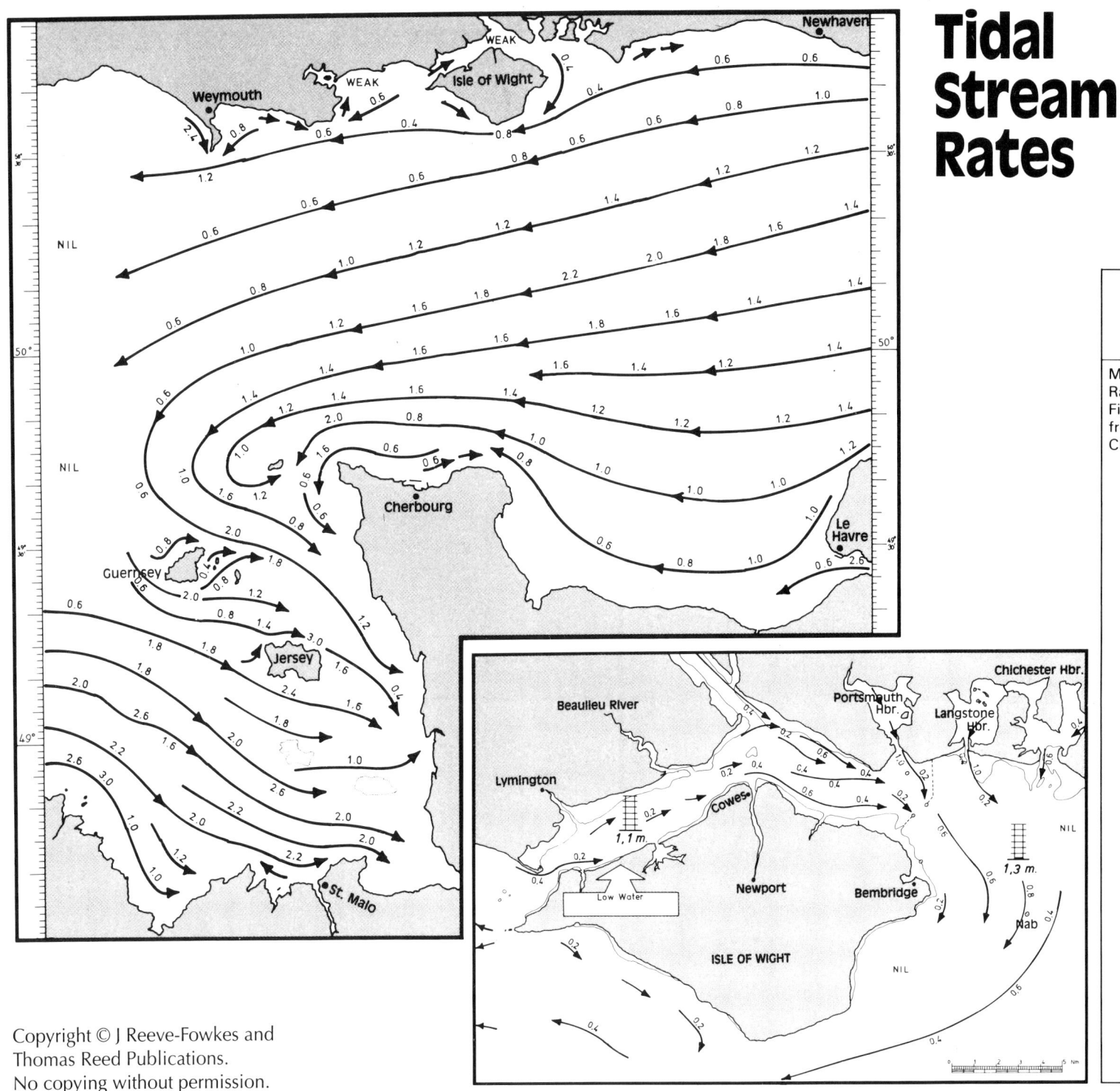

Stream Rate Conversion Table

Mean Rate Figure from Chart ▼	\multicolumn{11}{c}{Pencil-in height of HW Cherbourg — Read from column below pencil mark}
	4.8	5.0	5.2	5.4	5.6	5.8	6.0	6.2	6.4	6.6	6.8
0.2	0.1	0.1	0.2	0.2	0.2	0.2	0.2	0.2	0.3	0.3	0.3
0.4	0.2	0.3	0.3	0.3	0.4	0.4	0.4	0.5	0.5	0.6	0.6
0.6	0.4	0.4	0.5	0.5	0.6	0.6	0.6	0.7	0.7	0.8	0.9
0.8	0.5	0.5	0.6	0.7	0.7	0.8	0.9	1.0	1.0	1.1	1.2	1.2
1.0	0.6	0.7	0.8	0.8	0.9	1.0	1.1	1.2	1.3	1.4	1.5	1.5
1.2	0.7	0.8	0.9	1.0	1.1	1.2	1.3	1.4	1.5	1.6	1.7	1.9
1.4	0.8	0.9	1.1	1.2	1.3	1.4	1.6	1.7	1.8	1.9	2.0	2.2
1.6	0.9	1.1	1.2	1.4	1.5	1.6	1.8	1.9	2.1	2.2	2.3	2.5
1.8	1.0	1.2	1.4	1.5	1.7	1.8	2.0	2.1	2.3	2.5	2.6	2.8
2.0	1.2	1.3	1.5	1.7	1.9	2.0	2.2	2.4	2.6	2.7	2.9	3.1
2.2	1.3	1.5	1.7	1.9	2.1	2.2	2.4	2.6	2.8	3.0	3.2	3.4
2.4	1.4	1.6	1.8	2.0	2.2	2.5	2.7	2.9	3.1	3.3	3.5	3.7
2.6	1.5	1.8	2.0	2.2	2.4	2.7	2.9	3.1	3.3	3.6	3.8	4.0
2.8	1.6	1.9	2.1	2.4	2.6	2.9	3.1	3.3	3.6	3.8	4.1	4.3
3.0	1.8	2.0	2.3	2.5	2.8	3.1	3.3	3.6	3.8	4.1	4.4	4.6
3.2	1.9	2.2	2.4	2.7	3.0	3.3	3.5	3.8	4.1	4.4	4.7	4.9
3.4	2.0	2.3	2.6	2.9	3.2	3.5	3.8	4.1	4.4	4.7	5.0	5.3
3.6	2.1	2.4	2.7	3.1	3.4	3.7	4.0	4.3	4.6	4.9	5.2	5.6
3.8	2.2	2.6	2.9	3.2	3.6	3.9	4.2	4.5	4.9	5.2	5.5	5.9
4.0	2.3	2.7	3.0	3.4	3.7	4.1	4.4	4.8	5.1	5.5	5.8	6.2
4.2	2.5	2.8	3.2	3.6	3.9	4.3	4.7	5.0	5.4	5.8	6.1	6.5
4.4	2.6	3.0	3.3	3.7	4.1	4.5	4.9	5.3	5.6	6.0	6.4	6.8
4.6	2.7	3.1	3.5	3.9	4.3	4.7	5.1	5.5	5.9	6.3	6.7	7.1
4.8	2.8	3.2	3.6	4.1	4.5	4.9	5.3	5.7	6.2	6.6	7.0	7.4
5.0	2.9	3.4	3.8	4.2	4.7	5.1	5.5	6.0	6.4	6.9	7.3	7.7
5.2	3.0	3.5	4.0	4.4	4.9	5.3	5.8	6.2	6.7	7.1	7.6	8.0
5.4	3.2	3.6	4.1	4.6	5.0	5.5	6.0	6.5	6.9	7.4	7.9	8.3
5.6	3.3	3.8	4.3	4.7	5.2	5.7	6.2	6.7	7.2	7.7	8.2	8.6
5.8	3.4	3.9	4.4	4.9	5.4	5.9	6.4	6.9	7.4	7.9	8.5	9.0
6.0	3.5	4.0	4.6	5.1	5.6	6.1	6.7	7.2	7.7	8.2	8.7	9.3
6.2	3.6	4.2	4.7	5.3	5.8	6.3	6.9	7.4	8.0	8.5	9.0	9.6
6.4	3.8	4.3	4.9	5.4	6.0	6.5	7.1	7.7	8.2	8.8	9.3	9.9
6.6	3.9	4.4	5.0	5.6	6.2	6.7	7.3	7.9	8.5	9.0	9.6	10.2
6.8	4.0	4.6	5.2	5.8	6.4	6.9	7.5	8.1	8.7	9.3	9.9	10.5
7.0	4.1	4.7	5.3	5.9	6.6	7.2	7.8	8.4	9.0	9.6	10.2	10.8

Copyright © J Reeve-Fowkes and Thomas Reed Publications.
No copying without permission.

-3 3 hours before HW Cherbourg

Tidal Heights

Copyright © J Reeve-Fowkes and
Thomas Reed Publications.
No copying without permission.

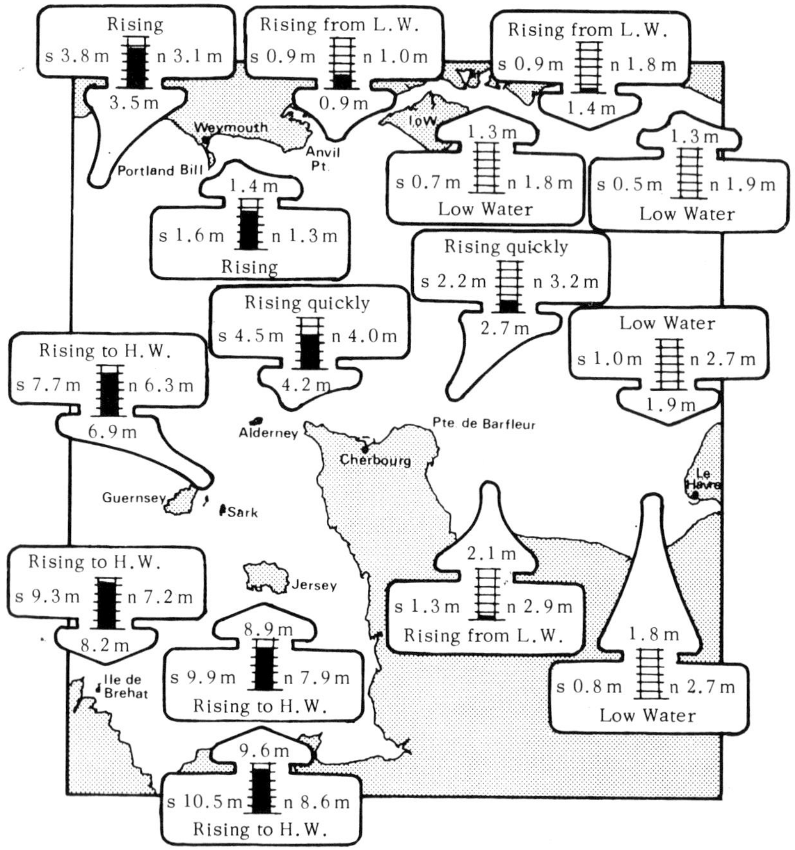

Tidal Heights (offshore)

The broad arrows apply to the time entered on the adjacent page. Each arrow gives the following information:

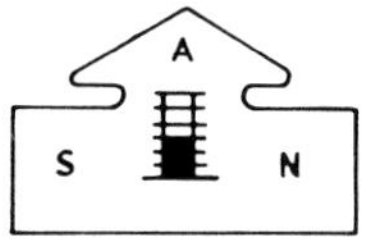

A Average Height of Tide. This is the height of tide, in metres, above Chart Datum, at the position indicated by the arrow. Although only an average height, this figure is sufficiently accurate for use for most coastal navigation.
S Height of Tide at Springs.
N Height of Tide at Neaps.
The Tidal Gauge gives a visual display of the approximate state of the tide with the vertical movement of tide described briefly above or below.

Tidal diagram labels

- Rising s 3.8 m n 3.1 m — 3.5 m
- Rising from L.W. s 0.9 m n 1.0 m — 0.9 m
- Rising from L.W. s 0.9 m n 1.8 m — 1.4 m
- 1.3 m
- 1.3 m
- s 0.7 m n 1.8 m Low Water
- s 0.5 m n 1.9 m Low Water
- s 1.6 m n 1.3 m Rising — 1.4 m
- Rising quickly s 2.2 m n 3.2 m — 2.7 m
- Rising quickly s 4.5 m n 4.0 m — 4.2 m
- Low Water s 1.0 m n 2.7 m — 1.9 m
- Rising to H.W. s 7.7 m n 6.3 m — 6.9 m
- Rising to H.W. s 9.3 m n 7.2 m — 8.2 m
- 2.1 m
- s 1.3 m n 2.9 m Rising from L.W.
- 1.8 m
- s 0.8 m n 2.7 m Low Water
- 8.9 m
- s 9.9 m n 7.9 m Rising to H.W.
- 9.6 m
- s 10.5 m n 8.6 m Rising to H.W.

Place labels: Weymouth, Portland Bill, Anvil Pt., Alderney, Cherbourg, Pte de Barfleur, Le Havre, Guernsey, Sark, Jersey, Ile de Bréhat

---

TIDAL HEIGHTS — PORTS & PLACES

Pencil-in height of ▶ HW Cherbourg	4.8	5.0	5.2	5.4	5.6	5.8	6.0	6.2	6.4	6.6	6.8
ENGLAND											
Lyme Regis	2.8	2.9	3.1	3.2	3.3	3.4	3.6	3.7	3.8	3.9	4.0	4.1
Bridport	2.9	3.0	3.0	3.1	3.2	3.3	3.4	3.5	3.6	3.7	3.9	4.0
Portland & Weymouth..	1.3	1.3	1.3	1.3	1.3	1.4	1.4	1.4	1.5	1.6	1.7	1.8
Lulworth Cove	1.3	1.4	1.4	1.5	1.6	1.6	1.7	1.7	1.8	1.9	2.0	2.1
Swanage	1.3	1.3	1.3	1.3	1.2	1.2	1.2	1.1	1.1	1.1	1.1	1.1
Poole entrance	1.2	1.2	1.2	1.2	1.1	1.1	1.1	1.1	1.1	1.0	1.0	0.9
Poole Town Quay	1.4	1.3	1.3	1.2	1.1	1.0	0.9	0.9	0.8	0.7	0.7	0.6
Christchurch appr'ch ..	0.8	0.8	0.8	0.8	0.8	0.8	0.7	0.6	0.5	0.4	0.4	0.3
Christchurch Hbr	0.8	0.8	0.8	0.8	0.8	0.8	0.8	0.7	0.7	0.7	0.7	0.7
Lymington	1.6	1.5	1.5	1.4	1.3	1.2	1.1	0.9	0.8	0.7	0.6	0.5
Yarmouth I. o. W.	1.7	1.6	1.6	1.5	1.5	1.4	1.3	1.2	1.1	1.0	0.9	0.8
Cowes I. o. W.	1.9	1.8	1.8	1.7	1.5	1.4	1.2	1.1	0.9	0.7	0.6	0.4
Sandown I. o. W.	1.8	1.7	1.7	1.6	1.4	1.3	1.1	1.0	0.8	0.7	0.6	0.4
Southampton	2.3	2.1	1.9	1.7	1.5	1.3	1.1	0.9	0.7	0.6	0.5	0.4
Portsmouth	2.0	1.9	1.7	1.6	1.4	1.3	1.1	1.0	0.8	0.6	0.5	0.4
Chichester entrance	2.1	1.9	1.7	1.5	1.4	1.2	1.0	0.9	0.7	0.6	0.5	0.4
Selsey Bill	2.1	1.9	1.7	1.5	1.3	1.2	1.0	0.8	0.6	0.5	0.4	0.1
Littlehampton Hbr	1.8	1.7	1.5	1.4	1.3	1.2	1.0	0.9	0.8	0.8	0.8	0.8
Littlehampton appr'ch ..	2.0	1.8	1.6	1.4	1.2	1.1	0.9	0.7	0.5	0.4	0.3	0.2
Shoreham	2.2	2.0	1.8	1.6	1.4	1.3	1.1	0.9	0.7	0.6	0.4	0.3
Brighton	2.2	2.0	1.8	1.6	1.4	1.2	1.0	0.8	0.6	0.4	0.3	0.1
Newhaven	2.2	2.0	1.8	1.6	1.4	1.1	0.9	0.7	0.5	0.4	0.2	0.1
FRANCE											
Le Havre	3.5	3.2	3.0	2.7	2.4	2.1	1.8	1.5	1.2	1.0	0.7	0.5
Honfleur	3.2	3.0	2.8	2.6	2.4	2.1	1.9	1.7	1.5	1.3	1.2	1.0
Trouville (Deauville)	3.5	3.2	3.0	2.7	2.4	2.1	1.9	1.6	1.3	1.1	0.9	0.7
Ouistreham	3.5	3.2	2.8	2.5	2.2	1.9	1.6	1.3	1.0	0.8	0.6	0.4
Courseulles	3.1	2.9	2.7	2.5	2.3	2.2	2.0	1.8	1.6	1.5	1.3	1.2
Arromanches	3.7	3.5	3.3	3.1	2.8	2.6	2.4	2.1	1.9	1.7	1.6	1.4
Port-en-Bessin	3.5	3.2	3.0	2.7	2.4	2.2	1.9	1.7	1.4	1.2	1.1	0.9
Saint-Vaast-la-Hougue..	3.1	2.9	2.7	2.5	2.3	2.2	2.0	1.8	1.6	1.4	1.2	1.0
Barfleur	3.4	3.3	3.1	3.0	2.9	2.7	2.6	2.4	2.3	2.1	2.0	1.8
Cherbourg	3.7	3.7	3.7	3.7	3.7	3.6	3.6	3.6	3.6	3.6	3.6	3.6
Omonville	4.0	4.0	4.0	4.0	4.0	4.0	4.0	4.0	4.0	4.0	4.0	4.0
Goury	5.7	5.8	5.8	5.9	5.9	6.0	6.0	6.1	6.1	6.1	6.2	6.2
Dielette	6.5	6.6	6.8	6.9	7.1	7.2	7.4	7.5	7.7	7.8	8.0	8.1
Carteret	7.3	7.6	7.8	8.1	8.3	8.6	8.8	9.1	9.3	9.5	9.8	10.0
Granville	8.8	9.1	9.5	9.8	10.1	10.4	10.8	11.1	11.4	11.7	11.9	12.2
Saint Malo	8.5	8.8	9.0	9.3	9.6	9.8	10.1	10.3	10.6	10.8	11.1	11.3
All Hbrs, St Brieuc Bay	7.8	8.3	8.6	9.0	9.3	9.7	10.1	10.4	10.8	11.0	11.3	11.5
Paimpol	7.1	7.4	7.8	8.1	8.5	8.8	9.2	9.5	9.9	10.2	10.5	10.8
Ile de Bréhat	7.6	7.9	8.1	8.4	8.6	8.9	9.1	9.4	9.6	9.8	10.0	10.2
Lezardrieux	7.2	7.5	7.7	8.0	8.3	8.5	8.8	9.0	9.3	9.5	9.8	10.0
ISLANDS OFF											
Braye, Alderney	3.9	4.0	4.2	4.3	4.4	4.5	4.7	4.8	4.9	5.0	5.2	5.3
St Peter Port & Sark ...	6.0	6.2	6.4	6.6	6.8	7.0	7.2	7.4	7.6	7.8	7.9	8.1
St Helier, Jersey	7.2	7.5	7.7	8.0	8.3	8.6	8.9	9.2	9.5	9.7	10.0	10.2
St Catherine, Jersey	7.1	7.4	7.6	7.9	8.1	8.4	8.6	8.9	9.1	9.3	9.5	9.7
Les Minquiers	7.8	8.1	8.3	8.6	8.9	9.1	9.4	9.6	9.9	10.1	10.3	10.5
Iles Chausey	8.9	9.2	9.4	9.7	10.0	10.3	10.6	10.9	11.2	11.4	11.7	11.9

Tidal Stream Rates

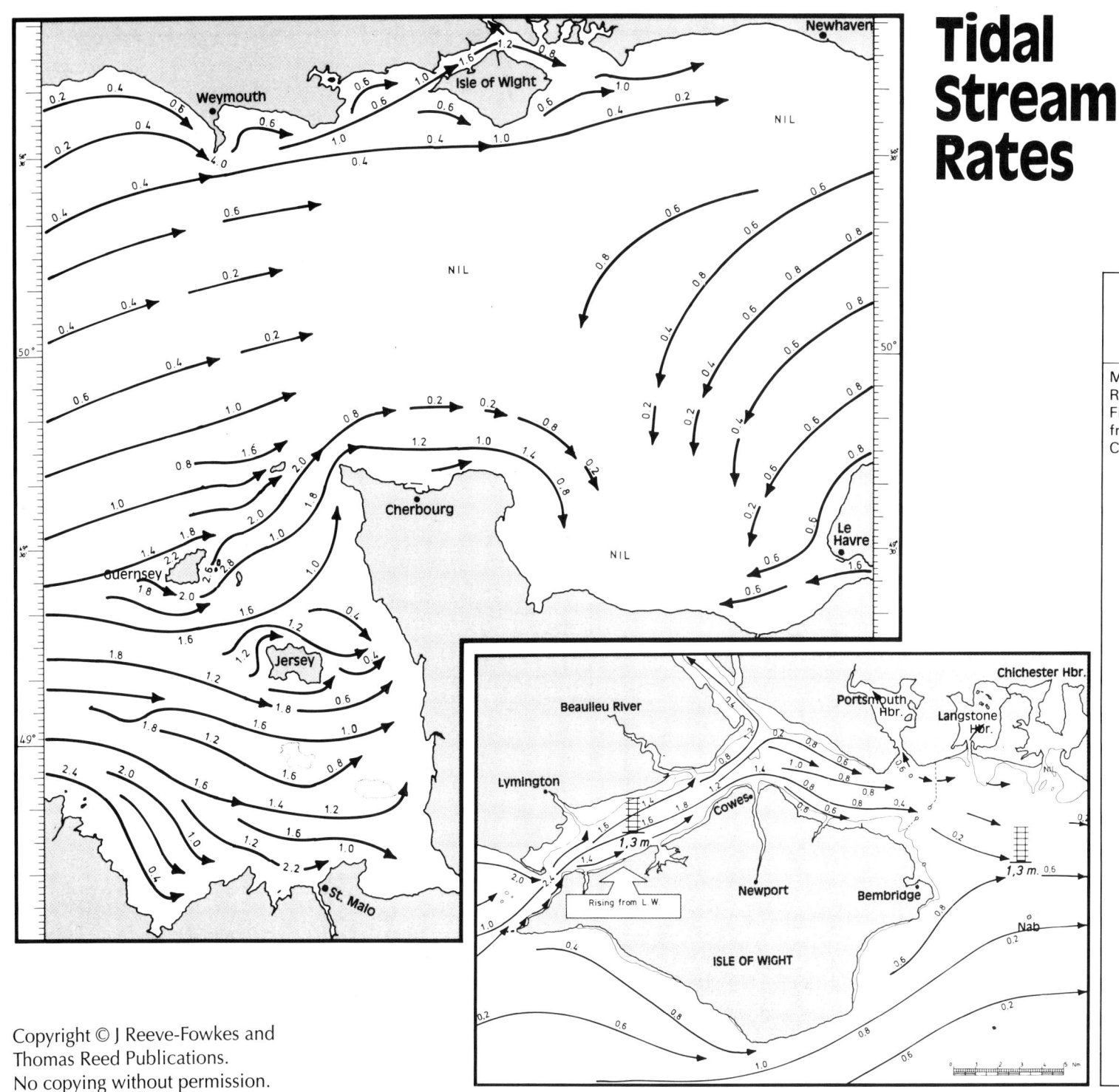

3 hours before HW Cherbourg

-3

Time (to be inserted)

Stream Rate Conversion Table

Mean Rate Figure from Chart ▼	\multicolumn{11}{c}{Pencil-in height of HW Cherbourg — Read from column below pencil mark}
	4.8	5.0	5.2	5.4	5.6	5.8	6.0	6.2	6.4	6.6	6.8
0.2	0.1	0.1	0.2	0.2	0.2	0.2	0.2	0.3	0.3	0.3	0.3
0.4	0.2	0.3	0.3	0.3	0.4	0.4	0.4	0.5	0.5	0.6	0.6
0.6	0.4	0.4	0.5	0.5	0.6	0.6	0.6	0.7	0.7	0.8	0.9
0.8	0.5	0.5	0.6	0.7	0.7	0.8	0.9	1.0	1.0	1.1	1.2	1.2
1.0	0.6	0.7	0.8	0.8	0.9	1.0	1.1	1.2	1.3	1.4	1.5	1.5
1.2	0.7	0.8	0.9	1.0	1.1	1.2	1.3	1.4	1.5	1.6	1.7	1.9
1.4	0.8	0.9	1.1	1.2	1.3	1.4	1.6	1.7	1.8	1.9	2.0	2.2
1.6	0.9	1.1	1.2	1.4	1.5	1.6	1.8	1.9	2.1	2.2	2.3	2.5
1.8	1.0	1.2	1.4	1.5	1.7	1.8	2.0	2.1	2.3	2.5	2.6	2.8
2.0	1.2	1.3	1.5	1.7	1.9	2.0	2.2	2.4	2.6	2.7	2.9	3.1
2.2	1.3	1.5	1.7	1.9	2.1	2.2	2.4	2.6	2.8	3.0	3.2	3.4
2.4	1.4	1.6	1.8	2.0	2.2	2.5	2.7	2.9	3.1	3.3	3.5	3.7
2.6	1.5	1.8	2.0	2.2	2.4	2.7	2.9	3.1	3.3	3.6	3.8	4.0
2.8	1.6	1.9	2.1	2.4	2.6	2.9	3.1	3.3	3.6	3.8	4.1	4.3
3.0	1.8	2.0	2.3	2.5	2.8	3.1	3.3	3.6	3.8	4.1	4.4	4.6
3.2	1.9	2.2	2.4	2.7	3.0	3.3	3.5	3.8	4.1	4.4	4.7	4.9
3.4	2.0	2.3	2.6	2.9	3.2	3.5	3.8	4.1	4.4	4.7	5.0	5.3
3.6	2.1	2.4	2.7	3.1	3.4	3.7	4.0	4.3	4.6	4.9	5.2	5.6
3.8	2.2	2.6	2.9	3.2	3.6	3.9	4.2	4.5	4.9	5.2	5.5	5.8
4.0	2.3	2.7	3.0	3.4	3.7	4.1	4.4	4.8	5.1	5.5	5.8	6.2
4.2	2.5	2.8	3.2	3.6	3.9	4.3	4.7	5.0	5.4	5.8	6.1	6.5
4.4	2.6	3.0	3.3	3.7	4.1	4.5	4.9	5.3	5.6	6.0	6.4	6.8
4.6	2.7	3.1	3.5	3.9	4.3	4.7	5.1	5.5	5.9	6.3	6.7	7.1
4.8	2.8	3.2	3.6	4.1	4.5	4.9	5.3	5.7	6.2	6.6	7.0	7.4
5.0	2.9	3.4	3.8	4.2	4.7	5.1	5.5	6.0	6.4	6.9	7.3	7.7
5.2	3.0	3.5	4.0	4.4	4.9	5.3	5.8	6.2	6.7	7.1	7.6	8.0
5.4	3.2	3.6	4.1	4.6	5.0	5.5	6.0	6.5	6.9	7.4	7.9	8.3
5.6	3.3	3.8	4.3	4.7	5.2	5.7	6.2	6.7	7.2	7.7	8.2	8.6
5.8	3.4	3.9	4.4	4.9	5.4	5.9	6.4	6.9	7.4	7.9	8.5	9.0
6.0	3.5	4.0	4.6	5.1	5.6	6.1	6.7	7.2	7.7	8.2	8.7	9.3
6.2	3.6	4.2	4.7	5.2	5.8	6.3	6.9	7.4	8.0	8.5	9.0	9.6
6.4	3.8	4.3	4.9	5.4	6.0	6.5	7.1	7.7	8.2	8.8	9.3	9.9
6.6	3.9	4.4	5.0	5.6	6.2	6.7	7.3	7.9	8.5	9.0	9.6	10.2
6.8	4.0	4.6	5.2	5.8	6.4	6.9	7.5	8.1	8.7	9.3	9.9	10.5
7.0	4.1	4.7	5.3	5.9	6.6	7.2	7.8	8.4	9.0	9.6	10.2	10.8

Copyright © J Reeve-Fowkes and Thomas Reed Publications.
No copying without permission.

-2
2 hours before HW Cherbourg

Tidal Heights

Copyright © J Reeve-Fowkes and
Thomas Reed Publications.
No copying without permission.

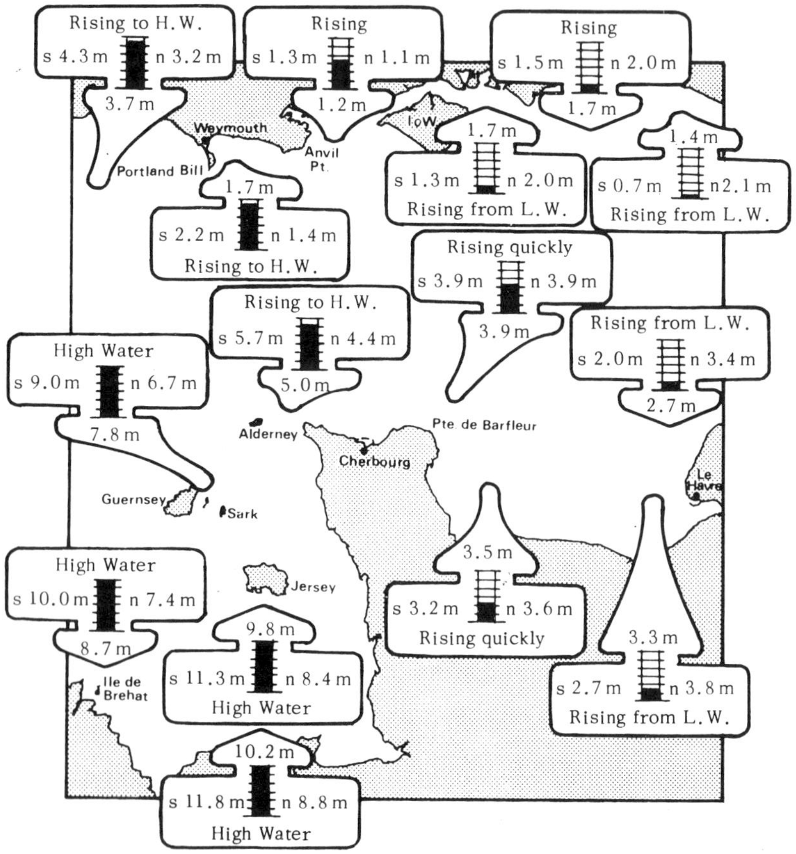

TIDAL HEIGHTS — PORTS & PLACES

Pencil-in height of ▶ HW Cherbourg	4.8	5.0	5.2	5.4	5.6	5.8	6.0	6.2	6.4	6.6	6.8
ENGLAND											
Lyme Regis..............	2.8	3.0	3.2	3.4	3.5	3.7	3.9	4.0	4.2	4.3	4.5	4.6
Bridport....................	2.7	2.9	3.1	3.3	3.4	3.6	3.8	3.9	4.1	4.3	4.4	4.6
Portland & Weymouth..	1.3	1.4	1.4	1.5	1.6	1.7	1.8	1.9	2.0	2.1	2.2	2.3
Lulworth Cove	1.3	1.4	1.6	1.7	1.8	1.9	2.0	2.1	2.2	2.4	2.5	2.7
Swanage	1.4	1.4	1.4	1.4	1.4	1.4	1.4	1.5	1.5	1.5	1.6	1.6
Poole entrance...........	1.3	1.3	1.3	1.3	1.4	1.4	1.4	1.5	1.5	1.5	1.5	1.5
Poole Town Quay.......	1.4	1.4	1.4	1.4	1.3	1.3	1.3	1.3	1.3	1.3	1.2	1.2
Christchurch appr'ch ...	0.8	0.9	0.9	1.0	1.0	1.1	1.1	1.1	1.1	1.1	1.1	1.1
Christchurch Hbr........	1.0	1.0	1.0	1.0	1.1	1.1	1.1	1.1	1.1	1.1	1.1	1.1
Lymington	1.6	1.6	1.6	1.6	1.5	1.5	1.5	1.4	1.4	1.4	1.3	1.3
Yarmouth I. o. W.........	1.7	1.7	1.7	1.7	1.7	1.7	1.7	1.6	1.6	1.6	1.5	1.5
Cowes I. o. W............	2.1	2.0	2.0	1.9	1.8	1.7	1.6	1.6	1.5	1.4	1.2	1.1
Sandown I. o. W.........	1.9	1.8	1.8	1.7	1.7	1.6	1.5	1.4	1.3	1.2	1.2	1.1
Southampton	2.3	2.2	2.2	2.1	2.0	1.9	1.9	1.8	1.7	1.6	1.6	1.5
Portsmouth...............	2.1	2.0	2.0	1.9	1.8	1.7	1.6	1.5	1.4	1.4	1.3	1.3
Chichester entrance.....	2.0	1.9	1.9	1.8	1.7	1.7	1.6	1.6	1.5	1.5	1.4	1.4
Selsey Bill.................	2.1	2.0	1.8	1.7	1.6	1.5	1.4	1.3	1.2	1.1	1.1	1.0
Littlehampton Hbr........	1.9	1.8	1.6	1.5	1.3	1.2	1.0	0.8	0.7	0.7	0.7	0.7
Littlehampton appr'ch ..	1.9	1.8	1.8	1.7	1.6	1.5	1.4	1.3	1.2	1.1	1.1	1.0
Shoreham..................	2.4	2.2	2.0	1.9	1.7	1.5	1.3	1.2	1.0	0.9	0.8	0.7
Brighton	2.4	2.2	2.1	1.8	1.7	1.5	1.3	1.2	1.0	0.9	0.7	0.6
Newhaven	2.4	2.2	2.0	1.8	1.6	1.4	1.2	1.0	0.8	0.7	0.5	0.4
FRANCE											
Le Havre	4.1	3.9	3.7	3.5	3.3	3.1	2.9	2.7	2.5	2.3	2.2	2.0
Honfleur	4.1	3.9	3.7	3.5	3.3	3.1	2.9	2.7	2.5	2.4	2.3	2.2
Trouville (Deauville)	4.0	3.9	3.9	3.8	3.7	3.6	3.6	3.5	3.4	3.3	3.2	3.1
Ouistreham	4.1	4.0	3.8	3.7	3.6	3.5	3.3	3.2	3.1	3.0	2.9	2.8
Courseulles	3.6	3.7	3.9	4.0	4.1	4.3	4.4	4.6	4.7	4.7	4.8	4.8
Arromanches	4.3	4.4	4.4	4.5	4.5	4.6	4.6	4.7	4.7	4.7	4.7	4.7
Port-en-Bessin............	4.1	4.1	4.1	4.1	4.1	4.1	4.1	4.1	4.1	4.0	4.0	3.9
Saint-Vaast-la-Hougue..	3.8	3.7	3.7	3.6	3.6	3.5	3.5	3.4	3.4	3.3	3.3	3.2
Barfleur	3.9	3.9	3.9	3.9	3.9	3.9	3.9	3.9	3.9	3.9	3.9	3.9
Cherbourg	4.2	4.3	4.5	4.6	4.7	4.8	4.9	5.0	5.1	5.2	5.3	5.4
Omonville	4.3	4.4	4.6	4.7	4.8	4.9	5.1	5.2	5.3	5.4	5.6	5.7
Goury	6.2	6.3	6.5	6.6	6.7	6.9	7.0	7.2	7.3	7.4	7.6	7.7
Dielette	6.7	7.0	7.4	7.7	8.0	8.3	8.6	8.9	9.2	9.4	9.7	9.9
Carteret	7.6	8.0	8.4	8.8	9.2	9.5	9.9	10.3	10.7	11.0	11.3	11.6
Granville...................	8.9	9.4	9.8	10.3	10.8	11.3	11.7	12.2	12.7	13.0	13.4	13.7
Saint Malo	8.4	8.9	9.3	9.8	10.2	10.7	11.1	11.6	12.0	12.3	12.6	12.9
All Hbrs, St Brieuc Bay	7.9	8.3	8.7	9.1	9.6	10.0	10.4	10.9	11.3	11.6	11.8	12.1
Paimpol	7.2	7.6	8.0	8.4	8.8	9.2	9.6	10.0	10.4	10.7	11.0	11.3
Ile de Bréhat	7.5	7.9	8.3	8.7	9.0	9.4	9.8	10.1	10.5	10.8	11.0	11.3
Lezardrieux	7.1	7.5	7.9	8.3	8.7	9.0	9.4	9.8	10.2	10.5	10.7	11.0
ISLANDS OFF											
Braye, Alderney...........	4.3	4.5	4.7	4.9	5.1	5.3	5.5	5.7	6.0	6.2	6.3	6.5
St Peter Port & Sark	6.2	6.5	6.9	7.2	7.5	7.8	8.2	8.5	8.8	9.0	9.3	9.5
St Helier, Jersey	7.5	7.9	8.3	8.7	9.2	9.6	10.0	10.5	10.9	11.3	11.6	12.0
St Catherine, Jersey	7.4	7.8	8.2	8.6	9.0	9.4	9.8	10.2	10.6	10.9	11.2	11.5
Les Minquiers	8.3	8.7	9.1	9.5	9.8	10.2	10.6	10.9	11.3	11.6	11.9	12.2
Iles Chausey	9.1	9.5	9.9	10.3	10.8	11.2	11.6	12.1	12.5	12.8	13.2	13.5

Tidal Heights (offshore)

The broad arrows apply to the time entered on the adjacent page. Each arrow gives the following information:

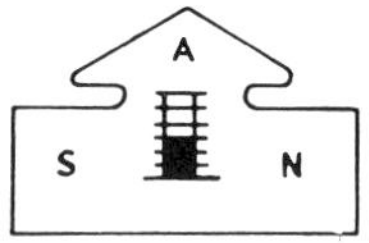

A Average Height of Tide. This is the height of tide, in metres, above Chart Datum, at the position indicated by the arrow. Although only an average height, this figure is sufficiently accurate for use for most coastal navigation.
S Height of Tide at Springs.
N Height of Tide at Neaps.
The Tidal Gauge gives a visual display of the approximate state of the tide with the vertical movement of tide described briefly above or below.

Map callouts:

- Rising to H.W. — s 4.3m n 3.2m — 3.7m
- Rising — s 1.3m n 1.1m — 1.2m
- Rising — s 1.5m n 2.0m — 1.7m
- s 1.3m n 2.0m — 1.7m — Rising from L.W.
- s 0.7m n 2.1m — 1.4m — Rising from L.W.
- Rising to H.W. — s 2.2m n 1.4m — 1.7m
- Rising quickly — s 3.9m n 3.9m — 3.9m
- Rising to H.W. — s 5.7m n 4.4m — 5.0m
- Rising from L.W. — s 2.0m n 3.4m — 2.7m
- High Water — s 9.0m n 6.7m — 7.8m
- High Water — s 10.0m n 7.4m — 8.7m
- s 3.2m n 3.6m — 3.5m — Rising quickly
- 3.3m — s 2.7m n 3.8m — Rising from L.W.
- s 11.3m n 8.4m — 9.8m — High Water
- s 11.8m n 8.8m — 10.2m — High Water

Weymouth, Anvil Pt., I o W, Portland Bill, Alderney, Cherbourg, Pte de Barfleur, Guernsey, Sark, Jersey, Ile de Bréhat, Le Havre

Tidal Stream Rates

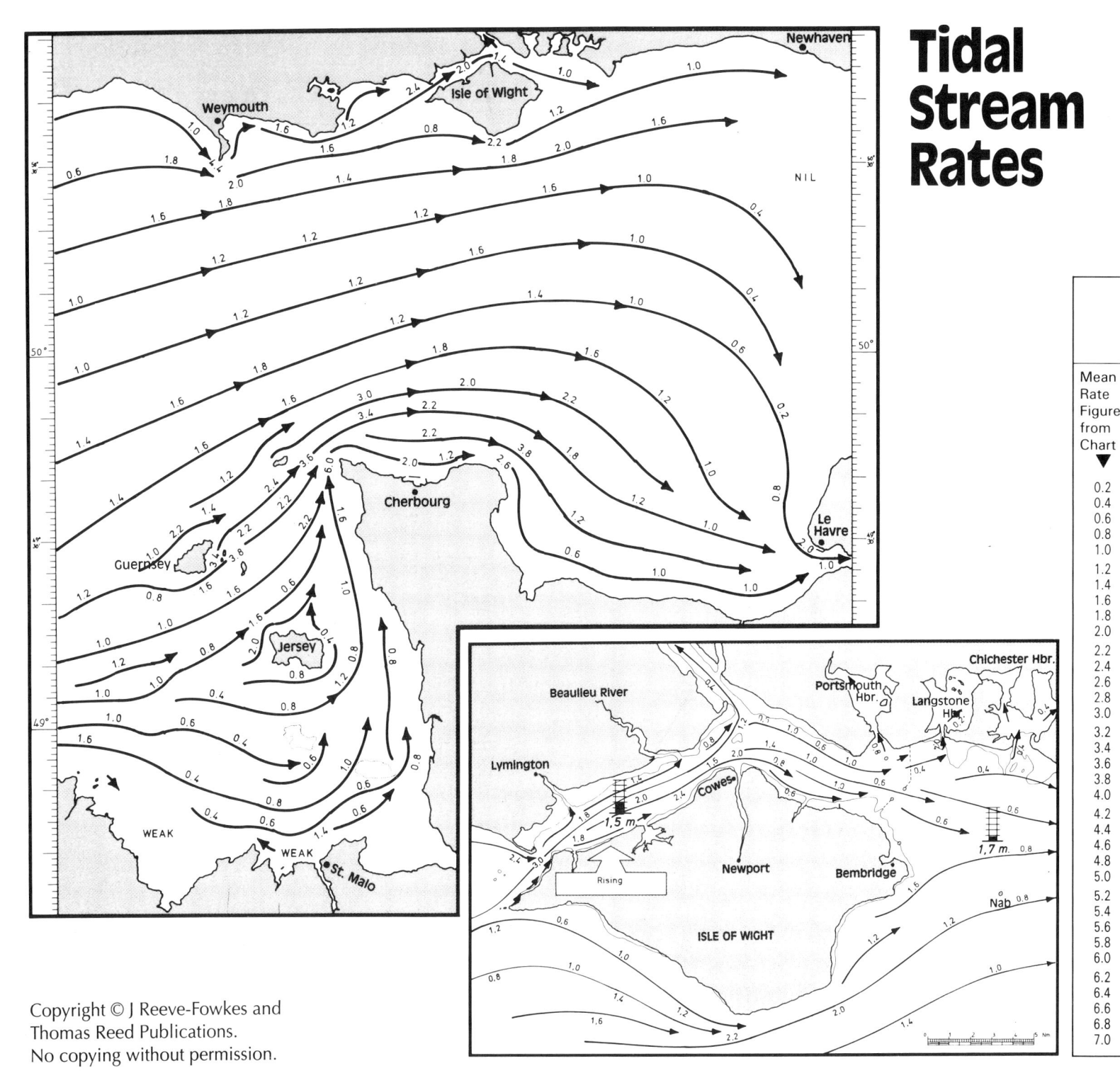

2 hours before HW Cherbourg **-2**

Time (to be inserted)

Stream Rate Conversion Table

Mean Rate Figure from Chart ▼	Pencil-in height of HW Cherbourg Read from column below pencil mark
	4.8 5.0 5.2 5.4 5.6 5.8 6.0 6.2 6.4 6.6 6.8
0.2	0.1 0.1 0.2 0.2 0.2 0.2 0.2 0.2 0.3 0.3 0.3 0.3
0.4	0.2 0.3 0.3 0.3 0.4 0.4 0.4 0.5 0.5 0.5 0.6 0.6
0.6	0.4 0.4 0.5 0.5 0.6 0.6 0.6 0.7 0.7 0.8 0.8 0.9
0.8	0.5 0.5 0.6 0.7 0.7 0.8 0.9 1.0 1.0 1.1 1.2 1.2
1.0	0.6 0.7 0.8 0.8 0.9 1.0 1.1 1.2 1.3 1.4 1.5 1.5
1.2	0.7 0.8 0.9 1.0 1.1 1.2 1.3 1.4 1.5 1.6 1.7 1.9
1.4	0.8 0.9 1.1 1.2 1.3 1.4 1.6 1.7 1.8 1.9 2.0 2.2
1.6	0.9 1.1 1.2 1.4 1.5 1.6 1.8 1.9 2.1 2.2 2.3 2.5
1.8	1.0 1.2 1.4 1.5 1.7 1.8 2.0 2.1 2.3 2.5 2.6 2.8
2.0	1.2 1.3 1.5 1.7 1.9 2.0 2.2 2.4 2.6 2.7 2.9 3.1
2.2	1.3 1.5 1.7 1.9 2.1 2.2 2.4 2.6 2.8 3.0 3.2 3.4
2.4	1.4 1.6 1.8 2.0 2.2 2.5 2.7 2.9 3.1 3.3 3.5 3.7
2.6	1.5 1.8 2.0 2.2 2.4 2.7 2.9 3.1 3.3 3.6 3.8 4.0
2.8	1.6 1.9 2.1 2.4 2.6 2.9 3.1 3.3 3.6 3.8 4.1 4.3
3.0	1.8 2.0 2.3 2.5 2.8 3.1 3.3 3.6 3.8 4.1 4.4 4.6
3.2	1.9 2.2 2.4 2.7 3.0 3.3 3.5 3.8 4.1 4.4 4.7 4.9
3.4	2.0 2.3 2.6 2.9 3.2 3.5 3.8 4.1 4.4 4.7 5.0 5.3
3.6	2.1 2.4 2.7 3.1 3.4 3.7 4.0 4.3 4.6 4.9 5.2 5.6
3.8	2.2 2.6 2.9 3.2 3.6 3.9 4.2 4.5 4.9 5.2 5.5 5.9
4.0	2.3 2.7 3.0 3.4 3.7 4.1 4.4 4.8 5.1 5.5 5.8 6.2
4.2	2.5 2.8 3.2 3.6 3.9 4.3 4.7 5.0 5.4 5.8 6.1 6.5
4.4	2.6 3.0 3.3 3.7 4.1 4.5 4.9 5.3 5.6 6.0 6.4 6.8
4.6	2.7 3.1 3.5 3.9 4.3 4.7 5.1 5.5 5.9 6.3 6.7 7.1
4.8	2.8 3.2 3.6 4.1 4.5 4.9 5.3 5.7 6.2 6.6 7.0 7.4
5.0	2.9 3.4 3.8 4.2 4.7 5.1 5.5 6.0 6.4 6.9 7.3 7.7
5.2	3.0 3.5 4.0 4.4 4.9 5.3 5.8 6.2 6.7 7.1 7.6 8.0
5.4	3.2 3.6 4.1 4.6 5.0 5.5 6.0 6.5 6.9 7.4 7.9 8.3
5.6	3.3 3.8 4.3 4.7 5.2 5.7 6.2 6.7 7.2 7.7 8.2 8.6
5.8	3.4 3.9 4.4 4.9 5.4 5.9 6.4 6.9 7.4 7.9 8.5 9.0
6.0	3.5 4.0 4.6 5.1 5.6 6.1 6.7 7.2 7.7 8.2 8.7 9.3
6.2	3.6 4.2 4.7 5.3 5.8 6.3 6.9 7.4 8.0 8.5 9.0 9.6
6.4	3.8 4.3 4.9 5.4 6.0 6.5 7.1 7.7 8.2 8.8 9.3 9.9
6.6	3.9 4.4 5.0 5.6 6.2 6.7 7.3 7.9 8.5 9.0 9.6 10.2
6.8	4.0 4.6 5.2 5.8 6.4 6.9 7.5 8.1 8.7 9.3 9.9 10.5
7.0	4.1 4.7 5.3 5.9 6.6 7.2 7.8 8.4 9.0 9.6 10.2 10.8

Copyright © J Reeve-Fowkes and Thomas Reed Publications.
No copying without permission.

125

Tidal Heights

-1 — 1 hour before HW Cherbourg

Copyright © J Reeve-Fowkes and Thomas Reed Publications. No copying without permission.

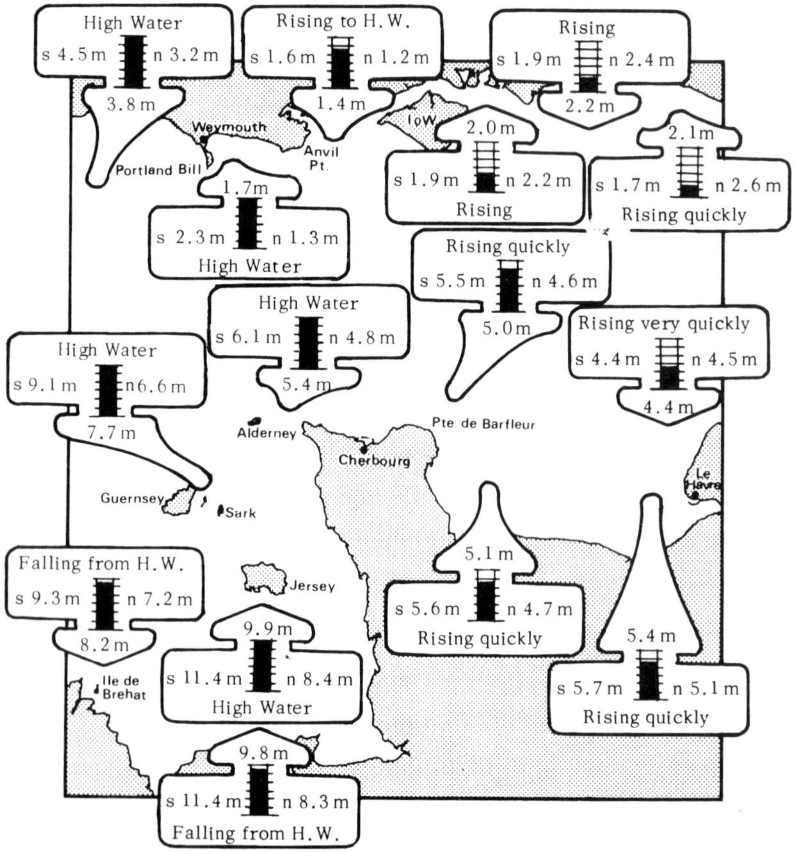

TIDAL HEIGHTS — PORTS & PLACES

Pencil-in height of ▶ HW Cherbourg	4.8	5.0	5.2	5.4	5.6	5.8	6.0	6.2	6.4	6.6	6.8
ENGLAND											
Lyme Regis..............	2.7	2.9	3.1	3.3	3.5	3.7	3.9	4.1	4.3	4.4	4.6	4.7
Bridport....................	2.6	2.8	3.0	3.2	3.4	3.5	3.7	3.9	4.1	4.3	4.4	4.6
Portland & Weymouth..	1.1	1.2	1.4	1.5	1.6	1.7	1.9	2.0	2.1	2.2	2.4	2.5
Lulworth Cove	1.2	1.3	1.5	1.6	1.7	1.9	2.0	2.2	2.3	2.5	2.6	2.8
Swanage	1.3	1.4	1.4	1.5	1.5	1.6	1.7	1.7	1.8	1.9	1.9	2.0
Poole entrance	1.3	1.4	1.4	1.5	1.5	1.6	1.7	1.7	1.8	1.8	1.9	1.9
Poole Town Quay........	1.5	1.5	1.5	1.5	1.6	1.6	1.7	1.7	1.8	1.8	1.8	1.8
Christchurch appr'ch ...	0.9	1.0	1.0	1.1	1.2	1.3	1.3	1.4	1.4	1.4	1.5	1.5
Christchurch Hbr.........	1.0	1.1	1.1	1.2	1.2	1.3	1.4	1.4	1.5	1.5	1.6	1.6
Lymington	1.7	1.7	1.7	1.7	1.7	1.7	1.7	1.8	1.8	1.8	1.8	1.8
Yarmouth I. o. W.	1.8	1.8	1.8	1.8	1.9	1.9	1.9	1.8	1.8	1.8	1.8	1.8
Cowes I. o. W.	2.1	2.1	2.1	2.1	2.0	2.0	2.0	2.0	2.0	1.9	1.8	1.7
Sandown I. o. W.	2.2	2.1	2.1	2.0	2.0	1.9	1.8	1.8	1.7	1.7	1.6	1.6
Southampton	2.3	2.3	2.3	2.3	2.2	2.2	2.2	2.1	2.1	2.1	2.0	2.0
Portsmouth	2.1	2.1	2.1	2.1	2.0	2.0	2.0	1.9	1.9	1.9	1.8	1.8
Chichester entrance.....	2.1	2.1	2.1	2.1	2.1	2.1	2.0	2.0	2.0	2.0	1.9	1.9
Selsey Bill................	2.1	2.1	2.1	2.1	2.1	2.1	2.0	2.0	2.0	1.9	1.9	1.8
Littlehampton Hbr........	2.1	2.0	2.0	1.9	1.8	1.8	1.7	1.7	1.6	1.6	1.6	1.6
Littlehampton appr'ch ...	2.1	2.1	2.1	2.1	2.1	2.1	2.0	2.0	2.0	2.0	1.9	1.9
Shoreham	2.7	2.6	2.4	2.3	2.2	2.1	1.9	1.8	1.7	1.6	1.6	1.5
Brighton	2.8	2.7	2.5	2.4	2.3	2.2	2.0	1.9	1.8	1.7	1.7	1.6
Newhaven	2.8	2.7	2.5	2.4	2.3	2.1	2.0	1.8	1.7	1.6	1.6	1.5
FRANCE											
Le Havre	5.1	5.1	5.1	5.1	5.2	5.2	5.2	5.3	5.3	5.3	5.3	5.3
Honfleur	5.2	5.2	5.2	5.2	5.3	5.3	5.3	5.4	5.4	5.4	5.5	5.5
Trouville (Deauville)	4.7	5.0	5.2	5.5	5.7	6.0	6.2	6.5	6.7	6.8	6.8	6.9
Ouistreham................	4.8	5.0	5.2	5.4	5.5	5.7	5.9	6.0	6.2	6.3	6.3	6.4
Courseulles...............	4.5	4.8	5.0	5.3	5.6	5.9	6.1	6.4	6.7	6.8	7.0	7.1
Arromanches	5.2	5.4	5.6	5.8	6.0	6.3	6.5	6.7	6.9	7.0	7.1	7.2
Port-en-Bessin	4.8	5.0	5.2	5.4	5.6	5.8	6.0	6.2	6.4	6.5	6.6	6.7
Saint-Vaast-la-Hougue..	4.3	4.4	4.6	4.7	4.8	4.9	5.0	5.1	5.2	5.3	5.3	5.4
Barfleur	4.4	4.5	4.7	4.8	4.9	5.0	5.2	5.3	5.4	5.5	5.6	5.7
Cherbourg	4.6	4.8	5.0	5.2	5.3	5.5	5.7	5.8	6.0	6.2	6.4	6.6
Omonville	4.7	4.8	5.0	5.1	5.3	5.4	5.6	5.7	5.9	6.1	6.3	6.5
Goury	6.3	6.5	6.7	6.9	7.1	7.4	7.6	7.8	8.0	8.2	8.3	8.5
Dielette	6.6	7.0	7.4	7.8	8.1	8.5	8.9	9.2	9.6	9.8	10.1	10.3
Carteret	7.6	8.0	8.4	8.8	9.2	9.5	9.9	10.3	10.7	11.0	11.3	11.6
Granville	8.6	9.1	9.5	10.0	10.5	10.9	11.4	11.8	12.3	12.6	12.9	13.2
Saint Malo	7.9	8.4	8.8	9.3	9.8	10.3	10.7	11.2	11.7	12.0	12.3	12.6
All Hbrs, St Brieuc Bay	7.7	8.0	8.4	8.7	9.1	9.4	9.8	10.1	10.5	10.7	11.0	11.2
Paimpol	6.9	7.2	7.6	7.9	8.3	8.6	9.0	9.3	9.7	10.0	10.2	10.5
Ile de Bréhat	7.1	7.4	7.8	8.1	8.5	8.8	9.2	9.5	9.9	10.2	10.4	10.7
Lezardrieux	7.0	7.3	7.7	8.0	8.3	8.6	9.0	9.3	9.6	9.9	10.1	10.4
ISLANDS OFF											
Braye, Alderney.........	4.4	4.6	4.8	5.0	5.3	5.5	5.7	6.0	6.2	6.4	6.7	6.9
St Peter Port & Sark	6.1	6.4	6.8	7.1	7.5	7.8	8.2	8.5	8.9	9.1	9.4	9.6
St Helier, Jersey	7.3	7.8	8.2	8.7	9.1	9.6	10.0	10.5	10.9	11.2	11.6	11.9
St Catherine, Jersey	7.3	7.8	8.2	8.7	9.2	9.6	10.0	10.5	11.0	11.4	11.7	12.1
Les Minquiers	8.2	8.6	9.0	9.4	9.8	10.1	10.5	10.9	11.6	11.9	12.2	—
Iles Chausey	8.8	9.2	9.6	10.0	10.5	10.9	11.3	11.8	12.2	12.5	12.8	13.1

Map callouts

- High Water — s 4.5 m · n 3.2 m — 3.8 m (Weymouth / Portland Bill)
- Rising to H.W. — s 1.6 m · n 1.2 m — 1.4 m (IoW)
- Rising — s 1.9 m · n 2.4 m — 2.2 m
- Rising — s 1.9 m · n 2.2 m — 2.0 m (Anvil Pt.)
- Rising quickly — s 1.7 m · n 2.6 m — 2.1 m
- High Water — s 2.3 m · n 1.3 m — 1.7 m
- Rising quickly — s 5.5 m · n 4.6 m — 5.0 m
- High Water — s 6.1 m · n 4.8 m — 5.4 m
- Rising very quickly — s 4.4 m · n 4.5 m — 4.4 m (Pte. de Barfleur)
- High Water — s 9.1 m · n 6.6 m — 7.7 m (Alderney / Cherbourg)
- Falling from H.W. — s 9.3 m · n 7.2 m — 8.2 m (Guernsey / Sark)
- Rising quickly — s 5.6 m · n 4.7 m — 5.1 m (Jersey)
- Rising quickly — s 5.7 m · n 5.1 m — 5.4 m (Le Havre)
- High Water — s 11.4 m · n 8.4 m — 9.9 m (Ile de Bréhat)
- Falling from H.W. — s 11.4 m · n 8.3 m — 9.8 m

Tidal Heights (offshore)

The broad arrows apply to the time entered on the adjacent page. Each arrow gives the following information:

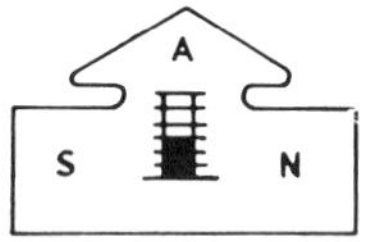

A Average Height of Tide. This is the height of tide, in metres, above Chart Datum, at the position indicated by the arrow. Although only an average height, this figure is sufficiently accurate for use for most coastal navigation.
S Height of Tide at Springs.
N Height of Tide at Neaps.
The Tidal Gauge gives a visual display of the approximate state of the tide with the vertical movement of tide described briefly above or below.

Tidal Stream Rates

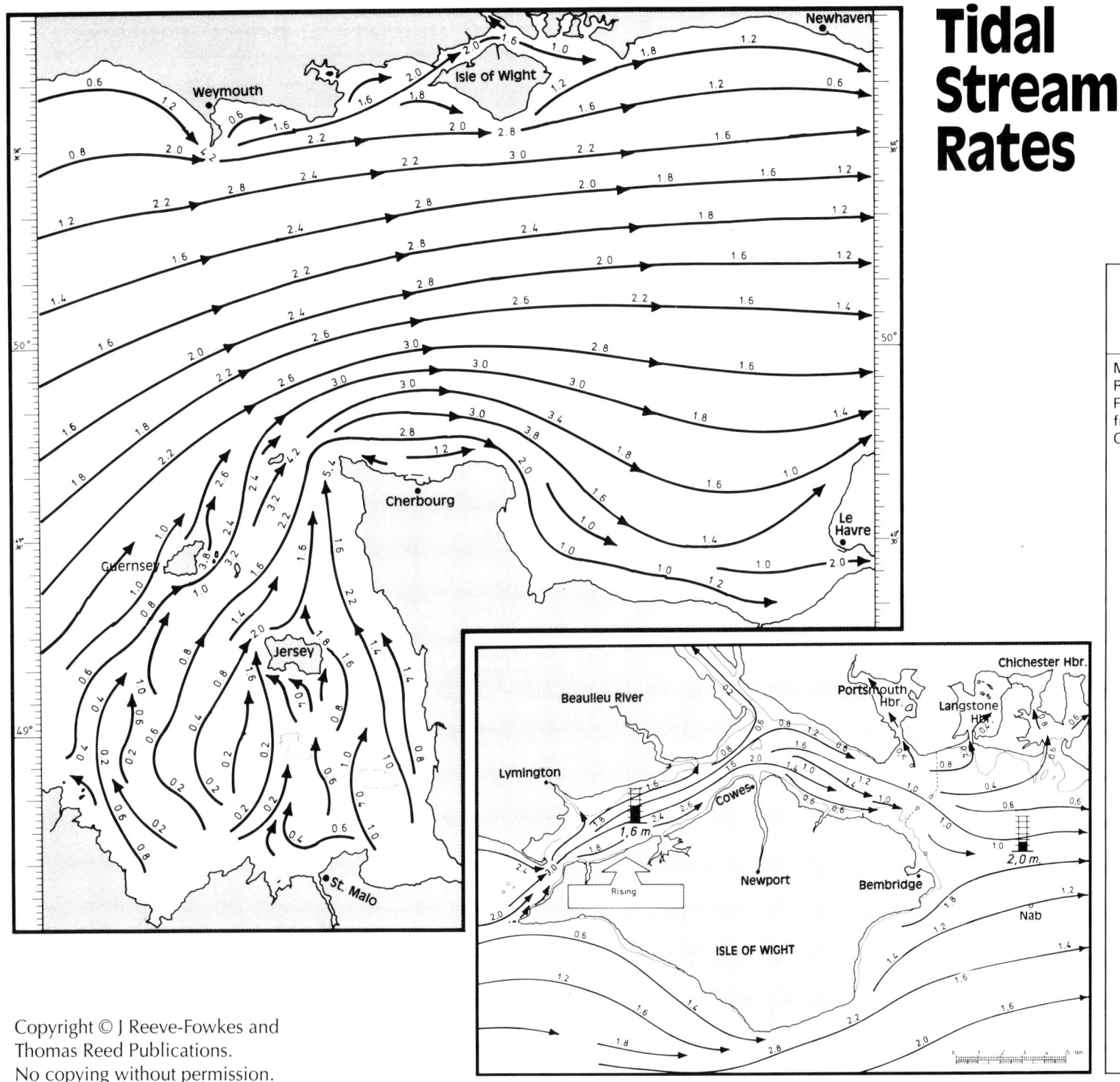

1 hour before HW Cherbourg **−1**

Time (to be inserted)

Stream Rate Conversion Table

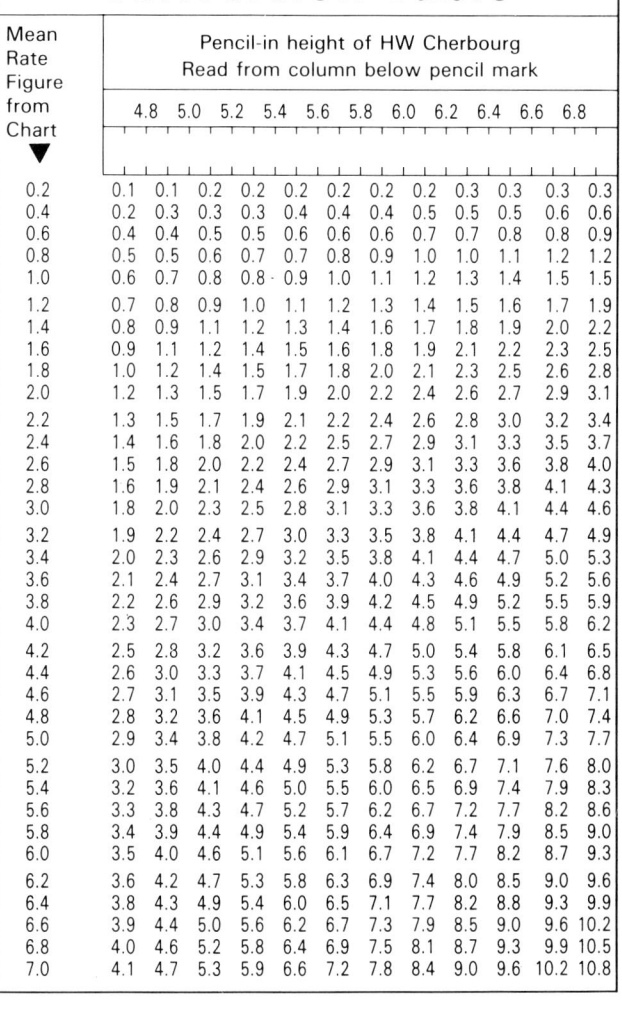

Mean Rate Figure from Chart ▼	\multicolumn{11}{c}{Pencil-in height of HW Cherbourg Read from column below pencil mark}
	4.8	5.0	5.2	5.4	5.6	5.8	6.0	6.2	6.4	6.6	6.8
0.2	0.1	0.1	0.2	0.2	0.2	0.2	0.2	0.2	0.3	0.3	0.3
0.4	0.2	0.3	0.3	0.3	0.4	0.4	0.4	0.5	0.5	0.5	0.6
0.6	0.4	0.4	0.5	0.5	0.6	0.6	0.6	0.7	0.7	0.8	0.8
0.8	0.5	0.5	0.6	0.7	0.7	0.8	0.9	1.0	1.0	1.1	1.2
1.0	0.6	0.7	0.8	0.8	0.9	1.0	1.1	1.2	1.3	1.4	1.5
1.2	0.7	0.8	0.9	1.0	1.1	1.2	1.3	1.4	1.5	1.6	1.7
1.4	0.8	0.9	1.1	1.2	1.3	1.4	1.6	1.7	1.8	1.9	2.0
1.6	0.9	1.1	1.2	1.4	1.5	1.6	1.8	1.9	2.1	2.2	2.3
1.8	1.0	1.2	1.4	1.5	1.7	1.8	2.0	2.1	2.3	2.5	2.6
2.0	1.2	1.3	1.5	1.7	1.9	2.0	2.2	2.4	2.6	2.7	2.9
2.2	1.3	1.5	1.7	1.9	2.1	2.2	2.4	2.6	2.8	3.0	3.2
2.4	1.4	1.6	1.8	2.0	2.2	2.5	2.7	2.9	3.1	3.3	3.5
2.6	1.5	1.8	2.0	2.2	2.4	2.7	2.9	3.1	3.3	3.6	3.8
2.8	1.6	1.9	2.1	2.4	2.6	2.9	3.1	3.3	3.6	3.8	4.1
3.0	1.8	2.0	2.3	2.5	2.8	3.1	3.3	3.6	3.8	4.1	4.4
3.2	1.9	2.2	2.4	2.7	3.0	3.3	3.5	3.8	4.1	4.4	4.7
3.4	2.0	2.3	2.6	2.9	3.2	3.5	3.8	4.1	4.4	4.7	5.0
3.6	2.1	2.4	2.7	3.1	3.4	3.7	4.0	4.3	4.6	4.9	5.2
3.8	2.2	2.6	2.9	3.2	3.6	3.9	4.2	4.5	4.9	5.2	5.5
4.0	2.3	2.7	3.0	3.4	3.7	4.1	4.4	4.8	5.1	5.5	5.8
4.2	2.5	2.8	3.2	3.6	3.9	4.3	4.7	5.0	5.4	5.8	6.1
4.4	2.6	3.0	3.3	3.7	4.1	4.5	4.9	5.3	5.6	6.0	6.4
4.6	2.7	3.1	3.5	3.9	4.3	4.7	5.1	5.5	5.9	6.3	6.7
4.8	2.8	3.2	3.6	4.1	4.5	4.9	5.3	5.7	6.2	6.6	7.0
5.0	2.9	3.4	3.8	4.2	4.7	5.1	5.5	6.0	6.4	6.9	7.3
5.2	3.0	3.5	4.0	4.4	4.9	5.3	5.8	6.2	6.7	7.1	7.6
5.4	3.2	3.6	4.1	4.6	5.0	5.5	6.0	6.5	6.9	7.4	7.9
5.6	3.3	3.8	4.3	4.7	5.2	5.7	6.2	6.7	7.2	7.7	8.2
5.8	3.4	3.9	4.4	4.9	5.4	5.9	6.4	6.9	7.4	7.9	8.5
6.0	3.5	4.0	4.6	5.1	5.6	6.1	6.7	7.2	7.7	8.2	8.7
6.2	3.6	4.2	4.7	5.2	5.8	6.3	6.9	7.4	8.0	8.5	9.0
6.4	3.8	4.3	4.9	5.4	6.0	6.5	7.1	7.7	8.2	8.8	9.3
6.6	3.9	4.4	5.0	5.6	6.2	6.7	7.3	7.9	8.5	9.0	9.6
6.8	4.0	4.6	5.2	5.8	6.4	6.9	7.5	8.1	8.7	9.3	9.9
7.0	4.1	4.7	5.3	5.9	6.6	7.2	7.8	8.4	9.0	9.6	10.2

Copyright © J Reeve-Fowkes and Thomas Reed Publications.
No copying without permission.

127

HW
HW Cherbourg

Tidal Heights

Copyright © J Reeve-Fowkes and
Thomas Reed Publications.
No copying without permission.

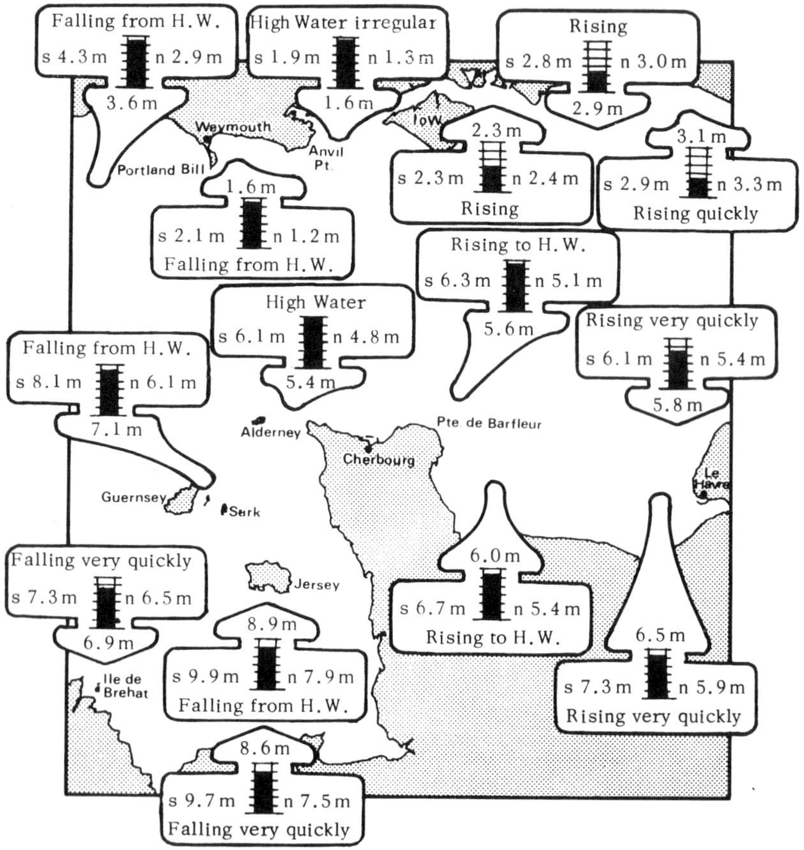

Tidal Heights (offshore)

The broad arrows apply to the time entered on the adjacent page. Each arrow gives the following information:

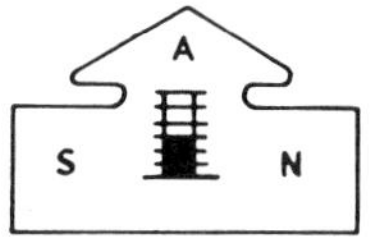

A Average Height of Tide. This is the height of tide, in metres, above Chart Datum, at the position indicated by the arrow. Although only an average height, this figure is sufficiently accurate for use for most coastal navigation.
S Height of Tide at Springs.
N Height of Tide at Neaps.
The Tidal Gauge gives a visual display of the approximate state of the tide with the vertical movement of tide described briefly above or below.

Offshore positions

Falling from H.W. — s 4.3 m n 2.9 m — 3.6 m
High Water irregular — s 1.9 m n 1.3 m — 1.6 m
Rising — s 2.8 m n 3.0 m — 2.9 m
Rising — s 2.3 m n 2.4 m — 2.3 m
Rising quickly — s 2.9 m n 3.3 m — 3.1 m
Falling from H.W. — s 2.1 m n 1.2 m — 1.6 m
Rising to H.W. — s 6.3 m n 5.1 m — 5.6 m
High Water — s 6.1 m n 4.8 m — 5.4 m
Rising very quickly — s 6.1 m n 5.4 m — 5.8 m
Falling from H.W. — s 8.1 m n 6.1 m — 7.1 m
Falling very quickly — s 7.3 m n 6.5 m — 6.9 m
Falling from H.W. — s 9.9 m n 7.9 m — 8.9 m
Rising to H.W. — s 6.7 m n 5.4 m — 6.0 m
Rising very quickly — s 7.3 m n 5.9 m — 6.5 m
Falling very quickly — s 9.7 m n 7.5 m — 8.6 m

Weymouth · Portland Bill · Anvil Pt. · IoW · Alderney · Cherbourg · Pte de Barfleur · Le Havre · Guernsey · Sark · Jersey · Ile de Bréhat

TIDAL HEIGHTS — PORTS & PLACES

Pencil-in height of HW Cherbourg ▶	4.8	5.0	5.2	5.4	5.6	5.8	6.0	6.2	6.4	6.6	6.8
ENGLAND											
Lyme Regis	3.8	3.9	3.9	4.0	4.0	4.1	4.1	4.2	4.2	4.3	4.5	4.6
Bridport	2.5	2.7	2.9	3.1	3.3	3.4	3.6	3.8	4.0	4.1	4.3	4.4
Portland & Weymouth	1.0	1.1	1.3	1.4	1.5	1.6	1.8	1.9	2.0	2.1	2.3	2.4
Lulworth Cove	1.1	1.2	1.4	1.5	1.6	1.7	1.9	2.0	2.1	2.3	2.4	2.6
Swanage	1.5	1.5	1.5	1.5	1.6	1.6	1.7	1.8	1.9	2.0	2.0	2.1
Poole entrance	1.3	1.4	1.4	1.5	1.5	1.6	1.7	1.9	2.0	2.0	2.1	2.1
Poole Town Quay	1.4	1.5	1.5	1.6	1.7	1.8	1.9	2.0	2.1	2.1	2.2	2.2
Christchurch appr'ch	1.0	1.1	1.1	1.2	1.3	1.4	1.5	1.6	1.7	1.7	1.8	1.8
Christchurch Hbr	1.1	1.2	1.2	1.3	1.4	1.5	1.6	1.6	1.7	1.7	1.8	1.8
Lymington	1.8	1.8	1.8	1.8	1.9	1.9	2.0	2.0	2.1	2.1	2.2	2.2
Yarmouth I. o. W.	1.8	1.9	1.9	2.0	2.0	2.1	2.1	2.1	2.1	2.1	2.2	2.2
Cowes I. o. W.	2.4	2.4	2.4	2.4	2.3	2.3	2.3	2.3	2.3	2.2	2.2	2.1
Sandown I. o. W.	2.4	2.4	2.4	2.4	2.3	2.3	2.3	2.3	2.3	2.3	2.3	2.3
Southampton	2.4	2.4	2.4	2.4	2.3	2.3	2.3	2.2	2.2	2.2	2.1	2.1
Portsmouth	2.4	2.4	2.4	2.4	2.3	2.3	2.3	2.2	2.2	2.2	2.2	2.2
Chichester entrance	2.4	2.4	2.4	2.4	2.4	2.4	2.4	2.4	2.4	2.4	2.3	2.3
Selsey Bill	2.4	2.4	2.4	2.4	2.4	2.4	2.3	2.3	2.3	2.3	2.2	2.2
Littlehampton Hbr	2.4	2.4	2.4	2.4	2.3	2.3	2.3	2.2	2.2	2.2	2.2	2.2
Littlehampton appr'ch	2.5	2.5	2.5	2.5	2.5	2.5	2.4	2.4	2.4	2.4	2.4	2.4
Shoreham	3.3	3.2	3.2	3.1	3.0	2.9	2.9	2.8	2.7	2.7	2.7	2.7
Brighton	3.3	3.3	3.3	3.2	3.2	3.1	3.1	3.0	3.0	3.0	2.9	2.9
Newhaven	3.4	3.3	3.3	3.2	3.1	3.1	3.0	3.0	2.9	2.9	2.9	2.9
FRANCE											
Le Havre	5.7	5.9	6.1	6.3	6.4	6.6	6.8	7.0	7.1	7.2	7.3	7.4
Honfleur	6.2	6.3	6.5	6.6	6.7	6.9	7.0	7.2	7.3	7.4	7.5	7.6
Trouville (Deauville)	5.6	5.9	6.1	6.4	6.6	6.9	7.1	7.4	7.6	7.7	7.8	8.0
Ouistreham	5.6	5.8	6.0	6.2	6.4	6.7	6.9	7.1	7.3	7.4	7.5	7.6
Courseulles	5.2	5.4	5.6	5.8	6.1	6.3	6.5	6.8	7.0	7.2	7.4	7.5
Arromanches	5.7	5.9	6.1	6.3	6.5	6.8	7.0	7.2	7.4	7.5	7.7	7.8
Port-en-Bessin	5.4	5.6	5.8	6.0	6.2	6.4	6.6	6.8	7.0	7.1	7.2	7.3
Saint-Vaast-la-Hougue	4.9	5.1	5.3	5.5	5.6	5.8	6.0	6.1	6.3	6.5	6.6	6.8
Barfleur	4.8	5.0	5.2	5.4	5.5	5.7	5.9	6.0	6.2	6.4	6.5	6.7
Cherbourg	4.7	4.9	5.1	5.3	5.5	5.7	5.9	6.1	6.3	6.5	6.7	6.9
Omonville	4.7	4.9	5.1	5.3	5.5	5.6	5.8	6.0	6.2	6.4	6.7	6.9
Goury	6.0	6.2	6.4	6.6	6.8	7.1	7.3	7.5	7.7	7.9	8.0	8.2
Dielette	6.3	6.6	7.0	7.3	7.6	7.9	8.2	8.5	8.8	9.0	9.1	9.3
Carteret	7.3	7.6	7.8	8.1	8.4	8.7	9.0	9.3	9.6	9.8	10.0	10.2
Granville	7.8	8.2	8.6	9.0	9.3	9.7	10.0	10.4	10.8	11.0	11.2	11.4
Saint Malo	7.2	7.6	8.0	8.4	8.8	9.1	9.5	9.9	10.3	10.5	10.7	10.9
All Hbrs, St Brieuc Bay	6.9	7.2	7.4	7.7	7.9	8.2	8.4	8.7	8.9	9.0	9.2	9.3
Paimpol	6.2	6.4	6.6	6.8	7.1	7.3	7.5	7.8	8.0	8.2	8.3	8.5
Ile de Bréhat	6.3	6.6	6.8	7.1	7.4	7.8	8.0	8.3	8.6	8.7	8.9	9.0
Lezardrieux	5.9	6.2	6.4	6.7	6.9	7.2	7.4	7.7	7.9	8.1	8.2	8.4
ISLANDS OFF											
Braye, Alderney	4.3	4.5	4.7	4.9	5.1	5.3	5.5	5.7	5.9	6.1	6.4	6.6
St Peter Port & Sark	5.9	6.1	6.3	6.6	6.9	7.1	7.4	7.6	7.9	8.1	8.3	8.5
St Helier, Jersey	7.0	7.3	7.7	8.0	8.3	8.7	9.0	9.4	9.7	10.0	10.2	10.5
St Catherine, Jersey	7.0	7.4	7.8	8.2	8.5	8.9	9.3	9.6	10.0	10.3	10.6	10.8
Les Minquiers	7.9	8.2	8.4	8.7	9.0	9.3	9.6	9.9	10.2	10.4	10.6	10.8
Iles Chausey	8.1	8.4	8.8	9.1	9.4	9.7	10.1	10.4	10.7	10.9	11.1	11.3

Tidal Stream Rates

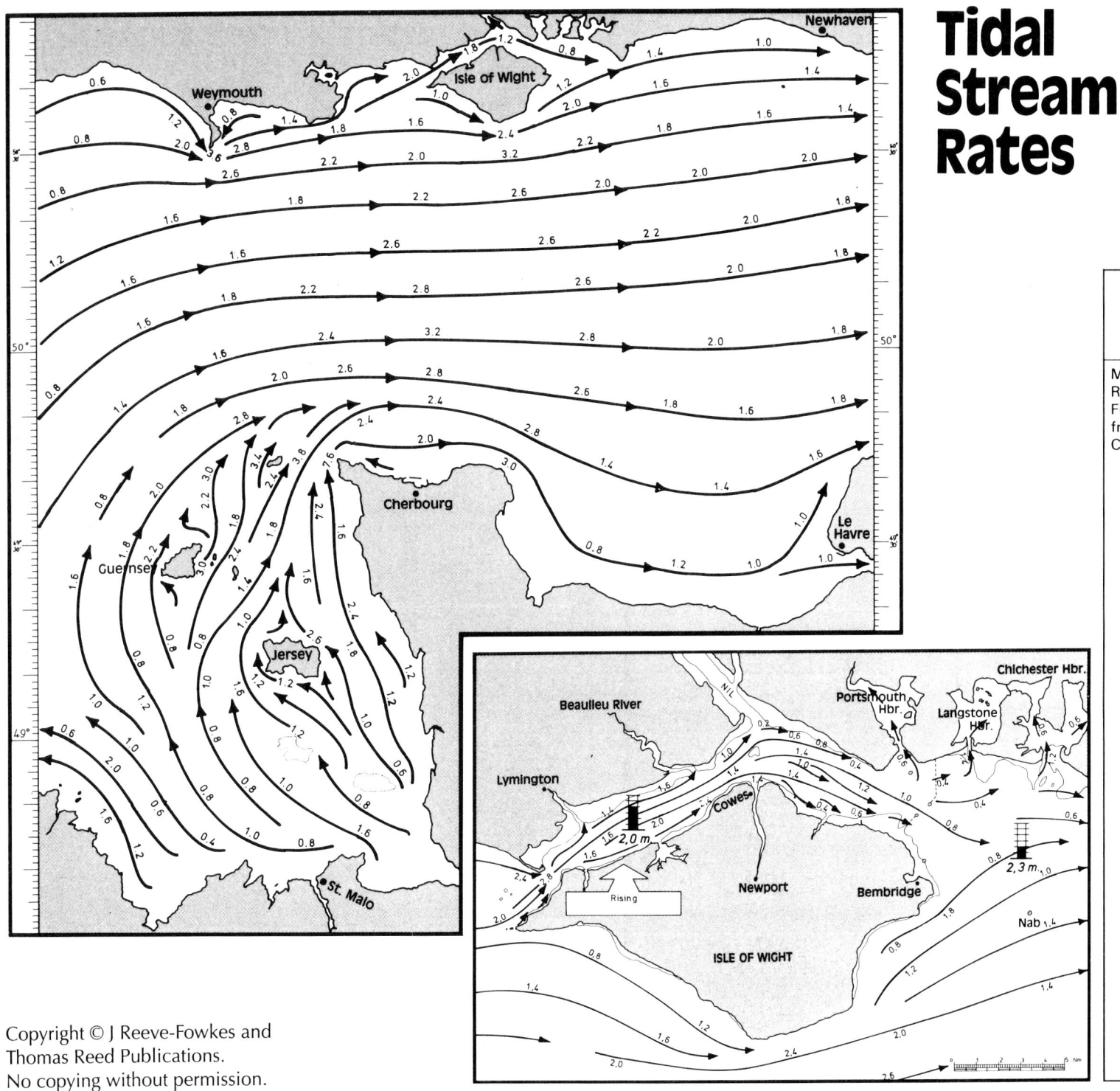

HW Cherbourg

HW

Time (to be inserted)

Stream Rate Conversion Table

Mean Rate Figure from Chart ▼	Pencil-in height of HW Cherbourg Read from column below pencil mark										
	4.8	5.0	5.2	5.4	5.6	5.8	6.0	6.2	6.4	6.6	6.8
0.2	0.1	0.1	0.2	0.2	0.2	0.2	0.2	0.2	0.3	0.3	0.3
0.4	0.2	0.3	0.3	0.3	0.4	0.4	0.4	0.5	0.5	0.5	0.6	0.6
0.6	0.4	0.4	0.5	0.5	0.6	0.6	0.6	0.7	0.7	0.8	0.8	0.9
0.8	0.5	0.5	0.6	0.7	0.7	0.8	0.9	1.0	1.0	1.1	1.2	1.2
1.0	0.6	0.7	0.8	0.8	0.9	1.0	1.1	1.2	1.3	1.4	1.5	1.5
1.2	0.7	0.8	0.9	1.0	1.1	1.2	1.3	1.4	1.5	1.6	1.7	1.9
1.4	0.8	0.9	1.1	1.2	1.3	1.4	1.6	1.7	1.8	1.9	2.0	2.2
1.6	0.9	1.1	1.2	1.4	1.5	1.6	1.8	1.9	2.1	2.2	2.3	2.5
1.8	1.0	1.2	1.4	1.5	1.7	1.8	2.0	2.1	2.3	2.5	2.6	2.8
2.0	1.2	1.3	1.5	1.7	1.9	2.0	2.2	2.4	2.6	2.7	2.9	3.1
2.2	1.3	1.5	1.7	1.9	2.1	2.2	2.4	2.6	2.8	3.0	3.2	3.4
2.4	1.4	1.6	1.8	2.0	2.2	2.5	2.7	2.9	3.1	3.3	3.5	3.7
2.6	1.5	1.8	2.0	2.2	2.4	2.7	2.9	3.1	3.3	3.6	3.8	4.0
2.8	1.6	1.9	2.1	2.4	2.6	2.9	3.1	3.3	3.6	3.8	4.1	4.3
3.0	1.8	2.0	2.3	2.5	2.8	3.1	3.3	3.6	3.8	4.1	4.4	4.6
3.2	1.9	2.2	2.4	2.7	3.0	3.3	3.5	3.8	4.1	4.4	4.7	4.9
3.4	2.0	2.3	2.6	2.9	3.2	3.5	3.8	4.1	4.4	4.7	5.0	5.3
3.6	2.1	2.4	2.7	3.1	3.4	3.7	4.0	4.3	4.6	4.9	5.2	5.6
3.8	2.2	2.6	2.9	3.2	3.6	3.9	4.2	4.5	4.9	5.2	5.5	5.9
4.0	2.3	2.7	3.0	3.4	3.7	4.1	4.4	4.8	5.1	5.5	5.8	6.2
4.2	2.5	2.8	3.2	3.6	3.9	4.3	4.7	5.0	5.4	5.8	6.1	6.5
4.4	2.6	3.0	3.3	3.7	4.1	4.5	4.9	5.3	5.6	6.0	6.4	6.8
4.6	2.7	3.1	3.5	3.9	4.3	4.7	5.1	5.5	5.9	6.3	6.7	7.1
4.8	2.8	3.2	3.6	4.1	4.5	4.9	5.3	5.7	6.2	6.6	7.0	7.4
5.0	2.9	3.4	3.8	4.2	4.7	5.1	5.5	6.0	6.4	6.9	7.3	7.7
5.2	3.0	3.5	4.0	4.4	4.9	5.3	5.8	6.2	6.7	7.1	7.6	8.0
5.4	3.2	3.6	4.1	4.6	5.0	5.5	6.0	6.5	6.9	7.4	7.9	8.3
5.6	3.3	3.8	4.3	4.7	5.2	5.7	6.2	6.7	7.2	7.7	8.2	8.6
5.8	3.4	3.9	4.4	4.9	5.4	5.9	6.4	6.9	7.4	7.9	8.5	9.0
6.0	3.5	4.0	4.6	5.1	5.6	6.1	6.7	7.2	7.7	8.2	8.7	9.3
6.2	3.6	4.2	4.7	5.2	5.8	6.3	6.9	7.4	8.0	8.5	9.0	9.6
6.4	3.8	4.3	4.9	5.4	6.0	6.5	7.1	7.7	8.2	8.8	9.3	9.9
6.6	3.9	4.4	5.0	5.6	6.2	6.7	7.3	7.9	8.5	9.0	9.6	10.2
6.8	4.0	4.6	5.2	5.8	6.4	6.9	7.5	8.1	8.7	9.3	9.9	10.5
7.0	4.1	4.7	5.3	5.9	6.6	7.2	7.8	8.4	9.0	9.6	10.2	10.8

Copyright © J Reeve-Fowkes and Thomas Reed Publications.
No copying without permission.

+1 — 1 hour after HW Cherbourg

Tidal Heights

Copyright © J Reeve-Fowkes and
Thomas Reed Publications.
No copying without permission.

Tidal Heights (offshore)

The broad arrows apply to the time entered on the adjacent page. Each arrow gives the following information:

A Average Height of Tide. This is the height of tide, in metres, above Chart Datum, at the position indicated by the arrow. Although only an average height, this figure is sufficiently accurate for use for most coastal navigation.
S Height of Tide at Springs.
N Height of Tide at Neaps.
The Tidal Gauge gives a visual display of the approximate state of the tide with the vertical movement of tide described briefly above or below.

Map diagram labels

- Falling — s 3.8 m / n 2.5 m — 3.1 m
- High Water irregular — s 1.9 m / n 1.3 m — 1.6 m
- Rising — s 4.0 m / n 3.7 m — 3.8 m
- 2.9 m — s 3.0 m / n 2.8 m — Rising
- 4.5 m — s 4.7 m / n 4.3 m — Rising quickly
- 1.3 m — s 1.7 m / n 1.0 m — Falling slowly
- High Water — s 6.5 m / n 5.2 m — 5.8 m
- Falling from H.W. — s 5.5 m / n 4.4 m — 4.9 m
- Rising to H.W. — s 7.3 m / n 6.1 m — 6.7 m
- Falling very quickly — s 6.4 m / n 5.5 m — 5.9 m
- Falling very quickly — s 5.1 m / n 5.6 m — 5.3 m
- 7.5 m — s 8.1 m / n 7.0 m — Falling very quickly
- 6.3 m — s 7.1 m / n 5.6 m — High Water
- 7.0 m — s 7.7 m / n 6.2 m — Rising to H.W.
- 7.1 m — s 7.7 m / n 6.5 m — Falling very quickly

Weymouth, Portland Bill, Anvil Pt., IoW, Alderney, Cherbourg, Pte. de Barfleur, Le Havre, Guernsey, Sark, Jersey, Ile de Bréhat

TIDAL HEIGHTS — PORTS & PLACES

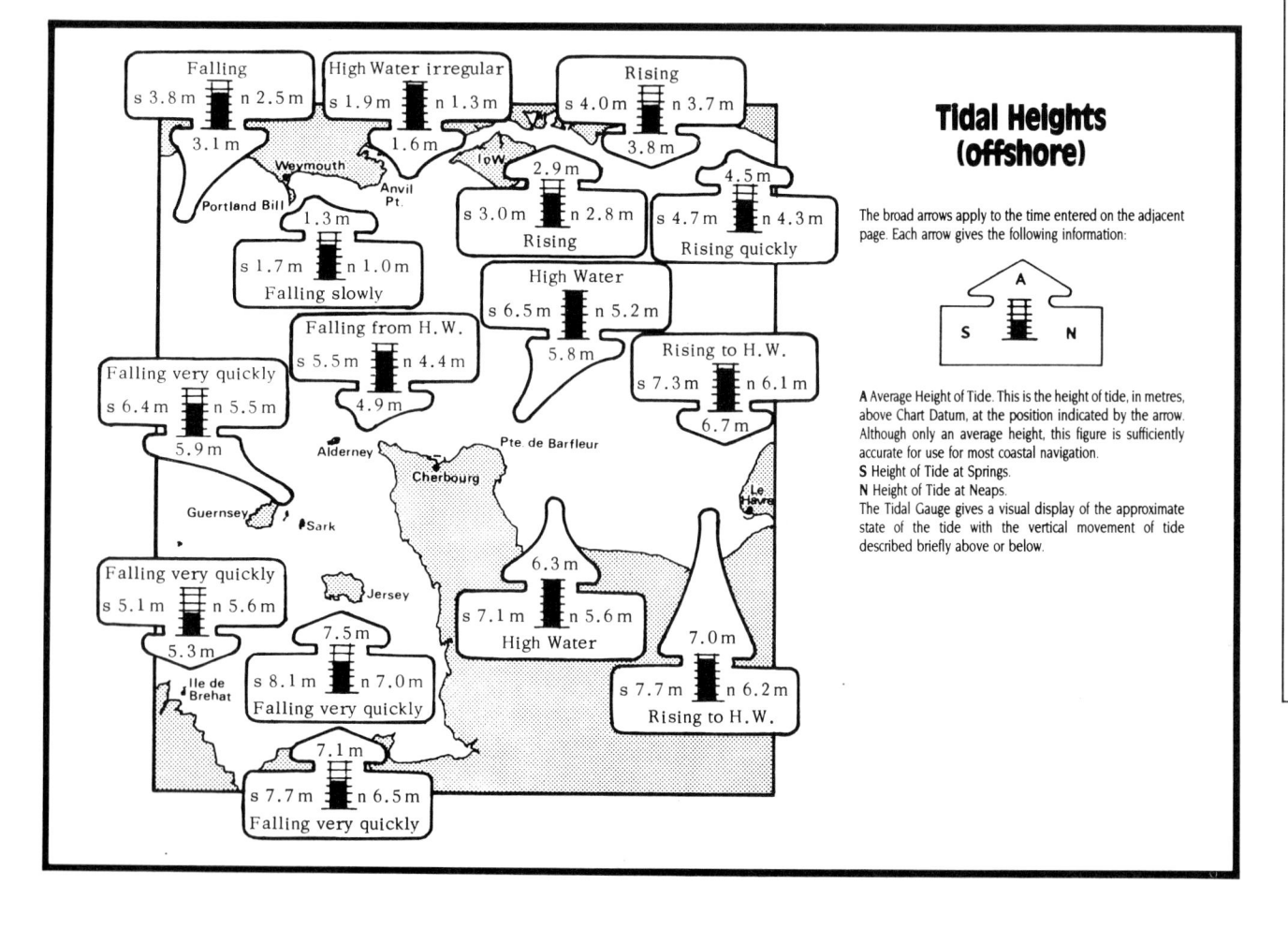

Pencil-in height of HW Cherbourg ▶	4.8	5.0	5.2	5.4	5.6	5.8	6.0	6.2	6.4	6.6	6.8
ENGLAND											
Lyme Regis	2.2	2.4	2.6	2.8	2.9	3.1	3.3	3.5	3.7	3.8	3.8	3.9
Bridport	2.1	2.3	2.5	2.7	2.8	3.0	3.2	3.3	3.5	3.6	3.8	3.9
Portland & Weymouth	0.9	1.0	1.0	1.1	1.2	1.3	1.4	1.5	1.6	1.7	1.8	1.9
Lulworth Cove	1.0	1.1	1.1	1.2	1.3	1.4	1.5	1.6	1.7	1.8	1.9	2.0
Swanage	1.5	1.5	1.5	1.5	1.6	1.6	1.7	1.8	1.9	1.9	1.9	2.0
Poole entrance	1.5	1.5	1.5	1.5	1.6	1.6	1.7	1.8	1.9	1.9	2.0	2.0
Poole Town Quay	1.4	1.5	1.5	1.6	1.6	1.7	1.9	2.0	2.2	2.2	2.3	2.3
Christchurch appr'ch	1.1	1.2	1.2	1.3	1.4	1.5	1.6	1.7	1.8	1.9	1.9	2.0
Christchurch Hbr	1.1	1.2	1.2	1.3	1.4	1.5	1.6	1.7	1.8	1.8	1.9	1.9
Lymington	2.1	2.1	2.1	2.1	2.2	2.2	2.3	2.3	2.4	2.4	2.5	2.5
Yarmouth I. o. W.	2.1	2.2	2.2	2.3	2.3	2.4	2.5	2.5	2.6	2.6	2.6	2.6
Cowes I. o. W.	2.8	2.8	2.8	2.8	2.8	2.8	2.9	2.9	3.0	3.0	3.0	3.0
Sandown I. o. W.	2.8	2.8	2.8	2.8	2.8	2.8	2.9	2.9	3.0	3.1	3.1	3.2
Southampton	2.9	2.9	2.9	2.9	2.9	2.9	2.8	2.8	2.8	2.8	2.8	2.8
Portsmouth	2.8	2.8	2.8	2.8	2.8	2.9	2.9	2.9	3.0	3.0	3.1	3.1
Chichester entrance	2.9	2.9	2.9	2.9	2.9	2.9	3.0	3.0	3.0	3.0	3.0	3.0
Selsey Bill	3.0	3.0	3.0	3.0	3.0	3.0	3.1	3.1	3.1	3.1	3.1	3.1
Littlehampton Hbr	3.2	3.1	3.1	3.0	3.0	2.9	2.9	2.8	2.8	2.8	2.8	2.8
Littlehampton appr'ch	3.1	3.1	3.1	3.1	3.2	3.2	3.2	3.3	3.3	3.3	3.4	3.4
Shoreham	3.8	3.9	3.9	4.0	4.0	4.1	4.1	4.2	4.2	4.2	4.3	4.3
Brighton	3.9	4.0	4.0	4.1	4.2	4.3	4.3	4.4	4.5	4.5	4.6	4.6
Newhaven	4.1	4.2	4.2	4.3	4.4	4.4	4.5	4.5	4.6	4.7	4.7	4.8
FRANCE											
Le Havre	6.1	6.3	6.5	6.7	6.9	7.1	7.3	7.5	7.7	7.8	8.0	8.1
Honfleur	6.3	6.5	6.7	6.9	7.1	7.2	7.4	7.6	7.8	7.9	8.1	8.2
Trouville (Deauville)	6.0	6.2	6.4	6.6	6.8	7.1	7.3	7.5	7.7	7.8	8.0	8.1
Ouistreham	5.8	6.0	6.2	6.4	6.6	6.9	7.1	7.3	7.5	7.6	7.8	7.9
Courseulles	5.3	5.5	5.7	5.9	6.2	6.4	6.6	6.9	7.1	7.2	7.4	7.5
Arromanches	5.8	6.0	6.2	6.4	6.6	6.9	7.1	7.3	7.5	7.6	7.8	7.9
Port-en-Bessin	5.6	5.8	6.0	6.2	6.4	6.5	6.7	6.9	7.1	7.2	7.3	7.4
Saint-Vaast-la-Hougue	5.1	5.3	5.5	5.7	5.9	6.0	6.2	6.4	6.6	6.8	7.0	7.2
Barfleur	4.9	5.1	5.3	5.5	5.7	5.8	6.0	6.2	6.4	6.6	6.8	7.0
Cherbourg	4.6	4.8	5.0	5.2	5.3	5.5	5.7	5.8	6.0	6.2	6.4	6.5
Omonville	4.4	4.6	4.8	5.0	5.1	5.3	5.5	5.6	5.8	6.0	6.2	6.3
Goury	5.6	5.7	5.9	6.0	6.1	6.2	6.4	6.5	6.6	6.7	6.8	6.9
Dielette	5.8	6.0	6.2	6.4	6.5	6.7	6.9	7.0	7.2	7.3	7.4	7.5
Carteret	6.6	6.7	6.9	7.0	7.2	7.3	7.5	7.6	7.8	7.9	8.0	8.1
Granville	7.1	7.3	7.5	7.7	7.8	8.0	8.2	8.3	8.5	8.6	8.7	8.8
Saint Malo	6.5	6.7	6.9	7.1	7.3	7.6	7.8	8.0	8.2	8.3	8.3	8.4
All Hbrs, St Brieuc Bay	6.2	6.3	6.3	6.4	6.4	6.5	6.5	6.6	6.7	6.7	6.7	6.7
Paimpol	5.3	5.4	5.4	5.5	5.6	5.6	5.7	5.8	5.8	5.8	5.9	5.9
Ile de Bréhat	5.5	5.6	5.8	5.9	6.1	6.2	6.4	6.5	6.6	6.7	6.8	6.8
Lezardrieux	5.1	5.2	5.2	5.3	5.4	5.4	5.5	5.5	5.6	5.6	5.6	5.6
ISLANDS OFF											
Braye, Alderney	3.9	4.0	4.2	4.3	4.4	4.6	4.7	4.9	5.0	5.1	5.3	5.4
St Peter Port & Sark	5.3	5.4	5.6	5.7	5.8	5.9	6.1	6.2	6.3	6.4	6.4	6.5
St Helier, Jersey	6.3	6.5	6.7	6.9	7.1	7.3	7.5	7.7	7.9	8.0	8.1	8.2
St Catherine, Jersey	6.5	6.7	6.9	7.1	7.3	7.6	7.8	8.0	8.2	8.3	8.5	8.6
Les Minquiers	7.1	7.2	7.4	7.5	7.6	7.7	7.8	7.9	8.0	8.1	8.2	8.3
Iles Chausey	7.3	7.4	7.6	7.7	7.9	8.0	8.2	8.3	8.5	8.6	8.7	8.8

Tidal Stream Rates

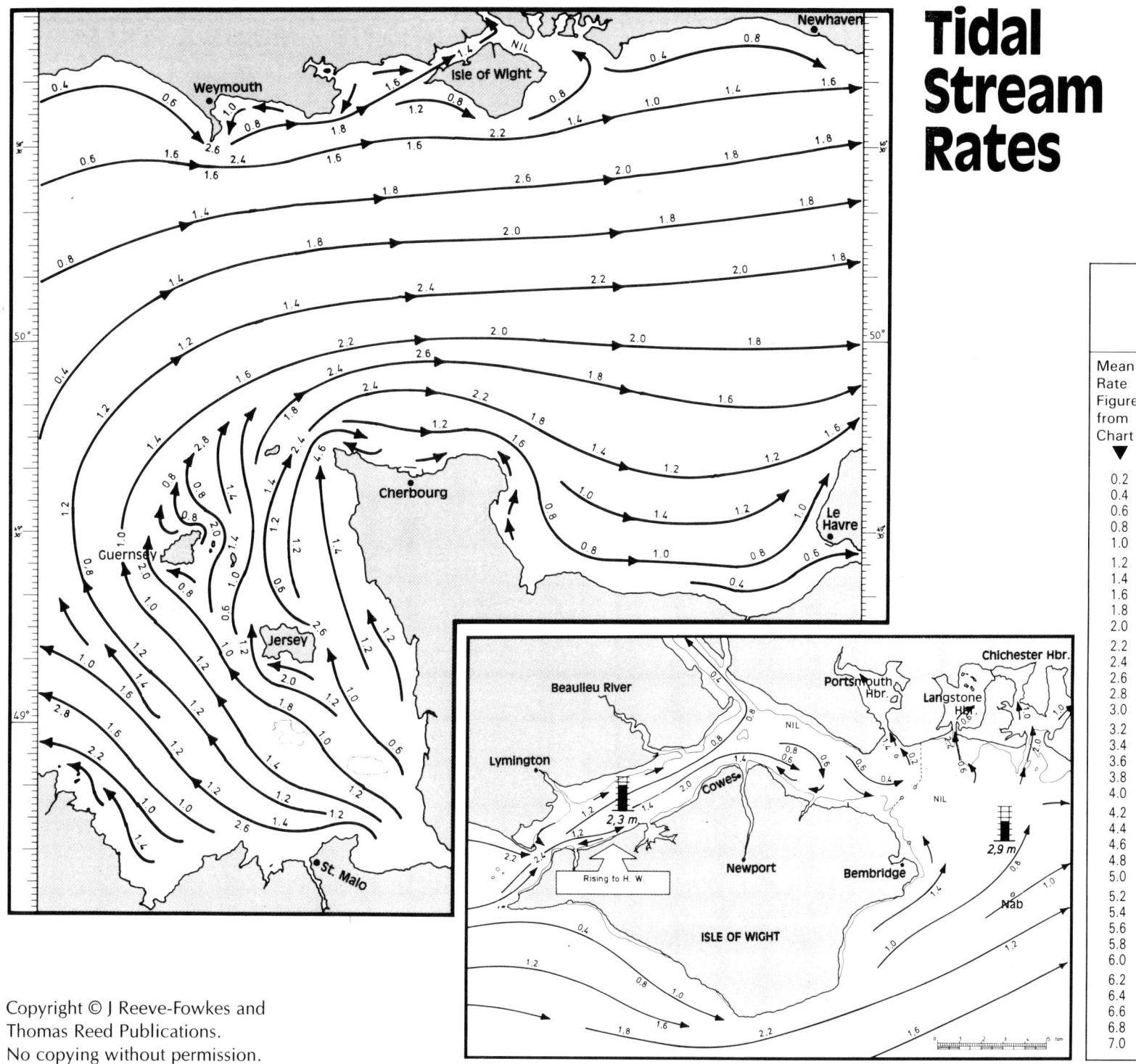

+1

1 hour after HW Cherbourg

Time (to be inserted)

Stream Rate Conversion Table

Mean Rate Figure from Chart ▼	Pencil-in height of HW Cherbourg Read from column below pencil mark										
	4.8	5.0	5.2	5.4	5.6	5.8	6.0	6.2	6.4	6.6	6.8
0.2	0.1	0.1	0.2	0.2	0.2	0.2	0.2	0.2	0.3	0.3	0.3
0.4	0.2	0.3	0.3	0.3	0.4	0.4	0.4	0.5	0.5	0.5	0.6
0.6	0.4	0.4	0.5	0.5	0.6	0.6	0.6	0.7	0.7	0.8	0.8
0.8	0.5	0.5	0.6	0.7	0.7	0.8	0.9	1.0	1.0	1.1	1.2
1.0	0.6	0.7	0.8	0.8	0.9	1.0	1.1	1.2	1.3	1.4	1.5
1.2	0.7	0.8	0.9	1.0	1.1	1.2	1.3	1.4	1.5	1.6	1.7
1.4	0.8	0.9	1.1	1.2	1.3	1.4	1.6	1.7	1.8	1.9	2.0
1.6	0.9	1.1	1.2	1.4	1.5	1.6	1.8	1.9	2.1	2.2	2.3
1.8	1.0	1.2	1.4	1.5	1.7	1.8	2.0	2.1	2.3	2.5	2.6
2.0	1.2	1.3	1.5	1.7	1.9	2.0	2.2	2.4	2.6	2.7	2.9
2.2	1.3	1.5	1.7	1.9	2.1	2.2	2.4	2.6	2.8	3.0	3.2
2.4	1.4	1.6	1.8	2.0	2.2	2.5	2.7	2.9	3.1	3.3	3.5
2.6	1.5	1.8	2.0	2.2	2.4	2.7	2.9	3.1	3.3	3.6	3.8
2.8	1.6	1.9	2.1	2.4	2.6	2.9	3.1	3.3	3.6	3.8	4.1
3.0	1.8	2.0	2.3	2.5	2.8	3.1	3.3	3.6	3.8	4.1	4.4
3.2	1.9	2.2	2.4	2.7	3.0	3.3	3.5	3.8	4.1	4.4	4.7
3.4	2.0	2.3	2.6	2.9	3.2	3.5	3.8	4.1	4.4	4.7	5.0
3.6	2.1	2.4	2.7	3.1	3.4	3.7	4.0	4.3	4.6	4.9	5.2
3.8	2.2	2.6	2.9	3.2	3.6	3.9	4.2	4.5	4.9	5.2	5.5
4.0	2.3	2.7	3.0	3.4	3.7	4.1	4.4	4.8	5.1	5.5	5.8
4.2	2.5	2.8	3.2	3.6	3.9	4.3	4.7	5.0	5.4	5.8	6.1
4.4	2.6	3.0	3.3	3.7	4.1	4.5	4.9	5.3	5.6	6.0	6.4
4.6	2.7	3.1	3.5	3.9	4.3	4.7	5.1	5.5	5.9	6.3	6.7
4.8	2.8	3.2	3.6	4.1	4.5	4.9	5.3	5.7	6.2	6.6	7.0
5.0	2.9	3.4	3.8	4.2	4.7	5.1	5.5	6.0	6.4	6.9	7.3
5.2	3.0	3.5	4.0	4.4	4.9	5.3	5.8	6.2	6.7	7.1	7.6
5.4	3.2	3.6	4.1	4.6	5.0	5.5	6.0	6.5	6.9	7.4	7.9
5.6	3.3	3.8	4.3	4.7	5.2	5.7	6.2	6.7	7.2	7.7	8.2
5.8	3.4	3.9	4.4	4.9	5.4	5.9	6.4	6.9	7.4	7.9	8.5
6.0	3.5	4.0	4.6	5.1	5.6	6.1	6.7	7.2	7.7	8.2	8.7
6.2	3.6	4.2	4.7	5.3	5.8	6.3	6.9	7.4	8.0	8.5	9.0
6.4	3.8	4.3	4.9	5.4	6.0	6.5	7.1	7.7	8.2	8.8	9.3
6.6	3.9	4.4	5.0	5.6	6.2	6.7	7.3	7.9	8.5	9.0	9.6
6.8	4.0	4.6	5.2	5.8	6.4	6.9	7.5	8.1	8.7	9.3	9.9
7.0	4.1	4.7	5.3	5.9	6.6	7.2	7.8	8.4	9.0	9.6	10.2

Copyright © J Reeve-Fowkes and Thomas Reed Publications.
No copying without permission.

+2
2 hours after HW Cherbourg

Tidal Heights

Copyright © J Reeve-Fowkes and Thomas Reed Publications.
No copying without permission.

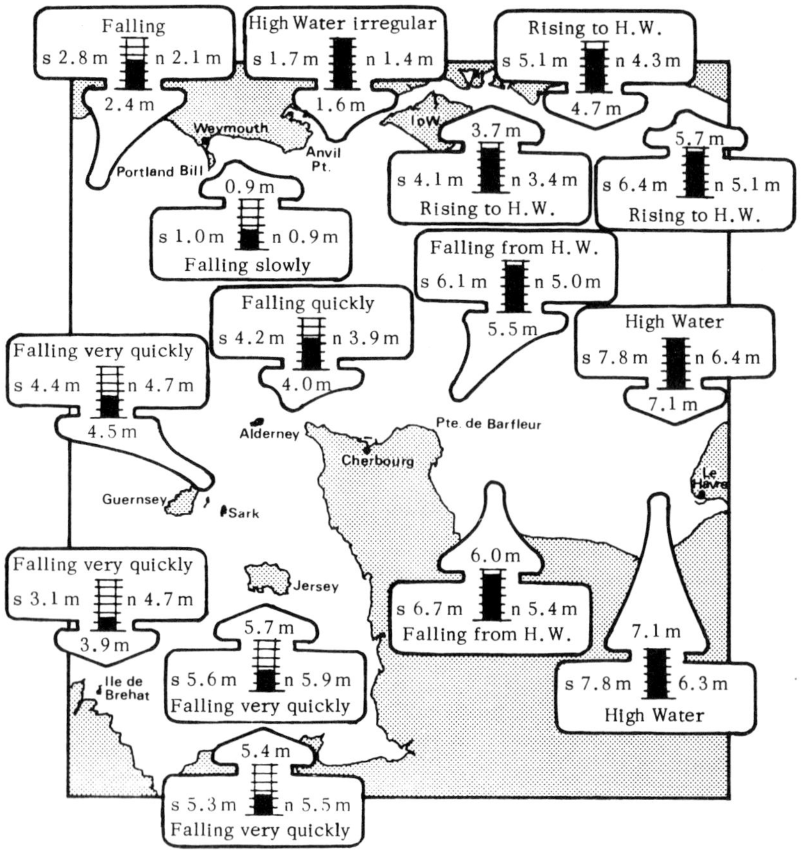

Tidal Heights (offshore)

The broad arrows apply to the time entered on the adjacent page. Each arrow gives the following information:

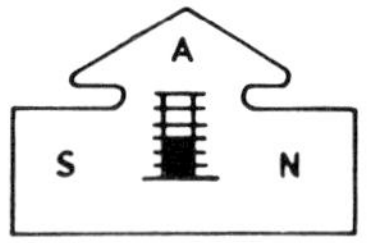

A Average Height of Tide. This is the height of tide, in metres, above Chart Datum, at the position indicated by the arrow. Although only an average height, this figure is sufficiently accurate for use for most coastal navigation.
S Height of Tide at Springs.
N Height of Tide at Neaps.
The Tidal Gauge gives a visual display of the approximate state of the tide with the vertical movement of tide described briefly above or below.

Map labels

- Falling — s 2.8 m — n 2.1 m — 2.4 m
- High Water irregular — s 1.7 m — n 1.4 m — 1.6 m
- Rising to H.W. — s 5.1 m — n 4.3 m — 4.7 m
- 3.7 m — s 4.1 m — n 3.4 m — Rising to H.W.
- 5.7 m — s 6.4 m — n 5.1 m — Rising to H.W.
- 0.9 m — s 1.0 m — n 0.9 m — Falling slowly
- Falling from H.W. — s 6.1 m — n 5.0 m — 5.5 m
- High Water — s 7.8 m — n 6.4 m — 7.1 m
- Falling quickly — s 4.2 m — n 3.9 m — 4.0 m
- Falling very quickly — s 4.4 m — n 4.7 m — 4.5 m
- Falling very quickly — s 3.1 m — n 4.7 m — 3.9 m
- 5.7 m — s 5.6 m — n 5.9 m — Falling very quickly
- 6.0 m — s 6.7 m — n 5.4 m — Falling from H.W.
- 7.1 m — s 7.8 m — 6.3 m — High Water
- 5.4 m — s 5.3 m — n 5.5 m — Falling very quickly

Place names: Weymouth, IoW, Anvil Pt., Portland Bill, Alderney, Cherbourg, Pte. de Barfleur, Le Havre, Guernsey, Sark, Jersey, Ile de Brehat

TIDAL HEIGHTS — PORTS & PLACES

Pencil-in height of HW Cherbourg ▶	4.8	5.0	5.2	5.4	5.6	5.8	6.0	6.2	6.4	6.6	6.8	
ENGLAND												
Lyme Regis	1.9	2.0	2.2	2.3	2.4	2.5	2.6	2.7	2.8	2.8	2.9	2.9
Bridport	1.7	1.8	2.0	2.1	2.2	2.4	2.5	2.6	2.7	2.8	2.8	2.9
Portland & Weymouth	0.8	0.8	0.8	0.8	0.9	0.9	0.9	1.0	1.0	1.1	1.1	1.2
Lulworth Cove	1.0	1.0	1.0	1.0	1.0	1.1	1.1	1.1	1.1	1.1	1.2	1.2
Swanage	1.5	1.5	1.5	1.5	1.5	1.5	1.6	1.6	1.6	1.7	1.7	1.7
Poole entrance	1.5	1.5	1.5	1.5	1.5	1.5	1.6	1.6	1.7	1.7	1.7	1.7
Poole Town Quay	1.6	1.6	1.6	1.6	1.6	1.6	1.7	1.9	2.0	2.0	2.1	2.1
Christchurch appr'ch	1.3	1.3	1.3	1.3	1.4	1.4	1.5	1.5	1.6	1.7	1.7	1.8
Christchurch Hbr	1.3	1.3	1.3	1.3	1.4	1.4	1.5	1.5	1.6	1.6	1.7	1.7
Lymington	2.2	2.3	2.3	2.4	2.4	2.5	2.6	2.7	2.8	2.9	2.9	3.0
Yarmouth I. o. W.	2.3	2.4	2.4	2.5	2.5	2.6	2.7	2.8	2.9	3.0	3.2	3.3
Cowes I. o. W.	3.1	3.2	3.2	3.3	3.3	3.4	3.5	3.7	3.8	3.8	3.9	3.9
Sandown I. o. W.	3.0	3.1	3.1	3.2	3.2	3.3	3.4	3.5	3.6	3.7	3.9	4.0
Southampton	3.4	3.5	3.5	3.6	3.7	3.7	3.8	3.8	3.9	4.0	4.0	4.1
Portsmouth	3.3	3.4	3.4	3.5	3.6	3.7	3.7	3.8	3.9	4.0	4.0	4.1
Chichester entrance	3.4	3.5	3.5	3.6	3.7	3.8	3.8	3.9	4.0	4.1	4.1	4.2
Selsey Bill	3.6	3.7	3.7	3.8	3.9	4.0	4.1	4.2	4.3	4.4	4.4	4.5
Littlehampton Hbr	3.8	3.8	3.8	3.8	3.9	3.9	3.9	4.0	4.0	4.1	4.1	4.2
Littlehampton appr'ch	3.7	3.8	4.0	4.1	4.2	4.3	4.4	4.5	4.6	4.7	4.7	4.8
Shoreham	4.4	4.5	4.7	4.8	4.9	5.1	5.2	5.4	5.5	5.6	5.7	5.8
Brighton	4.4	4.6	4.8	5.0	5.2	5.3	5.5	5.7	5.9	6.0	6.1	6.2
Newhaven	4.6	4.8	5.0	5.2	5.4	5.5	5.7	5.9	6.1	6.2	6.4	6.5
FRANCE												
Le Havre	6.2	6.4	6.6	6.8	7.0	7.2	7.4	7.6	7.8	7.9	8.1	8.2
Honfleur	6.3	6.5	6.7	6.9	7.0	7.2	7.4	7.5	7.7	7.9	8.0	8.2
Trouville (Deauville)	6.2	6.3	6.5	6.6	6.8	6.9	7.1	7.2	7.4	7.5	7.7	7.8
Ouistreham	5.9	6.1	6.3	6.5	6.7	6.9	7.1	7.3	7.5	7.6	7.8	7.9
Courseulles	5.2	5.4	5.6	5.8	6.0	6.2	6.4	6.6	6.8	6.9	7.1	7.2
Arromanches	5.8	6.0	6.2	6.4	6.6	6.8	7.0	7.2	7.4	7.5	7.7	7.8
Port-en-Bessin	5.5	5.7	5.9	6.1	6.2	6.4	6.6	6.7	6.9	7.0	7.1	7.2
Saint-Vaast-la-Hougue	5.0	5.1	5.3	5.4	5.6	5.7	5.9	6.0	6.2	6.4	6.5	6.7
Barfleur	4.8	4.9	5.1	5.2	5.4	5.5	5.7	5.8	6.0	6.2	6.3	6.5
Cherbourg	4.4	4.5	4.5	4.6	4.7	4.8	4.9	5.0	5.1	5.2	5.3	5.4
Omonville	4.2	4.3	4.3	4.4	4.5	4.6	4.7	4.8	4.9	5.0	5.0	5.1
Goury	5.1	5.1	5.1	5.1	5.1	5.2	5.2	5.2	5.2	5.2	5.1	5.1
Dielette	5.2	5.2	5.2	5.2	5.3	5.3	5.3	5.4	5.4	5.4	5.3	5.3
Carteret	5.8	5.8	5.8	5.8	5.7	5.7	5.7	5.6	5.6	5.6	5.5	5.5
Granville	6.3	6.2	6.2	6.1	6.1	6.0	6.0	5.9	5.9	5.8	5.7	5.6
Saint Malo	5.8	5.8	5.8	5.8	5.8	5.9	5.9	5.9	5.8	5.8	5.7	5.7
All Hbrs, St Brieuc Bay	5.5	5.4	5.2	5.1	5.0	4.9	4.7	4.6	4.5	4.4	4.2	4.1
Paimpol	4.6	4.5	4.3	4.2	4.1	4.0	3.9	3.8	3.7	3.5	3.4	3.2
Ile de Bréhat	4.7	4.7	4.7	4.7	4.7	4.8	4.8	4.8	4.8	4.7	4.7	4.6
Lezardrieux	4.4	4.3	4.1	4.0	3.9	3.8	3.7	3.6	3.5	3.4	3.2	3.1
ISLANDS OFF												
Braye, Alderney	3.6	3.6	3.6	3.6	3.7	3.7	3.7	3.8	3.8	3.9	3.9	4.0
St Peter Port & Sark	4.8	4.7	4.7	4.6	4.6	4.5	4.5	4.4	4.4	4.3	4.3	4.2
St Helier, Jersey	5.7	5.7	5.7	5.7	5.7	5.6	5.6	5.6	5.6	5.6	5.5	5.5
St Catherine, Jersey	6.0	6.0	6.0	6.0	6.0	5.9	5.9	5.9	5.9	5.9	5.9	5.9
Les Minquiers	6.1	6.1	6.1	6.1	6.1	6.0	6.0	6.0	6.0	6.0	6.0	6.0
Iles Chausey	6.3	6.3	6.3	6.3	6.3	6.3	6.3	6.3	6.3	6.2	6.2	6.1

Tidal Stream Rates

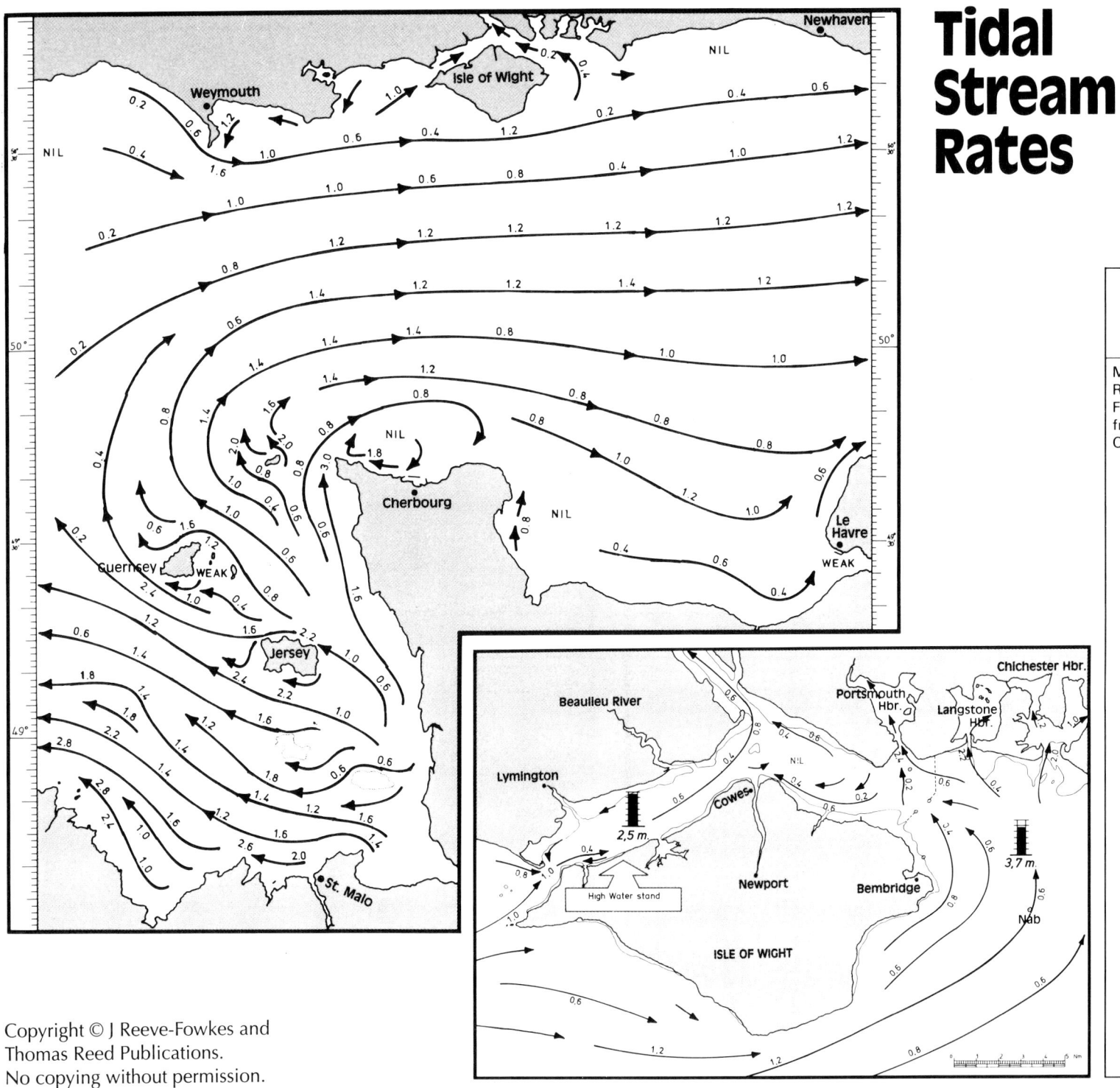

2 hours after HW Cherbourg

+2

Time (to be inserted)

Stream Rate Conversion Table

Mean Rate Figure from Chart ▼	\multicolumn{11}{c}{Pencil-in height of HW Cherbourg Read from column below pencil mark}
	4.8	5.0	5.2	5.4	5.6	5.8	6.0	6.2	6.4	6.6	6.8
0.2	0.1	0.1	0.2	0.2	0.2	0.2	0.2	0.2	0.3	0.3	0.3
0.4	0.2	0.3	0.3	0.3	0.4	0.4	0.4	0.5	0.5	0.6	0.6
0.6	0.4	0.4	0.5	0.5	0.6	0.6	0.7	0.7	0.8	0.8	0.9
0.8	0.5	0.5	0.6	0.7	0.7	0.8	0.9	1.0	1.1	1.2	1.2
1.0	0.6	0.7	0.8	0.8	0.9	1.0	1.1	1.2	1.3	1.4	1.5
1.2	0.7	0.8	0.9	1.0	1.1	1.2	1.3	1.4	1.5	1.6	1.7	1.9
1.4	0.8	0.9	1.1	1.2	1.3	1.4	1.6	1.7	1.8	1.9	2.0	2.2
1.6	0.9	1.1	1.2	1.4	1.5	1.6	1.8	1.9	2.1	2.2	2.3	2.5
1.8	1.0	1.2	1.4	1.5	1.7	1.8	2.0	2.1	2.3	2.5	2.6	2.8
2.0	1.2	1.3	1.5	1.7	1.9	2.0	2.2	2.4	2.6	2.7	2.9	3.1
2.2	1.3	1.5	1.7	1.9	2.1	2.2	2.4	2.6	2.8	3.0	3.2	3.4
2.4	1.4	1.6	1.8	2.0	2.2	2.5	2.7	2.9	3.1	3.3	3.5	3.7
2.6	1.5	1.8	2.0	2.2	2.4	2.7	2.9	3.1	3.3	3.6	3.8	4.0
2.8	1.6	1.9	2.1	2.4	2.6	2.9	3.1	3.3	3.6	3.8	4.1	4.3
3.0	1.8	2.0	2.3	2.5	2.8	3.1	3.3	3.6	3.8	4.1	4.4	4.6
3.2	1.9	2.2	2.4	2.7	3.0	3.3	3.5	3.8	4.1	4.4	4.7	4.9
3.4	2.0	2.3	2.6	2.9	3.2	3.5	3.8	4.1	4.4	4.7	5.0	5.3
3.6	2.1	2.4	2.7	3.1	3.4	3.7	4.0	4.3	4.6	4.9	5.2	5.6
3.8	2.2	2.6	2.9	3.2	3.6	3.9	4.2	4.5	4.9	5.2	5.5	5.9
4.0	2.3	2.7	3.0	3.4	3.7	4.1	4.4	4.8	5.1	5.5	5.8	6.2
4.2	2.5	2.8	3.2	3.6	3.9	4.3	4.7	5.0	5.4	5.8	6.1	6.5
4.4	2.6	3.0	3.3	3.7	4.1	4.5	4.9	5.3	5.6	6.0	6.4	6.8
4.6	2.7	3.1	3.5	3.9	4.3	4.7	5.1	5.5	5.9	6.3	6.7	7.1
4.8	2.8	3.2	3.6	4.1	4.5	4.9	5.3	5.7	6.2	6.6	7.0	7.4
5.0	2.9	3.4	3.8	4.2	4.7	5.1	5.5	6.0	6.4	6.9	7.3	7.7
5.2	3.0	3.5	4.0	4.4	4.9	5.3	5.8	6.2	6.7	7.1	7.6	8.0
5.4	3.2	3.6	4.1	4.6	5.0	5.5	6.0	6.5	6.9	7.4	7.9	8.3
5.6	3.3	3.8	4.3	4.7	5.2	5.7	6.2	6.7	7.2	7.7	8.2	8.6
5.8	3.4	3.9	4.4	4.9	5.4	5.9	6.4	6.9	7.4	7.9	8.5	9.0
6.0	3.5	4.0	4.6	5.1	5.6	6.1	6.7	7.2	7.7	8.2	8.7	9.3
6.2	3.6	4.2	4.7	5.2	5.8	6.3	6.9	7.4	8.0	8.5	9.0	9.6
6.4	3.8	4.3	4.9	5.4	6.0	6.5	7.1	7.7	8.2	8.8	9.3	9.9
6.6	3.9	4.4	5.0	5.6	6.2	6.7	7.3	7.9	8.5	9.0	9.6	10.2
6.8	4.0	4.6	5.2	5.8	6.4	6.9	7.5	8.1	8.7	9.3	9.9	10.5
7.0	4.1	4.7	5.3	5.9	6.6	7.2	7.8	8.4	9.0	9.6	10.2	10.8

Copyright © J Reeve-Fowkes and Thomas Reed Publications. No copying without permission.

+3 — 3 hours after HW Cherbourg

Tidal Heights

Copyright © J Reeve-Fowkes and
Thomas Reed Publications.
No copying without permission.

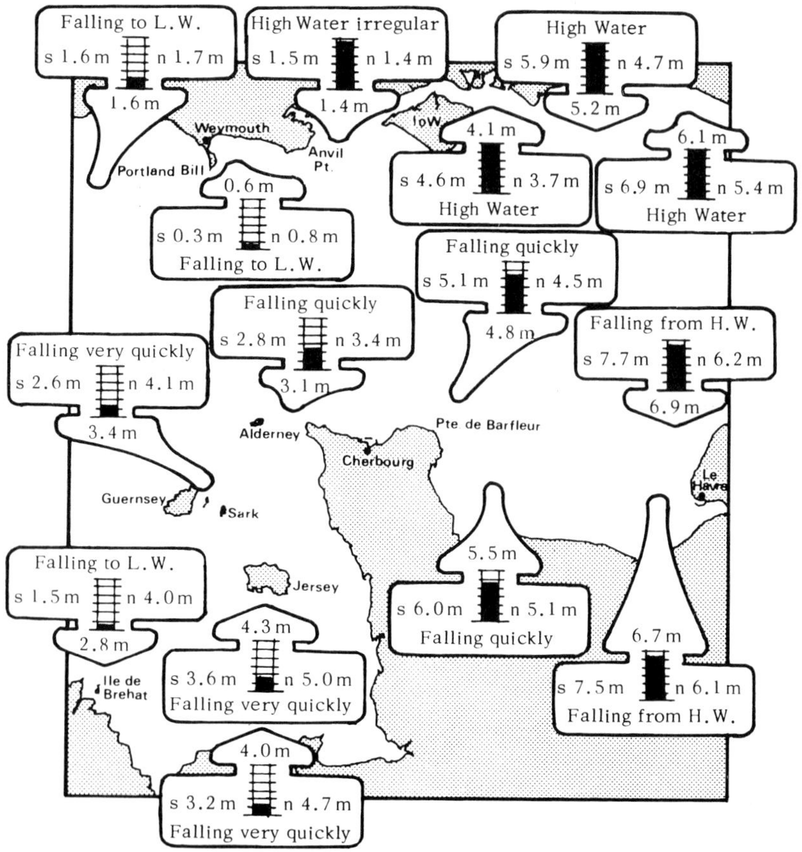

Tidal Heights (offshore)

The broad arrows apply to the time entered on the adjacent page. Each arrow gives the following information:

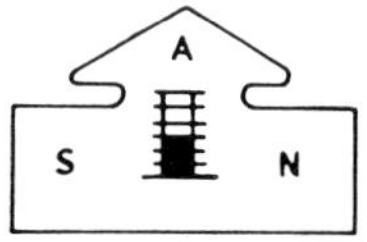

A Average Height of Tide. This is the height of tide, in metres, above Chart Datum, at the position indicated by the arrow. Although only an average height, this figure is sufficiently accurate for use for most coastal navigation.
S Height of Tide at Springs.
N Height of Tide at Neaps.
The Tidal Gauge gives a visual display of the approximate state of the tide with the vertical movement of tide described briefly above or below.

Offshore panels:
- Falling to L.W. — s 1.6 m / n 1.7 m — 1.6 m
- High Water irregular — s 1.5 m / n 1.4 m — 1.4 m
- High Water — s 5.9 m / n 4.7 m — 5.2 m
- 4.1 m — s 4.6 m / n 3.7 m — High Water
- 6.1 m — s 6.9 m / n 5.4 m — High Water
- 0.6 m — s 0.3 m / n 0.8 m — Falling to L.W.
- Falling quickly — s 5.1 m / n 4.5 m — 4.8 m
- Falling quickly — s 2.8 m / n 3.4 m — 3.1 m
- Falling from H.W. — s 7.7 m / n 6.2 m — 6.9 m
- Falling very quickly — s 2.6 m / n 4.1 m — 3.4 m
- Falling to L.W. — s 1.5 m / n 4.0 m — 2.8 m
- 4.3 m — s 3.6 m / n 5.0 m — Falling very quickly
- 5.5 m — s 6.0 m / n 5.1 m — Falling quickly
- 6.7 m — s 7.5 m / n 6.1 m — Falling from H.W.
- 4.0 m — s 3.2 m / n 4.7 m — Falling very quickly

TIDAL HEIGHTS — PORTS & PLACES

Pencil-in height of HW Cherbourg ▶	4.8	5.0	5.2	5.4	5.6	5.8	6.0	6.2	6.4	6.6	6.8
ENGLAND											
Lyme Regis	1.7	1.7	1.7	1.7	1.6	1.6	1.6	1.6	1.6	1.6	1.5	1.5
Bridport	1.6	1.6	1.6	1.6	1.5	1.5	1.5	1.4	1.4	1.3	1.3	1.2
Portland & Weymouth	0.8	0.7	0.7	0.6	0.6	0.5	0.5	0.4	0.4	0.4	0.4	0.4
Lulworth Cove	1.0	0.9	0.9	0.8	0.7	0.6	0.6	0.5	0.4	0.4	0.4	0.4
Swanage	1.5	1.5	1.5	1.5	1.5	1.5	1.5	1.4	1.4	1.4	1.5	1.5
Poole entrance	1.5	1.5	1.5	1.5	1.5	1.5	1.5	1.5	1.5	1.5	1.4	1.4
Poole Town Quay	1.7	1.7	1.7	1.7	1.7	1.7	1.7	1.7	1.7	1.7	1.7	1.7
Christchurch appr'ch	1.3	1.3	1.3	1.3	1.4	1.4	1.4	1.4	1.4	1.4	1.4	1.4
Christchurch Hbr	1.4	1.4	1.4	1.4	1.4	1.4	1.4	1.4	1.4	1.4	1.5	1.5
Lymington	2.4	2.5	2.5	2.6	2.6	2.7	2.8	2.8	2.9	3.0	3.0	3.1
Yarmouth I. o. W.	2.4	2.5	2.5	2.6	2.6	2.7	2.8	2.8	2.9	3.0	3.2	3.3
Cowes I. o. W.	3.3	3.4	3.4	3.5	3.7	3.8	3.9	4.1	4.2	4.3	4.3	4.4
Sandown I. o. W.	3.2	3.3	3.3	3.4	3.5	3.6	3.7	3.8	3.9	4.1	4.2	4.4
Southampton	3.5	3.6	3.8	3.9	4.0	4.1	4.3	4.4	4.5	4.6	4.7	4.8
Portsmouth	3.5	3.6	3.8	3.9	4.0	4.2	4.3	4.4	4.6	4.7	4.8	4.9
Chichester entrance	3.7	3.8	4.0	4.1	4.2	4.3	4.5	4.6	4.7	4.8	4.9	5.0
Selsey Bill	4.0	4.1	4.3	4.4	4.5	4.7	4.8	5.0	5.1	5.2	5.3	5.5
Littlehampton Hbr	3.9	4.1	4.3	4.5	4.6	4.8	5.0	5.1	5.3	5.4	5.5	5.6
Littlehampton appr'ch	4.2	4.4	4.6	4.8	4.9	5.1	5.3	5.4	5.6	5.7	5.9	6.0
Shoreham	4.7	4.9	5.1	5.3	5.4	5.6	5.8	5.9	6.1	6.3	6.4	6.6
Brighton	4.8	5.0	5.2	5.4	5.6	5.9	6.1	6.3	6.5	6.6	6.8	6.9
Newhaven	4.9	5.1	5.3	5.5	5.7	6.0	6.2	6.4	6.6	6.8	6.9	7.1
FRANCE											
Le Havre	6.0	6.2	6.4	6.6	6.8	7.1	7.3	7.5	7.7	7.8	8.0	8.1
Honfleur	6.3	6.5	6.7	6.9	7.1	7.2	7.4	7.6	7.8	7.9	8.1	8.2
Trouville (Deauville)	6.0	6.1	6.3	6.4	6.5	6.7	6.8	7.0	7.1	7.2	7.3	7.4
Ouistreham	5.7	5.9	6.1	6.3	6.4	6.6	6.8	6.9	7.1	7.2	7.3	7.4
Courseulles	5.2	5.3	5.3	5.4	5.5	5.6	5.7	5.8	5.9	6.0	6.1	6.2
Arromanches	5.6	5.7	5.9	6.0	6.1	6.2	6.4	6.5	6.6	6.7	6.8	6.9
Port-en-Bessin	5.5	5.6	5.6	5.7	5.8	5.9	5.9	6.0	6.1	6.2	6.2	6.3
Saint-Vaast-la-Hougue	4.6	4.7	4.7	4.8	4.9	5.0	5.1	5.2	5.2	5.3	5.4	5.5
Barfleur	4.4	4.5	4.5	4.6	4.7	4.8	4.9	5.0	5.1	5.2	5.3	
Cherbourg	3.9	3.9	3.9	3.9	4.0	4.0	4.0	4.1	4.1	4.1	4.1	
Omonville	3.8	3.8	3.8	3.8	3.8	3.7	3.7	3.7	3.7	3.7	3.7	
Goury	4.7	4.6	4.4	4.3	4.2	4.0	3.9	3.7	3.6	3.4	3.3	3.1
Dielette	4.6	4.5	4.3	4.2	4.1	3.9	3.8	3.6	3.5	3.3	3.2	
Carteret	5.1	4.9	4.7	4.5	4.3	4.2	4.0	3.9	3.7	3.5	3.4	3.2
Granville	5.7	5.4	5.2	4.9	4.7	4.4	4.2	3.9	3.7	3.5	3.3	3.1
Saint Malo	5.3	5.1	4.9	4.7	4.5	4.4	4.2	4.0	3.8	3.6	3.4	3.2
All Hbrs, St Brieuc Bay	5.0	4.7	4.5	4.2	3.9	3.6	3.2	3.0	2.7	2.4	2.2	1.9
Paimpol	4.1	3.8	3.6	3.3	3.0	2.7	2.5	2.2	1.9	1.6	1.4	1.1
Ile de Bréhat	4.2	4.1	3.9	3.8	3.6	3.5	3.3	3.2	3.0	2.8	2.7	2.5
Lezardrieux	3.9	3.6	3.4	3.1	2.8	2.6	2.3	2.1	1.8	1.5	1.3	1.0
ISLANDS OFF											
Braye, Alderney	3.2	3.1	3.1	3.0	2.9	2.8	2.8	2.7	2.6	2.5	2.5	2.4
St Peter Port & Sark	4.4	4.2	4.0	3.8	3.6	3.3	3.1	2.9	2.7	2.5	2.3	2.1
St Helier, Jersey	5.2	5.0	4.8	4.6	4.5	4.3	4.1	3.9	3.7	3.5	3.4	3.2
St Catherine, Jersey	5.4	5.2	5.0	4.8	4.6	4.5	4.3	4.1	3.9	3.7	3.6	3.4
Les Minquiers	5.5	5.2	5.0	4.7	4.5	4.2	4.0	3.8	3.5	3.3	3.2	3.0
Iles Chausey	5.6	5.4	5.2	5.0	4.8	4.6	4.4	4.2	4.0	3.8	3.6	3.4

Tidal Stream Rates

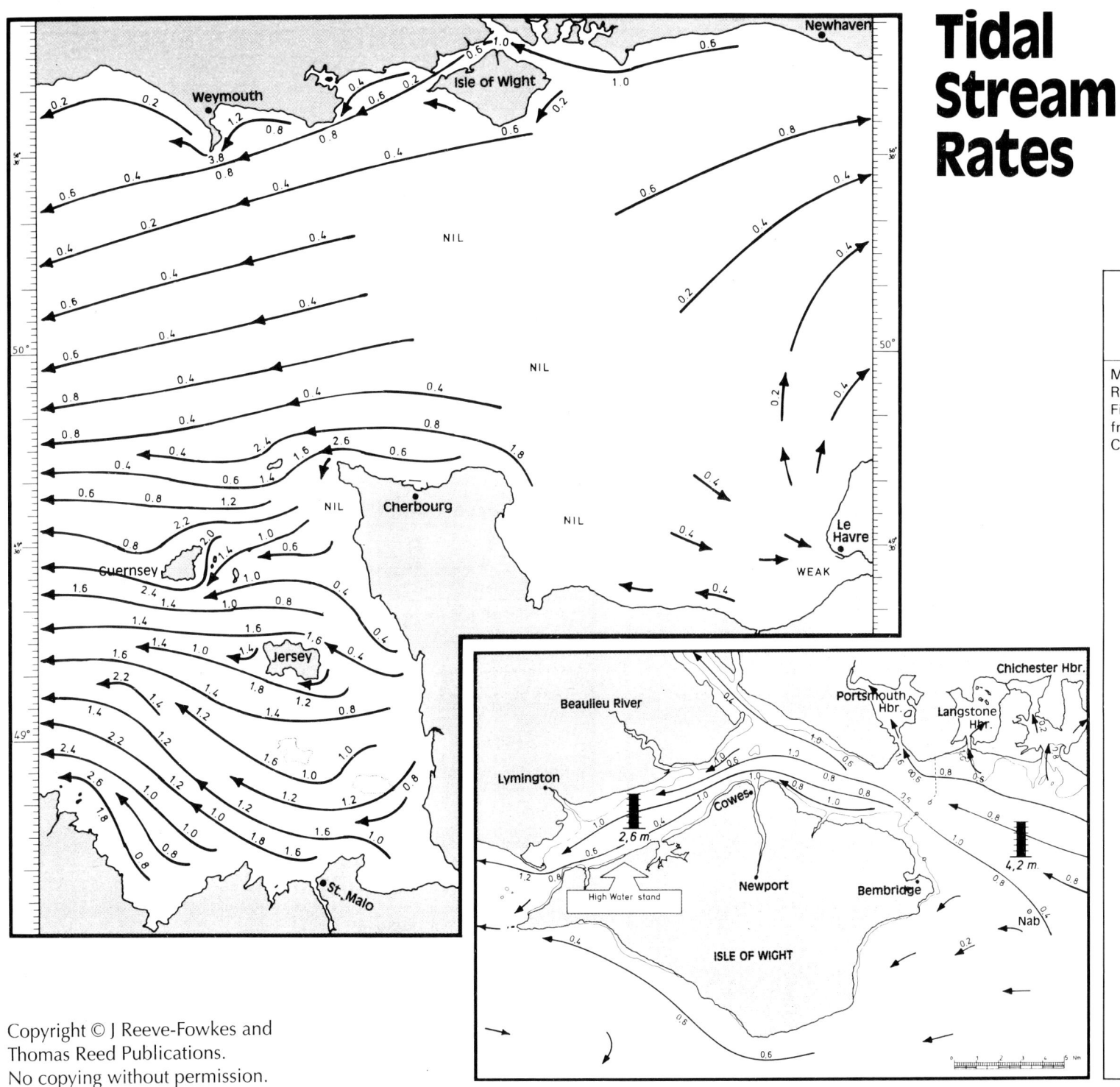

+3 — 3 hours after HW Cherbourg

Time (to be inserted)

Stream Rate Conversion Table

Mean Rate Figure from Chart ▼	\multicolumn{11}{c}{Pencil-in height of HW Cherbourg — Read from column below pencil mark}
	4.8	5.0	5.2	5.4	5.6	5.8	6.0	6.2	6.4	6.6	6.8
0.2	0.1	0.1	0.2	0.2	0.2	0.2	0.2	0.2	0.3	0.3	0.3
0.4	0.2	0.3	0.3	0.3	0.4	0.4	0.4	0.5	0.5	0.5	0.6
0.6	0.4	0.4	0.5	0.5	0.6	0.6	0.6	0.7	0.7	0.8	0.8	0.9
0.8	0.5	0.5	0.6	0.7	0.7	0.8	0.9	1.0	1.0	1.1	1.2	1.2
1.0	0.6	0.7	0.8	0.8	0.9	1.0	1.1	1.2	1.3	1.4	1.5	1.5
1.2	0.7	0.8	0.9	1.0	1.1	1.2	1.3	1.4	1.5	1.6	1.7	1.9
1.4	0.8	0.9	1.1	1.2	1.3	1.4	1.6	1.7	1.8	1.9	2.0	2.2
1.6	0.9	1.1	1.2	1.4	1.5	1.6	1.8	1.9	2.1	2.2	2.3	2.5
1.8	1.0	1.2	1.4	1.5	1.7	1.8	2.0	2.2	2.3	2.5	2.6	2.8
2.0	1.2	1.3	1.5	1.7	1.9	2.0	2.2	2.4	2.6	2.7	2.9	3.1
2.2	1.3	1.5	1.7	1.9	2.1	2.2	2.4	2.6	2.8	3.0	3.2	3.4
2.4	1.4	1.6	1.8	2.0	2.2	2.5	2.7	2.9	3.1	3.3	3.5	3.7
2.6	1.5	1.8	2.0	2.2	2.4	2.7	2.9	3.1	3.3	3.6	3.8	4.0
2.8	1.6	1.9	2.1	2.4	2.6	2.9	3.1	3.3	3.6	3.8	4.1	4.3
3.0	1.8	2.0	2.3	2.5	2.8	3.1	3.3	3.6	3.8	4.1	4.4	4.6
3.2	1.9	2.2	2.4	2.7	3.0	3.3	3.5	3.8	4.1	4.4	4.7	4.9
3.4	2.0	2.3	2.6	2.9	3.2	3.5	3.8	4.1	4.4	4.7	5.0	5.3
3.6	2.1	2.4	2.7	3.1	3.4	3.7	4.0	4.3	4.6	4.9	5.2	5.6
3.8	2.2	2.6	2.9	3.2	3.6	3.9	4.2	4.5	4.9	5.2	5.5	5.9
4.0	2.3	2.7	3.0	3.4	3.7	4.1	4.4	4.8	5.1	5.5	5.8	6.2
4.2	2.5	2.8	3.2	3.6	3.9	4.3	4.7	5.0	5.4	5.8	6.1	6.5
4.4	2.6	3.0	3.3	3.7	4.1	4.5	4.9	5.3	5.6	6.0	6.4	6.8
4.6	2.7	3.1	3.5	3.9	4.3	4.7	5.1	5.5	5.9	6.3	6.7	7.1
4.8	2.8	3.2	3.6	4.1	4.5	4.9	5.3	5.7	6.2	6.6	7.0	7.4
5.0	2.9	3.4	3.8	4.2	4.7	5.1	5.5	6.0	6.4	6.9	7.3	7.7
5.2	3.0	3.5	4.0	4.4	4.9	5.3	5.8	6.2	6.7	7.1	7.6	8.0
5.4	3.2	3.6	4.1	4.6	5.0	5.5	6.0	6.5	6.9	7.4	7.9	8.3
5.6	3.3	3.8	4.3	4.7	5.2	5.7	6.2	6.7	7.2	7.7	8.2	8.6
5.8	3.4	3.9	4.4	4.9	5.4	5.9	6.4	6.9	7.4	7.9	8.5	9.0
6.0	3.5	4.0	4.6	5.1	5.6	6.1	6.7	7.2	7.7	8.2	8.7	9.3
6.2	3.6	4.2	4.7	5.3	5.8	6.3	6.9	7.4	8.0	8.5	9.0	9.6
6.4	3.8	4.3	4.9	5.4	6.0	6.5	7.1	7.7	8.2	8.8	9.3	9.9
6.6	3.9	4.4	5.0	5.6	6.2	6.7	7.3	7.9	8.5	9.0	9.6	10.2
6.8	4.0	4.6	5.2	5.8	6.4	6.9	7.5	8.1	8.7	9.3	9.9	10.5
7.0	4.1	4.7	5.3	5.9	6.6	7.2	7.8	8.4	9.0	9.6	10.2	10.8

Copyright © J Reeve-Fowkes and Thomas Reed Publications.
No copying without permission.

135

+4
4 hours after HW Cherbourg

Tidal Heights

Copyright © J Reeve-Fowkes and
Thomas Reed Publications.
No copying without permission.

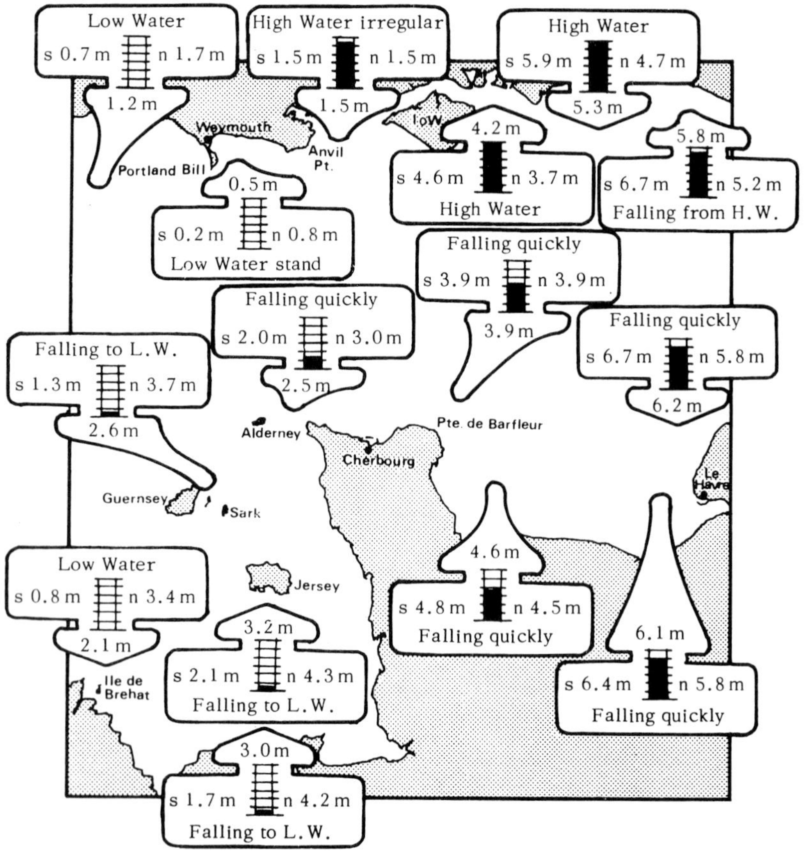

Tidal Heights (offshore)

The broad arrows apply to the time entered on the adjacent page. Each arrow gives the following information:

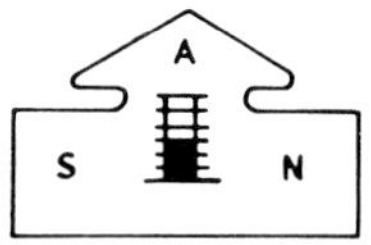

A Average Height of Tide. This is the height of tide, in metres, above Chart Datum, at the position indicated by the arrow. Although only an average height, this figure is sufficiently accurate for use for most coastal navigation.
S Height of Tide at Springs.
N Height of Tide at Neaps.
The Tidal Gauge gives a visual display of the approximate state of the tide with the vertical movement of tide described briefly above or below.

Offshore tidal gauges:
- Low Water — s 0.7m n 1.7m — 1.2m
- High Water irregular — s 1.5m n 1.5m — 1.5m
- High Water — s 5.9m n 4.7m — 5.3m
- 4.2m — s 4.6m n 3.7m — High Water
- 5.8m — s 6.7m n 5.2m — Falling from H.W.
- 0.5m — s 0.2m n 0.8m — Low Water stand
- Falling quickly — s 3.9m n 3.9m — 3.9m
- Falling quickly — s 2.0m n 3.0m — 2.5m
- Falling quickly — s 6.7m n 5.8m — 6.2m
- Falling to L.W. — s 1.3m n 3.7m — 2.6m
- Low Water — s 0.8m n 3.4m — 2.1m
- 3.2m — s 2.1m n 4.3m — Falling to L.W.
- 4.6m — s 4.8m n 4.5m — Falling quickly
- 6.1m — s 6.4m n 5.8m — Falling quickly
- 3.0m — s 1.7m n 4.2m — Falling to L.W.

TIDAL HEIGHTS — PORTS & PLACES

Pencil-in height of HW Cherbourg ▶	4.8	5.0	5.2	5.4	5.6	5.8	6.0	6.2	6.4	6.6	6.8
ENGLAND											
Lyme Regis	2.1	1.9	1.7	1.5	1.4	1.2	1.0	0.9	0.7	0.6	0.4	0.3
Bridport	1.8	1.7	1.5	1.4	1.2	1.1	0.9	0.8	0.6	0.5	0.4	0.3
Portland & Weymouth	0.9	0.8	0.8	0.7	0.6	0.5	0.4	0.3	0.2	0.2	0.1	0.1
Lulworth Cove	1.0	0.9	0.9	0.8	0.7	0.6	0.6	0.5	0.4	0.4	0.3	0.3
Swanage	1.7	1.6	1.6	1.5	1.4	1.3	1.3	1.4	1.4	1.4	1.5	1.5
Poole entrance	1.6	1.6	1.6	1.6	1.5	1.5	1.5	1.5	1.5	1.5	1.4	1.4
Poole Town Quay	1.8	1.8	1.8	1.8	1.8	1.8	1.7	1.7	1.6	1.6	1.6	1.6
Christchurch appr'ch	1.4	1.4	1.4	1.4	1.5	1.5	1.5	1.4	1.4	1.5	1.5	1.6
Christchurch Hbr	1.4	1.4	1.4	1.4	1.5	1.5	1.5	1.4	1.4	1.4	1.5	1.5
Lymington	2.4	2.5	2.5	2.6	2.6	2.7	2.8	2.8	2.9	3.0	3.0	3.1
Yarmouth I. o. W.	2.4	2.5	2.5	2.6	2.6	2.7	2.7	2.8	2.8	2.9	3.1	3.2
Cowes I. o. W.	3.3	3.4	3.4	3.5	3.6	3.7	3.8	4.0	4.1	4.2	4.2	4.3
Sandown I. o. W.	3.1	3.2	3.2	3.3	3.4	3.5	3.6	3.8	3.9	4.1	4.2	4.4
Southampton	3.6	3.7	3.7	3.8	3.9	4.0	4.1	4.2	4.3	4.4	4.5	4.6
Portsmouth	3.6	3.7	3.9	4.0	4.1	4.2	4.4	4.5	4.6	4.7	4.8	4.9
Chichester entrance	3.8	3.9	4.1	4.2	4.3	4.5	4.6	4.8	4.9	5.0	5.1	5.2
Selsey Bill	4.2	4.3	4.5	4.6	4.7	4.9	5.0	5.2	5.3	5.4	5.4	5.5
Littlehampton Hbr	4.0	4.2	4.4	4.6	4.7	4.9	5.1	5.2	5.4	5.5	5.7	5.8
Littlehampton appr'ch	4.3	4.4	4.6	4.7	4.9	5.0	5.2	5.3	5.5	5.6	5.8	5.9
Shoreham	4.6	4.8	5.0	5.2	5.3	5.5	5.7	5.8	6.0	6.1	6.3	6.4
Brighton	4.7	4.9	5.1	5.3	5.5	5.7	5.9	6.1	6.3	6.4	6.6	6.7
Newhaven	4.7	4.9	5.1	5.3	5.5	5.8	6.0	6.2	6.4	6.5	6.7	6.8
FRANCE											
Le Havre	5.8	5.9	6.1	6.2	6.4	6.5	6.7	6.8	7.0	7.1	7.1	7.2
Honfleur	5.9	6.0	6.2	6.3	6.5	6.6	6.8	6.9	7.1	7.2	7.3	7.4
Trouville (Deauville)	5.7	5.8	5.8	5.9	6.0	6.1	6.2	6.3	6.4	6.5	6.5	6.6
Ouistreham	5.5	5.6	5.6	5.7	5.7	5.8	5.8	5.9	5.9	5.9	6.0	6.0
Courseulles	4.8	4.8	4.8	4.8	4.8	4.8	4.8	4.8	4.8	4.8	4.8	4.8
Arromanches	5.3	5.3	5.3	5.3	5.3	5.3	5.3	5.3	5.3	5.3	5.4	5.4
Port-en-Bessin	5.1	5.1	5.1	5.1	5.0	5.0	5.0	4.9	4.9	4.9	4.8	4.8
Saint-Vaast-la-Hougue	4.0	4.0	4.0	4.0	4.1	4.1	4.1	4.2	4.2	4.2	4.2	4.2
Barfleur	3.9	3.9	3.9	3.9	3.9	3.9	3.9	3.9	3.9	3.9	3.9	3.9
Cherbourg	3.6	3.5	3.5	3.4	3.3	3.2	3.2	3.1	3.0	2.9	2.8	2.7
Omonville	3.4	3.3	3.3	3.2	3.1	3.0	2.9	2.8	2.7	2.6	2.4	2.3
Goury	4.3	4.0	3.8	3.5	3.3	3.0	2.8	2.5	2.3	2.0	1.8	1.5
Dielette	4.3	4.0	3.8	3.5	3.2	3.0	2.7	2.5	2.2	1.9	1.7	1.4
Carteret	4.7	4.4	4.0	3.7	3.4	3.1	2.8	2.5	2.2	1.9	1.7	1.4
Granville	5.3	4.9	4.5	4.1	3.7	3.4	3.0	2.6	2.2	1.9	1.5	1.2
Saint Malo	4.9	4.6	4.2	3.9	3.6	3.2	2.9	2.5	2.2	1.9	1.6	1.3
All Hbrs, St Brieuc Bay	4.7	4.3	3.9	3.5	3.1	2.7	2.3	1.9	1.5	1.2	0.8	0.5
Paimpol	3.8	3.4	3.0	2.6	2.2	1.9	1.5	1.1	0.7	0.4	0.1	-0.2
Ile de Bréhat	4.0	3.7	3.5	3.2	2.9	2.6	2.4	2.1	1.8	1.5	1.3	1.0
Lezardrieux	3.8	3.4	3.0	2.6	2.3	1.9	1.5	1.2	0.8	0.5	0.2	-0.1
ISLANDS OFF											
Braye, Alderney	3.0	2.8	2.6	2.4	2.3	2.1	1.9	1.8	1.6	1.4	1.3	1.1
St Peter Port & Sark	4.2	3.9	3.5	3.2	2.9	2.5	2.2	1.8	1.5	1.2	0.9	0.6
St Helier, Jersey	4.8	4.5	4.1	3.8	3.5	3.2	2.8	2.5	2.2	1.9	1.6	1.3
St Catherine, Jersey	5.1	4.8	4.4	4.1	3.7	3.4	3.0	2.7	2.3	2.0	1.7	1.4
Les Minquiers	4.8	4.5	4.1	3.8	3.4	3.1	2.7	2.4	2.0	1.7	1.5	1.2
Iles Chausey	5.1	4.8	4.4	4.1	3.8	3.4	3.1	2.7	2.4	2.1	1.8	1.5

Tidal Stream Rates

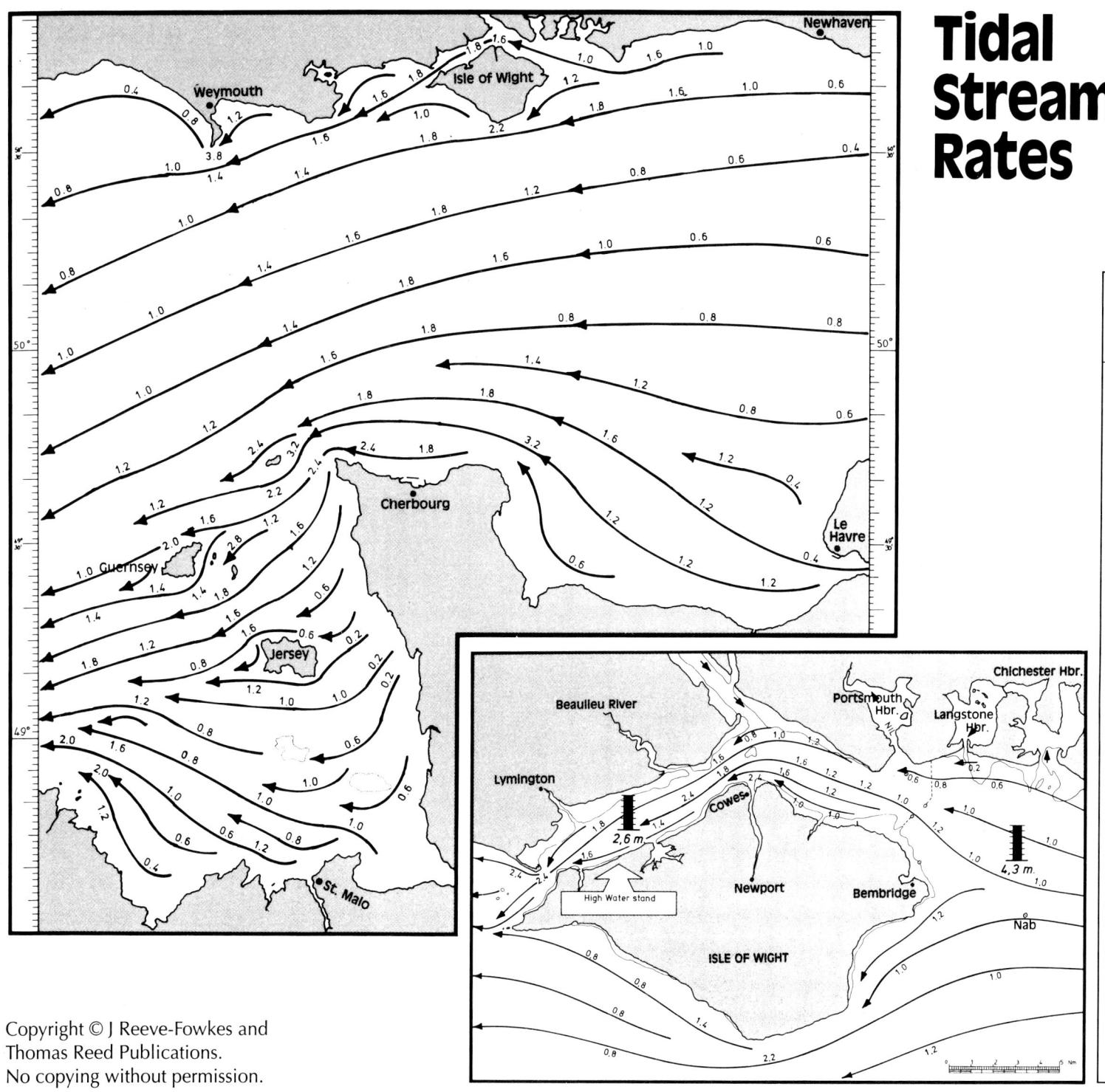

4 hours after HW Cherbourg

+4

Time (to be inserted)

Stream Rate Conversion Table

Mean Rate Figure from Chart ▼	\multicolumn{11}{c}{Pencil-in height of HW Cherbourg — Read from column below pencil mark}
	4.8	5.0	5.2	5.4	5.6	5.8	6.0	6.2	6.4	6.6	6.8
0.2	0.1	0.1	0.2	0.2	0.2	0.2	0.2	0.2	0.3	0.3	0.3
0.4	0.2	0.3	0.3	0.3	0.4	0.4	0.4	0.5	0.5	0.5	0.6
0.6	0.4	0.4	0.5	0.5	0.6	0.6	0.6	0.7	0.7	0.8	0.8	0.9
0.8	0.5	0.5	0.6	0.7	0.7	0.8	0.9	1.0	1.0	1.1	1.2	1.2
1.0	0.6	0.7	0.8	0.8	0.9	1.0	1.1	1.2	1.3	1.4	1.5	1.5
1.2	0.7	0.8	0.9	1.0	1.1	1.2	1.3	1.4	1.5	1.6	1.7	1.9
1.4	0.8	0.9	1.1	1.2	1.3	1.4	1.6	1.7	1.8	1.9	2.0	2.2
1.6	0.9	1.1	1.2	1.4	1.5	1.6	1.8	1.9	2.1	2.2	2.3	2.5
1.8	1.0	1.2	1.4	1.5	1.7	1.8	2.0	2.1	2.3	2.5	2.6	2.8
2.0	1.2	1.3	1.5	1.7	1.9	2.0	2.2	2.4	2.6	2.7	2.9	3.1
2.2	1.3	1.5	1.7	1.9	2.1	2.2	2.4	2.6	2.8	3.0	3.2	3.4
2.4	1.4	1.6	1.8	2.0	2.2	2.5	2.7	2.9	3.1	3.3	3.5	3.7
2.6	1.5	1.8	2.0	2.2	2.4	2.7	2.9	3.1	3.3	3.6	3.8	4.0
2.8	1.6	1.9	2.1	2.4	2.6	2.9	3.1	3.3	3.6	3.8	4.1	4.3
3.0	1.8	2.0	2.3	2.5	2.8	3.1	3.3	3.6	3.8	4.1	4.4	4.6
3.2	1.9	2.2	2.4	2.7	3.0	3.3	3.5	3.8	4.1	4.4	4.7	4.9
3.4	2.0	2.3	2.6	2.9	3.2	3.5	3.8	4.1	4.4	4.7	5.0	5.3
3.6	2.1	2.4	2.7	3.1	3.4	3.7	4.0	4.3	4.6	4.9	5.2	5.6
3.8	2.2	2.6	2.9	3.2	3.6	3.9	4.2	4.5	4.9	5.2	5.5	5.9
4.0	2.3	2.7	3.0	3.4	3.7	4.1	4.4	4.8	5.1	5.5	5.8	6.2
4.2	2.5	2.8	3.2	3.6	3.9	4.3	4.7	5.0	5.4	5.8	6.1	6.5
4.4	2.6	3.0	3.3	3.7	4.1	4.5	4.9	5.3	5.6	6.0	6.4	6.8
4.6	2.7	3.1	3.5	3.9	4.3	4.7	5.1	5.5	5.9	6.3	6.7	7.1
4.8	2.8	3.2	3.6	4.1	4.5	4.9	5.3	5.7	6.2	6.6	7.0	7.4
5.0	2.9	3.4	3.8	4.2	4.7	5.1	5.5	6.0	6.4	6.9	7.3	7.7
5.2	3.0	3.5	4.0	4.4	4.9	5.3	5.8	6.2	6.7	7.1	7.6	8.0
5.4	3.2	3.6	4.1	4.6	5.0	5.5	6.0	6.5	6.9	7.4	7.9	8.3
5.6	3.3	3.8	4.3	4.7	5.2	5.7	6.2	6.7	7.2	7.7	8.2	8.6
5.8	3.4	3.9	4.4	4.9	5.4	5.9	6.4	6.9	7.4	7.9	8.5	9.0
6.0	3.5	4.0	4.6	5.1	5.6	6.1	6.7	7.2	7.7	8.2	8.7	9.3
6.2	3.6	4.2	4.7	5.3	5.8	6.3	6.9	7.4	8.0	8.5	9.0	9.6
6.4	3.8	4.3	4.9	5.4	6.0	6.5	7.1	7.7	8.2	8.8	9.3	9.9
6.6	3.9	4.4	5.0	5.6	6.2	6.7	7.3	7.9	8.5	9.0	9.6	10.2
6.8	4.0	4.6	5.2	5.8	6.4	6.9	7.5	8.1	8.7	9.3	9.9	10.5
7.0	4.1	4.7	5.3	5.9	6.6	7.2	7.8	8.4	9.0	9.6	10.2	10.8

Copyright © J Reeve-Fowkes and Thomas Reed Publications.
No copying without permission.

137

+5
5 hours after HW Cherbourg

Tidal Heights

Copyright © J Reeve-Fowkes and
Thomas Reed Publications.
No copying without permission.

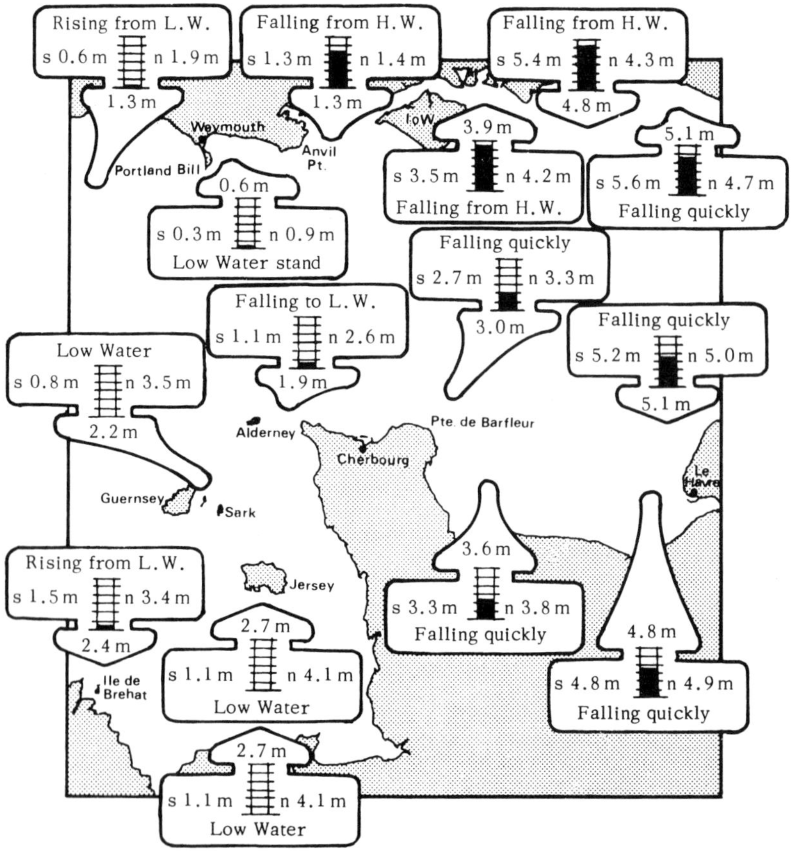

Tidal Heights (offshore)

The broad arrows apply to the time entered on the adjacent page. Each arrow gives the following information:

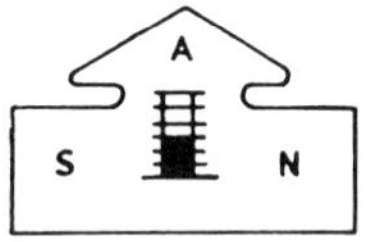

A Average Height of Tide. This is the height of tide, in metres, above Chart Datum, at the position indicated by the arrow. Although only an average height, this figure is sufficiently accurate for use for most coastal navigation.
S Height of Tide at Springs.
N Height of Tide at Neaps.
The Tidal Gauge gives a visual display of the approximate state of the tide with the vertical movement of tide described briefly above or below.

Map labels

- Rising from L.W. s 0.6m n 1.9m — 1.3 m
- Falling from H.W. s 1.3m n 1.4m — 1.3 m
- Falling from H.W. s 5.4m n 4.3m — 4.8 m
- 3.9 m
- Falling from H.W. s 3.5m n 4.2m
- Falling quickly s 5.6m n 4.7m — 5.1 m
- s 0.3m n 0.9m — Low Water stand — 0.6 m
- Falling quickly s 2.7m n 3.3m — 3.0 m
- Falling quickly s 5.2m n 5.0m — 5.1 m
- Falling to L.W. s 1.1m n 2.6m — 1.9 m
- Low Water s 0.8m n 3.5m — 2.2 m
- Rising from L.W. s 1.5m n 3.4m — 2.4 m
- 3.6 m
- Falling quickly s 3.3m n 3.8m
- Falling quickly s 4.8m n 4.9m — 4.8 m
- Low Water s 1.1m n 4.1m — 2.7 m
- Low Water s 1.1m n 4.1m — 2.7 m

Place names: Weymouth, Anvil Pt., IoW, Portland Bill, Alderney, Cherbourg, Pte. de Barfleur, Le Havre, Guernsey, Sark, Jersey, Ile de Brehat

TIDAL HEIGHTS — PORTS & PLACES

Pencil-in height of HW Cherbourg ▶	4.8	5.0	5.2	5.4	5.6	5.8	6.0	6.2	6.4	6.6	6.8
ENGLAND											
Lyme Regis..............	2.1	2.0	1.8	1.7	1.5	1.4	1.2	1.1	0.9	0.8	0.7	0.6
Bridport....................	2.0	1.9	1.7	1.6	1.4	1.3	1.1	1.0	0.8	0.6	0.5	0.3
Portland & Weymouth..	1.0	0.9	0.9	0.8	0.7	0.6	0.5	0.4	0.4	0.4	0.3	0.3
Lulworth Cove	1.1	1.0	1.0	0.9	0.8	0.7	0.7	0.6	0.5	0.5	0.4	0.4
Swanage	1.6	1.5	1.5	1.4	1.4	1.3	1.3	1.3	1.3	1.3	1.3	1.3
Poole entrance	1.5	1.5	1.5	1.5	1.5	1.5	1.5	1.5	1.5	1.5	1.4	1.4
Poole Town Quay........	1.8	1.8	1.8	1.8	1.8	1.8	1.8	1.7	1.7	1.7	1.7	1.7
Christchurch appr'ch ...	1.3	1.3	1.3	1.3	1.3	1.3	1.3	1.2	1.2	1.2	1.3	1.3
Christchurch Hbr........	1.2	1.2	1.2	1.3	1.3	1.3	1.3	1.3	1.3	1.3	1.4	1.4
Lymington	2.3	2.4	2.4	2.5	2.5	2.6	2.7	2.7	2.8	2.9	2.9	3.0
Yarmouth I. o. W.	2.3	2.4	2.4	2.5	2.5	2.6	2.6	2.7	2.7	2.8	2.9	3.0
Cowes I. o. W.	3.2	3.3	3.3	3.4	3.5	3.6	3.7	3.8	3.9	3.9	4.0	4.0
Sandown I. o. W.	2.8	2.9	2.9	3.0	3.2	3.3	3.4	3.4	3.5	3.6	3.8	3.9
Southampton	3.4	3.5	3.7	3.8	3.9	4.0	4.2	4.3	4.4	4.5	4.6	4.7
Portsmouth................	3.4	3.5	3.7	3.8	3.9	4.0	4.2	4.3	4.4	4.5	4.5	4.6
Chichester entrance.....	3.6	3.7	3.9	4.0	4.1	4.2	4.4	4.5	4.6	4.7	4.7	4.8
Selsey Bill.................	4.0	4.1	4.3	4.4	4.5	4.6	4.7	4.8	4.9	5.0	5.1	5.2
Littlehampton Hbr........	3.9	4.0	4.2	4.3	4.4	4.5	4.6	4.8	4.9	5.1	5.2	5.4	5.5
Littlehampton appr'ch ..	4.1	4.2	4.4	4.5	4.7	4.8	5.0	5.1	5.3	5.4	5.5	5.6
Shoreham	4.2	4.3	4.5	4.6	4.8	4.9	5.1	5.2	5.4	5.5	5.6	5.7
Brighton	4.3	4.4	4.6	4.7	4.9	5.0	5.2	5.3	5.5	5.6	5.7	5.8
Newhaven	4.3	4.4	4.6	4.7	4.8	5.0	5.1	5.3	5.4	5.5	5.7	5.8
FRANCE											
Le Havre	5.2	5.2	5.2	5.2	5.3	5.3	5.3	5.4	5.4	5.4	5.4	5.4
Honfleur	5.1	5.2	5.2	5.3	5.4	5.4	5.5	5.5	5.6	5.6	5.6	5.6
Trouville (Deauville)	5.1	5.0	5.0	4.9	4.8	4.7	4.6	4.5	4.4	4.4	4.3	4.3
Ouistreham	4.7	4.6	4.6	4.5	4.5	4.4	4.4	4.3	4.3	4.3	4.2	4.2
Courseulles...............	4.0	3.9	3.9	3.8	3.7	3.6	3.6	3.5	3.5	3.4	3.3	3.3
Arromanches	4.5	4.4	4.4	4.3	4.2	4.1	4.1	4.0	3.9	3.9	3.8	3.8
Port-en-Bessin.............	4.3	4.2	4.2	4.1	4.0	3.9	3.8	3.7	3.6	3.5	3.5	3.4
Saint-Vaast-la-Hougue..	3.5	3.4	3.4	3.3	3.3	3.2	3.2	3.1	3.1	3.0	3.0	2.9
Barfleur	3.4	3.3	3.3	3.2	3.1	3.0	3.0	2.9	2.8	2.7	2.5	2.4
Cherbourg	3.2	3.1	2.9	2.8	2.6	2.5	2.5	2.2	2.0	1.8	1.7	1.5
Omonville	3.2	3.0	2.8	2.6	2.4	2.3	2.1	1.9	1.7	1.5	1.3	1.1
Goury	4.0	3.7	3.3	3.0	2.7	2.4	2.0	1.7	1.4	1.1	0.7	0.4
Dielette	4.1	3.8	3.4	3.1	2.7	2.4	2.0	1.7	1.3	1.0	0.7	0.3
Carteret	4.5	4.1	3.7	3.3	2.9	2.6	2.2	1.8	1.4	1.1	0.7	0.4
Granville..................	5.3	4.8	4.2	3.7	3.2	2.7	2.2	1.7	1.2	0.8	0.5	0.1
Saint Malo	5.0	4.5	4.1	3.6	3.2	2.7	2.3	1.8	1.4	1.1	0.7	0.4
All Hbrs, St Brieuc Bay	4.7	4.3	3.9	3.5	3.1	2.6	2.2	1.8	1.4	1.1	0.7	0.4
Paimpol	3.9	3.5	3.1	2.7	2.3	1.8	1.4	1.0	0.6	0.3	-0.1	-0.4
Ile de Bréhat	4.6	4.2	3.8	3.4	2.9	2.5	2.1	1.6	1.2	0.9	0.6	0.3
Lezardrieux	3.9	3.6	3.2	2.9	2.6	2.3	1.9	1.6	1.3	1.0	0.7	0.4
ISLANDS OFF											
Braye, Alderney........	2.6	2.4	2.2	2.0	1.7	1.5	1.3	1.0	0.8	0.6	0.5	0.3
St Peter Port & Sark....	4.1	3.7	3.3	2.9	2.5	2.2	1.8	1.4	1.0	0.7	0.3	0.0
St Helier, Jersey	4.7	4.3	3.9	3.5	3.0	2.6	2.2	1.7	1.3	1.0	0.6	0.3
St Catherine, Jersey	4.9	4.4	4.0	3.5	3.1	2.6	2.2	1.7	1.3	1.0	0.6	0.3
Les Minquiers	4.6	4.2	3.8	3.4	3.0	2.5	2.1	1.7	1.3	1.0	0.7	0.4
Iles Chausey	5.0	4.6	4.2	3.8	3.3	2.9	2.5	2.0	1.6	1.2	0.9	0.5

Tidal Stream Rates

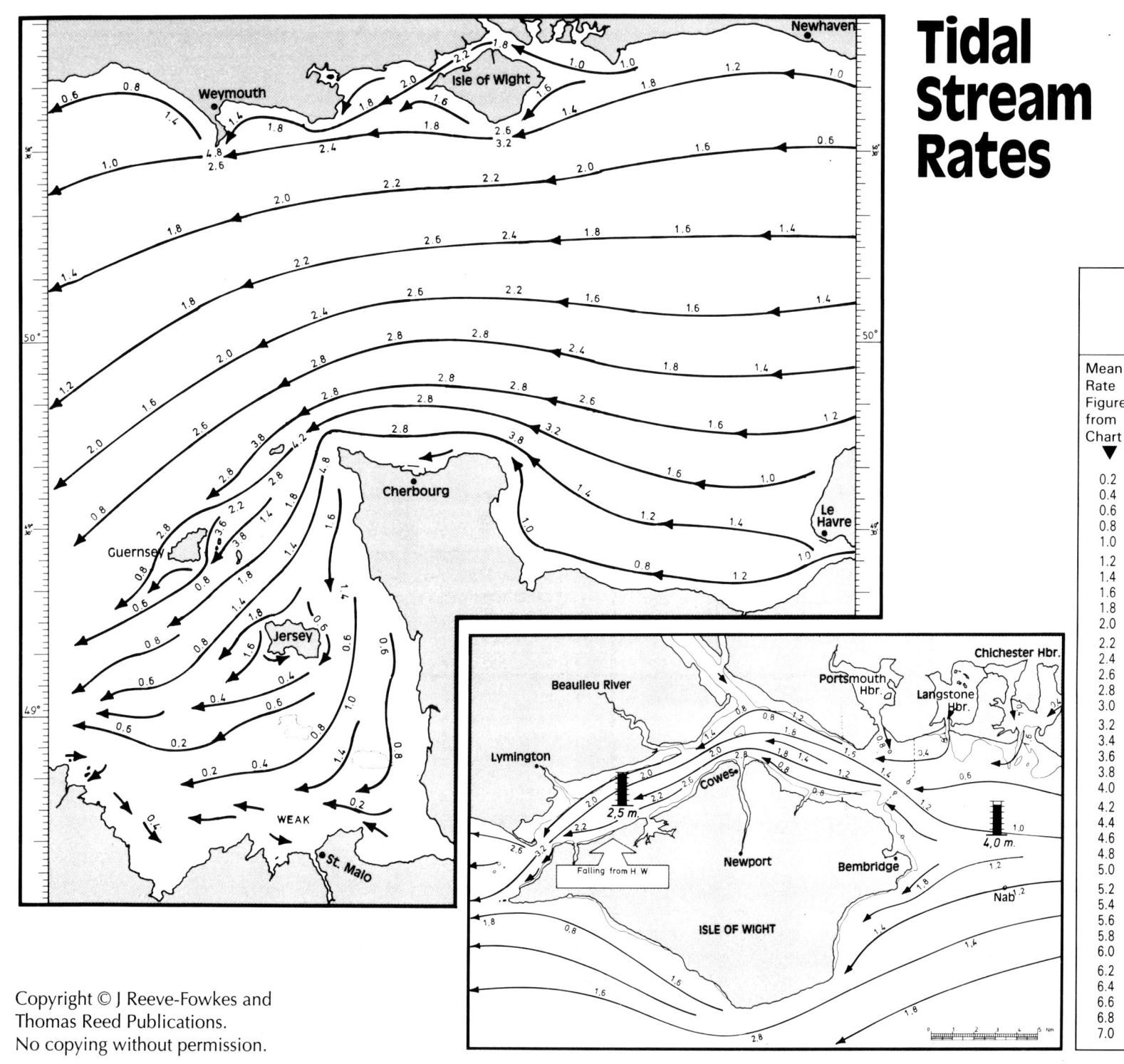

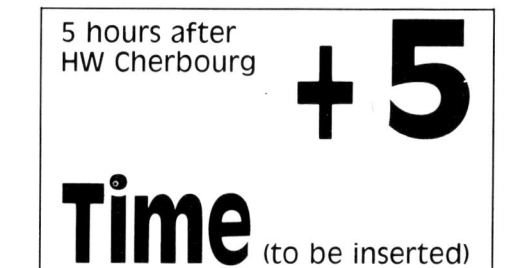

5 hours after HW Cherbourg **+5**

Time (to be inserted)

Stream Rate Conversion Table

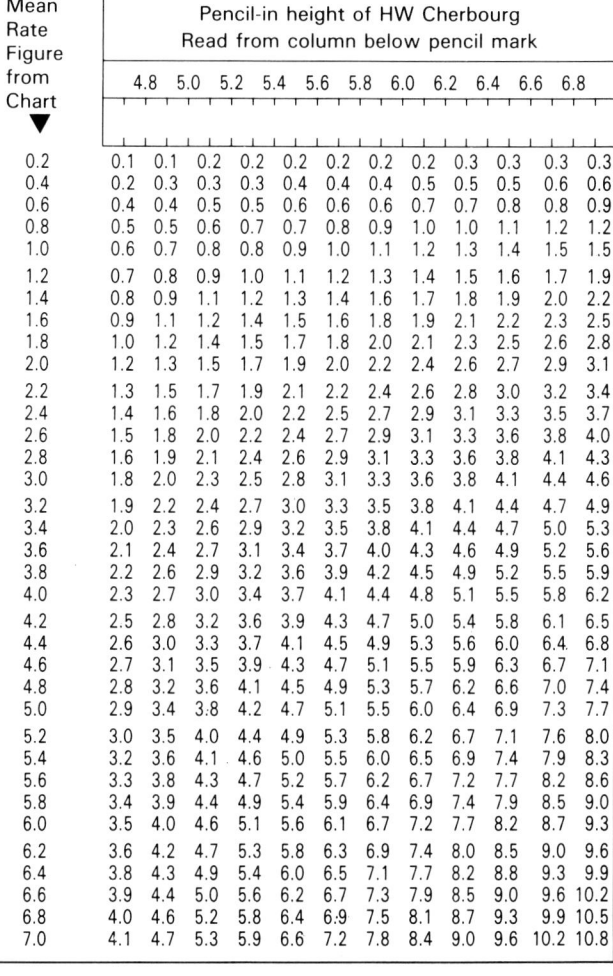

Mean Rate Figure from Chart ▼	\multicolumn{11}{c}{Pencil-in height of HW Cherbourg — Read from column below pencil mark}
	4.8	5.0	5.2	5.4	5.6	5.8	6.0	6.2	6.4	6.6	6.8
0.2	0.1	0.1	0.2	0.2	0.2	0.2	0.2	0.2	0.3	0.3	0.3
0.4	0.2	0.3	0.3	0.3	0.4	0.4	0.4	0.5	0.5	0.5	0.6
0.6	0.4	0.4	0.5	0.5	0.6	0.6	0.6	0.7	0.7	0.8	0.8
0.8	0.5	0.5	0.6	0.7	0.7	0.8	0.9	1.0	1.0	1.1	1.2
1.0	0.6	0.7	0.8	0.8	0.9	1.0	1.1	1.2	1.3	1.4	1.5
1.2	0.7	0.8	0.9	1.0	1.1	1.2	1.3	1.4	1.5	1.6	1.7
1.4	0.8	0.9	1.1	1.2	1.3	1.4	1.6	1.7	1.8	1.9	2.0
1.6	0.9	1.1	1.2	1.4	1.5	1.6	1.8	1.9	2.1	2.2	2.3
1.8	1.0	1.2	1.4	1.5	1.7	1.8	2.0	2.1	2.3	2.5	2.6
2.0	1.2	1.3	1.5	1.7	1.9	2.0	2.2	2.4	2.6	2.7	2.9
2.2	1.3	1.5	1.7	1.9	2.1	2.2	2.4	2.6	2.8	3.0	3.2
2.4	1.4	1.6	1.8	2.0	2.2	2.5	2.7	2.9	3.1	3.3	3.5
2.6	1.5	1.8	2.0	2.2	2.5	2.7	2.9	3.1	3.3	3.6	3.8
2.8	1.6	1.9	2.1	2.4	2.6	2.9	3.1	3.3	3.6	3.8	4.1
3.0	1.8	2.0	2.3	2.5	2.8	3.1	3.3	3.6	3.8	4.1	4.4
3.2	1.9	2.2	2.4	2.7	3.0	3.3	3.5	3.8	4.1	4.4	4.7
3.4	2.0	2.3	2.6	2.9	3.2	3.5	3.8	4.1	4.4	4.7	5.0
3.6	2.1	2.4	2.7	3.1	3.4	3.7	4.0	4.3	4.6	4.9	5.2
3.8	2.2	2.6	2.9	3.2	3.6	3.9	4.2	4.5	4.9	5.2	5.5
4.0	2.3	2.7	3.0	3.4	3.7	4.1	4.4	4.8	5.1	5.5	5.8
4.2	2.5	2.8	3.2	3.6	3.9	4.3	4.7	5.0	5.4	5.8	6.1
4.4	2.6	3.0	3.3	3.7	4.1	4.5	4.9	5.3	5.6	6.0	6.4
4.6	2.7	3.1	3.5	3.9	4.3	4.7	5.1	5.5	5.9	6.3	6.7
4.8	2.8	3.2	3.6	4.1	4.5	4.9	5.3	5.7	6.2	6.6	7.0
5.0	2.9	3.4	3.8	4.2	4.7	5.1	5.5	6.0	6.4	6.9	7.3
5.2	3.0	3.5	4.0	4.4	4.9	5.3	5.8	6.2	6.7	7.1	7.6
5.4	3.2	3.6	4.1	4.6	5.0	5.5	6.0	6.5	6.9	7.4	7.9
5.6	3.3	3.8	4.3	4.7	5.2	5.7	6.2	6.7	7.2	7.7	8.2
5.8	3.4	3.9	4.4	4.9	5.4	5.9	6.4	6.9	7.4	7.9	8.5
6.0	3.5	4.0	4.6	5.1	5.6	6.1	6.7	7.2	7.7	8.2	8.7
6.2	3.6	4.2	4.7	5.3	5.8	6.3	6.9	7.4	8.0	8.5	9.0
6.4	3.8	4.3	4.9	5.4	6.0	6.5	7.1	7.7	8.2	8.8	9.3
6.6	3.9	4.4	5.0	5.6	6.2	6.7	7.3	7.9	8.5	9.0	9.6
6.8	4.0	4.6	5.2	5.8	6.4	6.9	7.5	8.1	8.7	9.3	9.9
7.0	4.1	4.7	5.3	5.9	6.6	7.2	7.8	8.4	9.0	9.6	10.2

Copyright © J Reeve-Fowkes and Thomas Reed Publications. No copying without permission.

+6
6 hours after HW Cherbourg

Tidal Heights

Copyright © J Reeve-Fowkes and
Thomas Reed Publications.
No copying without permission.

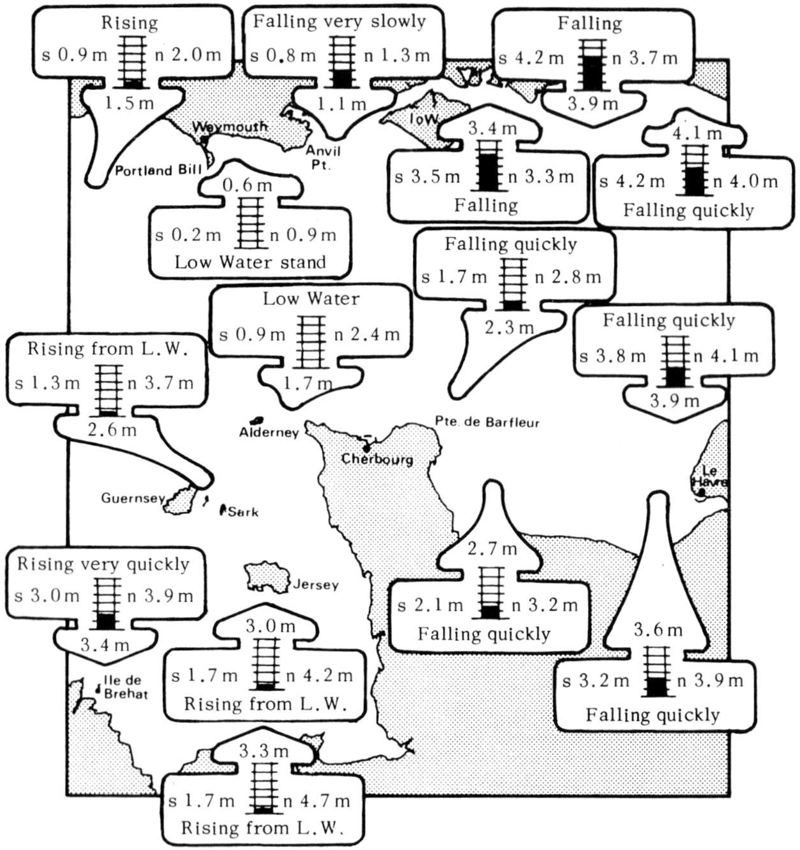

TIDAL HEIGHTS — PORTS & PLACES

Pencil-in height of ▶ HW Cherbourg	4.8	5.0	5.2	5.4	5.6	5.8	6.0	6.2	6.4	6.6	6.8
ENGLAND											
Lyme Regis..............	2.2	2.1	1.9	1.8	1.7	1.5	1.4	1.2	1.1	1.0	1.0	0.9
Bridport....................	2.1	2.0	1.8	1.7	1.6	1.5	1.3	1.2	1.1	1.0	1.0	0.9
Portland & Weymouth..	1.0	0.9	0.9	0.8	0.7	0.6	0.5	0.4	0.3	0.3	0.3	0.3
Lulworth Cove	1.1	1.0	1.0	0.9	0.8	0.7	0.6	0.5	0.4	0.4	0.3	0.3
Swanage	1.5	1.4	1.4	1.3	1.3	1.3	1.2	1.1	1.1	1.0	0.9	0.9
Poole entrance	1.4	1.4	1.4	1.4	1.3	1.3	1.2	1.2	1.1	1.0	1.0	0.9
Poole Town Quay........	1.6	1.6	1.6	1.6	1.6	1.6	1.6	1.5	1.5	1.5	1.5	1.5
Christchurch appr'ch ...	1.0	1.0	1.0	1.0	1.0	1.0	0.9	0.9	0.8	0.8	0.8	0.9
Christchurch Hbr.........	1.0	1.0	1.0	1.0	1.0	1.0	1.0	1.0	0.9	0.9	0.9	0.9
Lymington	2.2	2.2	2.2	2.2	2.3	2.3	2.3	2.4	2.4	2.4	2.5	2.5
Yarmouth I. o. W.	2.1	2.1	2.1	2.1	2.2	2.2	2.2	2.2	2.2	2.2	2.3	2.3
Cowes I. o. W.	2.8	2.9	2.9	3.0	3.0	3.1	3.2	3.3	3.4	3.4	3.4	3.4
Sandown I. o. W.	2.5	2.5	2.5	2.5	2.6	2.6	2.6	2.7	2.7	2.8	2.8	2.9
Southampton	3.0	3.1	3.3	3.4	3.5	3.7	3.8	4.0	4.1	4.2	4.2	4.3
Portsmouth	3.2	3.3	3.3	3.4	3.5	3.6	3.7	3.8	3.9	4.0	4.0	4.1
Chichester entrance.....	3.2	3.3	3.5	3.6	3.7	3.8	3.9	4.0	4.1	4.2	4.2	4.3
Selsey Bill.................	3.5	3.6	3.8	3.9	4.0	4.1	4.2	4.3	4.4	4.5	4.5	4.6
Littlehampton Hbr........	3.6	3.7	3.9	4.0	4.2	4.3	4.5	4.6	4.8	4.9	5.0	5.1
Littlehampton appr'ch ..	3.6	3.7	3.9	4.0	4.1	4.3	4.4	4.6	4.7	4.8	4.9	5.0
Shoreham	3.8	3.8	3.8	3.8	3.9	3.9	3.9	4.0	4.0	4.0	4.1	4.1
Brighton	3.8	3.8	3.8	3.8	3.9	3.9	3.9	4.0	4.0	4.0	4.1	4.1
Newhaven	3.8	3.8	3.8	3.8	3.9	3.9	3.9	4.0	4.0	4.0	4.1	4.1
FRANCE											
Le Havre	4.2	4.1	4.1	4.0	3.9	3.9	3.8	3.8	3.7	3.6	3.5	3.4
Honfleur	4.6	4.5	4.5	4.4	4.3	4.2	4.1	4.0	3.9	3.8	3.8	3.7
Trouville (Deauville)	4.2	4.1	3.9	3.8	3.7	3.6	3.4	3.3	3.2	3.1	3.0	2.9
Ouistreham................	3.9	3.8	3.6	3.5	3.4	3.2	3.1	2.9	2.8	2.7	2.6	2.5
Courseulles	3.2	3.1	2.9	2.8	2.7	2.6	2.4	2.3	2.2	2.1	2.0	1.9
Arromanches	3.8	3.7	3.5	3.4	3.3	3.1	3.0	2.8	2.7	2.6	2.5	2.4
Port-en-Bessin	3.6	3.5	3.3	3.2	3.0	2.9	2.7	2.6	2.4	2.3	2.1	2.0
Saint-Vaast-la-Hougue..	3.1	3.0	2.8	2.7	2.6	2.5	2.3	2.2	2.1	1.9	1.8	1.6
Barfleur	3.0	2.9	2.7	2.6	2.4	2.3	2.1	2.0	1.8	1.6	1.4	1.2
Cherbourg	3.0	2.8	2.6	2.4	2.2	1.9	1.7	1.5	1.3	1.1	0.8	0.6
Omonville	2.9	2.7	2.5	2.3	2.1	1.8	1.6	1.4	1.2	0.9	0.7	0.4
Goury	4.0	3.7	3.3	3.0	2.7	2.3	2.0	1.6	1.3	0.9	0.6	0.2
Dielette	4.4	4.0	3.6	3.2	2.9	2.5	2.1	1.8	1.4	1.1	0.7	0.4
Carteret	4.6	4.3	3.9	3.6	3.2	2.9	2.5	2.2	1.8	1.5	1.2	0.9
Granville	5.7	5.2	4.8	4.3	3.8	3.3	2.9	1.4	1.9	1.6	1.3	1.0
Saint Malo	5.6	5.1	4.7	4.2	3.7	3.2	2.7	2.2	1.7	1.4	1.1	0.8
All Hbrs, St Brieuc Bay	5.2	4.9	4.5	4.2	3.9	3.6	3.3	3.0	2.7	2.4	2.2	1.9
Paimpol....................	4.5	4.2	3.8	3.5	3.2	2.9	2.5	2.2	1.9	1.6	1.4	1.1
Ile de Bréhat	5.1	4.7	4.3	3.9	3.5	3.1	2.7	2.3	1.9	1.6	1.4	1.1
Lezardrieux	4.5	4.3	4.1	3.9	3.6	3.4	3.2	2.9	2.7	2.5	2.3	2.1
ISLANDS OFF											
Braye, Alderney...........	2.6	2.4	2.2	2.0	1.7	1.5	1.3	1.0	0.8	0.6	0.4	0.2
St Peter Port & Sark	4.2	3.9	3.5	3.2	2.9	2.5	2.2	1.8	1.5	1.2	1.0	0.7
St Helier, Jersey	4.8	4.4	4.0	3.6	3.3	2.9	2.5	2.2	1.8	1.5	1.1	0.8
St Catherine, Jersey	5.1	4.6	4.2	3.7	3.2	2.8	2.4	1.9	1.5	1.2	0.8	0.5
Les Minquiers	4.8	4.4	4.0	3.6	3.3	2.9	2.5	2.2	1.8	1.5	1.3	1.0
Iles Chausey	5.4	5.0	4.6	4.2	3.8	3.3	2.9	2.5	2.1	1.8	1.4	1.1

Tidal Heights (offshore)

The broad arrows apply to the time entered on the adjacent page. Each arrow gives the following information:

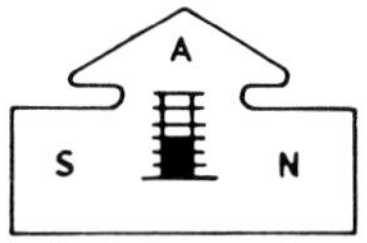

A Average Height of Tide. This is the height of tide, in metres, above Chart Datum, at the position indicated by the arrow. Although only an average height, this figure is sufficiently accurate for use for most coastal navigation.
S Height of Tide at Springs.
N Height of Tide at Neaps.
The Tidal Gauge gives a visual display of the approximate state of the tide with the vertical movement of tide described briefly above or below.

Rising
s 0.9 m n 2.0 m
1.5 m

Falling very slowly
s 0.8 m n 1.3 m
1.1 m

Falling
s 4.2 m n 3.7 m
3.9 m

3.4 m
s 3.5 m n 3.3 m
Falling

4.1 m
s 4.2 m n 4.0 m
Falling quickly

0.6 m
s 0.2 m n 0.9 m
Low Water stand

Falling quickly
s 1.7 m n 2.8 m
2.3 m

Low Water
s 0.9 m n 2.4 m
1.7 m

Falling quickly
s 3.8 m n 4.1 m
3.9 m

Rising from L.W.
s 1.3 m n 3.7 m
2.6 m

Rising very quickly
s 3.0 m n 3.9 m
3.4 m

3.0 m
s 1.7 m n 4.2 m
Rising from L.W.

2.7 m
s 2.1 m n 3.2 m
Falling quickly

3.6 m
s 3.2 m n 3.9 m
Falling quickly

3.3 m
s 1.7 m n 4.7 m
Rising from L.W.

Weymouth
Anvil Pt.
Portland Bill
I o W
Alderney
Pte. de Barfleur
Cherbourg
Guernsey
Sark
Jersey
Ile de Bréhat
Le Havre

Tidal Stream Rates

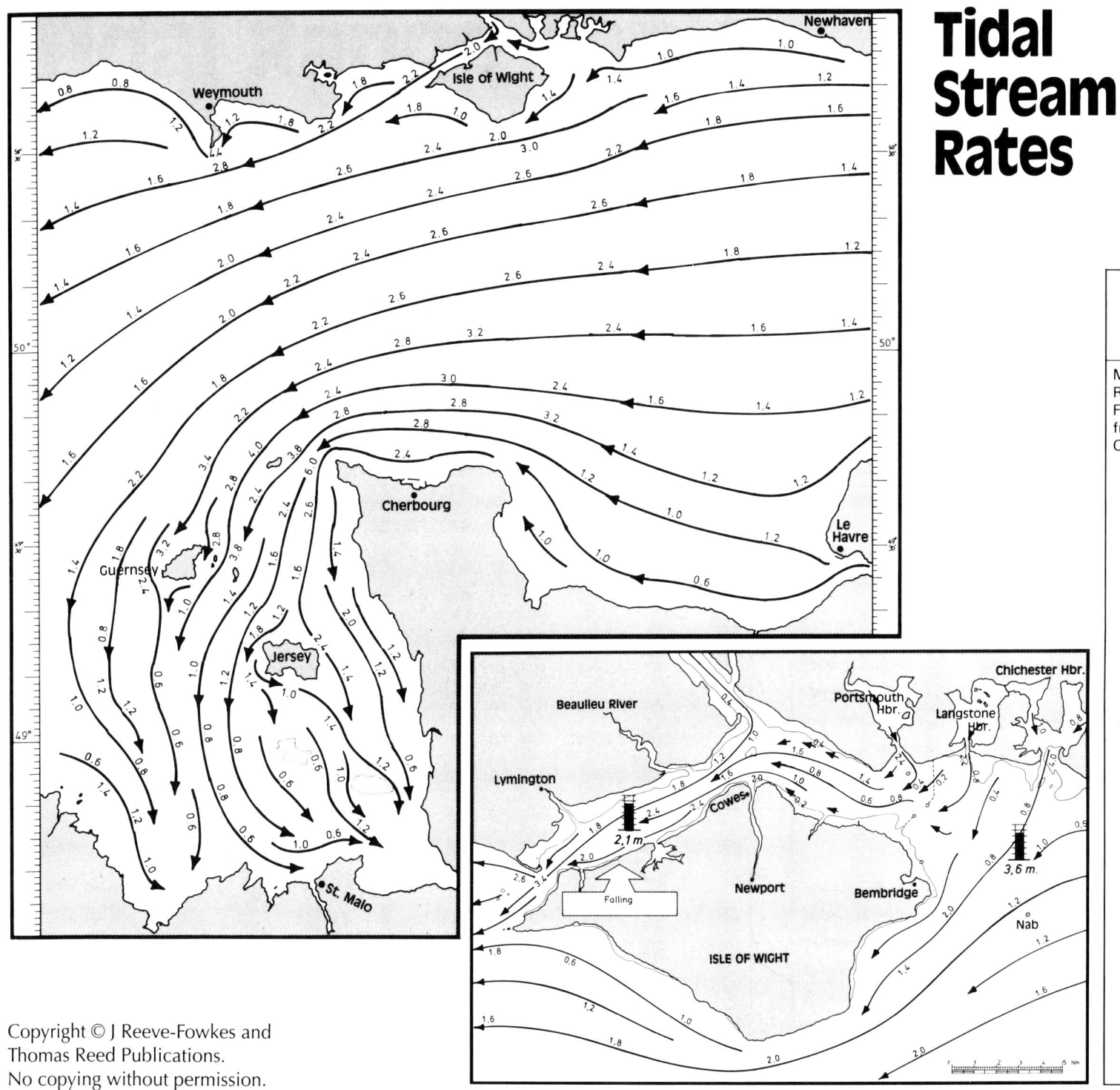

+6 6 hours after HW Cherbourg

Time (to be inserted)

Stream Rate Conversion Table

Mean Rate Figure from Chart ▼	Pencil-in height of HW Cherbourg Read from column below pencil mark										
	4.8	5.0	5.2	5.4	5.6	5.8	6.0	6.2	6.4	6.6	6.8
0.2	0.1	0.1	0.2	0.2	0.2	0.2	0.2	0.2	0.3	0.3	0.3
0.4	0.2	0.3	0.3	0.3	0.4	0.4	0.4	0.5	0.5	0.6	0.6
0.6	0.4	0.4	0.5	0.5	0.6	0.6	0.6	0.7	0.7	0.8	0.8
0.8	0.5	0.5	0.6	0.7	0.7	0.8	0.9	1.0	1.1	1.2	1.2
1.0	0.6	0.7	0.8	0.8	0.9	1.0	1.1	1.2	1.3	1.4	1.5	1.5
1.2	0.7	0.8	0.9	1.0	1.1	1.2	1.3	1.4	1.5	1.6	1.7	1.9
1.4	0.8	0.9	1.1	1.2	1.3	1.4	1.6	1.7	1.8	1.9	2.0	2.2
1.6	0.9	1.1	1.2	1.4	1.5	1.6	1.8	1.9	2.1	2.2	2.3	2.5
1.8	1.0	1.2	1.4	1.5	1.7	1.8	2.0	2.1	2.3	2.5	2.6	2.8
2.0	1.2	1.3	1.5	1.7	1.9	2.0	2.2	2.4	2.6	2.7	2.9	3.1
2.2	1.3	1.5	1.7	1.9	2.1	2.2	2.4	2.6	2.8	3.0	3.2	3.4
2.4	1.4	1.6	1.8	2.0	2.2	2.5	2.7	2.9	3.1	3.3	3.5	3.7
2.6	1.5	1.8	2.0	2.2	2.4	2.7	2.9	3.1	3.3	3.6	3.8	4.0
2.8	1.6	1.9	2.1	2.4	2.6	2.9	3.1	3.3	3.6	3.8	4.1	4.3
3.0	1.8	2.0	2.3	2.5	2.8	3.1	3.3	3.6	3.8	4.1	4.4	4.6
3.2	1.9	2.2	2.4	2.7	3.0	3.3	3.5	3.8	4.1	4.4	4.7	4.9
3.4	2.0	2.3	2.6	2.9	3.2	3.5	3.8	4.1	4.4	4.7	5.0	5.3
3.6	2.1	2.4	2.7	3.1	3.4	3.7	4.0	4.3	4.6	4.9	5.2	5.6
3.8	2.2	2.6	2.9	3.2	3.6	3.9	4.2	4.5	4.9	5.2	5.5	5.9
4.0	2.3	2.7	3.0	3.4	3.7	4.1	4.4	4.8	5.1	5.5	5.8	6.2
4.2	2.5	2.8	3.2	3.6	3.9	4.3	4.7	5.0	5.4	5.8	6.1	6.5
4.4	2.6	3.0	3.3	3.7	4.1	4.5	4.9	5.3	5.6	6.0	6.4	6.8
4.6	2.7	3.1	3.5	3.9	4.3	4.7	5.1	5.5	5.9	6.3	6.7	7.1
4.8	2.8	3.2	3.6	4.1	4.5	4.9	5.3	5.7	6.2	6.6	7.0	7.4
5.0	2.9	3.4	3.8	4.2	4.7	5.1	5.5	6.0	6.4	6.9	7.3	7.7
5.2	3.0	3.5	4.0	4.4	4.9	5.3	5.8	6.2	6.7	7.1	7.6	8.0
5.4	3.2	3.6	4.1	4.6	5.0	5.5	6.0	6.5	6.9	7.4	7.9	8.3
5.6	3.3	3.8	4.3	4.7	5.2	5.7	6.2	6.7	7.2	7.7	8.2	8.6
5.8	3.4	3.9	4.4	4.9	5.4	5.9	6.4	6.9	7.4	7.9	8.5	9.0
6.0	3.5	4.0	4.6	5.1	5.6	6.1	6.7	7.2	7.7	8.2	8.7	9.3
6.2	3.6	4.2	4.7	5.3	5.8	6.3	6.9	7.4	8.0	8.5	9.0	9.6
6.4	3.8	4.3	4.9	5.4	6.0	6.5	7.1	7.7	8.2	8.8	9.3	9.9
6.6	3.9	4.4	5.0	5.6	6.2	6.7	7.3	7.9	8.5	9.0	9.6	10.2
6.8	4.0	4.6	5.2	5.8	6.4	6.9	7.5	8.1	8.7	9.3	9.9	10.5
7.0	4.1	4.7	5.3	5.9	6.6	7.2	7.8	8.4	9.0	9.6	10.2	10.8

Copyright © J Reeve-Fowkes and Thomas Reed Publications.
No copying without permission.

The Yachtsman's Tidal Atlas
CHANNEL PORTS & APPROACHES

TIDAL STREAM RATES & TIDAL HEIGHTS
for the areas
The Solent and approaches
Portland Bill
Alderney and Cherbourg
Poole
Russel Channels
St. Helier approaches
St. Malo approaches
Ile de Bréhat
Le Havre
The Scilly Isles
Ile d'Ouessant and Chenal du Four

Section 1
The Solent and approaches
Portland Bill
Alderney and Cherbourg
Poole
Russel Channels
St. Helier approaches
St. Malo approaches
Ile de Brehat
Le Havre

PORTLAND RACE
An inshore passage between Portland Bill and the Race is possible in moderate weather, but careful timing is advised: these times are noted on the Tidal Stream Chartlet for Portland Bill.

ALDERNEY RACE
Passage through the race should if possible be avoided when wind against tide conditions prevail. On windless days passages south or southwest through the Alderney Race on the ebb stream will be comfortable. However, when heading north or northeast on the flood stream, small areas of turbulence occur as Alderney is approached and passed, coinciding with changes in the depth of water. As a yacht passes north of a line from Quenard Point to Cap de la Hague, observations by the author indicate an area of confused water which extends 6 or 7 miles northwards into the English Channel during the period −2 to +1½ hours HW Cherbourg: it is also likely that the rate of flood streams in this area exceeds predictions. These uncomfortable conditions can be avoided if a passage is planned so as to pass through the area at slack water.

THE SWINGE AND ORTAC CHANNEL
Race conditions with overfalls will prevail in these channels during both the flood and ebb and it is therefore advisable to negotiate them at slack water.

LE HAVRE
Streams in the Seine Maritime can be very much influenced by rainfall and in particular by the spate of water in the Spring which is caused by thawing snow in the mountains. The effect is to delay the flood stream and to reduce the effective speed of a vessel proceeding upstream, although it is usually possible even under these circumstances for a yacht to reach Rouen on a single tide.

6 hours before
HW Cherbourg

-6

Time (to be inserted)

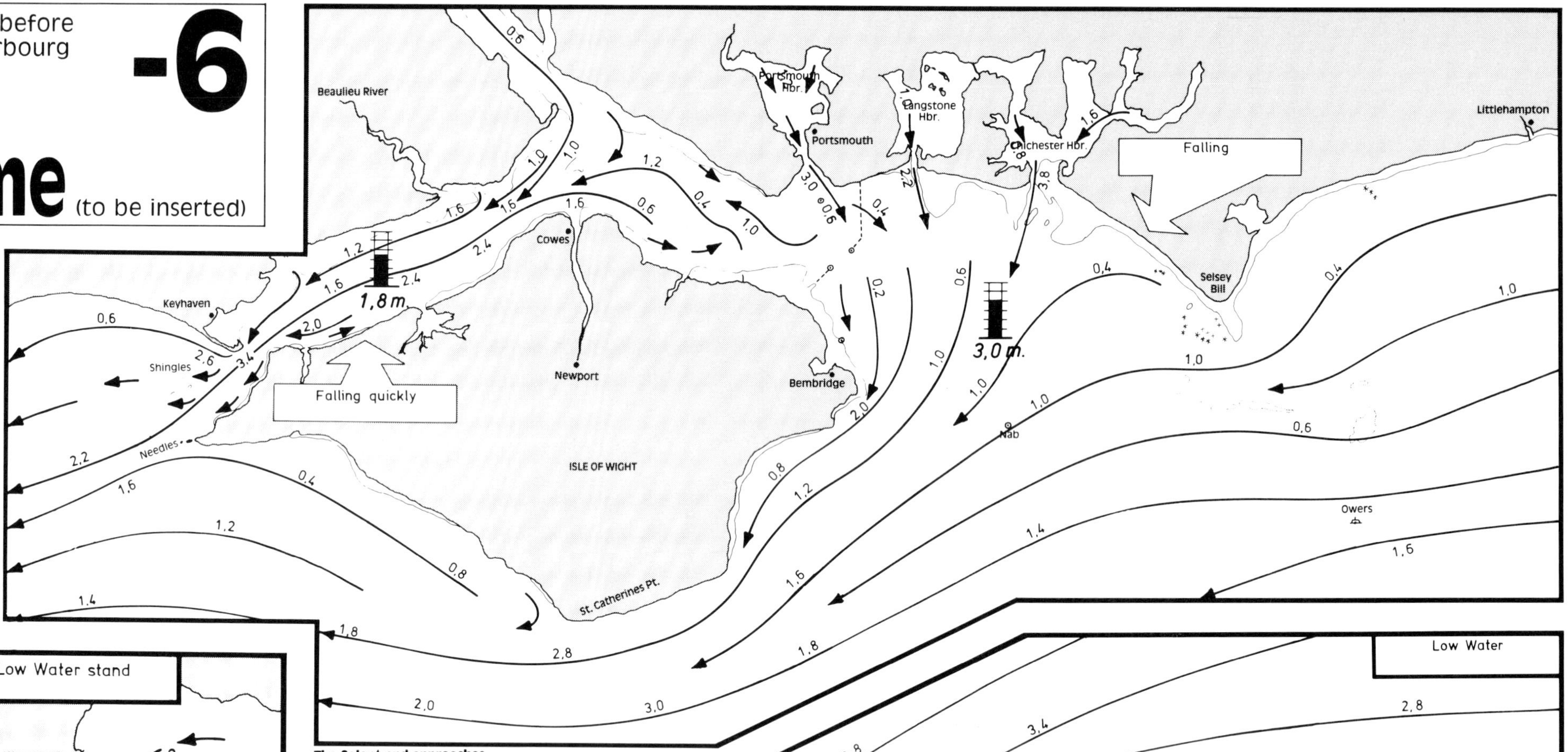

The Solent and approaches

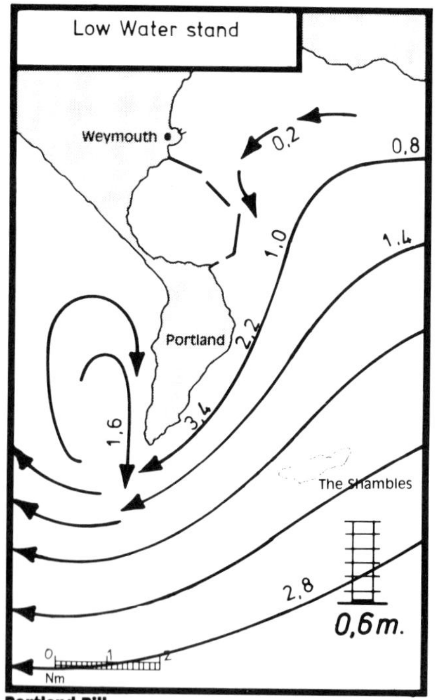

Portland Bill

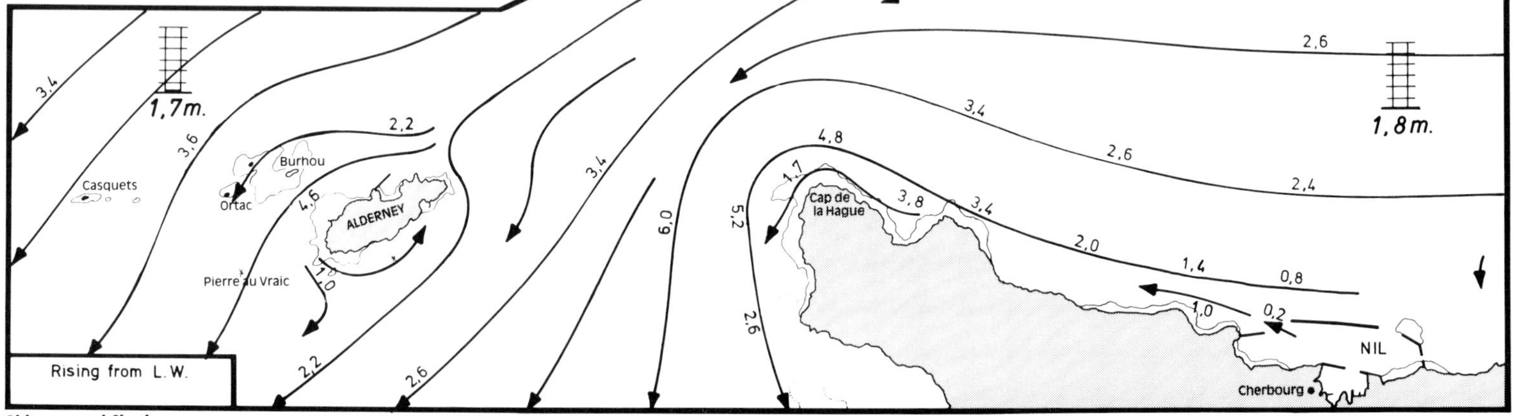

Alderney and Cherbourg

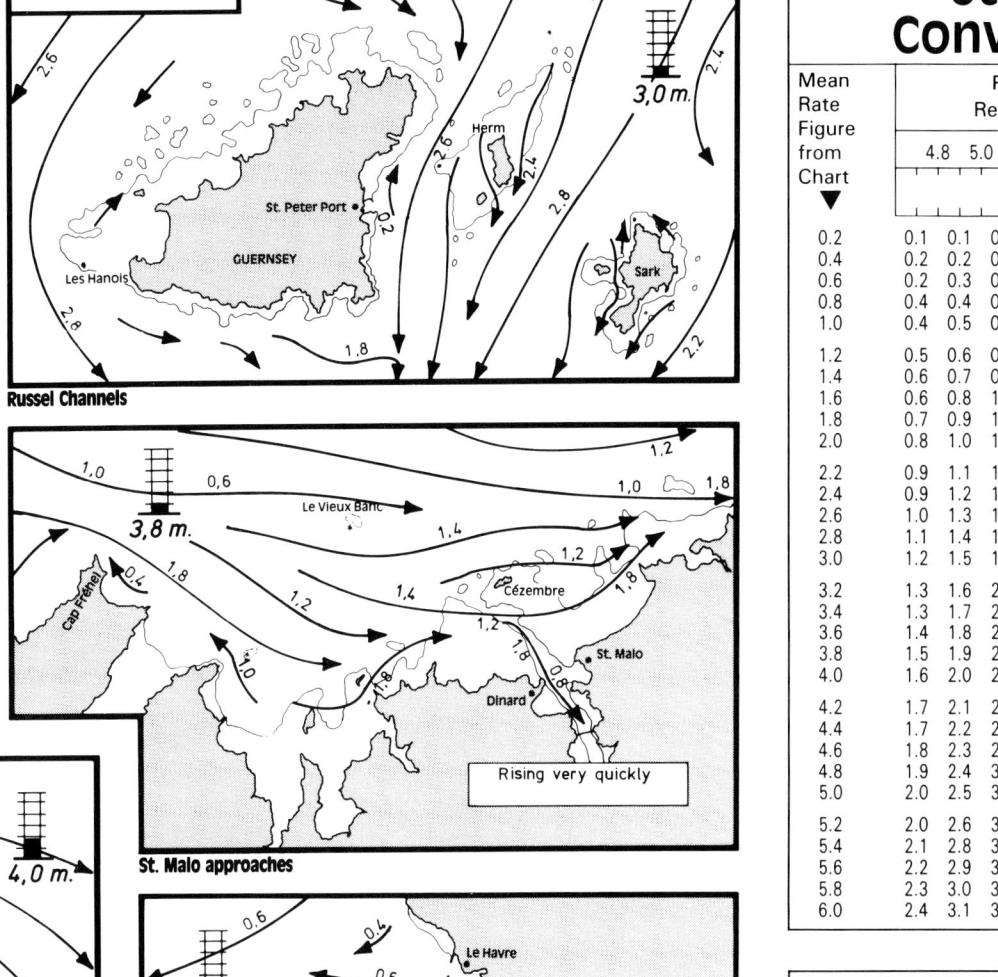

Stream Rate Conversion Table

-6

Mean Rate Figure from Chart ▼	Pencil-in height of HW Cherbourg Read from column below pencil mark											
	4.8	5.0	5.2	5.4	5.6	5.8	6.0	6.2	6.4	6.6	6.8
0.2	0.1	0.1	0.1	0.1	0.2	0.2	0.2	0.2	0.3	0.3	0.3
0.4	0.2	0.2	0.2	0.3	0.3	0.4	0.4	0.5	0.5	0.6	0.7
0.6	0.2	0.3	0.4	0.4	0.5	0.6	0.7	0.7	0.8	0.9	1.0
0.8	0.4	0.4	0.5	0.6	0.7	0.8	0.9	1.0	1.1	1.2	1.3
1.0	0.4	0.5	0.6	0.7	0.9	1.0	1.1	1.2	1.3	1.4	1.5
1.2	0.5	0.6	0.7	0.9	1.0	1.2	1.3	1.4	1.6	1.7	1.9
1.4	0.6	0.7	0.9	1.0	1.2	1.4	1.5	1.7	1.8	2.0	2.2
1.6	0.6	0.8	1.0	1.2	1.4	1.6	1.7	1.9	2.1	2.3	2.5
1.8	0.7	0.9	1.1	1.3	1.5	1.7	2.0	2.2	2.4	2.6	2.8
2.0	0.8	1.0	1.2	1.5	1.7	1.9	2.2	2.4	2.6	2.9	3.1
2.2	0.9	1.1	1.4	1.6	1.9	2.1	2.3	2.6	2.9	3.2	3.4
2.4	0.9	1.2	1.5	1.8	2.1	2.3	2.6	2.9	3.2	3.4	3.7
2.6	1.0	1.3	1.6	1.9	2.2	2.5	2.8	3.1	3.4	3.7	4.0
2.8	1.1	1.4	1.7	2.1	2.4	2.7	3.0	3.4	3.7	4.0	4.3
3.0	1.2	1.5	1.9	2.2	2.6	2.9	3.2	3.6	4.0	4.3	4.6
3.2	1.3	1.6	2.0	2.4	2.7	3.1	3.4	3.8	4.2	4.6	4.9
3.4	1.3	1.7	2.1	2.5	2.9	3.3	3.7	4.1	4.5	4.9	5.3
3.6	1.4	1.8	2.2	2.7	3.1	3.5	3.9	4.3	4.7	5.2	5.6
3.8	1.5	1.9	2.4	2.8	3.3	3.7	4.1	4.6	5.0	5.4	5.9
4.0	1.6	2.0	2.5	3.0	3.4	3.9	4.3	4.8	5.3	5.7	6.2
4.2	1.7	2.1	2.6	3.1	3.6	4.1	4.6	5.0	5.5	6.0	6.5
4.4	1.7	2.2	2.7	3.3	3.8	4.3	4.8	5.3	5.8	6.3	6.8
4.6	1.8	2.3	2.9	3.4	3.9	4.5	5.0	5.5	6.1	6.6	7.1
4.8	1.9	2.4	3.0	3.6	4.1	4.7	5.2	5.8	6.3	6.9	7.4
5.0	2.0	2.5	3.1	3.7	4.3	4.9	5.4	6.0	6.6	7.2	7.7
5.2	2.0	2.6	3.2	3.8	4.4	5.0	5.6	6.2	6.8	7.4	8.0
5.4	2.1	2.8	3.4	4.0	4.6	5.2	5.7	6.5	7.1	7.7	8.4
5.6	2.2	2.9	3.5	4.1	4.8	5.4	6.1	6.7	7.4	8.0	8.7
5.8	2.3	3.0	3.6	4.3	5.0	5.6	6.3	7.0	7.6	8.3	9.0
6.0	2.4	3.1	3.7	4.4	5.1	5.8	6.5	7.2	7.9	8.6	9.3

TIDAL HEIGHTS — PORTS & PLACES

Pencil-in height of HW Cherbourg ▶	4.8	5.0	5.2	5.4	5.6	5.8	6.0	6.2	6.4	6.6	6.8
Lymington (& Yarmouth approx)	1.9	1.9	1.9	1.9	1.9	1.9	1.9	1.9	1.9	1.9	1.9
Portsmouth (Chichester entrance & Cowes approx)	2.7	2.8	3.0	3.1	3.2	3.3	3.4	3.5	3.6	3.6	3.7
Cherbourg (& Omonville approx)	2.8	2.6	2.4	2.2	2.0	1.8	1.6	1.4	1.2	0.9	0.7
Braye, Alderney	2.7	2.5	2.3	2.1	1.8	1.6	1.4	1.1	0.9	0.7	0.6
Weymouth	0.9	0.8	0.8	0.7	0.6	0.5	0.5	0.4	0.3	0.3	0.2
Poole entrance	1.3	1.2	1.2	1.1	1.1	1.0	0.9	0.9	0.8	0.7	0.6
Poole Town Quay	1.6	1.5	1.5	1.4	1.4	1.4	1.3	1.3	1.2	1.1	1.1
St Peter Port & Sark	4.6	4.3	3.9	3.6	3.3	3.0	2.6	2.3	2.0	1.7	1.5
St Helier	5.5	5.1	4.7	4.3	3.9	3.4	3.0	2.6	2.2	1.9	1.6
St Malo	6.2	5.7	5.3	4.8	4.3	3.8	3.3	2.8	2.3	2.0	1.7
Lezardrieux	5.1	4.9	4.5	4.2	4.0	3.8	3.5	3.2	3.2	3.0	2.7
Paimpol	5.2	4.9	4.5	4.2	3.9	3.5	3.2	2.8	2.5	2.2	1.9
Le Havre	3.7	3.6	3.6	3.5	3.4	3.4	3.3	3.2	3.1	3.0	2.9

Copyright © J Reeve-Fowkes and Thomas Reed Publications.
No copying without permission.

5 hours before
HW Cherbourg

-5

Time (to be inserted)

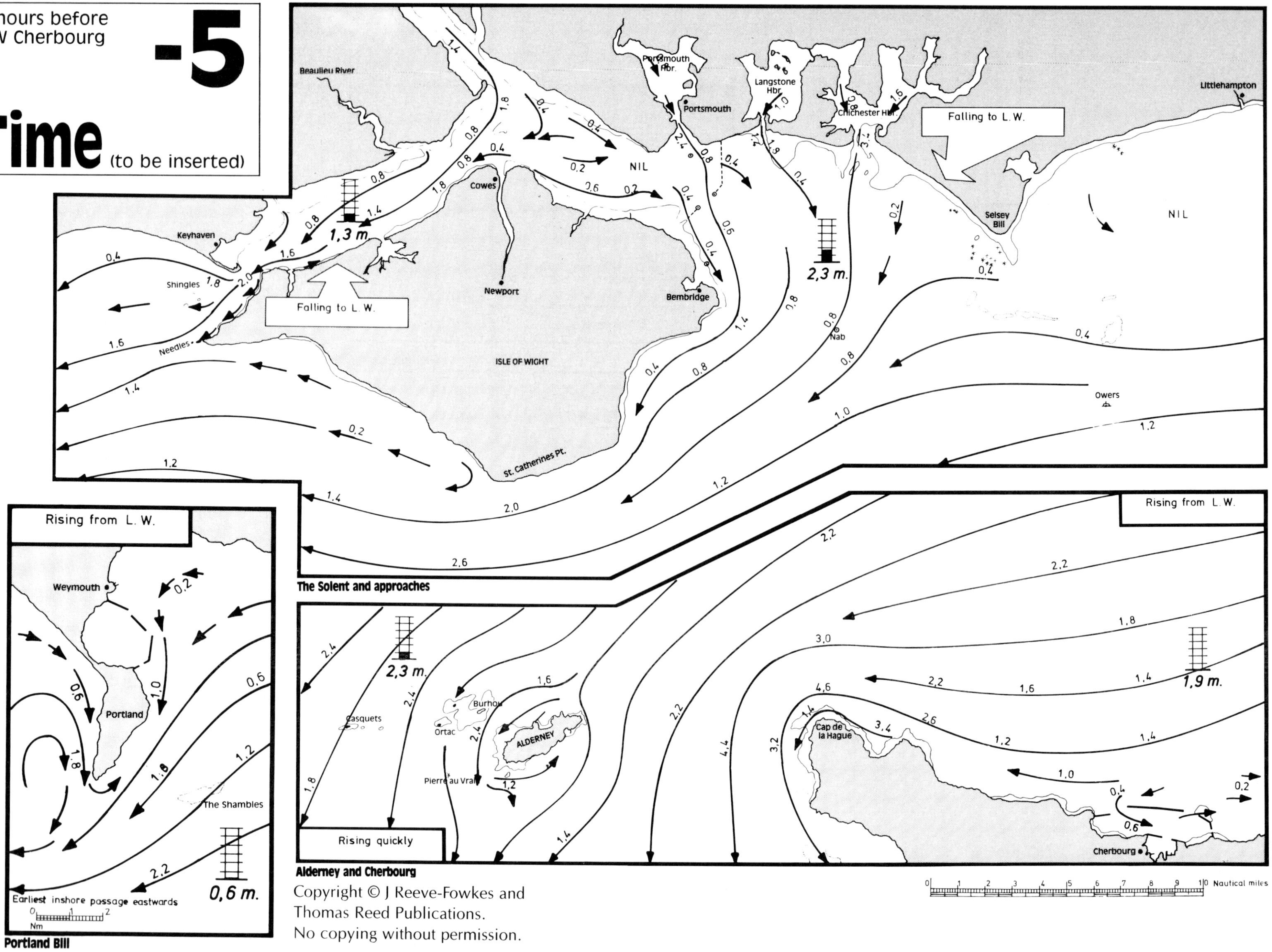

Stream Rate Conversion Table

−5

Mean Rate Figure from Chart ▼	Pencil-in height of HW Cherbourg Read from column below pencil mark										
	4.8	5.0	5.2	5.4	5.6	5.8	6.0	6.2	6.4	6.6	6.8
0.2	0.1	0.1	0.1	0.1	0.2	0.2	0.2	0.3	0.3	0.3	0.3
0.4	0.2	0.2	0.2	0.3	0.3	0.4	0.4	0.5	0.5	0.6	0.7
0.6	0.2	0.3	0.4	0.4	0.5	0.6	0.7	0.7	0.8	0.9	1.0
0.8	0.4	0.4	0.5	0.6	0.7	0.8	0.9	1.0	1.1	1.2	1.3
1.0	0.4	0.5	0.6	0.7	0.9	1.0	1.1	1.2	1.3	1.4	1.5	1.7
1.2	0.5	0.6	0.7	0.9	1.0	1.2	1.3	1.4	1.6	1.7	1.9	2.0
1.4	0.6	0.7	0.9	1.0	1.2	1.4	1.5	1.7	1.8	2.0	2.2	2.3
1.6	0.6	0.8	1.0	1.2	1.4	1.6	1.7	1.9	2.1	2.3	2.5	2.7
1.8	0.7	0.9	1.1	1.3	1.5	1.7	2.0	2.2	2.4	2.6	2.8	3.0
2.0	0.8	1.0	1.2	1.5	1.7	1.9	2.2	2.4	2.6	2.9	3.1	3.3
2.2	0.9	1.1	1.4	1.6	1.9	2.1	2.3	2.6	2.9	3.2	3.4	3.7
2.4	0.9	1.2	1.5	1.8	2.1	2.3	2.6	2.9	3.2	3.4	3.7	4.0
2.6	1.0	1.3	1.6	1.9	2.2	2.5	2.8	3.1	3.4	3.7	4.0	4.3
2.8	1.1	1.4	1.7	2.1	2.4	2.7	3.0	3.4	3.7	4.0	4.3	4.7
3.0	1.2	1.5	1.9	2.2	2.6	2.9	3.2	3.6	4.0	4.3	4.6	5.0
3.2	1.3	1.6	2.0	2.4	2.7	3.1	3.4	3.8	4.2	4.6	4.9	5.3
3.4	1.3	1.7	2.1	2.5	2.9	3.3	3.7	4.1	4.5	4.9	5.3	5.7
3.6	1.4	1.8	2.2	2.7	3.1	3.5	3.9	4.3	4.7	5.2	5.6	6.0
3.8	1.5	1.9	2.4	2.8	3.3	3.7	4.1	4.6	5.0	5.4	5.9	6.3
4.0	1.6	2.0	2.5	3.0	3.4	3.9	4.3	4.8	5.3	5.7	6.2	6.7
4.2	1.7	2.1	2.6	3.1	3.6	4.1	4.6	5.0	5.5	6.0	6.5	7.0
4.4	1.7	2.2	2.7	3.3	3.8	4.3	4.8	5.3	5.8	6.3	6.8	7.3
4.6	1.8	2.3	2.9	3.4	3.9	4.5	5.0	5.6	6.1	6.6	7.1	7.7
4.8	1.9	2.4	3.0	3.6	4.1	4.7	5.2	5.8	6.3	6.9	7.4	8.0
5.0	2.0	2.5	3.1	3.7	4.3	4.9	5.4	6.0	6.6	7.2	7.7	8.3
5.2	2.0	2.6	3.2	3.8	4.4	5.0	5.6	6.2	6.8	7.4	8.0	8.6
5.4	2.1	2.8	3.4	4.0	4.6	5.2	5.8	6.5	7.1	7.7	8.4	9.0
5.6	2.2	2.9	3.5	4.1	4.8	5.4	6.1	6.7	7.4	8.0	8.7	9.3
5.8	2.3	3.0	3.6	4.3	5.0	5.6	6.3	7.0	7.6	8.3	9.0	9.6
6.0	2.4	3.1	3.7	4.4	5.1	5.8	6.5	7.2	7.9	8.6	9.3	9.9

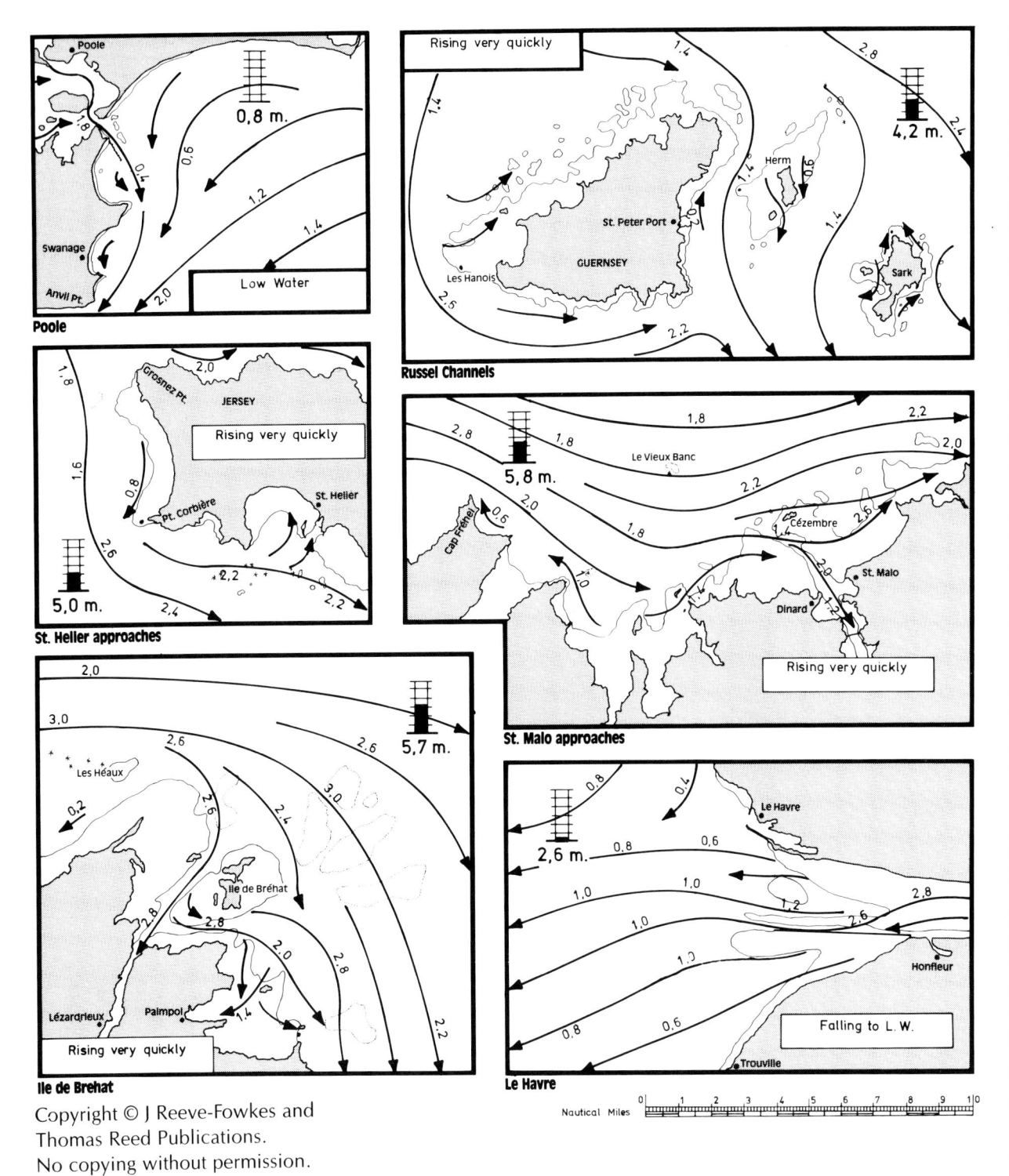

TIDAL HEIGHTS — PORTS & PLACES

Pencil-in height of HW Cherbourg ▶	4.8	5.0	5.2	5.4	5.6	5.8	6.0	6.2	6.4	6.6	6.8
Lymington (& Yarmouth approx)	1.7	1.6	1.6	1.5	1.5	1.4	1.3	1.3	1.2	1.1	1.1	1.0
Portsmouth (Chichester entrance & Cowes approx)	2.2	2.2	2.2	2.2	2.2	2.2	2.2	2.2	2.2	2.2	2.1	2.1
Cherbourg (& Omonville approx)	2.9	2.7	2.5	2.3	2.1	1.9	1.7	1.5	1.3	1.0	0.8	0.5
Braye, Alderney	3.0	2.9	2.7	2.6	2.5	2.3	2.2	2.0	1.9	1.8	1.7	1.6
Weymouth	1.0	0.9	0.9	0.8	0.7	0.6	0.5	0.4	0.3	0.3	0.2	0.2
Poole entrance	1.2	1.1	1.1	1.0	1.0	0.9	0.8	0.6	0.5	0.4	0.3	0.1
Poole Town Quay	1.5	1.4	1.4	1.3	1.3	1.2	1.1	0.9	0.8	0.7	0.7	0.6
St Peter Port & Sark	5.1	4.9	4.7	4.5	4.3	4.2	4.0	3.8	3.6	3.4	3.3	3.1
St Helier	6.2	5.9	5.7	5.4	5.2	4.9	4.7	4.4	4.2	4.1	3.9	3.8
St Malo	7.1	6.8	6.6	6.3	6.0	5.7	5.4	5.1	4.8	4.6	4.5	4.3
Lezardrieux	6.0	5.9	5.9	5.8	5.8	5.7	5.7	5.6	5.6	5.6	5.6	5.6
Paimpol	6.0	5.9	5.7	5.6	5.5	5.4	5.2	5.1	5.0	5.0	4.9	4.9
Le Havre	3.3	3.2	3.0	2.9	2.7	2.6	2.4	2.3	2.1	1.9	1.8	1.6

Copyright © J Reeve-Fowkes and Thomas Reed Publications.
No copying without permission.

4 hours before
HW Cherbourg

-4

Time (to be inserted)

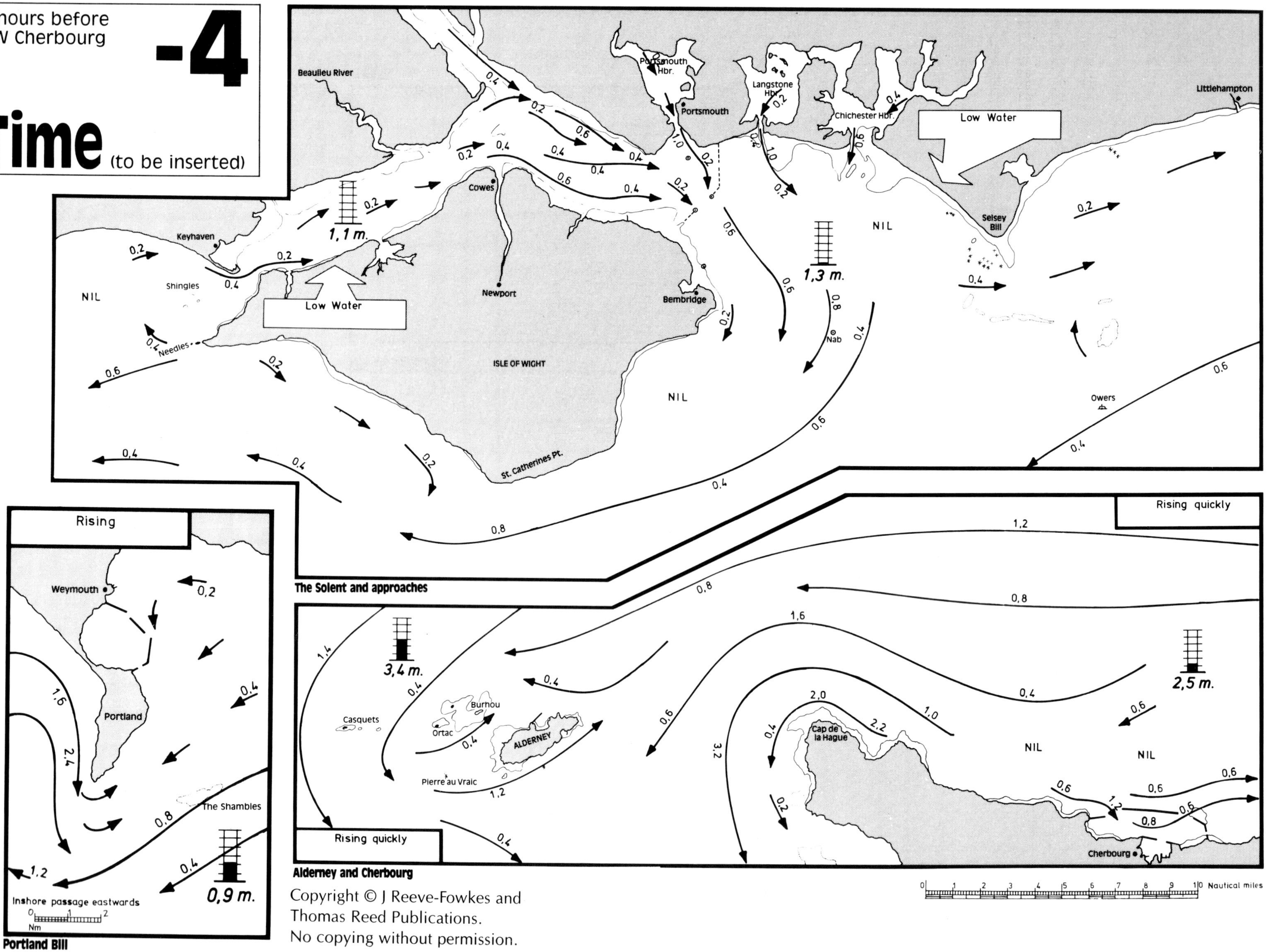

−4

Poole
0.8 m. — Rising from L.W.

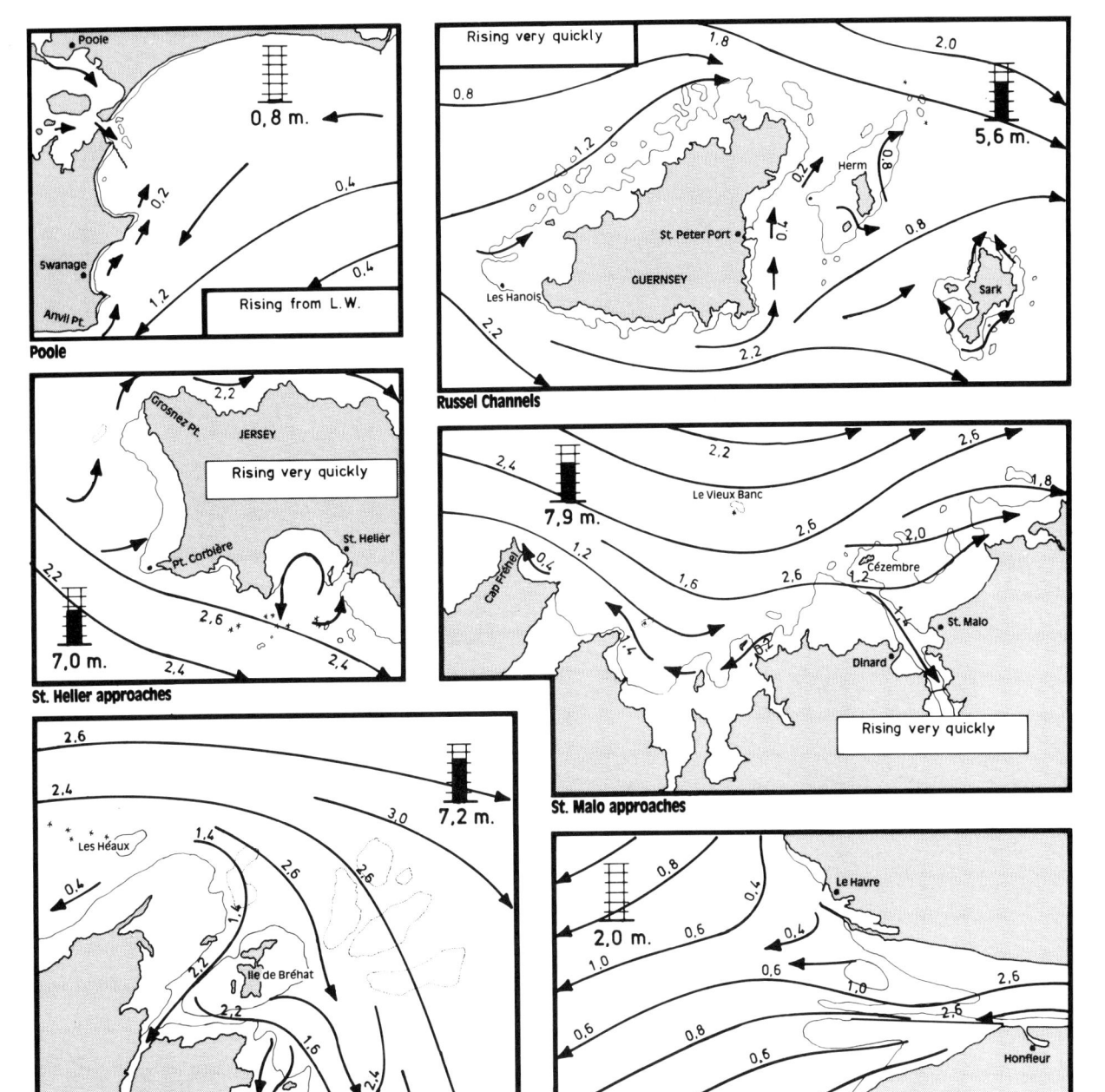

Russel Channels
5.6 m. — Rising very quickly

St. Helier approaches
7.0 m. — Rising very quickly (Jersey)

St. Malo approaches
7.9 m. — Rising very quickly

Ile de Brehat
7.2 m. — Rising very quickly

Le Havre
2.0 m. — Low Water

Copyright © J Reeve-Fowkes and Thomas Reed Publications.
No copying without permission.

Stream Rate Conversion Table

Mean Rate Figure from Chart ▼	Pencil-in height of HW Cherbourg — Read from column below pencil mark										
	4.8	5.0	5.2	5.4	5.6	5.8	6.0	6.2	6.4	6.6	6.8
0.2	0.1	0.1	0.1	0.1	0.2	0.2	0.2	0.2	0.3	0.3	0.3
0.4	0.2	0.2	0.2	0.3	0.3	0.4	0.4	0.5	0.5	0.6	0.7
0.6	0.2	0.3	0.4	0.4	0.5	0.6	0.7	0.7	0.8	0.9	1.0
0.8	0.4	0.4	0.5	0.6	0.7	0.8	0.9	1.0	1.1	1.2	1.3
1.0	0.4	0.5	0.6	0.7	0.9	1.0	1.1	1.2	1.3	1.4	1.5	1.7
1.2	0.5	0.6	0.7	0.9	1.0	1.2	1.3	1.4	1.6	1.7	1.9	2.0
1.4	0.6	0.7	0.9	1.0	1.2	1.4	1.5	1.7	1.8	2.0	2.2	2.3
1.6	0.6	0.8	1.0	1.2	1.4	1.6	1.7	1.9	2.1	2.3	2.5	2.7
1.8	0.7	0.9	1.1	1.3	1.5	1.7	2.0	2.2	2.4	2.6	2.8	3.0
2.0	0.8	1.0	1.2	1.5	1.7	1.9	2.2	2.4	2.6	2.9	3.1	3.3
2.2	0.9	1.1	1.4	1.6	1.9	2.1	2.3	2.6	2.9	3.2	3.4	3.7
2.4	0.9	1.2	1.5	1.8	2.1	2.3	2.6	2.9	3.2	3.4	3.7	4.0
2.6	1.0	1.3	1.6	1.9	2.2	2.5	2.8	3.1	3.4	3.7	4.0	4.3
2.8	1.1	1.4	1.7	2.1	2.4	2.7	3.0	3.4	3.7	4.0	4.3	4.7
3.0	1.2	1.5	1.9	2.2	2.6	2.9	3.2	3.6	4.0	4.3	4.6	5.0
3.2	1.3	1.6	2.0	2.4	2.7	3.1	3.4	3.8	4.2	4.6	4.9	5.3
3.4	1.3	1.7	2.1	2.5	2.9	3.3	3.7	4.1	4.5	4.9	5.3	5.7
3.6	1.4	1.8	2.2	2.7	3.1	3.5	3.9	4.3	4.7	5.2	5.6	6.0
3.8	1.5	1.9	2.4	2.8	3.3	3.7	4.1	4.6	5.0	5.4	5.9	6.3
4.0	1.6	2.0	2.5	3.0	3.4	3.9	4.3	4.8	5.3	5.7	6.2	6.7
4.2	1.7	2.1	2.6	3.1	3.6	4.1	4.6	5.0	5.5	6.0	6.5	7.0
4.4	1.7	2.2	2.7	3.3	3.8	4.3	4.8	5.3	5.8	6.3	6.8	7.3
4.6	1.8	2.3	2.9	3.4	3.9	4.5	5.0	5.5	6.1	6.6	7.1	7.7
4.8	1.9	2.4	3.0	3.6	4.1	4.7	5.2	5.8	6.3	6.9	7.4	8.0
5.0	2.0	2.5	3.1	3.7	4.3	4.9	5.4	6.0	6.6	7.2	7.7	8.3
5.2	2.0	2.6	3.2	3.8	4.4	5.0	5.6	6.2	6.8	7.4	8.0	8.6
5.4	2.1	2.8	3.4	4.0	4.6	5.2	5.7	6.5	7.1	7.7	8.4	9.0
5.6	2.2	2.9	3.5	4.1	4.8	5.4	6.1	6.7	7.4	8.0	8.7	9.3
5.8	2.3	3.0	3.6	4.3	5.0	5.6	6.3	7.0	7.6	8.3	9.0	9.6
6.0	2.4	3.1	3.7	4.4	5.1	5.8	6.5	7.2	7.9	8.6	9.3	9.9

TIDAL HEIGHTS — PORTS & PLACES

Pencil-in height of HW Cherbourg ▶	4.8	5.0	5.2	5.4	5.6	5.8	6.0	6.2	6.4	6.6	6.8
Lymington (& Yarmouth approx)	1.5	1.4	1.4	1.3	1.1	1.0	0.9	0.7	0.6	0.5	0.4	0.3
Portsmouth (Chichester entrance & Cowes approx)	2.0	1.9	1.7	1.6	1.4	1.3	1.1	1.0	0.8	0.7	0.6	0.5
Cherbourg (& Omonville approx)	3.2	3.1	2.9	2.8	2.7	2.5	2.4	2.2	2.1	1.9	1.8	1.6
Braye, Alderney	3.4	3.4	3.4	3.4	3.4	3.5	3.5	3.5	3.5	3.5	3.5	3.5
Weymouth	1.0	1.0	1.0	1.0	0.9	0.9	0.9	0.9	0.8	0.8	0.9	0.9
Poole entrance	1.2	1.1	1.1	1.0	1.0	0.9	0.8	0.7	0.6	0.5	0.3	0.2
Poole Town Quay	1.3	1.2	1.2	1.1	1.0	0.9	0.8	0.6	0.5	0.4	0.3	0.2
St Peter Port & Sark	5.6	5.6	5.6	5.6	5.6	5.7	5.7	5.7	5.7	5.7	5.8	5.8
St Helier	6.7	6.8	6.8	6.9	6.9	7.0	7.0	7.0	7.1	7.2	7.2	7.3
St Malo	7.9	7.9	7.9	7.9	7.9	8.0	8.0	8.0	8.1	8.1	8.1	8.2
Lezardrieux	6.6	6.7	6.9	7.0	7.1	7.3	7.4	7.6	7.7	7.8	8.0	8.1
Paimpol	6.7	6.8	7.0	7.1	7.3	7.4	7.6	7.7	7.9	8.0	8.2	8.3
Le Havre	3.1	2.9	2.7	2.5	2.2	2.0	1.8	1.5	1.3	1.1	0.9	0.7

3 hours before HW Cherbourg

-3

Time (to be inserted)

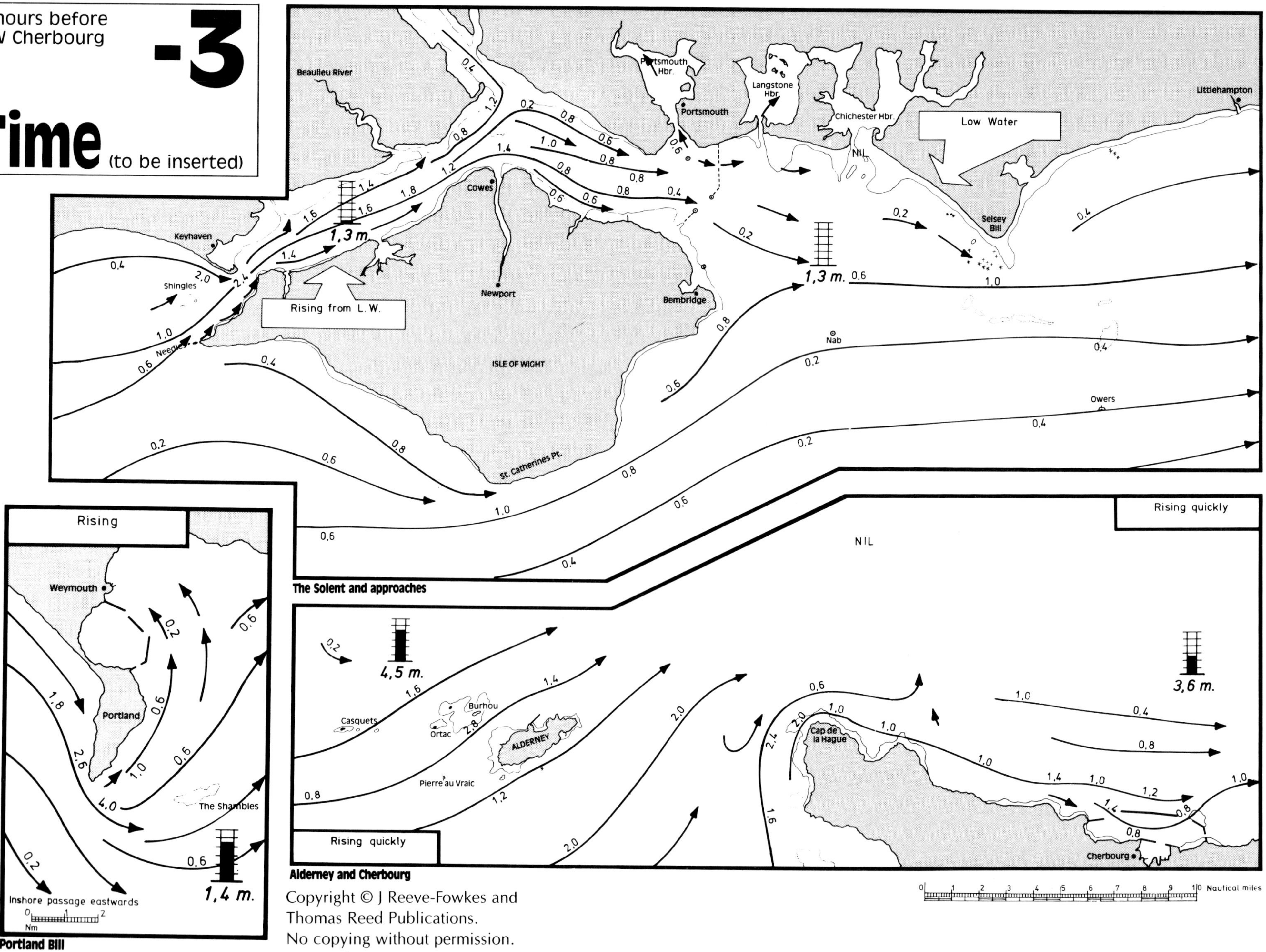

Beaulieu River

Portsmouth Hbr.

Portsmouth

Langstone Hbr.

Chichester Hbr.

Littlehampton

Low Water

0.4

1.2

0.2

0.8

0.8

0.6

1.0

0.6

NIL

1.4

0.8

0.8

Cowes

1.6

1.4

0.8

0.4

0.2

Selsey Bill

0.4

1.6

1.8

1.2

0.6

0.6

0.8

1,3 m.

0.2

1,3 m. 0.6

1.0

Keyhaven

0.4

2.0

Shingles

1.4

2.4

Rising from L.W.

Newport

Bembridge

1.0

Needles

0.6

0.8

Nab

0.4

ISLE OF WIGHT

0.6

0.2

Owers

0.4

0.4

0.2

0.6

0.8

0.2

St. Catherines Pt.

0.8

0.6

0.2

1.0

0.6

Rising quickly

0.6

NIL

0.4

The Solent and approaches

Rising

Weymouth

0.2

0.6

1.8

0.6

Portland

0.6

2.6

1.0

0.6

4.0

The Shambles

0.2

0.6

1,4 m.

Inshore passage eastwards

0   1   2
Nm

Portland Bill

0.2

4,5 m.

1.6

1.4

Casquets

Burhou

2.8

Ortac

ALDERNEY

0.6

1.0

1.0

Cap de la Hague

1.0

0.4

3,6 m.

0.8

2.4

1.0

Pierre au Vraic

1.2

2.0

1.4

1.0

1.0

1.4

1.0

0.8

Rising quickly

2.0

1.6

0.8

Cherbourg

Alderney and Cherbourg

Copyright © J Reeve-Fowkes and
Thomas Reed Publications.
No copying without permission.

0 1 2 3 4 5 6 7 8 9 10 Nautical miles

-3

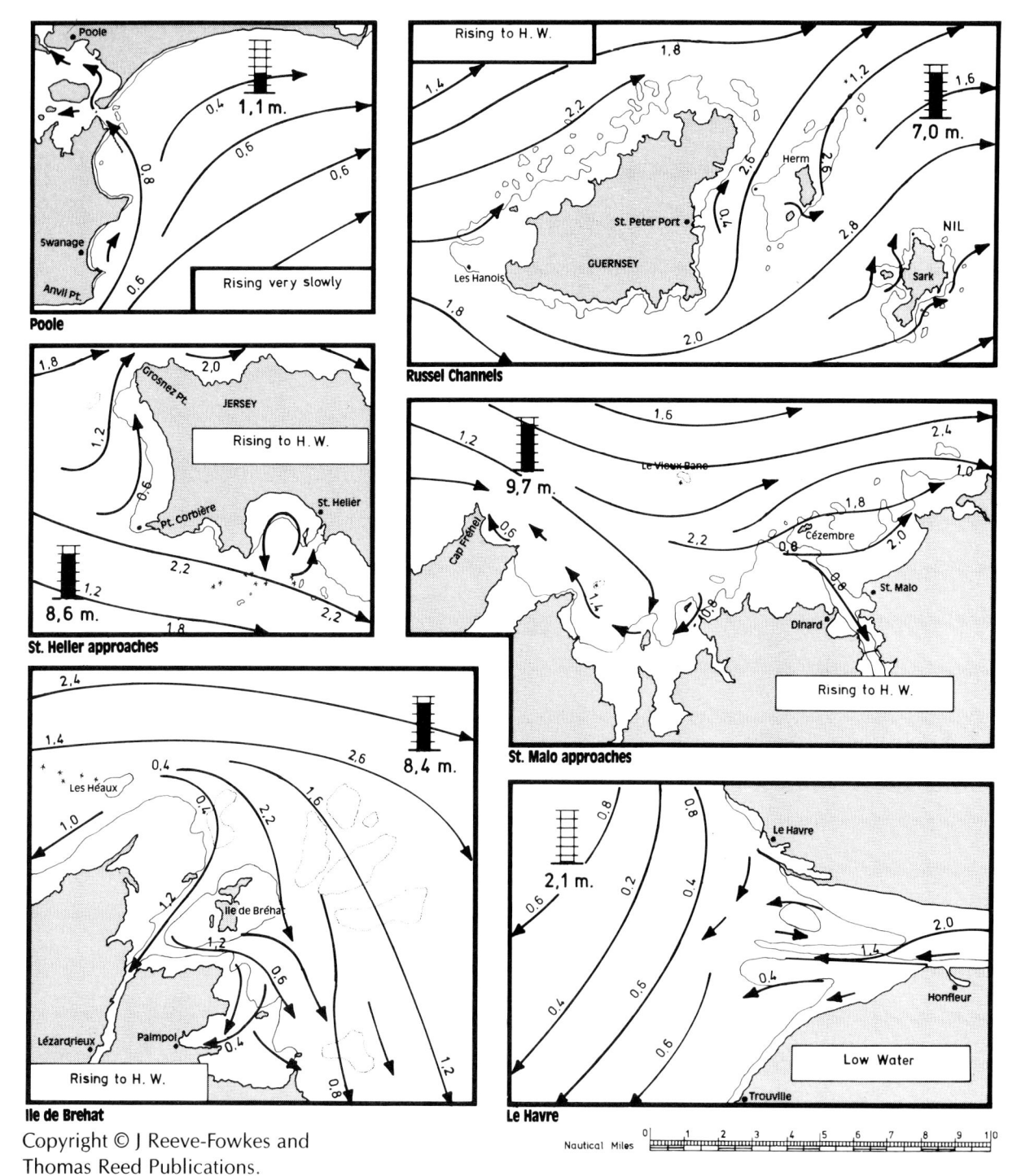

Stream Rate Conversion Table

Mean Rate Figure from Chart ▼	Pencil-in height of HW Cherbourg Read from column below pencil mark										
	4.8	5.0	5.2	5.4	5.6	5.8	6.0	6.2	6.4	6.6	6.8
0.2	0.1	0.1	0.1	0.1	0.2	0.2	0.2	0.3	0.3	0.3	0.3
0.4	0.2	0.2	0.2	0.3	0.3	0.4	0.4	0.5	0.5	0.6	0.7
0.6	0.2	0.3	0.4	0.4	0.5	0.6	0.7	0.7	0.8	0.9	1.0
0.8	0.4	0.4	0.5	0.6	0.7	0.8	0.9	1.0	1.1	1.2	1.3
1.0	0.4	0.5	0.6	0.8	0.9	1.0	1.1	1.2	1.3	1.4	1.7
1.2	0.5	0.6	0.7	0.9	1.0	1.2	1.3	1.4	1.6	1.7	1.9	2.0
1.4	0.6	0.7	0.9	1.0	1.2	1.4	1.5	1.7	1.8	2.0	2.2	2.3
1.6	0.6	0.8	1.0	1.2	1.4	1.6	1.7	1.9	2.1	2.3	2.5	2.7
1.8	0.7	0.9	1.1	1.3	1.5	1.7	2.0	2.2	2.4	2.6	2.8	3.0
2.0	0.8	1.0	1.2	1.5	1.7	1.9	2.2	2.4	2.6	2.9	3.1	3.3
2.2	0.9	1.1	1.4	1.6	1.9	2.1	2.3	2.6	2.9	3.2	3.4	3.7
2.4	0.9	1.2	1.5	1.8	2.1	2.3	2.6	2.9	3.2	3.4	3.7	4.0
2.6	1.0	1.3	1.6	1.9	2.2	2.5	2.8	3.1	3.4	3.7	4.0	4.3
2.8	1.1	1.4	1.7	2.1	2.4	2.7	3.0	3.4	3.7	4.0	4.3	4.7
3.0	1.2	1.5	1.9	2.2	2.6	2.9	3.2	3.6	4.0	4.3	4.6	5.0
3.2	1.3	1.6	2.0	2.4	2.7	3.1	3.4	3.8	4.2	4.6	4.9	5.3
3.4	1.3	1.7	2.1	2.5	2.9	3.3	3.7	4.1	4.5	4.9	5.3	5.7
3.6	1.4	1.8	2.2	2.7	3.1	3.5	3.9	4.3	4.7	5.2	5.6	6.0
3.8	1.5	1.9	2.4	2.8	3.3	3.7	4.1	4.6	5.0	5.4	5.9	6.3
4.0	1.6	2.0	2.5	3.0	3.4	3.9	4.3	4.8	5.3	5.7	6.2	6.7
4.2	1.7	2.1	2.6	3.1	3.6	4.1	4.5	5.0	5.5	6.0	6.5	7.0
4.4	1.7	2.2	2.7	3.3	3.8	4.3	4.8	5.3	5.8	6.3	6.8	7.3
4.6	1.8	2.3	2.9	3.4	3.9	4.5	5.0	5.5	6.1	6.6	7.1	7.7
4.8	1.9	2.4	3.0	3.6	4.1	4.7	5.2	5.8	6.3	6.9	7.4	8.0
5.0	2.0	2.5	3.1	3.7	4.3	4.9	5.4	6.0	6.6	7.2	7.7	8.3
5.2	2.0	2.6	3.2	3.8	4.4	5.0	5.6	6.2	6.8	7.4	8.0	8.6
5.4	2.1	2.8	3.4	4.0	4.6	5.2	5.7	6.5	7.1	7.7	8.4	9.0
5.6	2.2	2.9	3.5	4.1	4.8	5.4	6.1	6.7	7.4	8.0	8.7	9.3
5.8	2.3	3.0	3.6	4.3	5.0	5.6	6.3	7.0	7.6	8.3	9.0	9.6
6.0	2.4	3.1	3.7	4.4	5.1	5.8	6.5	7.2	7.9	8.6	9.3	9.9

TIDAL HEIGHTS — PORTS & PLACES

Pencil-in height of HW Cherbourg ▶	4.8	5.0	5.2	5.4	5.6	5.8	6.0	6.2	6.4	6.6	6.8
Lymington (& Yarmouth approx)	1.6	1.5	1.5	1.4	1.3	1.2	1.1	0.9	0.8	0.7	0.6	0.5
Portsmouth (Chichester entrance & Cowes approx)	2.0	1.9	1.7	1.6	1.4	1.3	1.1	1.0	0.8	0.7	0.5	0.4
Cherbourg (& Omonville approx)	3.7	3.7	3.7	3.7	3.7	3.6	3.6	3.6	3.6	3.6	3.6	3.6
Braye, Alderney	3.9	4.0	4.2	4.3	4.4	4.5	4.7	4.8	4.9	5.0	5.2	5.3
Weymouth	1.3	1.3	1.3	1.3	1.4	1.4	1.4	1.5	1.5	1.6	1.7	1.8
Poole entrance	1.2	1.2	1.2	1.2	1.1	1.1	1.1	1.1	1.1	1.0	1.0	0.9
Poole Town Quay	1.4	1.3	1.3	1.2	1.1	1.0	0.9	0.9	0.8	0.7	0.7	0.6
St Peter Port & Sark	6.0	6.2	6.4	6.6	6.8	7.0	7.2	7.4	7.6	7.8	7.9	8.1
St Helier	7.2	7.5	7.7	8.0	8.3	8.6	8.9	9.2	9.5	9.7	10.0	10.2
St Malo	8.5	8.8	9.0	9.3	9.6	9.8	10.1	10.3	10.6	10.8	11.1	11.3
Lezardrieux	7.2	7.5	7.7	8.0	8.3	8.5	8.8	9.0	9.3	9.5	9.9	10.2
Paimpol	7.1	7.4	7.8	8.1	8.5	8.8	9.2	9.5	9.9	10.2	10.5	10.8
Le Havre	3.5	3.2	3.0	2.7	2.4	2.1	1.8	1.5	1.2	1.0	0.7	0.5

Poole — Rising very slowly — 1.1 m.

St. Helier approaches — 8.6 m.

Ile de Bréhat — Rising to H.W. — 8.4 m.

Russel Channels — Rising to H.W. — 7.0 m.

St. Malo approaches — Rising to H.W. — 9.7 m.

Le Havre — Low Water — 2.1 m.

Copyright © J Reeve-Fowkes and Thomas Reed Publications.
No copying without permission.

153

2 hours before HW Cherbourg

-2

Time (to be inserted)

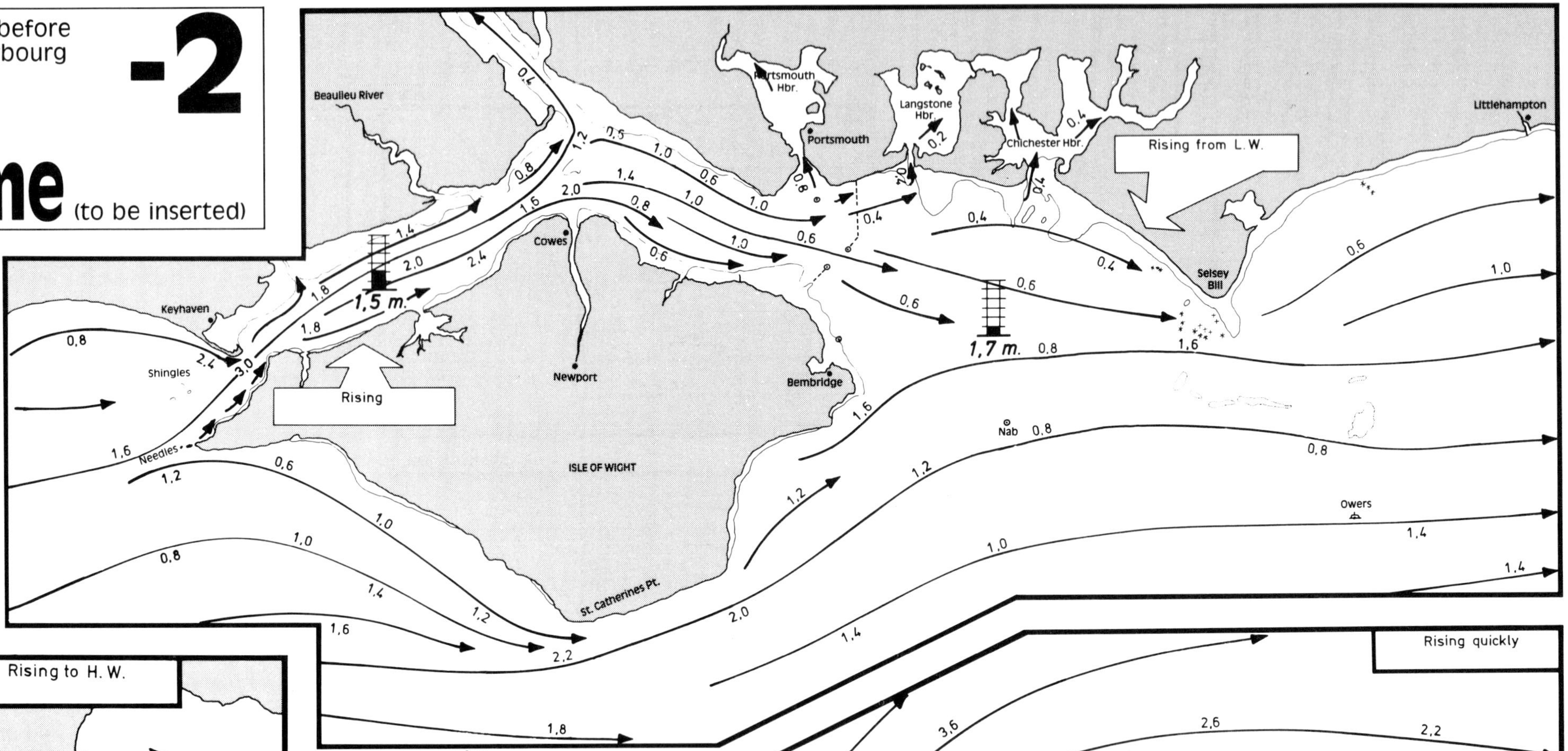

The Solent and approaches

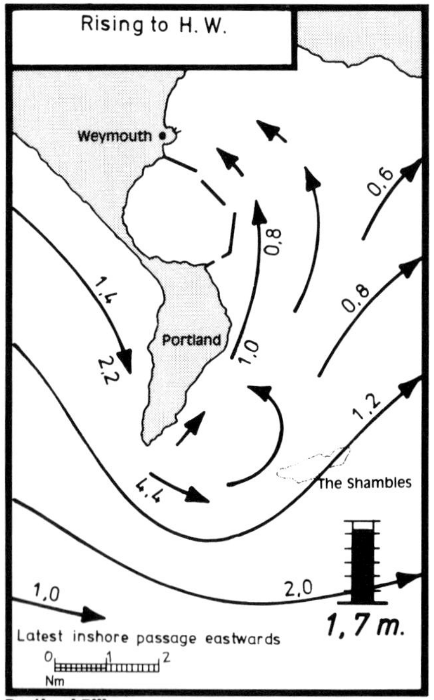

Portland Bill

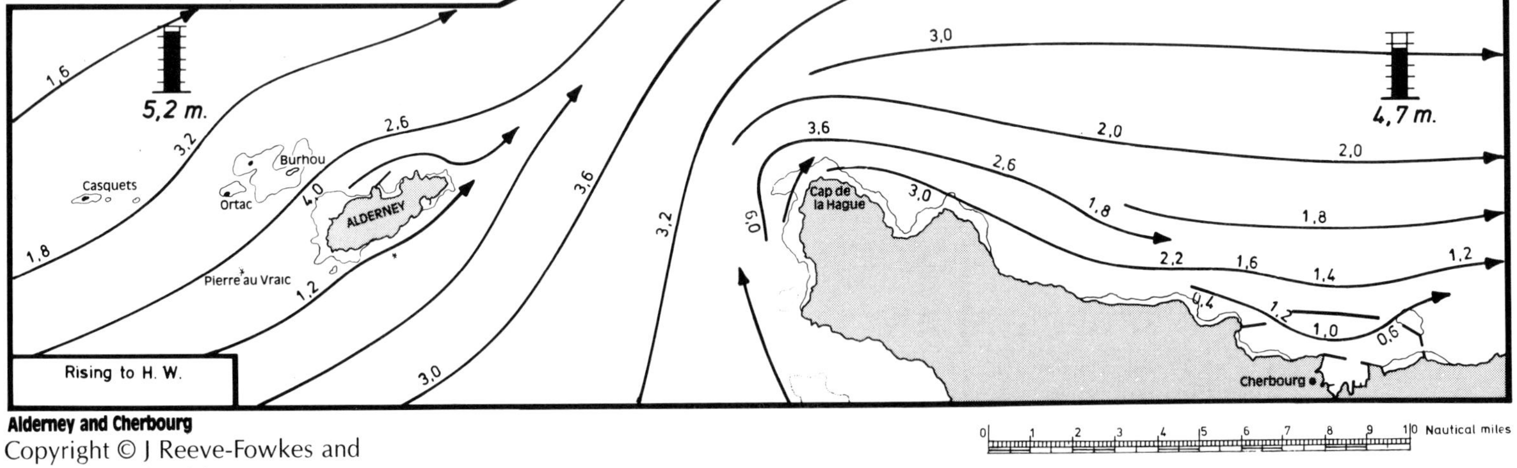

Alderney and Cherbourg

−2

Stream Rate Conversion Table

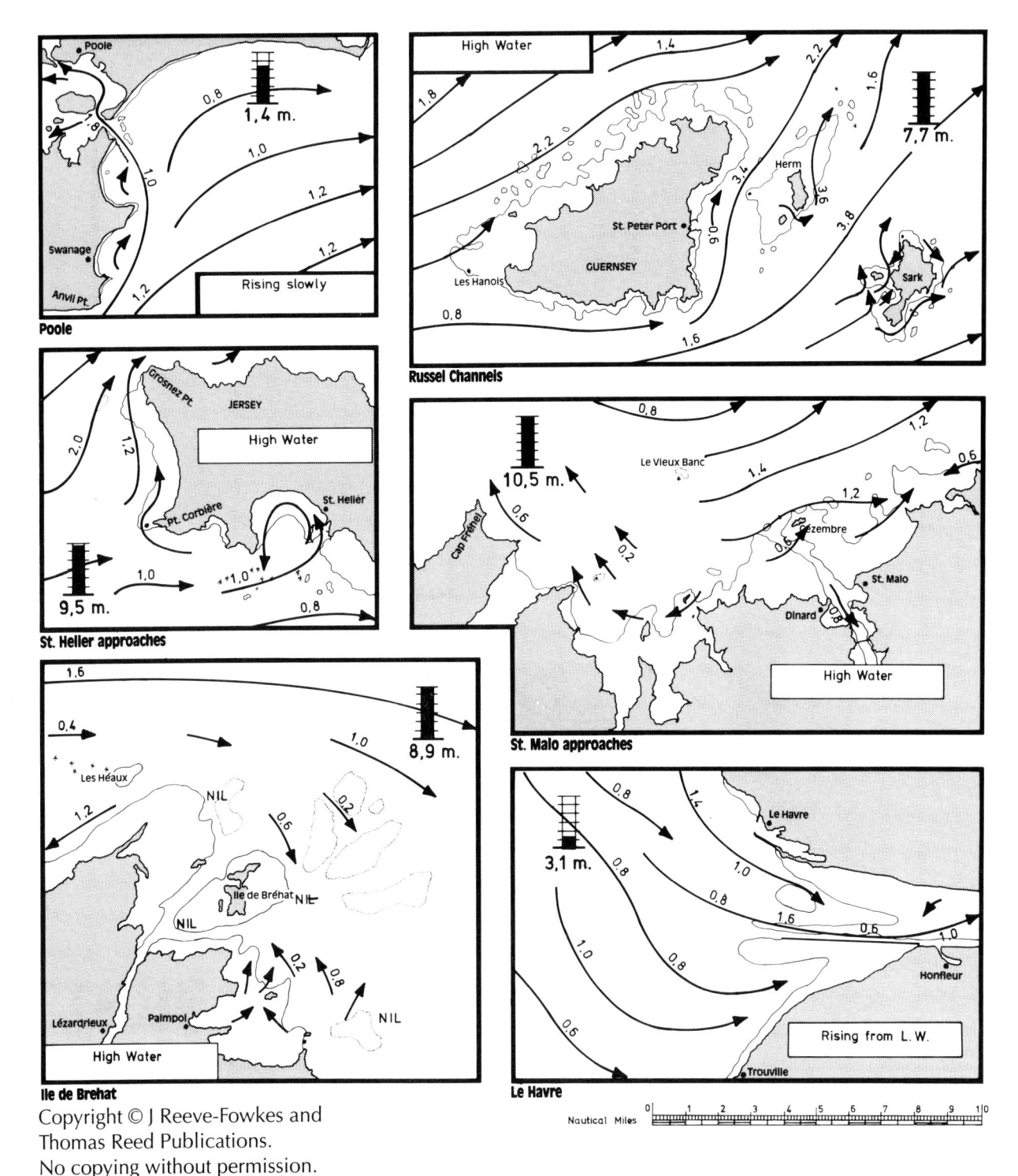

Mean Rate Figure from Chart ▼	Pencil-in height of HW Cherbourg Read from column below pencil mark										
	4.8	5.0	5.2	5.4	5.6	5.8	6.0	6.2	6.4	6.6	6.8
0.2	0.1	0.1	0.1	0.1	0.2	0.2	0.2	0.3	0.3	0.3	0.3
0.4	0.2	0.2	0.2	0.3	0.3	0.4	0.4	0.5	0.5	0.6	0.7
0.6	0.2	0.3	0.4	0.4	0.5	0.6	0.7	0.7	0.8	0.9	1.0
0.8	0.4	0.4	0.5	0.6	0.7	0.8	0.9	1.0	1.1	1.2	1.3
1.0	0.4	0.5	0.6	0.7	0.9	1.0	1.1	1.2	1.3	1.4	1.5
1.2	0.5	0.6	0.7	0.9	1.0	1.2	1.3	1.4	1.6	1.7	1.9	2.0
1.4	0.6	0.7	0.9	1.0	1.2	1.4	1.5	1.7	1.8	2.0	2.2	2.3
1.6	0.6	0.8	1.0	1.2	1.4	1.6	1.7	1.9	2.1	2.3	2.5	2.7
1.8	0.7	0.9	1.1	1.3	1.5	1.7	2.0	2.2	2.4	2.6	2.8	3.0
2.0	0.8	1.0	1.2	1.5	1.7	1.9	2.2	2.4	2.6	2.9	3.1	3.3
2.2	0.9	1.1	1.4	1.6	1.9	2.1	2.3	2.6	2.9	3.2	3.4	3.7
2.4	0.9	1.2	1.5	1.8	2.1	2.3	2.6	2.9	3.2	3.4	3.7	4.0
2.6	1.0	1.3	1.6	1.9	2.2	2.5	2.8	3.1	3.4	3.7	4.0	4.3
2.8	1.1	1.4	1.7	2.1	2.4	2.7	3.0	3.4	3.7	4.0	4.3	4.7
3.0	1.2	1.5	1.9	2.2	2.6	2.9	3.2	3.6	4.0	4.3	4.6	5.0
3.2	1.3	1.6	2.0	2.4	2.7	3.1	3.4	3.8	4.2	4.6	4.9	5.3
3.4	1.3	1.7	2.1	2.5	2.9	3.3	3.7	4.1	4.5	4.9	5.3	5.7
3.6	1.4	1.8	2.2	2.7	3.1	3.5	3.9	4.3	4.7	5.2	5.6	6.0
3.8	1.5	1.9	2.4	2.8	3.3	3.7	4.1	4.6	5.0	5.4	5.9	6.3
4.0	1.6	2.0	2.5	3.0	3.4	3.9	4.3	4.8	5.3	5.7	6.2	6.7
4.2	1.7	2.1	2.6	3.1	3.6	4.1	4.6	5.0	5.5	6.0	6.5	7.0
4.4	1.7	2.2	2.7	3.3	3.8	4.3	4.8	5.3	5.8	6.3	6.8	7.3
4.6	1.8	2.3	2.9	3.4	3.9	4.5	5.0	5.5	6.1	6.6	7.1	7.7
4.8	1.9	2.4	3.0	3.6	4.1	4.7	5.2	5.8	6.3	6.9	7.4	8.0
5.0	2.0	2.5	3.1	3.7	4.3	4.9	5.4	6.0	6.6	7.2	7.7	8.3
5.2	2.0	2.6	3.2	3.8	4.4	5.0	5.6	6.2	6.8	7.4	8.0	8.6
5.4	2.1	2.8	3.4	4.0	4.6	5.2	5.7	6.5	7.1	7.7	8.4	9.0
5.6	2.2	2.9	3.5	4.1	4.8	5.4	6.1	6.7	7.4	8.0	8.7	9.3
5.8	2.3	3.0	3.6	4.3	5.0	5.6	6.3	7.0	7.6	8.3	9.0	9.6
6.0	2.4	3.1	3.7	4.4	5.1	5.8	6.5	7.2	7.9	8.6	9.3	9.9

TIDAL HEIGHTS — PORTS & PLACES

Pencil-in height of HW Cherbourg ▶	4.8	5.0	5.2	5.4	5.6	5.8	6.0	6.2	6.4	6.6	6.8
Lymington (& Yarmouth approx)	1.6	1.6	1.6	1.6	1.5	1.5	1.5	1.4	1.4	1.3	1.3
Portsmouth (Chichester entrance & Cowes approx)	2.1	2.0	2.0	1.9	1.8	1.7	1.6	1.5	1.4	1.3	1.3
Cherbourg (& Omonville approx)	4.2	4.3	4.5	4.6	4.7	4.8	4.9	5.0	5.1	5.2	5.3	5.4
Braye, Alderney	4.3	4.5	4.7	4.9	5.1	5.3	5.5	5.7	5.9	6.1	6.3	6.5
Weymouth	1.3	1.4	1.4	1.5	1.6	1.7	1.8	1.9	2.0	2.1	2.2	2.3
Poole entrance	1.3	1.3	1.3	1.3	1.4	1.4	1.4	1.5	1.5	1.5	1.5
Poole Town Quay	1.4	1.4	1.4	1.4	1.3	1.3	1.3	1.3	1.3	1.2	1.2
St Peter Port & Sark	6.2	6.5	6.9	7.2	7.5	7.8	8.2	8.5	8.8	9.0	9.3	9.5
St Helier	7.5	7.9	8.3	8.7	9.2	9.6	10.0	10.5	10.9	11.3	11.6	12.0
St Malo	8.4	8.9	9.3	9.8	10.2	10.7	11.1	11.6	12.0	12.3	12.6	12.9
Lezardrieux	7.1	7.5	7.9	8.3	8.7	9.2	9.6	9.8	10.2	10.5	10.7	11.0
Paimpol	7.2	7.6	8.0	8.4	8.8	9.2	9.6	10.0	10.4	10.7	11.0	11.3
Le Havre	4.1	3.9	3.7	3.5	3.3	3.1	2.9	2.7	2.5	2.3	2.2	2.0

Poole — Rising slowly

Russel Channels — High Water — 7.7 m.

St. Helier approaches — High Water — 9.5 m.

St. Malo approaches — High Water — 10.5 m.

Ile de Bréhat — High Water — 8.9 m.

Le Havre — Rising from L.W. — 3.1 m.

Copyright © J Reeve-Fowkes and Thomas Reed Publications.
No copying without permission.

155

1 hour before HW Cherbourg

-1

Time (to be inserted)

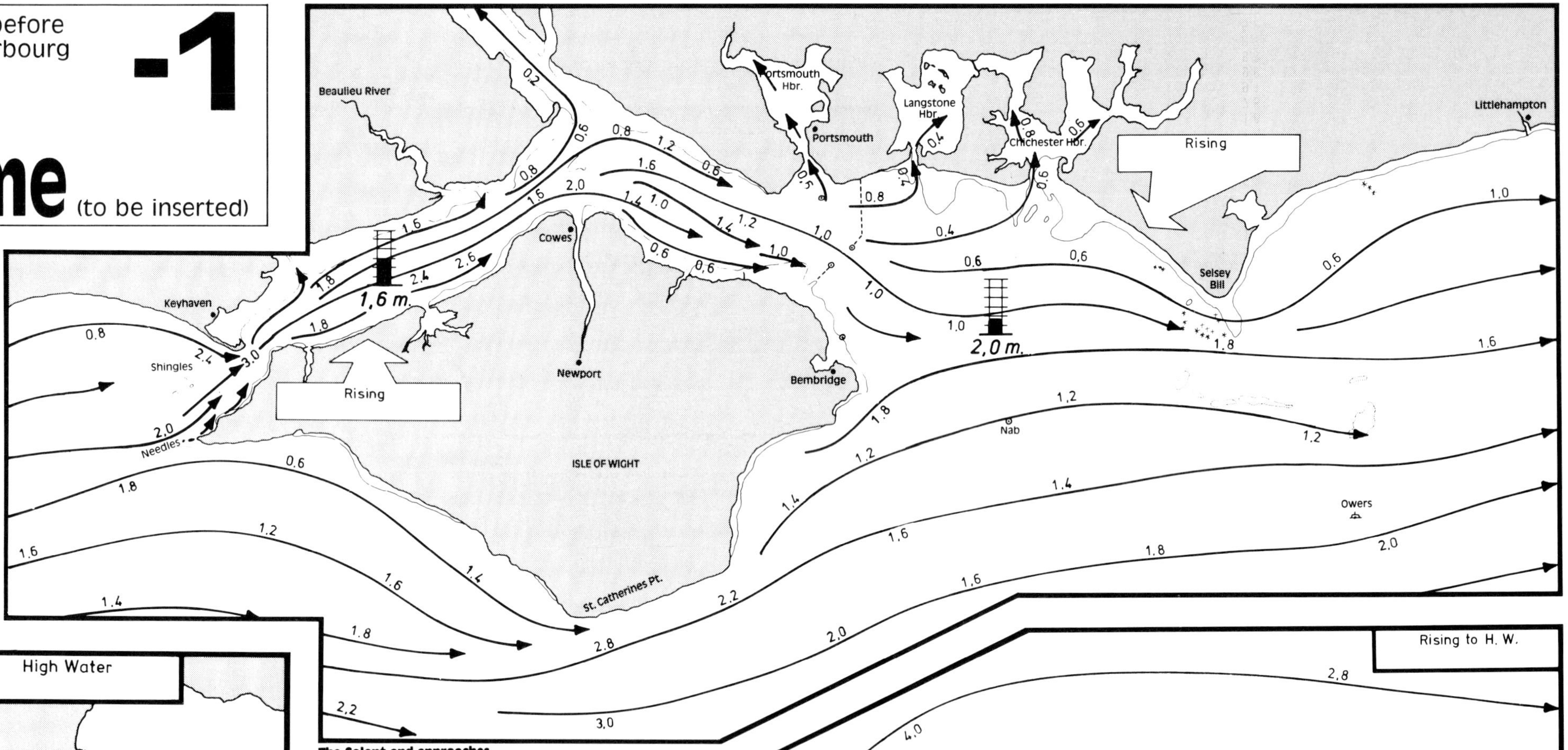

The Solent and approaches

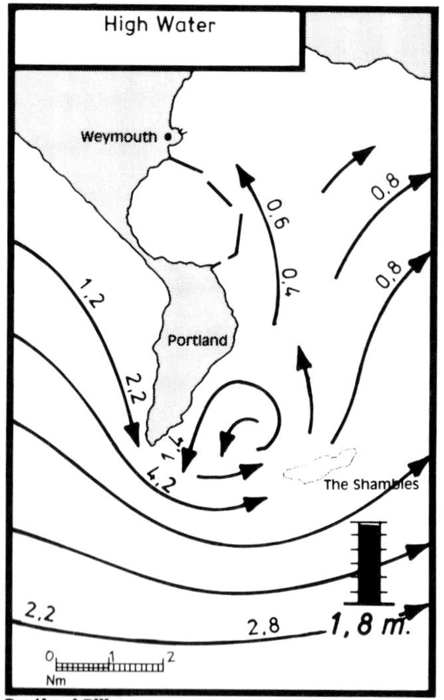

Portland Bill

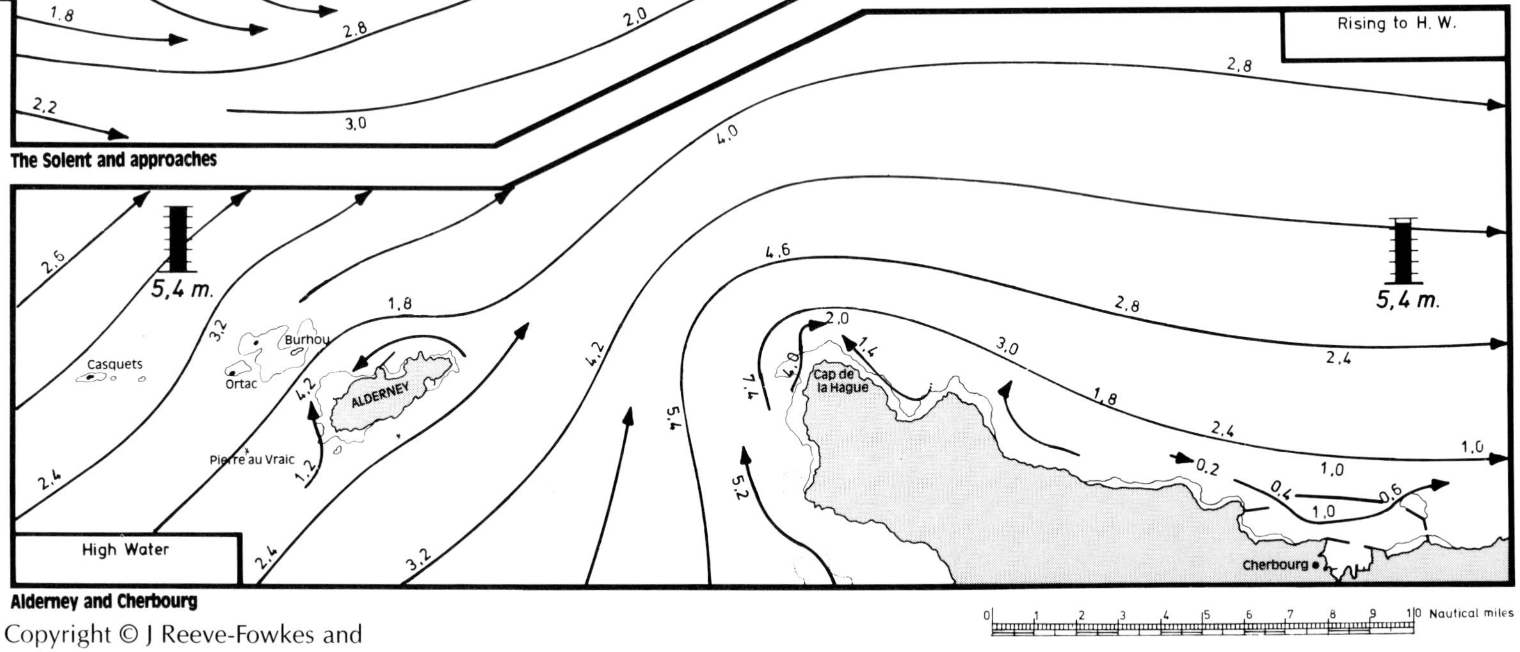

Alderney and Cherbourg

Stream Rate Conversion Table

Mean Rate Figure from Chart ▼	\multicolumn{11}{c}{Pencil-in height of HW Cherbourg Read from column below pencil mark}
	4.8	5.0	5.2	5.4	5.6	5.8	6.0	6.2	6.4	6.6	6.8
0.2	0.1	0.1	0.1	0.1	0.2	0.2	0.2	0.2	0.3	0.3	0.3
0.4	0.2	0.2	0.2	0.3	0.3	0.4	0.4	0.5	0.5	0.6	0.7
0.6	0.2	0.3	0.4	0.4	0.5	0.6	0.7	0.7	0.8	0.9	1.0
0.8	0.4	0.4	0.5	0.6	0.7	0.8	0.9	1.0	1.1	1.2	1.3
1.0	0.4	0.5	0.6	0.7	0.9	1.0	1.1	1.2	1.3	1.4	1.5	1.7
1.2	0.5	0.6	0.7	0.9	1.0	1.2	1.3	1.4	1.6	1.7	1.9	2.0
1.4	0.6	0.7	0.9	1.0	1.2	1.4	1.5	1.7	1.8	2.0	2.2	2.3
1.6	0.6	0.8	1.0	1.2	1.4	1.6	1.7	1.9	2.1	2.3	2.5	2.7
1.8	0.7	0.9	1.1	1.3	1.5	1.7	2.0	2.2	2.4	2.6	2.8	3.0
2.0	0.8	1.0	1.2	1.5	1.7	1.9	2.2	2.4	2.6	2.9	3.1	3.3
2.2	0.9	1.1	1.4	1.6	1.9	2.1	2.3	2.6	2.9	3.2	3.4	3.7
2.4	0.9	1.2	1.5	1.8	2.1	2.3	2.6	2.9	3.2	3.4	3.7	4.0
2.6	1.0	1.3	1.6	1.9	2.2	2.5	2.8	3.1	3.4	3.7	4.0	4.3
2.8	1.1	1.4	1.7	2.1	2.4	2.7	3.0	3.4	3.7	4.0	4.3	4.7
3.0	1.2	1.5	1.9	2.2	2.6	2.9	3.2	3.6	4.0	4.3	4.6	5.0
3.2	1.3	1.6	2.0	2.4	2.7	3.1	3.4	3.8	4.2	4.6	4.9	5.3
3.4	1.3	1.7	2.1	2.5	2.9	3.3	3.7	4.1	4.5	4.9	5.3	5.7
3.6	1.4	1.8	2.2	2.7	3.1	3.5	3.9	4.3	4.7	5.2	5.6	6.0
3.8	1.5	1.9	2.4	2.8	3.3	3.7	4.1	4.6	5.0	5.4	5.9	6.3
4.0	1.6	2.0	2.5	3.0	3.4	3.9	4.3	4.8	5.3	5.7	6.2	6.7
4.2	1.7	2.1	2.6	3.1	3.6	4.1	4.6	5.0	5.5	6.0	6.5	7.0
4.4	1.7	2.2	2.7	3.3	3.8	4.3	4.8	5.3	5.8	6.3	6.8	7.3
4.6	1.8	2.3	2.9	3.4	3.9	4.5	5.0	5.5	6.1	6.6	7.1	7.7
4.8	1.9	2.4	3.0	3.6	4.1	4.7	5.2	5.8	6.3	6.9	7.4	8.0
5.0	2.0	2.5	3.1	3.7	4.3	4.9	5.4	6.0	6.6	7.2	7.7	8.3
5.2	2.0	2.6	3.2	3.8	4.4	5.0	5.6	6.2	6.8	7.4	8.0	8.6
5.4	2.1	2.8	3.4	4.0	4.6	5.2	5.7	6.5	7.1	7.7	8.4	9.0
5.6	2.2	2.9	3.5	4.1	4.8	5.4	6.1	6.7	7.4	8.0	8.7	9.3
5.8	2.3	3.0	3.6	4.3	5.0	5.6	6.3	7.0	7.6	8.3	9.0	9.6
6.0	2.4	3.1	3.7	4.4	5.1	5.8	6.5	7.2	7.9	8.6	9.3	9.9

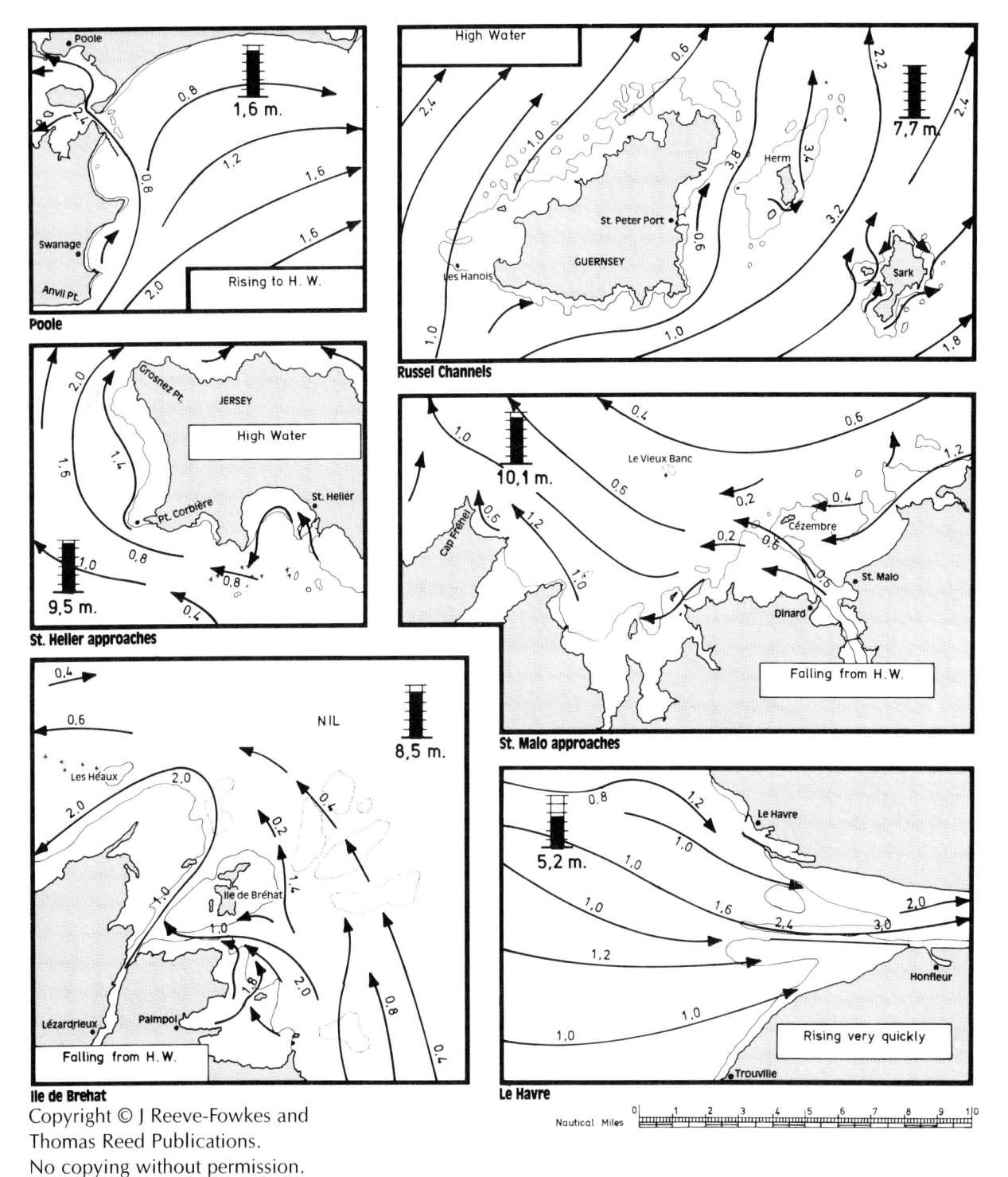

TIDAL HEIGHTS — PORTS & PLACES

Pencil-in height of HW Cherbourg ▶	4.8	5.0	5.2	5.4	5.6	5.8	6.0	6.2	6.4	6.6	6.8
Lymington (& Yarmouth approx)	1.7	1.7	1.7	1.7	1.7	1.7	1.7	1.7	1.8	1.8	1.8	1.8
Portsmouth (Chichester entrance & Cowes approx)	2.1	2.1	2.1	2.1	2.0	2.0	2.0	1.9	1.9	1.9	1.8	1.8
Cherbourg (& Omonville approx)	4.6	4.8	5.0	5.2	5.3	5.5	5.7	5.8	6.0	6.2	6.4	6.6
Braye, Alderney	4.4	4.6	4.8	5.0	5.3	5.5	5.7	6.0	6.2	6.4	6.7	6.9
Weymouth	1.2	1.3	1.5	1.6	1.7	1.9	2.0	2.2	2.3	2.5	2.6	2.8
Poole entrance	1.3	1.4	1.4	1.5	1.5	1.6	1.7	1.7	1.8	1.8	1.9	1.9
Poole Town Quay	1.5	1.5	1.5	1.5	1.6	1.6	1.7	1.7	1.7	1.8	1.8	1.8
St Peter Port & Sark	6.1	6.4	6.8	7.1	7.5	7.8	8.2	8.5	8.9	9.1	9.4	9.6
St Helier	7.3	7.8	8.2	8.7	9.1	9.6	10.0	10.5	10.9	11.2	11.6	11.9
St Malo	7.9	8.4	8.8	9.3	9.8	10.3	10.7	11.2	11.7	12.0	12.3	12.6
Lezardrieux	7.0	7.3	7.7	8.0	8.3	8.6	9.0	9.3	9.6	9.9	10.1	10.4
Paimpol	6.9	7.2	7.6	7.9	8.3	8.6	9.0	9.3	9.7	10.0	10.2	10.5
Le Havre	5.1	5.1	5.1	5.1	5.2	5.2	5.2	5.3	5.3	5.3	5.3	5.3

−1

Poole — Rising to H.W. — 1.6 m.

Russel Channels — High Water — 7.7 m.

St. Helier approaches — High Water — 9.5 m.

St. Malo approaches — Falling from H.W. — 10.1 m.

Ile de Brehat — Falling from H.W. — NIL — 8.5 m.

Le Havre — Rising very quickly — 5.2 m.

Copyright © J Reeve-Fowkes and Thomas Reed Publications.
No copying without permission.

HW Cherbourg

HW Time (to be inserted)

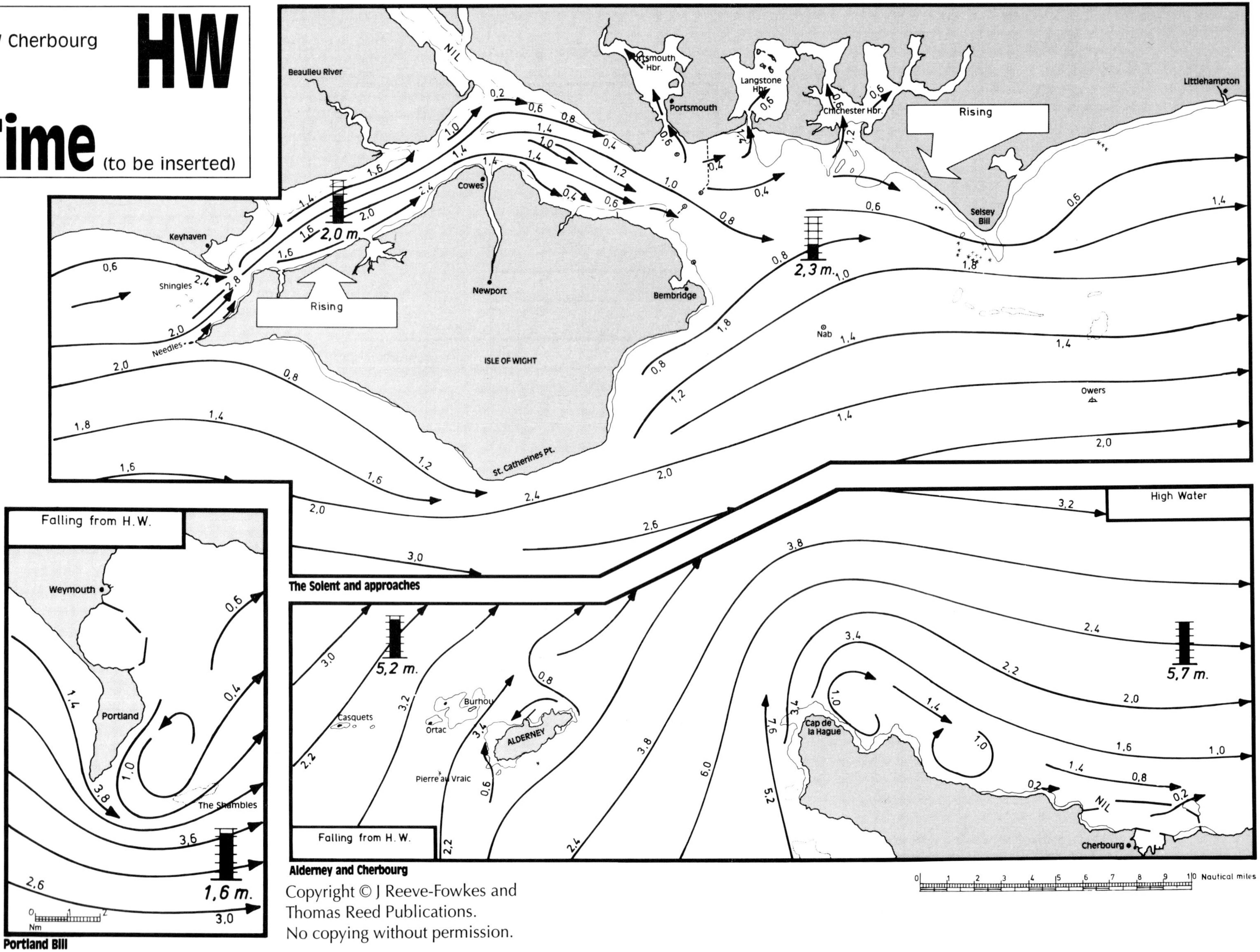

The Solent and approaches

NIL

Beaulieu River

Portsmouth Hbr.
Portsmouth
Langstone Hbr.
Chichester Hbr.
Littlehampton

Rising

Keyhaven
Cowes
Shingles
Needles
2,0 m

Newport
Bembridge
Selsey Bill

Rising

ISLE OF WIGHT
Nab
Owers

St. Catherines Pt.

2,3 m.

High Water

Falling from H.W.

Weymouth
Portland
The Shambles

1,6 m.

Portland Bill

Nm

Falling from H.W.

5,2 m.

Casquets
Ortac
Burhou
ALDERNEY
Pierre au Vraic

Cap de la Hague

5,7 m.

NIL
Cherbourg

Alderney and Cherbourg

Nautical miles

Copyright © J Reeve-Fowkes and
Thomas Reed Publications.
No copying without permission.

HW

Stream Rate Conversion Table

Mean Rate Figure from Chart ▼	\multicolumn{11}{c}{Pencil-in height of HW Cherbourg Read from column below pencil mark}
	4.8	5.0	5.2	5.4	5.6	5.8	6.0	6.2	6.4	6.6	6.8
0.2	0.1	0.1	0.1	0.1	0.2	0.2	0.2	0.2	0.3	0.3	0.3
0.4	0.2	0.2	0.2	0.3	0.3	0.4	0.4	0.5	0.5	0.6	0.7
0.6	0.2	0.3	0.4	0.4	0.5	0.6	0.7	0.7	0.8	0.9	1.0
0.8	0.4	0.4	0.5	0.6	0.7	0.8	0.9	1.0	1.1	1.2	1.3
1.0	0.4	0.5	0.6	0.7	0.9	1.0	1.1	1.2	1.3	1.5	1.7
1.2	0.5	0.6	0.7	0.9	1.0	1.2	1.3	1.4	1.6	1.7	1.9
1.4	0.6	0.7	0.9	1.0	1.2	1.4	1.5	1.7	1.8	2.0	2.2	2.3
1.6	0.6	0.8	1.0	1.2	1.4	1.6	1.7	1.9	2.1	2.3	2.5	2.7
1.8	0.7	0.9	1.1	1.3	1.5	1.7	2.0	2.2	2.4	2.6	2.8	3.0
2.0	0.8	1.0	1.2	1.5	1.7	1.9	2.2	2.4	2.6	2.9	3.1	3.3
2.2	0.9	1.1	1.4	1.6	1.9	2.1	2.3	2.6	2.9	3.2	3.4	3.7
2.4	0.9	1.2	1.5	1.8	2.1	2.3	2.6	2.9	3.2	3.4	3.7	4.0
2.6	1.0	1.3	1.6	1.9	2.2	2.5	2.8	3.1	3.4	3.7	4.0	4.3
2.8	1.1	1.4	1.7	2.1	2.4	2.7	3.0	3.4	3.7	4.0	4.3	4.7
3.0	1.2	1.5	1.9	2.2	2.6	2.9	3.2	3.6	4.0	4.3	4.6	5.0
3.2	1.3	1.6	2.0	2.4	2.7	3.1	3.4	3.8	4.2	4.6	4.9	5.3
3.4	1.3	1.7	2.1	2.5	2.9	3.3	3.7	4.1	4.5	4.9	5.3	5.7
3.6	1.4	1.8	2.2	2.7	3.1	3.5	3.9	4.3	4.7	5.2	5.6	6.0
3.8	1.5	1.9	2.4	2.8	3.3	3.7	4.1	4.6	5.0	5.4	5.9	6.3
4.0	1.6	2.0	2.5	3.0	3.4	3.9	4.3	4.8	5.3	5.7	6.2	6.7
4.2	1.7	2.1	2.6	3.1	3.6	4.1	4.6	5.0	5.5	6.0	6.5	7.0
4.4	1.7	2.2	2.7	3.3	3.8	4.3	4.8	5.3	5.8	6.3	6.8	7.3
4.6	1.8	2.3	2.9	3.4	3.9	4.5	5.0	5.5	6.1	6.6	7.1	7.7
4.8	1.9	2.4	3.0	3.6	4.1	4.7	5.2	5.8	6.3	6.9	7.4	8.0
5.0	2.0	2.5	3.1	3.7	4.3	4.9	5.4	6.0	6.6	7.2	7.7	8.3
5.2	2.0	2.6	3.2	3.8	4.4	5.0	5.6	6.2	6.8	7.4	8.0	8.6
5.4	2.1	2.8	3.4	4.0	4.6	5.2	5.7	6.5	7.1	7.7	8.4	9.0
5.6	2.2	2.9	3.5	4.1	4.8	5.4	6.1	6.7	7.4	8.0	8.7	9.3
5.8	2.3	3.0	3.6	4.3	5.0	5.6	6.3	7.0	7.6	8.3	9.0	9.6
6.0	2.4	3.1	3.7	4.4	5.1	5.8	6.5	7.2	7.9	8.6	9.3	9.9

TIDAL HEIGHTS — PORTS & PLACES

Pencil-in height of HW Cherbourg ▶	4.8	5.0	5.2	5.4	5.6	5.8	6.0	6.2	6.4	6.6	6.8
Lymington (& Yarmouth approx)	1.8	1.9	1.9	2.0	2.0	2.1	2.1	2.1	2.1	2.2	2.2
Portsmouth (Chichester entrance & Cowes approx)	2.4	2.4	2.4	2.4	2.3	2.3	2.3	2.2	2.2	2.2	2.2
Cherbourg (& Omonville approx)	4.7	4.9	5.1	5.3	5.5	5.7	5.9	6.1	6.3	6.5	6.7	6.9
Braye, Alderney	4.3	4.5	4.7	4.9	5.1	5.3	5.5	5.7	5.9	6.1	6.4	6.6
Weymouth	1.0	1.1	1.3	1.4	1.5	1.6	1.8	1.9	2.0	2.1	2.3	2.4
Poole entrance	1.3	1.4	1.4	1.5	1.5	1.6	1.7	1.9	2.0	2.0	2.1	2.1
Poole Town Quay	1.4	1.5	1.5	1.6	1.7	1.8	1.9	2.0	2.1	2.1	2.2	2.2
St Peter Port & Sark	5.9	6.1	6.3	6.6	6.9	7.1	7.4	7.6	7.9	8.1	8.3	8.5
St Helier	7.0	7.3	7.7	8.0	8.3	8.7	9.0	9.4	9.7	10.0	10.2	10.5
St Malo	7.2	7.6	8.0	8.4	8.8	9.1	9.5	9.9	10.3	10.5	10.7	10.9
Lezardrieux	5.9	6.2	6.4	6.7	6.9	7.2	7.4	7.7	7.9	8.1	8.2	8.4
Paimpol	6.2	6.4	6.6	6.8	7.1	7.3	7.5	7.8	8.0	8.3	8.7	9.0
Le Havre	5.7	5.9	6.1	6.3	6.4	6.6	6.8	7.0	7.1	7.2	7.3	7.4

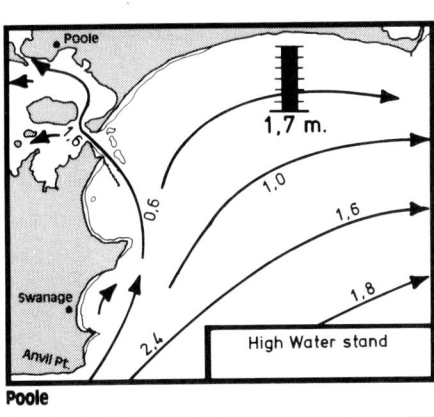

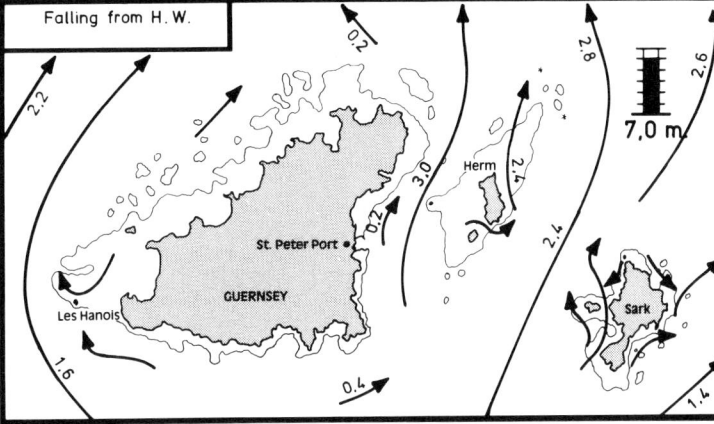

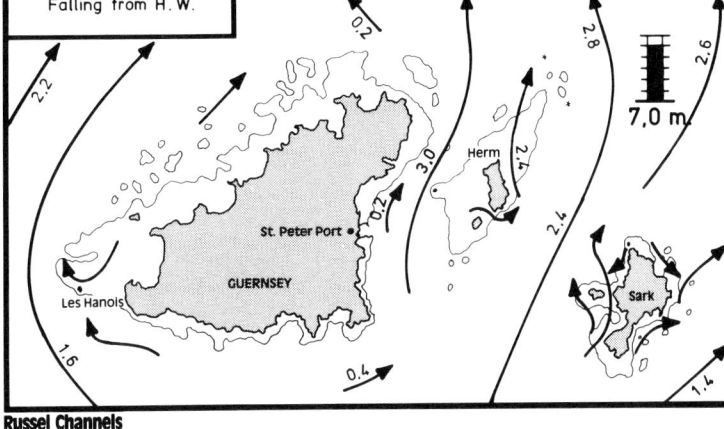

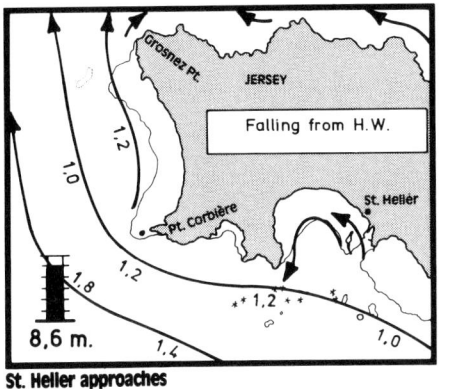

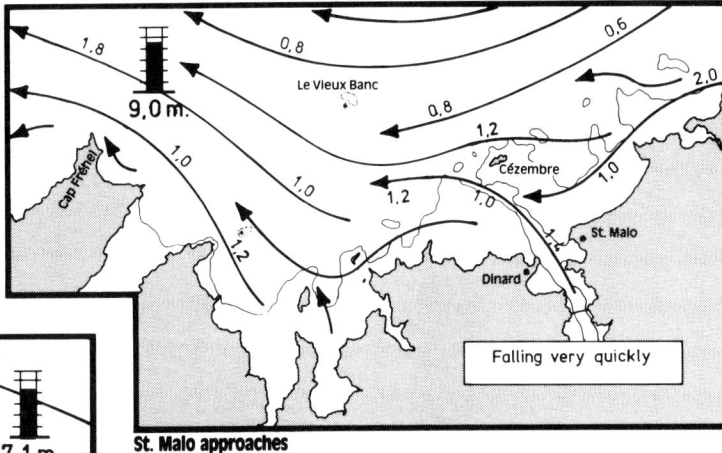

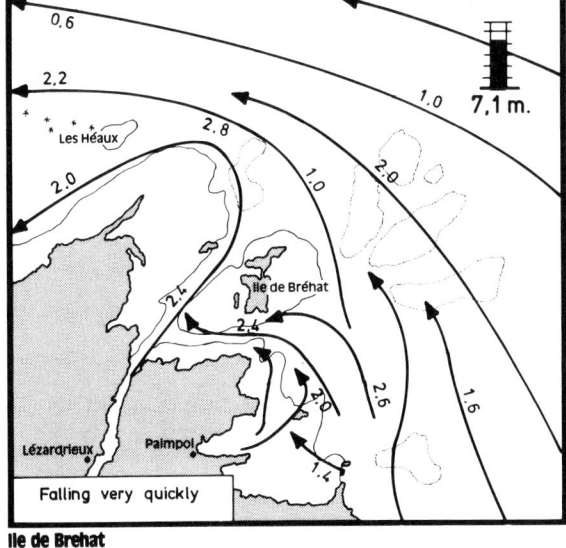

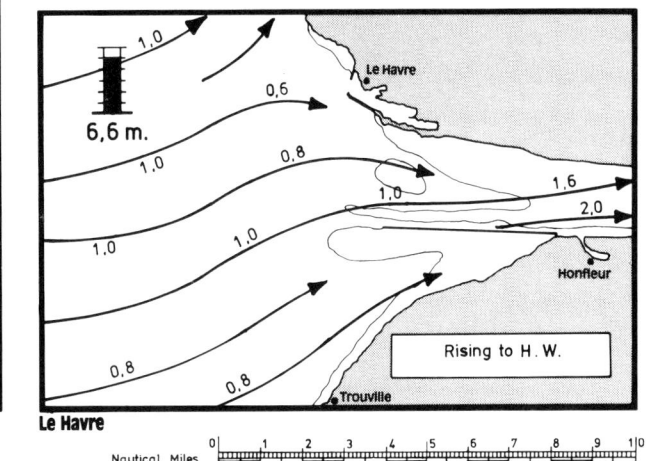

Copyright © J Reeve-Fowkes and Thomas Reed Publications.
No copying without permission.

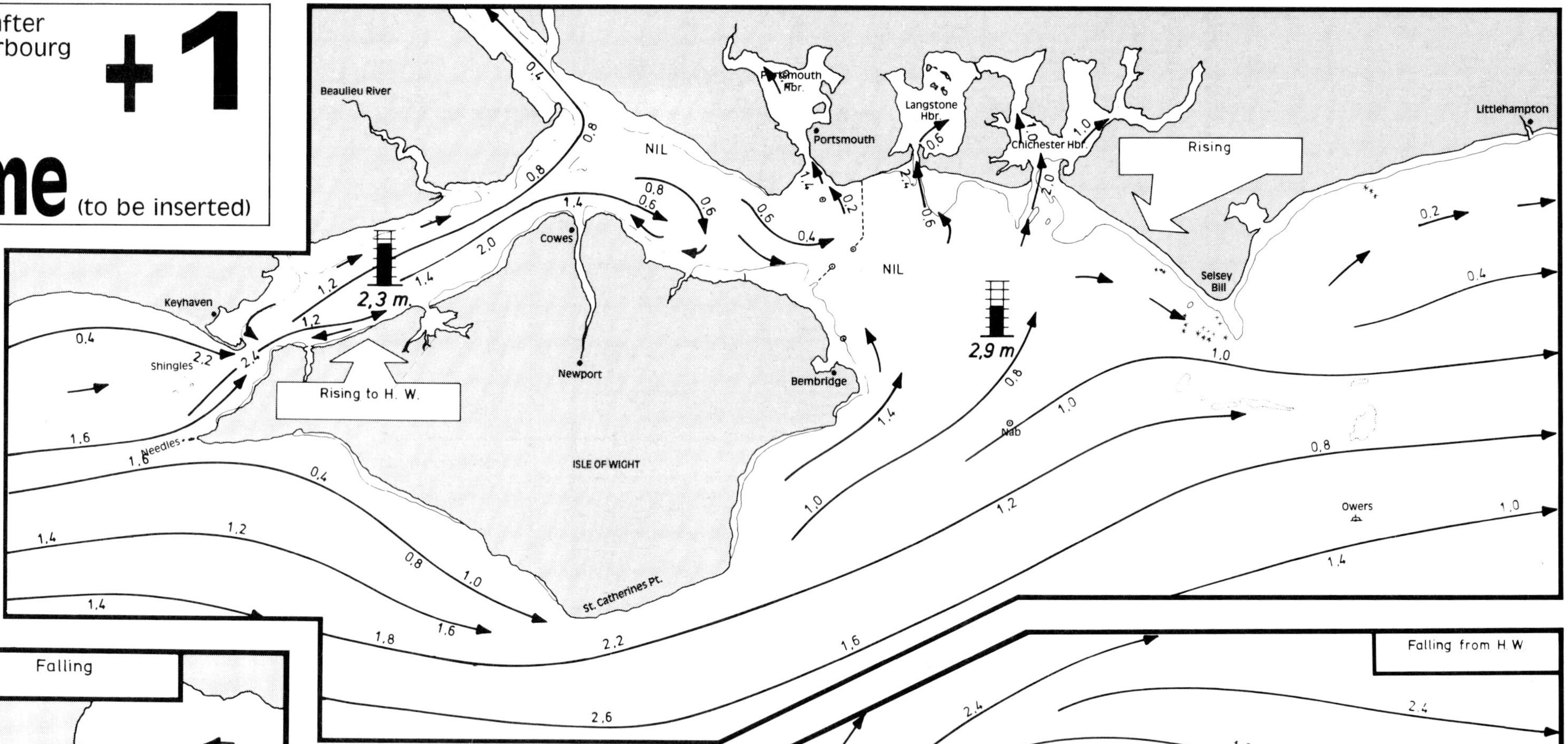

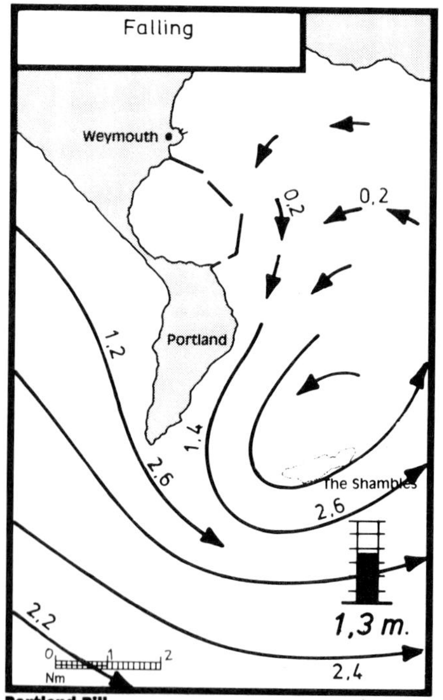

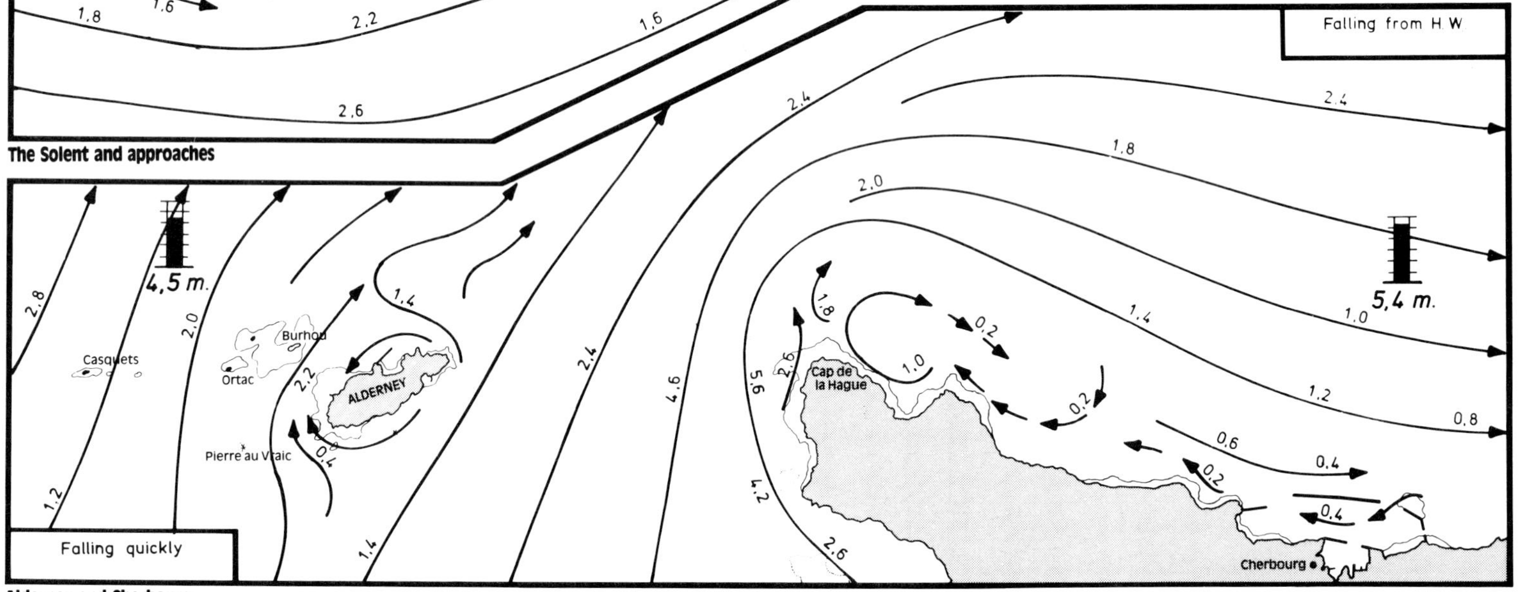

+1

Stream Rate Conversion Table

Mean Rate Figure from Chart	Pencil-in height of HW Cherbourg Read from column below pencil mark										
	4.8	5.0	5.2	5.4	5.6	5.8	6.0	6.2	6.4	6.6	6.8
0.2	0.1	0.1	0.1	0.1	0.2	0.2	0.2	0.3	0.3	0.3	0.3
0.4	0.2	0.2	0.2	0.3	0.3	0.4	0.5	0.5	0.6	0.6	0.7
0.6	0.2	0.3	0.4	0.4	0.5	0.6	0.7	0.7	0.8	0.9	1.0
0.8	0.4	0.4	0.5	0.6	0.7	0.8	0.9	1.0	1.1	1.2	1.3
1.0	0.4	0.5	0.6	0.7	0.9	1.0	1.1	1.2	1.3	1.4	1.5	1.7
1.2	0.5	0.6	0.7	0.9	1.0	1.2	1.3	1.4	1.6	1.7	1.9	2.0
1.4	0.6	0.7	0.9	1.0	1.2	1.4	1.5	1.7	1.8	2.0	2.2	2.3
1.6	0.6	0.8	1.0	1.2	1.4	1.6	1.7	1.9	2.1	2.3	2.5	2.7
1.8	0.7	0.9	1.1	1.3	1.5	1.7	2.0	2.2	2.4	2.6	2.8	3.0
2.0	0.8	1.0	1.2	1.5	1.7	1.9	2.2	2.4	2.6	2.9	3.1	3.3
2.2	0.9	1.1	1.4	1.6	1.9	2.1	2.3	2.6	2.9	3.2	3.4	3.7
2.4	0.9	1.2	1.5	1.8	2.1	2.3	2.6	2.9	3.2	3.4	3.7	4.0
2.6	1.0	1.3	1.6	1.9	2.2	2.5	2.8	3.1	3.4	3.7	4.0	4.3
2.8	1.1	1.4	1.7	2.1	2.4	2.7	3.0	3.4	3.7	4.0	4.3	4.7
3.0	1.2	1.5	1.9	2.2	2.6	2.9	3.2	3.6	4.0	4.3	4.6	5.0
3.2	1.3	1.6	2.0	2.4	2.7	3.1	3.4	3.8	4.2	4.6	4.9	5.3
3.4	1.3	1.7	2.1	2.5	2.9	3.3	3.7	4.1	4.5	4.9	5.3	5.7
3.6	1.4	1.8	2.2	2.7	3.1	3.5	3.9	4.3	4.7	5.2	5.6	6.0
3.8	1.5	1.9	2.4	2.8	3.3	3.7	4.1	4.6	5.0	5.4	5.9	6.3
4.0	1.6	2.0	2.5	3.0	3.4	3.9	4.3	4.8	5.3	5.7	6.2	6.7
4.2	1.7	2.1	2.6	3.1	3.6	4.1	4.6	5.0	5.5	6.0	6.5	7.0
4.4	1.7	2.1	2.7	3.3	3.8	4.3	4.8	5.3	5.8	6.3	6.8	7.3
4.6	1.8	2.3	2.9	3.4	3.9	4.5	5.0	5.5	6.1	6.6	7.1	7.7
4.8	1.9	2.4	3.0	3.6	4.1	4.7	5.2	5.8	6.3	6.9	7.4	8.0
5.0	2.0	2.5	3.1	3.7	4.3	4.9	5.4	6.0	6.6	7.2	7.7	8.3
5.2	2.0	2.6	3.2	3.8	4.4	5.0	5.6	6.2	6.8	7.4	8.0	8.6
5.4	2.1	2.8	3.4	4.0	4.6	5.2	5.7	6.5	7.1	7.7	8.4	9.0
5.6	2.2	2.9	3.5	4.1	4.8	5.4	6.1	6.7	7.4	8.0	8.7	9.3
5.8	2.3	3.0	3.6	4.3	5.0	5.6	6.3	7.0	7.6	8.3	9.0	9.6
6.0	2.4	3.1	3.7	4.4	5.1	5.8	6.5	7.2	7.9	8.6	9.3	9.9

TIDAL HEIGHTS — PORTS & PLACES

Pencil-in height of HW Cherbourg ▶	4.8	5.0	5.2	5.4	5.6	5.8	6.0	6.2	6.4	6.6	6.8
Lymington (& Yarmouth approx)	2.1	2.1	2.1	2.1	2.2	2.2	2.3	2.4	2.4	2.5	2.5
Portsmouth (Chichester entrance & Cowes approx)	2.8	2.8	2.8	2.8	2.9	2.9	2.9	3.0	3.0	3.1	3.1
Cherbourg (& Omonville approx)	4.6	4.8	5.0	5.2	5.3	5.5	5.7	5.8	6.0	6.2	6.4	6.5
Braye, Alderney	3.9	4.0	4.2	4.3	4.4	4.6	4.7	4.9	5.0	5.1	5.3	5.4
Weymouth	0.9	1.0	1.0	1.1	1.2	1.3	1.4	1.5	1.6	1.7	1.8	1.9
Poole entrance	1.5	1.5	1.5	1.5	1.6	1.6	1.7	1.8	1.8	1.9	2.0	2.0
Poole Town Quay	1.4	1.5	1.5	1.6	1.6	1.7	1.9	2.0	2.2	2.2	2.3	2.3
St Peter Port & Sark	5.3	5.4	5.6	5.7	5.8	5.9	6.1	6.2	6.3	6.4	6.4	6.5
St Helier	6.3	6.5	6.7	6.9	7.1	7.3	7.5	7.7	7.9	8.0	8.1	8.2
St Malo	6.5	6.7	6.9	7.1	7.3	7.6	7.8	8.0	8.2	8.3	8.3	8.4
Lezardrieux	5.1	5.2	5.3	5.3	5.4	5.4	5.5	5.5	5.6	5.6	5.6
Paimpol	5.3	5.4	5.4	5.5	5.6	5.6	5.7	5.7	5.8	5.8	5.9	5.9
Le Havre	6.1	6.3	6.5	6.7	6.9	7.1	7.3	7.5	7.7	7.8	8.0	8.1

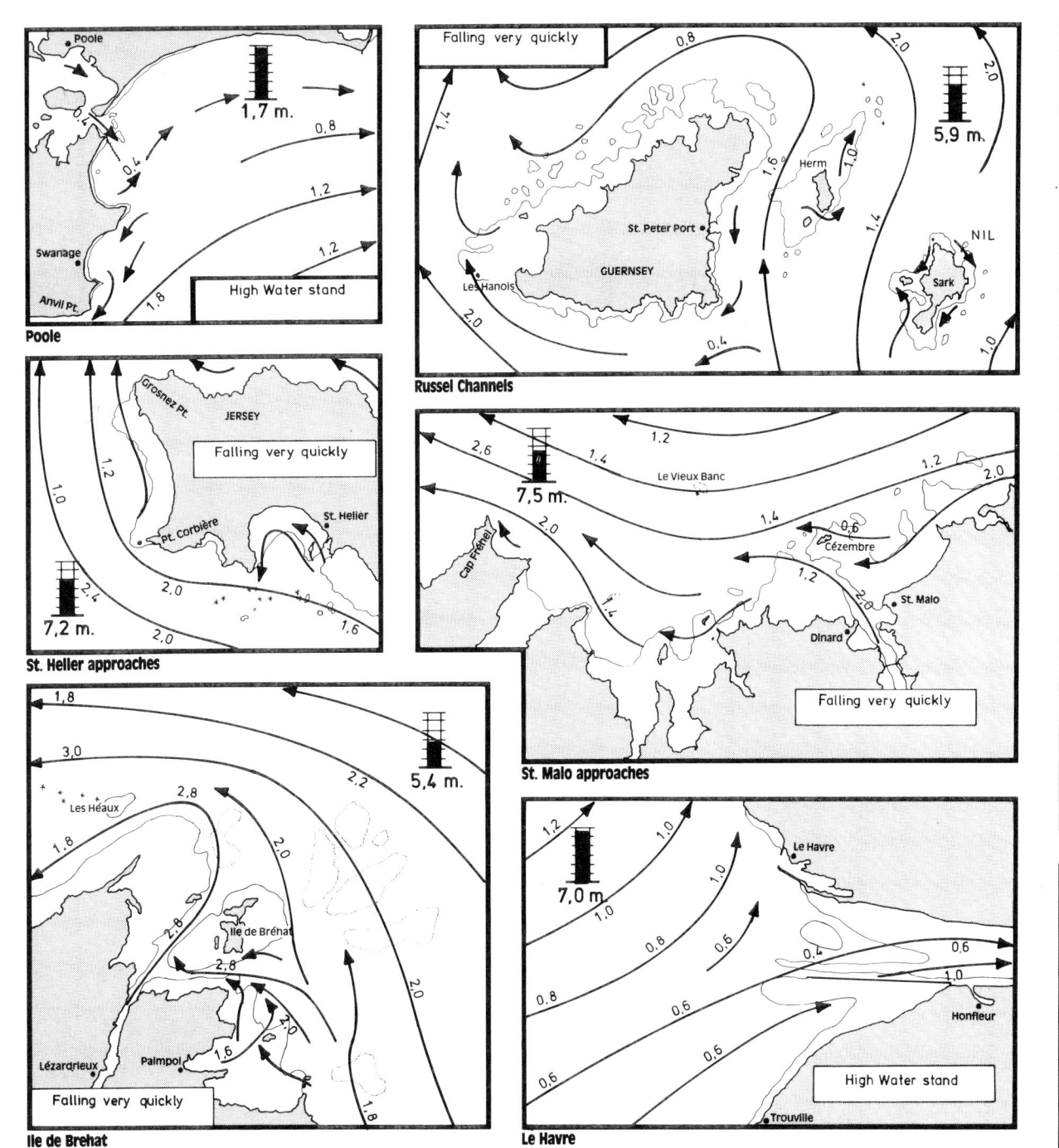

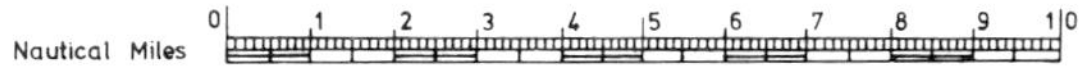

Copyright © J Reeve-Fowkes and Thomas Reed Publications.
No copying without permission.

2 hours after HW Cherbourg

+2

Time (to be inserted)

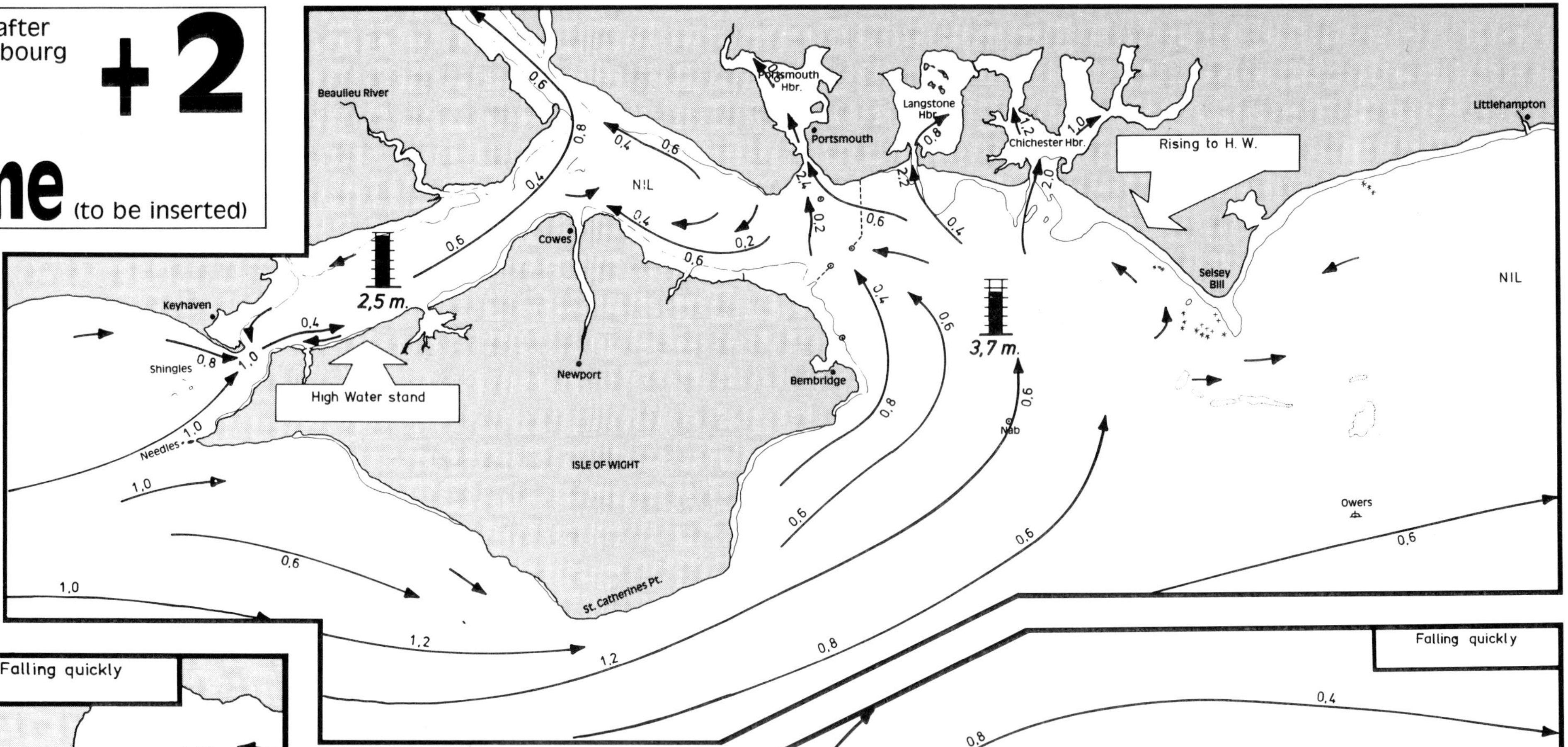

Beaulieu River

0.6

0.8

0.4

0.6

0.4

NIL

0.4

Cowes

0.6

2,5 m.

High Water stand

Keyhaven

0.4

0.8

1.0

Shingles

0.8

1.0

Needles 1.0

Newport

ISLE OF WIGHT

1.0

1.0

0.6

St. Catherines Pt.

1.2

1.2

Portsmouth Hbr.

Portsmouth

Langstone Hbr.

1.2

1.0

Chichester Hbr.

0.8

2.4

0.2

2.2

0.6

0.2

0.4

2.0

Rising to H. W.

Littlehampton

Selsey Bill

NIL

0.4

0.6

0.4

0.6

0.8

0.6

3,7 m.

Nab

0.5

Owers

0.5

0.8

0.6

0.5

The Solent and approaches

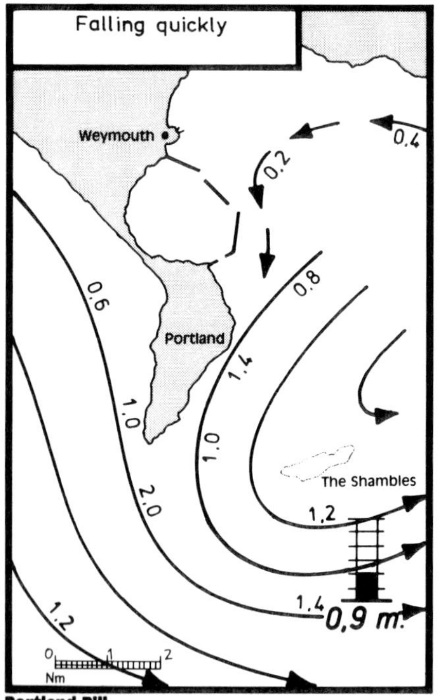

Falling quickly

0.4

Falling quickly

Weymouth

0.2

0.4

0.6

0.8

0.8

1.4

Portland

1.0

2.0

The Shambles

1.2

1.4

0.9 m.

1.2

0

Nm

1 2

Portland Bill

2.0

3,7 m.

Casquets

1.0

Burhou

Ortac 0.6

ALDERNEY

1.8

1.0

Pierre au Vraic 0.8

Falling quickly

0.4

0.8

0.8

3.2

1.8

2.4

1.8

2.8

1.8

1.2

Cap de la Hague

2.4

1.0

1.0

NIL

NIL

4,8 m.

NIL

0.2

0.2

0.6

0.4

1.8

Cherbourg

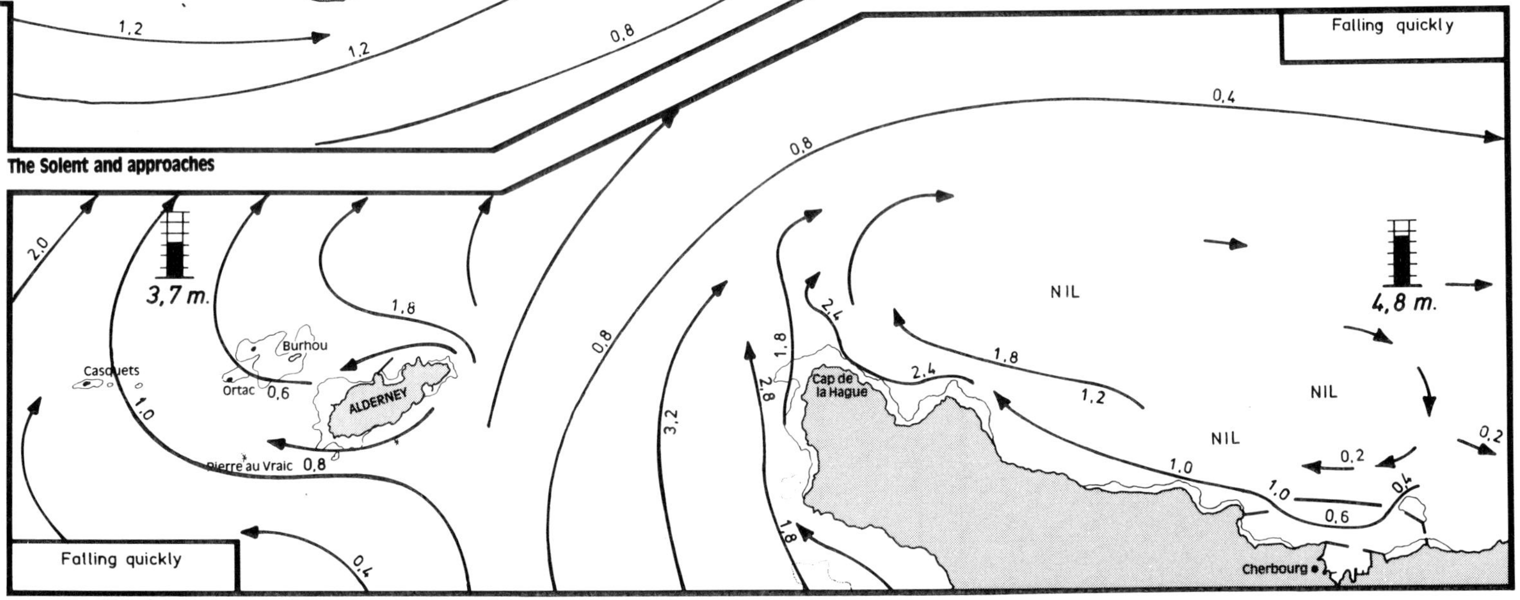

Alderney and Cherbourg

Copyright © J Reeve-Fowkes and
Thomas Reed Publications.
No copying without permission.

0 1 2 3 4 5 6 7 8 9 10 Nautical miles

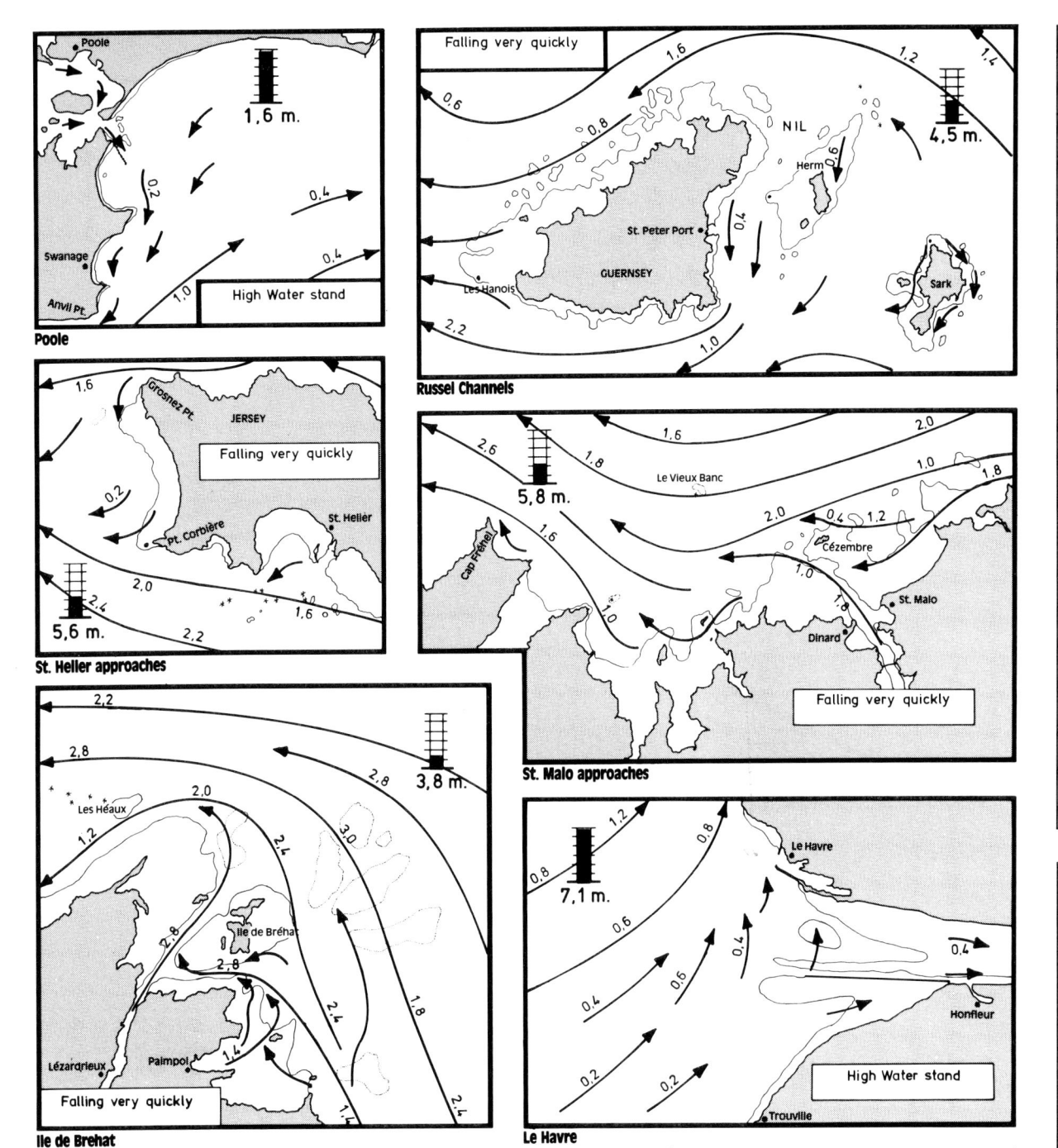

Stream Rate Conversion Table

+2

Mean Rate Figure from Chart ▼	Pencil-in height of HW Cherbourg Read from column below pencil mark											
	4.8	5.0	5.2	5.4	5.6	5.8	6.0	6.2	6.4	6.6	6.8
0.2	0.1	0.1	0.1	0.1	0.2	0.2	0.2	0.2	0.3	0.3	0.3
0.4	0.2	0.2	0.2	0.3	0.3	0.4	0.4	0.5	0.5	0.6	0.7
0.6	0.2	0.3	0.4	0.4	0.5	0.6	0.7	0.7	0.8	0.9	0.9	1.0
0.8	0.4	0.4	0.5	0.6	0.7	0.8	0.9	1.0	1.1	1.2	1.3
1.0	0.4	0.5	0.6	0.7	0.9	1.0	1.1	1.2	1.3	1.4	1.5	1.7
1.2	0.5	0.6	0.7	0.9	1.0	1.2	1.3	1.4	1.6	1.7	1.9	2.0
1.4	0.6	0.7	0.9	1.0	1.2	1.4	1.5	1.7	1.8	2.0	2.2	2.3
1.6	0.6	0.8	1.0	1.2	1.4	1.6	1.7	1.9	2.1	2.3	2.5	2.7
1.8	0.7	0.9	1.1	1.3	1.5	1.7	2.0	2.2	2.4	2.6	2.8	3.0
2.0	0.8	1.0	1.2	1.5	1.7	1.9	2.2	2.4	2.6	2.9	3.1	3.3
2.2	0.9	1.1	1.4	1.6	1.9	2.1	2.3	2.6	2.9	3.2	3.4	3.7
2.4	0.9	1.2	1.5	1.8	2.1	2.3	2.6	2.9	3.2	3.4	3.7	4.0
2.6	1.0	1.3	1.6	1.9	2.2	2.5	2.8	3.1	3.4	3.7	4.0
2.8	1.1	1.4	1.7	2.1	2.4	2.7	3.0	3.4	3.7	4.0	4.3	4.7
3.0	1.2	1.5	1.9	2.2	2.6	2.9	3.2	3.6	4.0	4.3	4.6	5.0
3.2	1.3	1.6	2.0	2.4	2.7	3.1	3.4	3.8	4.2	4.6	4.9	5.3
3.4	1.3	1.7	2.1	2.5	2.9	3.3	3.7	4.1	4.5	4.9	5.3	5.7
3.6	1.4	1.8	2.2	2.7	3.1	3.5	3.9	4.3	4.7	5.2	5.6	6.0
3.8	1.5	1.9	2.4	2.8	3.3	3.7	4.1	4.6	5.0	5.4	5.9	6.3
4.0	1.6	2.0	2.5	3.0	3.4	3.9	4.3	4.8	5.3	5.7	6.2	6.7
4.2	1.7	2.1	2.6	3.1	3.6	4.1	4.5	5.0	5.5	6.0	6.5	7.0
4.4	1.7	2.2	2.7	3.3	3.8	4.3	4.8	5.3	5.8	6.3	6.8	7.3
4.6	1.8	2.3	2.9	3.4	3.9	4.5	5.0	5.5	6.1	6.6	7.1	7.7
4.8	1.9	2.4	3.0	3.6	4.1	4.7	5.2	5.8	6.3	6.9	7.4	8.0
5.0	2.0	2.5	3.1	3.7	4.3	4.9	5.4	6.0	6.6	7.2	7.7	8.3
5.2	2.0	2.6	3.2	3.8	4.4	5.0	5.6	6.2	6.8	7.4	8.0	8.6
5.4	2.1	2.8	3.4	4.0	4.6	5.2	5.7	6.5	7.1	7.7	8.4	9.0
5.6	2.2	2.9	3.5	4.1	4.8	5.4	6.1	6.7	7.4	8.0	8.7	9.3
5.8	2.3	3.0	3.6	4.3	5.0	5.6	6.3	7.0	7.6	8.3	9.0	9.6
6.0	2.4	3.1	3.7	4.4	5.1	5.8	6.5	7.2	7.9	8.6	9.3	9.9

TIDAL HEIGHTS — PORTS & PLACES

Pencil-in height of HW Cherbourg ▶	4.8	5.0	5.2	5.4	5.6	5.8	6.0	6.2	6.4	6.6	6.8
Lymington (& Yarmouth approx)	2.2	2.3	2.3	2.4	2.4	2.5	2.6	2.7	2.8	2.9	3.0
Portsmouth (Chichester entrance & Cowes approx)	3.3	3.4	3.4	3.5	3.6	3.7	3.7	3.8	3.9	4.0	4.1
Cherbourg (& Omonville approx)	4.4	4.5	4.5	4.6	4.7	4.8	4.9	5.0	5.1	5.2	5.3	5.4
Braye, Alderney	3.6	3.6	3.6	3.6	3.7	3.7	3.7	3.8	3.8	3.9	4.0
Weymouth	0.8	0.8	0.8	0.8	0.9	0.9	0.9	1.0	1.0	1.1	1.1	1.2
Poole entrance	1.5	1.5	1.5	1.5	1.5	1.5	1.6	1.6	1.7	1.7	1.7
Poole Town Quay	1.6	1.6	1.6	1.6	1.6	1.6	1.7	1.9	2.0	2.0	2.1
St Peter Port & Sark	4.8	4.7	4.7	4.6	4.6	4.5	4.5	4.4	4.4	4.3	4.3	4.2
St Helier	5.7	5.7	5.7	5.7	5.7	5.6	5.6	5.6	5.6	5.5	5.5
St Malo	5.8	5.8	5.8	5.8	5.8	5.9	5.9	5.9	5.8	5.8	5.7	5.7
Lezardrieux	4.4	4.3	4.1	4.0	3.9	3.9	3.8	3.7	3.6	3.5	3.4
Paimpol	4.6	4.5	4.3	4.2	4.1	4.0	3.9	3.8	3.7	3.5	3.4	3.2
Le Havre	6.2	6.4	6.6	6.8	7.0	7.2	7.4	7.6	7.8	7.9	8.1	8.2

Copyright © J Reeve-Fowkes and Thomas Reed Publications.
No copying without permission.

3 hours after
HW Cherbourg

+3

Time (to be inserted)

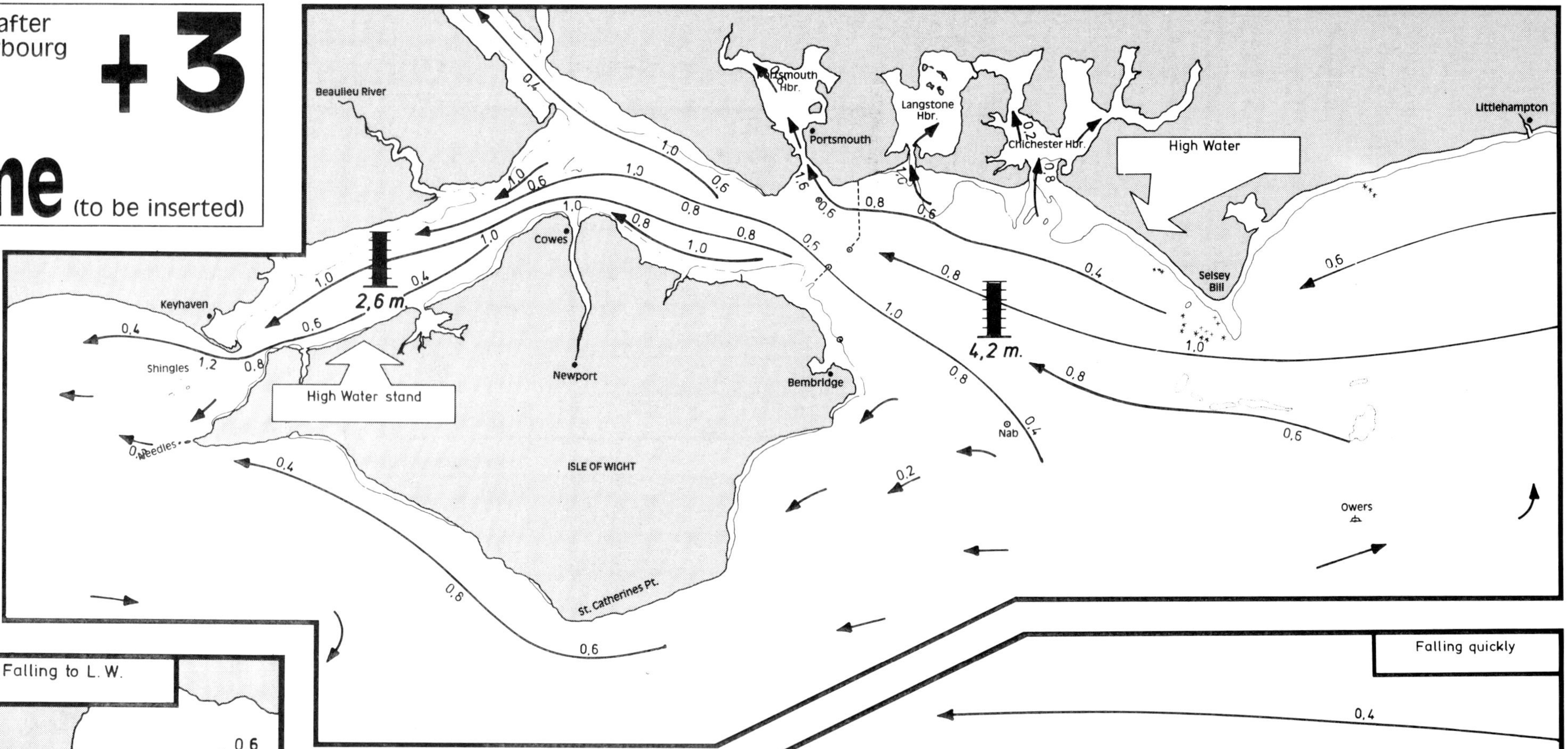

The Solent and approaches

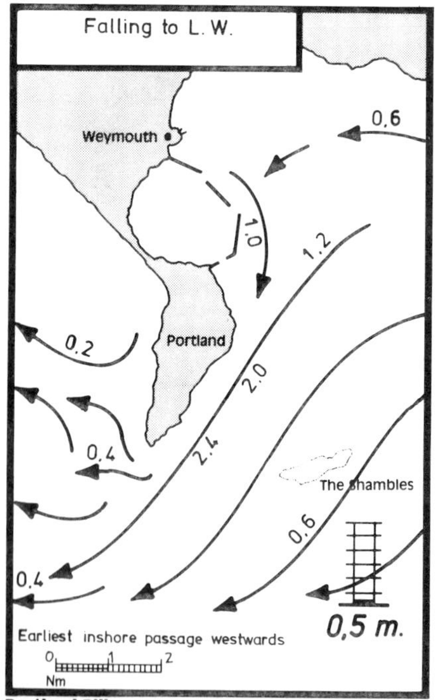

Portland Bill

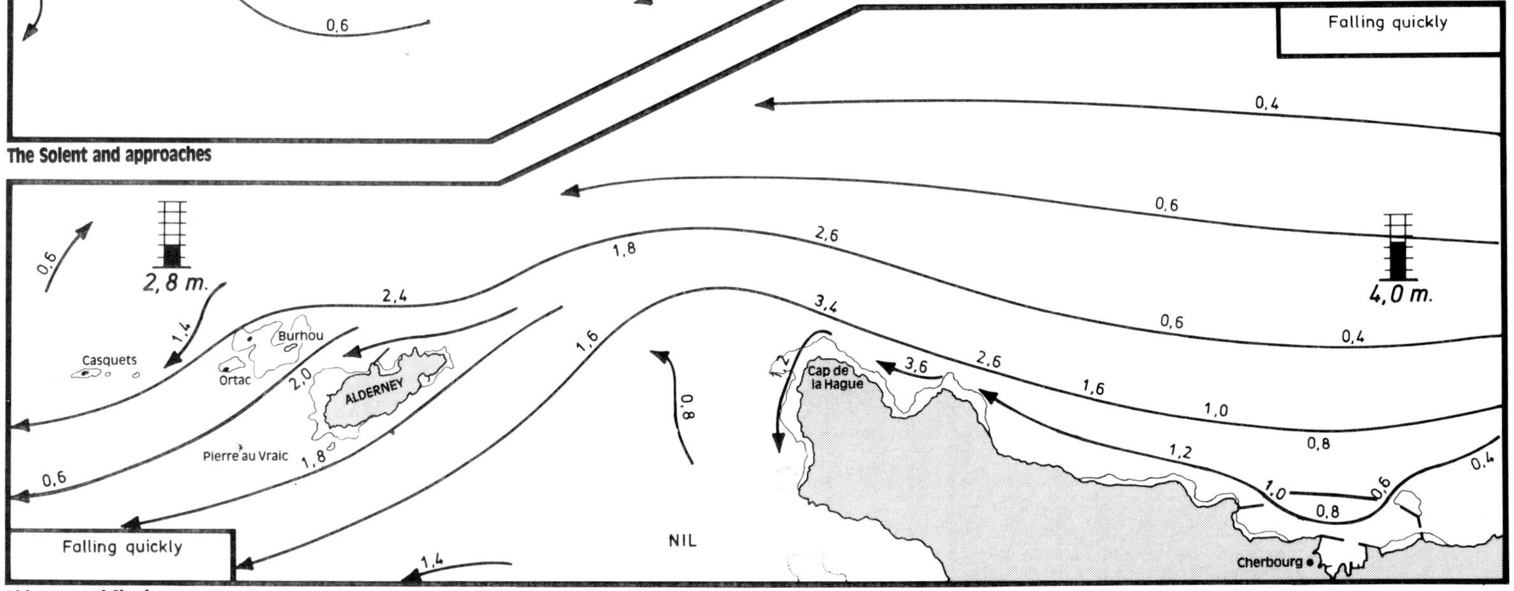

Alderney and Cherbourg

0 1 2 3 4 5 6 7 8 9 10 Nautical miles

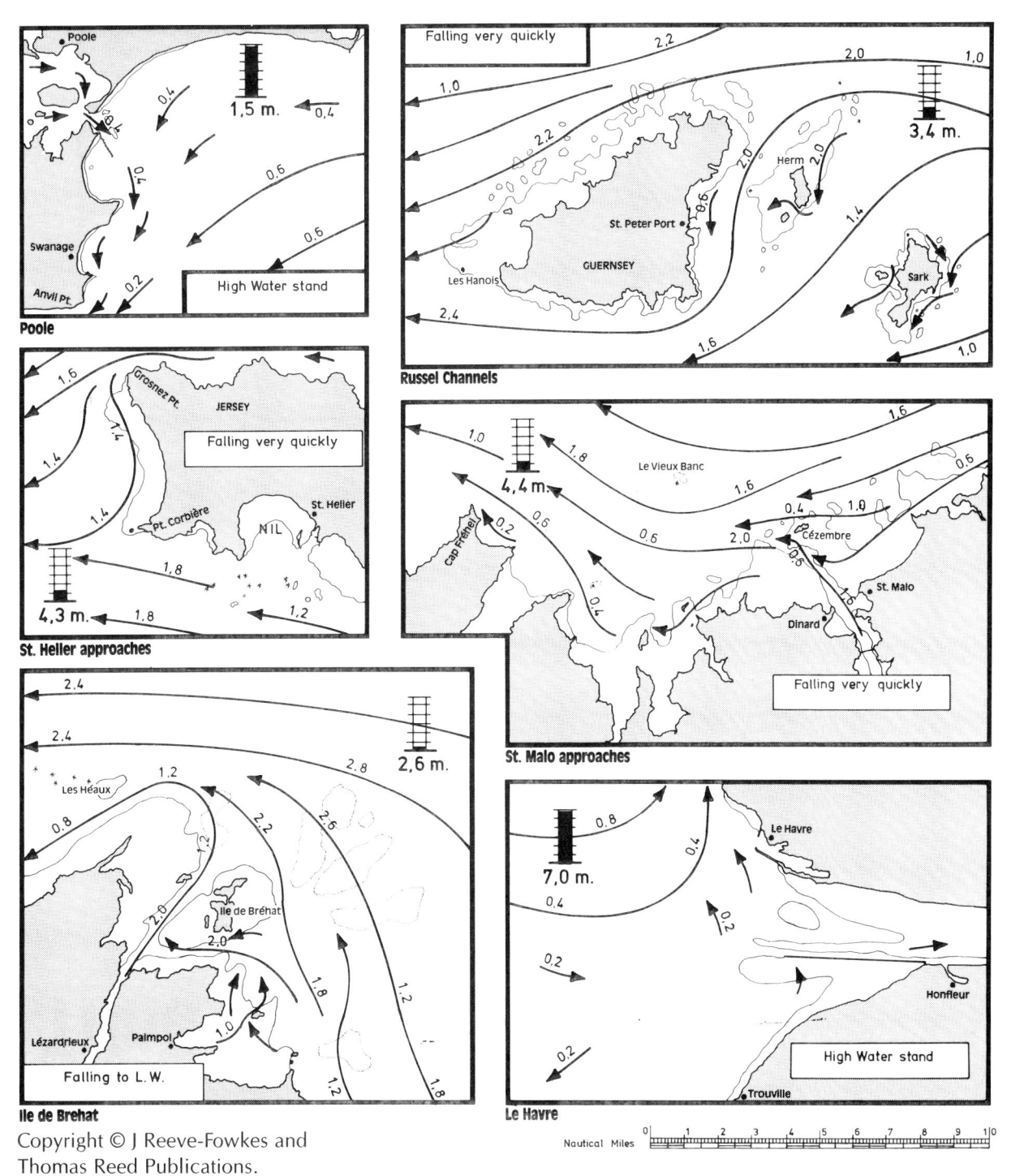

+3

Poole
- 1,5 m. High Water stand
- Falling very quickly

Russel Channels
- 3,4 m.
- Guernsey, St. Peter Port, Les Hanois, Herm, Sark

St. Helier approaches
- 4,3 m.
- Grosnez Pt., Jersey, Pt. Corbière, St. Helier
- Falling very quickly
- NIL

St. Malo approaches
- 4,4 m.
- Le Vieux Banc, Cap Fréhel, Cézembre, St. Malo, Dinard
- Falling very quickly

Ile de Bréhat
- 2,6 m.
- Les Héaux, Île de Bréhat, Lézardrieux, Paimpol
- Falling to L.W.

Le Havre
- 7,0 m.
- Le Havre, Honfleur, Trouville
- High Water stand

Copyright © J Reeve-Fowkes and Thomas Reed Publications.
No copying without permission.

Nautical Miles 0–10

Stream Rate Conversion Table

Mean Rate Figure from Chart	Pencil-in height of HW Cherbourg — Read from column below pencil mark										
	4.8	5.0	5.2	5.4	5.6	5.8	6.0	6.2	6.4	6.6	6.8
0.2	0.1	0.1	0.1	0.1	0.2	0.2	0.2	0.2	0.3	0.3	0.3
0.4	0.2	0.2	0.2	0.3	0.3	0.4	0.4	0.5	0.5	0.6	0.7
0.6	0.2	0.3	0.4	0.4	0.5	0.6	0.7	0.7	0.8	0.9	1.0
0.8	0.4	0.4	0.5	0.6	0.7	0.8	0.9	1.0	1.1	1.2	1.3
1.0	0.4	0.5	0.6	0.7	0.9	1.0	1.1	1.2	1.3	1.4	1.5	1.7
1.2	0.5	0.6	0.7	0.9	1.0	1.2	1.3	1.4	1.6	1.7	1.9	2.0
1.4	0.6	0.7	0.9	1.0	1.2	1.4	1.5	1.7	1.8	2.0	2.2	2.3
1.6	0.6	0.8	1.0	1.2	1.4	1.6	1.7	1.9	2.1	2.3	2.5	2.7
1.8	0.7	0.9	1.1	1.3	1.5	1.7	2.0	2.2	2.4	2.6	2.8	3.0
2.0	0.8	1.0	1.2	1.5	1.7	1.9	2.2	2.4	2.6	2.9	3.1	3.3
2.2	0.9	1.1	1.4	1.6	1.9	2.1	2.3	2.6	2.9	3.2	3.4	3.7
2.4	0.9	1.2	1.5	1.8	2.1	2.3	2.6	2.9	3.2	3.4	3.7	4.0
2.6	1.0	1.3	1.6	1.9	2.2	2.5	2.8	3.1	3.4	3.7	4.0	4.3
2.8	1.1	1.4	1.7	2.1	2.4	2.7	3.0	3.4	3.7	4.0	4.3	4.7
3.0	1.2	1.5	1.9	2.2	2.6	2.9	3.2	3.6	4.0	4.3	4.6	5.0
3.2	1.3	1.6	2.0	2.4	2.7	3.1	3.4	3.8	4.2	4.6	4.9	5.3
3.4	1.3	1.7	2.1	2.5	2.9	3.3	3.7	4.1	4.5	4.9	5.3	5.7
3.6	1.4	1.8	2.2	2.7	3.1	3.5	3.9	4.3	4.7	5.2	5.6	6.0
3.8	1.5	1.9	2.4	2.8	3.3	3.7	4.1	4.6	5.0	5.4	5.9	6.3
4.0	1.6	2.0	2.5	3.0	3.4	3.9	4.3	4.8	5.3	5.7	6.2	6.7
4.2	1.7	2.1	2.6	3.1	3.6	4.1	4.6	5.0	5.5	6.0	6.5	7.0
4.4	1.7	2.2	2.7	3.3	3.8	4.3	4.8	5.3	5.8	6.3	6.8	7.3
4.6	1.8	2.3	2.9	3.4	3.9	4.5	5.0	5.5	6.1	6.6	7.1	7.7
4.8	1.9	2.4	3.0	3.6	4.1	4.7	5.2	5.8	6.3	6.9	7.4	8.0
5.0	2.0	2.5	3.1	3.7	4.3	4.9	5.4	6.0	6.6	7.2	7.7	8.3
5.2	2.0	2.6	3.2	3.8	4.4	5.0	5.6	6.2	6.8	7.4	8.0	8.6
5.4	2.1	2.8	3.4	4.0	4.6	5.2	5.7	6.5	7.1	7.7	8.4	9.0
5.6	2.2	2.9	3.5	4.1	4.8	5.4	6.1	6.7	7.4	8.0	8.7	9.3
5.8	2.3	3.0	3.6	4.3	5.0	5.6	6.3	7.0	7.6	8.3	9.0	9.6
6.0	2.4	3.1	3.7	4.4	5.1	5.8	6.5	7.2	7.9	8.6	9.3	9.9

TIDAL HEIGHTS — PORTS & PLACES

Pencil-in height of HW Cherbourg	4.8	5.0	5.2	5.4	5.6	5.8	6.0	6.2	6.4	6.6	6.8
Lymington (& Yarmouth approx)	2.4	2.5	2.5	2.6	2.6	2.7	2.8	2.8	2.9	3.0	3.0	3.1
Portsmouth (Chichester entrance & Cowes approx)	3.5	3.6	3.8	3.9	4.0	4.2	4.3	4.5	4.6	4.7	4.8	4.9
Cherbourg (& Omonville approx)	3.9	3.9	3.9	3.9	4.0	4.0	4.0	4.1	4.1	4.1	4.1
Braye, Alderney	3.2	3.1	3.1	3.0	2.9	2.8	2.8	2.7	2.6	2.5	2.5	2.4
Weymouth	0.8	0.7	0.7	0.6	0.6	0.5	0.5	0.4	0.4	0.4	0.4	0.4
Poole entrance	1.5	1.5	1.5	1.5	1.5	1.5	1.5	1.5	1.5	1.5	1.4	1.4
Poole Town Quay	1.7	1.7	1.7	1.7	1.7	1.7	1.7	1.7	1.7	1.7	1.7	1.7
St Peter Port & Sark	4.4	4.2	4.0	3.8	3.6	3.3	3.1	2.9	2.7	2.5	2.3	2.1
St Helier	5.2	5.0	4.8	4.6	4.4	4.3	4.1	3.9	3.7	3.5	3.4	3.2
St Malo	5.3	5.1	4.9	4.7	4.5	4.4	4.2	4.0	3.8	3.6	3.4	3.2
Lezardrieux	3.9	3.6	3.4	3.1	2.8	2.6	2.3	2.1	1.8	1.5	1.3	1.0
Paimpol	4.1	3.8	3.6	3.3	3.0	2.7	2.5	2.2	1.9	1.6	1.4	1.1
Le Havre	6.0	6.3	6.4	6.6	6.8	7.1	7.3	7.5	7.7	7.8	8.0	8.1

4 hours after HW Cherbourg

+4

Time (to be inserted)

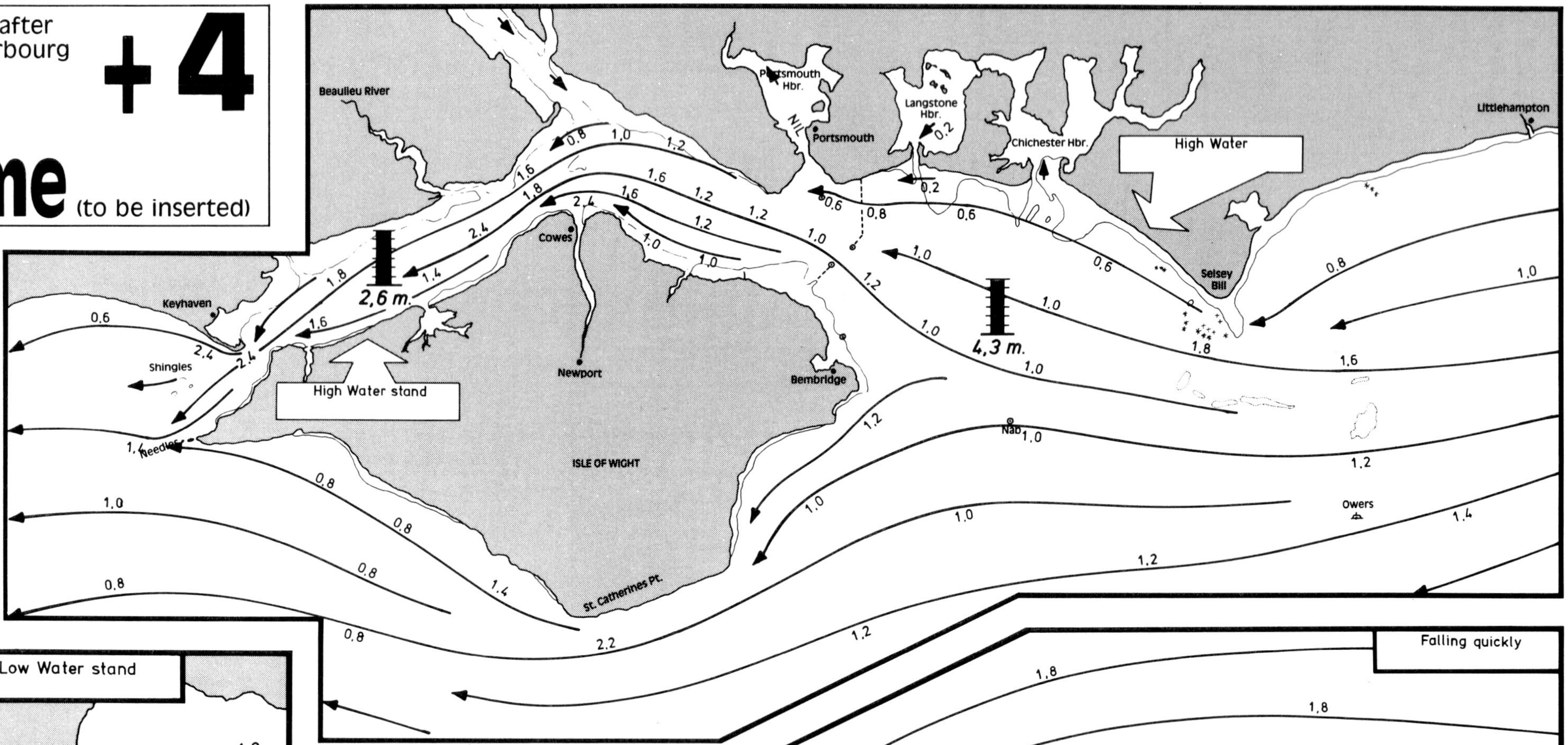

Beaulieu River

Littlehampton

Portsmouth Hbr.

Langstone Hbr. 0.2

Chichester Hbr.

High Water

0.8 1.0 1.2

NIL

Portsmouth

0.6 0.8 0.6

1.6

1.8

2.4

2.4 1.6

1.2 1.2

Cowes

1.6 1.2 1.0

Selsey Bill 0.8

1.0

1.0

2.6 m.

1.4

1.0 1.0

0.6

1.0

4,3 m.

1.8

1.0

Keyhaven

0.6

2.4

2.4

1.6

Shingles

High Water stand

Newport

Bembridge

1.2

1.0

Nab 1.0

1.6

1.2

Needles

1.0

ISLE OF WIGHT

0.8

1.0

0.8

0.8

Owers

1.4

0.8

0.8

St. Catherines Pt.

1.0

1.0

1.2

0.8

2.2

1.2

Falling quickly

1.8

The Solent and approaches

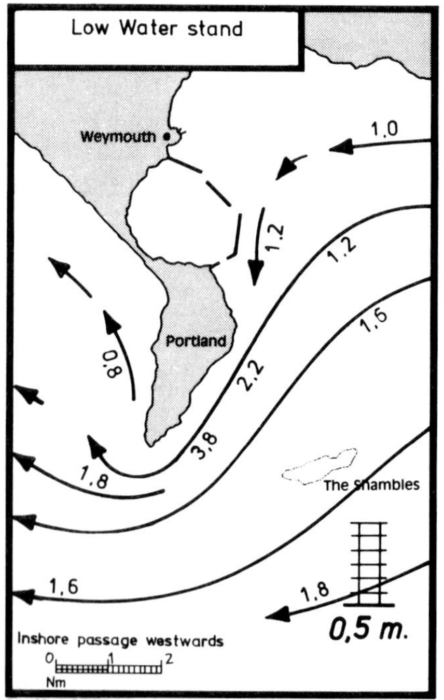

1.8

Low Water stand

Weymouth

1.0

3.0

1.6

1.2

1.2

1.2

1.8

1.4

1.2

0.8

2.8

2,1 m.

Burhou

2.4

3.8

3,2 m.

Portland

0.8

2.2

Casquets

Ortac

ALDERNEY

3.2

3.8

3.4

4.4

1.4

Cap de la Hague

4.4

3.8

1.6

1.8

1.4

1.8

2.2

Pierre au Vraic

2.4

2.4

1.4

1.0

1.0

The Shambles

1.6

1.8

0,5 m.

Falling quickly

2.4

2.2

1.4

0.6

Cherbourg

Inshore passage westwards

0 Nm 2

Portland Bill

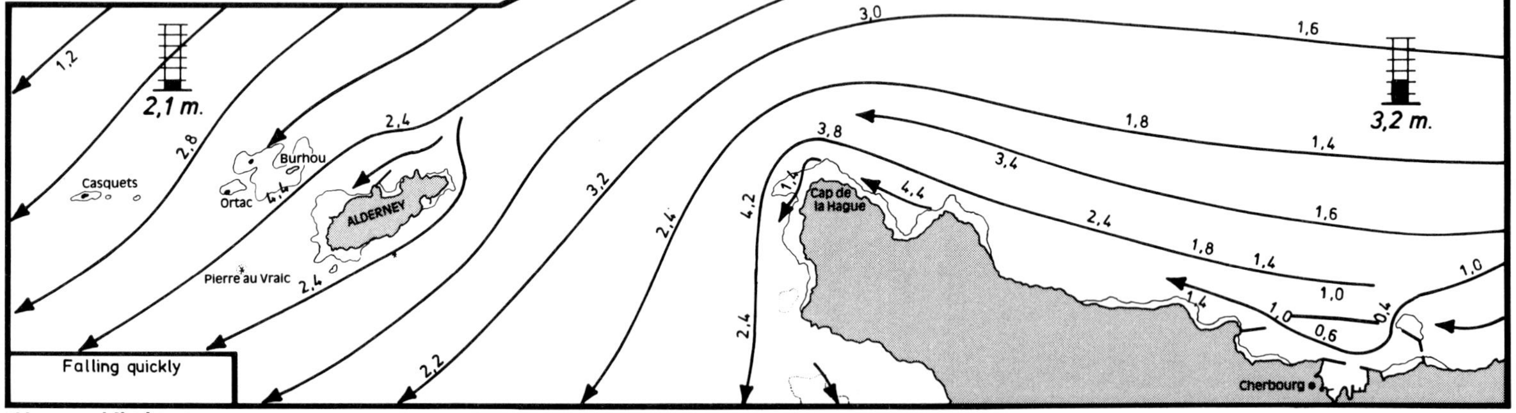

Alderney and Cherbourg

Copyright © J Reeve-Fowkes and
Thomas Reed Publications.
No copying without permission.

0 1 2 3 4 5 6 7 8 9 10 Nautical miles

+4

Stream Rate Conversion Table

Mean Rate Figure from Chart ▼	Pencil-in height of HW Cherbourg Read from column below pencil mark										
	4.8	5.0	5.2	5.4	5.6	5.8	6.0	6.2	6.4	6.6	6.8
0.2	0.1	0.1	0.1	0.1	0.2	0.2	0.2	0.2	0.3	0.3	0.3
0.4	0.2	0.2	0.2	0.3	0.3	0.4	0.4	0.5	0.5	0.6	0.7
0.6	0.2	0.3	0.4	0.4	0.5	0.6	0.7	0.7	0.8	0.9	1.0
0.8	0.4	0.4	0.5	0.6	0.7	0.8	0.9	1.0	1.1	1.2	1.3
1.0	0.4	0.5	0.6	0.7	0.9	1.0	1.1	1.2	1.3	1.4	1.5
1.2	0.5	0.6	0.7	0.9	1.0	1.2	1.3	1.4	1.6	1.7	1.9	2.0
1.4	0.6	0.7	0.9	1.0	1.2	1.4	1.5	1.7	1.8	2.0	2.2	2.3
1.6	0.6	0.8	1.0	1.2	1.4	1.6	1.7	1.9	2.1	2.3	2.5	2.7
1.8	0.7	0.9	1.1	1.3	1.5	1.7	2.0	2.2	2.4	2.6	2.8	3.0
2.0	0.8	1.0	1.2	1.5	1.7	1.9	2.2	2.4	2.6	2.9	3.1	3.3
2.2	0.9	1.1	1.4	1.6	1.9	2.1	2.3	2.6	2.9	3.4	3.7
2.4	0.9	1.2	1.5	1.8	2.1	2.3	2.6	2.9	3.2	3.4	3.7	4.0
2.6	1.0	1.3	1.6	1.9	2.2	2.5	2.8	3.1	3.4	3.7	4.0	4.3
2.8	1.1	1.4	1.7	2.1	2.4	2.7	3.0	3.4	3.7	4.0	4.3	4.7
3.0	1.2	1.5	1.9	2.2	2.6	2.9	3.2	3.6	4.0	4.3	4.6	5.0
3.2	1.3	1.6	2.0	2.4	2.7	3.1	3.4	3.8	4.2	4.6	4.9	5.3
3.4	1.3	1.7	2.1	2.5	2.9	3.3	3.7	4.1	4.5	4.9	5.3	5.7
3.6	1.4	1.8	2.2	2.7	3.1	3.5	3.9	4.3	4.7	5.2	5.6	6.0
3.8	1.5	1.9	2.4	2.8	3.3	3.7	4.1	4.6	5.0	5.4	5.9	6.3
4.0	1.6	2.0	2.5	3.0	3.4	3.9	4.3	4.8	5.3	5.7	6.2	6.7
4.2	1.7	2.1	2.6	3.1	3.6	4.1	4.6	5.0	5.5	6.0	6.5	7.0
4.4	1.7	2.2	2.7	3.3	3.8	4.3	4.8	5.3	5.8	6.3	6.8	7.3
4.6	1.8	2.3	2.9	3.4	3.9	4.5	5.0	5.5	6.1	6.6	7.1	7.7
4.8	1.9	2.4	3.0	3.6	4.1	4.7	5.2	5.8	6.3	6.9	7.4	8.0
5.0	2.0	2.5	3.1	3.7	4.3	4.9	5.4	6.0	6.6	7.2	7.7	8.3
5.2	2.0	2.6	3.2	3.8	4.4	5.0	5.6	6.2	6.8	7.4	8.0	8.6
5.4	2.1	2.8	3.4	4.0	4.6	5.2	5.7	6.5	7.1	7.7	8.4	9.0
5.6	2.2	2.9	3.5	4.1	4.8	5.4	6.1	6.7	7.4	8.0	8.7	9.3
5.8	2.3	3.0	3.6	4.3	5.0	5.6	6.3	7.0	7.6	8.3	9.0	9.6
6.0	2.4	3.1	3.7	4.4	5.1	5.8	6.5	7.2	7.9	8.6	9.3	9.9

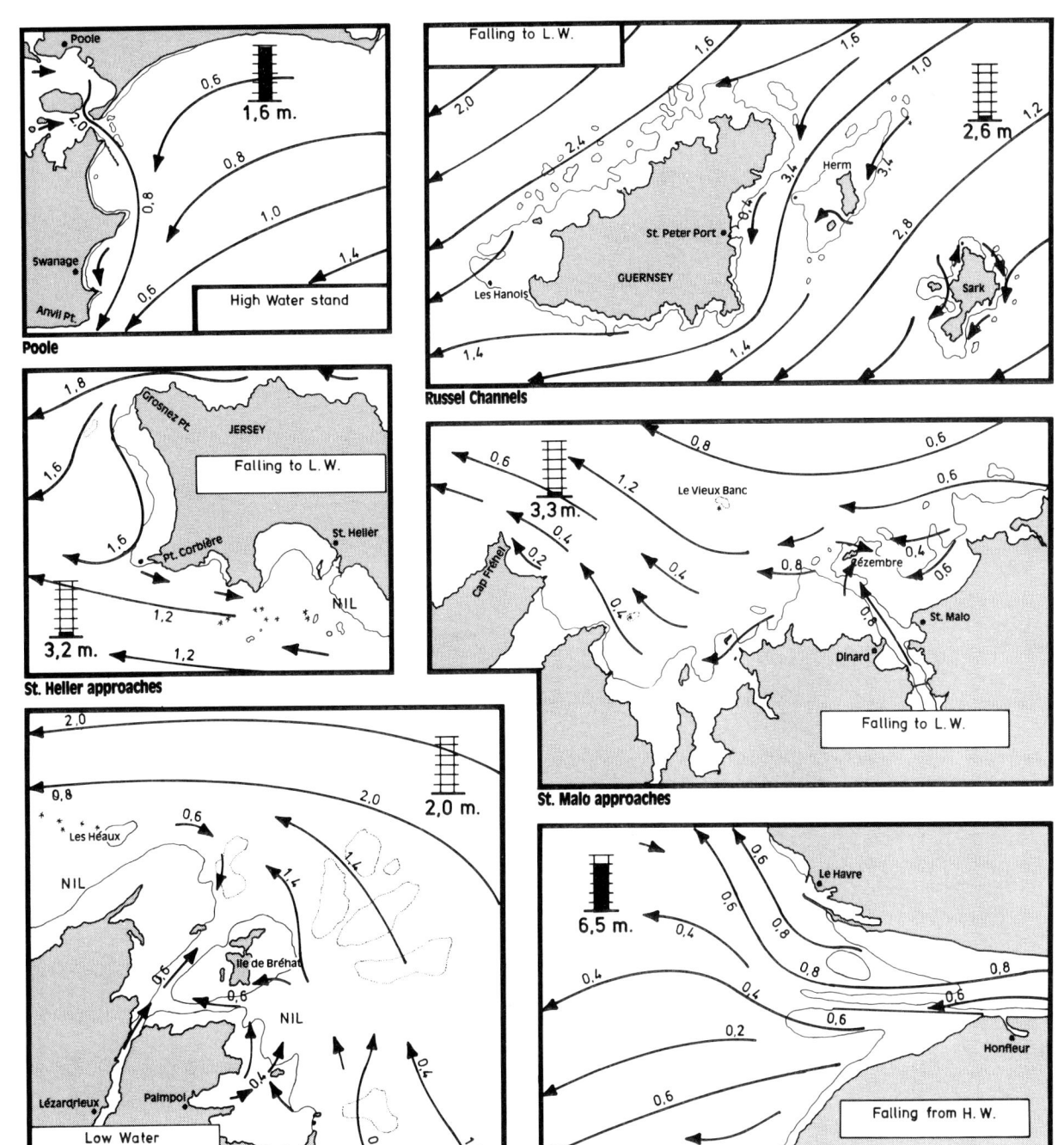

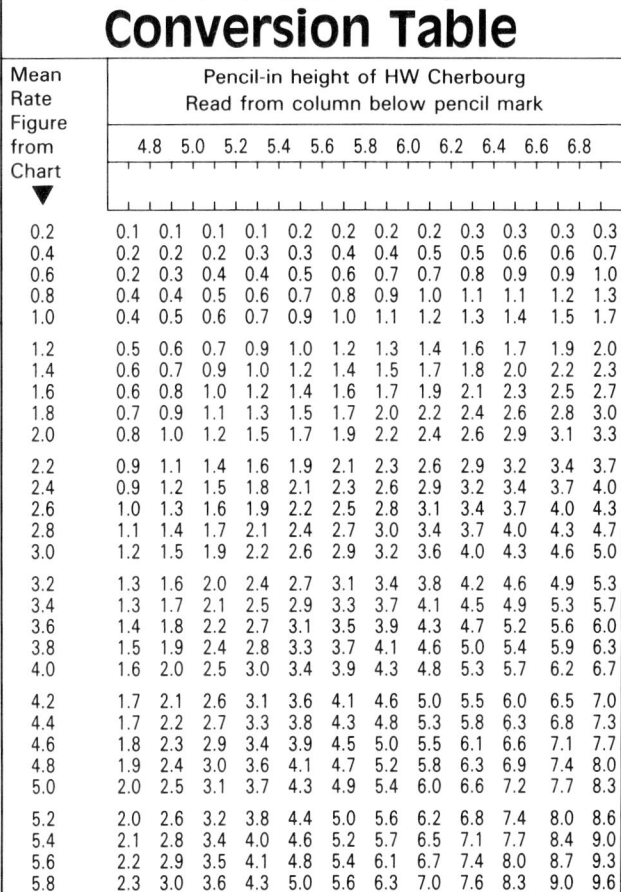

TIDAL HEIGHTS — PORTS & PLACES

Pencil-in height of HW Cherbourg ▶	4.8	5.0	5.2	5.4	5.6	5.8	6.0	6.2	6.4	6.6	6.8
Lymington (& Yarmouth approx)	2.4	2.5	2.5	2.6	2.6	2.7	2.8	2.8	2.9	3.0	3.0	3.1
Portsmouth (Chichester entrance & Cowes approx)	3.6	3.7	3.9	4.0	4.1	4.2	4.4	4.5	4.6	4.7	4.8	4.9
Cherbourg (& Omonville approx)	3.6	3.5	3.5	3.4	3.3	3.2	3.2	3.1	3.0	2.9	2.8	2.7
Braye, Alderney	3.0	2.8	2.6	2.4	2.3	2.1	1.9	1.8	1.6	1.4	1.3	1.1
Weymouth	0.9	0.8	0.8	0.7	0.6	0.5	0.4	0.3	0.2	0.2	0.1	0.1
Poole entrance	1.6	1.6	1.6	1.6	1.5	1.5	1.5	1.5	1.5	1.5	1.4	1.4
Poole Town Quay	1.8	1.8	1.8	1.8	1.8	1.8	1.7	1.7	1.6	1.6	1.6	1.6
St Peter Port & Sark	4.2	3.9	3.5	3.2	2.9	2.5	2.2	1.8	1.5	1.2	0.9	0.6
St Helier	4.8	4.5	4.1	3.8	3.5	3.2	2.8	2.5	2.2	1.9	1.6	1.3
St Malo	4.9	4.6	4.2	3.9	3.6	3.2	2.9	2.5	2.2	1.9	1.6	1.3
Lezardrieux	3.8	3.4	3.0	2.6	2.3	1.9	1.5	1.2	0.8	0.5	0.2	-0.1
Paimpol	3.8	3.4	3.0	2.6	2.2	1.9	1.5	1.1	0.7	0.4	0.1	-0.2
Le Havre	5.8	5.9	6.1	6.2	6.4	6.5	6.7	6.8	7.0	7.1	7.1	7.2

Copyright © J Reeve-Fowkes and Thomas Reed Publications.
No copying without permission.

5 hours after
HW Cherbourg

+5

Time (to be inserted)

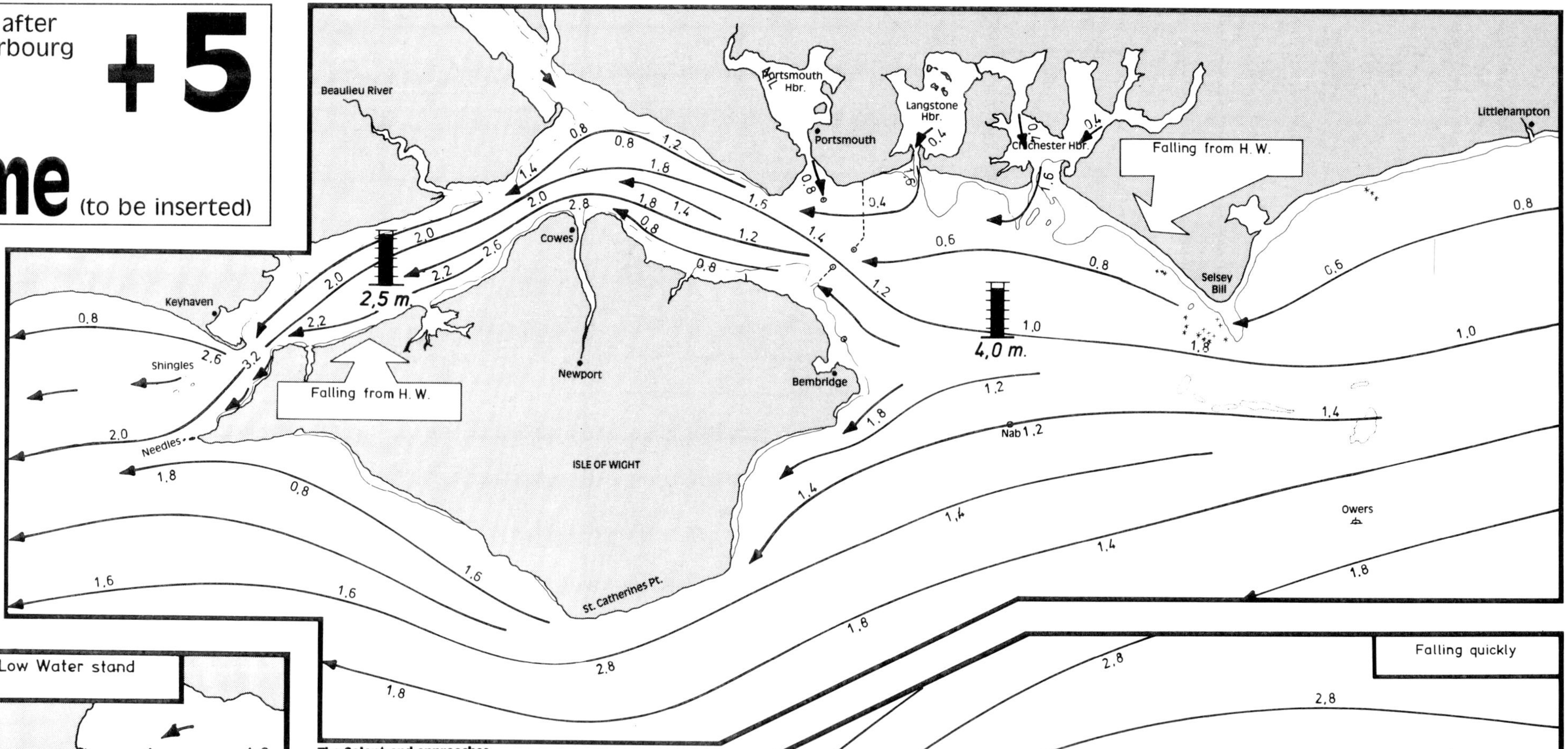

The Solent and approaches

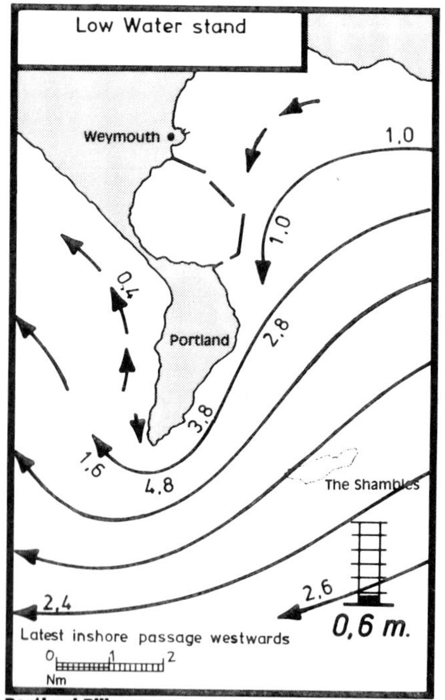

Portland Bill

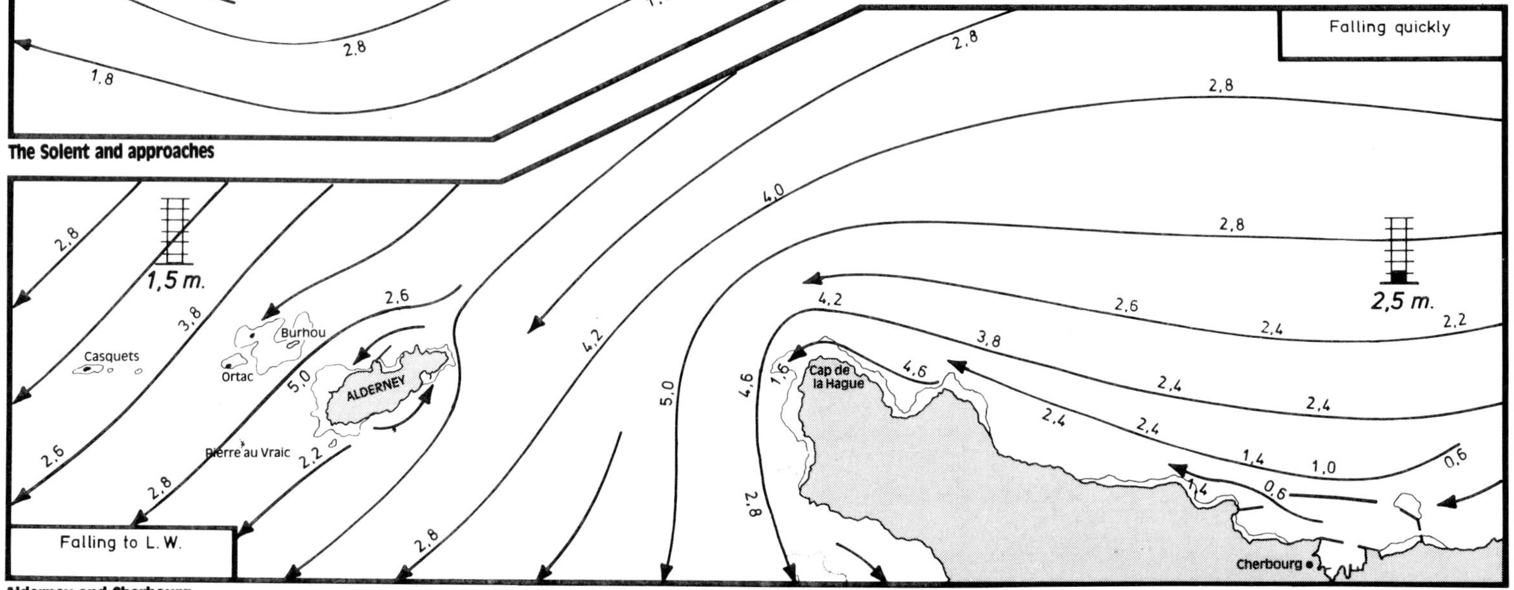

Alderney and Cherbourg

0 1 2 3 4 5 6 7 8 9 10 Nautical miles

+5

Stream Rate Conversion Table

Mean Rate Figure from Chart ▼	Pencil-in height of HW Cherbourg Read from column below pencil mark										
	4.8	5.0	5.2	5.4	5.6	5.8	6.0	6.2	6.4	6.6	6.8
0.2	0.1	0.1	0.1	0.1	0.2	0.2	0.2	0.2	0.3	0.3	0.3
0.4	0.2	0.2	0.2	0.3	0.3	0.4	0.4	0.5	0.5	0.6	0.7
0.6	0.2	0.3	0.4	0.4	0.5	0.6	0.7	0.7	0.8	0.9	1.0
0.8	0.4	0.4	0.5	0.6	0.7	0.8	0.9	1.0	1.1	1.2	1.3
1.0	0.4	0.5	0.6	0.9	1.0	1.1	1.2	1.3	1.4	1.5	1.7
1.2	0.5	0.6	0.7	0.9	1.0	1.2	1.3	1.4	1.6	1.7	1.9	2.0
1.4	0.6	0.7	0.9	1.0	1.2	1.4	1.5	1.7	1.8	2.0	2.2	2.3
1.6	0.6	0.8	1.0	1.2	1.4	1.6	1.7	1.9	2.1	2.3	2.5	2.7
1.8	0.7	0.9	1.1	1.3	1.5	1.7	2.0	2.2	2.4	2.6	2.8	3.0
2.0	0.8	1.0	1.2	1.5	1.7	1.9	2.2	2.4	2.6	2.9	3.1	3.3
2.2	0.9	1.1	1.4	1.6	1.9	2.1	2.3	2.6	2.9	3.2	3.4	3.7
2.4	0.9	1.2	1.5	1.8	2.1	2.3	2.6	2.9	3.2	3.4	3.7	4.0
2.6	1.0	1.3	1.6	1.9	2.2	2.5	2.8	3.1	3.4	3.7	4.0	4.3
2.8	1.1	1.4	1.7	2.1	2.4	2.7	3.0	3.4	3.7	4.0	4.3	4.7
3.0	1.2	1.5	1.9	2.2	2.6	2.9	3.2	3.6	4.0	4.3	4.6	5.0
3.2	1.3	1.6	2.0	2.4	2.7	3.1	3.4	3.8	4.2	4.6	4.9	5.3
3.4	1.3	1.7	2.1	2.5	2.9	3.3	3.7	4.1	4.5	4.9	5.3	5.7
3.6	1.4	1.8	2.2	2.7	3.1	3.5	3.9	4.3	4.7	5.2	5.6	6.0
3.8	1.5	1.9	2.4	2.8	3.3	3.7	4.1	4.6	5.0	5.4	5.9	6.3
4.0	1.6	2.0	2.5	3.0	3.4	3.9	4.3	4.8	5.3	5.7	6.2	6.7
4.2	1.7	2.1	2.6	3.1	3.6	4.1	4.6	5.0	5.5	6.0	6.5	7.0
4.4	1.7	2.2	2.7	3.3	3.8	4.3	4.8	5.3	5.8	6.3	6.8	7.3
4.6	1.8	2.3	2.9	3.4	3.9	4.5	5.0	5.5	6.1	6.6	7.1	7.7
4.8	1.9	2.4	3.0	3.6	4.1	4.7	5.2	5.8	6.3	6.9	7.4	8.0
5.0	2.0	2.5	3.1	3.7	4.3	4.9	5.4	6.0	6.6	7.2	7.7	8.3
5.2	2.0	2.6	3.2	3.8	4.4	5.0	5.6	6.2	6.8	7.4	8.0	8.6
5.4	2.1	2.8	3.4	4.0	4.6	5.2	5.7	6.5	7.1	7.7	8.4	9.0
5.6	2.2	2.9	3.5	4.1	4.8	5.4	6.1	6.7	7.4	8.0	8.7	9.3
5.8	2.3	3.0	3.6	4.3	5.0	5.6	6.3	7.0	7.6	8.3	9.0	9.6
6.0	2.4	3.1	3.7	4.4	5.1	5.8	6.5	7.2	7.9	8.6	9.3	9.9

TIDAL HEIGHTS — PORTS & PLACES

Pencil-in height of HW Cherbourg ▶	4.8	5.0	5.2	5.4	5.6	5.8	6.0	6.2	6.4	6.6	6.8
Lymington (& Yarmouth approx)	2.3	2.4	2.4	2.5	2.5	2.6	2.7	2.7	2.8	2.9	3.0
Portsmouth (Chichester entrance & Cowes approx)	3.4	3.5	3.7	3.8	3.9	4.0	4.2	4.3	4.4	4.5	4.6
Cherbourg (& Omonville approx)	3.2	3.1	2.9	2.8	2.6	2.5	2.3	2.2	2.0	1.8	1.7	1.5
Braye, Alderney	2.6	2.4	2.2	2.0	1.7	1.5	1.3	1.0	0.8	0.6	0.5	0.3
Weymouth	1.0	0.9	0.9	0.8	0.7	0.6	0.6	0.5	0.4	0.4	0.3	0.3
Poole entrance	1.5	1.5	1.5	1.5	1.5	1.5	1.5	1.5	1.5	1.5	1.4	1.4
Poole Town Quay	1.8	1.8	1.8	1.8	1.8	1.8	1.8	1.7	1.7	1.7	1.7
St Peter Port & Sark	4.1	3.7	3.3	2.9	2.5	2.2	1.8	1.4	1.0	0.7	0.3	0.0
St Helier	4.7	4.3	3.9	3.5	3.0	2.6	2.2	1.7	1.3	1.0	0.6	0.3
St Malo	5.0	4.5	4.1	3.6	3.2	2.7	2.3	1.8	1.4	1.1	0.7	0.4
Lezardrieux	3.9	3.6	3.2	2.9	2.6	2.3	1.9	1.6	1.3	1.0	0.7	0.4
Paimpol	3.9	3.5	3.1	2.7	2.3	1.8	1.4	1.0	0.6	0.3	0.0	−0.4
Le Havre	5.2	5.2	5.2	5.2	5.3	5.3	5.3	5.4	5.4	5.4	5.4

Poole — Falling from H.W.
St. Helier approaches
Ile de Brehat — Rising from L.W.
Russel Channels — Low Water
St. Malo approaches — Low Water
Le Havre — Falling quickly

Copyright © J Reeve-Fowkes and Thomas Reed Publications.
No copying without permission.

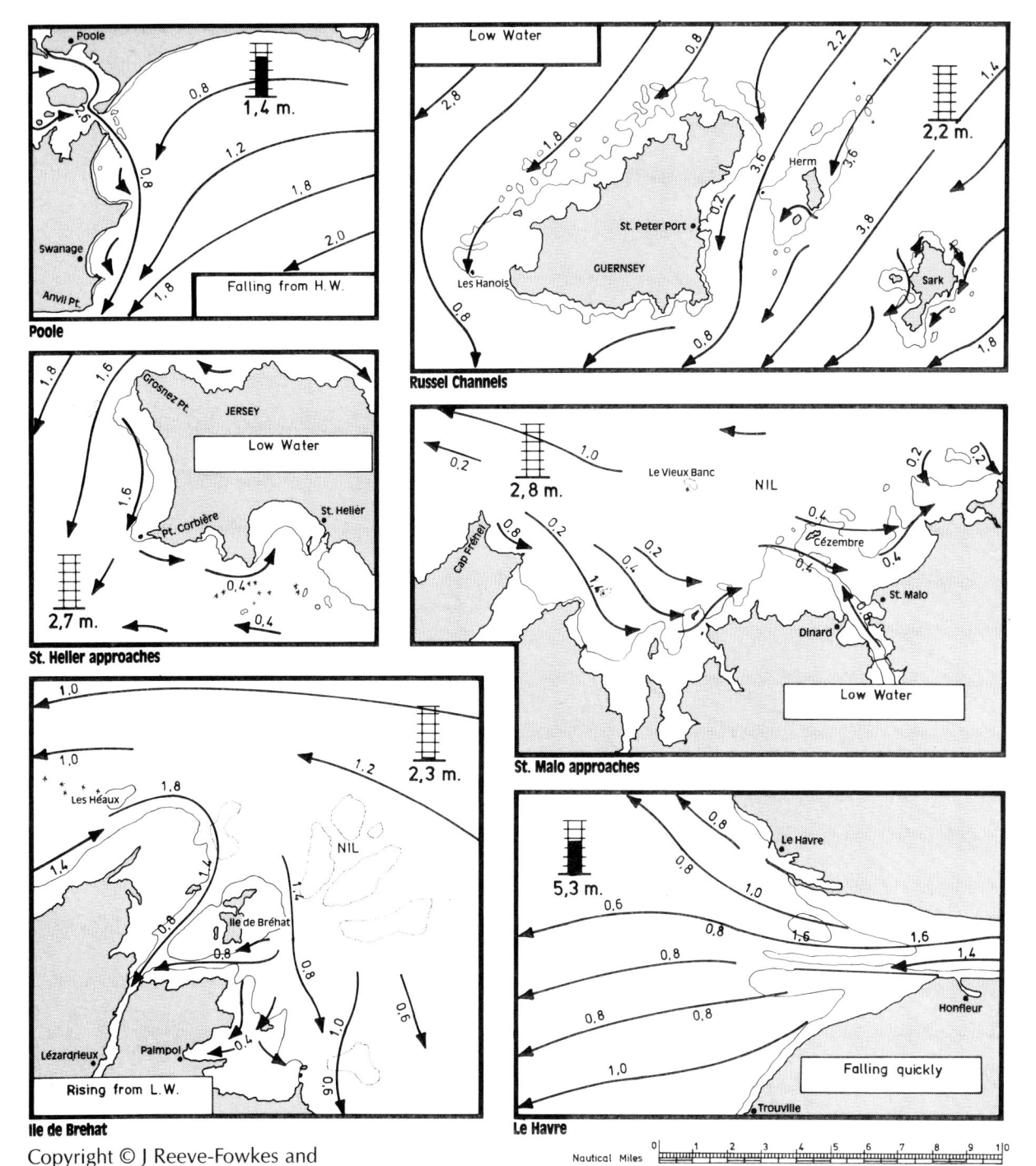

Nautical Miles 0 1 2 3 4 5 6 7 8 9 10

169

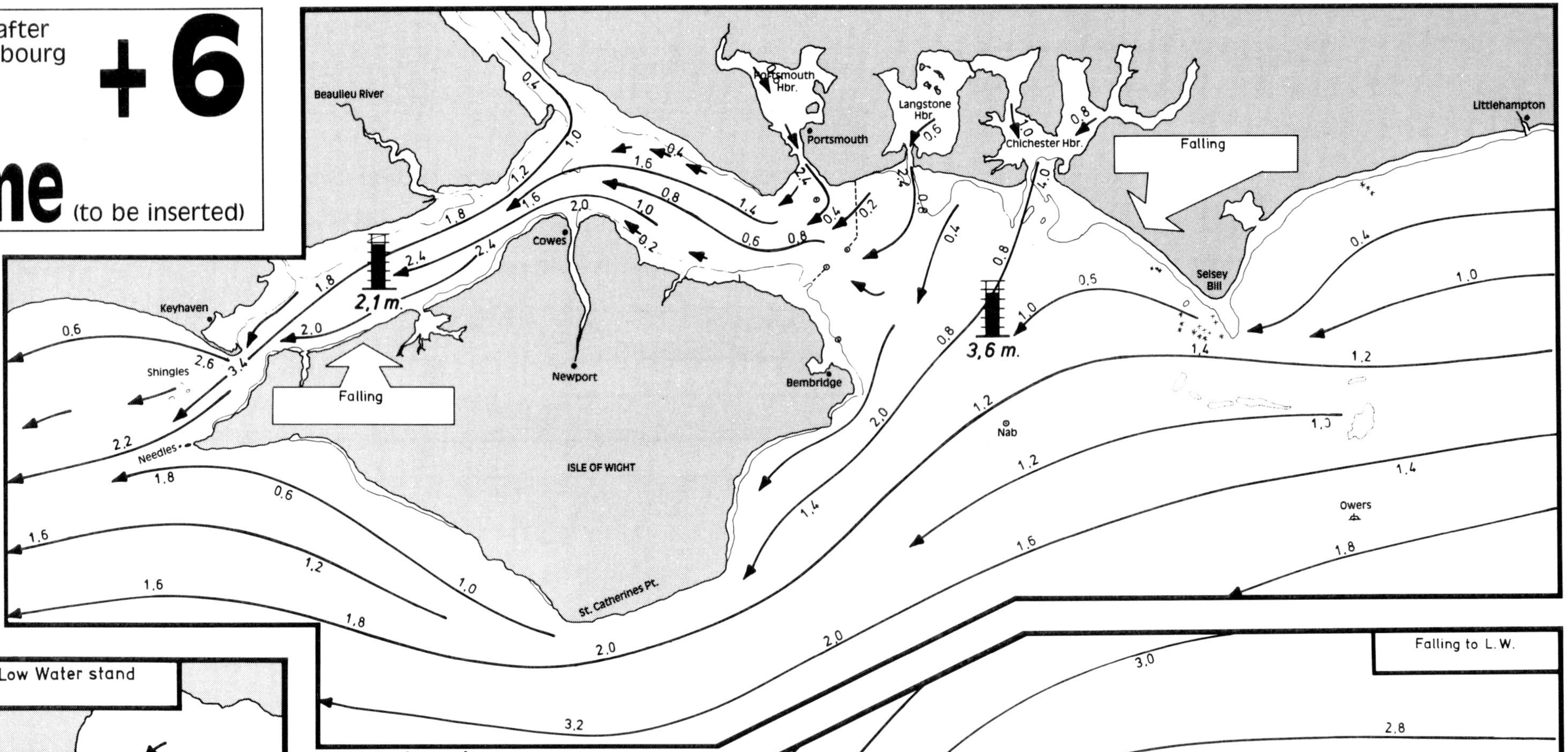

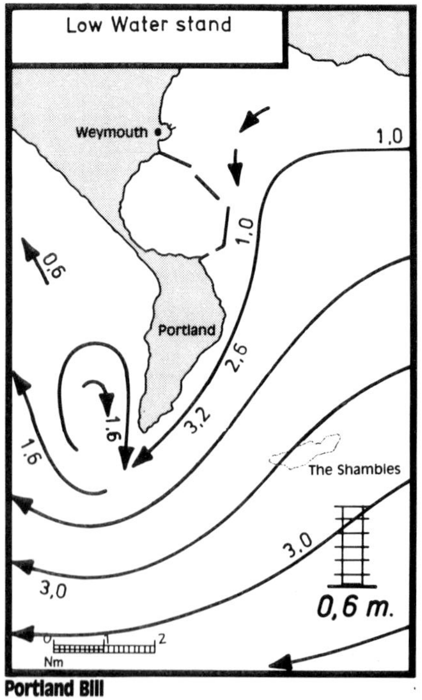

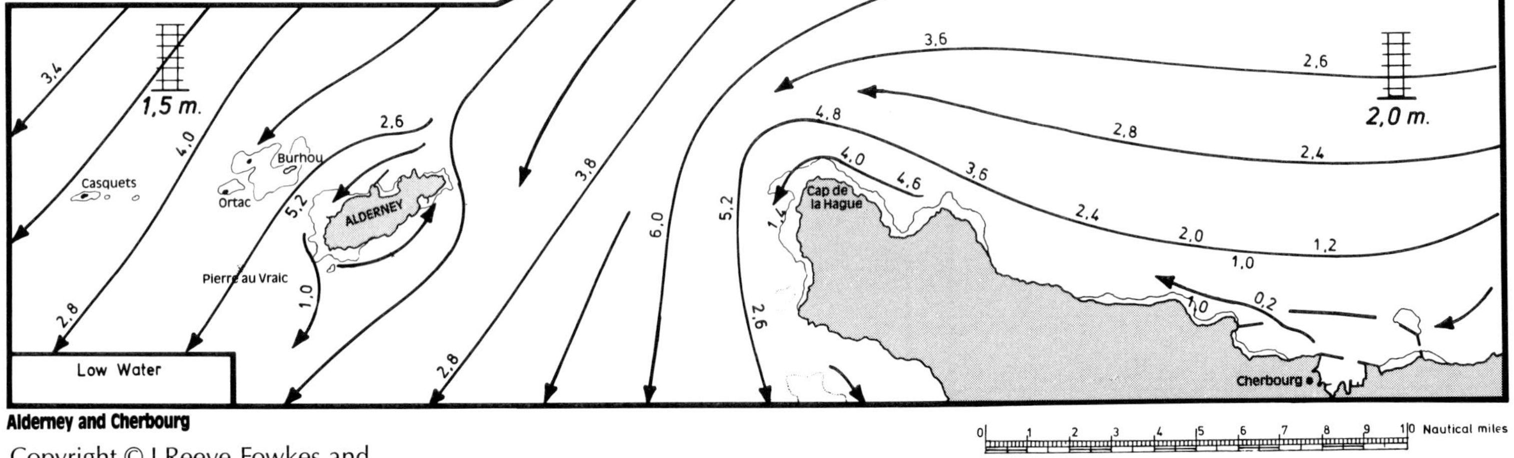

+6

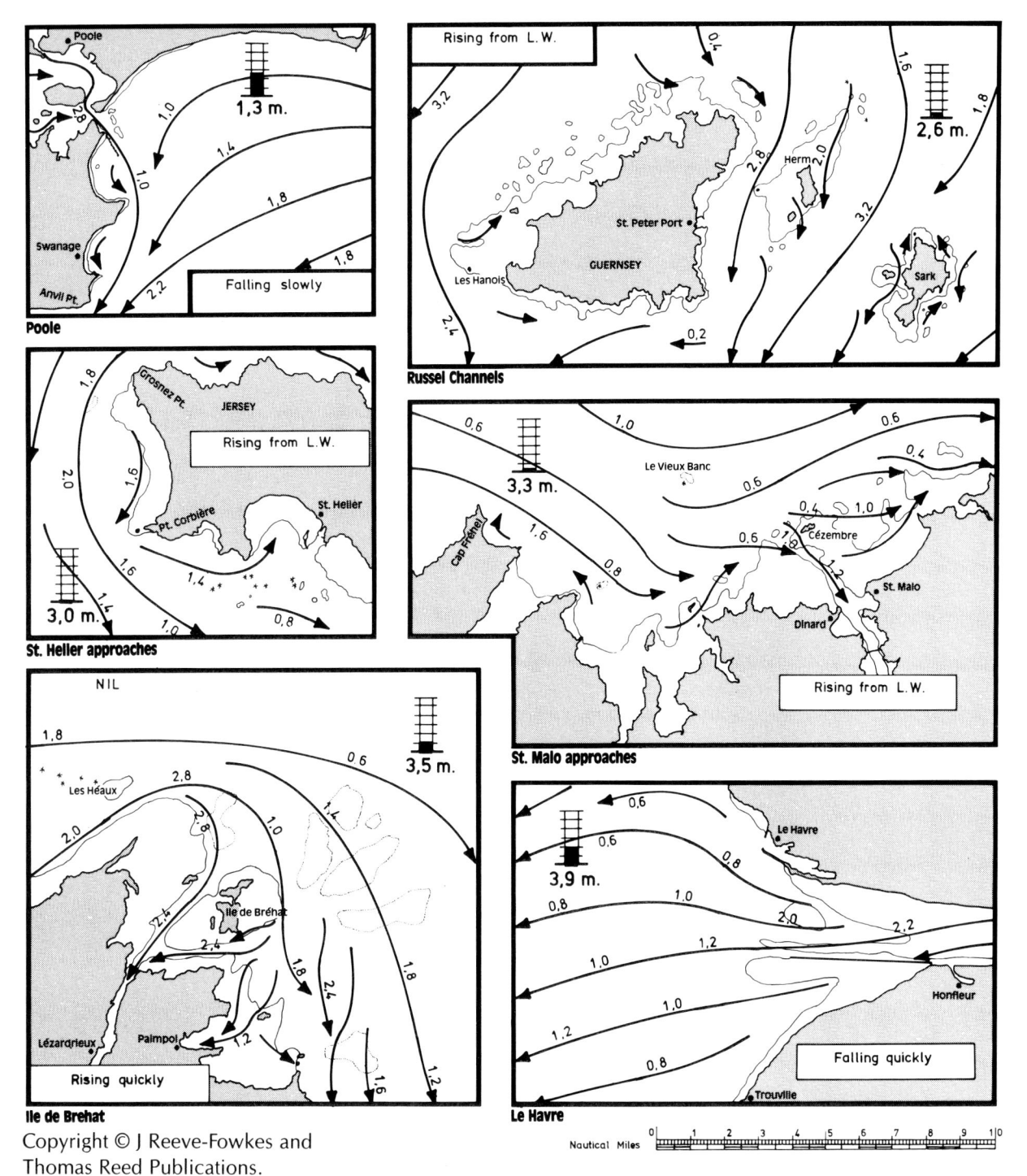

Stream Rate Conversion Table

Mean Rate Figure from Chart ▼	Pencil-in height of HW Cherbourg Read from column below pencil mark										
	4.8	5.0	5.2	5.4	5.6	5.8	6.0	6.2	6.4	6.6	6.8
0.2	0.1	0.1	0.1	0.1	0.2	0.2	0.2	0.2	0.3	0.3	0.3
0.4	0.2	0.2	0.2	0.3	0.3	0.4	0.4	0.5	0.5	0.6	0.7
0.6	0.2	0.3	0.4	0.4	0.5	0.6	0.7	0.7	0.8	0.9	1.0
0.8	0.4	0.4	0.5	0.6	0.7	0.8	0.9	1.0	1.1	1.2	1.3
1.0	0.4	0.5	0.6	0.7	0.9	1.0	1.1	1.2	1.3	1.4	1.5	1.7
1.2	0.5	0.6	0.7	0.9	1.0	1.2	1.3	1.4	1.6	1.7	1.9	2.0
1.4	0.6	0.7	0.9	1.0	1.2	1.4	1.5	1.7	1.8	2.0	2.2	2.3
1.6	0.6	0.8	1.0	1.2	1.4	1.6	1.7	1.9	2.1	2.3	2.5	2.7
1.8	0.7	0.9	1.1	1.3	1.5	1.7	2.0	2.2	2.4	2.6	2.8	3.0
2.0	0.8	1.0	1.2	1.5	1.7	1.9	2.2	2.4	2.6	2.9	3.1	3.3
2.2	0.9	1.1	1.4	1.6	1.9	2.1	2.3	2.6	2.9	3.2	3.4	3.7
2.4	0.9	1.2	1.5	1.8	2.1	2.3	2.6	2.9	3.2	3.4	3.7	4.0
2.6	1.0	1.3	1.6	1.9	2.2	2.5	2.8	3.1	3.4	3.7	4.0	4.3
2.8	1.1	1.4	1.7	2.1	2.4	2.7	3.0	3.4	3.7	4.0	4.3	4.7
3.0	1.2	1.5	1.9	2.2	2.6	2.9	3.2	3.6	4.0	4.3	4.6	5.0
3.2	1.3	1.6	2.0	2.4	2.7	3.1	3.4	3.8	4.2	4.6	4.9	5.3
3.4	1.3	1.7	2.1	2.5	2.9	3.3	3.7	4.1	4.5	4.9	5.3	5.7
3.6	1.4	1.8	2.2	2.7	3.1	3.5	3.9	4.3	4.7	5.2	5.6	6.0
3.8	1.5	1.9	2.4	2.8	3.3	3.7	4.1	4.6	5.0	5.4	5.9	6.3
4.0	1.6	2.0	2.5	3.0	3.4	3.9	4.3	4.8	5.3	5.7	6.2	6.7
4.2	1.7	2.1	2.6	3.1	3.6	4.1	4.6	5.0	5.5	6.0	6.5	7.0
4.4	1.7	2.2	2.7	3.3	3.8	4.3	4.8	5.3	5.8	6.3	6.8	7.3
4.6	1.8	2.3	2.9	3.4	3.9	4.5	5.0	5.5	6.1	6.6	7.1	7.7
4.8	1.9	2.4	3.0	3.6	4.1	4.7	5.2	5.8	6.3	6.9	7.4	8.0
5.0	2.0	2.5	3.1	3.7	4.3	4.9	5.4	6.0	6.6	7.2	7.7	8.3
5.2	2.0	2.6	3.2	3.8	4.4	5.0	5.6	6.2	6.8	7.4	8.0	8.6
5.4	2.1	2.8	3.4	4.0	4.6	5.2	5.7	6.5	7.1	7.7	8.4	9.0
5.6	2.2	2.9	3.5	4.1	4.8	5.4	6.1	6.7	7.4	8.0	8.7	9.3
5.8	2.3	3.0	4.3	5.0	5.6	6.3	7.0	7.6	8.3	9.0	9.6
6.0	2.4	3.1	3.7	4.4	5.1	5.8	6.5	7.2	7.9	8.6	9.3	9.9

TIDAL HEIGHTS — PORTS & PLACES

Pencil-in height of HW Cherbourg ▶	4.8	5.0	5.2	5.4	5.6	5.8	6.0	6.2	6.4	6.6	6.8
Lymington (& Yarmouth approx)	2.2	2.2	2.2	2.2	2.3	2.3	2.3	2.4	2.4	2.4	2.5	2.5
Portsmouth (Chichester entrance & Cowes approx)	3.2	3.3	3.3	3.4	3.5	3.6	3.7	3.8	3.9	4.0	4.0	4.1
Cherbourg (& Omonville approx)	3.0	2.8	2.6	2.4	2.2	1.9	1.7	1.5	1.3	1.1	0.8	0.6
Braye, Alderney	2.6	2.4	2.2	2.0	1.7	1.5	1.3	1.0	0.8	0.6	0.4	0.2
Weymouth	1.0	0.9	0.9	0.8	0.7	0.6	0.5	0.4	0.3	0.3	0.3	0.3
Poole entrance	1.4	1.4	1.4	1.4	1.3	1.3	1.2	1.2	1.1	1.0	1.0	0.9
Poole Town Quay	1.6	1.6	1.6	1.6	1.6	1.6	1.5	1.5	1.5	1.5	1.5
St Peter Port & Sark	4.2	3.9	3.5	3.2	2.9	2.5	2.2	1.8	1.5	1.2	0.9	0.7
St Helier	4.8	4.4	4.0	3.6	3.3	2.9	2.5	2.1	1.8	1.5	1.0	0.8
St Malo	5.6	5.1	4.7	4.2	3.8	3.3	2.9	2.5	2.2	1.7	1.4	1.1	0.8
Lezardrieux	4.5	4.3	4.1	3.9	3.6	3.3	3.2	2.9	2.7	2.5	2.3	2.1
Paimpol	4.5	4.3	3.8	3.5	3.2	2.9	2.5	2.2	1.9	1.6	1.4	1.1
Le Havre	4.2	4.1	4.1	4.0	3.9	3.9	3.8	3.8	3.7	3.6	3.5	3.4

Copyright © J Reeve-Fowkes and Thomas Reed Publications.
No copying without permission.

Section 2

The Scilly Isles
Ile d'Ouessant and Chenal du Four

ILE D'OUESSANT AND CHENAL DU FOUR
The channels between Ile d'Ouessant and the mainland are beset with dangers and with strong and sometimes violent streams, particularly when wind is opposed to tide. The Passage du Fromveur on the south-eastern side of Ile d'Ouessant has very fast streams, attaining 8 or 9 knots at maximum springs, and the seas can be very turbulent. The Chenal du Four, close to the mainland, is the usual passage for yachtsmen. All the other channels between the Passage du Fromveur and Chenal du Four should only be attempted with local knowledge and in good weather. Winds from a northerly quarter substantially increase the velocity of the south-going ebb streams through all these channels.

6 hours before HW Cherbourg **-6**

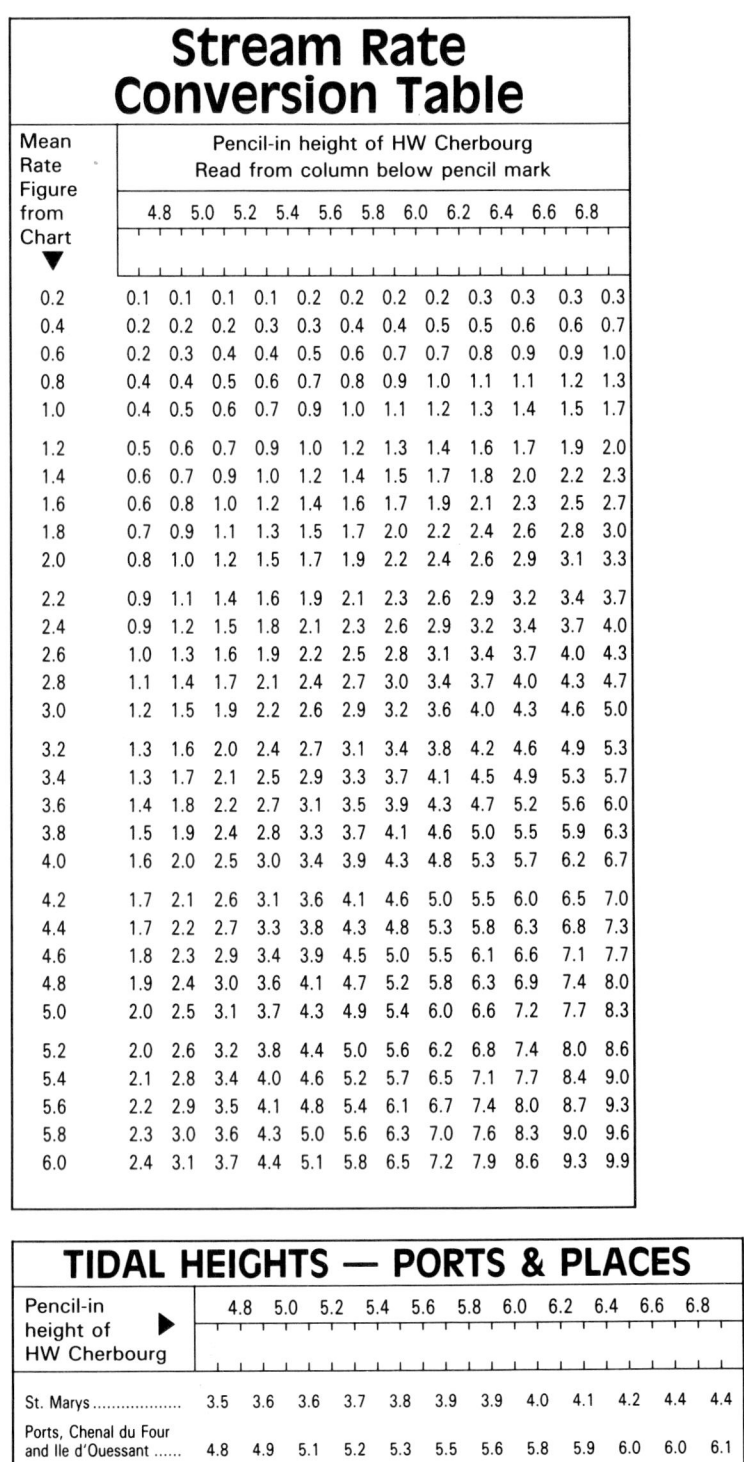

Time (to be inserted)

Copyright © J Reeve-Fowkes and
Thomas Reed Publications.
No copying without permission.

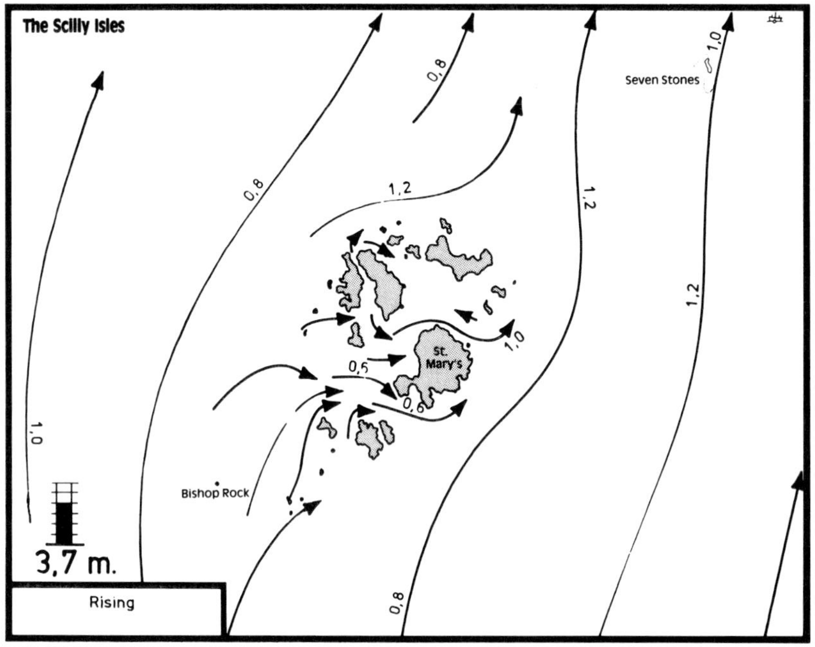

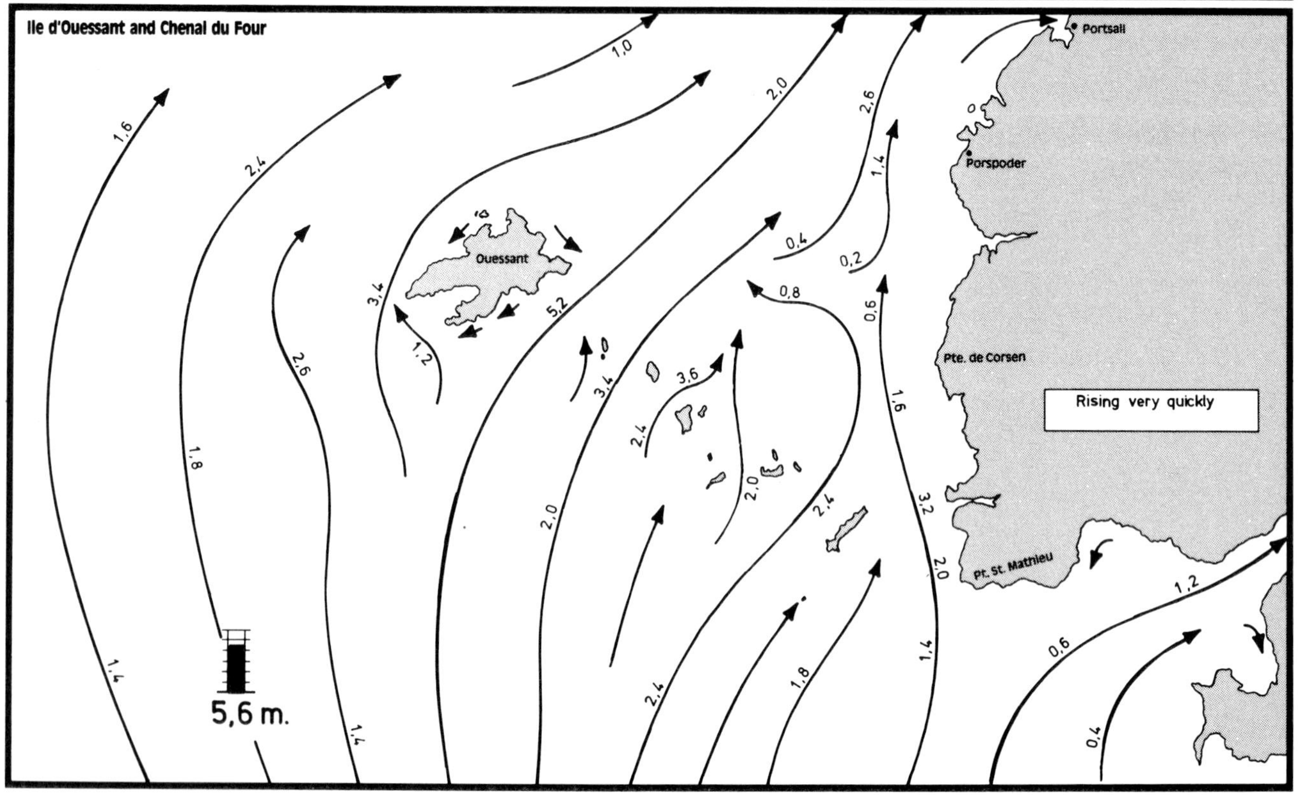

The Scilly Isles

3,7 m.
Rising

Ile d'Ouessant and Chenal du Four

5,6 m.

Rising very quickly

Stream Rate Conversion Table

Mean Rate Figure from Chart ▼	Pencil-in height of HW Cherbourg Read from column below pencil mark										
	4.8	5.0	5.2	5.4	5.6	5.8	6.0	6.2	6.4	6.6	6.8
0.2	0.1	0.1	0.1	0.1	0.2	0.2	0.2	0.2	0.3	0.3	0.3	0.3
0.4	0.2	0.2	0.2	0.3	0.3	0.4	0.4	0.5	0.5	0.6	0.6	0.7
0.6	0.2	0.3	0.4	0.4	0.5	0.6	0.7	0.7	0.8	0.9	0.9	1.0
0.8	0.4	0.4	0.5	0.6	0.7	0.8	0.9	1.0	1.1	1.1	1.2	1.3
1.0	0.4	0.5	0.6	0.7	0.9	1.0	1.1	1.2	1.3	1.4	1.5	1.7
1.2	0.5	0.6	0.7	0.9	1.0	1.2	1.3	1.4	1.6	1.7	1.9	2.0
1.4	0.6	0.7	0.9	1.0	1.2	1.4	1.5	1.7	1.8	2.0	2.2	2.3
1.6	0.6	0.8	1.0	1.2	1.4	1.6	1.7	1.9	2.1	2.3	2.5	2.7
1.8	0.7	0.9	1.1	1.3	1.5	1.7	2.0	2.2	2.4	2.6	2.8	3.0
2.0	0.8	1.0	1.2	1.5	1.7	1.9	2.2	2.4	2.6	2.9	3.1	3.3
2.2	0.9	1.1	1.4	1.6	1.9	2.1	2.3	2.6	2.9	3.2	3.4	3.7
2.4	0.9	1.2	1.5	1.8	2.1	2.3	2.6	2.9	3.2	3.4	3.7	4.0
2.6	1.0	1.3	1.6	1.9	2.2	2.5	2.8	3.1	3.4	3.7	4.0	4.3
2.8	1.1	1.4	1.7	2.1	2.4	2.7	3.0	3.4	3.7	4.0	4.3	4.7
3.0	1.2	1.5	1.9	2.2	2.6	2.9	3.2	3.6	4.0	4.3	4.6	5.0
3.2	1.3	1.6	2.0	2.4	2.7	3.1	3.4	3.8	4.2	4.6	4.9	5.3
3.4	1.3	1.7	2.1	2.5	2.9	3.3	3.7	4.1	4.5	4.9	5.3	5.7
3.6	1.4	1.8	2.2	2.7	3.1	3.5	3.9	4.3	4.7	5.2	5.6	6.0
3.8	1.5	1.9	2.4	2.8	3.3	3.7	4.1	4.6	5.0	5.5	5.9	6.3
4.0	1.6	2.0	2.5	3.0	3.4	3.9	4.3	4.8	5.3	5.7	6.2	6.7
4.2	1.7	2.1	2.6	3.1	3.6	4.1	4.6	5.0	5.5	6.0	6.5	7.0
4.4	1.7	2.2	2.7	3.3	3.8	4.3	4.8	5.3	5.8	6.3	6.8	7.3
4.6	1.8	2.3	2.9	3.4	3.9	4.5	5.0	5.5	6.1	6.6	7.1	7.7
4.8	1.9	2.4	3.0	3.6	4.1	4.7	5.2	5.8	6.3	6.9	7.4	8.0
5.0	2.0	2.5	3.1	3.7	4.3	4.9	5.4	6.0	6.6	7.2	7.7	8.3
5.2	2.0	2.6	3.2	3.8	4.4	5.0	5.6	6.2	6.8	7.4	8.0	8.6
5.4	2.1	2.8	3.4	4.0	4.6	5.2	5.7	6.5	7.1	7.7	8.4	9.0
5.6	2.2	2.9	3.5	4.1	4.8	5.4	6.1	6.7	7.4	8.0	8.7	9.3
5.8	2.3	3.0	3.6	4.3	5.0	5.6	6.3	7.0	7.6	8.3	9.0	9.6
6.0	2.4	3.1	3.7	4.4	5.1	5.8	6.5	7.2	7.9	8.6	9.3	9.9

TIDAL HEIGHTS — PORTS & PLACES

Pencil-in height of HW Cherbourg ▶	4.8	5.0	5.2	5.4	5.6	5.8	6.0	6.2	6.4	6.6	6.8
St. Marys	3.5	3.6	3.6	3.7	3.8	3.9	3.9	4.0	4.1	4.2	4.4	4.4
Ports, Chenal du Four and Ile d'Ouessant	4.8	4.9	5.1	5.2	5.3	5.5	5.6	5.8	5.9	6.0	6.0	6.1

5 hours before HW Cherbourg −5

Time (to be inserted)

Copyright © J Reeve-Fowkes and Thomas Reed Publications.
No copying without permission.

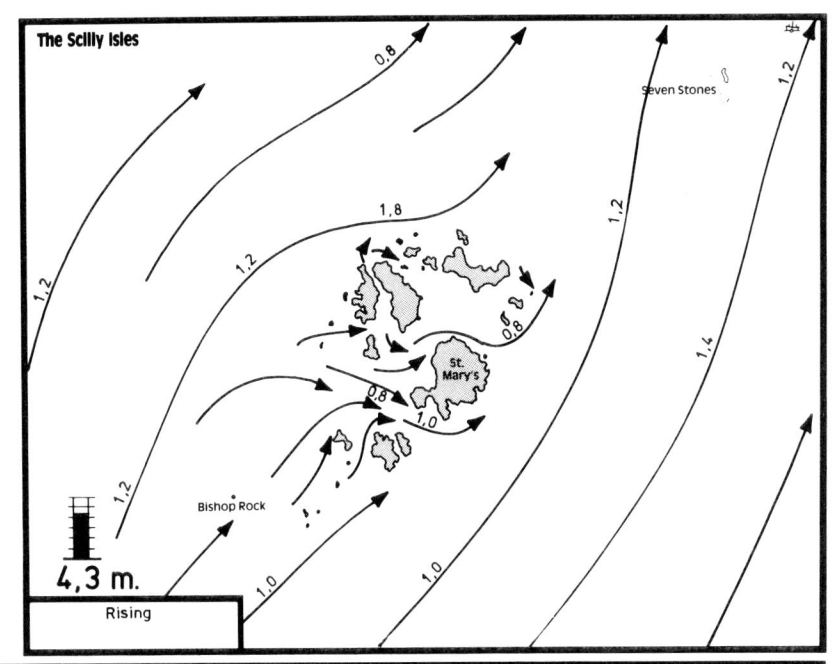

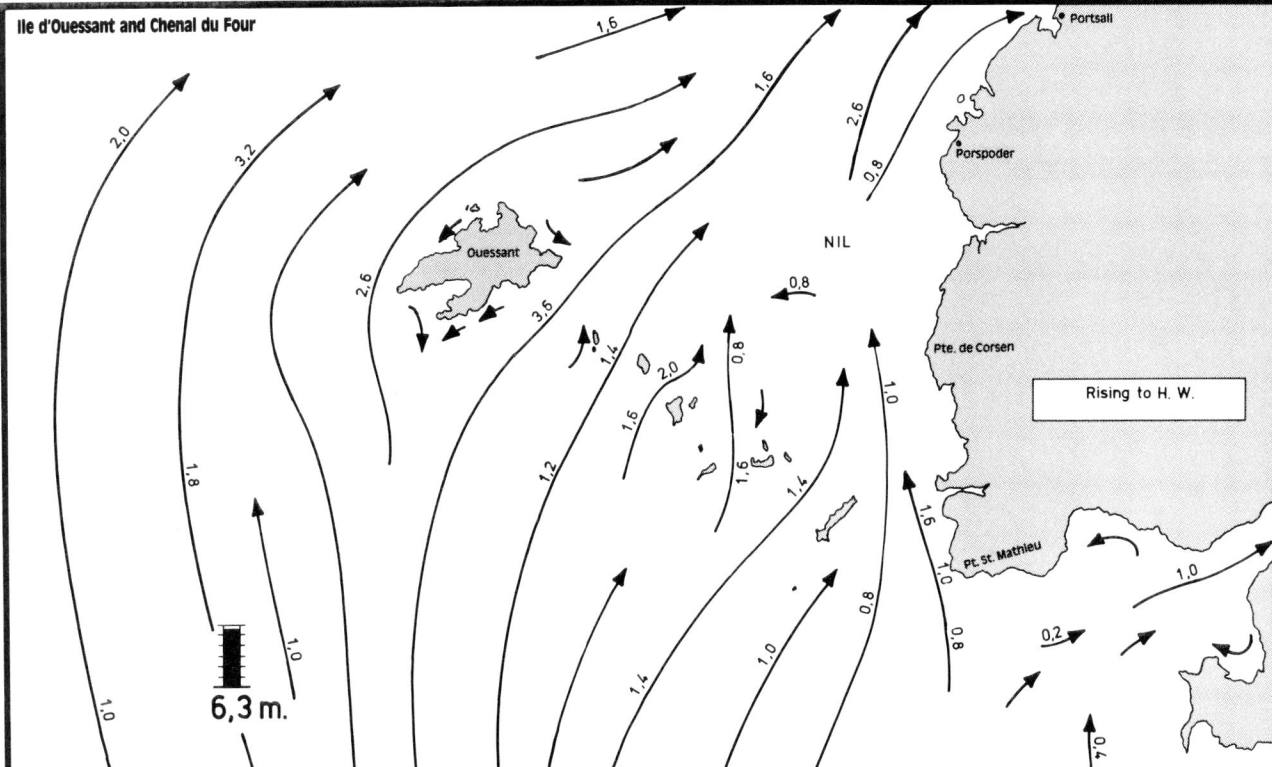

The Scilly Isles
- Seven Stones
- St. Mary's
- Bishop Rock
- 4,3 m. Rising
- 0–5 Nautical Miles

Ile d'Ouessant and Chenal du Four
- Portsall
- Porspoder
- Ouessant
- NIL
- Pte. de Corsen
- Pt. St. Mathieu
- Rising to H.W.
- 6,3 m.

Stream Rate Conversion Table

Mean Rate Figure from Chart	\multicolumn{11}{c}{Pencil-in height of HW Cherbourg Read from column below pencil mark}
	4.8	5.0	5.2	5.4	5.6	5.8	6.0	6.2	6.4	6.6	6.8
0.2	0.1	0.1	0.1	0.1	0.2	0.2	0.2	0.2	0.3	0.3	0.3
0.4	0.2	0.2	0.2	0.3	0.3	0.4	0.4	0.5	0.5	0.6	0.7
0.6	0.2	0.3	0.4	0.4	0.5	0.6	0.7	0.7	0.8	0.9	1.0
0.8	0.4	0.4	0.5	0.6	0.7	0.8	0.9	1.0	1.1	1.2	1.3
1.0	0.4	0.5	0.6	0.7	0.9	1.0	1.1	1.2	1.3	1.5	1.7
1.2	0.5	0.6	0.7	0.9	1.0	1.2	1.3	1.4	1.6	1.7	1.9	2.0
1.4	0.6	0.7	0.9	1.0	1.2	1.4	1.5	1.7	1.8	2.0	2.2	2.3
1.6	0.6	0.8	1.0	1.2	1.4	1.6	1.7	1.9	2.1	2.3	2.5	2.7
1.8	0.7	0.9	1.1	1.3	1.5	1.7	2.0	2.2	2.4	2.6	2.8	3.0
2.0	0.8	1.0	1.2	1.5	1.7	1.9	2.2	2.4	2.6	2.9	3.1	3.3
2.2	0.9	1.1	1.4	1.6	1.9	2.1	2.3	2.6	2.9	3.2	3.4	3.7
2.4	0.9	1.2	1.5	1.8	2.1	2.3	2.6	2.9	3.2	3.4	3.7	4.0
2.6	1.0	1.3	1.6	1.9	2.2	2.5	2.8	3.1	3.4	3.7	4.0	4.3
2.8	1.1	1.4	1.7	2.1	2.4	2.7	3.0	3.4	3.7	4.0	4.3	4.7
3.0	1.2	1.5	1.9	2.2	2.6	2.9	3.2	3.6	4.0	4.3	4.6	5.0
3.2	1.3	1.6	2.0	2.4	2.7	3.1	3.4	3.8	4.2	4.6	4.9	5.3
3.4	1.3	1.7	2.1	2.5	2.9	3.3	3.7	4.1	4.5	4.9	5.3	5.7
3.6	1.4	1.8	2.2	2.7	3.1	3.5	3.9	4.3	4.7	5.2	5.6	6.0
3.8	1.5	1.9	2.4	2.8	3.3	3.7	4.1	4.6	5.0	5.5	5.9	6.3
4.0	1.6	2.0	2.5	3.0	3.4	3.9	4.3	4.8	5.3	5.7	6.2	6.7
4.2	1.7	2.1	2.6	3.1	3.6	4.1	4.6	5.0	5.5	6.0	6.5	7.0
4.4	1.7	2.2	2.7	3.3	3.8	4.3	4.8	5.3	5.8	6.3	6.8	7.3
4.6	1.8	2.3	2.9	3.4	3.9	4.5	5.0	5.5	6.1	6.6	7.1	7.7
4.8	1.9	2.4	3.0	3.6	4.1	4.7	5.2	5.8	6.3	6.9	7.4	8.0
5.0	2.0	2.5	3.1	3.7	4.3	4.9	5.4	6.0	6.6	7.2	7.7	8.3
5.2	2.0	2.6	3.2	3.8	4.4	5.0	5.6	6.2	6.8	7.4	8.0	8.6
5.4	2.1	2.8	3.4	4.0	4.6	5.2	5.7	6.5	7.1	7.7	8.4	9.0
5.6	2.2	2.9	3.5	4.1	4.8	5.4	6.1	6.7	7.4	8.0	8.7	9.3
5.8	2.3	3.0	3.6	4.3	5.0	5.6	6.3	7.0	7.6	8.3	9.0	9.6
6.0	2.4	3.1	3.7	4.4	5.1	5.8	6.5	7.2	7.9	8.6	9.3	9.9

TIDAL HEIGHTS — PORTS & PLACES

Pencil-in height of HW Cherbourg	4.8	5.0	5.2	5.4	5.6	5.8	6.0	6.2	6.4	6.6	6.8
St. Marys	3.6	3.8	4.0	4.2	4.3	4.5	4.7	4.8	5.0	5.1	5.3	5.4
Ports, Chenal du Four and Ile d'Ouessant	5.2	5.4	5.6	5.8	6.1	6.3	6.5	6.8	7.0	7.1	7.3	7.4

4 hours before HW Cherbourg **-4**

Time (to be inserted)

Copyright © J Reeve-Fowkes and
Thomas Reed Publications.
No copying without permission.

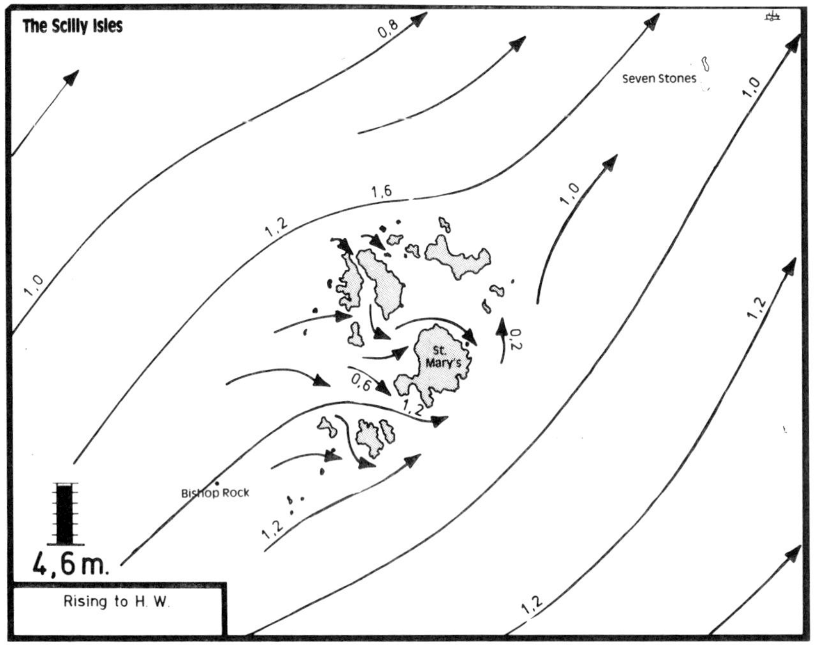

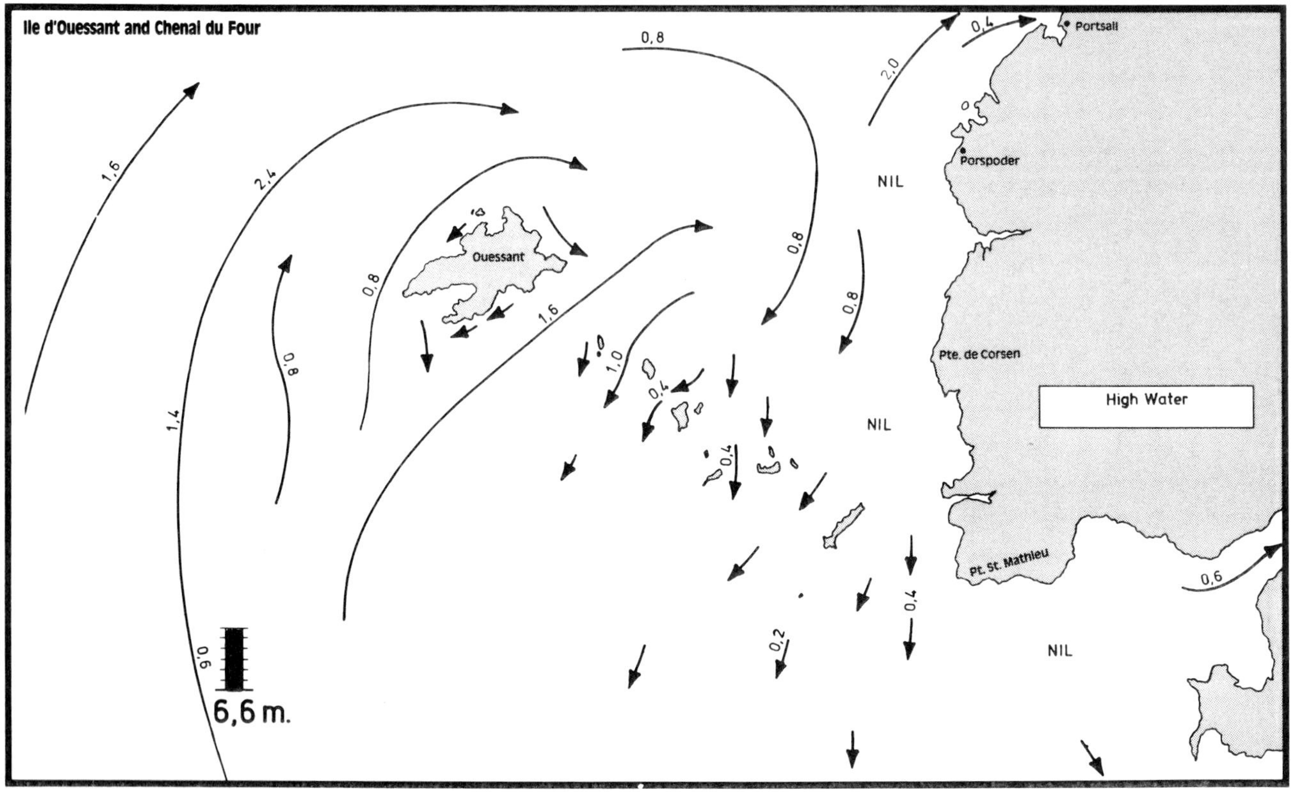

The Scilly Isles

0.8, Seven Stones, 1.0, 1.6, 1.2, 1.0, 1.0, 1.2, St. Mary's, 0.2, 0.6, 1.2, Bishop Rock, 1.2

4,6 m.

Rising to H.W.

0 — 5
Nautical Miles

Ile d'Ouessant and Chenal du Four

0.8, 2.0, Portsall, NIL, Porspoder, Ouessant, 0.8, 0.8, 1.6, 0.8, 1.0, 0.4, Pte. de Corsen, **High Water**, NIL, 0.4, 0.2, Pt. St. Mathieu, 0.6, NIL, 1.6, 2.4, 0.8, 1.4, 0.6

6,6 m.

Stream Rate Conversion Table

Mean Rate Figure from Chart ▼	Pencil-in height of HW Cherbourg Read from column below pencil mark											
	4.8	5.0	5.2	5.4	5.6	5.8	6.0	6.2	6.4	6.6	6.8	
0.2	0.1	0.1	0.1	0.1	0.2	0.2	0.2	0.2	0.3	0.3	0.3	0.3
0.4	0.2	0.2	0.2	0.3	0.3	0.4	0.4	0.5	0.5	0.6	0.6	0.7
0.6	0.2	0.3	0.4	0.4	0.5	0.6	0.7	0.7	0.8	0.9	0.9	1.0
0.8	0.4	0.4	0.5	0.6	0.7	0.8	0.9	1.0	1.1	1.1	1.2	1.3
1.0	0.4	0.5	0.6	0.7	0.9	1.0	1.1	1.2	1.3	1.4	1.5	1.7
1.2	0.5	0.6	0.7	0.9	1.0	1.2	1.3	1.4	1.6	1.7	1.9	2.0
1.4	0.6	0.7	0.9	1.0	1.2	1.4	1.5	1.7	1.8	2.0	2.2	2.3
1.6	0.6	0.8	1.0	1.2	1.4	1.6	1.7	1.9	2.1	2.3	2.5	2.7
1.8	0.7	0.9	1.1	1.3	1.5	1.7	2.0	2.2	2.4	2.6	2.8	3.0
2.0	0.8	1.0	1.2	1.5	1.7	1.9	2.2	2.4	2.6	2.9	3.1	3.3
2.2	0.9	1.1	1.4	1.6	1.9	2.1	2.3	2.6	2.9	3.2	3.4	3.7
2.4	0.9	1.2	1.5	1.8	2.1	2.3	2.6	2.9	3.2	3.4	3.7	4.0
2.6	1.0	1.3	1.6	1.9	2.2	2.5	2.8	3.1	3.4	3.7	4.0	4.3
2.8	1.1	1.4	1.7	2.1	2.4	2.7	3.0	3.4	3.7	4.0	4.3	4.7
3.0	1.2	1.5	1.9	2.2	2.6	2.9	3.2	3.6	4.0	4.3	4.6	5.0
3.2	1.3	1.6	2.0	2.4	2.7	3.1	3.4	3.8	4.2	4.6	4.9	5.3
3.4	1.3	1.7	2.1	2.5	2.9	3.3	3.7	4.1	4.5	4.9	5.3	5.7
3.6	1.4	1.8	2.2	2.7	3.1	3.5	3.9	4.3	4.7	5.2	5.6	6.0
3.8	1.5	1.9	2.4	2.8	3.3	3.7	4.1	4.6	5.0	5.5	5.9	6.3
4.0	1.6	2.0	2.5	3.0	3.4	3.9	4.3	4.8	5.3	5.7	6.2	6.7
4.2	1.7	2.1	2.6	3.1	3.6	4.1	4.6	5.0	5.5	6.0	6.5	7.0
4.4	1.7	2.2	2.7	3.3	3.8	4.3	4.8	5.3	5.8	6.3	6.8	7.3
4.6	1.8	2.3	2.9	3.4	3.9	4.5	5.0	5.5	6.1	6.6	7.1	7.7
4.8	1.9	2.4	3.0	3.6	4.1	4.7	5.2	5.8	6.3	6.9	7.4	8.0
5.0	2.0	2.5	3.1	3.7	4.3	4.9	5.4	6.0	6.6	7.2	7.7	8.3
5.2	2.0	2.6	3.2	3.8	4.4	5.0	5.6	6.2	6.8	7.4	8.0	8.6
5.4	2.1	2.8	3.4	4.0	4.6	5.2	5.7	6.5	7.1	7.7	8.4	9.0
5.6	2.2	2.9	3.5	4.1	4.8	5.4	6.1	6.7	7.4	8.0	8.7	9.3
5.8	2.3	3.0	3.6	4.3	5.0	5.6	6.3	7.0	7.6	8.3	9.0	9.6
6.0	2.4	3.1	3.7	4.4	5.1	5.8	6.5	7.2	7.9	8.6	9.3	9.9

TIDAL HEIGHTS — PORTS & PLACES

Pencil-in height of HW Cherbourg ▶	4.8	5.0	5.2	5.4	5.6	5.8	6.0	6.2	6.4	6.6	6.8
St. Marys	3.9	4.1	4.3	4.5	4.7	4.9	5.1	5.3	5.5	5.7	5.9	6.1
Ports, Chenal du Four and Ile d'Ouessant	5.3	5.6	5.8	6.1	6.3	6.6	6.8	7.1	7.3	7.5	7.6	7.8

3 hours before HW Cherbourg   **−3**

Time (to be inserted)

Copyright © J Reeve-Fowkes and Thomas Reed Publications.
No copying without permission.

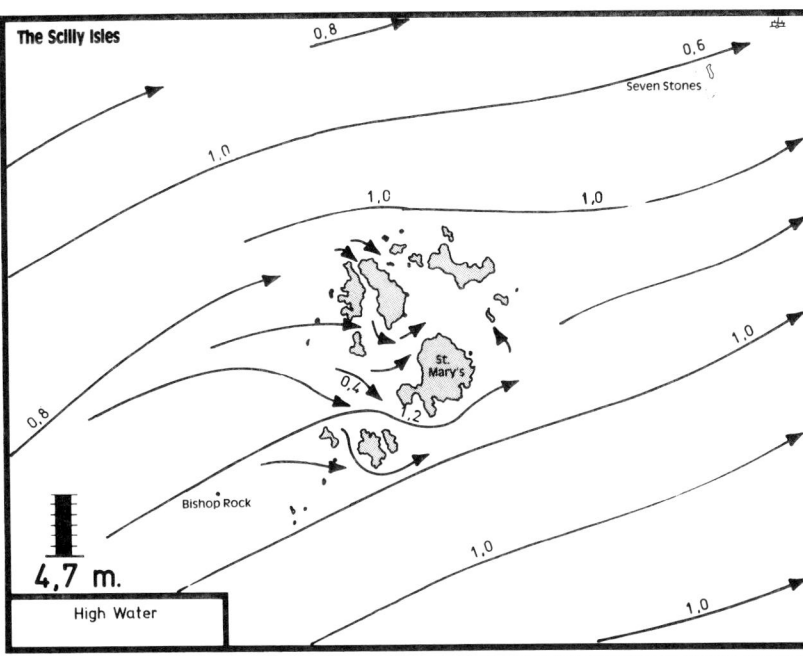

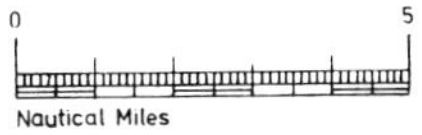

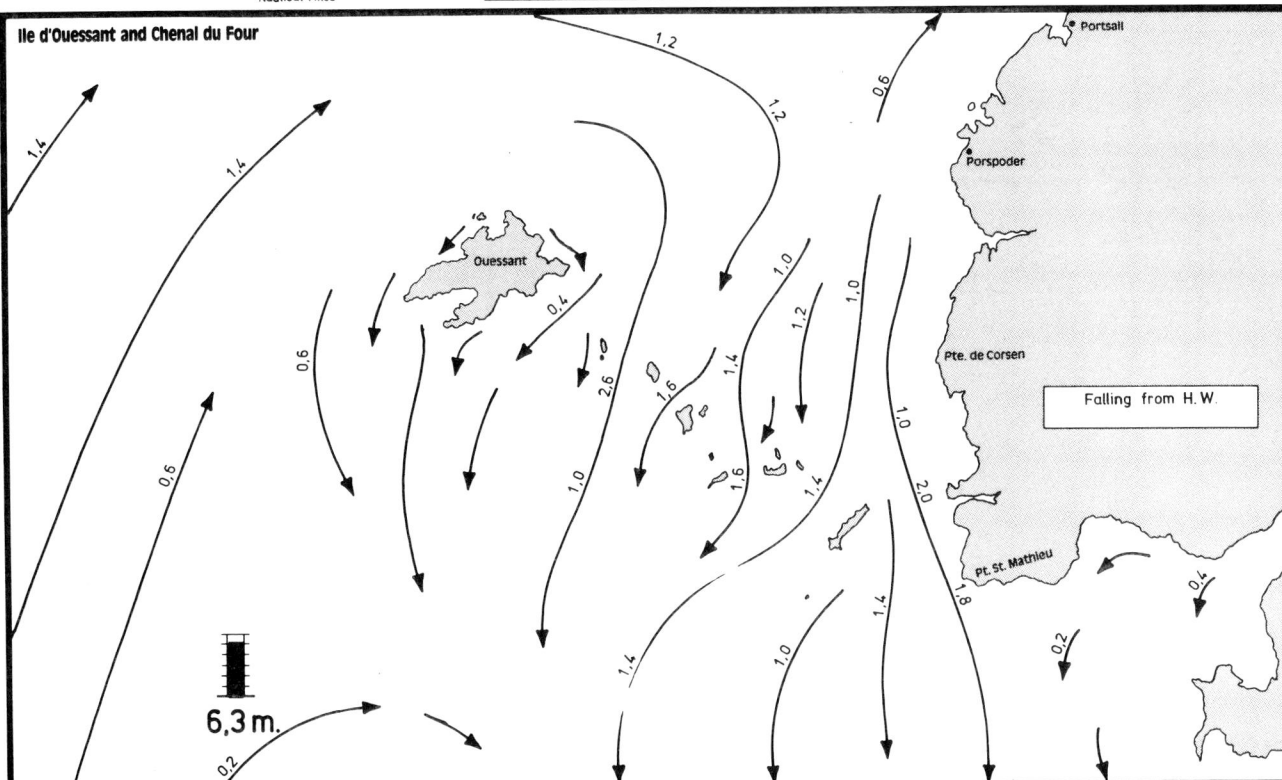

The Scilly Isles — High Water — 4.7 m.

Ile d'Ouessant and Chenal du Four — Falling from H.W. — 6.3 m.

Stream Rate Conversion Table

Mean Rate Figure from Chart ▼	\multicolumn{11}{c}{Pencil-in height of HW Cherbourg Read from column below pencil mark}
	4.8	5.0	5.2	5.4	5.6	5.8	6.0	6.2	6.4	6.6	6.8
0.2	0.1	0.1	0.1	0.1	0.2	0.2	0.2	0.2	0.3	0.3	0.3
0.4	0.2	0.2	0.2	0.3	0.3	0.4	0.4	0.5	0.5	0.6	0.7
0.6	0.2	0.3	0.4	0.4	0.5	0.6	0.7	0.7	0.8	0.9	1.0
0.8	0.4	0.4	0.5	0.6	0.7	0.8	0.9	1.0	1.1	1.2	1.3
1.0	0.4	0.5	0.6	0.7	0.9	1.0	1.1	1.2	1.3	1.4	1.5	1.7
1.2	0.5	0.6	0.7	0.9	1.0	1.2	1.3	1.4	1.6	1.7	1.9	2.0
1.4	0.6	0.7	0.9	1.1	1.2	1.4	1.5	1.7	1.8	2.0	2.2	2.3
1.6	0.6	0.8	1.0	1.2	1.4	1.6	1.7	1.9	2.1	2.3	2.5	2.7
1.8	0.7	0.9	1.1	1.3	1.5	1.7	2.0	2.2	2.4	2.6	2.8	3.0
2.0	0.8	1.0	1.2	1.5	1.7	1.9	2.2	2.4	2.6	2.9	3.1	3.3
2.2	0.9	1.1	1.4	1.6	1.9	2.1	2.3	2.6	2.9	3.2	3.4	3.7
2.4	0.9	1.2	1.5	1.8	2.1	2.3	2.6	2.9	3.2	3.4	3.7	4.0
2.6	1.0	1.3	1.6	1.9	2.2	2.5	2.8	3.1	3.4	3.7	4.0	4.3
2.8	1.1	1.4	1.7	2.1	2.4	2.7	3.0	3.4	3.7	4.0	4.3	4.7
3.0	1.2	1.5	1.9	2.2	2.6	2.9	3.2	3.6	4.0	4.3	4.6	5.0
3.2	1.3	1.6	2.0	2.4	2.7	3.1	3.4	3.8	4.2	4.6	4.9	5.3
3.4	1.3	1.7	2.1	2.5	2.9	3.3	3.7	4.1	4.5	4.9	5.3	5.7
3.6	1.4	1.8	2.2	2.7	3.1	3.5	3.9	4.4	4.7	5.2	5.6	6.0
3.8	1.5	1.9	2.4	2.8	3.3	3.7	4.1	4.6	5.0	5.5	5.9	6.3
4.0	1.6	2.0	2.5	3.0	3.4	3.9	4.3	4.8	5.3	5.7	6.2	6.7
4.2	1.7	2.1	2.6	3.1	3.6	4.1	4.6	5.0	5.5	6.0	6.5	7.0
4.4	1.7	2.2	2.7	3.3	3.8	4.3	4.8	5.3	5.8	6.3	6.8	7.3
4.6	1.8	2.3	2.9	3.4	3.9	4.5	5.0	5.5	6.1	6.6	7.1	7.7
4.8	1.9	2.4	3.0	3.6	4.1	4.7	5.2	5.8	6.3	6.9	7.4	8.0
5.0	2.0	2.5	3.1	3.7	4.3	4.9	5.4	6.0	6.6	7.2	7.7	8.3
5.2	2.0	2.6	3.2	3.8	4.4	5.0	5.6	6.2	6.8	7.4	8.0	8.6
5.4	2.1	2.8	3.4	4.0	4.6	5.2	5.7	6.5	7.1	7.7	8.4	9.0
5.6	2.2	2.9	3.5	4.1	4.8	5.4	6.1	6.7	7.4	8.0	8.7	9.3
5.8	2.3	3.0	3.6	4.3	5.0	5.6	6.3	7.0	7.6	8.3	9.0	9.6
6.0	2.4	3.1	3.7	4.4	5.1	5.8	6.5	7.2	7.9	8.6	9.3	9.9

TIDAL HEIGHTS — PORTS & PLACES

Pencil-in height of HW Cherbourg ▶	4.8	5.0	5.2	5.4	5.6	5.8	6.0	6.2	6.4	6.6	6.8
St. Marys	4.0	4.2	4.4	4.6	4.8	5.1	5.3	5.5	5.7	5.9	6.1	6.3
Ports, Chenal du Four and Ile d'Ouessant	5.3	5.5	5.7	5.9	6.1	6.3	6.5	6.7	6.9	7.0	7.2	7.3

177

2 hours before HW Cherbourg

-2

Time (to be inserted)

Copyright © J Reeve-Fowkes and Thomas Reed Publications.
No copying without permission.

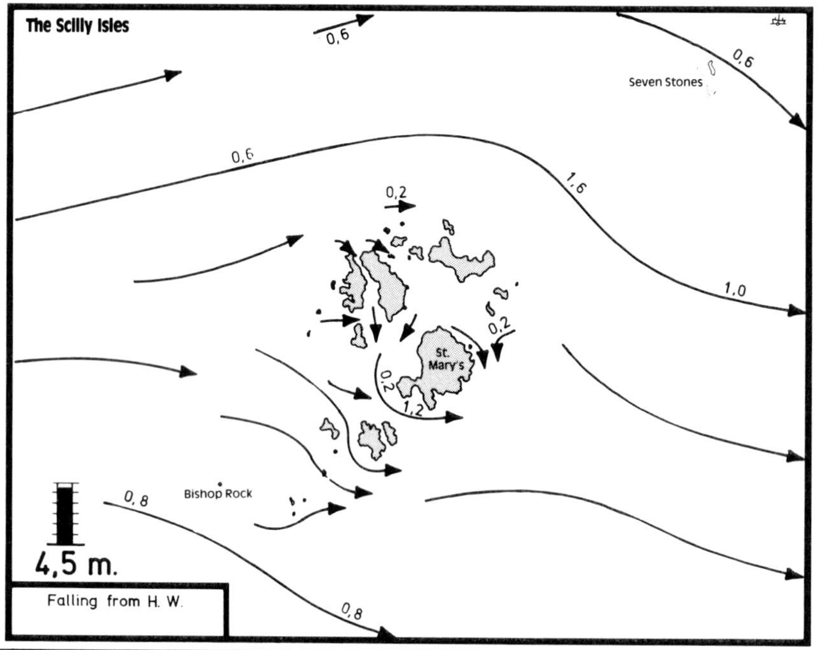

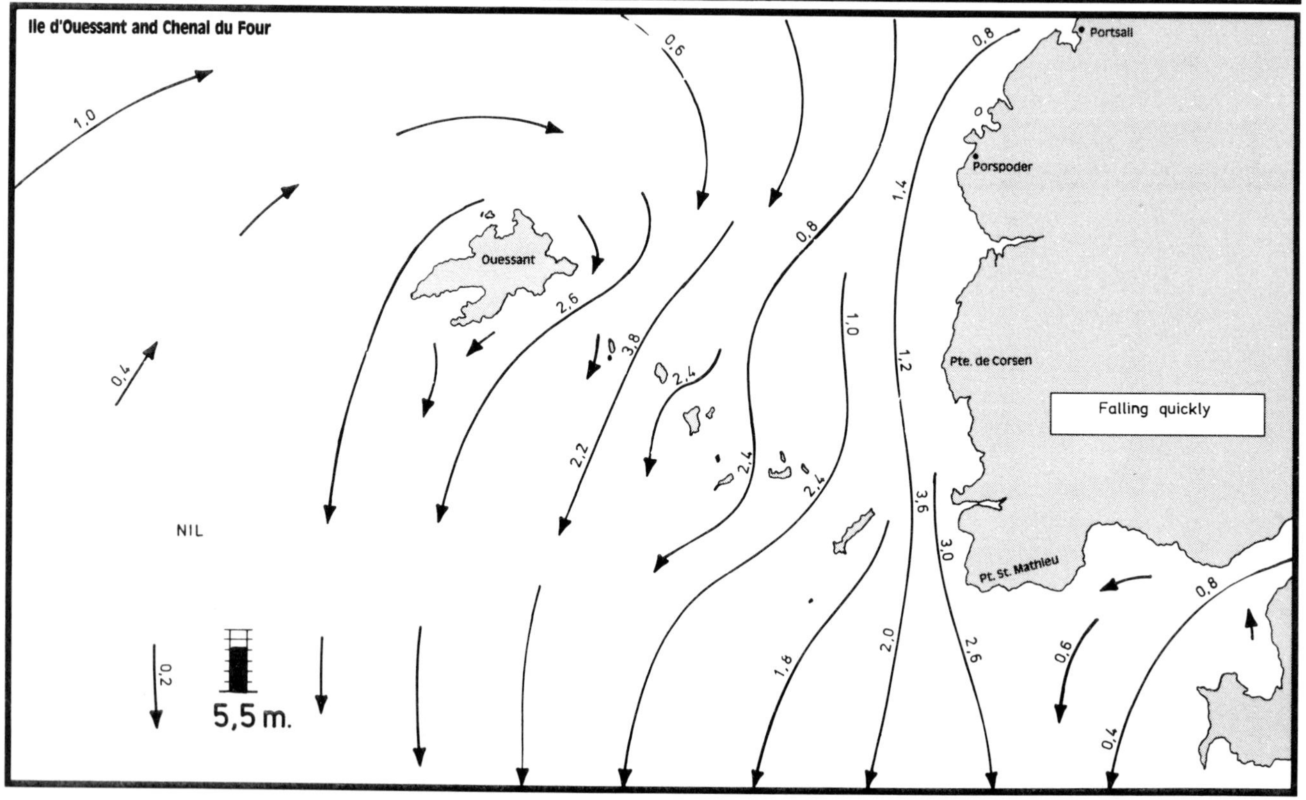

The Scilly Isles

Seven Stones

St. Mary's

Bishop Rock

0,6 0,6 0,2 1,6 1,0 0,6 0,2 0,2 1,2 0,8 0,8

4,5 m.

Falling from H. W.

0 — Nautical Miles — 5

Ile d'Ouessant and Chenal du Four

Portsall

Porspoder

Ouessant

Pte. de Corsen

Pt. St. Mathieu

Falling quickly

NIL

1.0 0.4 0.6 0.8 0.8 2.6 1.4 1.2 1.0 0.2 2.4 3.8 2.2 2.4 2.4 3.6 3.0 1.6 0.2 2.6 0.6 0.8 0.4

0.2

5,5 m.

Stream Rate Conversion Table

| Mean Rate Figure from Chart ▼ | Pencil-in height of HW Cherbourg — Read from column below pencil mark | | | | | | | | | | |
	4.8	5.0	5.2	5.4	5.6	5.8	6.0	6.2	6.4	6.6	6.8
0.2	0.1	0.1	0.1	0.1	0.2	0.2	0.2	0.2	0.3	0.3	0.3	0.3
0.4	0.2	0.2	0.2	0.3	0.3	0.4	0.4	0.5	0.5	0.6	0.6	0.7
0.6	0.2	0.3	0.4	0.4	0.5	0.6	0.7	0.7	0.8	0.9	0.9	1.0
0.8	0.4	0.4	0.5	0.6	0.7	0.8	0.9	1.0	1.1	1.1	1.2	1.3
1.0	0.4	0.5	0.6	0.7	0.9	1.0	1.1	1.2	1.3	1.4	1.5	1.7
1.2	0.5	0.6	0.7	0.9	1.0	1.2	1.3	1.4	1.6	1.7	1.9	2.0
1.4	0.6	0.7	0.9	1.0	1.2	1.4	1.5	1.7	1.8	2.0	2.2	2.3
1.6	0.6	0.8	1.0	1.2	1.4	1.6	1.7	1.9	2.1	2.3	2.5	2.7
1.8	0.7	0.9	1.1	1.3	1.5	1.7	2.0	2.2	2.4	2.6	2.8	3.0
2.0	0.8	1.0	1.2	1.5	1.7	1.9	2.2	2.4	2.6	2.9	3.1	3.3
2.2	0.9	1.1	1.4	1.6	1.9	2.1	2.3	2.6	2.9	3.2	3.4	3.7
2.4	0.9	1.2	1.5	1.8	2.1	2.3	2.6	2.9	3.2	3.4	3.7	4.0
2.6	1.0	1.3	1.6	1.9	2.2	2.5	2.8	3.1	3.4	3.7	4.0	4.3
2.8	1.1	1.4	1.7	2.1	2.4	2.7	3.0	3.4	3.7	4.0	4.3	4.7
3.0	1.2	1.5	1.9	2.2	2.6	2.9	3.2	3.6	4.0	4.3	4.6	5.0
3.2	1.3	1.6	2.0	2.4	2.7	3.1	3.4	3.8	4.2	4.6	4.9	5.3
3.4	1.3	1.7	2.1	2.5	2.9	3.3	3.7	4.1	4.5	4.9	5.3	5.7
3.6	1.4	1.8	2.2	2.7	3.1	3.5	3.9	4.3	4.7	5.2	5.6	6.0
3.8	1.5	1.9	2.4	2.8	3.3	3.7	4.1	4.6	5.0	5.5	5.9	6.3
4.0	1.6	2.0	2.5	3.0	3.4	3.9	4.3	4.8	5.3	5.7	6.2	6.7
4.2	1.7	2.1	2.6	3.1	3.6	4.1	4.6	5.0	5.5	6.0	6.5	7.0
4.4	1.7	2.2	2.7	3.3	3.8	4.3	4.8	5.3	5.8	6.3	6.8	7.3
4.6	1.8	2.3	2.9	3.4	3.9	4.5	5.0	5.5	6.1	6.6	7.1	7.7
4.8	1.9	2.4	3.0	3.6	4.1	4.7	5.2	5.8	6.3	6.9	7.4	8.0
5.0	2.0	2.5	3.1	3.7	4.3	4.9	5.4	6.0	6.6	7.2	7.7	8.3
5.2	2.0	2.6	3.2	3.8	4.4	5.0	5.6	6.2	6.8	7.4	8.0	8.6
5.4	2.1	2.8	3.4	4.0	4.6	5.2	5.7	6.5	7.1	7.7	8.4	9.0
5.6	2.2	2.9	3.5	4.1	4.8	5.4	6.1	6.7	7.4	8.0	8.7	9.3
5.8	2.3	3.0	3.6	4.3	5.0	5.6	6.3	7.0	7.6	8.3	9.0	9.6
6.0	2.4	3.1	3.7	4.4	5.1	5.8	6.5	7.2	7.9	8.6	9.3	9.9

TIDAL HEIGHTS — PORTS & PLACES

Pencil-in height of HW Cherbourg ▶	4.8	5.0	5.2	5.4	5.6	5.8	6.0	6.2	6.4	6.6	6.8
St. Marys	3.8	4.0	4.2	4.4	4.6	4.7	4.9	5.1	5.3	5.5	5.7	5.9
Ports, Chenal du Four and Ile d'Ouessant	4.8	4.9	5.1	5.2	5.3	5.5	5.6	5.7	5.8	5.9	5.9	6.0

1 hour before HW Cherbourg −1

Time (to be inserted)

Copyright © J Reeve-Fowkes and Thomas Reed Publications.
No copying without permission.

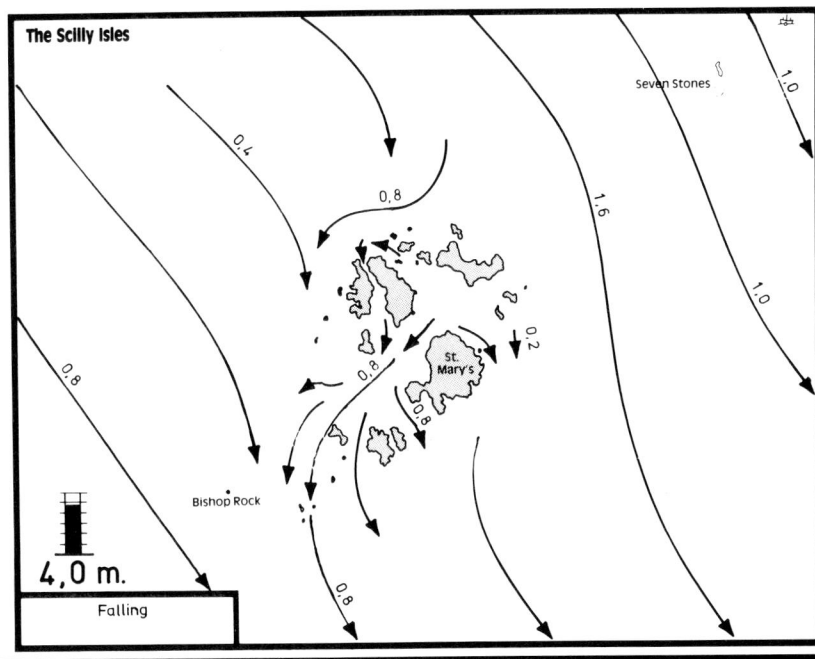

The Scilly Isles

Seven Stones

St. Mary's

Bishop Rock

4,0 m. Falling

0 — 5 Nautical Miles

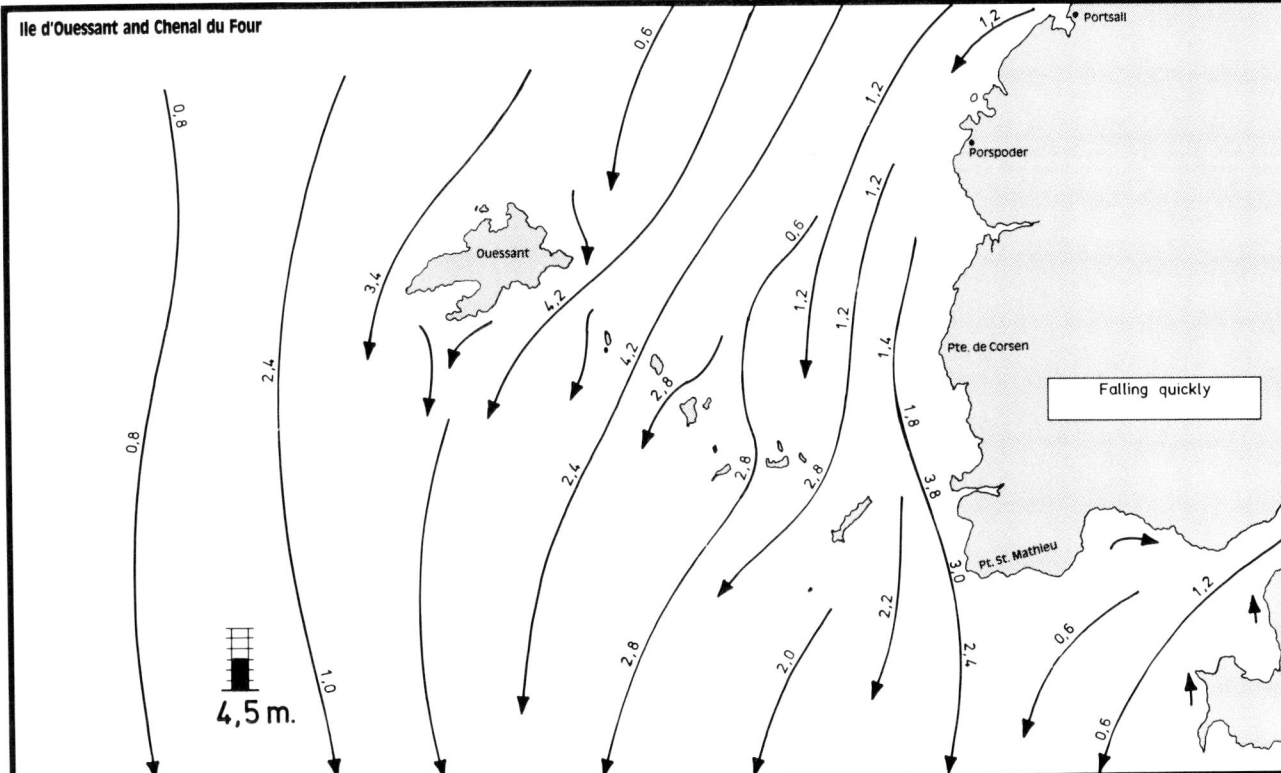

Ile d'Ouessant and Chenal du Four

Portsall
Porspoder
Ouessant
Pte. de Corsen
Falling quickly
Pt. St. Mathieu

4,5 m.

Stream Rate Conversion Table

Mean Rate Figure from Chart	Pencil-in height of HW Cherbourg Read from column below pencil mark										
	4.8	5.0	5.2	5.4	5.6	5.8	6.0	6.2	6.4	6.6	6.8
0.2	0.1	0.1	0.1	0.1	0.2	0.2	0.2	0.2	0.3	0.3	0.3	0.3
0.4	0.2	0.2	0.2	0.3	0.3	0.4	0.4	0.5	0.5	0.6	0.6	0.7
0.6	0.2	0.3	0.4	0.4	0.5	0.6	0.7	0.7	0.8	0.9	0.9	1.0
0.8	0.4	0.4	0.5	0.6	0.7	0.8	0.9	1.0	1.1	1.1	1.2	1.3
1.0	0.4	0.5	0.6	0.7	0.9	1.0	1.1	1.2	1.3	1.4	1.5	1.7
1.2	0.5	0.6	0.7	0.9	1.0	1.2	1.3	1.4	1.6	1.7	1.9	2.0
1.4	0.6	0.7	0.9	1.0	1.2	1.4	1.5	1.7	1.8	2.0	2.2	2.3
1.6	0.6	0.8	1.0	1.2	1.4	1.6	1.7	1.9	2.1	2.3	2.5	2.7
1.8	0.7	0.9	1.1	1.3	1.5	1.7	2.0	2.2	2.4	2.6	2.8	3.0
2.0	0.8	1.0	1.2	1.5	1.7	1.9	2.2	2.4	2.6	2.9	3.1	3.3
2.2	0.9	1.1	1.4	1.6	1.9	2.1	2.3	2.6	2.9	3.2	3.4	3.7
2.4	0.9	1.2	1.5	1.8	2.1	2.3	2.6	2.9	3.2	3.4	3.7	4.0
2.6	1.0	1.3	1.6	1.9	2.2	2.5	2.8	3.1	3.4	3.7	4.0	4.3
2.8	1.1	1.4	1.7	2.1	2.4	2.7	3.0	3.4	3.7	4.0	4.3	4.7
3.0	1.2	1.5	1.9	2.2	2.6	2.9	3.2	3.6	4.0	4.3	4.6	5.0
3.2	1.3	1.6	2.0	2.4	2.7	3.1	3.4	3.8	4.2	4.6	4.9	5.3
3.4	1.3	1.7	2.1	2.5	2.9	3.3	3.7	4.1	4.5	4.9	5.3	5.7
3.6	1.4	1.8	2.2	2.7	3.1	3.5	3.9	4.3	4.7	5.2	5.6	6.0
3.8	1.5	1.9	2.4	2.8	3.3	3.7	4.1	4.6	5.0	5.5	5.9	6.3
4.0	1.6	2.0	2.5	3.0	3.4	3.9	4.3	4.8	5.3	5.7	6.2	6.7
4.2	1.7	2.1	2.6	3.1	3.6	4.1	4.6	5.0	5.5	6.0	6.5	7.0
4.4	1.7	2.2	2.7	3.3	3.8	4.3	4.8	5.3	5.8	6.3	6.8	7.3
4.6	1.8	2.3	2.9	3.4	3.9	4.5	5.0	5.5	6.1	6.6	7.1	7.7
4.8	1.9	2.4	3.0	3.6	4.1	4.7	5.2	5.8	6.3	6.9	7.4	8.0
5.0	2.0	2.5	3.1	3.7	4.3	4.9	5.4	6.0	6.6	7.2	7.7	8.3
5.2	2.0	2.6	3.2	3.8	4.4	5.0	5.6	6.2	6.8	7.4	8.0	8.6
5.4	2.1	2.8	3.4	4.0	4.6	5.2	5.7	6.5	7.1	7.7	8.4	9.0
5.6	2.2	2.9	3.5	4.1	4.8	5.4	6.1	6.7	7.4	8.0	8.7	9.3
5.8	2.3	3.0	3.6	4.3	5.0	5.6	6.3	7.0	7.6	8.3	9.0	9.6
6.0	2.4	3.1	3.7	4.4	5.1	5.8	6.5	7.2	7.9	8.6	9.3	9.9

TIDAL HEIGHTS — PORTS & PLACES

Pencil-in height of HW Cherbourg ▶	4.8	5.0	5.2	5.4	5.6	5.8	6.0	6.2	6.4	6.6	6.8
St. Marys	3.5	3.6	3.8	3.9	4.1	4.2	4.4	4.5	4.7	4.8	5.0	5.1
Ports, Chenal du Four and Ile d'Ouessant	4.4	4.4	4.4	4.4	4.4	4.5	4.5	4.5	4.5	4.5	4.4	4.4

HW Cherbourg **HW**

Time (to be inserted)

Copyright © J Reeve-Fowkes and
Thomas Reed Publications.
No copying without permission.

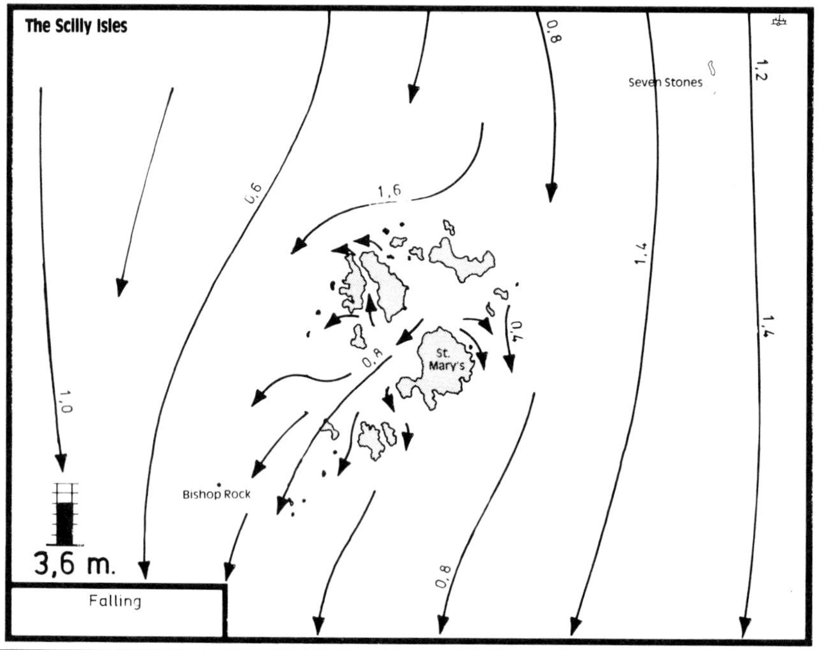

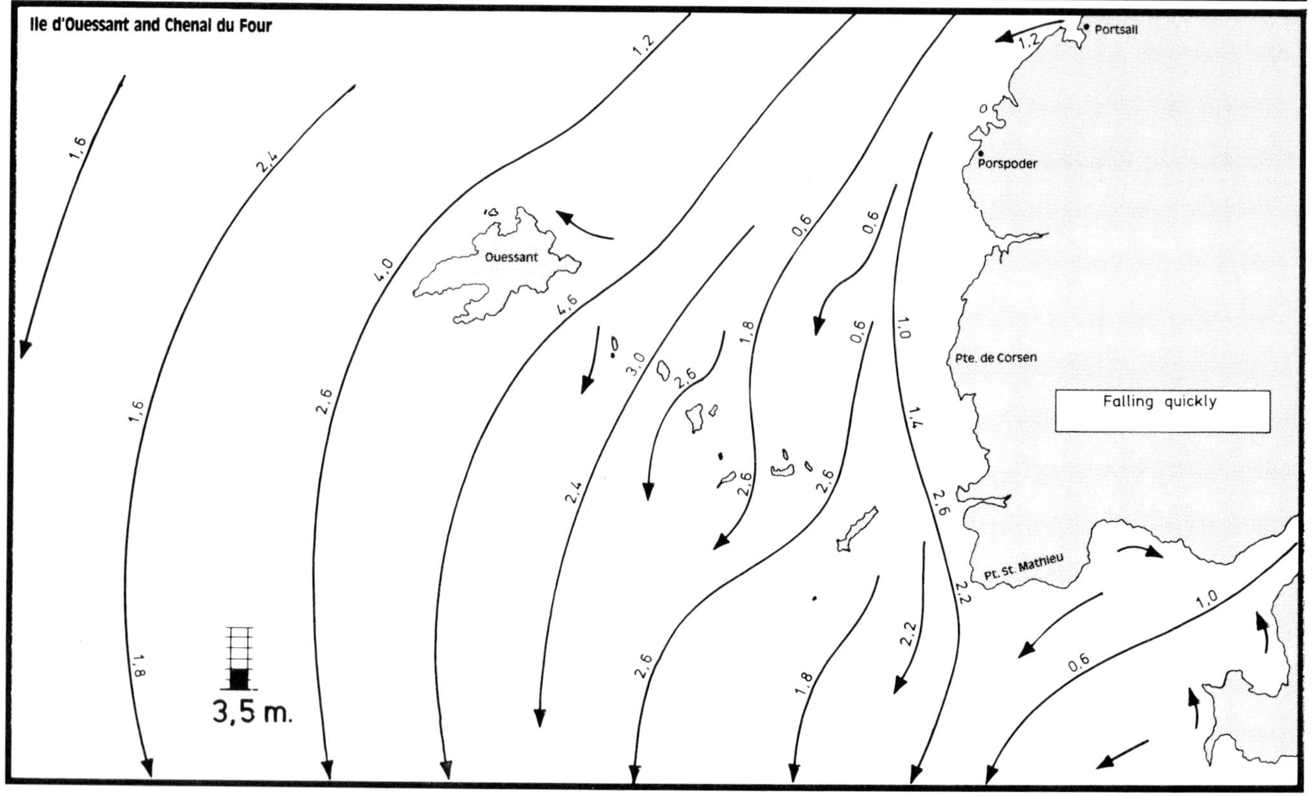

The Scilly Isles

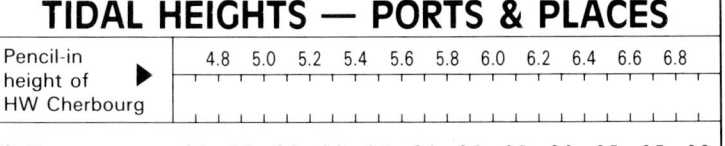

Seven Stones · St. Mary's · Bishop Rock

Falling — 3,6 m.

0 Nautical Miles 5

Ile d'Ouessant and Chenal du Four

Portsall · Porspoder · Ouessant · Pte. de Corsen · Pt. St. Mathieu

Falling quickly — 3,5 m.

Stream Rate Conversion Table

Mean Rate Figure from Chart ▼	Pencil-in height of HW Cherbourg — Read from column below pencil mark											
	4.8	5.0	5.2	5.4	5.6	5.8	6.0	6.2	6.4	6.6	6.8	7.0
0.2	0.1	0.1	0.1	0.1	0.2	0.2	0.2	0.2	0.3	0.3	0.3	0.3
0.4	0.2	0.2	0.2	0.3	0.3	0.4	0.4	0.5	0.5	0.6	0.6	0.7
0.6	0.2	0.3	0.4	0.4	0.5	0.6	0.7	0.7	0.8	0.9	0.9	1.0
0.8	0.4	0.4	0.5	0.6	0.7	0.8	0.9	1.0	1.1	1.1	1.2	1.3
1.0	0.4	0.5	0.6	0.7	0.9	1.0	1.1	1.2	1.3	1.4	1.5	1.7
1.2	0.5	0.6	0.7	0.9	1.0	1.2	1.3	1.4	1.6	1.7	1.9	2.0
1.4	0.6	0.7	0.9	1.0	1.2	1.4	1.5	1.7	1.8	2.0	2.2	2.3
1.6	0.6	0.8	1.0	1.2	1.4	1.6	1.7	1.9	2.1	2.3	2.5	2.7
1.8	0.7	0.9	1.1	1.3	1.5	1.7	2.0	2.2	2.4	2.6	2.8	3.0
2.0	0.8	1.0	1.2	1.5	1.7	1.9	2.2	2.4	2.6	2.9	3.1	3.3
2.2	0.9	1.1	1.4	1.6	1.9	2.1	2.3	2.6	2.9	3.2	3.4	3.7
2.4	0.9	1.2	1.5	1.8	2.1	2.3	2.6	2.9	3.2	3.4	3.7	4.0
2.6	1.0	1.3	1.6	1.9	2.2	2.5	2.8	3.1	3.4	3.7	4.0	4.3
2.8	1.1	1.4	1.7	2.1	2.4	2.7	3.0	3.4	3.7	4.0	4.3	4.7
3.0	1.2	1.5	1.9	2.2	2.6	2.9	3.2	3.6	4.0	4.3	4.6	5.0
3.2	1.3	1.6	2.0	2.4	2.7	3.1	3.4	3.8	4.2	4.6	4.9	5.3
3.4	1.3	1.7	2.1	2.5	2.9	3.3	3.7	4.1	4.5	4.9	5.3	5.7
3.6	1.4	1.8	2.2	2.7	3.1	3.5	3.9	4.3	4.7	5.2	5.6	6.0
3.8	1.5	1.9	2.4	2.8	3.3	3.7	4.1	4.6	5.0	5.5	5.9	6.3
4.0	1.6	2.0	2.5	3.0	3.4	3.9	4.3	4.8	5.3	5.7	6.2	6.7
4.2	1.7	2.1	2.6	3.1	3.6	4.1	4.6	5.0	5.5	6.0	6.5	7.0
4.4	1.7	2.2	2.7	3.3	3.8	4.3	4.8	5.3	5.8	6.3	6.8	7.3
4.6	1.8	2.3	2.9	3.4	3.9	4.5	5.0	5.5	6.1	6.6	7.1	7.7
4.8	1.9	2.4	3.0	3.6	4.1	4.7	5.2	5.8	6.3	6.9	7.4	8.0
5.0	2.0	2.5	3.1	3.7	4.3	4.9	5.4	6.0	6.6	7.2	7.7	8.3
5.2	2.0	2.6	3.2	3.8	4.4	5.0	5.6	6.2	6.8	7.4	8.0	8.6
5.4	2.1	2.8	3.4	4.0	4.6	5.2	5.7	6.5	7.1	7.7	8.4	9.0
5.6	2.2	2.9	3.5	4.1	4.8	5.4	6.1	6.7	7.4	8.0	8.7	9.3
5.8	2.3	3.0	3.6	4.3	5.0	5.6	6.3	7.0	7.6	8.3	9.0	9.6
6.0	2.4	3.1	3.7	4.4	5.1	5.8	6.5	7.2	7.9	8.6	9.3	9.9

TIDAL HEIGHTS — PORTS & PLACES

Pencil-in height of HW Cherbourg ▶	4.8	5.0	5.2	5.4	5.6	5.8	6.0	6.2	6.4	6.6	6.8	7.0
St. Marys	3.1	3.2	3.2	3.3	3.4	3.4	3.5	3.5	3.6	3.7	3.7	3.8
Ports, Chenal du Four and Ile d'Ouessant	3.9	3.8	3.8	3.7	3.6	3.5	3.4	3.3	3.2	3.1	2.9	2.8

1 hour after HW Cherbourg +1

Time (to be inserted)

Copyright © J Reeve-Fowkes and Thomas Reed Publications.
No copying without permission.

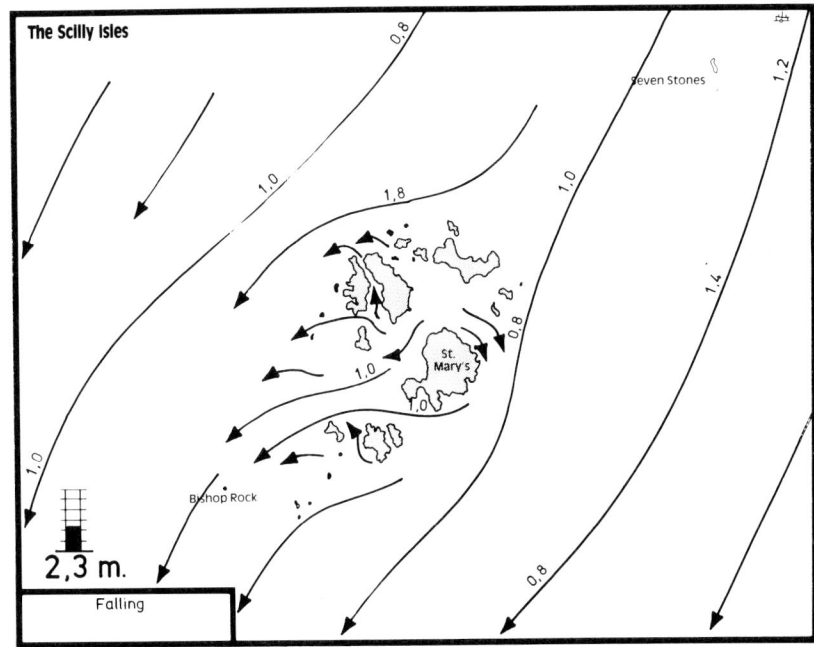

The Scilly Isles
Seven Stones
St. Mary's
Bishop Rock
2,3 m. Falling
0—5 Nautical Miles

Ile d'Ouessant and Chenal du Four
Portsall
Ouessant
Porspoder
Pte. de Corsen
Falling to L.W.
Pt. St. Mathieu
2,7 m.

Stream Rate Conversion Table

Mean Rate Figure from Chart	Pencil-in height of HW Cherbourg — Read from column below pencil mark										
	4.8	5.0	5.2	5.4	5.6	5.8	6.0	6.2	6.4	6.6	6.8
0.2	0.1	0.1	0.1	0.1	0.2	0.2	0.2	0.2	0.3	0.3	0.3
0.4	0.2	0.2	0.2	0.3	0.3	0.4	0.4	0.5	0.5	0.6	0.7
0.6	0.2	0.3	0.4	0.4	0.5	0.6	0.7	0.7	0.8	0.9	1.0
0.8	0.4	0.4	0.5	0.6	0.7	0.8	0.9	1.0	1.1	1.2	1.3
1.0	0.4	0.5	0.6	0.7	0.9	1.0	1.1	1.2	1.3	1.4	1.5	1.7
1.2	0.5	0.6	0.7	0.9	1.0	1.2	1.3	1.4	1.6	1.7	1.9	2.0
1.4	0.6	0.7	0.9	1.0	1.2	1.4	1.5	1.7	1.8	2.0	2.2	2.3
1.6	0.6	0.8	1.0	1.2	1.4	1.6	1.7	1.9	2.1	2.3	2.5	2.7
1.8	0.7	0.9	1.1	1.3	1.5	1.7	2.0	2.2	2.4	2.6	2.8	3.0
2.0	0.8	1.0	1.2	1.5	1.7	1.9	2.2	2.4	2.6	2.9	3.1	3.3
2.2	0.9	1.1	1.4	1.6	1.9	2.1	2.3	2.6	2.9	3.2	3.4	3.7
2.4	0.9	1.2	1.5	1.8	2.1	2.3	2.6	2.9	3.2	3.4	3.7	4.0
2.6	1.0	1.3	1.6	1.9	2.2	2.5	2.8	3.1	3.4	3.7	4.0	4.3
2.8	1.1	1.4	1.7	2.1	2.4	2.7	3.0	3.4	3.7	4.0	4.3	4.7
3.0	1.2	1.5	1.9	2.2	2.6	2.9	3.2	3.6	4.0	4.3	4.6	5.0
3.2	1.3	1.6	2.0	2.4	2.7	3.1	3.4	3.8	4.2	4.6	4.9	5.3
3.4	1.3	1.7	2.1	2.5	2.9	3.3	3.7	4.1	4.5	4.9	5.3	5.7
3.6	1.4	1.8	2.2	2.7	3.1	3.5	3.9	4.3	4.7	5.2	5.6	6.0
3.8	1.5	1.9	2.4	2.8	3.3	3.7	4.1	4.6	5.0	5.5	5.9	6.3
4.0	1.6	2.0	2.5	3.0	3.4	3.9	4.3	4.8	5.3	5.7	6.2	6.7
4.2	1.7	2.1	2.6	3.1	3.6	4.1	4.6	5.0	5.5	6.0	6.5	7.0
4.4	1.7	2.2	2.7	3.3	3.8	4.3	4.8	5.3	5.8	6.3	6.8	7.3
4.6	1.8	2.3	2.9	3.4	3.9	4.5	5.0	5.5	6.1	6.6	7.1	7.7
4.8	1.9	2.4	3.0	3.6	4.1	4.7	5.2	5.8	6.3	6.9	7.4	8.0
5.0	2.0	2.5	3.1	3.7	4.3	4.9	5.4	6.0	6.6	7.2	7.7	8.3
5.2	2.0	2.6	3.2	3.8	4.4	5.0	5.6	6.2	6.8	7.4	8.0	8.6
5.4	2.1	2.8	3.4	4.0	4.6	5.2	5.7	6.5	7.1	7.7	8.4	9.0
5.6	2.2	2.9	3.5	4.1	4.8	5.4	6.1	6.7	7.4	8.0	8.7	9.3
5.8	2.3	3.0	3.6	4.3	5.0	5.6	6.3	7.0	7.6	8.3	9.0	9.6
6.0	2.4	3.1	3.7	4.4	5.1	5.8	6.5	7.2	7.9	8.6	9.3	9.9

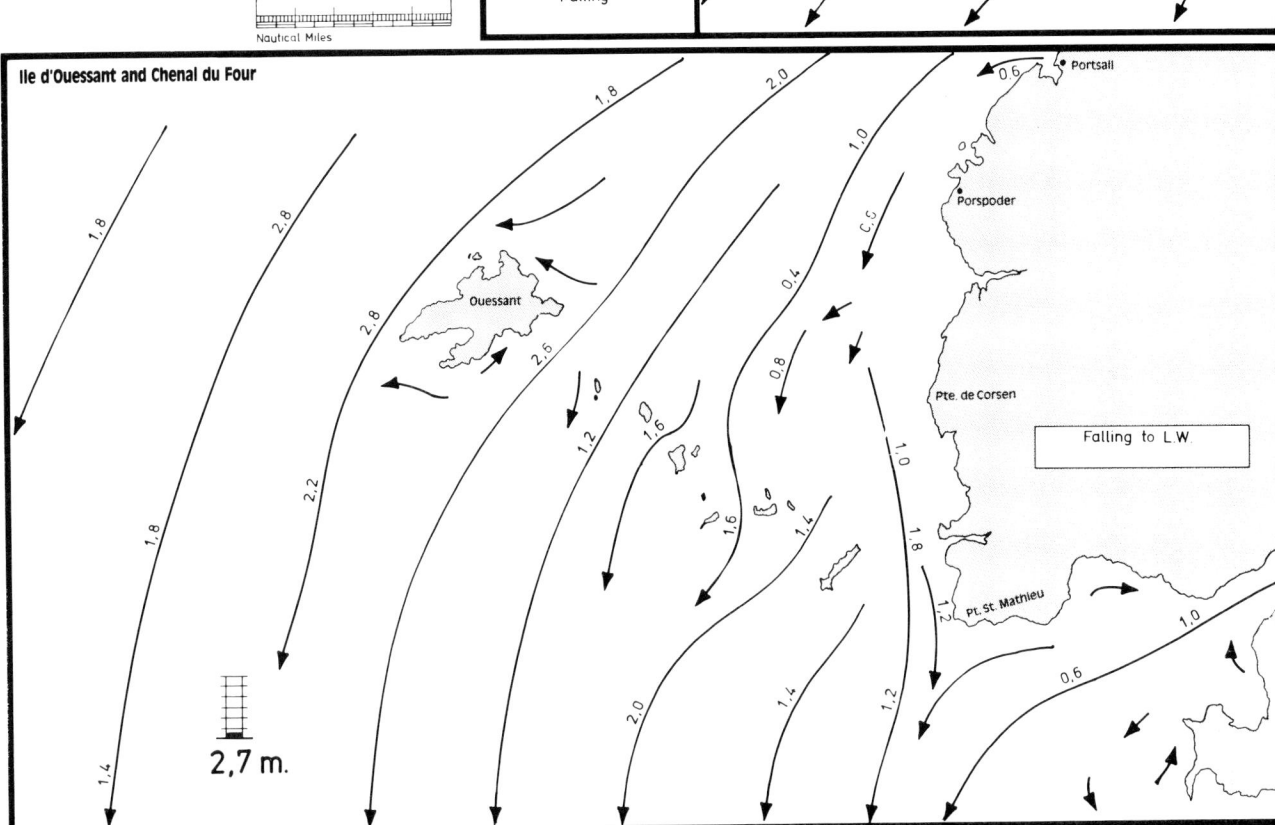

TIDAL HEIGHTS — PORTS & PLACES

Pencil-in height of HW Cherbourg ▶	4.8	5.0	5.2	5.4	5.6	5.8	6.0	6.2	6.4	6.6	6.8
St. Marys	2.6	2.6	2.6	2.6	2.5	2.5	2.5	2.4	2.4	2.4	2.3
Ports, Chenal du Four and Ile d'Ouessant	3.5	3.3	3.1	2.9	2.8	2.6	2.4	2.3	2.1	1.9	1.7	1.5

2 hours after HW Cherbourg +2

Time (to be inserted)

Copyright © J Reeve-Fowkes and
Thomas Reed Publications.
No copying without permission.

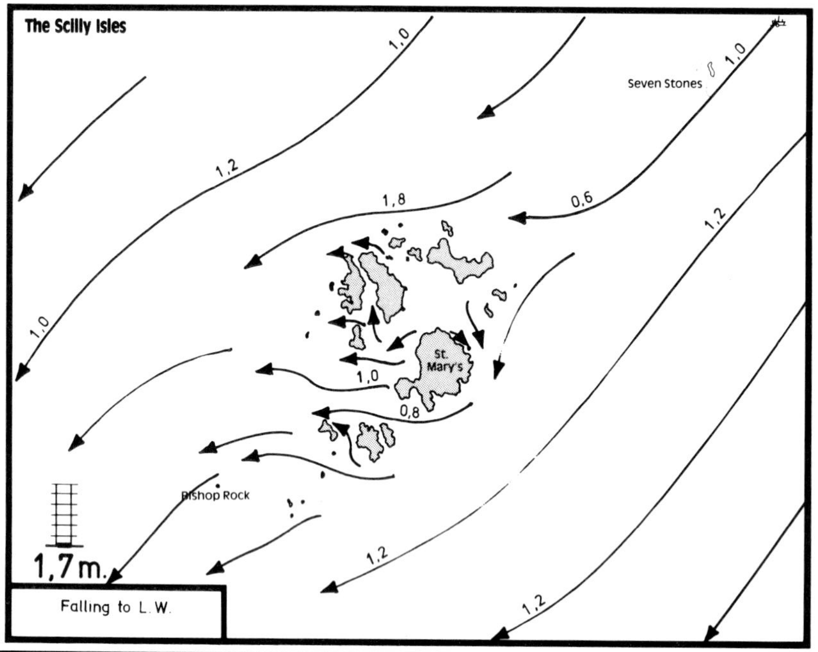

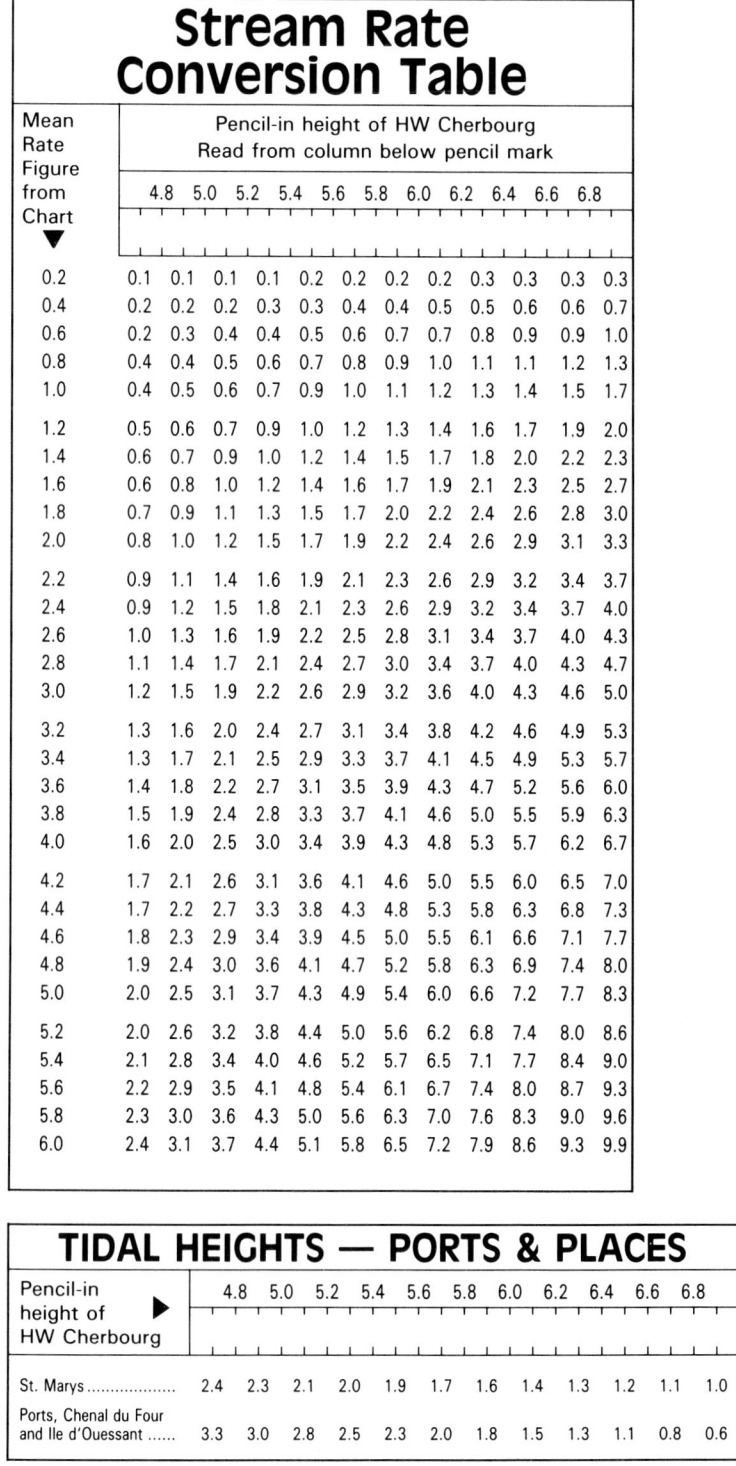

The Scilly Isles

Seven Stones

St. Mary's

Bishop Rock

1,7 m.
Falling to L.W.

0 — 5
Nautical Miles

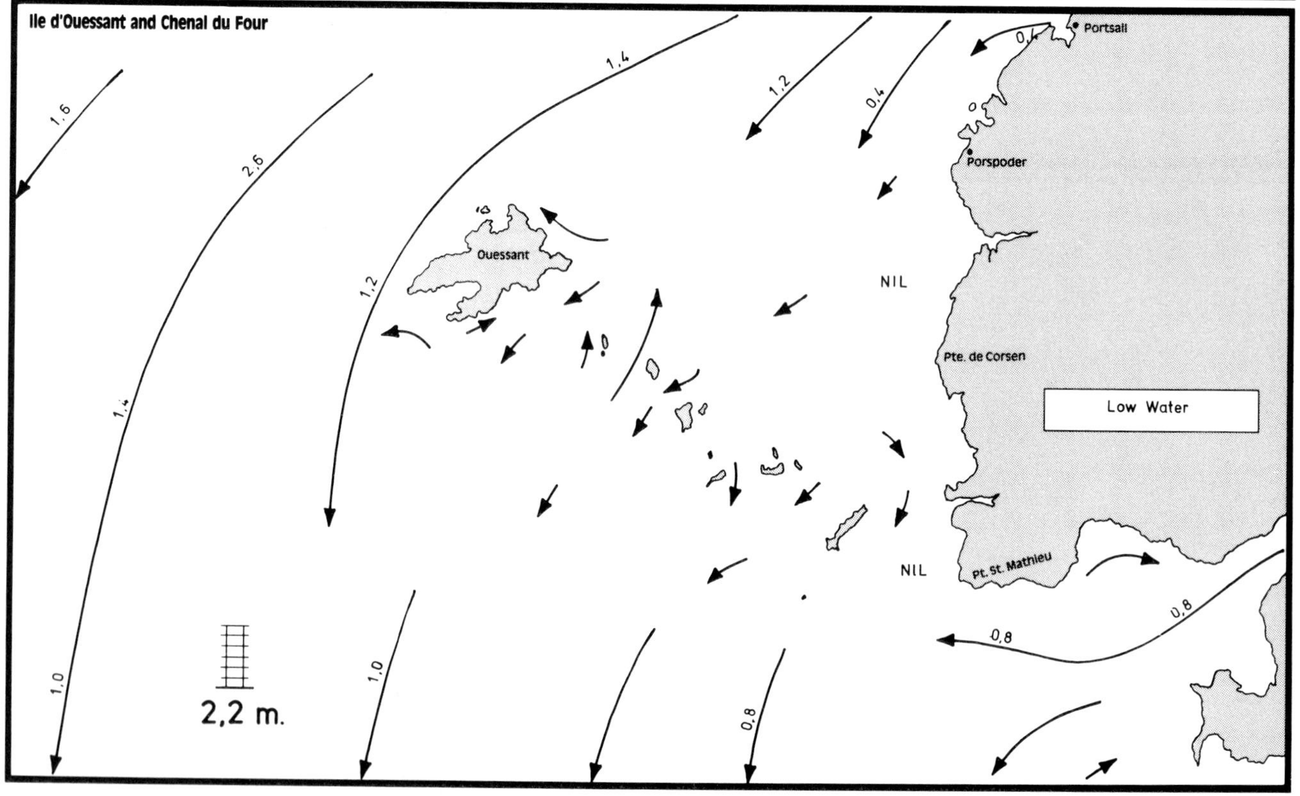

Ile d'Ouessant and Chenal du Four

Portsall
Porspoder
Ouessant
NIL
Pte. de Corsen
Low Water
NIL
Pt. St. Mathieu

2,2 m.

Stream Rate Conversion Table

Mean Rate Figure from Chart ▼	Pencil-in height of HW Cherbourg Read from column below pencil mark										
	4.8	5.0	5.2	5.4	5.6	5.8	6.0	6.2	6.4	6.6	6.8
0.2	0.1	0.1	0.1	0.1	0.2	0.2	0.2	0.2	0.3	0.3	0.3	0.3
0.4	0.2	0.2	0.2	0.3	0.3	0.4	0.4	0.5	0.5	0.6	0.6	0.7
0.6	0.2	0.3	0.4	0.4	0.5	0.6	0.7	0.7	0.8	0.9	0.9	1.0
0.8	0.4	0.4	0.5	0.6	0.7	0.8	0.9	1.0	1.1	1.1	1.2	1.3
1.0	0.4	0.5	0.6	0.7	0.9	1.0	1.1	1.2	1.3	1.4	1.5	1.7
1.2	0.5	0.6	0.7	0.9	1.0	1.2	1.3	1.4	1.6	1.7	1.9	2.0
1.4	0.6	0.7	0.9	1.0	1.2	1.4	1.5	1.7	1.8	2.0	2.2	2.3
1.6	0.6	0.8	1.0	1.2	1.4	1.6	1.7	1.9	2.1	2.3	2.5	2.7
1.8	0.7	0.9	1.1	1.3	1.5	1.7	2.0	2.2	2.4	2.6	2.8	3.0
2.0	0.8	1.0	1.2	1.5	1.7	1.9	2.2	2.4	2.6	2.9	3.1	3.3
2.2	0.9	1.1	1.4	1.6	1.9	2.1	2.3	2.6	2.9	3.2	3.4	3.7
2.4	0.9	1.2	1.5	1.8	2.1	2.3	2.6	2.9	3.2	3.4	3.7	4.0
2.6	1.0	1.3	1.6	1.9	2.2	2.5	2.8	3.1	3.4	3.7	4.0	4.3
2.8	1.1	1.4	1.7	2.1	2.4	2.7	3.0	3.4	3.7	4.0	4.3	4.7
3.0	1.2	1.5	1.9	2.2	2.6	2.9	3.2	3.6	4.0	4.3	4.6	5.0
3.2	1.3	1.6	2.0	2.4	2.7	3.1	3.4	3.8	4.2	4.6	4.9	5.3
3.4	1.3	1.7	2.1	2.5	2.9	3.3	3.7	4.1	4.5	4.9	5.3	5.7
3.6	1.4	1.8	2.2	2.7	3.1	3.5	3.9	4.3	4.7	5.2	5.6	6.0
3.8	1.5	1.9	2.4	2.8	3.3	3.7	4.1	4.6	5.0	5.5	5.9	6.3
4.0	1.6	2.0	2.5	3.0	3.4	3.9	4.3	4.8	5.3	5.7	6.2	6.7
4.2	1.7	2.1	2.6	3.1	3.6	4.1	4.6	5.0	5.5	6.0	6.5	7.0
4.4	1.7	2.2	2.7	3.3	3.8	4.3	4.8	5.3	5.8	6.3	6.8	7.3
4.6	1.8	2.3	2.9	3.4	3.9	4.5	5.0	5.5	6.1	6.6	7.1	7.7
4.8	1.9	2.4	3.0	3.6	4.1	4.7	5.2	5.8	6.3	6.9	7.4	8.0
5.0	2.0	2.5	3.1	3.7	4.3	4.9	5.4	6.0	6.6	7.2	7.7	8.3
5.2	2.0	2.6	3.2	3.8	4.4	5.0	5.6	6.2	6.8	7.4	8.0	8.6
5.4	2.1	2.8	3.4	4.0	4.6	5.2	5.7	6.5	7.1	7.7	8.4	9.0
5.6	2.2	2.9	3.5	4.1	4.8	5.4	6.1	6.7	7.4	8.0	8.7	9.3
5.8	2.3	3.0	3.6	4.3	5.0	5.6	6.3	7.0	7.6	8.3	9.0	9.6
6.0	2.4	3.1	3.7	4.4	5.1	5.8	6.5	7.2	7.9	8.6	9.3	9.9

TIDAL HEIGHTS — PORTS & PLACES

Pencil-in height of HW Cherbourg ▶	4.8	5.0	5.2	5.4	5.6	5.8	6.0	6.2	6.4	6.6	6.8
St. Marys	2.4	2.3	2.1	2.0	1.9	1.7	1.6	1.4	1.3	1.2	1.1	1.0
Ports, Chenal du Four and Ile d'Ouessant	3.3	3.0	2.8	2.5	2.3	2.0	1.8	1.5	1.3	1.1	0.8	0.6

3 hours after HW Cherbourg +3

Time (to be inserted)

Copyright © J Reeve-Fowkes and Thomas Reed Publications.
No copying without permission.

The Scilly Isles

1,3 m. Low Water

Ile d'Ouessant and Chenal du Four

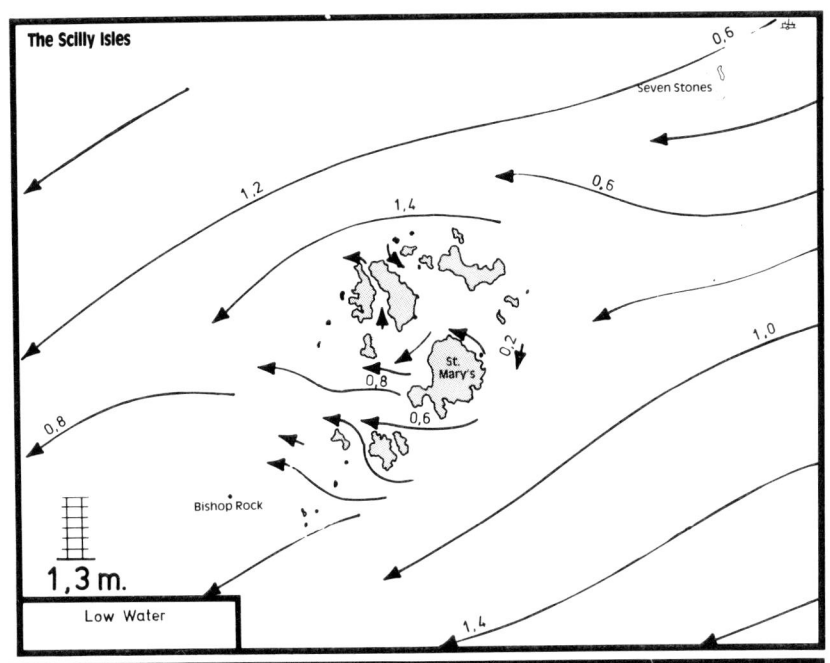

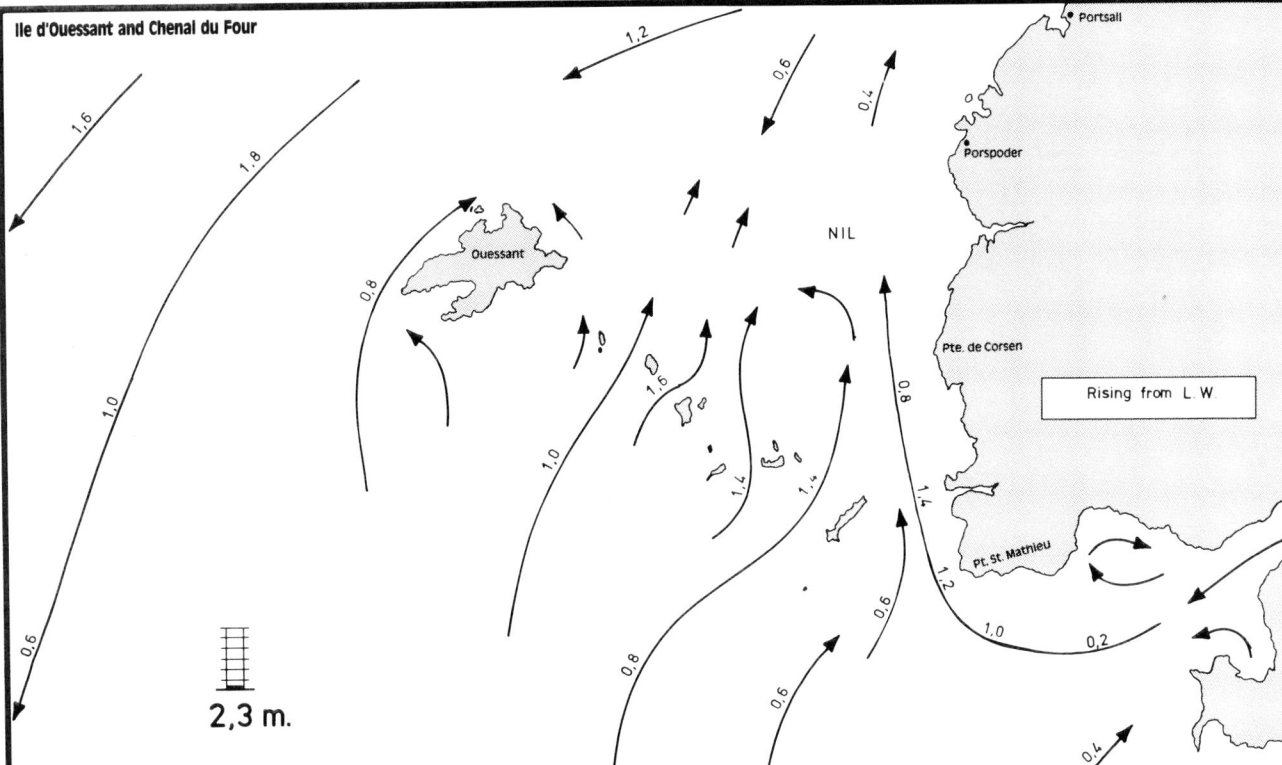

2,3 m.

Rising from L.W.

Stream Rate Conversion Table

Mean Rate Figure from Chart	Pencil-in height of HW Cherbourg Read from column below pencil mark										
	4.8	5.0	5.2	5.4	5.6	5.8	6.0	6.2	6.4	6.6	6.8
0.2	0.1	0.1	0.1	0.1	0.2	0.2	0.2	0.2	0.3	0.3	0.3
0.4	0.2	0.2	0.2	0.3	0.3	0.4	0.4	0.5	0.5	0.6	0.7
0.6	0.2	0.3	0.4	0.4	0.5	0.6	0.7	0.7	0.8	0.9	1.0
0.8	0.4	0.4	0.5	0.6	0.7	0.8	0.9	1.0	1.1	1.2	1.3
1.0	0.4	0.5	0.6	0.7	0.9	1.0	1.1	1.2	1.3	1.4	1.5	1.7
1.2	0.5	0.6	0.7	0.9	1.0	1.2	1.3	1.4	1.6	1.7	1.9	2.0
1.4	0.6	0.7	0.9	1.0	1.2	1.4	1.5	1.7	1.8	2.0	2.2	2.3
1.6	0.6	0.8	1.0	1.2	1.4	1.6	1.7	1.9	2.1	2.3	2.5	2.7
1.8	0.7	0.9	1.1	1.3	1.5	1.7	2.0	2.2	2.4	2.6	2.8	3.0
2.0	0.8	1.0	1.2	1.5	1.7	1.9	2.2	2.4	2.6	2.9	3.1	3.3
2.2	0.9	1.1	1.4	1.6	1.9	2.1	2.3	2.6	2.9	3.2	3.4	3.7
2.4	0.9	1.2	1.5	1.8	2.1	2.3	2.6	2.9	3.2	3.4	3.7	4.0
2.6	1.0	1.3	1.6	1.9	2.2	2.5	2.8	3.1	3.4	3.7	4.0	4.3
2.8	1.1	1.4	1.7	2.1	2.4	2.7	3.0	3.4	3.7	4.0	4.3	4.7
3.0	1.2	1.5	1.9	2.2	2.6	2.9	3.2	3.6	4.0	4.3	4.6	5.0
3.2	1.3	1.6	2.0	2.4	2.7	3.1	3.4	3.8	4.2	4.6	4.9	5.3
3.4	1.3	1.7	2.1	2.5	2.9	3.3	3.7	4.1	4.5	4.9	5.3	5.7
3.6	1.4	1.8	2.2	2.7	3.1	3.5	3.9	4.3	4.7	5.2	5.6	6.0
3.8	1.5	1.9	2.4	2.8	3.3	3.7	4.1	4.6	5.0	5.5	5.9	6.3
4.0	1.6	2.0	2.5	3.0	3.4	3.9	4.3	4.8	5.3	5.7	6.2	6.7
4.2	1.7	2.1	2.6	3.1	3.6	4.1	4.6	5.0	5.5	6.0	6.5	7.0
4.4	1.7	2.2	2.7	3.3	3.8	4.3	4.8	5.3	5.8	6.3	6.8	7.3
4.6	1.8	2.3	2.9	3.4	3.9	4.5	5.0	5.5	6.1	6.6	7.1	7.7
4.8	1.9	2.4	3.0	3.6	4.1	4.7	5.2	5.8	6.3	6.9	7.4	8.0
5.0	2.0	2.5	3.1	3.7	4.3	4.9	5.4	6.0	6.6	7.2	7.7	8.3
5.2	2.0	2.6	3.2	3.8	4.4	5.0	5.6	6.2	6.8	7.4	8.0	8.6
5.4	2.1	2.8	3.4	4.0	4.6	5.2	5.7	6.5	7.1	7.7	8.4	9.0
5.6	2.2	2.9	3.5	4.1	4.8	5.4	6.1	6.7	7.4	8.0	8.7	9.3
5.8	2.3	3.0	3.6	4.3	5.0	5.6	6.3	7.0	7.6	8.3	9.0	9.6
6.0	2.4	3.1	3.7	4.4	5.1	5.8	6.5	7.2	7.9	8.6	9.3	9.9

TIDAL HEIGHTS — PORTS & PLACES

Pencil-in height of HW Cherbourg ▶	4.8	5.0	5.2	5.4	5.6	5.8	6.0	6.2	6.4	6.6	6.8
St. Marys	2.3	2.1	1.9	1.7	1.5	1.3	1.1	0.9	0.7	0.6	0.4	0.3
Ports, Chenal du Four and Ile d'Ouessant	3.1	2.9	2.7	2.5	2.3	2.0	1.8	1.6	1.4	1.2	0.9	0.7

4 hours after HW Cherbourg +4

Time (to be inserted)

Copyright © J Reeve-Fowkes and Thomas Reed Publications.
No copying without permission.

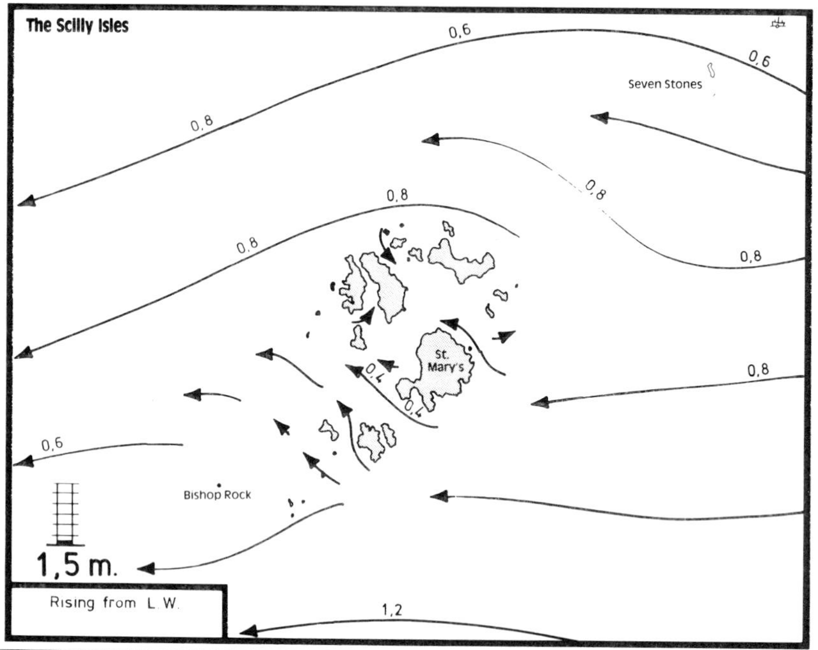

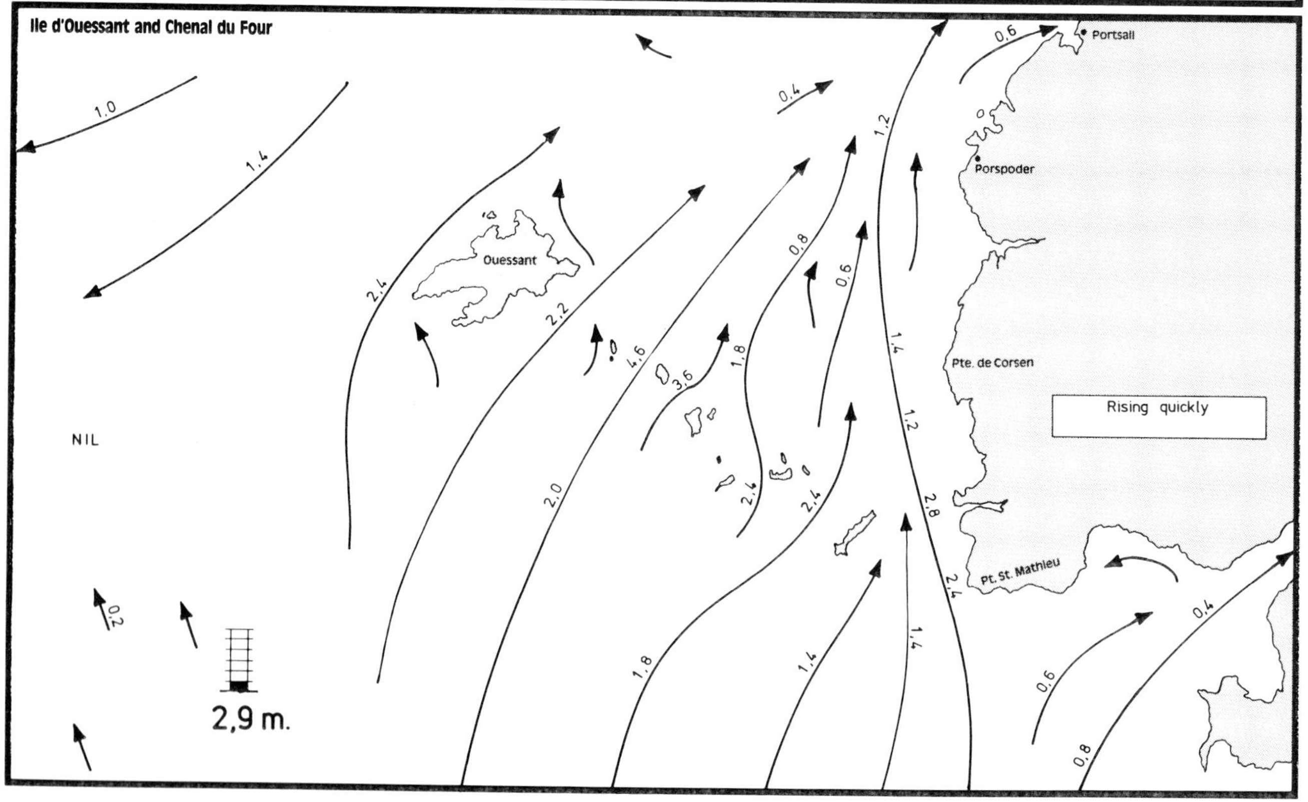

The Scilly Isles

Seven Stones

0.6
0.6
0.8
0.8
0.8
0.8
0.8
0.8
0.6
St. Mary's
0.4
0.4
0.6
0.4

1,5 m.
Rising from L.W.
1.2

Ile d'Ouessant and Chenal du Four

Portsall
0.6
0.4
1.2
Porspoder
1.0
1.4
0.4
2.4
Ouessant
2.2
0.8
0.6
4.6
3.6
1.8
Pte. de Corsen
1.4
1.2
NIL
Rising quickly
2.0
2.6
2.6
2.4
2.8
0.2
2.4
Pt. St. Mathieu
1.8
1.4
1.4
0.4
0.6
2,9 m.
0.8

0   Nautical Miles   5

Stream Rate Conversion Table

Mean Rate Figure from Chart ▼	Pencil-in height of HW Cherbourg Read from column below pencil mark											
	4.8	5.0	5.2	5.4	5.6	5.8	6.0	6.2	6.4	6.6	6.8
0.2	0.1	0.1	0.1	0.1	0.2	0.2	0.2	0.2	0.3	0.3	0.3	0.3
0.4	0.2	0.2	0.2	0.3	0.3	0.4	0.4	0.5	0.5	0.6	0.6	0.7
0.6	0.2	0.3	0.4	0.4	0.5	0.6	0.7	0.7	0.8	0.9	0.9	1.0
0.8	0.4	0.4	0.5	0.6	0.7	0.8	0.9	1.0	1.1	1.1	1.2	1.3
1.0	0.4	0.5	0.6	0.7	0.9	1.0	1.1	1.2	1.3	1.4	1.5	1.7
1.2	0.5	0.6	0.7	0.9	1.0	1.2	1.3	1.4	1.6	1.7	1.9	2.0
1.4	0.6	0.7	0.9	1.0	1.2	1.4	1.5	1.7	1.8	2.0	2.2	2.3
1.6	0.6	0.8	1.0	1.2	1.4	1.6	1.7	1.9	2.1	2.3	2.5	2.7
1.8	0.7	0.9	1.1	1.3	1.5	1.7	2.0	2.2	2.4	2.6	2.8	3.0
2.0	0.8	1.0	1.2	1.5	1.7	1.9	2.2	2.4	2.6	2.9	3.1	3.3
2.2	0.9	1.1	1.4	1.6	1.9	2.1	2.3	2.6	2.9	3.2	3.4	3.7
2.4	0.9	1.2	1.5	1.8	2.1	2.3	2.6	2.9	3.2	3.4	3.7	4.0
2.6	1.0	1.3	1.6	1.9	2.2	2.5	2.8	3.1	3.4	3.7	4.0	4.3
2.8	1.1	1.4	1.7	2.1	2.4	2.7	3.0	3.4	3.7	4.0	4.3	4.7
3.0	1.2	1.5	1.9	2.2	2.6	2.9	3.2	3.6	4.0	4.3	4.6	5.0
3.2	1.3	1.6	2.0	2.4	2.7	3.1	3.4	3.8	4.2	4.6	4.9	5.3
3.4	1.3	1.7	2.1	2.5	2.9	3.3	3.7	4.1	4.5	4.9	5.3	5.7
3.6	1.4	1.8	2.2	2.7	3.1	3.5	3.9	4.3	4.7	5.2	5.6	6.0
3.8	1.5	1.9	2.4	2.8	3.3	3.7	4.1	4.6	5.0	5.5	5.9	6.3
4.0	1.6	2.0	2.5	3.0	3.4	3.9	4.3	4.8	5.3	5.7	6.2	6.7
4.2	1.7	2.1	2.6	3.1	3.6	4.1	4.6	5.0	5.5	6.0	6.5	7.0
4.4	1.7	2.2	2.7	3.3	3.8	4.3	4.8	5.3	5.8	6.3	6.8	7.3
4.6	1.8	2.3	2.9	3.4	3.9	4.5	5.0	5.5	6.1	6.6	7.1	7.7
4.8	1.9	2.4	3.0	3.6	4.1	4.7	5.2	5.8	6.3	6.9	7.4	8.0
5.0	2.0	2.5	3.1	3.7	4.3	4.9	5.4	6.0	6.6	7.2	7.7	8.3
5.2	2.0	2.6	3.2	3.8	4.4	5.0	5.6	6.2	6.8	7.4	8.0	8.6
5.4	2.1	2.8	3.4	4.0	4.6	5.2	5.7	6.5	7.1	7.7	8.4	9.0
5.6	2.2	2.9	3.5	4.1	4.8	5.4	6.1	6.7	7.4	8.0	8.7	9.3
5.8	2.3	3.0	3.6	4.3	5.0	5.6	6.3	7.0	7.6	8.3	9.0	9.6
6.0	2.4	3.1	3.7	4.4	5.1	5.8	6.5	7.2	7.9	8.6	9.3	9.9

TIDAL HEIGHTS — PORTS & PLACES

Pencil-in height of HW Cherbourg ▶	4.8	5.0	5.2	5.4	5.6	5.8	6.0	6.2	6.4	6.6	6.8
St. Marys	2.3	2.1	2.0	1.9	1.7	1.6	1.4	1.3	1.1	1.0	0.8	0.7
Ports, Chenal du Four and Ile d'Ouessant	3.4	3.3	3.1	3.0	2.9	2.7	2.6	2.4	2.3	2.1	2.0	1.8

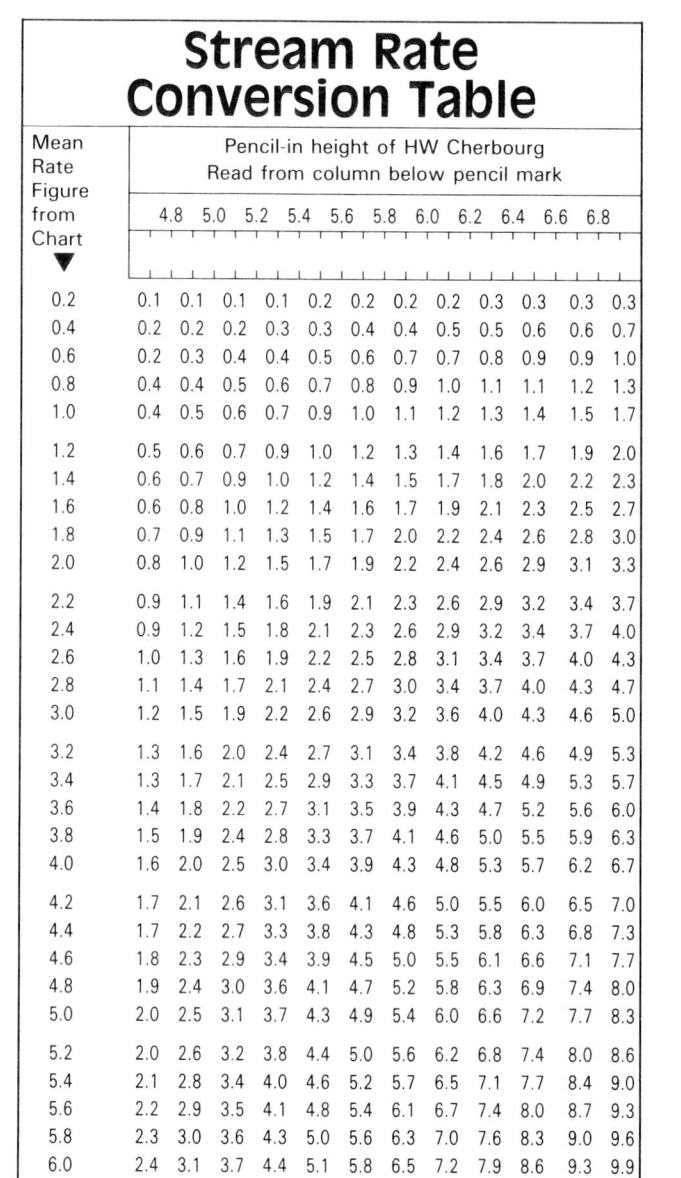

5 hours after HW Cherbourg +5

Time (to be inserted)

Copyright © J Reeve-Fowkes and Thomas Reed Publications.
No copying without permission.

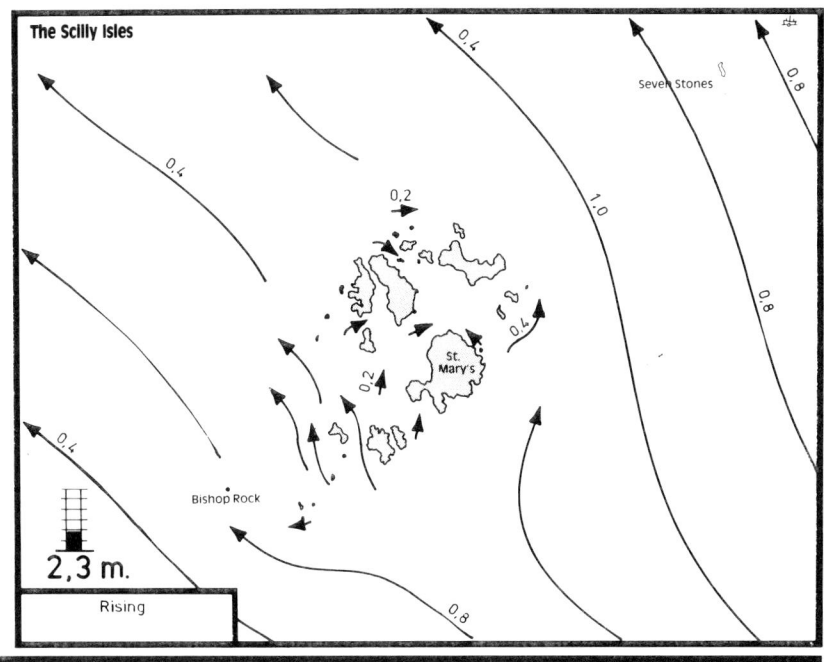

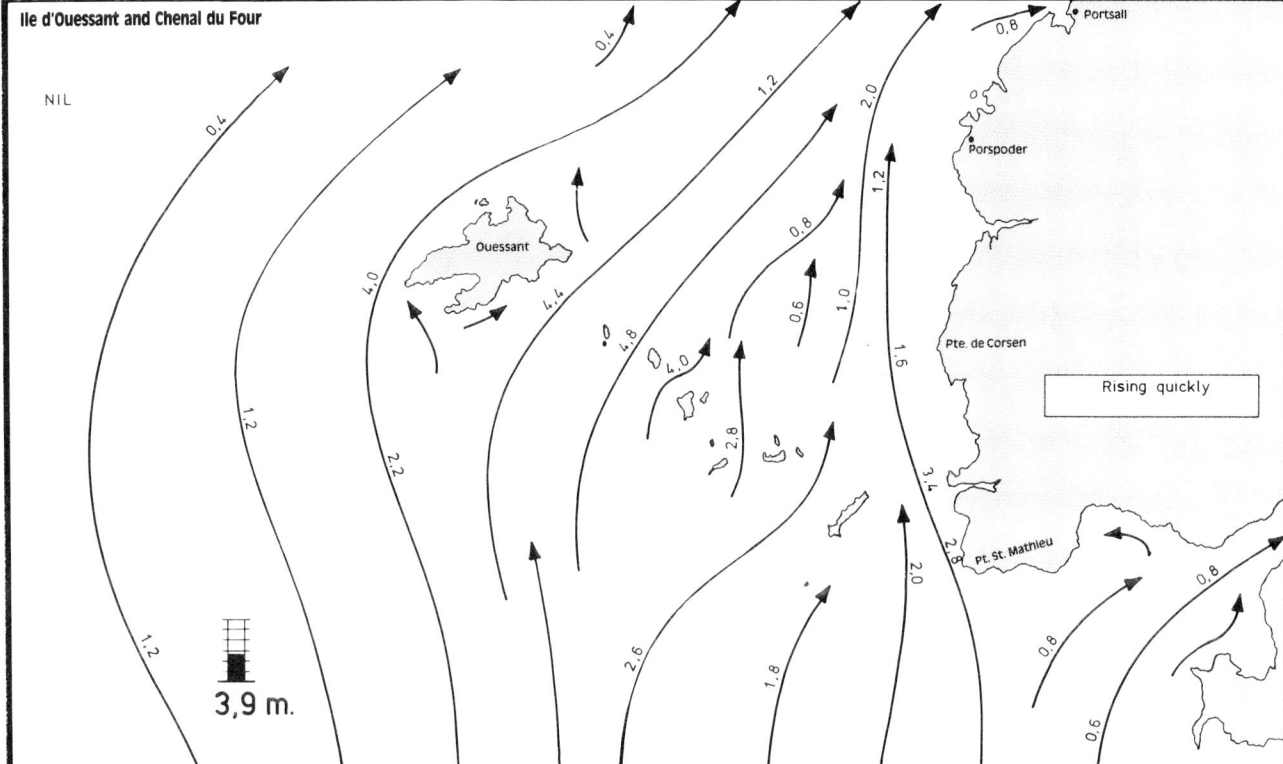

The Scilly Isles — 2,3 m. Rising

Ile d'Ouessant and Chenal du Four — 3,9 m. Rising quickly

Stream Rate Conversion Table

Mean Rate Figure from Chart	Pencil-in height of HW Cherbourg — Read from column below pencil mark										
	4.8	5.0	5.2	5.4	5.6	5.8	6.0	6.2	6.4	6.6	6.8
0.2	0.1	0.1	0.1	0.1	0.2	0.2	0.2	0.2	0.3	0.3	0.3
0.4	0.2	0.2	0.2	0.3	0.3	0.4	0.4	0.5	0.5	0.6	0.7
0.6	0.2	0.3	0.4	0.4	0.5	0.6	0.7	0.7	0.8	0.9	1.0
0.8	0.4	0.4	0.5	0.6	0.7	0.8	0.9	1.0	1.1	1.2	1.3
1.0	0.4	0.5	0.6	0.7	0.9	1.0	1.1	1.2	1.3	1.4	1.5	1.7
1.2	0.5	0.6	0.7	0.9	1.0	1.2	1.3	1.4	1.6	1.7	1.9	2.0
1.4	0.6	0.7	0.9	1.0	1.2	1.4	1.5	1.7	1.8	2.0	2.2	2.3
1.6	0.6	0.8	1.0	1.2	1.4	1.6	1.7	1.9	2.1	2.3	2.5	2.7
1.8	0.7	0.9	1.1	1.3	1.5	1.7	2.0	2.2	2.4	2.6	2.8	3.0
2.0	0.8	1.0	1.2	1.5	1.7	1.9	2.2	2.4	2.6	2.9	3.1	3.3
2.2	0.9	1.1	1.4	1.6	1.9	2.1	2.3	2.6	2.9	3.2	3.4	3.7
2.4	0.9	1.2	1.5	1.8	2.1	2.3	2.6	2.9	3.2	3.4	3.7	4.0
2.6	1.0	1.3	1.6	1.9	2.2	2.5	2.8	3.1	3.4	3.7	4.0	4.3
2.8	1.1	1.4	1.7	2.1	2.4	2.7	3.0	3.4	3.7	4.0	4.3	4.7
3.0	1.2	1.5	1.9	2.2	2.6	2.9	3.2	3.6	4.0	4.3	4.6	5.0
3.2	1.3	1.6	2.0	2.4	2.7	3.1	3.4	3.8	4.2	4.6	4.9	5.3
3.4	1.3	1.7	2.1	2.5	2.9	3.3	3.7	4.1	4.5	4.9	5.3	5.7
3.6	1.4	1.8	2.2	2.7	3.1	3.5	3.9	4.3	4.7	5.2	5.6	6.0
3.8	1.5	1.9	2.4	2.8	3.3	3.7	4.1	4.6	5.0	5.5	5.9	6.3
4.0	1.6	2.0	2.5	3.0	3.4	3.9	4.3	4.8	5.3	5.7	6.2	6.7
4.2	1.7	2.1	2.6	3.1	3.6	4.1	4.6	5.0	5.5	6.0	6.5	7.0
4.4	1.7	2.2	2.7	3.3	3.8	4.3	4.8	5.3	5.8	6.3	6.8	7.3
4.6	1.8	2.3	2.9	3.4	3.9	4.5	5.0	5.5	6.1	6.6	7.1	7.7
4.8	1.9	2.4	3.0	3.6	4.1	4.7	5.2	5.8	6.3	6.9	7.4	8.0
5.0	2.0	2.5	3.1	3.7	4.3	4.9	5.4	6.0	6.6	7.2	7.7	8.3
5.2	2.0	2.6	3.2	3.8	4.4	5.0	5.6	6.2	6.8	7.4	8.0	8.6
5.4	2.1	2.8	3.4	4.0	4.6	5.2	5.7	6.5	7.1	7.7	8.4	9.0
5.6	2.2	2.9	3.5	4.1	4.8	5.4	6.1	6.7	7.4	8.0	8.7	9.3
5.8	2.3	3.0	3.6	4.3	5.0	5.6	6.3	7.0	7.6	8.3	9.0	9.6
6.0	2.4	3.1	3.7	4.4	5.1	5.8	6.5	7.2	7.9	8.6	9.3	9.9

TIDAL HEIGHTS — PORTS & PLACES

Pencil-in height of HW Cherbourg	4.8	5.0	5.2	5.4	5.6	5.8	6.0	6.2	6.4	6.6	6.8
St. Marys	2.7	2.6	2.6	2.5	2.5	2.4	2.4	2.3	2.3	2.3	2.2	2.2
Ports, Chenal du Four and Ile d'Ouessant	3.8	3.8	3.8	3.8	3.8	3.8	3.8	3.8	3.8	3.8	3.7	3.6

6 hours after HW Cherbourg +6

Time (to be inserted)

Copyright © J Reeve-Fowkes and
Thomas Reed Publications.
No copying without permission.

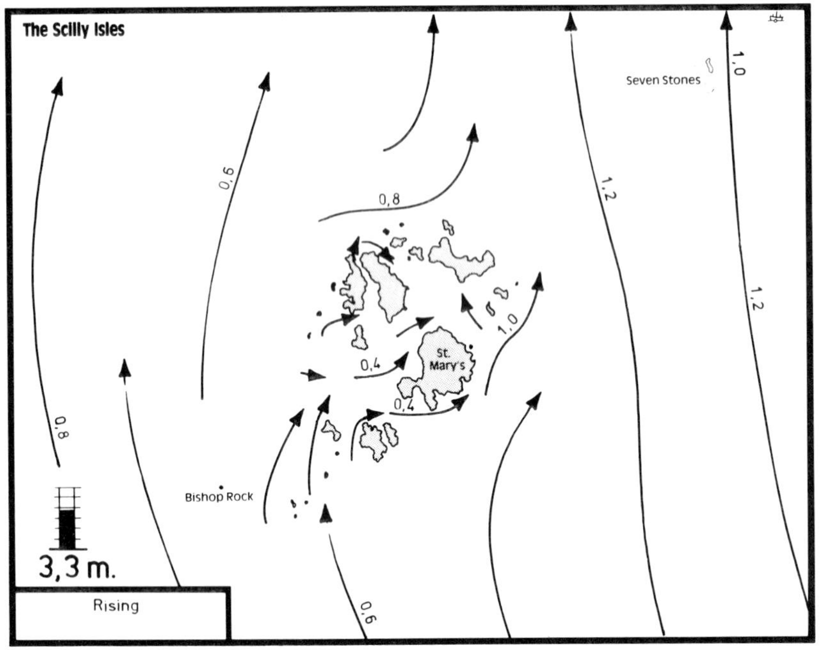

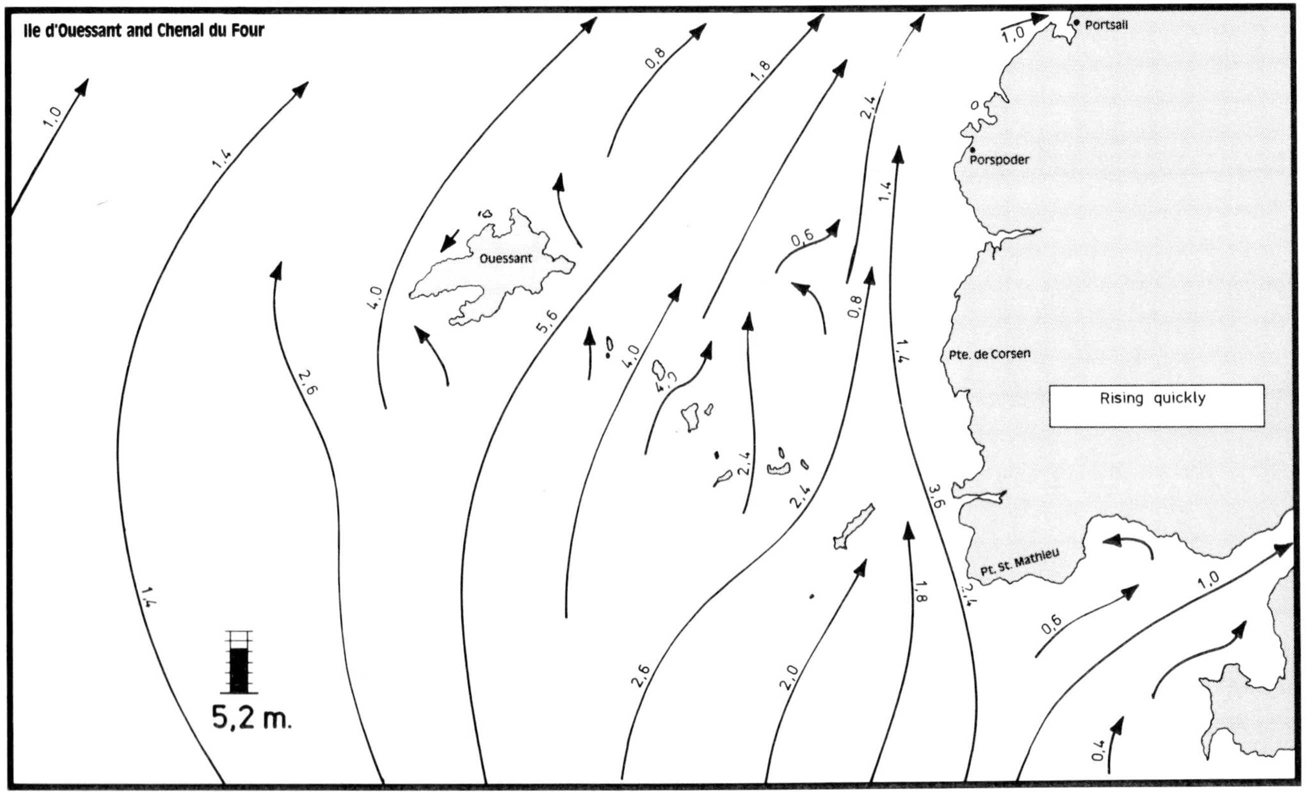

The Scilly Isles

Seven Stones

St. Mary's

Bishop Rock

0
5
Nautical Miles

3,3 m.
Rising

Ile d'Ouessant and Chenal du Four

Portsall
Porspoder
Ouessant
Pte. de Corsen
Rising quickly
Pt. St. Mathieu

5,2 m.

Stream Rate Conversion Table

Mean Rate Figure from Chart ▼	Pencil-in height of HW Cherbourg Read from column below pencil mark											
	4.8	5.0	5.2	5.4	5.6	5.8	6.0	6.2	6.4	6.6	6.8
0.2	0.1	0.1	0.1	0.1	0.2	0.2	0.2	0.2	0.3	0.3	0.3	0.3
0.4	0.2	0.2	0.2	0.3	0.3	0.4	0.4	0.5	0.5	0.6	0.6	0.7
0.6	0.2	0.3	0.4	0.4	0.5	0.6	0.7	0.7	0.8	0.9	0.9	1.0
0.8	0.4	0.4	0.5	0.6	0.7	0.8	0.9	1.0	1.1	1.1	1.2	1.3
1.0	0.4	0.5	0.6	0.7	0.9	1.0	1.1	1.2	1.3	1.4	1.5	1.7
1.2	0.5	0.6	0.7	0.9	1.0	1.2	1.3	1.4	1.6	1.7	1.9	2.0
1.4	0.6	0.7	0.9	1.0	1.2	1.4	1.5	1.7	1.8	2.0	2.2	2.3
1.6	0.6	0.8	1.0	1.2	1.4	1.6	1.7	1.9	2.1	2.3	2.5	2.7
1.8	0.7	0.9	1.1	1.3	1.5	1.7	2.0	2.2	2.4	2.6	2.8	3.0
2.0	0.8	1.0	1.2	1.5	1.7	1.9	2.2	2.4	2.6	2.9	3.1	3.3
2.2	0.9	1.1	1.4	1.6	1.9	2.1	2.3	2.6	2.9	3.2	3.4	3.7
2.4	0.9	1.2	1.5	1.8	2.1	2.3	2.6	2.9	3.2	3.4	3.7	4.3
2.6	1.0	1.3	1.6	1.9	2.2	2.5	2.8	3.1	3.4	3.7	4.0	4.3
2.8	1.1	1.4	1.7	2.1	2.4	2.7	3.0	3.4	3.7	4.0	4.3	4.7
3.0	1.2	1.5	1.9	2.2	2.6	2.9	3.2	3.6	4.0	4.3	4.6	5.0
3.2	1.3	1.6	2.0	2.4	2.7	3.1	3.4	3.8	4.2	4.6	4.9	5.3
3.4	1.3	1.7	2.1	2.5	2.9	3.3	3.7	4.1	4.5	4.9	5.3	5.7
3.6	1.4	1.8	2.2	2.7	3.1	3.5	3.9	4.3	4.7	5.2	5.6	6.0
3.8	1.5	1.9	2.4	2.8	3.3	3.7	4.1	4.6	5.0	5.5	5.9	6.3
4.0	1.6	2.0	2.5	3.0	3.4	3.9	4.3	4.8	5.3	5.7	6.2	6.7
4.2	1.7	2.1	2.6	3.1	3.6	4.1	4.6	5.0	5.5	6.0	6.5	7.0
4.4	1.7	2.2	2.7	3.3	3.8	4.3	4.8	5.3	5.8	6.3	6.8	7.3
4.6	1.8	2.3	2.9	3.4	3.9	4.5	5.0	5.5	6.1	6.6	7.1	7.7
4.8	1.9	2.4	3.0	3.6	4.1	4.7	5.2	5.8	6.3	6.9	7.4	8.0
5.0	2.0	2.5	3.1	3.7	4.3	4.9	5.4	6.0	6.6	7.2	7.7	8.3
5.2	2.0	2.6	3.2	3.8	4.4	5.0	5.6	6.2	6.8	7.4	8.0	8.6
5.4	2.1	2.8	3.4	4.0	4.6	5.2	5.7	6.5	7.1	7.7	8.4	9.0
5.6	2.2	2.9	3.5	4.1	4.8	5.4	6.1	6.7	7.4	8.0	8.7	9.3
5.8	2.3	3.0	3.6	4.3	5.0	5.6	6.3	7.0	7.6	8.3	9.0	9.6
6.0	2.4	3.1	3.7	4.4	5.1	5.8	6.5	7.2	7.9	8.6	9.3	9.9

TIDAL HEIGHTS — PORTS & PLACES

Pencil-in height of HW Cherbourg ▶	4.8	5.0	5.2	5.4	5.6	5.8	6.0	6.2	6.4	6.6	6.8
St. Marys	3.1	3.2	3.2	3.3	3.4	3.5	3.5	3.6	3.7	3.8	3.9	4.0
Ports, Chenal du Four and Ile d'Ouessant	4.3	4.4	4.6	4.8	4.9	5.0	5.2	5.3	5.4	5.5	5.6	5.6

Tidal Ranges

Tidal Ranges

Tidal range is the difference in the height between low water and the preceding or succeeding high water. Knowing the range of a particular tide can be useful when calculating lengths of chain or warp to lay when anchoring, for instance when a vessel has to be left unattended for a period. Tidal Range also needs to be known for computing rates of streams if you are using Admiralty tidal stream atlases; although the figures provided here are approximate only, they will be adequate for this purpose if tide tables for the various Standard Ports are not carried aboard.

Remember that Tidal Range figures are not related to Chart Datum in any way and have no connection with Heights of Tides.

INSTRUCTIONS FOR THE USE OF THE TIDAL RANGE TABLES

1. From the Cherbourg tide table extract the height of HW Cherbourg at a HW time nearest to the required time. Mark this height in pencil on the scale at the top of the Tidal Range Table, opposite; use a vertical arrow or other similar mark.

2. From the place listed in the left-hand column of the table, read across the table to the column underneath your pencilled mark on the top scale. If the pencil mark is between two columns, interpolate between the figures shown in each column. The figure thus found is the range of the tide in metres at that place for that particular tide (Diagram G).

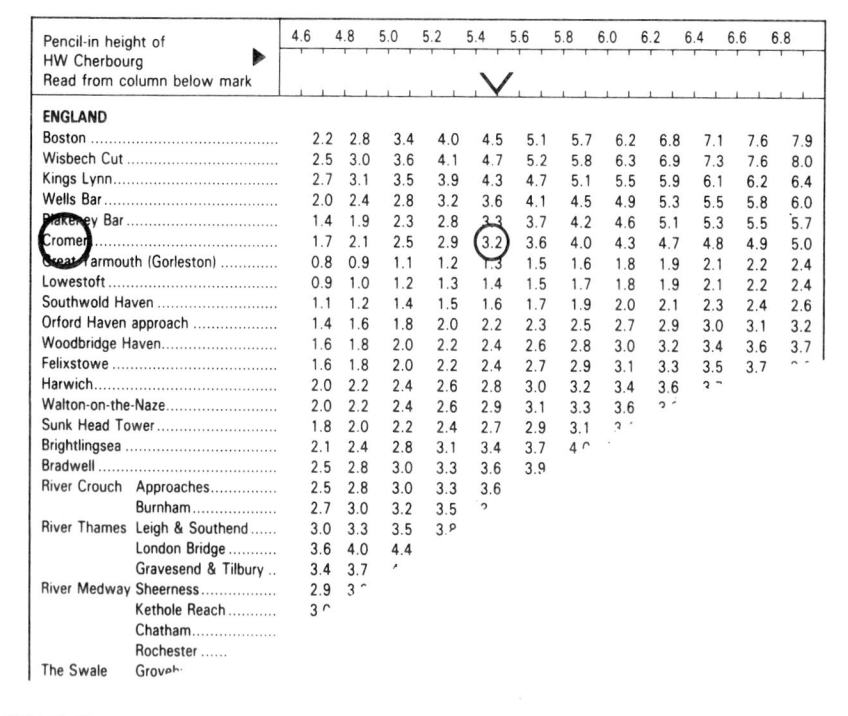

Pencil-in height of HW Cherbourg Read from column below mark ▶	4.6	4.8	5.0	5.2	5.4	5.6	5.8	6.0	6.2	6.4	6.6	6.8
ENGLAND												
Boston	2.2	2.8	3.4	4.0	4.5	5.1	5.7	6.2	6.8	7.1	7.6	7.9
Wisbech Cut	2.5	3.0	3.6	4.1	4.7	5.2	5.8	6.3	6.9	7.3	7.6	8.0
Kings Lynn	2.7	3.1	3.5	3.9	4.3	4.7	5.1	5.5	5.9	6.1	6.2	6.4
Wells Bar	2.0	2.4	2.8	3.2	3.6	4.1	4.5	4.9	5.3	5.5	5.8	6.0
Blakeney Bar	1.4	1.9	2.3	2.8	3.3	3.7	4.2	4.6	5.1	5.3	5.5	5.7
Cromer	1.7	2.1	2.5	2.9	3.2	3.6	4.0	4.3	4.7	4.8	4.9	5.0
Great Yarmouth (Gorleston)	0.8	0.9	1.1	1.2	1.3	1.5	1.6	1.8	1.9	2.1	2.2	2.4
Lowestoft	0.9	1.0	1.2	1.3	1.4	1.5	1.7	1.8	1.9	2.1	2.2	2.4
Southwold Haven	1.1	1.2	1.4	1.5	1.6	1.7	1.9	2.0	2.1	2.3	2.4	2.6
Orford Haven approach	1.4	1.6	1.8	2.0	2.2	2.3	2.5	2.7	2.9	3.0	3.1	3.2
Woodbridge Haven	1.6	1.8	2.0	2.2	2.4	2.6	2.8	3.0	3.2	3.4	3.6	3.7
Felixstowe	1.6	1.8	2.0	2.2	2.4	2.7	2.9	3.1	3.3	3.5	3.7	
Harwich	2.0	2.2	2.4	2.6	2.8	3.0	3.2	3.4	3.6			
Walton-on-the-Naze	2.0	2.2	2.4	2.6	2.9	3.1	3.3	3.6				
Sunk Head Tower	1.8	2.0	2.2	2.4	2.7	2.9	3.1					
Brightlingsea	2.1	2.4	2.8	3.1	3.4	3.7	4.0					
Bradwell	2.5	2.8	3.0	3.3	3.6	3.9						
River Crouch Approaches	2.5	2.8	3.0	3.3	3.6							
Burnham	2.7	3.0	3.2	3.5								
River Thames Leigh & Southend	3.0	3.3	3.5	3.8								
London Bridge	3.6	4.0	4.4									
Gravesend & Tilbury	3.4	3.7										
River Medway Sheerness	2.9	3.0										
Kethole Reach	3.0											
Chatham												
Rochester												
The Swale Grovehill												

DIAGRAM G:
Range of tide at Cromer equals 3.2m.

Tidal Range Tables – Western Channel

Pencil-in height of HW Cherbourg Read from column below mark	4.6	4.8	5.0	5.2	5.4	5.6	5.8	6.0	6.2	6.4	6.6	6.8
WALES												
Portmadoc	1.9	2.2	2.6	2.9	3.2	3.5	3.8	4.1	4.4	4.7	5.1	5.4
Pwllheli & Barmouth	1.7	2.0	2.4	2.7	3.0	3.3	3.7	4.0	4.3	4.6	4.8	5.1
Aberdovey	1.6	1.9	2.3	2.6	2.9	3.3	3.6	4.0	4.3	4.6	4.8	5.1
Aberystwth	1.3	1.7	2.1	2.5	2.8	3.2	3.6	3.9	4.3	4.6	4.9	5.2
New Quay	1.2	1.6	2.0	2.4	2.7	3.1	3.5	3.8	4.2	4.5	4.8	5.1
Fishguard (& Port Cardigan approx.)	0.9	1.3	1.7	2.1	2.4	2.8	3.2	3.5	3.9	4.2	4.5	4.8
MILFORD HAVEN	1.9	2.4	3.0	3.5	4.1	4.6	5.2	5.7	6.3	6.7	7.2	7.6
Tenby & Saundersfoot	2.3	3.0	3.6	4.3	4.9	5.6	6.2	6.9	7.5	8.0	8.5	9.0
Burry Inlet approach	2.9	3.5	4.1	4.7	5.3	6.0	6.6	7.2	7.8	8.3	8.8	9.3
Swansea	3.1	3.8	4.4	5.1	5.8	6.5	7.2	7.9	8.6	9.1	9.6	10.1
Port of Neath approach	3.2	3.9	4.5	5.2	5.9	6.6	7.2	7.9	8.6	9.1	9.6	10.1
Port Talbot & Porthcawl	3.0	3.7	4.5	5.2	5.9	6.6	7.4	8.1	8.8	9.4	10.0	10.6
Barry	3.9	4.8	5.6	6.5	7.3	8.2	9.0	9.9	10.7	11.2	11.7	12.2
CARDIFF & Penarth	4.3	5.1	5.9	6.7	7.6	8.4	9.2	10.1	10.9	11.5	12.1	12.7
Newport	4.8	5.7	6.5	7.4	8.3	9.2	10.1	11.0	11.9	12.4	13.0	13.5
IRELAND												
Arklow	0.4	0.5	0.5	0.6	0.6	0.7	0.7	0.8	0.8	0.9	0.9	1.0
Rosslare	0.4	0.5	0.7	0.8	1.0	1.1	1.3	1.4	1.6	1.8	1.9	2.1
Waterford Harbour entrance	1.9	2.1	2.3	2.5	2.7	3.0	3.2	3.4	3.6	3.8	3.9	4.1
Youghal	1.8	2.0	2.2	2.4	2.7	2.9	3.1	3.4	3.6	3.8	3.9	4.1
Ballycotton	1.8	2.0	2.3	2.4	2.7	2.9	3.1	3.4	3.6	3.8	3.9	4.1
Cork	1.7	2.0	2.2	2.5	2.8	3.1	3.3	3.6	3.9	4.1	4.3	4.5
Cobh	1.6	1.9	2.1	2.4	2.6	2.9	3.1	3.4	3.6	3.8	4.0	4.2
Kinsale (& Baltimore Bay approx.)	1.4	1.7	1.9	2.2	2.5	2.7	3.0	3.2	3.5	3.7	3.9	4.1
ENGLAND												
Avonmouth	5.2	6.1	6.9	7.8	8.7	9.6	10.5	11.4	12.3	12.8	13.4	13.9
Clevedon	4.9	5.8	6.6	7.5	8.4	9.3	10.1	11.0	11.9	12.4	13.0	13.5
Weston-super-Mare	5.3	6.0	6.8	7.5	8.3	9.0	9.8	10.5	11.3	11.7	12.2	12.6
Burnham	5.2	6.0	6.8	7.6	8.4	9.1	9.9	10.7	11.5	11.9	12.4	12.8
Watchet	4.0	4.8	5.6	6.4	7.2	8.1	8.9	9.7	10.5	11.0	11.4	11.9
Minehead	3.4	4.2	5.0	5.8	6.6	7.5	8.3	9.1	9.9	10.4	10.8	11.3
Porlock Bay	3.5	4.2	5.0	5.7	6.5	7.2	8.0	8.7	9.5	9.9	10.3	10.7
Ilfracombe	2.8	3.5	4.3	5.0	5.7	6.4	7.1	7.8	8.5	9.1	9.7	10.3
Appledore	2.7	3.3	3.9	4.5	5.0	5.6	6.3	6.7	7.3	7.8	8.2	8.7
Clovelly	2.7	3.3	3.9	4.5	5.1	5.6	6.2	6.8	7.4	7.9	8.3	8.8
Bude	2.2	2.8	3.4	4.0	4.5	5.1	5.7	6.2	6.8	7.3	7.7	8.2
Boscastle	2.1	2.6	3.2	3.7	4.2	4.8	5.2	5.9	6.4	6.8	7.3	7.7
Padstow (& Newquay approx.)	2.2	2.7	3.3	3.8	4.3	4.9	5.3	6.0	6.5	6.9	7.4	7.8
St. Ives Bay	1.7	2.2	2.8	3.3	3.8	4.4	4.8	5.5	6.0	6.4	6.9	7.3
Lundy Island	2.3	2.9	3.5	4.1	4.7	5.4	6.0	6.6	7.2	7.7	8.2	8.7
St. Mary's, Scilly Isles	1.7	2.1	2.5	2.9	3.3	3.8	4.2	4.6	5.0	5.3	5.7	6.0

Pencil-in height of HW Cherbourg Read from column below mark	4.6	4.8	5.0	5.2	5.4	5.6	5.8	6.0	6.2	6.4	6.6	6.8
Newlyn, Penzance & Porthleven	1.8	2.2	2.6	3.0	3.3	3.7	4.1	4.2	4.8	5.1	5.4	5.7
Coverack, Falmouth & Helford R.	1.7	2.1	2.5	2.9	3.2	3.6	4.0	4.3	4.7	5.0	5.2	5.5
Mevagissey, Fowey & Looe	1.7	2.1	2.5	2.9	3.3	3.6	4.0	4.4	4.8	5.1	5.4	5.7
PLYMOUTH, Whitsand Bay & Yealm R.	1.6	2.0	2.4	2.8	3.2	3.5	3.9	4.3	4.7	5.0	5.3	5.6
Salcombe	1.4	1.8	2.2	2.6	3.0	3.4	3.2	4.2	4.6	4.9	5.2	5.5
Dartmouth	1.2	1.6	2.0	2.4	2.8	3.2	3.6	4.0	4.4	4.7	5.1	5.4
Brixham, Torquay & Teignmouth	1.1	1.5	1.9	2.3	2.7	3.0	3.4	3.8	4.2	4.5	4.9	5.2
Exmouth approaches	1.0	1.4	1.8	2.2	2.5	2.9	3.3	3.6	4.0	4.3	4.7	5.0
Lyme Regis	0.9	1.2	1.6	1.9	2.3	2.6	3.0	3.3	3.7	3.9	4.2	4.4
Bridport	0.9	1.2	1.6	1.9	2.2	2.5	2.9	3.2	3.5	3.8	4.0	4.3
Portland & Weymouth	0.4	0.6	0.8	1.0	1.2	1.3	1.5	1.7	1.9	2.1	2.2	2.4
Lulworth Cove	0.3	0.5	0.7	0.9	1.1	1.4	1.6	1.8	2.0	2.2	2.4	2.6
Swanage	0.3	0.4	0.6	0.7	0.8	0.9	1.0	1.3	1.5	1.7	1.8	2.0
Poole entrance	0.4	0.5	0.5	0.6	0.6	0.7	1.0	1.2	1.5	1.7	1.8	2.0
Poole Town	0.5	0.6	0.6	0.7	0.8	0.9	1.2	1.4	1.7	1.8	2.0	2.2
Christchurch approaches	0.5	0.6	0.6	0.7	0.8	0.9	1.2	1.6	1.9	2.0	2.1	2.2
Christchurch Harbour	0.6	0.7	0.7	0.8	0.8	0.9	1.1	1.2	1.4	1.5	1.5	1.6
CHANNEL ISLANDS												
Braye Harbour, Alderney	1.8	2.3	2.7	3.2	3.7	4.1	4.6	5.0	5.5	5.9	6.4	6.8
St. Peter Port (Guernsey) & Sark	2.1	2.8	3.6	4.3	5.0	5.8	6.5	7.3	8.0	8.6	9.1	9.7
St. Helier (Jersey)	2.7	3.6	4.4	5.3	6.2	7.1	8.0	8.9	9.8	10.5	11.2	11.9
St. Catherine (Jersey)	2.4	3.3	4.3	5.2	6.1	7.1	8.0	9.0	9.9	10.6	11.4	12.1
Les Minquiers	3.8	4.6	5.4	6.2	7.0	7.8	8.6	9.4	10.2	10.8	11.4	12.0
FRANCE												
CHERBOURG	1.9	2.3	2.7	3.1	3.5	4.0	4.4	4.8	5.2	5.7	6.1	6.6
Omonville	1.8	2.2	2.6	3.0	3.4	3.9	4.3	4.7	5.1	5.6	6.1	6.6
Goury	2.4	2.9	3.5	4.0	4.5	5.1	5.6	6.2	6.7	7.2	7.8	8.3
Dielette	2.6	3.3	4.1	4.8	5.5	6.2	7.0	7.7	8.4	9.0	9.6	10.2
Iles Chausey	4.0	4.9	5.7	6.6	7.5	8.4	9.3	10.2	11.1	11.8	12.5	13.2
Carteret	3.2	4.0	4.8	5.6	6.4	7.2	8.0	8.8	9.6	10.2	10.9	11.5
Granville	3.6	4.6	5.6	6.6	7.6	8.6	9.6	10.6	11.6	12.3	13.0	13.7
SAINT MALO	3.4	4.3	5.3	6.2	7.1	8.0	9.0	9.9	10.8	11.5	12.1	12.8
Erquy, Dahouet, Le Légué, Binic, Portrieux	3.2	4.1	4.9	5.8	6.6	7.5	8.3	9.2	10.0	10.6	11.2	11.8
Paimpol	3.4	4.2	5.0	5.8	6.6	7.5	8.3	9.1	9.9	10.6	11.2	11.9
Ile de Bréhat (Port-Clos)	3.3	4.0	4.8	5.5	6.2	7.0	7.7	8.5	9.2	9.8	10.4	11.0
Lezardrieux	3.4	4.1	4.9	5.6	6.4	7.1	7.9	8.6	9.4	10.0	10.6	11.2
Tréguier	3.0	3.7	4.5	5.2	5.9	6.7	7.4	8.2	8.9	9.4	9.9	10.4
Ploumanach	2.7	3.4	4.0	4.7	5.3	6.0	6.6	7.3	7.9	8.4	8.9	9.4
Morlaix & Anse de Primel	2.5	3.2	3.8	4.5	5.1	5.8	6.4	7.1	7.7	8.3	8.8	9.4
Roscoff & Ile de Batz	2.6	3.2	3.8	4.4	5.1	5.7	6.3	7.0	7.6	8.1	8.5	9.0
L'Aberwrach & L'Aberbenoit	2.2	2.8	3.4	4.0	4.6	5.1	5.7	6.3	6.9	7.4	7.8	8.3
Portsal	2.3	2.8	3.4	3.9	4.4	5.0	5.5	6.1	6.6	7.1	7.6	8.1
Ports, Chenal du Four & Ouessant	2.2	2.7	3.1	3.6	4.1	4.6	5.1	5.6	6.1	6.5	7.0	7.4
BREST	2.0	2.5	3.1	3.6	4.1	4.6	5.1	5.6	6.1	6.5	6.9	7.3
Camaret & Douarnenez	1.9	2.4	2.8	3.3	3.8	4.2	4.7	5.1	5.6	6.0	6.4	6.8

Tidal Range Tables – Eastern Channel

Pencil-in height of HW Cherbourg ▶ Read from column below mark	4.6	4.8	5.0	5.2	5.4	5.6	5.8	6.0	6.2	6.4	6.6	6.8
ENGLAND												
Boston	2.2	2.8	3.4	4.0	4.5	5.1	5.7	6.2	6.8	7.1	7.6	7.9
Wisbech Cut	2.5	3.0	3.6	4.1	4.7	5.2	5.8	6.3	6.9	7.3	7.6	8.0
Kings Lynn	2.7	3.1	3.5	3.9	4.3	4.7	5.1	5.5	5.9	6.1	6.2	6.4
Wells Bar	2.0	2.4	2.8	3.2	3.6	4.1	4.5	4.9	5.3	5.5	5.8	6.0
Blakeney Bar	1.4	1.9	2.3	2.8	3.3	3.7	4.2	4.6	5.1	5.3	5.5	5.7
Cromer	1.7	2.1	2.5	2.9	3.2	3.6	4.0	4.3	4.7	4.8	4.9	5.0
Great Yarmouth (Gorleston)	0.8	0.9	1.1	1.2	1.3	1.5	1.6	1.8	1.9	2.1	2.2	2.4
Lowestoft	0.9	1.0	1.2	1.3	1.4	1.5	1.7	1.8	1.9	2.1	2.2	2.4
Southwold Haven	1.1	1.2	1.4	1.5	1.6	1.7	1.9	2.0	2.1	2.3	2.4	2.6
Orford Haven approach	1.4	1.6	1.8	2.0	2.2	2.3	2.5	2.7	2.9	3.0	3.1	3.2
Woodbridge Haven	1.6	1.8	2.0	2.2	2.4	2.6	2.8	3.0	3.2	3.4	3.6	3.7
Felixstowe	1.6	1.8	2.0	2.2	2.4	2.7	2.9	3.1	3.3	3.5	3.7	3.9
Harwich	2.0	2.2	2.4	2.6	2.8	3.0	3.2	3.4	3.6	3.7	3.9	4.0
Walton-on-the-Naze	2.0	2.2	2.4	2.6	2.9	3.1	3.3	3.6	3.8	4.0	4.2	4.4
Sunk Head Tower	1.8	2.0	2.2	2.4	2.7	2.9	3.1	3.4	3.6	3.8	4.0	4.2
Brightlingsea	2.1	2.4	2.8	3.1	3.4	3.7	4.0	4.3	4.6	4.8	5.1	5.5
Bradwell	2.5	2.8	3.0	3.3	3.6	3.9	4.2	4.5	4.8	5.0	5.3	5.5
River Crouch Approaches	2.5	2.8	3.0	3.3	3.6	3.9	4.2	4.5	4.8	5.1	5.4	5.7
Burnham	2.7	3.0	3.2	3.5	3.8	4.1	4.4	4.7	5.0	5.3	5.5	5.8
River Thames Leigh & Southend	3.0	3.3	3.5	3.8	4.1	4.4	4.6	4.9	5.2	5.5	5.9	6.2
London Bridge	3.6	4.0	4.4	4.8	5.1	5.5	5.9	6.2	6.6	7.0	7.3	7.7
Gravesend & Tilbury	3.4	3.7	4.1	4.4	4.7	5.0	5.4	5.7	6.0	6.4	6.9	7.3
River Medway Sheerness	2.9	3.2	3.4	3.7	4.0	4.3	4.5	4.8	5.1	5.4	5.8	6.1
Kethole Reach	3.0	3.3	3.5	3.8	4.1	4.4	4.7	5.0	5.3	5.6	5.8	6.1
Chatham	3.0	3.3	3.7	4.0	4.3	4.6	5.0	5.3	5.6	5.9	6.2	6.5
Rochester	3.0	3.3	3.7	4.0	4.3	4.6	5.0	5.3	5.6	6.0	6.4	6.8
The Swale Grovehurst	2.9	3.2	3.4	3.7	4.0	4.3	4.6	4.9	5.2	5.6	5.9	6.3
Whitstable approaches	2.7	3.0	3.2	3.5	3.8	4.1	4.4	4.7	4.9	5.1	5.4	5.6
Shivering Sand Tower	2.4	2.7	2.9	3.2	3.5	3.8	4.0	4.3	4.6	5.0	5.3	5.7
Edinburgh Channels	2.2	2.5	2.7	3.0	3.3	3.6	3.8	4.1	4.4	4.6	4.8	5.0
Margate	2.1	2.4	2.6	2.9	3.2	3.5	3.7	4.0	4.3	4.5	4.7	4.9
Ramsgate	2.2	2.5	2.7	3.0	3.3	3.6	3.9	4.2	4.5	4.7	5.0	5.2
The Downs	2.5	2.8	3.2	3.5	3.9	4.2	4.6	4.9	5.3	5.6	6.0	6.3
DOVER	2.7	3.1	3.5	3.9	4.3	4.7	5.1	5.5	5.9	6.2	6.6	6.9
Folkestone	3.1	3.5	3.9	4.3	4.7	5.2	5.6	6.0	6.4	6.7	7.1	7.4
Dungeness	3.3	3.8	4.2	4.7	5.2	5.6	6.1	6.5	7.0	7.4	7.8	8.2
Rye approaches	3.1	3.6	4.0	4.5	5.0	5.4	5.9	6.3	6.8	7.2	7.6	8.0
Newhaven	2.7	3.1	3.5	3.9	4.4	4.8	5.2	5.7	6.1	6.4	6.7	7.0
Brighton	2.6	3.0	3.4	3.8	4.2	4.7	5.1	5.5	5.9	6.2	6.5	6.8
Shoreham	2.5	2.9	3.3	3.7	4.0	4.4	4.8	5.1	5.5	5.8	6.0	6.3
Littlehampton approaches	2.2	2.5	2.9	3.2	3.5	3.8	4.2	4.5	4.8	5.0	5.2	5.4
Littlehampton Harbour	2.4	2.7	3.1	3.2	3.5	3.8	4.2	4.5	4.8	5.0	5.2	5.4

Pencil-in height of HW Cherbourg ▶ Read from column below mark	4.6	4.8	5.0	5.2	5.4	5.6	5.8	6.0	6.2	6.4	6.6	6.8
Selsey Bill	2.1	2.4	2.8	3.1	3.4	3.7	4.1	4.4	4.7	4.9	5.1	5.3
Chichester entrance	1.7	2.0	2.4	2.7	3.0	3.3	3.6	3.9	4.2	4.4	4.6	4.8
PORTSMOUTH	1.5	1.8	2.2	2.5	2.8	3.1	3.5	3.8	4.1	4.3	4.4	4.6
Southampton	1.4	1.7	2.1	2.4	2.7	3.0	3.4	3.7	4.0	4.2	4.4	4.6
Sandown I. o W.	1.0	1.3	1.5	1.8	2.1	2.4	2.7	2.9	3.2	3.5	3.8	4.1
Cowes I. o W.	1.2	1.5	1.7	2.0	2.2	2.5	2.8	3.1	3.4	3.6	3.9	4.1
Yarmouth I. o W.	0.8	0.9	1.1	1.2	1.4	1.5	1.7	1.9	2.1	2.3	2.6	2.8
Lymington	0.6	0.8	1.0	1.2	1.5	1.7	1.9	2.1	2.3	2.5	2.6	2.8
HOLLAND												
Den Helder	1.0	1.1	1.1	1.2	1.3	1.4	1.4	1.5	1.6	1.6	1.6	1.6
IJmuiden	1.1	1.2	1.2	1.3	1.4	1.5	1.6	1.7	1.8	1.9	1.9	2.0
Scheveningen	1.2	1.3	1.3	1.4	1.5	1.6	1.6	1.7	1.8	1.9	1.9	2.0
Hoek van Holland	1.2	1.3	1.3	1.4	1.5	1.6	1.6	1.7	1.8	1.8	1.9	1.9
Rotterdam	1.4	1.5	1.5	1.6	1.6	1.7	1.7	1.8	1.8	1.8	1.9	1.9
Haringvlietsluizen	1.4	1.5	1.5	1.6	1.7	1.8	1.8	1.9	2.0	2.0	2.0	2.0
Flushing	2.6	2.8	3.0	3.2	3.4	3.7	3.9	4.1	4.3	4.4	4.6	4.7
Terneuzen	2.9	3.1	3.3	3.5	3.8	4.0	4.2	4.5	4.7	4.8	5.0	5.1
BELGIUM												
Antwerp	3.6	3.9	4.1	4.4	4.6	4.9	5.1	5.4	5.6	5.8	6.0	6.2
Zeebrugge	2.4	2.7	2.9	3.2	3.5	3.8	4.0	4.3	4.6	4.8	4.9	5.1
Ostende	2.7	3.0	3.2	3.5	3.8	4.0	4.3	4.5	4.8	4.9	5.1	5.2
Nieuwpoort	2.8	3.1	3.3	3.6	3.9	4.1	4.4	4.6	4.9	5.1	5.2	5.4
FRANCE												
Dunkerque	3.0	3.3	3.5	3.8	4.1	4.4	4.6	4.9	5.2	5.4	5.5	5.7
Gravelines	3.2	3.5	3.7	4.0	4.3	4.6	4.9	5.2	5.5	5.7	5.8	6.0
Calais	3.4	3.7	4.1	4.4	4.8	5.1	5.5	5.8	6.2	6.4	6.6	6.8
Boulogne	3.9	4.4	5.0	5.5	6.0	6.5	7.0	7.5	8.0	8.3	8.7	9.0
Etaples	3.7	4.2	4.8	5.3	5.8	6.3	6.9	7.4	7.9	8.1	8.4	8.6
Somme Estuary	4.3	4.9	5.5	6.1	6.6	7.2	7.8	8.3	8.9	9.1	9.3	9.5
Le Tréport	4.3	4.8	5.4	5.9	6.5	7.0	7.6	8.1	8.7	8.9	9.2	9.4
Dieppe	3.8	4.4	5.0	5.6	6.2	6.7	7.3	7.9	8.5	8.8	9.2	9.5
Saint-Valery-en-Caux	4.0	4.5	4.9	5.4	5.9	6.4	6.9	7.4	7.9	8.2	8.4	8.7
Fécamp	3.2	3.7	4.1	4.6	5.1	5.6	6.0	6.5	7.0	7.3	7.7	8.0
LE HAVRE	2.9	3.4	3.8	4.3	4.8	5.2	5.7	6.1	6.6	7.0	7.3	7.7
Honfleur	3.2	3.6	4.0	4.4	4.9	5.3	5.7	6.2	6.6	6.9	7.2	7.5
Trouville (Deauville)	2.9	3.4	3.8	4.3	4.8	5.3	5.7	6.2	6.7	7.0	7.4	7.7
Ouistreham	2.9	3.4	3.8	4.3	4.8	5.3	5.7	6.2	6.7	7.0	7.4	7.7
Courseulles	2.6	3.1	3.5	4.0	4.4	4.9	5.3	5.8	6.2	6.5	6.9	7.2
Arromanches	2.6	3.1	3.5	4.0	4.5	4.9	5.4	5.8	6.3	6.6	7.0	7.3
Port-en-Bessin	2.7	3.1	3.5	3.9	4.4	4.8	5.2	5.7	6.1	6.4	6.8	7.1
Saint-Vaast-la-Hougue	2.5	2.9	3.3	3.7	4.1	4.5	4.9	5.3	5.7	6.2	6.6	7.1
Barfleur	2.2	2.6	3.0	3.4	3.8	4.2	4.6	5.0	5.4	5.8	6.3	6.7

Tidal Range Tables – Central Channel

Pencil-in height of HW Cherbourg Read from column below mark ▶	4.6	4.8	5.0	5.2	5.4	5.6	5.8	6.0	6.2	6.4	6.6	6.8
ENGLAND												
Lyme Regis	0.9	1.2	1.6	1.9	2.3	2.6	3.0	3.3	3.7	3.9	4.2	4.4
Bridport	0.9	1.2	1.6	1.9	2.2	2.5	2.9	3.2	3.5	3.8	4.0	4.3
Portland & Weymouth	0.4	0.6	0.8	1.0	1.2	1.3	1.5	1.7	1.9	2.1	2.2	2.4
Lulworth Cove	0.3	0.5	0.7	0.9	1.1	1.4	1.6	1.8	2.0	2.2	2.4	2.6
Swanage	0.3	0.4	0.6	0.7	0.8	0.9	1.0	1.3	1.5	1.7	1.8	2.0
Poole entrance	0.4	0.5	0.5	0.6	0.6	0.7	1.0	1.2	1.5	1.7	1.8	2.0
Poole Town Quay	0.5	0.6	0.6	0.7	0.8	0.9	1.2	1.4	1.7	1.8	2.0	2.2
Christchurch appr'ch	0.5	0.6	0.6	0.7	0.8	0.9	1.2	1.6	1.9	2.0	2.1	2.2
Christchurch Hbr	0.6	0.7	0.7	0.8	0.8	0.9	1.1	1.2	1.4	1.5	1.5	1.6
Lymington	0.6	0.8	1.0	1.2	1.5	1.7	1.9	2.1	2.3	2.5	2.6	2.8
Yarmouth I. o. W.	0.8	0.9	1.1	1.2	1.4	1.5	1.7	1.9	2.1	2.3	2.6	2.8
Cowes I. o. W.	1.2	1.5	1.7	2.0	2.2	2.5	2.8	3.1	3.4	3.6	3.9	4.1
Sandown I. o. W.	1.0	1.3	1.5	1.8	2.1	2.4	2.7	2.9	3.2	3.5	3.8	4.1
Southampton	1.4	1.7	2.1	2.4	2.7	3.0	3.4	3.7	4.0	4.2	4.4	4.6
Portsmouth	1.5	1.8	2.2	2.5	2.8	3.1	3.5	3.8	4.1	4.3	4.4	4.6
Chichester entrance	1.7	2.0	2.4	2.7	3.0	3.3	3.6	3.9	4.2	4.4	4.6	4.8
Selsey Bill	2.1	2.4	2.8	3.1	3.4	3.7	4.1	4.4	4.7	4.9	5.1	5.3
Littlehampton Hbr	2.2	2.5	2.9	3.2	3.5	3.8	4.2	4.5	4.8	5.0	5.2	5.4
Littlehampton appr'ch	2.4	2.7	3.1	3.4	3.8	4.1	4.5	4.8	5.2	5.4	5.7	5.9
Shoreham	2.5	2.9	3.3	3.7	4.0	4.4	4.8	5.1	5.5	5.8	6.0	6.3
Brighton	2.6	3.0	3.4	3.8	4.2	4.7	5.1	5.5	5.9	6.2	6.5	6.8
Newhaven	2.7	3.1	3.5	3.9	4.4	4.8	5.2	5.7	6.1	6.4	6.7	7.0

Pencil-in height of HW Cherbourg Read from column below mark ▶	4.6	4.8	5.0	5.2	5.4	5.6	5.8	6.0	6.2	6.4	6.6	6.8
FRANCE												
Le Havre	2.9	3.4	3.8	4.3	4.8	5.2	5.7	6.1	6.6	7.0	7.3	7.7
Honfleur	3.2	3.6	4.0	4.4	4.9	5.3	5.7	6.2	6.6	6.9	7.2	7.5
Trouville (Deauville)	2.9	3.4	3.8	4.3	4.8	5.3	5.7	6.2	6.7	7.0	7.4	7.7
Ouistreham	2.9	3.4	3.8	4.3	4.8	5.3	5.7	6.2	6.7	7.0	7.4	7.7
Courseulles	2.6	3.1	3.6	4.0	4.4	4.9	5.3	5.8	6.2	6.5	6.9	7.2
Arromanches	2.6	3.1	3.5	4.0	4.5	4.9	5.4	5.8	6.3	6.6	7.0	7.3
Port-en-Bessin	2.7	3.1	3.5	3.9	4.4	4.8	5.2	5.7	6.1	6.4	6.8	7.1
Saint-Vaast-la-Hougue	2.5	2.9	3.3	3.7	4.1	4.5	4.9	5.3	5.7	6.2	6.6	7.1
Barfleur	2.2	2.6	3.0	3.4	3.8	4.2	4.6	5.0	5.4	5.8	6.3	6.7
Cherbourg	1.9	2.3	2.7	3.1	3.5	4.0	4.4	4.8	5.2	5.7	6.1	6.6
Omonville	1.8	2.2	2.6	3.0	3.4	3.9	4.3	4.7	5.1	5.6	6.1	6.6
Goury	2.4	2.9	3.5	4.0	4.5	5.1	5.6	6.2	6.7	7.2	7.8	8.3
Dielette	2.6	3.3	4.1	4.8	5.5	6.2	7.0	7.7	8.4	9.0	9.6	10.2
Carteret	3.2	4.0	4.8	5.6	6.4	7.2	8.0	8.8	9.6	10.2	10.9	11.5
Granville	3.6	4.6	5.6	6.6	7.6	8.6	9.6	10.6	11.6	12.3	13.0	13.7
Saint Malo	3.4	4.3	5.3	6.2	7.1	8.0	9.0	9.9	10.8	11.5	12.1	12.8
All Hbrs, St Brieuc Bay	3.2	4.1	4.9	5.8	6.6	7.5	8.3	9.2	10.0	10.6	11.2	11.8
Paimpol	3.4	4.2	5.0	5.8	6.6	7.5	8.3	9.1	9.9	10.6	11.2	11.9
Ile de Bréhat	3.3	4.0	4.8	5.5	6.2	7.0	7.7	8.5	9.2	9.8	10.4	11.0
Lezardrieux	3.4	4.1	4.9	5.6	6.4	7.1	7.9	8.6	9.4	10.0	10.6	11.1
ISLANDS OFF												
Braye, Alderney	1.8	2.3	2.7	3.2	3.7	4.1	4.6	5.0	5.5	5.9	6.4	6.8
St Peter Port & Sark	2.1	2.8	3.6	4.3	5.0	5.8	6.5	7.3	8.0	8.6	9.1	9.7
St Helier, Jersey	2.7	3.6	4.4	5.3	6.2	7.1	8.0	8.9	9.8	10.5	11.2	11.9
St Catherine, Jersey	2.4	3.3	4.3	5.2	6.2	7.0	8.0	9.0	9.9	10.4	11.4	12.1
Les Minquiers	3.8	4.6	5.4	6.2	7.0	7.8	8.6	9.4	10.2	10.8	11.4	12.0
Iles Chausey	4.0	4.9	5.7	6.6	7.5	8.4	9.3	10.2	11.1	11.8	12.5	13.2

Index

Accumulated sets and drifts 42
Actual rates 42
Amphidromic 13
Apparent tide-wind 47
Apparent wind 46
Apparent wind, total 47
Awash 13
Back-bearings 30
Barometric pressure 27
Chart datum 13
Charts 16
Computation of rates 17
Conjunction 8
Conversion tables 23
Course achieved 32
Course setting 30
Course setting, the shortest distance ... 40
Course-to-steer 30
Cross-track error 52
Currents 9
Currents, wind-induced 26
Curves, spring and neap 18
Diamonds, tidal 16
Dipping distance 13
Distance off 13
Drift 11
Ebb 9
Eddies 10
Electronics 52
Exposed heights 13
Flood 9
GPS 52
Gravitational pull 8
HAT 12
Heading 32

Height, high water 13
Height of tide 18
Heights, drying 13
Heights, tidal 18
Inset 11
IRPCS 43
LAT 12
Lee-bowing 47
Leeway 31
Making 13
Mean levels 12
Mean rates 42
MHW 12
MHWN 12
MHWS 12
ML 12
MLW 12
MLWN 12
MLWS 12
MSL 12
MTL 12
Neaps 12
Nil 9
Opposition 8
Origin, data 23
Origin, tides 8
Overfalls 10
Passages, coastal 34
Passages cross-channel 41
Passages, windward 48
Phases, moon 8
Position-fixing, electronic 52
Publications 16
Races 10
Rainfall 27
Range 11
Rate 8
Rectilinear streams 9

Rhumb line 52
Rips 10
Rise 13
Rotary streams 9
Seastate 47
Secondary ports 13
Set 11
Sets and drifts, accumulated 42
Single-port phasing 22
Soundings 18
Slack 9
Springs 12
Stand 11
Standard port 13
Stay-on-track 52
Streams and currents 9
Surges 27
Tacking angle 31
Tacking – track estimating 31
Taking off 13
Tidal diamonds 16
Tidal height calculation 19
Tidal heights 18
Tide-gate 37
Tide-wind 47
Total apparent wind 46
Total tacking angle 32
Track 30
Track estimating 31
Traffic separation zones 43
Transits 30
True wind 46
Twelfths rule 19
Waves 26
Weak 9
Wind, apparent 46
Wind, true 46
Windward tactics 48